KT-399-765

UNDERSTANDING

MANAGEMENT

UNDERSTANDING

MANAGEMENT

RICHARD L. DAFT

VANDERBILT UNIVERSITY

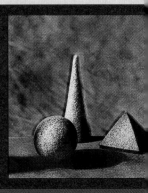

THE DRYDEN PRESS
HARCOURT BRACE COLLEGE PUBLISHERS

Fort Worth   Philadelphia   San Diego   New York   Austin   San Antonio
Toronto   Montreal   London   Sydney   Tokyo

Acquisitions Editor	Ruth Rominger
Developmental Editor	Traci Keller
Project Editor	Jon Gregory
Designer	Linda Wooton Miller
Production Manager	Kelly Cordes
Marketing Manager	Lisé Johnson
Photo/Permissions Editors	Elizabeth Banks, Avery Hallowell, Louise Karkoutli
Copy Editor	Michael Ferreira
Indexer	Leoni McVey
Compositor	GTS Graphics, Inc.
Text Type	10/12 Palatino

Copyright © 1995 by Harcourt Brace & Company

All rights reserved. No part of this publication may be reproduced or transmitted in any form or by any means, electronic or mechanical, including photocopy, recording, or any information storage and retrieval system, without permission in writing from the publisher.

Requests for permission to make copies of any part of the work should be mailed to: Permissions Department, Harcourt Brace & Company, 6277 Sea Harbor Drive, Orlando, Florida 32887-6777.

Some material in this work was previously published in MANAGEMENT, Third Edition, copyright 1994, 1991, 1988 by The Dryden Press. All rights reserved.

Permission acknowledgments and photo credits appear on page P-1, which constitutes a continuation of the copyright page.

Address for Editorial Correspondence:
The Dryden Press
301 Commerce Street, Suite 3700
Fort Worth, TX 76102

Address for Orders:
The Dryden Press
6277 Sea Harbor Drive
Orlando, FL 32887-6777
1-800-782-4479 or 1-800-433-0001 (in Florida)

ISBN: 0-03-098582-X

Library of Congress Catalog Card Number: 94-76162

Printed in the United States of America

4 5 6 7 8 9 0 1 2 3   048   9 8 7 6 5 4 3 2 1

The Dryden Press
Harcourt Brace College Publishers

● PREFACE

My vision for *Understanding Management* is to create the best and most relevant textbook available for students and teachers who are interested in small- and medium-sized local organizations. Unlike traditional management textbooks, this book does not rely on abstract theories and company examples applicable only to top managers of billion-dollar corporations. To achieve the vision of appealing to students who "work for a living in typical companies," this textbook contains two distinctive qualities:

- Management concepts are absolutely current and up-to-date, and they are selected for relevance to the large student audience interested in real management problems in local companies. The management concepts are also applicable to readers with interests in small business and entrepreneurship. The concepts have been enhanced with an easy-to-understand writing style, and many practical examples are woven into the text.

- Case applications, boxed items, photo captions, and end-of-chapter materials are heavily oriented toward middle management and supervisory issues in smaller companies and away from the "top management of Fortune 500 companies" perspective applicable to M.B.A. students in select schools. Vivid illustrations of real organizational issues appeal to people at all levels in companies of all sizes. Not only are these teaching aids current and practical, they reinforce the vision of the book by illustrating companies and management situations that students can identify with.

This first edition of *Understanding Management* brings the working world of management to the student, including emerging management trends, through the following features:

- Each chapter begins with a real-life problem faced by an organization manager. A Management Solution ends each chapter with an examination of how managers have used chapter concepts to solve a problem.

- All chapters have been written with emphasis on entrepreneurship.

- An emphasis on supervisory decision making is thoroughly integrated within the text.

- Line and midlevel managers' planning process and MIS needs are given complete, focused coverage.

■ Substantial material on diversity, international issues, total quality management, and the history of management gives the student a solid background for further study.

ORGANIZATION

The chapter sequence in *Understanding Management* is organized around the management functions of planning, organizing, leading, and controlling. These four functions effectively encompass both management research and characteristics of the manager's job.

Part I introduces the world of management, including the nature of the manager's job, historical perspectives on management, and the influence of the environment on organizations and management. Chapter 3, "Managing in a Global Environment," provides students with a fundamental understanding of issues relevant to the remaining chapters.

Part II presents three chapters on planning. The first chapter describes ethics and corporate responsibility, which play increasingly important roles in today's complex business environment. Subsequent chapters describe organizational goal setting, planning and implementation, and the decision-making process, including the use of information systems in decision making.

Part III focuses on organizing processes. These chapters describe the fundamentals of organizing, structural designs for promoting innovation and change, and the design and use of the human resource function. Chapter 11 is devoted to the significant organizing function of managing diverse employees.

Part IV concentrates on leadership. The section begins with a description of leadership and paves the way for the subsequent topics of employee motivation, communication, and management of teams.

Part V describes the controlling functions of management, including quality control and productivity, the design of control systems, and service management.

The appendixes include supplementary material on career management and management science aids for decision making. Appendix A, "Career Management," describes both individual and organizational strategies for managing careers, and it includes a substantial section on managing individual stress and burnout. Appendix B, "Management Science Aids for Planning and Decision Making," contains the quantitative material that many instructors use to expand on the more qualitative decision approaches described in Chapter 7. The quantitative approaches of linear programming, break-even analysis, forecasting, PERT charting, and decision tree analysis are all covered in Appendix B.

SPECIAL FEATURES

One major goal of this book is to offer better ways of using the textbook medium to convey management knowledge to the reader. To this end, the book includes several special features.

CHAPTER OUTLINE AND OBJECTIVES.   Each chapter begins with a clear statement of learning objectives and an outline of its contents. These devices provide an overview of what is to come and can also be used by students to see whether they understand and have retained important points.

MANAGEMENT PROBLEM/SOLUTION.   Each chapter begins with a real-life problem faced by organization managers. The problem pertains to the topic of the chapter and will heighten students' interest in chapter concepts. The problem is resolved at the end of the chapter, where chapter concepts guiding the management's actions are highlighted.

CONTEMPORARY EXAMPLES.   Every chapter of the textbook contains a number of examples of management situations. These are placed at strategic points in the chapter and are designed to demonstrate the application of concepts to specific companies. The examples include well-known companies as well as lesser-known companies and not-for-profit organizations. They put students in immediate touch with the real world of organizations so that they can appreciate the value of management concepts.

LEADING EDGE.   This boxed feature explores how leading companies, when faced with new challenges, use innovative ideas to compete in both the domestic and global marketplaces.

MANAGER'S SHOPTALK.   These boxed items contain issues of special interest to management students. They may describe a contemporary topic or problem relevant to chapter content, or they may contain a diagnostic questionnaire or special example of how managers handle a problem. These boxes will heighten student interest in the subject matter and provide an auxiliary view of management issues not typically available in textbooks.

FOCUS BOXES.   These boxed items pertain to topics such as ethics and not-for-profit organizations. Their purpose is to help students integrate these topics with other concepts in the book. Too often such topics are presented in chapters unconnected to other materials. Yet concepts in almost every chapter have implications for ethics, not-for-profit organizations, and smaller companies. The focus boxes are referenced in the chapter to help students understand the relevance of the chapter material for these important management topics.

GLOSSARIES.   Learning the management vocabulary is essential to understanding contemporary management. This process is facilitated in three ways. First, key concepts are boldfaced and completely defined where they first appear in the text. Second, brief definitions are set out in the margin for easy review and follow-up. Third, a glossary summarizing all key terms and definitions appears at the end of the book for handy reference.

EXHIBITS.   Many aspects of management are research based, and some concepts are abstract and theoretical. To enhance students' awareness and understanding of these concepts, many exhibits are included throughout the book. These exhibits consolidate key points, indicate relationships among variables, and illustrate concepts visually. They also make effective use of color to enhance their imagery and appeal.

MANAGEMENT IN PRACTICE EXERCISES. End-of-chapter exercises called either "Management in Practice: Experiential Exercise" or "Management in Practice: Ethical Dilemma" provide a self-test for students and an opportunity to experience management issues in a personal way. Many exercises also provide an opportunity for students to work in teams.

CHAPTER SUMMARY AND DISCUSSION QUESTIONS. Each chapter closes with a summary of key points that students should retain. The discussion questions are a complementary learning tool that will enable students to check their understanding of key issues, think beyond basic concepts, and determine areas that require further study. The summary and discussion questions help students discriminate between main and supporting points and provide mechanisms for self-teaching.

CASES FOR ANALYSIS. One brief but substantive end-of-chapter case provides an opportunity for student analysis and class discussion. These cases provide an opportunity for students to apply concepts to real events and to sharpen their diagnostic skills for management problem solving.

SUPPLEMENTARY MATERIALS

Many instructors face large classes with limited resources, and supplementary materials provide a way to expand and improve the students' learning experience. The learning package provided with *Understanding Management* was specifically designed to meet the needs of instructors facing a variety of teaching conditions and to enhance management students' experience of the subject.

INSTRUCTOR'S MANUAL
The Instructor's Manual has been prepared to provide fundamental support to new professors teaching the course and innovative new material for experienced professors. Prepared by Bonnie Chavez of Santa Barbara City College and Tom Shaughnessy of Illinois Central Community College, the manual features detailed lecture outlines with examples and information for integrating into the text. Additional support includes annotated learning objectives, answers to chapter discussion questions, case discussion suggestions, and video teaching notes. "Unique Perspectives" discuss current news articles for further study and reference.

TEST BANK
The test bank, written by William Vincent of Santa Barbara City College and David Murphy of Madisonville Community College, contains more than 1,000 all-new multiple-choice and true/false questions with more essay, matching, and minicase questions for additional support. Each

question has been rated by difficulty level and is designated as either factual or application so that instructors can provide a balanced set of questions in student exams.

COMPUTERIZED TEST BANKS AND REQUESTEST

The test bank is available in computerized form for both DOS and Macintosh systems and is free to adopters. The computerized test bank allows instructors to select and edit test items from the printed test banks as well as add an unlimited number of their own questions. As many as 99 versions of each test can be custom printed. Adopters can also request customized tests with Dryden's special service, RequesTest. When a requester calls the toll-free number, 1-800-447-9457, Dryden will compile test questions according to a requester's criteria, then either mail or fax the test master to the user within 48 hours.

TRANSPARENCY ACETATES AND MASTERS

About 60 four-color transparency acetates and more than 75 transparency masters from text art are available to adopters. Masters and acetates are accompanied by detailed teaching notes that include summaries of key concepts and discussion questions for in-class use.

STUDY GUIDE

This guide is invaluable for helping students master management concepts. Prepared by Hal Babson and Murray Brunton of Columbus State Community College, the study guide provides a summary of major concepts, exercises, and questions for key terms and concepts for a traditional review of chapter material. This is followed by situation analysis, "just-suppose" scenarios, personal learning experiences, and journal entry suggestions to allow for more critical thinking and writing practice. An integrated case with critical analysis questions continues throughout the guide and could be used as homework or in class.

COMPUTER SIMULATIONS

Io Enterprises, created by Chad Lewis et al., is a computer-assisted classroom activity that emphasizes basic organizational and management concepts and applications. In-class simulations offer students challenging opportunities to practice people skills such as dealing with staff problems and building teams. *Chopsticks Company*, a simulation written by Eugene Calvasina of Auburn University at Montgomery, places students in the manager's role and requires them to make decisions about key areas of the business. This is an interactive simulation designed to offer students the opportunity to learn how decisions affect an organization.

SUPPLEMENTAL MODULES

Supplemental written modules in the areas of natural environment, diversity, quality, and working as a team are available to augment text coverage and to address the needs of schools whose management principles courses emphasize any of these areas. The natural environment module is accompanied by a video program featuring various business responses to a concern for the environment.

EXPERIENTIAL EXERCISES AND CASES

Two separate supplements are available for those instructors looking for additional experiential exercises or cases to use in the classroom. *Management: A Case Approach* and *Management: An Experiential Approach* are both authored by Lawrence R. Jauch and Sally A. Coltrin, and each is supported by an instructor's manual.

MANAGEMENT SKILLS SOFTWARE

This excellent student software by Eric Sandburg provides students with interactive exercises coordinated with each part of the book. It includes modules on such topics as decision making, leadership, delegation, ethics, diversity, sexual harassment, budgeting, entrepreneurship, and career planning. After completing one or more questionnaires or activities, students can use the software program to help measure their current level of awareness and capabilities and then obtain personalized advice for improving various options and skills.

MANAGEMENT QUARTERLY REPORT

Adopters may subscribe to a quarterly video series from The Dryden Press. The video series will include recent news from the world of business. These quarterly segments may be used in the classroom to provide current examples of management principles at work.

LASER DISC

The Dryden Press Management laser disc includes graphic and textual elements from the textbook and support materials integrated with video and animation sequences to provide a dynamic, easy-to-use multimedia presentation of management principles.

● ACKNOWLEDGMENTS

It was gratifying to work with the Fort Worth team of dedicated professionals at The Dryden Press, who were committed to the vision of producing the best management textbook ever. I am grateful to Ruth Rominger for her creative ideas, assistance, and vision for this text. Lisé Johnson provided keen market knowledge and innovative ideas for instructional support. Traci Keller helped the manuscript process flow smoothly and made sure all the pieces fit. Linda Miller created a rich and elegant book design. Michael Ferreira provided the right touch of copyediting. Kelly Cordes coordinated the production team. Cheryl Hauser and Jon Gregory provided superb project coordination and made excellent suggestions to overcome obstacles and keep the project moving on schedule. These people brought enormous caring and commitment to this textbook, and I am deeply grateful to each of them.

Here at Vanderbilt I want to extend special appreciation to Rita Carswell. Rita helped me make the transition to Vanderbilt, and we have worked together almost five years. I also want to acknowledge an intellectual debt to my colleagues, Bruce Barry, Tom Mahoney, Rich Oliver and Greg Stewart. Thanks also to Dean Marty Geisel, who supported this project and maintained a positive scholarly atmosphere here at the Owen School.

Another group of people who made a major contribution to this textbook were the management experts who provided advice, reviews, answers to surveys, and suggestions for changes, insertions, and clarifications. They participated in a focus group in which many of the ideas that shape this textbook were first discussed and fine-tuned. I consider them my advisory panel and deeply appreciate their commitment to excellence.

Judy Bulin
Monroe Community College

Barry Burns
Houston Community College

Bonnie Chavez
Santa Barbara City College

Phyllis Goodman
College of DuPage

Rudy Stippec
Tarrant County Junior College—South Campus

Understanding Management also benefited from the valuable input of management instructors throughout the country. I would especially like to thank those who responded to our questions about how they teach management and who reviewed various parts of the manuscript:

Hal Babson
Columbus State Community College
Barbara Barrett
Merrimac Community College
Kathy Daruty
Pierce College
Helen Davis
University of Kentucky
Joe Galdiano
Normandale Community College
Jenna Johannpeter
Belleville Area College—Granite City Campus
Betty Ann Kirk
Tallahassee Community College
Chad Lewis
Everett Community College
Tom Shaughnessy
Illinois Central Community College
Darrell Thompson
Mountainview College
Bill Vincent
Santa Barbara City College
James H. White
North Lake College

I would like to extend personal thanks to the many dedicated authors
who contributed to the extensive supplement package for the textbook.
Bill Vincent and David Murphy have written a wonderful test bank. Bonnie Chavez and Tom Shaughnessy have made the instructor's manual a
valuable tool with critical teaching features. Hal Babson and Murray
Brunton worked to add value to the Study Guide and make it crucial to
full success in the course. Eric Sandburg has added tremendous career
assessment opportunities for students with his Management Software

I also want to acknowledge my daughters, Danielle and Amy, and
their husbands, Brian and Gary, for their love and support. We have
developed a wonderful understanding and appreciation for one another,
reached in part through the joy of skiing together in Santa Fe. Thanks
also to B.J. and Kaitlyn for their warmth, silliness and laughter that
brightens my life during our days together.

Finally, I'd like to pay tribute to my assistants DeeGee Lester, Sean
Lanham, and Carol Cirulli, who put enormous energy into this textbook.
DeeGee brought her innate enthusiasm and sense of humor, along with
a professor's eye and a student's ear, to the project. She provided major
assistance with the copyedited manuscript and galley proofs. Carol and
Sean dug out cases and provided many ideas and suggestions for materials that would illustrate concepts in smaller business settings. DeeGee,
Carol, and Sean were a wonderful team, and the textbook would not
have achieved its excellence without them.

RICHARD L. DAFT
Nashville, Tennessee
August 1994

THE DRYDEN PRESS SERIES IN MANAGEMENT

Anthony, Perrewe, and Kacmar
Strategic Human Resource Management

Bartlett
Cases in Strategic Management for Business

Bedeian
Management
Third Edition

Bedeian and Zammuto
Organizations: Theory and Design

Bereman and Lengnick-Hall, Mark
Compensation Decision Making: A Computer-Based Approach

Bracker, Montanari, and Morgan
Cases in Strategic Management

Calvasina and Barton
Chopstick Company: A Business Simulation

Costin
Readings in Total Quality Management

Czinkota, Ronkainen, and Moffett
International Business
Third Edition

Czinkota, Ronkainen, Moffett, and Moynihan
Global Business

Daft
Management
Third Edition

Daft
Understanding Management

Dessler
Managing Organizations in an Era of Change

Eckert, Ryan, and Ray
Small Business: An Entrepreneur's Plan
Third Edition

Etienne-Hamilton
Operations Strategies for Competitive Advantage: Text and Cases

Finch and Luebbe
Operations Management: Competing in a Changing Environment

Foegen
Business Plan Guidebook
Revised Edition

Gaither
Production and Operations Management
Sixth Edition

Gatewood and Feild
Human Resource Selection
Third Edition

Gold
Exploring Organizational Behavior: Cases, Readings, and Experiences

Greenhaus
Career Management
Second Edition

Harris and DeSimone
Human Resource Development

Higgins and Vincze
Strategic Management: Text and Cases
Fifth Edition

Hills, Bergmann, and Scarpello
Compensation Decision Making
Second Edition

Hodgetts
Management: Theory, Process, and Practice

Hodgetts
Modern Human Relations at Work
Fifth Edition

Hodgetts and Kroeck
Personnel and Human Resource Management

Hodgetts and Kuratko
Effective Small Business Management
Fourth Edition

Holley and Jennings
The Labor Relations Process
Fifth Edition

Jauch and Coltrin
The Managerial Experience: Cases and Exercises
Sixth Edition

Kemper
Experiencing Strategic Management

Kindler and Ginsburg
Transformational Change in Organizations

Kirkpatrick and Lewis
Effective Supervision: Preparing for the 21st Century

Kuehl and Lambing
Small Business: Planning and Management
Third Edition

Kuratko and Hodgetts
Entrepreneurship: A Contemporary Approach
Third Edition

Kuratko and Welsch
Entrepreneurial Strategy: Text and Cases

Lee
Introduction to Management Science
Second Edition

Lengnick-Hall, Cynthia, and Hartman
Experiencing Quality

Lewis
Io Enterprises Simulation

Long and Arnold
The Power of Environmental Partnerships

McMullen and Long
Developing New Ventures: The Entrepreneurial Option

Matsuura
International Business: A New Era

Montanari, Morgan, and Bracker
Strategic Management: A Choice Approach

Morgan
Managing for Success

Northcraft and Neale
Organizational Behavior: A Management Challenge
Second Edition

Penderghast
Entrepreneurial Simulation Program

Sandburg
Career Design Software

Shipley and Ruthstrom
Cases in Operations Management

Sower, Motwani, and Savoie
Classic Readings in Operations Management

Van Matre
Foundations of TQM: A Readings Book

Vecchio
Organizational Behavior
Third Edition

Walton
Corporate Encounters: Law, Ethics, and the Business Environment

Zikmund
Business Research Methods
Fourth Edition

THE HARCOURT BRACE COLLEGE OUTLINE SERIES

Pentico
Management Science

Pierson
Introduction to Business Information Systems

Sigband
Business Communication

● ABOUT THE AUTHOR

Richard L. Daft, Ph.D., holds the Ralph Owen Chair in Management at Vanderbilt University, where he specializes in the study of organization theory and management. Dr. Daft is a Fellow of the Academy of Management and has served on the editorial boards of *Academy of Management Journal*, *Administrative Science Quarterly*, and *Journal of Management Education*. He is the associate editor-in-chief of *Organization Science* and served for three years as associate editor of *Administrative Science Quarterly*.

Professor Daft has authored or coauthored six books, including *Organization Theory and Design* (West Publishing, 1992) and *What to Study: Generating and Developing Research Questions* (Sage, 1982). He has also authored dozens of scholarly articles, papers, and chapters. His work has been published in *Administrative Science Quarterly*, *Academy of Management Journal*, *Academy of Management Review*, *Strategic Management Journal*, *Journal of Management*, *Accounting Organizations and Society*, *Management Science*, *MIS Quarterly*, *California Management Review*, and *Organizational Behavior Teaching Review*. Professor Daft has been awarded several government research grants to pursue studies of organization design, organizational innovation and change, strategy implementation, and organizational information processing.

Dr. Daft also is an active teacher and consultant. He has taught management, organizational change, organizational behavior, organizational theory, and leadership. He has been actively involved in management development and consulting for many companies and government organizations, including the American Banking Association, Bell Canada, NL Baroid, Tenneco, and the United States Air Force.

BRIEF CONTENTS

CONTENTS

PART I
INTRODUCTION TO
MANAGEMENT   2

● CHAPTER 7
MANAGERIAL DECISION MAKING   198

PART III
ORGANIZING   234

● CHAPTER 8
STRUCTURAL AND FUNDAMENTALS OF ORGANIZING   236

● **CHAPTER 18**
  OPERATIONS AND SERVICE MANAGEMENT   560

UNDERSTANDING

MANAGEMENT

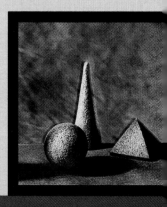

PHOTO PROVIDED COURTESY OF IDS FINANCIAL SERVICES, INC.

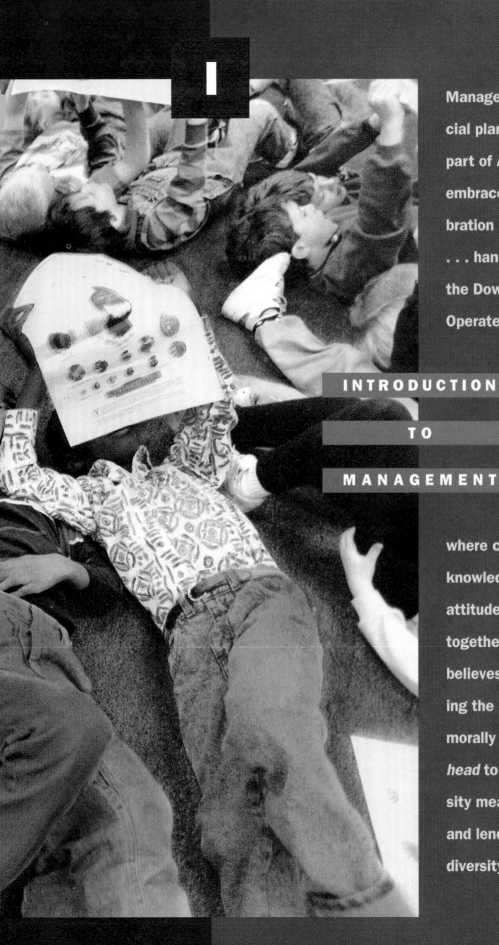

INTRODUCTION

TO

MANAGEMENT

Management at IDS, a financial planning company and part of American Express, embraces diversity as a celebration of "hearts . . . heads . . . hands." IDS cosponsors the Downtown Open School. Operated by Minneapolis Public Schools, this child-centered, bilingual (English and Spanish) school offers free classes where children acquire the knowledge, skills, and positive attitudes to solve problems together. IDS management believes "Diversity means having the *heart* to do what's morally correct . . . using your *head* to recognize that diversity means good business . . . and lending a *hand* to make diversity happen."

THE NATURE OF MANAGEMENT

1

CHAPTER OUTLINE

LEARNING OBJECTIVES

After studying this chapter, you should be able to

- Define management and give examples of successful managers.

- Describe the four management functions and the type of management activity associated with each.

- Explain the difference between efficiency and effectiveness and their importance for organizational performance.

- Describe differences in management functions by hierarchical level.

- Define functional, general, and project managers.

- Describe conceptual, human, and technical skills and their relevance for managers and nonmanagers.

- Define ten roles that managers perform in organizations.

- Describe characteristics of managerial success and the issues managers must prepare for in the future.

When Rudy Cedillo was named manager of the Luby's cafeteria on the north side of downtown San Antonio, he had his work cut out for him. As the manager of one of the largest and busiest outlets in the chain, his responsibilities would include selecting the menu, ordering food supplies from local wholesalers, and taking all the necessary steps to ensure that a hefty percentage of sales ended up on the company's bottom line. The hours were likely to be backbreaking, with work days starting as early as 7 AM and sometimes not ending until 9:30 PM. ∎ Since Luby's does not pay its managers a base salary, Cedillo's income would depend exclusively on profit-sharing. This incentive would be all he needed to make sure his managerial skills were at their best. In order for Cedillo to do well, he would have to make sure customers were satisfied, employees were productive, and the food quality and service were unsurpassed. What management techniques could Cedillo use to succeed in his new job? If you were offered the same position, would you accept?[1]

Few students have heard of Rudy Cedillo. Most are unfamiliar with the management actions needed to sustain a division with a reputation as thriving, inspired, and productive. The management problem at Luby's represents a situation that is repeated daily for managers in hundreds of organizations. Successful departments and successful organizations do not just happen—they are managed to be that way. Every organization has problems and challenges, and every organization needs skilled management.

Managers like Rudy Cedillo have the opportunity to make a difference. Lee Iacocca made a difference at Chrysler Corporation when he rescued it from bankruptcy by reducing internal costs, developing new products, and gaining concessions from lenders, the union, and the government. Iacocca transformed Chrysler again by implementing a strategy for developing a new generation of LH cars, which appeared beginning in 1993.[2] General William Creech made a difference to the huge Tactical Air Command of the U.S. Air Force when he reversed a sortie rate (number of flights flown with tactical aircraft) that had been declining 7.8 percent every year. Within a year of Creech's appointment, the sortie rate increased 11.2 percent and continued to rise at that rate for five years without additional people or resources. Kelly Johnson made a difference to an

CEO Linda Wachner's management style has helped make Warnaco, a once-quiet apparel maker, into a Fortune 500 company. Wachner's "Do It Now!" philosophy permeates the entire company. Even Wachner herself can be found from the stitchroom to the showroom, giving Warnaco a competitive edge in the traditionally tough apparel markets.

ailing satellite program at Lockheed. Launch effectiveness had been running 12.5 percent, was way behind schedule and over budget, and, as Johnson discovered, one subcontractor was using an astronomical 1,271 inspectors. Within a year, Johnson had the program back on schedule, improved launch effectiveness to 98 percent, and reduced the number of inspectors to 35.[3] On the international level, Nobuhiko Kawamoto, the new president of Honda, made a difference by shaking up the legendary Honda organization. His drastic reorganization included a move away from the traditional Japanese decision making by consensus. Early results indicate that his changes have provided significant gains in efficiency via improved communications and speedier decision making throughout the company's 38-country manufacturing empire.[4]

These managers are not unusual. Every day managers solve difficult problems, turn organizations around, and achieve astonishing performances. Every organization needs skilled managers to be successful. However, managers can make a difference in a negative direction too. Poor judgment, personal vanity, or greed can cause corporate disaster. For example, Harding Lawrence of Braniff Airlines was responsible for a misguided strategy of rapid national and international expansion. In addition, his domineering, bullying behavior alienated executives and employees. His influence launched Braniff on a flight path to bankruptcy.[5] Robert Fomon gained absolute power at E. F. Hutton. Acting like a feudal lord, he banished traditional organization structure, budgets, and planning, thereby initiating the lingering death of an old-line brokerage firm.[6] In another case, Robert Schoellhorn guided Abbott Laboratories to unprecedented profits, and then became obsessed with rewarding himself for company success. He accumulated money and hefty perks, including pricey "his-and-her" corporate jets used only by Schoellhorn and his wife. His self-serving behavior had sufficient negative impact that the board of directors had to let him go.[7]

This book introduces and explains the process of management with an emphasis on mid-level management and small-business management. By analyzing examples of successful and not-so-successful managers and reviewing studies of management techniques and styles, you will learn the fundamentals of management. The problems Cedillo faces with Luby's are not unusual for middle managers. By the end of this chapter, you will already understand the approach Cedillo must take to keep his division on track. By the end of this book, you will understand fundamental management skills for planning, organization, leading, and controlling a department or an entire organization. In the remainder of this chapter, we will define management and look at the roles and activities of managers in today's organizations.

● THE DEFINITION OF MANAGEMENT

What do managers like Lee Iacocca, General Creech, and Rudy Cedillo have in common? They get things done through their organizations. One management scholar, Mary Parker Follett, described management as "the art of getting things done through people."[8]

Peter Drucker, a noted management theorist, explains that managers give direction to their organizations, provide leadership, and decide how to use organizational resources to accomplish goals.[9] Getting things done through people and other resources and providing direction and leadership are what managers do. These activities apply not only to top executives such as Lee Iacocca or General Creech, but also to a new lieutenant in charge of a TAC maintenance squadron, a supervisor in the Ontario plant that makes Plymouth minivans, and Rudy Cedillo as new manager at Luby's. Moreover, management often is considered universal because it uses organizational resources to accomplish goals and attain high performance in all types of profit and not-for-profit organizations. Thus, our definition of management is as follows:

> **Management** is the attainment of organizational goals in an effective and efficient manner through planning, organizing, leading, and controlling organizational resources.

Two ideas are important in this definition: (1) the four functions of planning, organizing, leading, and controlling; and (2) the attainment of organizational goals in an effective and efficient manner. The management process of using resources to attain goals is illustrated in Exhibit 1.1. Although some management theorists identify additional management functions, such as staffing, communicating, or decision making, those additional functions will be discussed as subsets of the four primary functions in Exhibit 1.1. Chapters of this book are devoted to the multiple activities and skills associated with each function, as well as to the environment, global competitiveness, and ethics which influence how managers perform these functions. The next section begins with a brief overview of the four functions.

management

The attainment of organizational goals in an effective and efficient manner through planning, organizing, leading, and controlling organizational resources.

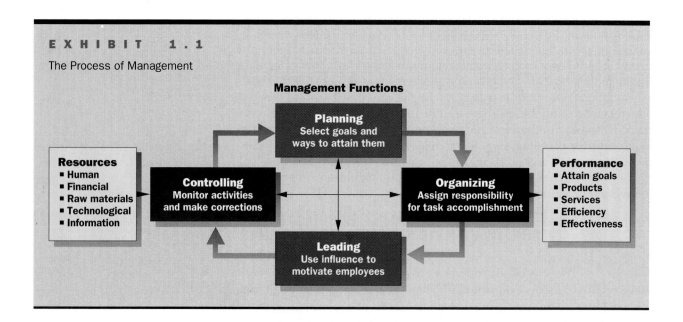

E X H I B I T   1 . 1

The Process of Management

● THE FOUR MANAGEMENT FUNCTIONS

PLANNING

Planning defines where the organization wants to be in the future and how it will get there. **Planning** means defining goals for future organizational performance and deciding on the tasks and resources needed to attain them. Senior managers at Chase Manhattan Bank decided to make it the number one service-quality bank in the world and, through extensive planning, to develop a worldwide network of branch banks, to implement a sophisticated foreign exchange system, and to offer a state-of-the art electronic funds transfer system. General Creech successfully turned around the Tactical Air Command because he had a specific plan including targets for improved sortie rates and techniques for achieving these new rates.

A lack of planning—or poor planning—can hurt an organization's performance. For example, the market share of Ashton-Tate Corporation, a PC software giant ranked in the big three of the industry, tumbled sharply as a consequence of planning errors attributed to chief executive Edward Esber, Jr. Critics cite the combination of Esber's lack of vision in perceiving market direction, a weak planning effort that left too many bugs in the *dBASEV* software introduction, and failed efforts to develop other software products. Planning is a major reason for the sharp decline in Ashton-Tate's market share and revenue growth rate, producing the company's first net loss of $30 million.[10]

Poor planning is also a major factor in many small business failures. Even those businesses which undergo rapid early growth often succumb to poor growth planning or inadequate financial planning. Two out of every three new business start-ups fail within the first five years which reflects the need for a strong, ongoing program of planning beyond developing the initial business plan.

planning
The management function concerned with defining goals for future organizational performance and deciding on the tasks and resource use needed to attain them.

ORGANIZING

Organizing typically follows planning and reflects how the organization tries to accomplish the plan. **Organizing** involves assigning tasks, grouping tasks into departments, and allocating resources to departments. For example, large companies such as Sears and Xerox have undergone structural reorganizations to accommodate their changing plans. General Creech accomplished his plan for TAC's improved sortie rate mainly through decentralization and the development of small, independent maintenance units—a drastic departure from the traditional structure which had encouraged centralization and consolidation of Air Force resources. Kelly Johnson used organizing wizardry at Lockheed to reduce the number of subcontractor inspectors from 1,271 to 35 while still achieving the objective of improved launch effectiveness. Indeed, his organizing was so good that the Air Force insisted that a competitor be allowed to

organizing
The management function concerned with assigning tasks, grouping tasks into departments, and allocating resources to departments.

visit Johnson's team. The competitor used 3,750 people to perform a similar task and was years behind and way over budget. Johnson's organization was on schedule and under budget—and with only 126 people.[11] Honeywell managers reorganized new product development into "tiger teams" consisting of marketing, engineering, and design employees. The new structural design reduced the time to produce a new thermostat from 4 years to 12 months.[12] Many companies today are following Honeywell's lead by using teams that have more responsibility for self-management. Reorganizing into teams is a major trend in North America.

Likewise, weak organizing facilitated the destruction of Braniff Airlines under Harding Lawrence. Braniff did not have enough departments and offices to handle passengers and airplanes for the new national and international routes Lawrence grabbed during deregulation of the airline industry. Braniff needed an enormous amount of money to set up a structure to fit its strategy. Even before its expansion Braniff lacked a strong internal structure with clearly defined roles for accomplishing tasks. The structure produced a group of "yes men" who deferred to Lawrence's every decision.[13]

LEADING

leading

The management function that involves the use of influence to motivate employees to achieve the organization's goals.

The third management function is to provide leadership for employees. **Leading** is the use of influence to motivate employees to achieve organizational goals. Leading means communicating goals to employees

David L. Dworkin, CEO of the Broadway department store chain, has directed a face-lift of the once-dowdy stores and is engendering a casual and creative corporate culture by relaxing the dress code.

At Compaq Computer Corporation, manufacturing managers Doug Johns and Greg Petsch arranged a rousing parade throughout the plant, complete with bagpipe band and signs of personal thanks for a job well done. By acknowledging employee efforts, these managers lead employees to go beyond the norm.

throughout the organization and infusing them with the desire to perform at a high level. Leading involves motivating entire departments and divisions as well as those individuals working immediately with the manager.

Managers such as Lee Iacocca are exceptional leaders. They are able to communicate their vision throughout the organization and energize employees into action. General Creech was a leader when he improved the motivation of aircraft maintenance technicians in hundreds of maintenance squadrons. The maintenance technicians previously had been neglected in favor of pilots. To improve motivation, Creech set up highly visible bulletin boards displaying pictures of the maintenance crew chiefs, improved their living quarters, and established decent maintenance facilities, complete with paintings and wall murals. He introduced competition among the newly independent maintenance squadrons and created trophy rooms to hold the plaques and other prizes won in maintenance competitions. This prominent display of concern for maintenance specialists greatly increased their motivation to keep the planes flying.

When current Maryland Governor William Donald Schaefer was mayor of Baltimore, he saw a city of dirty parks, housing violations, abandoned cars, dead trees, and uncollected trash. Schaefer involved citizens in a local ownership program that helped to pay for and maintain city services. More importantly, he motivated city workers to clean up the mess through a number of techniques including action memos that were blunt and direct: "Get the trash off East Lombard Street," "Broken pavement at 1700 Carey," "Abandoned car at 2900 Remington." One action memo said, "There is an abandoned car . . . but I'm not telling you where it is." City crews ran around for a week and towed several hundred cars.[14]

Leadership can have a negative side, too as exemplified by Harding Lawrence. His leadership of Braniff was said to contribute to employees' *demotivation*. Lawrence won notoriety on Braniff's Flight 6, which he took weekly to visit his wife, who worked in New York City:

> His tantrums on Flight 6 are legend. On one flight a stewardess served him an entire selection of condiments with his meal instead of asking him which one he preferred. He slammed his fist into the plate, splattering food on the surrounding seats of the first-class cabin. "Don't you ever assume what I want!" he screamed.
>
> "On several occasions flight attendants came to me in tears, fearful of losing their jobs," says Ed Clements, former director of flight attendant services at Braniff. "I was sickened by what he was doing to the employees."
>
> Lawrence's appearance on an aircraft was likely to arouse two emotions in the crew: fear and hatred.[15]

Inevitably, dissatisfied employees led to dissatisfied customers. Marketing surveys indicated that Braniff was unpopular with many of its passengers. Without a loyal customer base, successful expansion and high performance proved impossible.[16]

CONTROLLING

controlling

The management function concerned with monitoring employees' activities, keeping the organization on track toward its goals, and making corrections as needed.

Controlling is the fourth function in the management process. **Controlling** means monitoring employees' activities, determining whether the organization is on target toward its goals, and making corrections as necessary. Managers must ensure that the organization is moving toward its goals. Controlling often involves using an information system to advise managers on performance and a reward system for recognizing employees who make progress toward goals. For example, Domino's Pizza Distribution Company measures over 1,200 franchises weekly. A phone survey of customers determines the quality of service at each franchise which is reported to management. Compensation for all employees is based on the results. Expected performance levels are reviewed every six months and set slightly higher for the next six months. The control system then monitors whether employees achieve the higher targets.

One reason for organization failure is that managers either are not serious about control or lack control information. Robert Fomon, a longtime autocratic chief executive of E. F. Hutton, refused to set up control systems because he wanted to supervise senior management personally. At one time he reviewed the salaries and bonuses of more than 1,000 employees, but Hutton grew too big for his personal supervision. To achieve profit goals managers got involved in an undetected check-kiting scheme, and the firm pleaded guilty to 2,000 counts of mail and wire fraud. Other undetected behaviors included $900,000 in travel and entertainment expenses for one executive in one year and the listing of women from escort services as temporary secretarial help. This lack of control led to Fomon's demise. E. F. Hutton never fully recovered.[17]

⬤ ORGANIZATIONAL PERFORMANCE

The other part of our definition of management is the attainment of organizational goals in an efficient and effective manner. One reason management is so important is that organizations are so important. In an industrialized society where complex technologies dominate, organizations bring together knowledge, people, and raw materials to perform tasks that one individual could not do alone. Without organizations, how could 17,000 airline flights a day be accomplished without an accident, electricity produced from large dams or nuclear power generators, millions of automobiles manufactured, or hundreds of films, videos, and records made available for our entertainment? Organizations pervade our society. Most college students will work in an organization—perhaps Columbia/HCA Health Care Corporation, Dillard's Department Stores, or UPS. College students already are members of organizations, such as a university, junior college, YMCA, church, fraternity, or sorority. College students also deal with organizations every day: to renew a driver's license, to be treated in a hospital emergency room, buy food from a supermarket, to eat in a restaurant, or to buy new clothes. Managers are responsible for these organizations and for seeing that resources are used wisely to attain organizational goals.

Our formal definition of an **organization** is a social entity that is goal directed and deliberately structured. *Social entity* means being made up of two or more people. *Goal directed* means designed to achieve some outcome, such as make a profit (Boeing, Mack Trucks), win pay increases for members (AFL-CIO), meet spiritual needs (Methodist church), or provide social satisfaction (college sorority). *Deliberately structured* means that tasks are divided and responsibility for their performance assigned to organization members. This definition applies to both profit and not-for-profit organizations. Vickery Stoughton runs Toronto General Hospital and manages a $200 million budget. He endures intense public scrutiny, heavy government regulation, and daily crises of life and death. Hamilton Jordan, formerly President Carter's chief of staff, created a new organization called the Association of Tennis Professionals to take control of the professional tennis circuit. John and Marie Bouchard launched a small business called Wild Things that sells goods for outdoor activities. Small, offbeat, and not-for-profit organizations are more numerous than large, visible corporations—and just as important to society.

Based on our definition of management, the manager's responsibility is to coordinate resources in an effective and efficient manner to accomplish the organization's goals. Organizational **effectiveness** is the degree to which the organization achieves a stated objective. It means that the organization succeeds in accomplishing what it tries to do. Organizational effectiveness means providing a product or service that customers value.

organization

A social entity that is goal directed and deliberately structured.

effectiveness

The degree to which the organization achieves a stated objective.

efficiency

The use of minimal resources—raw materials, money, and people—to produce a desired volume of output.

Organizational **efficiency** refers to the amount of resources used to achieve an organizational goal. It is based on how much raw materials, money, and people are necessary for producing a given volume of output. Efficiency can be calculated as the amount of resources used to produce a product or service.

Efficiency and effectiveness can both be high in the same organization. Consider the impact of Dick Dauch, vice-president of manufacturing at Chrysler. His leadership allowed a startling increase in efficiency. Chrysler now can build 8,000 cars and trucks per day compared with only 4,500 a few years ago. The number of worker-hours per vehicle has shrunk from 175 to 102. Resources are used more efficiently: Worker absenteeism is down sharply. New technology has transformed the assembly line.[18] Likewise, management efforts at Stanley Works, the 140-year-old toolmaker, to increase automation and employee training and to establish quality circles and decision-making worker teams led to a scrap rate reduction from 15 percent to 3 percent.[19] In addition to increasing efficiency, managers at Chrysler and Stanley Works improved effectiveness as reflected in product quality, revenues, and profits.

Managers in other organizations, especially service firms, are improving efficiency, too. Labor shortages in the Midwest and northeastern United States have prompted managers to find labor-saving tricks. Burger King and Taco Bell restaurants let customers serve themselves drinks. Sleep Inn hotels have a washer and dryer installed behind the desk so that clerks can launder sheets and towels while waiting on customers.[20] McDonald's is experimenting with a grill that cooks hamburgers on both sides at once to improve efficiency, and to improve effectiveness with respect to the environment, it is experimenting with new food waste controls, decomposable packaging, and expanded recycling.[21]

performance

The organization's ability to attain its goals by using resources in an efficient and effective manner.

The ultimate responsibility of managers, then, is to achieve high **performance**, which is the attainment of organizational goals by using resources in an efficient and effective manner. Two examples of extraordinary management performance in the entertainment industry—Garth Brooks and the Grateful Dead—are described in the Leading Edge box. Whether managers are responsible for the organization as a whole (as with Garth Brooks or the Grateful Dead), or for a single department or division (as with Rudy Cedillo at Luby's), their ultimate responsibility is performance. Harold Geneen, a legendary manager who transformed ITT into one of the world's largest and best-run corporations, explained it this way:

> I think it is an immutable law in business that words are words, explanations are explanations, promises are promises—but only performance is reality. Performance alone is the best measure of your confidence, competence, and courage. Only performance gives you the freedom to grow as yourself.
>
> Just remember that: *performance is your reality*. Forget everything else. That is why my definition of a manager is what it is: one who turns in the performance. No alibis to others or to one's self will change that. And when you have performed well, the world will remember it, when everything else is forgotten. And most importantly, so will you.[22]

GARTH BROOKS AND THE GRATEFUL DEAD

LEADING edge

Garth Brooks and the Grateful Dead represent astonishing success stories during a recessionary period when record companies are not promoting new recordings, and stars such as Elton John and Hammer have reduced or cut their tours. Garth Brooks sits atop both country and pop charts with sales of 20 million albums, and the Grateful Dead is once again "Knocking on Heaven's Door," in the number-one position as touring's most popular act after nearly three decades of performances. These two organizations achieve startling efficiency and effectiveness.

Why so much success? One answer is management skills. Garth Brooks has been working on a master's degree in business and believes in human skills, employing a variation of MBWA (management by walking around). Brooks does in-store appearances to learn what customers want. He also has a knack for building support among employees. According to comanager Pam Lewis, "Garth was willing to go to the warehouses. He understands the importance of the people who are loading the trucks, the people shrink-wrapping the product, the truck drivers. He reaches these people and makes them a believer."

The Grateful Dead is another story of superb management. The group listens to customers. Most rock bands forbid tape-recording at concerts to prevent copyright infringement, yet the Dead ropes off a portion of the concert floor just for "tapeheads." The Dead's 50 employees are fully empowered, with large doses of job enrichment, few rules and procedures, and ownership of their jobs. Staff members earn large salaries and attractive benefits (life and medical insurance, trust funds for children), and they share in concert profits. Staff members feel part of the business, and turnover is low in an industry known for its instability.

Management counts. Garth Brooks and the Grateful Dead have organizations with powerful cultures, significant visions, and the motivation of human energy that set great organizations apart. ■

SOURCE: David E. Bowen and Caren Siehl, "Sweet Music: Grateful Employees, Grateful Customers, 'Grate' Profits," *Journal of Management Inquiry* (June 1992), 154–156; Robert K. Oermann, "Marketing Breaks Brooks away from Competition," *The Tennessean*, July 15, 1992, E1, E4; and Janice C. Simpson, "The Bands of Summer," *Time*, August 3, 1992, 66–67.

● MANAGEMENT TYPES

The four management functions must be performed in all organizations. But not all managers' jobs are the same. Managers are responsible for different departments, work at different levels in the hierarchy, and meet different requirements for achieving high performance. For example, Mary Lee Bowen is a middle manager at Rubbermaid and is responsible for teams that create new home organization and bath accessories products. Phillip Knight is chief executive officer for Nike, world leader in sports shoe design and manufacturing.[23] Both are managers, and both must contribute to planning, organizing, leading, and controlling their organizations—but in different amounts and ways.

VERTICAL DIFFERENCES

An important determinant of the manager's job is hierarchical level. Three levels in the hierarchy are illustrated in Exhibit 1.2. **Top managers** are at

top manager

A manager who is at the top of the organizational hierarchy and responsible for the entire organization.

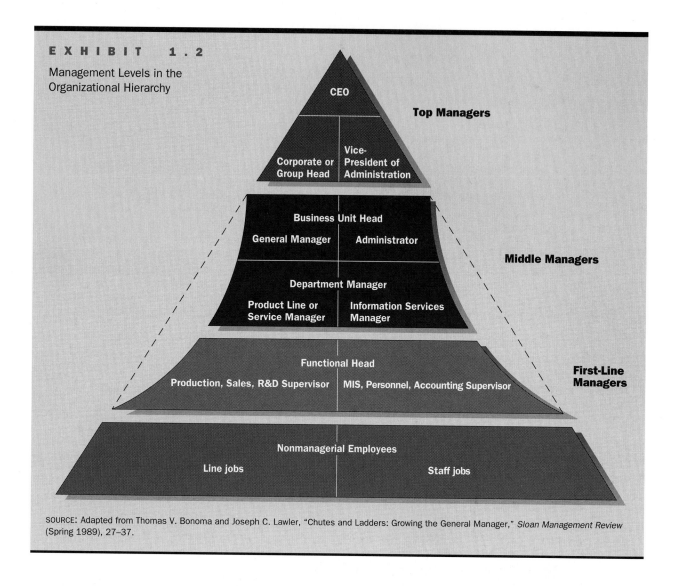

EXHIBIT 1.2

Management Levels in the Organizational Hierarchy

CEO

Top Managers

Corporate or Group Head | Vice-President of Administration

Business Unit Head

General Manager | Administrator

Middle Managers

Department Manager

Product Line or Service Manager | Information Services Manager

Functional Head

Production, Sales, R&D Supervisor | MIS, Personnel, Accounting Supervisor

First-Line Managers

Nonmanagerial Employees

Line jobs | Staff jobs

SOURCE: Adapted from Thomas V. Bonoma and Joseph C. Lawler, "Chutes and Ladders: Growing the General Manager," *Sloan Management Review* (Spring 1989), 27–37.

middle manager

A manager who works at the middle levels of the organization and is responsible for major departments.

the top of the hierarchy and are responsible for the entire organization. They have such titles as president, chairperson, executive director, chief executive officer (CEO), and executive vice-president. Top managers are responsible for setting organizational goals, defining strategies for achieving them, monitoring and interpreting the external environment, and making decisions that affect the entire organization. They look to the long-term future and concern themselves with general environmental trends and the organization's overall success. They also influence internal corporate culture.

Middle managers work at middle levels of the organization and are responsible for business units and major departments. Examples of middle managers are department head, division head, manager of quality control, and director of the research lab. Middle managers typically have two or more management levels beneath them. They are responsible for implementing the overall strategies and policies defined by top managers.

Middle managers are concerned with the near future, are expected to establish good relationships with peers around the organization, encourage teamwork, and resolve conflicts.

Recent trends in corporate restructuring and downsizing have made the middle manager's job difficult. Many companies have become lean and efficient by laying off middle managers, and by slashing middle management levels. Traditional pyramidal organization charts are flattening, allowing information to flow quickly from top to bottom and decisions to be made with the greater speed necessary in today's highly competitive global marketplace. The shrinking middle management is illustrated in Exhibit 1.2. For example, Eastman Kodak recently cut middle management by 30 percent and reduced its middle management levels from seven to three. The Medical Systems Group at General Electric cut middle management by 35 percent. These reductions increase the work load for remaining managers and contribute to job insecurity and a decline in opportunities for promotion. However, these cuts have improved the efficiency and performance of many corporations via improved responsiveness to customers, speed in new product development, and increased profits.[24]

First-line managers are directly responsible for the production of goods and services. They are the first or second level of management and have such titles as supervisor, line manager, section chief, and office manager. They are responsible for groups of nonmanagement employees. Their primary concern is the application of rules and procedures to achieve efficient production, provide technical assistance, and motivate subordinates. The time horizon at this level is short, with the emphasis on accomplishing day-to-day objectives.

An illustration of how the four functional activities differ for the three management levels is shown in Exhibit 1.3. Managers at all levels perform all four functions, but in different amounts. Planning and organizing the

first-line manager

A manager who is at the first or second management level and directly responsible for the production of goods and services.

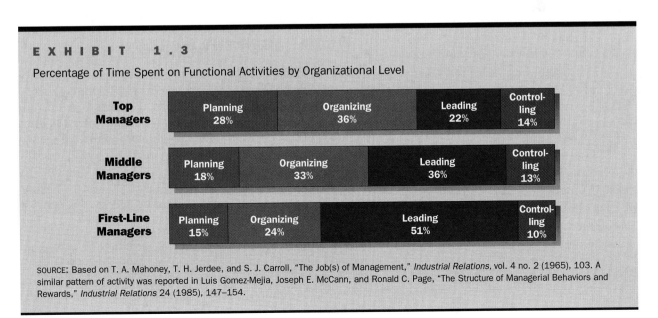

E X H I B I T   1 . 3

Percentage of Time Spent on Functional Activities by Organizational Level

Top Managers
- Planning 28%
- Organizing 36%
- Leading 22%
- Controlling 14%

Middle Managers
- Planning 18%
- Organizing 33%
- Leading 36%
- Controlling 13%

First-Line Managers
- Planning 15%
- Organizing 24%
- Leading 51%
- Controlling 10%

SOURCE: Based on T. A. Mahoney, T. H. Jerdee, and S. J. Carroll, "The Job(s) of Management," *Industrial Relations*, vol. 4 no. 2 (1965), 103. A similar pattern of activity was reported in Luis Gomez-Mejia, Joseph E. McCann, and Ronald C. Page, "The Structure of Managerial Behaviors and Rewards," *Industrial Relations* 24 (1985), 147–154.

firm are primarily the province of top managers, with the time devoted to these tasks decreasing for middle managers and first-line managers. Leading, in contrast, is highest for first-line managers because more time is spent directing and supervising subordinates than at higher management levels. A primary concern of first-line managers is the leadership and motivation of technical employees. Controlling is similar for all three levels, with somewhat more time devoted by middle and top managers.

HORIZONTAL DIFFERENCES

The other major difference in management jobs occurs horizontally across the organization. **Functional managers** are responsible for departments that perform a single functional task and have employees with similar training and skills. Functional departments include advertising, sales, finance, personnel, manufacturing, and accounting. Line managers are responsible for the manufacturing and marketing departments that make or sell the product or service. Staff managers are in charge of departments such as finance and personnel that support line departments.

　General managers are responsible for several departments that perform different functions. A general manager is responsible for a self-contained division, such as a Dillard's department store, and for all of the functional departments within it. **Project managers** also have general management responsibility, because they coordinate people across several departments to accomplish a specific project. Companies as diverse as consumer products and aerospace firms, for example, use project managers to coordinate people from marketing, manufacturing, finance, and production when a new product—breakfast cereal, guidance system—is developed. General and project managers require significant human skills, because they coordinate a variety of people to attain project or division goals.

functional manager

A manager who is responsible for a department that performs a single functional task and has employees with similar training and skills.

general manager

A manager who is responsible for several departments that perform different functions.

project manager

A manager who coordinates people across several departments to accomplish a specific project.

● MANAGEMENT SKILLS

A manager's job is diverse and complex and, as we shall see throughout this book, requires a range of skills. Although some management theorists propose a long list of skills, the necessary skills for planning, organizing, leading, and controlling can be summarized in three categories that are especially important: conceptual, human, and technical.[25] As illustrated in Exhibit 1.4, all managers need each skill, but the amounts differ by hierarchical level.

CONCEPTUAL SKILLS

conceptual skill

The cognitive ability to see the organization as a whole and the relationship among its parts.

Conceptual skill is the cognitive ability to see the organization as a whole and the relationship among its parts. Conceptual skill involves the manager's thinking and planning abilities. It involves knowing where one's department fits into the total organization and how the organization fits into the industry and the community. It means the ability to think "strategically"—to take the broad, long-term view.

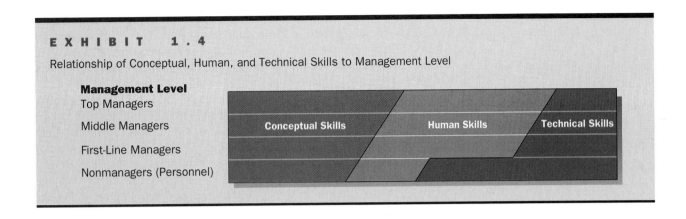

E X H I B I T   1 . 4

Relationship of Conceptual, Human, and Technical Skills to Management Level

Management Level
Top Managers

Middle Managers

First-Line Managers

Nonmanagers (Personnel)

Conceptual Skills   Human Skills   Technical Skills

Conceptual skills are needed by all managers, but they are especially important for managers at the top. Top managers must perceive significant elements in a situation and broad, conceptual patterns. For example, Microsoft Corporation, the giant software company, reflects the conceptual skills of its founder and chairman, Bill Gates. Overall business goals are clearly stated and effectively communicated throughout the company, which contributes to Microsoft's leadership reputation and billion dollar revenues. While actively participating in and coordinating small units devoted to functional areas such as programming and marketing, Gates spreads his concept for Microsoft by delegating to a cadre of strong managers. As Scott Oki, senior vice-president for U.S. sales and marketing, pointed out, "Each part of the company has a life of its own now, but Bill [Gates] is the glue that holds it all together."[26]

As managers move up the hierarchy, they must develop conceptual skills or their promotability will be limited. A senior engineering manager who is mired in technical matters rather than thinking strategically will not perform well at the top of the organization. Many of the responsibilities of top managers, such as decision making, resource allocation, and innovation, require a broad view.

HUMAN SKILLS

Human skill is the manager's ability to work with and through other people and to work effectively as a group member. This skill is demonstrated in the way a manager relates to other people, including the ability to motivate, facilitate, coordinate, lead, communicate, and resolve conflicts. A manager with human skills allows subordinates to express themselves without fear of ridicule and encourages participation. A manager with human skills likes other people and is liked by them. Barry Merkin, chairman of Dresher, Inc., the largest U.S. manufacturer of brass beds, is a cheerleader for his employees. He visits the plant floor and uses humor and hoopla to motivate them. Employees may have buckets of fried chicken served to them by supervisors wearing chef's hats.

Managers who lack human skills often are abrupt, critical, and unsympathetic toward others. Harding Lawrence of Braniff, described earlier, did not excel in human skills. Another example is the executive who

human skill

The ability to work with and through other people and to work effectively as a group member.

walked into a subordinate's office and insisted on talking to him. When the subordinate tried to explain that he was occupied, the manager snarled, "I don't give a damn. I said I wanted to see you now."[27] Managers without human skills are insensitive and arrogant. They often make other people feel stupid and resentful.

In recent years, the awareness of human skills has increased. Books such as *In Search of Excellence* and *A Passion for Excellence* stress the need for managers to take care of the human side of the organization. Excellent companies and excellent managers do not take people for granted. For example, former auto racer Roger Penske purchased struggling Detroit Diesel Corporation from General Motors and stressed the importance of a "team concept"—**t**eamwork, **e**ffort, **a**ttitude, and **m**anagement. Penske focused on people, answering questions from hundreds of employees and meeting regularly with union workers. Because of Penske's use of his people skills to motivate workers toward speedy and courteous response to customers, the Penske team's share of heavy truck engine sales rose 25 percent in its first year.[28] Effective managers are cheerleaders, facilitators, coaches, and nurturers. They build through people. Effective human skills enable managers to unleash subordinates' energy and help them grow as future managers.

TECHNICAL SKILLS

technical skill

The understanding of and proficiency in the performance of specific tasks.

Technical skill is the understanding of and proficiency in the performance of specific tasks. Technical skill includes mastery of the methods, techniques, and equipment involved in specific functions such as engineering, manufacturing, or finance. Technical skill also includes specialized knowledge, analytical ability, and the competent use of tools and techniques to solve problems in that specific discipline.

Technical skills are most important at lower organizational levels. Many managers get promoted into their first management jobs by having excellent technical skills. However, these skills are less important than human and conceptual skills as managers move up the hierarchy.

MAKING THE TRANSITION

As illustrated in Exhibit 1.4, the major difference between nonmanagers and managers is the shift from reliance on technical skills to focus on human skills. This is a difficult transition, because high achievement in the technical area may have been the basis for promotion to a supervisory position. New managers often mistakenly continue to rely on technical skills rather than concentrate on working with others, motivating employees, and building a team. Indeed, some people fail to become managers at all because they let technical skills take precedence over human skills.

Consider Peter Martin, who has a bachelor's degree and has worked for five years as a computer programmer for an oil company. In four short years, he has more new software programs to his credit than anyone else in the department. He is highly creative and widely respected. However, Pete is impulsive and has little tolerance for those whose work is less creative. Pete does not offer to help coworkers, and they are reluctant to ask because he often "puts them down." Pete is also slow to cooperate with other departments in meeting their needs, because he works primarily to enhance his own software-writing ability. He spends evenings and weekends working on his programs. Pete is a hardworking technical employee, but he sees little need to worry about other people.

Pete received high merit raises but was passed over for promotion and does not understand why. His lack of interpersonal skills, inconsideration for coworkers, and failure to cooperate with other departments severely limit his potential as a supervisor. Pete has great technical skills, but his human skills simply are inadequate for making the transition from worker to supervisor. Until Pete is ready to work on human skills, he has little chance of being promoted.

● WHAT IS IT LIKE TO BE A MANAGER?

So far we have described how managers perform four basic functions that help ensure that organizational resources are used to attain high levels of performance. These tasks require conceptual, human, and technical skills. Unless someone has actually performed managerial work, it is hard to understand exactly what managers do on an hour-by-hour, day-to-day basis. The manager's job is so diverse that a number of studies have been undertaken in an attempt to describe exactly what happens. The question of what managers actually do to plan, organize, lead, and control was answered by Henry Mintzberg, who followed managers around and recorded all of their activities.[29] He developed a description of managerial work that included three general characteristics and ten roles. These characteristics and roles have been supported in subsequent research.[30]

MANAGER ACTIVITIES

One of the most interesting findings about managerial activities is how busy managers are and how hectic the average workday can be.

MANAGERIAL ACTIVITY IS CHARACTERIZED BY VARIETY, FRAGMENTATION, AND BREVITY.[31] The manager's involvements are so widespread and voluminous that there is little time for quiet reflection. The average time spent on any one activity is less than nine minutes. Managers shift gears quickly. Significant crises are interspersed with trivial events in no predictable sequence.[32] One example of the morning activities for a typical general manager, Janet Howard, follows. Note the frequent interruptions, brevity, and variety.

7:30 AM   Janet arrives at work, unpacks her briefcase, and begins to plan her day.

7:37 AM   A subordinate, Morgan Cook, arrives and stops in Janet's office to discuss a dinner party the previous night and to review the cost-benefit analysis her department is working up for a proposed microcomputer.

7:45 AM	Janet's secretary, Pat, motions for Janet to pick up the telephone. "Janet, they had serious water damage at the downtown office last night. A pipe broke, causing about $50,000 damage. Everything will be back in shape in three days. Thought you should know."
8:00 AM	Another subordinate, Tim Birdwell, stops by. They chat about the water damage. Tim tells a joke. Tim and Morgan both leave, laughing at the story.
8:10 AM	Pat brings in the mail. She also asks instructions for typing a report Janet gave her yesterday.
8:17 AM	The mail includes an unsolicited proposal for a microcomputer from a prospective vendor and a clipped *Fortune* article about strategic decision making from Janet's boss.
8:30 AM	Janet gets a phone call from the accounting manager, who is returning a call from the day before. They talk about an accounting report.
8:45 AM	Janet leaves early to attend a regular 9:00 AM meeting in her boss's office. She tours the office area and informally chats with people before the meeting starts.
9:45 AM	Janet arrives back at her office, and a Mr. Nance is ushered in. Mr. Nance complains that a sales manager mistreats his employees and something must be done. Janet rearranges her schedule to investigate this claim.
10:05 AM	Janet returns to the mail. One letter is from an irate customer who is unhappy with the product and feels the sales engineer was unresponsive. Janet dictates a helpful, restrained reply.
10:20 AM	Pat brings in phone messages. Janet makes two phone calls and receives one. She goes back to the mail and papers on her desk.
10:35 AM	Another subordinate stops by with a question about how to complete forms requesting a maternity leave.
10:45 AM	Janet receives an urgent phone call from Larry Baldwin. They go back and forth talking about lost business, unhappy subordinates, a potential promotion, and what should be done. It is a long conversation, with much exchange of both official information and gossip.
11:15 AM	Janet decides to skip lunch, preferring to eat an apple in her office so she will have some time to plan divisional goals for the next six months.[33]

THE MANAGER PERFORMS A GREAT DEAL OF WORK AT AN UNRELENTING PACE.[34]   Managers' work is fast paced and requires great energy. The managers observed by Mintzberg processed 36 pieces of mail each day, attended 8 meetings, and took a tour through the building or plant. As soon as a manager's daily calendar is set, unexpected disturbances erupt. New meetings are required. During time away from the office, executives catch up on work-related reading and paperwork.

Sloan Wilson, author of *The Man in the Gray Flannel Suit*, had an opportunity to work with top managers from several companies. He tried to understand how these people had become so famous, rich, and successful.

They had no special advantages or influence, because each was a self-made person.

> So what was the secret? As I attempted to work around the clock on the many projects they undertook in addition to their real jobs, one simple answer came to me: raw energy. Super-abundant, inexhaustible energy—that was the one thing all these very successful men had.
>
> They were people who enthusiastically could undertake the fifth rewriting of a speech on education at three in the morning when they were up against a deadline, fly across the continent to deliver it and fly back again, working out of a briefcase on a plane all the time. And when they got to their offices, they were fresh and eager to see what their engagement calendar had to offer for the day and evening ahead. I never understood how they did it, and I was never able to keep up with them.[35]

MANAGER ROLES

Mintzberg's observations and subsequent research indicate that diverse manager activities can be organized into ten roles.[36] A **role** is a set of expectations for a manager's behavior. The ten roles are divided into three categories: interpersonal, information, and decisional. Each role represents activities that managers undertake to ultimately accomplish the functions of planning, organizing, leading, and controlling. The ten roles and brief examples are provided in Exhibit 1.5 on page 24.

role
A set of expectations for one's behavior.

INTERPERSONAL ROLES.   Interpersonal roles pertain to relationships with others and are related to the human skills described earlier. The *figurehead* role involves handling ceremonial and symbolic activities for the department or organization. The manager represents the organization in his or her formal managerial capacity as the head of the unit. The presentation of employee awards by a division manager at Taco Bell is an example of the figurehead role. The *leader* role encompasses relationships with subordinates, including motivation, communication, and influence. The *liaison* role pertains to the development of information sources both inside and outside the organization. An example is a face-to-face discussion between a controller and plan supervisor to resolve a misunderstanding about the budget.

INFORMATIONAL ROLES.   Informational roles describe the activities used to maintain and develop an information network. General managers spend about 75 percent of their time talking to other people. The *monitor* role involves seeking current information from many sources. The manager acquires information from others and scans written materials to stay well informed. One manager at a Canadian insurance company takes a turn at the switchboard every 40 days, plugging directly into customer and employee satisfaction.[37] The *disseminator* role is just the opposite: The manager transmits current information to others, both inside and outside the organization, who can use it. Managers do not hoard information; they pass it around to others. The *spokesperson* role pertains to official statements to people outside the organization about company policies, actions, or plans. For example, Lod Cook, chairman of Atlantic Richfield Company, talked to environmentalists about his backing of a ten-year ban on drilling in certain areas off the California coast, spoke in favor of a gas tax

Category	Role	Activity
EXHIBIT 1.5 Ten Manager Roles		
Interpersonal	**Figurehead**	Perform ceremonial and symbolic duties such as greeting visitors, signing legal documents.
	Leader	Direct and motivate subordinates; train, counsel, and communicate with subordinates.
	Liaison	Maintain information links both inside and outside organization; use mail, phone calls, meetings.
Informational	**Monitor**	Seek and receive information, scan periodicals and reports, maintain personal contacts.
	Disseminator	Forward information to other organization members; send memos and reports, make phone calls.
	Spokesperson	Transmit information to outsiders through speeches, reports, memos.
Decisional	**Entrepreneur**	Initiate improvement projects; identify new ideas, delegate idea responsibility to others.
	Disturbance handler	Take corrective action during disputes or crises; resolve conflicts among subordinates; adapt to environmental crises.
	Resource allocator	Decide who gets resources; schedule, budget, set priorities.
	Negotiator	Represent department during negotiation of union contracts, sales, purchases, budgets; represent departmental interests.

SOURCE: Adapted from Henry Mintzberg, The Nature of Managerial Work (New York: Harper & Row, 1973), 92–93, and Henry Mintzberg, "Managerial Work: Analysis from Observation," *Management Science* 18 (1971), B97–B110.

hike, and helped Arco proudly trumpet its price freeze during the buildup for the war in the Persian Gulf. Cook's figurehead activities not only show Arco's enlightenment but contribute to increased gasoline sales as well.[38]

DECISIONAL ROLES.   Decisional roles pertain to those events about which the manager must make a choice. These roles often require conceptual as well as human skills. The *entrepreneur* role involves the initiation of change. Managers are constantly thinking about the future and how to get there.[39] Managers become aware of problems and search for improvement projects that will correct them. One manager studied by Mintzberg had 50 improvement projects going simultaneously. The *disturbance handler* role involves resolving conflicts among subordinates or between the manager's department and other departments. For example, the division manager for a large furniture manufacturer got involved in a personal dispute between two section heads. One section head was let go because he did not fit the team. The *resource allocator* role pertains to decisions about how to allocate people, time, equipment, budget, and other resources to attain desired outcomes. The manager must decide which projects receive budget allocations, which of several customer complaints receive priority, and even how to spend his or her own time. The *negotiator* role involves formal

"Great Balls of Foil!" Reynolds Metals executives enjoy the figurehead role as they marvel at a portion of the 1,464 miles of recycled aluminum foil collected by schoolchildren in the Great Balls of Foil annual recycling contest.

negotiations and bargaining to attain outcomes for the manager's unit of responsibility. For example, the manager meets and formally negotiates with others—a supplier about a late delivery, the controller about the need for additional budget resources, or the union about a worker grievance during the normal workday.

SMALL BUSINESS

One interesting finding is that managers in small businesses tend to emphasize different roles than managers in large corporations. In small firms, the most important role is spokesperson, because managers must promote the small, growing company to the outside world. The entrepreneur role is also very important in small businesses, because managers must be creative and help their organizations develop new ideas to be competitive. Anita Roddick's commitment to environmental and social causes, as well as "natural" skin care products, appealed to the growing concerns of customers and Roddick's abilities as both spokesperson and entrepreneur helped to catapult the Body Shop from one small shop to a global competitor.

Small-business managers tend to rate lower on the leader role and on information-processing roles compared with counterparts in large corporations. In large firms, the most important role is resource allocator and the least important is entrepreneur.[40] The Leading Edge box illustrates the unique roles of the small business manager.

● MANAGING FOR THE FUTURE

One final question: How do you learn to be a manager for the year 2000 in an uncertain and rapidly changing world? More specifically, how does a course in management or a college degree in business prepare you to become a manager ready to face the challenges of the twenty-first century?

LEADING edge

HARBOR SWEETS, INC

Benneville Strohecker created Harbor Sweets candy company in his basement in 1973. Today it is a $2.5 million dollar business, based in Salem, Massachusetts, and Strohecker is proud to have built an organization that ignores convention. The majority of his workforce is part time. As we will see later in Chapter 11, the workforce is composed of a diverse group of teenagers, old-agers, the handicapped, and immigrants from Laos to the Dominican Republic.

Strohecker pays his 150 employees about what they could make at McDonald's, but without any benefits other than paid vacations. Employees do receive a small profit-sharing plan and discounted candy. Since a sweet tooth tends to be a seasonal urge that centers around holidays, many workers are laid off in the spring and summer.

If you think these employees feel like exploited stepchildren, think again. Harbor Sweets attracts smart, dedicated people who stay around. Three-quarters of the employees return after layoffs, and 40 percent have been around for three or more years. Strohecker sums up the key to the company's success and the essence of his management style: "There would be no Harbor Sweets without trust. But I believe it's not just being nice. Relying on trust is good business."

A lofty sentiment, and Strohecker means it. In an age of background checks and integrity profiles, he still "hires by gut." Trust extended to allowing employees to fill out their own time cards. Only recently, at the request of employees, were time clocks installed at Harbor Sweets.

As an extension of the value system and integrity of the company, every employee at Harbor Sweets is also expected to be a quality controller. "They're encouraged to reject anything that comes to them from another operation that doesn't look like the best piece of candy in the world," says Strohecker.

On occasion, Strohecker has deviated from reliance on trust. He once brought in a consultant group to increase plant efficiency. What at first seemed prudent and reasonable turned out to be expensive and self-defeating. "We threw the whole system out," Strohecker says, "because the very fact that we were measuring is not the culture of Harbor Sweets." Instead, he told his people to work as hard as they could; they responded, and the former sense of freedom was restored. A similar scenario evolved when a financial consultant wanted to present Strohecker some benefit options. He suggested going to the employees directly. The astonished consultant was certain Strohecker had lost his mind, and that his employees would plunder him. He was wrong on both counts. "They came out with a recommended package that was probably more conservative than what we would have given them," says Strohecker.

How long Harbor Sweets can continue with its present level of employee flexibility is uncertain. For now, Strohecker seems to have struck a workable balance in a company that can only be described as an anachronism. Confident that the company and its philosophy will survive without him, Strohecker has turned over day-to-day management to chief operating officer Phyllis LeBlanc, but has stayed on as chief executive officer. Even though trust may top the list of soon-to-be extinct management techniques, it seems to be working quite well. "I invented all of this," Strohecker says, "but workers are so much better than I am." ◼

SOURCE: Anne Driscoll, "Candy Man of the People," *Boston Globe*, March 29, 1992; Tracy E. Benson, "In Trust We Manage," *Industry Week*, March 4, 1991, 26–27; and Martha Mangelsdorf, "Managing the New Work Force," *INC.*, January 1990, 78–83. Company sources.

LEARNING MANAGEMENT SKILLS

Management is both an art and a science. It is an art because many skills cannot be learned from a textbook. Management takes practice, just like golf, tennis, or volleyball. Studying a book helps, but this is not enough.

Many skills, especially the human and, to some extent, the conceptual skills, and roles such as leader, spokesperson, disturbance handler, and negotiator, take practice. These skills are learned through experience.

Management is also a science because a growing body of knowledge and objective facts describes management and how to attain organizational performance. The knowledge is acquired through systematic research and can be conveyed through teaching and textbooks. Systematic knowledge about planning, organizing, and control system design, for example, helps managers understand the skills they need, the types of roles they must perform, and the techniques needed to manage organizations. Harding Lawrence of Braniff and Robert Fomon of E. F. Hutton relied solely on their experience and intuition, and they made grave mistakes.

Becoming a successful manager requires a blend of formal learning and practice, of science and art. Practice alone used to be enough to learn how to manage, but no longer. Formal course work in management can help a manager become more competent and be prepared for the challenges of the future. The study of management enables people to see and understand things about organizations that others cannot. Training that helps one acquire the conceptual, human, and technical skills necessary for management will be an asset.

MANAGEMENT SUCCESS AND FAILURE

A few clues about the importance of acquiring management skills were uncovered by the Center for Creative Leadership in Greensboro, North Carolina.[41] This study compared 21 derailed executives with 20 executives who had arrived at the top of the company. The derailed executives were successful people who had been expected to go far but reached a plateau, were fired, or were forced to retire early. Successful and derailed managers were similar in many ways. They were bright, worked hard, and excelled in a technical area such as accounting or engineering.

The most striking difference between the two groups was the ability to use human skills. Only 25 percent of the derailed group were described as having good ability with people, whereas 75 percent of those who had arrived at the top had such skill. The managers who arrived were sensitive to others and did not have negative qualities such as abrasiveness, aloofness, or arrogance. The successful managers also developed conceptual skills and were able to think strategically, that is, take a broad, long-term view. For example, one derailed manager was a superb engineer who got bogged down in details and tended to lose composure under stress. Another manager was known as cold and arrogant, but once he realized these limits to his career, he changed almost overnight. He made a genuine effort to develop better human skills—and succeeded.

PREPARING FOR THE YEAR 2000

Over the next few years, new forces are going to shape managerial careers. Managers will have to rely heavily on human skills and conceptual skills, but they will apply them in new ways. Major changes on the horizon for which managers must prepare include paradigm shifts, chaos theory, workplace diversity, and globalization.

paradigm

A mind-set that presents a fundamental way of thinking, perceiving, and understanding the world.

PARADIGM SHIFTS.   A **paradigm** is a mind-set that presents a fundamental way of thinking, perceiving, and understanding the world. Changing one's management paradigm is extremely difficult yet is becoming important in a world of rapidly changing products, technologies, and management techniques. Not too many years ago, Swiss companies made the best watches in the world, cornering 65 percent of sales and 80 percent of profits. A paradigm shift in the fundamental rules of watchmaking from mechanical to electronic dropped Swiss market share to 10 percent and profits to less than 20 percent. Another shift is in the speed with which work must be accomplished. Ford, Honda, and Chrysler have cut the time to develop a new car from five years to three, thus demanding new ways of thinking and organizing. The Limited retail chain rushes new fashions into its stores in less than 60 days, compared to six months for competitors. Another fundamental management shift is toward the belief that companies can be managed best by empowering people to manage themselves.[42]

CHAOS THEORY.   The new science of chaos theory reveals the existence of randomness and disorder within larger patterns of order. This means that day-to-day events for most organizations are random and unpredictable. Chaos theory will be associated with a paradigm shift away from the belief that managers can predict and control future events toward a management philosophy that organizations must become fluid, adaptable, and stay connected to customers and the environment on a day-to-day basis. Managers may become less concerned with detailed planning and control, orienting themselves instead toward facilitating teams and managing overall patterns, not day-to-day events.[43]

WORKPLACE DIVERSITY.   The increasing diversity of people within organizations is reflected in several ways. The number of male students going into business education has been stable since the mid-1970s. The increase of students has been accounted for by women, who now constitute 45 percent of all bachelor's degrees in business. By the year 2000, most new hires will be women or African-American, Hispanic, or Asian men. Organizations must learn to welcome diverse people into their upper ranks. Different people offer varying styles. Some research indicates, for example, that women have a different, and often superior, management style with an emphasis on empowerment, information-sharing, and other interactive skills. Managers must learn to motivate and lead different types of people and to attract the best people from these groups. U.S.-born white males will make up only about 15 percent of the new entrants into the labor force.[44]

MERGERS AND ACQUISITIONS.   Mergers and acquisitions have a major impact on managerial careers and will continue through the 1990s. During the 1980s, more than 10,000 companies changed hands, and over 2 million people saw their jobs disappear. Mergers and reorganizations are seen as an opportunity for companies to become more efficient, but they require new management responses. Managers have to be flexible enough to work for different bosses within new corporate cultures. Lifetime loyalty to a single firm may be a thing of the past. Downsizing middle management ranks requires managers to produce in ways that are highly visible and guarantee job mobility.[45]

NOT-FOR-PROFIT ORGANIZATIONS.   Not-for-profit organizations represent a major source of management talent and innovation. The Salvation Army, Girl Scouts, universities, city governments, hospitals, public schools, symphonies, and art museums all require superb management. Many not-for-profit organizations have been leaders in creating a sense of purpose and mission that motivates employees, encouraging workers to innovate and try new ideas, using boards and committees drawn from community members, and trimming long vertical hierarchies.[46]

GLOBALIZATION.   Managers need to think globally because companies are enmeshed with foreign competitors, suppliers, and customers. By one estimate, industrial countries on average import nearly 40 percent of the parts used in domestic manufacturing. Foreign companies have strong influence in the United States and Canada, with many citizens working for foreign employers. Some experts feel that globalization presents a management challenge because the United States is losing worldwide market share in important product areas.

The 12 nations of the European Union will reduce long-standing barriers to the transfer of goods, financing, and people across their borders. This true common market will be substantially larger than the United States, thereby allowing European companies to grow large and powerful and to become more competitive on the global stage. U.S. companies are trying to get a foothold in Europe now to avoid potential barriers in the future. In addition, the North American Free Trade Agreement reduces the trade barriers in North America, creating another common market. These rapid developments are changing the global picture, forcing managers to think internationally.[47]

Successful managers of tomorrow will be able to cross borders, will be good at languages, and will understand cultural differences. Right now executive recruiting organizations are searching worldwide for managers to take assignments in global organizations. Global experience is a prize asset of the managers of tomorrow.[48]

Strength through *diversity* is reflected in the faces of these Dow Chemical employees, and in Dow's vision of welcoming and valuing the contributions of each of its 61,000 employees around the world. These Los Angeles workers represent 11 countries, and each person brings a unique perspective and range of experience that benefits the entire organization.

SUMMARY AND MANAGEMENT SOLUTION

This chapter introduced a number of important concepts about management. High performance requires the efficient and effective use of organizational resources through the four management functions of planning, organizing, leading, and controlling.

Their importance differs somewhat by hierarchical level. Top and middle managers are most concerned with planning and place greater emphasis on organizing and controlling. First-line managers focus more on leading. To perform the four functions, managers need three skills—conceptual, human, and technical. Conceptual skills are more important at the top of the hierarchy; human skills are important at all levels; and technical skills are most important for first-line managers.

Two characteristics of managerial work also were explained in the chapter: (1) Managerial activities involve variety, fragmentation, and brevity; and (2) managers perform a great deal of work at an unrelenting pace. Managers also are expected to perform activities associated with ten roles: the interpersonal roles of figurehead, leader, and liaison; the informational roles of monitor, disseminator, and spokesperson; and the decisional roles of entrepreneur, disturbance handler, resource allocator, and negotiator.

Rudy Cedillo was well equipped to handle the challenges of his new management job. Luby's puts its managers through a rigorous selection and training process, and only the very best reach the top. The San Antonio-based cafeteria chain usually picks applicants who are just out of college and have no experience in food services. "It's easier for us to teach a person who doesn't know anything," says Wayne Shirley, director of management training. Candidates then are sent to the company's 12-week boot camp, where they learn the management essentials of planning, organizing, leading, and controlling. Those who make it through the training work for years as assistant and then associate managers before getting their own cafeteria.

The job is a big one, but so is the payoff. Managers get 20 to 25 percent of the location's profits, with salaries averaging well over $100,000 a year. There also is plenty of opportunity to move up the corporate ladder. Cedillo managed a Luby's in Albuquerque, New Mexico, before moving to the bigger and more lucrative location in San Antonio. Cedillo knows that if he works hard, his potential is limitless. Luby's CEO Ralph "Pete" Erben was once a cafeteria manager.[49]

Typically, managers who succeed have excellent human skills. In the future, managers will need even greater human skills as well as conceptual skills to deal with the pressing issues of paradigm shifts, chaos, workplace diversity, managers, and globalization.

DISCUSSION QUESTIONS

1. Assume you are a research engineer at a petrochemical company, collaborating with a marketing manager on a major product modification. You notice that every memo you receive from her has been copied to senior management. At every company function, she spends time talking to the big shots. You are also aware that sometimes when you are slaving away over the project, she is playing golf with senior managers. What is your evaluation of her behavior?

2. What similarities do you see among the four management functions of planning, organizing, leading, and controlling? Do you think these functions are related—that is, is a manager who performs well in one function likely to perform well in the others?

3. Why did a top manager such as Harding Lawrence at Braniff fail while a top manager such as General Creech of Tactical Air Command succeed? Which of the four management functions best explains this difference? Discuss.

4. What is the difference between efficiency and effectiveness? Which is more important for performance? Can an organization succeed in both simultaneously?

5. What changes in management functions and skills occur as one is promoted from a nonmanagement to a management position? How can managers acquire the new skills?

6. If managerial work is characterized by variety, fragmentation, and brevity, how do managers perform basic management functions such as planning, which would seem to require reflection and analysis?

7. A college professor told her students, "The purpose of a management course is to teach students *about* management, not to teach them to be managers." Do you agree or disagree with this statement? Discuss.

8. What does it mean to say that management is both an art and a science? Discuss.

9. In the Center for Creative Leadership study, many managers made it to the middle and upper levels of the organization before derailing. How do you think managers got so far if they had flaws that prevented them from reaching the top?

10. How should the teaching of management change to prepare future managers to deal with work-force diversity? Do you think diversity will have a more substantial impact on organizations than globalization will?

MANAGEMENT IN PRACTICE: EXPERIENTIAL EXERCISE

● TEST YOUR HUMAN SKILLS

The 60 questions that follow will help you evaluate your human skills compared with those of current managers. Be honest in your responses. Your instructor will provide you with information about the meaning of your responses.

Circle the letter, as illustrated here, that represents your acceptance or rejection of the statements that follow.

Strongly disagree:	Ⓓ	d	?	a	A
Moderately disagree:	D	ⓓ	?	a	A
Sometimes yes/no:	D	d	⑦	a	A
Moderately agree:	D	d	?	ⓐ	A

1. You have been elected or promoted to several leadership positions in your school/work/community/church involvements.

    D   d   ?   a   A

2. You have impeccably good manners, and people comment on your courteous behavior time and again.

    D   d   ?   a   A

3. You feel comfortable and at ease when others make you the center of attention.   D   d   ?   a   A

4. It irritates you when others treat life as nothing more than a game.   D   d   ?   a   A

5. You love old things, poetry, going out to the country, and being alone.   D   d   ?   a   A

6. You would love to make a citizen's arrest of someone honking his or her horn needlessly or disturbing the peace.   D   d   ?   a   A

7. You are good at praising others and give credit readily when credit is due.   D   d   ?   a   A

8. When you deal with people, you tread softly and give them the "kid glove" treatment.   D   d   ?   a   A

9. You allow people to manipulate and boss you around too much.   D   d   ?   a   A

10. In the end, with every liaison established primarily for ambition's sake, you have to give away a bit of your "soul."   D   d   ?   a   A

11. You have a knack for harmonizing the seemingly irreconcilable.   D   d   ?   a   A

12. You believe that nothing gets done properly unless you do it yourself.   D   d   ?   a   A

13. You seem to possess a natural charm and easily win people over.   D   d   ?   a   A

14. In large or new social situations, you are poised, relaxed, and self-assured.   D   d   ?   a   A

15. You have a real capacity for selling yourself to others.   D   d   ?   a   A

16. You really dislike others teasing or making fun of you.   D   d   ?   a   A

17. You feel a natural and real warmth toward all people.   D   d   ?   a   A

18. You have little patience for human ignorance and incompetence.   D   d   ?   a   A

19. You will usually give others the benefit of the doubt rather than argue openly with them.   D   d   ?   a   A

20. You seldom (or never) say anything to others without considering how they may receive it.   D   d   ?   a   A

21. When friends ask you out, you usually go, even when you would prefer your privacy.   D   d   ?   a   A

22. You stay on the lookout for people who can promote your advancement.   D   d   ?   a   A

23. You have a talent for diffusing tension and anger when situations are strained.   D   d   ?   a   A

24. You usually end up doing other people's jobs in addition to your own.   D   d   ?   a   A

25. You go out of your way to introduce yourself and start up conversation with strangers.   D   d   ?   a   A

26. You have a special magnetism that attracts people to you.   D   d   ?   a   A

27. You go out of your way to make sure other people recognize your accomplishments.   D   d   ?   a   A

28. You have an ability to see humor in situations many people overlook.   D   d   ?   a   A

29. If people are not doing a good job, you believe they should be fired.   D   d   ?   a   A

30. There are a lot of things you would change about people if you had your way.   D   d   ?   a   A

31. Others find you very easy to get along with and easy to work with.   D   d   ?   a   A

32. You freely tell others what you think is wrong with them.   D   d   ?   a   A

33. You dislike having to deal with conflict situations requiring confrontation.   D   d   ?   a   A

34. You realize you have to compete for promotions as much on the basis of politics as on merit.   D   d   ?   a   A

35. If invited to venture an opinion around a hot issue, you usually seek a conciliatory or middle position.   D   d   ?   a   A

36. The average person avoids responsibilities and must be strongly directed to work effectively.   D   d   ?   a   A

37. You are an all-around type who can "hit it off" with just about anyone.	D	d	?	a	A
38. You go out of your way to create a lasting first impression when meeting new people.	D	d	?	a	A
39. You pretend to be shy or quiet to avoid attention.	D	d	?	a	A
40. It is very hard to "ruffle your feathers" or "get your back up."	D	d	?	a	A
41. Until you get to know people, you tend to act distant or aloof.	D	d	?	a	A
42. You have little patience for people who ask irrelevant and elementary questions.	D	d	?	a	A
43. You find it easy to seek the advice and counsel of others, as opposed to doing something all on your own.	D	d	?	a	A
44. You are quick to criticize and discount the foolish opinions and actions of people you cannot stand.	D	d	?	a	A
45. You will usually wait for someone else to complain about something that displeases you.	D	d	?	a	A
46. You accept that cultivating your coworkers and bosses is often necessary in getting ahead.	D	d	?	a	A
47. You are a masterful strategist at deftly maneuvering others toward your views.	D	d	?	a	A
48. You prefer to make all the important decisions and then expect others to carry them out.	D	d	?	a	A
49. You avoid superficial "cocktail" talk whenever possible.	D	d	?	a	A
50. Others find you exciting and are swept along by your personal manner.	D	d	?	a	A
51. You are really worried about making people jealous or envious of your accomplishments.	D	d	?	a	A
52. You exude an optimistic appreciation of life that says "all is well."	D	d	?	a	A
53. You have little sympathy for the "dumb messes" people get themselves into.	D	d	?	a	A
54. When dealing with others, you have a very easygoing, "laid-back" style.	D	d	?	a	A
55. You usually have no difficulty collaborating or going along with the majority opinion.	D	d	?	a	A
56. Head-on, direct, "tell it as it is" confrontation is your style of relating to people.	D	d	?	a	A
57. When a quarrel takes place between you and others, you usually give in first.	D	d	?	a	A
58. You are a person who is particularly adept at currying special favors when you want something.	D	d	?	a	A
59. You have a facility for altering your opinions and viewpoints and adopting new value standards.	D	d	?	a	A
60. If there are ten ways of correctly doing a job, you would press to have it done your way.	D	d	?	a	A

CASE FOR ANALYSIS

COMPUTER SPECIALISTS, INC.

Computer Specialist, Inc. (CSI), a real company, achieved sales of about $3 million by providing computer programmers and system designers under contract to clients. The major client is a well-known bank in western Pennsylvania for whom CSI writes programs for its MasterCard and VISA applications.

While on vacation, Warren Rodgers, CEO of CSI, was informed that a star programmer entered the wrong set of instructions into the bank's computer. The mistake caused roughly 500,000 credit cards to be wrongly invalidated, and several thousand cards were quickly confiscated by automatic teller machines. Bank officers were furious, evicting the programmer from the premises and going to the press with the story. The story appeared on the evening news and in the morning newspaper, with the blame placed on CSI.

Two senior managers at CSI, the director of human resources and the marketing director, did not get involved in solving the problem because they had little technical grounding in the bank's data-processing system and no desire to step into this mess. The star programmer was sent home, where she was getting the cold shoulder from CSI managers and the bank. The bank blamed CSI for the fiasco and started demands for financial concessions. CSI's chief competitors were running CSI's name into the ground. They were telling other clients that CSI was totally responsible for the problem.

Before reading on, think for a moment about what you would do if you were Warren Rodgers returning from vacation. Rodgers' response went something like this: (1) Call the star employee at home to let her know that he was behind her 100 percent. This sent the right signal to other programmers and to the bank about her value. (2) Rectifying this problem was made the top management priority for the next few weeks. All available employees were at that bank making amends. Everyone—bank managers, secretaries—was taken to lunch. If any CSI employee was in the area, he or she walked through the bank to show a presence so that bank officials would know the problem was not being avoided. (3) Rodgers did not make a financial settlement with the bank. Instead, he offered a reduced rate for programmers, thereby increasing the number of CSI programmers at the bank. This effectively scuttled the rumor that CSI caused the problem. (4) The managers who failed to take immediate action are no longer with CSI. Managers are now promoted from within, and everyone must have some data-processing experience and be willing to get involved with customers in a proactive mode.

● QUESTIONS

1. How would you evaluate Rodgers' response to the crisis? Do you consider him a good manager?
2. How would you rate Rodgers on conceptual, human, and technical skills?
3. Do the managerial roles revealed in this case seem consistent with the small-business managers described in the text?

SOURCE: Based on Warren Rodgers, "My Terrible Vacation," INC., February 1988, 116–117.

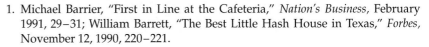

REFERENCES

1. Michael Barrier, "First in Line at the Cafeteria," *Nation's Business*, February 1991, 29–31; William Barrett, "The Best Little Hash House in Texas," *Forbes*, November 12, 1990, 220–221.

2. Kathleen Kerwin and James B. Treece, "Detroit's Big Chance," *Business Week*, June 29, 1992, 82–90; Wendy Zellner, "Chrysler's Next Generation," *Business Week*, December 19, 1988, 52–55.

3. Tom Peters and Nancy Austin, *A Passion for Excellence: The Leadership Difference* (New York: Random House, 1985).

4. Alex Taylor III, "A U.S. Style Shakeup at Honda," *Fortune*, December 30, 1991, 115–120.

5. Byron Harris, "The Man Who Killed Braniff," *Texas Monthly*, July 1982, 116–120, 183–189.

6. Brett Duval Fromson, "The Slow Death of E. F. Hutton," *Fortune*, February 29, 1988, 82–88.

7. John A. Byrne, William C. Symonds, and Julia Flynn Syler, "CEO Disease: Egotism Can Breed Corporate Disaster—and the Malady Is Spreading," *Business Week*, April 1, 1991, 52–60.

8. James A. F. Stoner and R. Edward Freeman, *Management*, 4th ed. (Englewood Cliffs, N.J.: Prentice-Hall, 1989).

9. Peter F. Drucker, *Management Tasks, Responsibilities, Practices* (New York: Harper & Row, 1974).

10. G. Pascal Zachary, "How Ashton-Tate Lost Its Leadership in PC Software Arena," *The Wall Street Journal*, April 11, 1990, A1, A12.

11. Peters and Austin, *A Passion for Excellence*, 11–12.

12. John Bussey and Douglas R. Sease, "Manufacturers Strive to Slice Time Needed to Develop Products," *The Wall Street Journal*, February 23, 1988, 1, 13.

13. Harris, "The Man Who Killed Braniff."

14. Peters and Austin, *A Passion for Excellence*.

15. Harris, "The Man Who Killed Braniff," 118–120.

16. Ibid.

17. Fromson, "The Slow Death of E. F. Hutton."

18. Alex Taylor III, "Lee Iacocca's Production Whiz," *Fortune*, June 22, 1987, 36–44.

19. Eric Calonius, "Smart Moves by Quality Champs," *Fortune*, special 1991 issue—The New American Century, 24–28.

20. David Wessell, "With Labor Scarce, Service Firms Strive to Raise Productivity," *The Wall Street Journal*, June 1, 1989, A1, A8.

21. Frank Edward Allen, "McDonald's Launches Plan to Cut Waste," *The Wall Street Journal*, April 17, 1991, B1.

22. Harold Geneen and Alvin Moscow, *Managing* (Garden City, N.Y.: Doubleday, 1984), 285.

23. Calonius, "Smart Moves by Quality Champs."

24. Carol Hymowitz, "When Firms Slash Middle Management, Those Spared Often Bear a Heavy Load," *The Wall Street Journal*, April 5, 1990, B1.

25. Robert L. Katz, "Skills of an Effective Administrator," *Harvard Business Review* 52 (September–October 1974), 90–102.

26. Brenton Schlender, "How Bill Gates Keeps the Magic Going," *Fortune*, June 18, 1990, 82–89.

27. Morgan W. McCall, Jr., and Michael M. Lombardo, "Off the Track: Why and How Successful Executives Get Derailed" (Technical Report No. 21, Center for Creative Leadership, Greensboro, N.C., January 1983).

28. Joseph B. White, "How Detroit Diesel, Out from under GM, Turned around Fast," *The Wall Street Journal*, August 16, 1991, A1, A8.

29. Henry Mintzberg, *The Nature of Managerial Work* (New York: Harper & Row, 1973).

30. Robert E. Kaplan, "Trade Routes: The Manager's Network of Relationships," *Organizational Dynamics* (Spring 1984), 37–52; Rosemary Stewart, "The Nature of Management: A Problem for Management Education," *Journal of Management Studies* 21 (1984) 323–330; John P. Kotter, "What Effective General Managers Really Do," *Harvard Business Review* (November–December 1982), 156–167; Morgan W. McCall, Jr., Ann M. Morrison, and

Robert L. Hannan, "Studies of Managerial Work: Results and Methods" (Technical Report No. 9, Center for Creative Leadership, Greensboro, N.C., 1978).

31. Henry Mintzberg, "Managerial Work: Analysis from Observation," *Management Science* 18 (1971), B97–B110.

32. Alan Deutschman, "The CEO's Secret of Managing Time," *Fortune*, June 1, 1992, 135–146.

33. Based on Carol Saunders and Jack William Jones, "Temporal Sequences in Information Acquisition for Decision Making: A Focus on Source and Medium," *Academy of Management Review* 15 (1990), 29–46; and John P. Kotter, "What Effective General Managers Really Do," *Harvard Business Review* (November–December 1982), 156–167; Mintzberg, "Managerial Work."

34. Mintzberg, "Managerial Work."

35. Sloan Wilson, "What Do Successful Men Have in Common? Raw Energy," *Houston Chronicle*, March 30, 1980, section 6, 11.

36. Lance B. Kurke and Howard E. Aldrich, "Mintzberg Was Right!: A Replication and Extension of *The Nature of Managerial Work*," *Management Science* 29 (1983), 975–984; Cynthia M. Pavett and Alan W. Lau, "Managerial Work: The Influence of Hierarchical Level and Functional Specialty," *Academy of Management Journal* 26 (1983), 170–177; Colin P. Hales, "What Do Managers Do? A Critical Review of the Evidence," *Journal of Management Studies* 23 (1986), 88–115.

37. Wendy Trueman, "CEO Isolation and How to Fight It," *Canadian Business*, July 1991, 28–32.

38. Ronald Grover, "Lod Cook: Mixing Oil and PR," *Business Week*, October 8, 1990, 110–116.

39. Harry S. Jonas III, Ronald E. Fry, and Suresh Srivastva, "The Office of the CEO: Understanding the Executive Experience," *Academy of Management Executive* 4 (August 1990), 36–48.

40. Martha E. Mangelsdorf, "Big vs. Small," *INC.*, May 1989, 22; Joseph G. P. Paolillo, "The Manager's Self-Assessment of Managerial Roles: Small vs. Large Firms," *American Journal of Small Business* (January/March 1984), 61–62.

41. McCall and Lombardo, "Off the Track"; and Carol Hymowitz, "Five Main Reasons Why Managers Fail," *The Wall Street Journal*, May 2, 1988, 21.

42. Joel Arthur Barker, *Future Edge* (New York: William Morrow, 1992).

43. James Gleick, *Chaos: Making a New Science* (New York: Viking, 1987).

44. Janice Castro, "Get Set: Here They Come!" *Time*, Fall 1990 special issue, 50–51; Carol Hymowitz, "Day in the Life of Tomorrow's Manager," *The Wall Street Journal*, March 20, 1989, B1; and Amanda Troy Segal, "Corporate Women," *Business Week*, June 8, 1992, 74–78.

45. Brian Bremner, "The Age of Consolidation," *Business Week*, October 14, 1991, 86–94.

46. John A. Byrne, "Profiting from the Nonprofits," *Business Week*, March 26, 1990, 66–74; and Michael Ryval, "Born-Again Bureaucrats," *Canadian Business*, November 1991, 64–71.

47. "Readying for the Global Bazaar," *Management Review*, September 1989, 18–19.

48. Bob Hagerty, "Firms in Europe Try to Find Executives Who Can Cross Borders in a Single Bound," *The Wall Street Journal*, January 25, 1991, B1; and Shawn Tully, "The Hunt for the Global Manager," *Fortune*, May 21, 1990, 140–144.

49. Barrier, "First in Line at the Cafeteria"; and Barrett, "The Best Little Hash House in Texas."

FOUNDATIONS OF MANAGEMENT UNDERSTANDING

2

CHAPTER OUTLINE

LEARNING OBJECTIVES

After studying this chapter, you should be able to

- Understand how historical forces in society have influenced the practice of management.

- Identify and explain major developments in the history of management thought.

- Describe the major components of the classical management perspective.

- Describe the major components of the human resource management perspective.

- Discuss the quantitative management perspective.

- Explain the major concepts of systems theory.

- Discuss the basic concepts underlying contingency views.

- Describe the recent influences of global competition on management in North America.

n the early 1980s, CPA Gregg L. Foster was the number two executive in his firm and was ready to start enjoying some of the fruits of a half lifetime of labor. Instead, he started acting like a man pushing people aside to get a seat on the Titanic. Foster entered a deal in 1983 to purchase the Elyria Foundry, a maker of heavy metal engine frames, pump housings, and air conditioner compressor valves. Although the 85-year-old iron foundry had once been a leader in its industry, it was now struggling for survival. The company, based outside of Cleveland, employed only 107 people, was running at under 15 percent of capacity, and had lost $3 million on annual revenues of only $4 million. To put things in perspective, everything that Foster put up, borrowed, and obtained as collateral from the seller did not quite come up to the last three months' losses. Still, Foster was betting he could beat the odds and save Elyria from an almost certain demise by blending historical lessons with new management techniques. ■ Faced with a dying industry, deep-rooted union problems, aging equipment, and a prolonged recession for heavy machinery, Foster had a formidable challenge awaiting him. Do you think a historical analysis would be a help or hindrance in overcoming the forces working against Elyria? What strategies do you believe Foster should employ to revive the company? Or has he simply taken on too much?[1]

Why should history matter to corporate managers like Gregg Foster of Elyria? The foundry's success may well hinge on Foster's bets about historical trends and the company's ability to capitalize on the cycles of economic growth and new product introductions that have persisted for almost 100 years. A historical perspective matters to executives, because it is a way of thinking, a way of searching for patterns and determining whether they recur across time periods. A historical perspective provides a context or environment in which to interpret problems. Only then does a major problem take on real meaning, reveal its severity, and point the way toward management actions.[2]

A study of the past contributes to understanding both the present and the future. It is a way of learning: learning from others' mistakes so as not to repeat them; learning from others' successes so as to repeat them in the appropriate situation; and, most of all, learning to understand why things happen to improve things in the future.

For example, such companies as Polaroid, Consolidated Edison, and Wells Fargo Bank have all asked historians to research their pasts. Managers want to know their corporate roots. Polaroid's W-3 plant in Waltham, Massachusetts, started out as a model of efficiency, but over the years productivity dropped and relations with workers soured. A corporate historian was hired to interview employees and examine old records. He pieced together how managers had imposed ever tighter controls over the years that lowered workers' morale.[3] Or consider the signing of Randy Travis, now a country music superstar, by Warner Brothers. Country music had been invaded by pop music influence, and industry managers wanted more pop in the country sound to appeal to younger audiences. Martha Sharp, a vice-president for Warner Brothers, loved Travis's voice and used a cycle-of-history argument on her bosses. She argued that based on historical patterns, a traditional country sound would reemerge, and Travis would be in the forefront. Her argument won, Travis was signed, and he led a resurgence in country music.[4]

This chapter provides an overview of how managers' philosophies have changed over the years. This foundation of management understanding illustrates that the value of studying management lies not in learning current facts and research but in developing a perspective that will facilitate the broad, long-term view needed for management success.

● HISTORICAL FORCES SHAPING MANAGEMENT

Studying history does not mean merely arranging events in chronological order; it means developing an understanding of the impact of societal forces on organizations. Studying history is a way to achieve strategic thinking, see the big picture, and improve conceptual skills. We will start by examining how social, political, and economic forces have influenced organizations and the practice of management.[5]

Social forces refer to those aspects of a culture that guide and influence relationships among people. What do people value? What do people need? What are the standards of behavior among people? These forces shape what is known as the *social contract*, which refers to the unwritten, common rules and perceptions about relationships among people and between employees and management. Expressions such as "a man's as good as his word" and "a day's work for a day's pay" convey such perceptions.

Political forces refer to the influence of political and legal institutions on people and organizations. Political forces include basic assumptions underlying the political system, such as the desirability of self-government, property rights, contract rights, the definition of justice, and the determination of innocence or guilt of a crime. Further, political forces determine managers' rights relative to those of owners, customers, suppliers, and workers as well as other publics with whom the organization must interact. For example, deregulation is a political force that has influenced the way of doing business in the banking and airline industries. Managers can understand deregulation by studying the regulations' original impact on corporations and how new regulations changed the market.

social forces

The aspects of a culture that guide and influence relationships among people—their values, needs, and standards of behavior.

political forces

The influence of political and legal institutions on people and organizations.

Lewis Hine's famous 1911 "Breaker Boys" photograph raised public outcry, and social, political, and economic forces all played a part in the passage of laws forbidding child labor. While bent in a back-breaking position and breathing coal dust, these boys picked impurities from coals 12 to 14 hours a day, six days a week, for $.75 a day.

economic forces
Forces that affect the availability, production, and distribution of a society's resources among competing users.

Economic forces pertain to the availability, production, and distribution of resources in a society. Governments, military agencies, churches, schools, and business organizations in every society require resources to achieve their objectives, and economic forces influence the allocation of scarce resources. Resources may be human or material, fabricated or natural, physical or conceptual, but over time they are scarce and must be allocated among competing users. Economic scarcity is often the stimulus for technological innovation with which to increase resource availability. The perfection of the moving assembly line at Ford in 1913 cut the number of worker-hours needed for assembling a Model T from 12 to 1.5. Ford doubled its daily pay rate to $5, shortened working hours, and cut the price of Model Ts until its market share reached 57 percent in 1923.

The Manager's Shop Talk box gives an example of how social and economic forces affected business decisions at Blue Bird Body Co.

● CLASSICAL PERSPECTIVE

The practice of management can be traced to 3000 B.C. to the first government organizations developed by the Sumerians and Egyptians, but the formal study of management is relatively recent.[6] The early study of management as we know it today began with what is now called the *classical perspective*.

classical perspective
A management perspective that emerged during the nineteenth and early twentieth centuries that emphasized a rational, scientific approach to the study of management and sought to make organizations efficient operating machines.

The **classical perspective** on management emerged during the nineteenth and early twentieth centuries. It was based on management experiences from manufacturing, transportation, and communication industries, which were heavily staffed by engineers. Firms tended to be small or composed of departments or divisions consisting of small groups. Most organizations produced only one line of product or service. Further, major educational, social, and cultural differences existed among owners, managers, and workers.

The factory system that began to appear in the 1800s posed management challenges that earlier organizations had not encountered. Problems arose in tooling the plants, organizing managerial structure, training employees (many of them non–English-speaking immigrants), scheduling complex manufacturing operations, and dealing with increased labor dissatisfaction and resulting strikes. These problems offset the factory system's increased efficiency brought about by interchangeable parts, standardization of products, division of labor, and improved rail transportation.

Traditional small, family-owned industrial plants with an average work force of eight employees in 1870 found the rapid growth in the late nineteenth century to be overwhelming. For example, McCormick Harvester Works of Chicago began in the 1840s with 23 employees. By 1884 it had a monstrous 12-acre plant employing 1,300 workers. A nostalgic longing for the "old and pleasant relations" of the small family-owned business failed to deal effectively with mounting labor grievances. The unhappy results were strikes and, ultimately, the disastrous Haymarket strike and violent labor riot in Chicago in May 1886.[7]

BLUE BIRD BODY COMPANY

Blue Bird Body Company is a family-run business with a firm hold on its leading position in the highly competitive school bus manufacturing business. A. Laurence Luce founded Blue Bird in 1932, and his sons George, Albert, and Joe assumed control in 1962. The company has five plants in the United States and Canada, and is the nation's largest maker of school buses. Blue Bird sells around 15,000 buses a year.

The sons learned their business, and the value of a dollar from their Depression-era father. He could cost the component parts of manufacturing a bus almost to the penny. In an industry where flinty-eyed state or local school boards scrutinize bids for the lowest-cost producer, such lessons helped earn Blue Bird one sale in three in the U.S. market.

Still, the company was a dichotomy. Old-world ways of making a company a community and the emphasis on religious beliefs comingled with the double edge cut of technology and competition. Engineers at Blue Bird availed themselves of the latest computer-aided technology systems. On their way to lunch they passed by the company's ten "Beliefs of the Blue Bird Company," opening with, "We will continue to build our companies on the

foundations of Christianity and the free enterprise system."

The eldest son, George Luce, forced nothing on anyone, but he did not make apologies either. The one-time missionary liked the old American shop environment, and could not see much future for it given the U.S. trend toward service businesses. "After all," he said, "somebody has got to make something for the service economy to work on. You have to create a product first."

Whether right or wrong in their viewpoints, nothing calcified the foresight of George or brothers Albert, Jr., and Joseph. Despite their aging eyes, they noted the ebbing numbers of school-age children and correctly predicted an eventual flattening in the demand for school buses. They coincidentally noted longer life spans and an increase in retirees with disposable income. In response, they began producing what are called Blue Bird Wanderlodges.

Called "Birds," these luxury vehicles ranged between 31 and 40 feet, traveled up to 1,200 miles on 200 gallons of fuel, and featured amenities like microwaves, satellite dishes, and VCRs. Priced at between $250,000 and $350,000, the Wanderlodges made up a large portion of sales and nearly half the profits for the company. Customers included a couple of foreign kings, Hussein of Jordan and Fahd of Saudi Arabia, and a couple of U.S.

kings, Johnny Cash and the late John Wayne.

The Luce brothers opened the board to nonfamily directors and hired Paul Glaske in 1986, the first company president from outside the family. Three brothers who used to hold their board meetings around the water cooler thought Glaske was the needed bridge between generations. "Blue Bird is really what an American company should be," said Glaske, "the type of company I can be proud to be associated with." The three sons in line to take over company oprations eventually left to persue other interests, however. A few months after George's death in 1991, the remaining brothers decided to sell Blue Bird. In addition to the $400 million dollar price tag, Glaske made his management position part of the deal. He also got assurances that there would be no shakeups or meddling from Manhattan executives either. The purchaser, Merrill Lynch Capital Partners, provided the response Glaske hoped for, "Look, we don't know how to build buses and we don't want to know. Whatever you need to do to make that company succeed is what we want you to do." ■

SOURCE: Scott Thurston, "Bus Maker Severs Ties to Founder," *Atlanta Journal & Constitution*, July 19, 1992; and Rita Koselka, "It was important to Father and Mother, and it's important to us," *Forbes*, October 6, 1986, 88–95.

In light of such events and in response to the myriad new problems facing management throughout industrial America, managers developed and tested solutions to the mounting challenges. The evolution of modern management, called the *classical perspective*, thus began. This perspective contains three subfields, each with a slightly different emphasis: scientific management, bureaucratic organization, and administrative principles.[8]

SCIENTIFIC MANAGEMENT

Organizations' somewhat limited success in achieving improvements in labor productivity led a young engineer to suggest that the problem lay more in poor management practices than in labor. Frederick Winslow Taylor (1856–1915) insisted that management itself would have to change and, further, that the manner of change could be determined only by scientific study; hence, the label **scientific management** emerged. Taylor suggested that decisions based on rules of thumb and tradition be replaced with precise procedures developed after careful study of individual situations.

While working at the Midvale Steel Company in Philadelphia, Taylor began experimenting with management methods, procedures, and practices. Taylor wrote frequently, had others write under his name, and consulted with businesses to encourage utilization of his ideas.[9] However, it was after the Eastern Railroad Rate Case hearings before the House of Representatives that his work really caught on. The attorney for the shippers, Louis D. Brandeis, used the term *scientific management* and successfully argued the shippers' side of the issue for using these techniques. The popular press picked up the term, and Taylor and his ideas became heralded as the way to prosperity for the United States.[10]

Taylor's approach is illustrated by the unloading of iron from rail cars and reloading finished steel for the Bethlehem Steel plant in 1898. Taylor calculated that with correct movements, tools, and sequencing, each man was capable of loading 47.5 tons per day instead of the typical 12.5 tons. He also worked out an incentive system that paid each man $1.85 a day for meeting the new standard, an increase from the previous rate of $1.15. Productivity at Bethlehem Steel shot up overnight.

Although known as the "father of scientific management," Taylor was not alone in this area. Henry Gantt, an associate of Taylor's, developed the *Gantt Chart*—a bar graph that measures planned and completed work along each stage of production by time elapsed. Two other important pioneers in this area were the husband-and-wife team of Frank B. and Lillian M. Gilbreth. Frank B. Gilbreth (1868–1924) pioneered time and motion study and arrived at many of his management techniques independently of Taylor. He stressed efficiency and was known for his quest for the "one best way" to do work. Although Gilbreth is known for his early work with bricklayers, his work had great impact on medical surgery by drastically reducing the time patients spent on the operating table. Surgeons were able to save countless lives through the application of time and motion study. Lillian M. Gilbreth (1878–1972) was more interested in the human aspect of work. When her husband died at the age of 56, she had 12 children ages 2 to 19. The undaunted "first lady of management" went right on with her work. She presented a paper in place of her late husband, continued their seminars and con-

scientific management

A subfield of the classical management perspective that emphasized scientifically determined changes in management practices as the solution to improving labor productivity.

Frederick Winslow Taylor (1856–1915)
Taylor's theory that labor productivity could be improved by scientifically determined management practices earned him the status of "father of scientific management."

sulting, lectured, and eventually became a professor at Purdue University.[11] She pioneered in the field of industrial psychology and made substantial contributions to personnel management.

The basic ideas of scientific management are shown in Exhibit 2.1. To use this approach, managers should develop standard methods for doing each job, select workers with the appropriate abilities, train workers in the standard methods, support workers and eliminate interruptions, and provide wage incentives.

Although scientific management improved productivity, its failure to deal with the social context and workers' needs led to increased conflict between managers and employees. Under this system, workers often felt exploited. This was in sharp contrast to the harmony and cooperation that Taylor and his followers had envisioned.

BUREAUCRATIC ORGANIZATIONS

A systematic approach developed in Europe that looked at the organization as a whole is the **bureaucratic organizations** approach, a subfield within the classical perspective. Max Weber (1864–1920), a German theorist, introduced most of the concepts on bureaucratic organizations.[12]

During the late 1800s, many European organizations were managed on a "personal," family-like basis. Employees were loyal to a single individual rather than to the organization or its mission. The dysfunctional consequence of this management practice was that resources were used to realize individual desires rather than organizational goals. Employees in effect owned the organization and used resources for their own gain rather than to serve clients. Weber envisioned organizations that would be managed on an impersonal, rational basis. This form of organization was called a *bureaucracy*. Exhibit 2.2 summarizes the six characteristics of bureaucracy as specified by Weber.

Weber believed that an organization based on rational authority would be more efficient and adaptable to change because continuity is

Lillian M. Gilbreth (1878–1972)
Frank B. Gilbreth (1868–1924)
This husband-and-wife team contributed to the principles of scientific management. His development of time and motion studies and her work in industrial psychology pioneered many of today's management and human resource techniques.

bureaucratic organizations

A subfield of the classical management perspective that emphasized management on an impersonal, rational basis through elements such as clearly defined authority and responsibility, formal recordkeeping, and separation of management and ownership.

General Approach
- Developed standard method for performing each job.
- Selected workers with appropriate abilities for each job.
- Trained workers in standard method.
- Supported workers by planning their work and eliminating interruptions.
- Provided wage incentives to workers for increased output.

Contributions
- Demonstrated the importance of compensation for performance.
- Initiated the careful study of tasks and jobs.
- Demonstrated the importance of personnel selection and training.

Criticisms
- Did not appreciate the social context of work and higher needs of workers.
- Did not acknowledge variance among individuals.
- Tended to regard workers as uninformed and ignored their ideas and suggestions.

EXHIBIT 2.1

Characteristics of Scientific Management

E X H I B I T   2 . 2

Characteristics of Weberian
Bureaucracy

SOURCE: Adapted from A. M. Henderson
and Talcott Parsons, eds. and trans.,
Max Weber, *The Theory of Social and
Economic Organizations* (New York:
Free Press, 1947), 328–337.

Elements of Bureaucracy

1. Labor is divided with clear definitions of authority and responsibility that are legitimized as official duties.
2. Positions are organized in a hierarchy of authority, with each position under the authority of a higher one.
3. All personnel are selected and promoted based on technical qualifications, which are assessed by examination or according to training and experience.
4. Administrative acts and decisions are recorded in writing. Recordkeeping provides organizational memory and continuity over time.
5. Management is separate from the ownership of the organization.
6. Managers are subject to rules and procedures that will ensure reliable, predictable behavior. Rules are impersonal and uniformly applied to all employees.

Max Weber
(1864–1920)
The German theorist's concepts on
bureaucratic organizations have contributed to the efficiency of many of
today's corporations.

related to formal structure and positions rather than to a particular person, who may leave or die. To Weber, rationality in organizations meant employee selection and advancement based on competence rather than on "whom you know." The organization relies on rules and written records for continuity. The manager depends not on his or her personality for successfully giving orders but on the legal power invested in the managerial position.

The term *bureaucracy* has taken on a negative meaning in today's organizations and is associated with endless rules and red tape. We have all been frustrated by waiting in long lines or following seemingly silly procedures. On the other hand, rules and other bureaucratic procedures provide a standard way of dealing with employees. Everyone gets equal treatment, and everyone knows what the rules are. This has enabled many organizations to become extremely efficient. Consider United Parcel Service, also called the "Brown Giant" for the color of the packages it delivers.

 U N I T E D   P A R C E L   S E R V I C E

United Parcel Service took on the U.S. Postal Service at its own game—and won. UPS specializes in the delivery of small packages. Why has the Brown Giant been so successful? One important reason is the concept of bureaucracy. UPS is bound up in rules and regulations. There are safety rules for drivers, loaders, clerks, and managers. Strict dress codes are enforced—no beards; hair cannot touch the collar; mustaches must be trimmed evenly; and no sideburns. Rules specify cleanliness standards for buildings and other properties. No eating or drinking is permitted at employee desks. Every manager is given bound copies of policy books and expected to use them regularly.

UPS also has a well-defined division of labor. Each plant consists of specialized drivers, loaders, clerks, washers, sorters, and maintenance personnel. UPS thrives on written records. Daily worksheets specify performance goals and work output. Daily employee quotas and achievements are recorded on a weekly and monthly basis.

Technical qualification is the criterion for hiring and promotion. The UPS policy book says the leader is expected to have the knowledge and capacity to justify the position of leadership. Favoritism is forbidden. The bureaucratic model works just fine at UPS, "the tightest ship in the shipping business."[13] ∎

ADMINISTRATIVE PRINCIPLES

Another major subfield within the classical perspective is known as the **administrative principles** approach. Whereas scientific management focused on the productivity of the individual worker, the administrative principles approach focused on the total organization. The contributors to this approach included Henri Fayol, Mary Parker Follett, and Chester I. Barnard.

Henri Fayol (1841–1925) was a French mining engineer who worked his way up to the head of a major mining group known as Comambault. Comambault survives today as part of Le Creusot-Loire, the largest mining and metallurgical group in central France. In his later years, Fayol wrote down his concepts on administration, based largely on his own management experiences.[14]

In his most significant work, *General and Industrial Management*, Fayol discussed 14 general principles of management, several of which are part of management philosophy today. For example:

- *Unit of command.* Each subordinate receives orders from one—and only one—superior.
- *Division of work.* Managerial and technical work are amenable to specialization to produce more and better work with the same amount of effort.
- *Unity of direction.* Similar activities in an organization should be grouped together under one manager.
- *Scalar chain.* A chain of authority extends from the top to the bottom of the organization and should include every employee.

Fayol felt that these principles could be applied in any organizational setting. He also identified five basic functions or elements of management: planning, organizing, commanding, coordinating, and controlling. These functions underlie much of the general approach to today's management theory.

Mary Parker Follett (1868–1933) was trained in philosophy and political science at what today is Radcliffe College. She applied herself in many fields, including social psychology and management. She wrote of the importance of common superordinate goals for reducing conflict in organizations.[15] Her work was popular with businesspeople of her day but was often overlooked by management scholars.[16] Follett's ideas served as a contrast to scientific management and are reemerging as applicable for modern managers dealing with rapid changes in today's global environment. Her approach to leadership stressed the importance of people rather than engineering techniques. She offered the pithy admonition, "Don't Hug Your Blueprints," and analyzed the dynamics of management-organization interactions. Follett addressed issues that

administrative principles
A subfield of the classical management perspective that focused on the total organization rather than the individual worker, delineating the management functions of planning, organizing, commanding, coordinating, and controlling.

Mary Parker Follett
(1868–1933)
Follett was a major contributor to the *administrative principles* approach to management. Her emphasis on worker participation and shared goals among managers was embraced by many businesspeople of the day, and has been recently "rediscovered" by corporate America.

are timely in the 1990s, such as ethics, power, and how to lead in a way that encourages employees to give their best. The concepts of empowerment, facilitating rather than controlling employees, and allowing employees to act depending on the authority of the situation opened new areas for theoretical study by Chester Barnard and others.[17]

Chester I. Barnard (1886–1961) studied economics at Harvard but failed to receive a degree because he lacked a course in laboratory science. He went to work in the statistical department of AT&T and in 1927 became president of New Jersey Bell. One of Barnard's significant contributions was the concept of the informal organization. The *informal organization* occurs in all formal organizations and includes cliques and naturally occurring social groupings. Barnard argued that organizations are not machines and informal relationships are powerful forces that can help the organization if properly managed. Another significant contribution was the *acceptance theory of authority*, which states that people have free will and can choose whether to follow management orders. People typically follow orders because they perceive positive benefit to themselves, but they do have a choice. Managers should treat employees properly because their acceptance of authority may be critical to organization success in important situations.[18]

The overall classical perspective as an approach to management was very powerful and gave companies fundamental new skills for establishing high productivity and effective treatment of employees. Indeed, America surged ahead of the world in management techniques, and other countries, especially Japan, borrowed heavily from American ideas following World War II, when General Douglas MacArthur summoned Homer Sarasohn, Charles Protzman, and Frank Polkingham to teach management fundamentals to the Japanese. Those lessons were reinforced by a second wave of Americans, including W. Edwards Deming and J. M. Juran.

● HUMAN RESOURCE PERSPECTIVE

America has always had a spirit of human equality. However, this spirit has not always been translated into practice when it comes to power sharing between managers and workers. The **human resource perspective** has recognized and directly responded to social pressures for enlightened treatment of employees. The early work on industrial psychology and personnel selection received little attention because of the prominence of scientific management. However, a series of studies at a Chicago electric company changed all that.

human resource perspective

A management perspective that emerged around the late nineteenth century that emphasized enlightened treatment of workers and power sharing between managers and employees.

THE HAWTHORNE STUDIES

Beginning about 1895, a struggle developed between manufacturers of gas and electric lighting fixtures for control of the residential and industrial market.[19] By 1909 electric lighting had begun to win, but the increasingly efficient electric fixtures used less total power. The electric companies began a campaign to convince industrial users that they needed more light to get more productivity. When advertising did not work, the industry began using experimental tests to demonstrate their argument. Managers were skeptical about the results, so the Committee on Industrial Lighting (CIL) was set up to run the tests. To further add to the tests' credibility, Thomas Edison was made honorary chairman of the CIL. In one test location—the Hawthorne plant of the Western Electric Company—some interesting events occurred. These and subsequent experiments have come to be known as the **Hawthorne studies**.

The major part of this work involved four experimental and three control groups. In all, five different "tests" were conducted. These pointed to the importance of factors *other* than illumination in affecting productivity. To more carefully examine these factors, numerous other experiments were conducted.[20] These were the first Relay Assembly Test Room, the second Relay Assembly Group, the Mica Splitting Group, the Typewriting Group, and the Bank Wiring Observation Room. The results of the most famous study, the first Relay Assembly Test Room (RATR) experiment, were extremely controversial. Under the guidance of two Harvard professors, Elton Mayo and Fritz Roethlisberger, the RATR studies lasted nearly six years (May 10, 1927, to May 4, 1933) and involved 24 separate experimental periods. So many factors were changed and so many unforeseen factors uncontrolled that scholars disagree on the factors that truly contributed to the general increase in performance over that period. Most early interpretations, however, agreed on one thing: Money was not the cause of the increased output.[21] Recent analyses of the experiments, however, suggest that money may well have been the single most important factor.[22] An interview with one of the original participants revealed that just getting into the experimental group had meant a huge increase in income.[23]

These new data clearly show that money mattered a great deal at Hawthorne, but it was not recognized at the time of the experiments. Then it was felt that the factor that best explained increased output was "human relations." Employees' output increased sharply when managers treated them in a positive manner. These findings were published and started a revolution in worker treatment for improving organizational productivity. To be historically accurate, money was probably the best explanation for increases in output, but at that time experimenters believed the explanation was human relations. Despite the inaccurate interpretation of the data, the findings provided the impetus for the human relations movement. That movement shaped management theory and practice for well over a quarter-century, and the belief that human relations is the best approach for increasing productivity persists today. See the Manager's Shoptalk box for a number of management innovations that have become popular over the years.

THE HUMAN RELATIONS MOVEMENT

One reason that "human relations" interpretation may have been so readily attached to the Hawthorne studies was the Great Depression. An unprecedented number of people were out of work. Emerging social forces supported people's humanitarian efforts to help one another. The

Hawthorne studies

A series of experiments on worker productivity begun in 1924 at the Hawthorne plant of Western Electric Company in Illinois; attributed employees' increased output to managers' better treatment of them during the study.

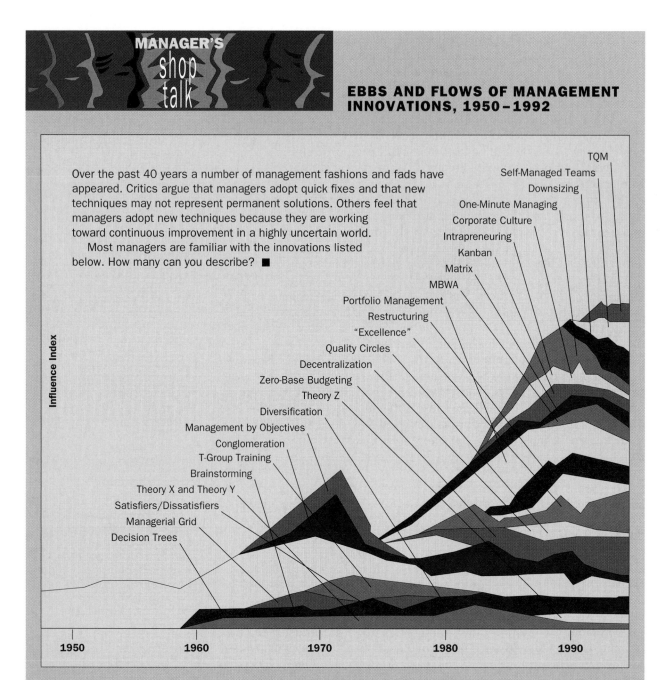

MANAGER'S
shop talk

EBBS AND FLOWS OF MANAGEMENT INNOVATIONS, 1950–1992

Over the past 40 years a number of management fashions and fads have appeared. Critics argue that managers adopt quick fixes and that new techniques may not represent permanent solutions. Others feel that managers adopt new techniques because they are working toward continuous improvement in a highly uncertain world.

Most managers are familiar with the innovations listed below. How many can you describe? ■

Influence Index

TQM
Self-Managed Teams
Downsizing
One-Minute Managing
Corporate Culture
Intrapreneuring
Kanban
Matrix
MBWA
Portfolio Management
Restructuring
"Excellence"
Quality Circles
Decentralization
Zero-Base Budgeting
Theory Z
Diversification
Management by Objectives
Conglomeration
T-Group Training
Brainstorming
Theory X and Theory Y
Satisfiers/Dissatisfiers
Managerial Grid
Decision Trees

1950   1960   1970   1980   1990

SOURCE: Adapted from Fig. 1.3, Richard Tanner Pascale, *Managing on the Edge* (New York: Touchstone/Simon & Schuster, 1990) 20. Copyright © 1990 by Richard Pascale. Reprinted by permission of Simon & Schuster, Inc.

human relations movement

A movement in management thinking and practice that emphasized satisfaction of employees' basic needs as the key to increased worker productivity.

human relations movement initially espoused a "dairy farm" view of management—contented cows give more milk, so satisfied workers will give more work. Gradually, views with deeper content began to emerge. Two of the best-known contributors to the human relations movement were Abraham Maslow and Douglas McGregor.

Abraham Maslow (1908–1970), a practicing psychologist, observed that his patients' problems usually stemmed from an inability to satisfy many of their needs. Thus, he generalized his work and suggested a hierarchy of needs. Maslow's hierarchy started with physiological needs and progressed to safety, belongingness, esteem, and, finally, self-actualization needs. Chapter 13 discusses his ideas in greater detail.

Douglas McGregor (1906–1964) had become frustrated with the early simplistic human relations notions while president of Antioch College in Ohio. He challenged both the classical perspective and the early human relations assumptions about human behavior. Based on his experiences as a manager and consultant, his training as a psychologist, and the work of Maslow, McGregor formulated his Theory X and Theory Y, which are explained in Exhibit 2.3.[24] McGregor believed that the classical perspective was based on Theory X assumptions about workers. He also felt that a slightly modified version of Theory X fit early human relations ideas. In other words, human relations ideas did not go far enough. McGregor proposed Theory Y as a more realistic view of workers for guiding management thinking.

The point of Theory Y is that organizations can take advantage of the imagination and intellect of all their employees. Employees will exercise self-control and will contribute to organizational objectives when given the opportunity. A few companies today still use Theory X management, but many are trying Theory Y techniques. With one of the best financial track records in the banking industry, University Bank and Trust has practiced Theory Y from its company's beginning.

Assumptions of Theory X
- The average human being has an inherent dislike of work and will avoid it if possible....
- Because of the human characteristic of dislike for work, most people must be coerced, controlled, directed, or threatened with punishment to get them to put forth adequate effort toward the achievement of organizational objectives....
- The average human being prefers to be directed, wishes to avoid responsibility, has relatively little ambition, wants security above all.

Assumptions of Theory Y
- The expenditure of physical and mental effort in work is as natural as play or rest. The average human being does not inherently dislike work....
- External control and the threat of punishment are not the only means for bringing about effort toward organizational objectives. A person will exercise self-direction and self-control in the service of objectives to which he or she is committed....
- The average human being learns, under proper conditions, not only to accept but to seek responsibility....
- The capacity to exercise a relatively high degree of imagination, ingenuity, and creativity in the solution of organizational problems is widely, not narrowly, distributed in the population.
- Under the conditions of modern industrial life, the intellectual potentialities of the average human being are only partially utilized.

E X H I B I T   2 . 3

Theory X and Theory Y

SOURCE: Douglas McGregor, *The Human Side of Enterprise* (New York: McGraw-Hill, 1960), 33–48.

UNIVERSITY NATIONAL BANK & TRUST COMPANY

Banks are notorious for playing by the rules. Everyone from senior vice presidents on down typically has a set of policies and procedures they are required to follow. At University National Bank & Trust Company, in Palo Alto, California, the opposite is true. Employees are encouraged to think for themselves, and those who expect to find answers in a manual are searching in vain "What will kill this company first is a bunch of people running around with their noses stuck in rule books and manuals," says Carl Schmitt, who founded the small community bank in 1980.

In order to ensure that even the most mundane jobs are challenging, Schmitt allows his 100-plus employees to take responsibility for their actions. Each teller, for example, has the authority to decide whether or not to cash a check, and the criteria are entirely subjective. Schmitt extends the policy further through a program he calls a "bank within a bank." These minibanks, made up of small teams headed by a senior vice president, oversee their own customers and loan portfolios. They even write letters on their own letterhead. In addition to having almost unlimited leeway in making day-to-day decisions, employees also receive generous pay, lucrative benefits, and the option to participate in a modified stock ownership plan. It is not surprising that turnover is low.

In a field dominated by pinstripes and conservative approaches, Schmitt's unconventional style may raise eyebrows, but it also breeds results. University National's return on assets exceeds the U.S. bank average by 45 percent. According to *Barron's,* the bank enjoys a seldom seen combination of robust reserves and almost no nonperforming loans. Perhaps this is why Schmitt is not shy about proclaiming the bank's unusual approach to the world. The license plates on the bank's courier trucks read: "UNBANK."[25] ■

behavioral sciences approach

A subfield of the human resource management perspective that applied social science in an organizational context, drawing from economics, psychology, sociology, and other disciplines.

BEHAVIORAL SCIENCES APPROACH

The word *science* is the keyword in the **behavioral sciences approach** (see Exhibit 2.4). Systematic research is the basis for theory development

---

EXHIBIT 2.4

The Behavioral Sciences Approach

General Approach
- Applies social science in an organizational context.
- Draws from an interdisciplinary research base, including anthropology, economics, psychology, and sociology.

Contributions
- Has improved our understanding of and practical applications for organizational processes such as motivation, communication, leadership, and group processes.
- Regards members of organizations as full human beings, not as tools.

Criticisms
- Because findings are increasingly complex, practical applications often are tried incorrectly or not at all.
- Some concepts run counter to common sense, thus inviting managers' rejection.

and testing, and its results form the basis for practical applications. The behavioral sciences approach can be seen in practically every organization. When General Electric conducts research to determine the best set of tests, interviews, and employee profiles to use when selecting new employees, it is employing behavioral science techniques. Emery Air Freight has utilized reinforcement theory to improve the incentives given to workers and increase the performance of many of its operations. When Westinghouse trains new managers in the techniques of employee motivation, most of the theories and findings are rooted in behavioral science research.

In the behavioral sciences, economics and sociology have significantly influenced the way today's managers approach organizational strategy and structure. Psychology has influenced management approaches to motivation, communication, leadership, and the overall field of personnel management. The conclusions from the tremendous body of behavioral science research are much like those derived from the natural sciences. Although we understand more, that understanding is not simple. Scholars have learned much about the behavior of people at work, but they have also learned that organizational processes are astonishingly complex.

All of the remaining chapters of this book contain research findings and applications that can be attributed to the behavioral sciences approach to the study of organizations and management. The Manager's Shoptalk box (page 50) shows the trend of new management concepts from the behavioral sciences. Note the increase in concepts about 1970 and then again from 1980 until the present. The increasing intensity of global competition has produced great interest in improved behavioral approaches to management. The continued development of new management techniques can be expected in the future.

● MANAGEMENT SCIENCE PERSPECTIVE

World War II caused many management changes. The massive and complicated problems associated with modern global warfare presented managerial decision makers with the need for more sophisticated tools than ever before. The **management science perspective** emerged to treat those problems. This view is distinguished for its application of mathematics, statistics, and other quantitative techniques to management decision making and problem solving. During World War II, groups of mathematicians, physicists, and other scientists were formed to solve military problems. Because those problems frequently involved moving massive amounts of materials and large numbers of people quickly and efficiently, the techniques had obvious applications to large-scale business firms.[26]

Operations research grew directly out of the World War II groups (called *operational research teams* in Great Britain and *operations research teams* in the United States).[27] It consists of mathematical model building and other applications of quantitative techniques to managerial problems.

management science perspective

A management perspective that emerged after World War II and applied mathematics, statistics, and other quantitative techniques to managerial problems.

Operations management refers to the field of management that specializes in the physical production of goods or services. Operations management specialists use quantitative techniques to solve manufacturing problems. Some of the commonly used methods are forecasting, inventory modeling, linear and nonlinear programming, queuing theory, scheduling, simulation and breakeven analysis.

Management information systems (MIS) is the most recent subfield of the management science perspective. These systems are designed to provide relevant information to managers in a timely and cost-efficient manner. The advent of the high-speed digital computer opened up the full potential of this area for management.

Many of today's organizations have departments of management science specialists to help solve quantitatively based problems. When Sears used computer models to minimize its inventory costs, it was applying a quantitative approach to management. When AT&T performed network analysis to speed up and control the construction of new facilities and switching systems, it was employing management science tools.

One specific technique used in many organizations is queuing theory. *Queuing theory* uses mathematics to calculate how to provide services that will minimize the waiting time of customers. Queuing theory has been used to analyze the traffic flow through the Lincoln Tunnel and to determine the number of toll booths and traffic officers for a toll road. Queuing theory was used to develop the single waiting line for tellers used in many banks. Wesley Long Community Hospital in Greensboro, North Carolina, used queuing theory to analyze the telemetry system used in wireless cardiac monitors. The analysis helped the hospital acquire the precise number of telemetry units needed to safely monitor all patients without overspending scarce resources.[28]

● CONTEMPORARY EXTENSIONS

Each of the three major management perspectives is still in use today. The Leading Edge box describes one example of a company that uses the human relations approach. The most prevalent is the human resource perspective, but even it has been undergoing change in recent years. Two major contemporary extensions of this perspective are systems theory and the contingency view. Examination of each will allow a fuller appreciation of the state of management thinking today.

SYSTEMS THEORY

system

A set of interrelated parts that function as a whole to achieve a common purpose.

systems theory

An extension of the human resources perspective that describes organizations as open systems that are characterized by entropy, synergy, and subsystem interdependence.

A **system** is a set of interrelated parts that function as a whole to achieve a common purpose.[29] A system functions by acquiring inputs from the external environment, transforming them in some way, and discharging outputs back to the environment. Exhibit 2.5 shows the basic **systems theory** of organizations. Here there are five components: inputs, a transformation process, outputs, feedback, and the environment. *Inputs* are the material, human, financial, or information resources used to produce goods or services. The *transformation process* is management's use of pro-

GRANITE ROCK COMPANY

Granite Rock Co. of Watsonville, California, has been owned and operated by the Woolpert family for more than 90 years. However, by the late 1980s, other similar family operations were being absorbed by conglomerates. The state of California was tightening industrial, air, and water regulations, and customers were clamoring for higher quality materials and more responsive service. Computer technology that would automate quarry work and concrete production was on the horizon, but at substantial cost. The asphalt, concrete, and retail building supply business was in transition. Granite Rock would need to find new ways of doing business amidst a host of changes and well-financed predators.

Bruce Woolpert, a joint CEO with his brother Steve, had spent eight years with Hewlett-Packard and he did not see why Granite Rock could not be as efficient and customer-oriented as HP. He decided the first step in that process was to get as much information flowing into the company as possible. While other high-tech manufacturers charted a dozen internal process controls, Granite Rock kept track of one hundred. He started asking customers to rate the company against competitors, and even issued "report cards" so that they could register their evaluations.

Woolpert also began picking up information on his own. He visited cement plants and the quarry, and inquired what workers liked and did not like about their jobs, their company, and even other companies. He established communication from the top management down to the quarry workers, and encouraged feedback in the other direction. He took a human relations approach, setting up teams of managers and hourly workers and giving them the latitude to analyze and act on matters within their departments. The joint merger of the groups increased input and united the company's 400 white- and blue-collar employees.

Employee education has been another unifying factor at Granite Rock. Woolpert has emphasized ongoing training, bringing in instructional speakers and urging employees to attend seminars on company time. Putting management and rank-and-file in the same classrooms, and the same hotels out of town, has reinforced a sense of common purpose. "I think Bruce wants us all to get a little smarter," says Ray Morgan, a supervisor and 20-year employee. "We're allowed to learn anything we can." The company also pays for employees to attend courses at the local college.

Technology and training have made Granite Rock the region's low-cost producer of crushed rock with annual sales of more than $90 million. The work force is highly motivated, and quality and service levels allow it to charge a 6 percent premium for concrete and asphalt and still increase market share. In Chapter 12, we will see exactly how Granite Rock inspires such fierce loyalty among its employees that few leave except to retire. ■

SOURCE: Edward Welles, "How're We Doing?" *INC.*, May 1991, 80–83; John Case, "The Change Masters," *INC.*, March 1992, 58–70; Company sources.

duction technology to change the inputs into outputs. *Outputs* include the organization's products and services. *Feedback* is knowledge of the results that influence the selection of inputs during the next cycle of the process. The *environment* surrounding the organization includes the social, political, and economic forces noted earlier in this chapter.

Some ideas in systems theory have had substantial impact on management thinking. These include open and closed systems, entropy, synergy, and subsystem interdependencies.[30]

Open systems must interact with the environment to survive; **closed systems** need not. In the classical and management science perspectives,

open system
A system that interacts with the external environment.

closed system
A system that does not interact with the external environment

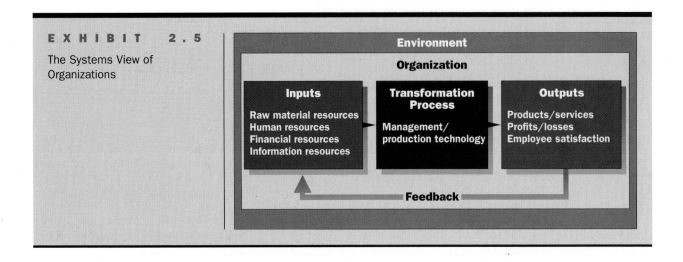

EXHIBIT   2.5

The Systems View of
Organizations

---

organizations were frequently thought of as closed systems. In the management science perspective, closed system assumptions—the absence of external disturbances—are sometimes used to simplify problems for quantitative analysis. In reality, however, all organizations are open systems and the cost of ignoring the environment may be failure. A prison tries to seal itself off from its environment; yet it must receive prisoners from the environment, obtain supplies from the environment, recruit employees from the environment, and ultimately release prisoners back to the environment.

Entropy is a universal property of systems and refers to their tendency to run down and die. If a system does not receive fresh inputs and energy from its environment, it will eventually cease to exist. Organizations must monitor their environments, adjust to changes, and continuously bring in new inputs in order to survive and prosper. Managers try to design the organization/environment interfaces to reduce entropy.

Synergy means that the whole is greater than the sum of its parts. When an organization is formed, something new comes into the world. Management, coordination, and production that did not exist before are now present. Organizational units working together can accomplish more than those same units working alone. The sales department depends on production, and vice versa.

Subsystems are parts of a system that depend on one another. Changes in one part of the organization affect other parts. The organization must be managed as a coordinated whole. Managers who understand subsystem interdependence are reluctant to make changes that do not recognize subsystem impact on the organization as a whole. Consider the management decision to remove time clocks from the Alcan Plant in Canada.

entropy

The tendency for a system to run down and die.

synergy

The concept that the whole is greater than the sum of its parts.

subsystems

Parts of a system that depend on one another for their functioning.

 ALCAN ALUMINUM LIMITED

A personnel specialist proposed that time clocks be removed from the shop floor. The shop managers agreed but after a few months, several problems emerged. A few workers began to show up late, or leave early, or stay away too long at lunch.

Supervisors had new demands placed on them to observe and record when workers came and left. They were responsible for reprimanding workers, which led to antagonistic relationships between supervisors and employees. As a consequence, the plant manager found it necessary to reduce the supervisors' span of control. Supervisors were unable to manage as many people because of the additional responsibility.

As Alcan managers discovered, the simple time clock was interdependent with many other parts of the organization system. The time clock influenced worker tardiness and absenteeism, closeness of supervision, the quality of the relationship between supervisors and workers, and span of management. The organization system was more complex than the personnel specialist had realized when he proposed the idea of removing time clocks.[31] ■

CONTINGENCY VIEW

The second contemporary extension to management thinking is the contingency view. The classical perspective assumed a *universalist* view. Management concepts were thought to be universal, that is, whatever worked—leader style, bureaucratic structure—in one organization would work in another. It proposed the discovery of "one-best-way" management principles that applied the same techniques to every organization. In business education, however, an alternative view exists. This is the *case* view, in which each situation is believed to be unique. There are no universal principles to be found, and one learns about management by experiencing a large number of case problem situations. Managers face the task of determining what methods will work in every new situation.

To integrate these views the **contingency view** has emerged, as illustrated in Exhibit 2.6.[32] Here neither of the above views is seen as entirely correct. Instead, certain contingencies, or variables, exist for helping management identify and understand situations. The contingency view means that a manager's response depends on identifying key

contingency view

An extension of the human resource perspective in which the successful resolution of organizational problems is thought to depend on managers' identification of key variables in the situation at hand.

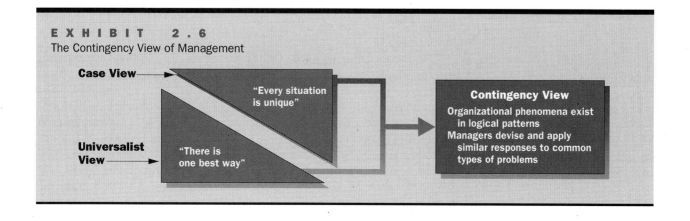

E X H I B I T   2 . 6
The Contingency View of Management

Case View → "Every situation is unique"

Universalist View → "There is one best way"

Contingency View
Organizational phenomena exist in logical patterns
Managers devise and apply similar responses to common types of problems

contingencies in an organizational situation. For example, a consultant may mistakenly recommend the same management-by-objectives (MBO) system for a manufacturing firm that was successful in a school system. A central government agency may impose the same rules on a welfare agency that it did in a worker's compensation office. A large corporation may take over a chain of restaurants and impose the same organizational charts and financial systems that are used in a banking division. The contingency view tells us that what works in one setting may not work in another. Management's job is to search for important contingencies. When managers learn to identify important patterns and characteristics of their organizations, they can then fit solutions to those characteristics.

Industry is one important contingency. Management practice in a rapidly changing industry will be very different from that in a stable one. Other important contingencies that managers must understand are manufacturing technology and international cultures. For example, several major banks, such as Manufacturers Hanover Corporation, misunderstood the nature of making loans to developing countries. As these big banks raised loan-loss reserves to cope with the prospect of bad international loans, their balance sheet was weakened to the extent that they had to stop expansion into new regions and new business activities. Having been through this experience, managers in the future will know how to handle this contingency in the international financial environment.[33]

● RECENT HISTORICAL TRENDS

The historical forces that influence management perspective continue to change and influence the practice of management. The most striking change now affecting management is international competition. This important trend has social, political, and economic consequences for organizations.

INDUSTRIAL GLOBALIZATION

The domain of business now covers the entire planet, where Reeboks, stock markets, fax machines, television, personal computers, and T-shirts intermingle across national boundaries. The world of commerce is becoming wired like an integrated circuit, with no nation left out of the loop.

The impact on firms in the United States and Canada has been severe. International competition has raised the standard of performance in quality, cost, productivity, and response times.[34] As a result, the United States and Canada have seen a decline in worldwide market share in traditional products. Moreover, as recently as 1975, the U.S. balance of payments was close to zero. In recent years it has been hundreds of billions of dollars in the red.[35] Likewise, the business world is reeling under the impact of recent historical events—the breakup of the Soviet Union and the opening of markets among its former republics and throughout the former Eastern bloc; the long-awaited arrival of Europe '92 with its lowering of internal trade boundaries; and the rush to the formation of a North American trade alliance. All of this means a new set of opportunities and upheavals for companies that strive to meet global competitive standards.

Globalization causes the need for innovation and new levels of customer service. Companies must shorten the time for developing new products, and new products must account for a larger percentage of total income because international competitors are relentless innovators.[36] Winning companies in the 1990s must provide extraordinary service. The CEO of one home electronics retailer is gearing up to provide international service through computerized files. If someone has a problem, he or she just calls the company and a computer screen shows the product's serial number, warranty information, whether parts are in stock, and when it can be repaired.[37]

Although managers have tried many techniques and ideas in recent years, two management trends that seem significant in response to international competition are the adoption of Japanese management practices and the renewed efforts to achieve excellence in product and service quality.

JAPANESE MANAGEMENT PRACTICES

In recent years, Japanese management practices have been thought to create more efficient and more effective companies, while American efficiency has been criticized and the American worker described as "lazy"

Believing its people to be the key to excellence, The Stanley Works adapts well to *Japanese-style management practices*, which emphasize teamwork, trust, and empowerment. Team leaders, like those pictured here at Stanley's Richmond, Virginia, consumer hardware facility, are elected on a 9-month rotation, and meet daily to set schedules and sequence production. The results of effective teamwork are quality, improved service, new products, and expanded "reach" for Stanley into the 135 countries in which its products are sold.

by Japanese Diet leader Yosio Sakurauchi. Japanese products—whether motorcycles, automobiles, or VCRs—garner praise as the world's standard in high quality and low price. The problem for U.S. companies was dramatized a few years ago by the visit of American executives of General Motors' Buick division who had visited a Buick car dealership in Japan:

> The operation appeared to be a massive repair facility, so they asked how he had built up such a large service business. He explained with some embarrassment that this was not a repair facility at all but rather a reassembly operation where newly delivered cars were disassembled and rebuilt to Japanese standards. While many Japanese admire the American automobile, they would never accept the low quality with which they are put together.[38]

How was American management expected to compete with NEC, Nissan, Sanyo, Sony, Toyota, and Kawasaki? Answers have been suggested in William Ouchi's *Theory Z* and Richard Pascale and Anthony Athos' *The Art of Japanese Management*.[39] The success of Japanese firms is often attributed to their group orientation. The Japanese culture focuses on trust and intimacy within the group and family. In North America, in contrast, the basic cultural orientation is toward individual rights and achievements. These differences in the two societies are reflected in how companies are managed.

Exhibit 2.7 illustrates differences in the management approaches used in America and Japan. American organizations are characterized as Type A and Japanese organizations Type J. However, it is impractical to take a management approach based on the culture of one country and apply it directly to that of another country. **Theory Z** proposes a hybrid form of management that incorporates techniques from both Japanese and North American management practices. Type Z is a blend of American and Japanese characteristics that can be used to revitalize and strengthen corporate cultures in North America.[40]

As illustrated in Exhibit 2.7, the Type Z organization uses the Japanese characteristic of long-term employment, which means that employees become familiar with the organization and are committed to and fully integrated into it. The Theory Z hybrid also adopts the Japanese approach of slow evaluation and promotion for employees. Likewise, the highly specialized American convention of a narrow career path is modified to reflect career training in multiple departments and functions.

In the Theory Z approach, control over employees combines the U.S. preference for explicit and precise performance measures and the Japanese approach to control based on social values. The Theory Z hybrid also encourages the Japanese characteristic of consensual decision making—that is, managers discuss among themselves and with subordinates until everyone is in agreement. Responsibility for outcomes, however, is based on the American approach of rewarding individuals. Finally, Theory Z adopts the Japanese holistic concern for employees' total personal lives.[41]

Theory Z

A management perspective that incorporates techniques from both Japanese and North American management practices.

ACHIEVING EXCELLENCE

Spurred by ideas from Japanese management and global competition, American managers have reawakened an interest in attaining high-

EXHIBIT   2.7

Characteristics of Theory Z Management

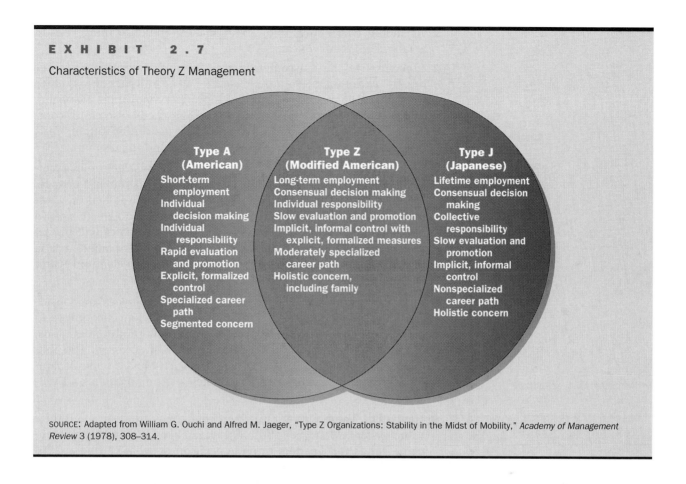

Type A (American)
Short-term employment
Individual decision making
Individual responsibility
Rapid evaluation and promotion
Explicit, formalized control
Specialized career path
Segmented concern

Type Z (Modified American)
Long-term employment
Consensual decision making
Individual responsibility
Slow evaluation and promotion
Implicit, informal control with explicit, formalized measures
Moderately specialized career path
Holistic concern, including family

Type J (Japanese)
Lifetime employment
Consensual decision making
Collective responsibility
Slow evaluation and promotion
Implicit, informal control
Nonspecialized career path
Holistic concern

SOURCE: Adapted from William G. Ouchi and Alfred M. Jaeger, "Type Z Organizations: Stability in the Midst of Mobility," *Academy of Management Review* 3 (1978), 308–314.

quality products through human resource management. The most notable publication in this area is *In Search of Excellence* by Peters and Waterman.[42] The book reported a study of U.S. companies, including Digital Equipment, 3M, Bechtel, Dow, Johnson & Johnson, Disney, Fluor, Caterpillar, Procter & Gamble, and McDonald's. These companies showed above-average performance for several years, and Peters and Waterman's research sought to uncover why. The findings revealed eight **excellence characteristics** that reflected these companies' management values and corporate culture.

excellence characteristics

A group of eight features found to typify the highest-performing U.S. companies.

  1 Bias toward Action. Successful companies value action, doing, and implementation. They do not talk problems to death or spend all their time creating exotic solutions. The CEO of a computer peripherals company put it this way: "We tell our people to make at least 10 mistakes a day. If you are not making 10 mistakes a day, you are not trying hard enough."[43] H. Ross Perot, after selling his company, EDS, to General Motors and serving on GM's board, remarked on the action differences between the two companies: "The first EDSer to see a snake kills it. At GM, the first thing you do is organize a committee on snakes. Then you bring in a consultant who knows a lot about snakes. The third thing you do is talk about it for a year."[44]

2 Closeness to the Customer. Successful companies are customer driven. A dominant value is customer need satisfaction, whether through excellent service or through product innovation. Managers often call customers directly and learn their needs. Successful companies value sales and service overkill. J. Willard Marriott, Sr., read every single customer complaint card—raw and unsummarized.

3 Autonomy and Entrepreneurship. Organization structure in excellent corporations is designed to encourage innovation and change. Technical people are located near marketing people so that they can lunch together. Organizational units are kept small to create a sense of belonging and adaptability. W. L. Gore & Associates will not let a plant grow larger than about 150 employees. Companies such as IBM, 3M, and Hewlett-Packard give freedom to idea champions and venture groups to generate creative new products.

4 Productivity through People. Rank-and-file employees are considered the roots of quality and productivity. People are encouraged to participate in production, marketing, and new-product decisions. Conflicting ideas are encouraged rather than suppressed. The ability to move ahead by consensus preserves trust and a sense of family, increases motivation, and facilitates both innovation and efficiency.

5 Hands On, Value Driven. Excellent companies are clear about their value system. Managers and employees alike know what the company stands for. Leaders provide a vision of what can be accomplished and give employees a sense of purpose and meaning. Leaders are willing to roll up their sleeves and become involved in problems at all levels.

6 Sticking to the Knitting. Successful firms stay close to the business they know and understand. Successful firms are highly focused. For example, Boeing, Intel, and Genentech confine themselves to a single product line of commercial aircraft, integrated circuits, and genetic engineering, respectively. Successful companies do what they know best.

7 Simple Form, Lean Staff. The underlying structural form and systems of excellent companies are elegantly simple, and few personnel are employed in staff positions. Large companies are subdivided into small divisions that allow each to do its job. For example, when Jack Reichert took over Brunswick Corporation, the headquarters' staff was reduced from 560 to 230 people. The vertical hierarchy was reduced to only five layers of management.[45]

8 Simultaneous Loose-Tight Properties. This may seem like a paradox, but excellent companies use tight controls in some areas and loose controls in others. Tight, centralized control is used for the firm's core values. At McDonald's, no exceptions are made to the core values of quality, service, cleanliness, and value. At IBM, top management will tolerate no disagreement with the cultural value of respect for the individual. Yet in other areas employees are free to experiment, to be flexible, to innovate, and to take risks in ways that will help the organization achieve its goals.

In Peters and Waterman's original study and subsequent research, not every company scored high on all eight values, but a preponderance of these values was often part of their management culture. One company that displays many characteristics of excellence is McDonald's.

 MCDONALD'S CORPORATION

Who would have thought it? That opening day in April 1955, the sales receipts totalled only $366.12. It rained in Des Plaines, Illinois, but it has been sunshine and, you guessed it, golden arches, ever since. Thirty-eight years and untold billions of burgers and bucks later, McDonald's is still going strong. Here are some reasons why:

McDonald's does burgers best, and that is what it sticks to. Diversification and acquisitions do not enter the picture. Handle small details properly and big problems are minimized. Managers need to know their business; they do not get to the corporate office until they've sold some Big Macs and fries. Bureaucracy is usually bad, one-on-one communication is better, and decision making at the lowest possible level is best. Certain distinctions are critical: planning is thinking, preparing is doing.

Soothsayers need not apply either. At McDonald's, preparation for the future means looking at the here and now. If it is acceptable, analyze how you arrived there, and take similar steps for the future. However, recognize when change is required. Customers will tell you. When a mistake occurs, acknowledge it and adapt in a hurry.

Senior vice-president Shelby Yastrow offers insight into the company's view of risk takers: "In 11 years with the company, I've never seen anybody held back for taking a chance of making a mistake, but I've seen people's careers sidetracked because they couldn't make a decision or because they played it safe."[46] ■

Excellence guidelines and Japanese management practices are not a panacea for all companies. Indeed, some of the high-performance companies originally studied are no longer performing well.[47] But the general approach seems more than a passing fad. These ideas reflect management's response to international competitive forces that have increased the need to fully utilize all employees. They represent a major new trend in the international environment.

SUMMARY AND MANAGEMENT SOLUTION

The practice of management has changed in response to historical conditions. The importance of this chapter is to outline the evolution of management so that present and future managers can understand where we are now and continue to progress toward better management. The evolution of management perspectives is summarized in Exhibit 2.8.

Three major forces that affect management are social, political, and economic. These forces have influenced management from ancient times to the present. These forces also shape individual companies, as CEO Gregg Foster found as he analyzed the 85-year history of Elyria Foundry. Social and political forces that influenced union strength and economic forces such as recession had direct impact on Elyria's performance.

The three major perspectives on management that have evolved since the late 1800s are the classical perspective, the human resource perspective, and the management science perspective. Each perspective has several specialized subfields. Two recent extensions of management perspectives are systems theory and contingency views. The most recent historical force affecting management is industrial globalization. The higher standards of quality, productivity, and responsiveness have caused a renewed concern for the full participation of people within organizations. The most recent trend in management has been to adopt Japanese management practices and to create the widespread desire for achieving excellence in North American organizations.

An historical analysis would reveal the strengths that had enabled Elyria Foundry to survive for nearly a century, along with the weaknesses that had contributed to the company's near demise. Foster was aware of the dangerous relics of the past when he began mapping out the company's future. Noting that a corporate atmosphere pervaded and ownership was missing, he abolished country clubs, cars, and other perks. Disdaining the high overhead associated with the seniority-based,

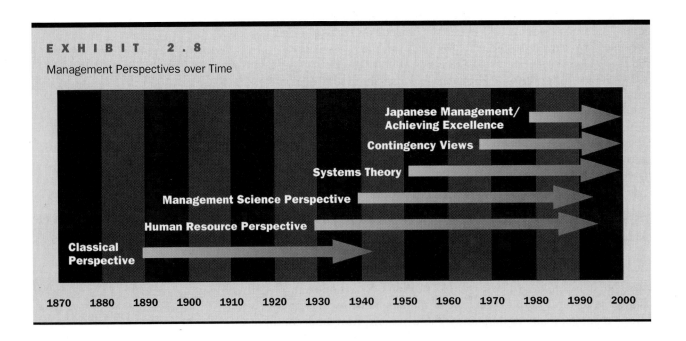

EXHIBIT   2 . 8

Management Perspectives over Time

specialized-job union shop, Foster and two advisers selected a general supervisor and three plant supervisors. The supervisors in turn picked the 100 best candidates among those who had applied to be rehired by the new owner. The union charged he was trying to bust them; Foster countered that employee benefits were of no use if workers did not have jobs. The plant voted decisively to dump its bargaining agent shortly thereafter. At the end of the year, Foster personally passed out small, but hugely symbolic profit-sharing checks. Since then, employee turnover has been practically zero. Foster ushered in the new era by renovating parts of the foundry that had not been updated since Hoover was president. Before long, productivity was up, labor costs were down, and the company was growing. By the end of 1984, sales at Elyria had tripled; sales doubled again four years later. In 1991, the company employed 265 workers and had sales of close to $28 million. All of this growth was achieved in the midst of a deep recession in what was regarded as a dying industry.[48]

DISCUSSION QUESTIONS

1. Why is it important to understand the different perspectives and approaches to management theory that have evolved throughout the history of organizations?
2. A recent article in *Fortune* magazine commented about the death of socialism around the world and the resurgence of capitalist economies. What impact will the trend away from socialism in other countries have on management in North America?
3. How do societal forces influence the practice and theory of management? Do you think management techniques are a response to these forces?
4. What change in management emphasis has been illustrated by the interest in "Japanese management" and "achieving excellence"?
5. What is the behavioral science approach? How does it differ from earlier approaches to management?
6. Explain the basic idea underlying the contingency view and provide an example.
7. Contrast open and closed systems. Can you give an example of each? Can a closed system survive?
8. Why can an event such as the Hawthorne studies be a major turning point in the history of management even if the idea is later shown to be in error? Discuss.
9. Identify the major components of systems theory. Is this perspective primarily internal or external?
10. Which approach to management thought is most appealing to you? Why?
11. Do you think management theory will ever be as precise as theories in the fields of physics, chemistry, or experimental psychology? Why or why not?

MANAGEMENT IN PRACTICE: EXPERIENTIAL EXERCISE ●

● ARE YOU COSMOPOLITAN?

One historical shift occurring in employee attitudes is the extent to which their allegiance is to their organization or to their profession. In recent years, salaried professionals, such as engineers, accountants, and lawyers, work within organizations, but express more loyalty to professional standards than to organizational rules and norms. To identify your own work orientation, answer the eight questions below. Use a scale 1 to 5, with 1 representing "strongly disagree"; 2, "somewhat disagree"; 3, "neutral"; 4, "somewhat agree"; and 5, "strongly agree."

____ 1. You believe it is the right of the professional to make his or her own decisions about what is to be done on the job.

____ 2. You believe a professional should stay in an individual staff role regardless of the income sacrifice.

____ 3. You have no interest in moving up to a top administrative post.

____ 4. You believe that professionals are better evaluated by professional colleagues than by management.

____ 5. Your friends tend to be members of your profession.

____ 6. You would rather be known or get credit for your work outside rather than inside the company.

____ 7. You would feel better making a contribution to society than to your organization.

____ 8. Managers have no right to place time and cost schedules on professional contributors.

This scale indicates the extent to which your work orientation is that of a "cosmopolitan" or a "local." A cosmopolitan identifies with the career profession, and a local identifies with the employing organization. A score between 30 and 40 indicates a cosmopolitan work orientation, between 10 and 20 is a local orientation, and between 20 and 30 represents a mixed orientation.

Discuss the pros and cons of each orientation for organizations and employees. What conflicts are likely to occur when "cosmopolitan" professionals work for a company?

SOURCE: Joseph A. Raelin, *The Clash of Cultures, Managers and Professionals* (Harvard Business School Press, 1986).

CASE FOR ANALYSIS ●

CITY PRIDE BAKERY

In 1989, Continental Baking Company closed the Braun Bakery, which has been in Pittsburgh, Pennsylvania, for a century, and moved to a more efficient plant in Philadelphia. The bakery's 110 employees, many of whom had worked there between 10 and 20 years, were angry. At a gathering at their union hall one Saturday, some employees suggested they ought to start their own bakery. And that's exactly what they did.

By the fall, the workers had hired a consultant, gotten the Pennsylvania Department of Commerce to chip in $100,000 for feasibility studies and the creation of a business plan, and conducted focus groups to determine the potential of launching a new brand of home-baked bread in Pittsburgh. Then a new consultant named Daniel Curtis came along and threw cold water over most of the plan.

Curtis told them that establishing a name against big bakery operations was not only a gamble, but it would cost millions that the upstart organization did not have. However, he had an idea that he thought would work. He advised them to look into private labeling. The large bakeries make less money there, and you can meet them head on and beat them.

Private labels are breads that individual supermarkets sell under their own name. "This is the dumbest industry," says Curtis. "Bakers produce a perishable product, and if it's not sold, they take it back." At the Gold Medal Bakery in Fall River, Massachusetts Curtis had raised revenues from $4 million to $20 million in two years, primarily by convincing supermarkets to use private labeling and then showing them how best to market the product. Using what he had learned at Gold Medal, Curtis saw an opportunity for fledgling City Pride Bakery to carve out a niche. In October 1990, he moved from California to Pittsburgh to take over as CEO of the company.

With the strategy defined, City Pride targeted supermarkets, and with a 46 percent market share, Giant Eagle Markets Company got the first call. The supermarket chain was doing $13.5 million in private label bread business, and none of its three suppliers were even located in Pennsylvania. The competitors took two to three days to deliver; Curtis promised bread would be on the shelf the day it was baked. He offered to provide in-store merchandisers to help with displays and product rotations, and margins between

35 to 55 percent. That level of service and those margins exceeded the industry norm by as much as 35 percent. Curtis tried to strike a chord of regional pride with the chain as well. Noting that they were all members of the same community, he pointed out the good-will benefits that could be reaped by doing business with the little, local bakery that got up off the deck and reinvented itself. In July 1991, Giant Eagle entered an agreement to buy from City Pride.

Around the early part of 1992, City Pride began grinding into life. Several potential hurdles remained, however. Workers had agreed to work for 28 percent less than the regional wage scale in exchange for promised ownership down the road. No less than three unions were involved, and labor strife could put an end to production. The equipment used was potentially in need of costly repairs. Raw materials in baking can fluctuate wildly; a move in the wrong direction could cripple a start-up. City Pride would be extremely reliant on Giant Eagle in the first year, and big chains are always shopping for a better price deal.

● **Q U E S T I O N S**

1. Do you think City Pride Bakery will be able to overcome the historical forces that had led to the demise of its predecessor, Braun Bakery? Why or why not?
2. Which management approach described in this chapter would best describe Curtis' approach at City Pride?
3. Curtis moved his family to Pittsburgh and sank $200,000 of his own money into City Pride. Was it a wise decision, or a reckless gamble?

SOURCE: Leslie Brokaw, "Fast Rising," *INC.*, August 1992, 64–73.

REFERENCES ●

1. Robert Mamis, "Man of Iron," *INC.*, January 1992, 56–59.

2. Alan M. Kantro, ed., "Why History Matters to Managers," *Harvard Business Review* 64 (January–February 1986), 81–88.

3. Susan Dentzer, "Profiting from the Past," *Newsweek*, May 10, 1982, 73–74.

4. Kim Heron, "Randy Travis: Making Country Music Hot Again," *The New York Times Magazine*, June 25, 1989, 28–58.

5. Daniel A. Wren, *The Evolution of Management Thought*, 2d ed. (New York: Wiley, 1979), 6–8. Much of the discussion of these forces comes from Arthur M. Schlesinger, *Political and Social History of the United States, 1829–1925* (New York: Macmillan, 1925), and Homer C. Hockett, *Political and Social History of the United States, 1492–1828* (New York: Macmillan, 1925).

6. Daniel A. Wren, "Management History: Issues and Ideas for Teaching and Research," *Journal of Management* 13 (1987), 339–350.

7. R. J. Wilson, J. Gilbert, S. Nissenbaum, K. O. Cupperman, and D. Scott, "The Climax of the Industrial Revolution: The Haymarket: Strike and Violence in Chicago," *The Pursuit of Liberty*, vol. II, 2nd ed. (Belmont, Calif.: Wadsworth, 1990), 607–609.

8. The following is based on Wren, *Evolution of Management Thought*, Chapters 4, 5; and Claude S. George, Jr., *The History of Management Thought* (Englewood Cliffs, N.J.: Prentice-Hall, 1968), Chapter 4.

9. Charles D. Wrege and Ann Marie Stoka, "Cooke Creates a Classic: The Story behind F. W. Taylor's Principles of Scientific Management," *Academy of Management Review* (October 1978), 736–749.

10. John F. Mee, "Pioneers of Management," *Advanced Management—Office Executive* (October 1962), 26–29; and W. J. Arnold and the editors of *Business Week*, *Milestones in Management* (New York: McGraw-Hill, vol. I, 1965; vol. II, 1966).

11. Wren, *Evolution of Management Thought*, 171; and George, *History of Management Thought*, 103–104.

12. Max Weber, *General Economic History*, trans. Frank H. Knight (London: Allen & Unwin, 1927); Max Weber, *The Protestant Ethic and the Spirit of Capitalism*,

trans. Talcott Parsons (New York: Scribner, 1930); and Max Weber, *The Theory of Social and Economic Organizations*, ed. and trans. A. M. Henderson and Talcott Parsons (New York: Free Press, 1947).

13. "UPS," *The Atlanta Journal and Constitution*, April 26, 1992, H1; Richard L. Daft, *Organization Theory and Design*, 3d ed. (St. Paul, Minn.: West, 1989), 181–182; and Kathy Goode, Betty Hahn, and Cindy Seibert, "United Parcel Service: The Brown Giant" (Unpublished manuscript, Texas A&M University, 1981).

14 Henri Fayol, *Industrial and General Administration*, trans. J. A. Coubrough (Geneva: International Management Institute, 1930); Henri Fayol, *General and Industrial Management*, trans. Constance Storrs (London: Pitman and Sons, 1949); and Arnold, "Milestones in Management."

15. Mary Parker Follett, *The New State: Group Organization: The Solution of Popular Government* (London: Longmans, Green, 1918); and Mary Parker Follett, *Creative Experience* (London: Longmans, Green, 1924).

16. Henry C. Metcalf and Lyndall Urwick, eds., *Dynamic Administration: The Collected Papers of Mary Parker Follett* (New York: Harper & Row, 1940), and Arnold, "Milestones in Management."

17. Mary Parker Follett, *The New State* (London: Longmans, Green, 1924), and *Dymanic Administration* (London: Sir Isaac Pitman, 1941).

18. William B. Wolf, *How to Understand Management: An Introduction to Chester I. Barnard* (Los Angeles: Lucas Brothers, 1968); and David D. Van Fleet, "The Need-Hierarchy and Theories of Authority," *Human Relations* 9 (Spring 1982), 111–118.

19. Charles D. Wrege, "Solving Mayo's Mystery: The First Complete Account of the Origin of the Hawthorne Studies—The Forgotten Contributions of Charles E. Snow and Homer Hibarger" (Paper presented to the Management History Division of the Academy of Management, August 1976).

20. Ronald G. Greenwood, Alfred A. Bolton, and Regina A. Greenwood, "Hawthorne a Half Century Later: Relay Assembly Participants Remember," *Journal of Management* 9 (Fall/Winter 1983), 217–231.

21. F. J. Roethlisberger, W. J. Dickson, and H. A. Wright, *Management and the Worker* (Cambridge, Mass.: Harvard University Press, 1939).

22. H. M. Parson, "What Happened at Hawthorne?" *Science* 183 (1974), 922–932.

23. Greenwood, Bolton, and Greenwood, "Hawthorne a Half Century Later," 219–221.

24. Douglas McGregor, *The Human Side of Enterprise* (New York: McGraw-Hill, 1960), 16–18.

25. Elizabeth Conlin, "Small Business," *INC.*, March 1991, 60–66.

26. Mansel G. Blackford and K. Austin Kerr, *Business Enterprise in American History* (Boston: Houghton Mifflin, 1986), Chapters 10, 11; and Alex Groner and the editors of *American Heritage* and *Business Week*, *The American Heritage History of American Business and Industry* (New York: American Heritage Publishing, 1972), Chapter 9.

27. Larry M. Austin and James R. Burns, *Management Science* (New York: Macmillan, 1985).

28. Tom Scott and William A. Hailey, "Queue Modeling Aids Economic Analysis at Health Center," *Industrial Engineering* (February 1981), 56–61.

29. Ludwig von Bertalanffy, Carl G. Hempel, Robert E. Bass, and Hans Jonas, "General Systems Theory: A New Approach to Unity of Science," *Human*

Biology 23 (December 1951), 302–361; and Kenneth E. Boulding, "General Systems Theory—The Skeleton of Science," *Management Science* 2 (April 1956), 197–208.

30. Fremont E. Kast and James E. Rosenzweig, "General Systems Theory: Applications for Organization and Management," *Academy of Management Journal* (December 1972), 447–465.

31. Daft, *Organization Theory*, 16–17.

32. Fred Luthans, "The Contingency Theory of Management: A Path Out of the Jungle," *Business Horizons* 16 (June 1973), 62–72; and Fremont E. Kast and James E. Rosenzweig, *Contingency Views of Organization and Management* (Chicago: Science Research Associates, 1973).

33. Robert Gunther, "Major Banks' Increases in Loan-Loss Reserves May Cramp Expansion," *The Wall Street Journal*, July 29, 1987, 1, 10.

34. Koh Sera, "Corporate Globalization: A New Trend," *Academy of Management Executive* 6 no. 1 (1992), 89–96; and B. Joseph White, "The Internationalization of Business: One Company's Response," *Academy of Management Executive* 2 (1988), 29–32.

35. Arnoldo C. Hax, "Building the Firm of the Future," *Sloan Management Review* (Spring 1989), 75–82.

36. Tom Peters, "Prometheus Barely Unbound," *Academy of Management Executive* 4 (November 1990), 70–84.

37. Brian Dumaine, "What the Leaders of Tomorrow See," *Fortune*, July 3, 1989, 48–62.

38. William Ouchi, *Theory Z: How American Business Can Meet the Japanese Challenge* (Reading, Mass.: Addison-Wesley, 1981).

39. Ouchi, *Theory Z*; and R. Pascale and A. Athos, *The Art of Japanese Management: Applications for American Executives* (New York: Simon and Schuster, 1981).

40. William G. Ouchi and Alfred M. Jaeger, "Type Z Organizations: Stability in the Midst of Mobility," *Academy of Management Review* 3 (1978), 305–314.

41. Ibid.

42. Thomas J. Peters and Robert H. Waterman, Jr., *In Search of Excellence: Lessons from America's Best-Run Companies* (New York: Harper & Row, 1982); Tom Peters and Nancy Austin, *A Passion for Excellence: The Leadership Difference* (New York: Random House, 1985); and Tom Peters, "Putting Excellence into Management," *Business Week*, July 21, 1980, 196–201.

43. Tom Peters, "An Excellent Question," *INC.*, December 1984, 155–162.

44. "Ross Perot's Crusade," *Business Week*, October 6, 1986, 60–65.

45. "A Slimmed-Down Brunswick Is Proving Wall Street Wrong," *Business Week*, May 28, 1984, 90–98.

46. Debi Sue Edmund, "The Secret Behind the Big Mac? It's Simple!" *Management Review* (May 1990), 32–33; and Penny Moser, "The McDonald's Mystique," *Fortune*, July 4, 1988, 112–116.

47. "Who's Excellent Now?" *Business Week*, November 5, 1984, 76+; Daniel T. Carroll, "A Disappointing Search for Excellence," *Harvard Business Review* 61 (November–December 1983), 78–79+; Jeremiah J. Sullivan, "A Critique of Theory Z," *Academy of Management Review* (January 1983), 132–142; and William Bowen, "Lessons from behind the Kimono," *Fortune*, June 15, 1981, 247–250.

48. Robert Mamis, "Man of Iron."

MANAGING IN A GLOBAL ENVIRONMENT

3

CHAPTER OUTLINE

LEARNING OBJECTIVES

After studying this chapter, you should be able to

- Describe the emerging borderless world.

- Define international management and explain how it differs from the management of domestic business operations.

- Indicate how dissimilarities in the economic, sociocultural, and legal-political environments throughout the world can affect business operations.

- Describe market entry strategies that businesses use to develop foreign markets.

- Describe the characteristics of a multinational corporation and the generic strategies available to them.

- Explain the strategic approaches used by multinational corporations.

Florod Corporation One's chief executive Rod Waters had never been too concerned about competitors. As the maker of laser erasers that clean up photomasks used in making integrated circuits, the small Gardena, California, company dominated a highly specialized field. However, in 1980, Waters received a rude awakening; Japan's Nippon Electric Company Ltd. entered the market. Waters suddenly found himself competing in an international marketplace without ever leaving the United States. ■ At the time, Florod was selling laser erasers for $100,000 a copy; those produced by Nippon were $13,000 cheaper. That was not even the worst part. Waters' own rating system graded the NEC as offering consistently better quality. In such a limited market, this sort of news made the rounds quickly. Florod's bank seized the company's cash to offset its credit line, and paychecks to employees that had not already been laid off bounced. ■ What were Waters' options? How do you think they should have been prioritized in order for Florod to meet day-to-day needs, while still staying focused on the long-term challenge from the huge, overseas competitor?[1]

Florod Corporation One is a well-established company facing enormous challenges on both domestic and international levels. Large companies such as IBM, Coca-Cola, and General Motors rely on international business for a substantial portion of sales and profits. However, increasing numbers of small companies, such as Atlanta Saw Company, and Molex Inc. are active in the export boom. These companies face special problems in trying to tailor their products and business management to the unique needs of foreign countries—but if they succeed, the whole world is their marketplace.

How important is international business to the study of management? *If you are not thinking international, you are not thinking business management.* It's that serious. As you read this page, ideas, takeover plans, capital investments, business strategies, Reeboks, services, and T-shirts are traveling around the planet by telephone, fax, and overnight mail.

If you think you are isolated from global influence, think again. As the Florod managers learned, no business is immune to international competition. Overnight, a foreign company may launch a competitive assault on your industry. A few years ago, U.S. firms made 85 percent of the world's memory chips and were unassailable, or so they thought. However, soon Japan had a 75 percent share of the world market, with the U.S. share at only 15 percent.

Even if you will not budge from your hometown, your company may be purchased by English, Japanese, or German firms tomorrow. Employees of CBS Records, Firestone, and Standard Oil are among the growing number of U.S. employees working for foreign bosses. In addition, Japan alone can be expected to purchase about 200 small- and medium-size American companies each year, while continuing to hire additional American workers in expanding U.S. plants. The November 1993 approval of NAFTA (North American Free Trade Agreement) will force companies throughout the United States to reevaluate the potential hazards and benefits of free trade and expanded markets. Many companies may promote managers with international experience and foreign language ability. In recent years, foreign-born managers with international experience have been appointed to run such companies as DuPont, Coca-Cola, and Heinz.[2]

This chapter introduces basic concepts about the global environment and international management. First, we consider the difficulty managers have operating in an increasingly borderless world. We will address challenges—economic, legal-political, and sociocultural—facing companies within the global business environment. Then we will discuss multinational corporations and touch on the various types of strategies and techniques needed for entering and succeeding in foreign markets.

● A BORDERLESS WORLD

Why would Florod chief executive Rod Waters want to consider a global strategy? Conventional wisdom is that companies involved in global industries must play the global game. If a company doesn't think globally, someone else will. Companies failing to keep up will be swallowed up. As its competitors rush toward globalization with acquisitions, mergers, and alliances, Florod risks continued losses in its domestic market share and bankruptcy unless it has the capacity to meet client needs and compete with foreign companies in both product and price.

International companies increasingly find that globalization provides a competitive edge at all stages of developing, manufacturing, and marketing products. A global approach to development enabled Otis Elevator, Inc., to use research centers in five countries during development of its customized Elevonic 411, saving an estimated $10 million in design costs and cutting in half the normal elevator development time.[3] The reality of today's borderless companies is illustrated in the Manager's Shoptalk box.

Corporations can participate in the international arena on a variety of levels. An example of a small company's entry into the global arena can be seen in the Leading Edge box. The process of globalization typically passes through four distinct stages.

MANAGER'S shop talk

BUY AMERICAN!

Under vocal pressure to "Buy American!" the town council of Greece, New York, voted in January 1992 to reject the purchase of a Japanese Komatsu excavator in favor of a John Deere model that cost $15,000 more. The council supported the patriotic principle of supporting American jobs. Only later did council members discover that 95 percent of the Komatsu models were made in the United States through a Japanese-American joint venture headquartered in Illinois. Meanwhile, only the engine of the John Deere was built in the United States. The excavator itself was made in Japan through Deere's joint venture with Hitachi. Today's consumers must face the complexity of a seemingly borderless international market.

The 1980s marked a pivotal period during which national boundaries began blurring with regard to the development, manufacture, and marketing of products. Industries such as chemicals, tires, steel, and building supplies have been reshaped by international dynamics. As Robert Reich of Harvard noted, "Every industrialized country is moving in the same direction, toward an industrial base that is global in ownership and orientation."

Americans find it increasingly difficult to buy purely American products. The Mercury Tracer parked outside may come from Mexico, while a neighbor's Nissan may have been built in Smyrna, Tennessee. By 1990, approximately 40 percent of Japanese cars sold in the United States were built in America by American workers. In the clothing industry, American consumers are likely to find their Van Heusen shirts with a "Made in Thailand" label and their Nike warmup suits made in Malaysia. As the production and marketing of goods become more global, consumers around the world will struggle with questions of quality and value for their money versus patriotic support for the home team.

For the town council of Greece, New York, the question of how to benefit America is difficult—buy the product with an American name or the product built by American workers? "We would like to purchase American-made equipment and keep Americans on the job," said Roger Boily, a supervisor for Greece. "But it becomes a very complicated issue." His town council eventually canceled the John Deere order and decided to rent the Komatsu excavator to clear a creek and prevent the flooding of a man's home. That grateful man didn't stop to ask whether the machine was American or Japanese. ■

SOURCE: James S. Hirsch and Dana Milbank, "'Buy American' Is Easier Said Than Done," *The Wall Street Journal*, January 28, 1992, B1, B5; Bradley A. Stertz, "New York Car Dealers Hope to Put Some Drive into 'Too Lazy' Workers," *The Wall Street Journal*, January 28, 1992, B1, B5; and Hillary Appleman, "Buying 'Made in USA' Not So Easy," *Nashville Tennessean*, January 26, 1992, 1E.

When Arden C. Sims was hired at Globe Metallurgical in 1984, the company was a wholly unremarkable division of a large steel conglomerate with more than its share of problems. Over the next several years, Sims battled unions, redesigned operations, and severed a 34-year relationship with a sales and marketing representative. He even pulled a few shifts cleaning out the furnace at the company's Beverly, Ohio, plant. He eventually led a leveraged buyout of the company.

In the process of transforming Cleveland, Ohio-based Globe Metallurgical into a global competitor in the specialty metals industry, Sims pinpointed the reasons for operating inefficiencies, for disappearing manufacturing jobs, and how both management-designed factory jobs and union-dictated shop rules were a sure recipe for uncompetitive labor costs.

Throughout all the adversity, Sims maintained a three-point strategy. To survive short term, Globe had to become a high-quality, low-cost leader in the industry. To distinguish itself technologically, Globe would have to actively pursue R&D. Achieving these objectives would lay the groundwork for Sims' vision of the future: the ability to compete effectively in overseas markets. In 1988, Globe received the Malcolm Baldrige National Quality Award. The following year the company was awarded the first Shigeo Shingo Prize for Manufacturing Excellence. "I felt we were now ready to compete with the best in the world," Sims said. "I considered the last five years of Globe's organizational transformation as preparation for going overseas."

Entry into European markets turned out to be easier than the Pacific Rim. Globe's 1989 acquisition of the British company Material & Methods (M&M), a world-class metals engineering firm, provided an early foothold in both the United Kingdom and Eastern Europe. Globe furnished some clout of its own in the Western European market, enabling M&M to compete with high-quality alloys that were competitively priced. A 1989 market share of 1 percent grew to 20 percent by 1992.

Asia was harder, and Japan harder still, but Sims viewed the latter as a linchpin since it was the largest market in the region. He also thought he had identified a weakness Globe could exploit. "I believe the Japanese will eventually exit specialty metals because Japanese power rates are so high and the processes they use are expensive and inefficient," Sims says. "I think we can be the future first-choice supplier in Japan."

It will not be easy, at least if some of Globe's early overtures are any indication. Sims thinks that for $120 million Globe can take on a $2 billion supplier, provided he can get customers to try his product. This is easier said than done. Most giant Japanese foundries like Toyota, Nissan, Kubota, and Komatsu produce no more than four products. Globe's marketing representatives can tout 180 to meet virtually every need at the highest quality levels. Most of the companies listen politely, but orders are hard to come by. Globe has made progress using local sales agents at smaller foundries. One plant that did test Globe's offering found it superior in quality. The company shipped around 3,000 tons to 20 foundries in 1992, or about 7 percent of the total Japanese market.

Globe has lived up to its name by setting priorities and following markets where the greatest opportunities lie, even if they happen to be far across the water. As you will see in Chapter 16, the company proves that the benchmark of the future is to produce the highest quality products possible. ∎

SOURCE: "Globe Goes Global," *World Trade*, March 1993; Bruce Rayner, "Trial-By-Fire Transformation," *Harvard Business Review*, May–June 1992, 117–129; and "Does the Baldrige Award Really Work," *Harvard Business Review*, January–February 1992, 126–127.

1 In the *domestic stage*, market potential is limited to the home country with all production and marketing facilities located at home. Managers may be aware of the global environment and may want to consider foreign involvement.

2 In the *international stage*, exports increase, and the company usually adopts a *multidomestic* approach, probably using an international division to deal with the marketing of products in several countries individually.

3 In the *multinational stage*, the company has marketing and production facilities located in many countries, with more than one-third of its sales outside the home country. Companies typically have a single home country, although they may opt for a *binational* approach, whereby two parent companies in separate countries maintain ownership and control. Examples are Unilever and the Royal Dutch/Shell Group, both of which are based in the United Kingdom and the Netherlands.

4 Finally, the *global* (or *stateless*) *stage* of corporate international development transcends any single home country. These corporations operate in true global fashion, making sales and acquiring resources in whatever country offers the best opportunities and lowest cost. At this stage, ownership, control, and top management tend to be dispersed among several nationalities.[4]

As the number of "stateless" corporations increases, so too the awareness of national borders decreases, as reflected by the frequency of foreign participation at the management level. Rising managers are expected to know a second or third language and to have international experience. Consider the makeup of global companies in today's environment. Nestlé (Switzerland) personifies the stateless corporation with 98 percent of sales and 96 percent of employees outside the home country. Nestlé's CEO is German and half of the company's general managers are non-Swiss. U.S. firms also show a growing international flavor. At CRC International, one-third of the officers are foreign nationals, while Heinz has an Irish citizen as CEO and a mixed board. At a British firm, ICI, 40 percent of the top 170 executives are non-British. Meanwhile, German companies such as Hoechst and BASF rely on local managers to run foreign operations.[5]

In recent years, a major player in the global game has been ABB (Asea Brown Boveri). This company generates over $25 billion in revenues and employs 240,000 in Europe, North and South America, Asia, and India. CEO Percy Barnevik points out that ABB has no geographical center. With a Swedish CEO, a Zurich headquarters, a multinational board, and posting financial results in American dollars, ABB is "a company with many homes."[6]

● THE INTERNATIONAL BUSINESS ENVIRONMENT

International management is the management of business operations conducted in more than one country. The fundamental tasks of business management, including the financing, production, and distribution of products and services, do not change in any substantive

international management
The management of business operations conducted in more than one country.

way when a firm is transacting business across international borders. The basic management functions of planning, organizing, leading, and controlling are the same whether a company operates domestically or internationally. However, managers will experience greater difficulties and risks when performing these management functions on an international scale. For example:

- Managers at one American company were shaken when they discovered that the brand name of the cooking oil they had introduced in Latin America translated into Spanish as "jackass oil."

- Still another company tried to sell its toothpaste in Southeast Asia by stressing that it whitens teeth. Managers were chagrined to discover that local people chew betel nut to blacken their teeth because they find the result attractive.[7]

- One company stamped "OK" on each page of its catalog. In many parts of South America, OK is a vulgar gesture. Six months were lost because the company had to reprint the catalogs.

What should managers of emerging global companies look for to avoid obvious international mistakes? When comparing one country with another, the economic, legal-political, and sociocultural sectors present the greatest difficulties. Key factors to understand in the international environment are summarized in Exhibit 3.1.

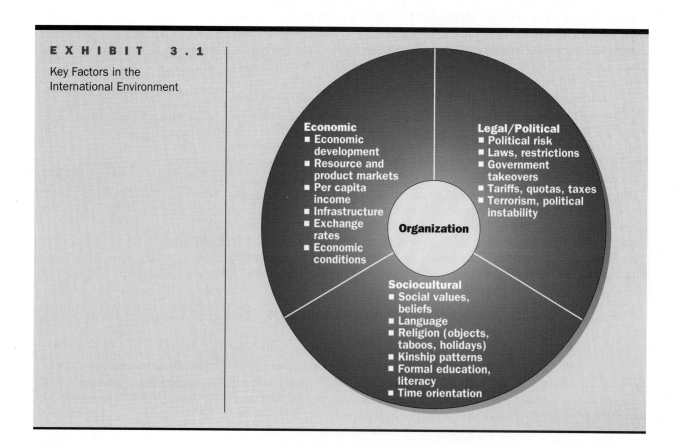

EXHIBIT   3.1

Key Factors in the
International Environment

Economic
- Economic development
- Resource and product markets
- Per capita income
- Infrastructure
- Exchange rates
- Economic conditions

Legal/Political
- Political risk
- Laws, restrictions
- Government takeovers
- Tariffs, quotas, taxes
- Terrorism, political instability

Organization

Sociocultural
- Social values, beliefs
- Language
- Religion (objects, taboos, holidays)
- Kinship patterns
- Formal education, literacy
- Time orientation

● THE ECONOMIC ENVIRONMENT

The economic environment represents the economic conditions in the country where the international organization operates. This part of the environment includes such factors as economic development; resource and product markets; infrastructure; exchange rates; and inflation, interest rates, and economic growth.

ECONOMIC DEVELOPMENT. Economic development differs widely among the countries and regions of the world. Countries can be categorized as either "developing" or "developed." The developing countries are referred to as *less-developed countries (LDCs)*. The criterion traditionally used to classify countries as developed or developing is *per capita income*, which is the income generated by the nation's production of goods and services divided by total population. The developing countries have low per capita incomes. LDCs generally are in the Southern Hemisphere, including Africa and South America, whereas developed countries tend to be in the Northern Hemisphere, including North America, Europe, and Japan.[8]

Most international business firms are based in the developed countries. They show a preference for confining their operations to the wealthier and economically advanced nations. However, based on the number of prospective customers, developing countries constitute an immense and largely untapped market.

INFRASTRUCTURE. A country's physical facilities that support economic activities make up its **infrastructure,** which includes transportation facilities such as airports, highways, and railroads; energy-producing facilities such as utilities and power plants; and communication facilities such as telephone lines and radio stations. Companies operating in LDCs must contend with lower levels of technology and perplexing logistical, distribution, and communication problems.

infrastructure

A country's physical facilities that support economic activities.

RESOURCE AND PRODUCT MARKETS. When operating in another country, company managers must evaluate the market demand for their products. If market demand is high, managers may choose to export products to that country. To develop manufacturing plants, however, resource markets for providing needed raw materials and labor must also be available. For example, the greatest challenge for McDonald's restaurants overseas is to obtain supplies of everything from potatoes to hamburger buns to plastic straws. Often supplies that meet McDonald's exacting standards are unavailable. The hamburger bun was the most difficult item to procure in Britain because local bakeries would not meet the company's standards. In Thailand, McDonald's actually helped farmers cultivate Idaho russet potatoes of sufficient quality to produce their golden french fries.[9]

EXCHANGE RATES. *Exchange rates* are the rate at which one country's currency is exchanged for another country's. Changes in the exchange rate can have major implications for the profitability of international operations.[10] For example, assume that the American dollar is exchanged for 8 French francs. If the dollar increases in value to 10 francs, U.S. goods will be more expensive in France because it will take more francs to buy a dollar's worth of U.S. goods. It will be more difficult to export American goods to France, and profits will be slim. If the dollar drops to a value of 6 francs, on the other hand, U.S. goods will be cheaper in France and can be exported at a profit.

● THE LEGAL-POLITICAL ENVIRONMENT

Businesses must deal with unfamiliar political systems when they go international, as well as with more government supervision and regulation. Government officials and the general public often view foreign companies as outsiders or even intruders and are suspicious of their impact on economic independence and political sovereignty. Some of the major legal-political concerns affecting international business are political risk, political instability, and laws and restrictions.

political risk

A company's risk of loss of assets, earning power, or managerial control due to politically motivated events or actions by host governments.

POLITICAL RISK.   A company's **political risk** is defined as its risk of loss of assets, earning power, or managerial control due to politically based events or actions by host governments.[11] Political risk includes government takeovers of property and acts of violence directed against a firm's properties or employees. Because such acts are not uncommon, companies must formulate special plans and programs to guard against unexpected losses. For example, Hercules, Inc., a large chemical company, has increased the number of security guards at several of its European plants. Because of a rumored protest, Monsanto Corporation canceled a ceremony to celebrate the opening of a new plant in England.[12]

POLITICAL INSTABILITY.   Another frequently cited problem for international companies is political instability, which includes riots, revolu-

Otis Elevator Company implements its international advantage in the design and production of the Elevonic 411, shown here. This state-of-the-art elevator system is created from parts and technology developed by its global subsidiaries.

tions, civil disorders, and frequent changes in government. Political instability increases uncertainty. Companies moving into former Soviet republics face continued instability because of changing government personnel and political philosophies. For example, Czechoslovakian hero and playwright Vaclav Havel, initially selected president by voters in a celebration of freedom, had already been replaced by mid-1992. The Czech government peacefully coped with nationalist tensions in Slovakia and in 1993 separated into two countries. The former Yugoslavia, by contrast, has broken up into a shooting war among ethnic groups.

For global companies, the threat of violence is strongest among those nations with political, ethnic, or religious upheaval. In the first seven months of 1991, BRI (Business Risk International), a security consulting firm, reported 1,236 bombings, 382 assassinations, and 103 kidnappings. Western businesses are often targeted to gain publicity for the "cause" and to damage the local economy. In recent years, Peruvian insurgents targeted companies such as Kentucky Fried Chicken and Pizza Hut. BRI compiles an annual list of the ten riskiest countries for business. Peru (with over 500 incidents in 1990) topped the 1991 listing, which included El Salvador, India, Turkey, Colombia, the Philippines, Sri Lanka, and Nicaragua, as well as two European countries—Spain and Northern Ireland.[13]

LAWS AND REGULATIONS.   Government laws and regulations differ from country to country and make manufacturing and sales a true challenge for international firms. Host governments have myriad laws concerning libel statutes, consumer protection, information and labeling, employment and safety, and wages. International companies must learn these rules and regulations and abide by them. After years of Communist mismanagement, markets in Eastern Europe with 100 million consumer households have been opened, creating both potential payoffs and pitfalls for global managers. Within months of the fall of communism, companies such as Volkswagen (Germany), Suzuki (Japan), Pilkington (Britain), General Electric (United States), and Sanofi (France) entered a variety of partnerships and acquisitions with companies in Poland, Czechoslovakia, and Hungary. However, there are still questions about emerging laws and regulations. Despite Western money and know-how, factory closures, shortages, and rising unemployment attest to the difficulty of movement toward free market economies.[14]

A major effort to deal with challenges in international manufacturing and service is described in Manager's Shoptalk ("Isomania"). Meanwhile, the most visible changes in legal-political factors grow out of the emerging international trade alliance system. Consider, for example, the impact of the European Union (EU) and the North American Free Trade Agreement (NAFTA).

EUROPEAN UNION

Formed in 1958 to improve the economic and social conditions among its members, the European Community (EC) has since expanded to a 12-nation alliance. This alliance is now called the European Union (EU). In the early 1980s, Europeans initiated steps to create a powerful single

"ISOMANIA"

A new "mania" is just reaching American shores. The latest mania sweeping the world involves no rock musicians, no sound systems or touring dates. "ISOmania" is the result of the rush to meet new international quality standards (ISO 9000) set up in the late 1980s by the blue-suit crowd at the International Organization for Standardization. ISO 9000, endorsed by more than 50 countries, including the United States, provides uniform quality-standards guidelines for manufacturing and service organizations.

International corporations are demanding that suppliers "get on board," and the catch-phrase, "Are you 'registered'?" is suddenly on the lips of big-name companies and knowledgeable customers. By 1993, more than 20,000 companies in the EU claimed ISO 9000 registration, while the United States lagged far behind with only 621 companies. A recent Grant-Thorton survey showed that 48 percent of top managers at U.S. companies were unfamiliar with ISO. "The U.S. is starting to wake up, but it's starting from way back in the pack," one Grant Thorton partner admitted.

Realization of the importance of ISO in international markets has American companies scurrying to achieve certification, and registrars are being mobbed with applications. For example, General Electric's plastics division set a June 1993 certification deadline for all vendors. Motorola, despite its reputation for quality as a former Baldrige Award winner, has likewise pursued ISO registration.

One of the strengths of ISO 9000 is the registration process itself, whereby a company's manufacturing and service processes (including design, training, marketing, packaging, record-keeping, and testing) are subjected to a rigorous third-party audit before certification is awarded. Periodic audits occur thereafter. Although it is expensive, the process of preparing for the audit increases company awareness of problems and obsolete practices and leads to greater efficiency.

Small companies such as AEC Engineering, Inc. of Minneapolis (with only 65 employees) are likewise finding benefits in ISO 9000 registration through elimination of "waste and repetition." In addition to meeting international quality standards, small companies can improve their competitive value as suppliers and beat what promises to be a stampede for certification five or six years down the road.

These regulations are an "attempt to streamline" the quality process through a common language, according to consultant Beth Summers. But U.S. reluctance to participate perplexes experts who believe American corporations will postpone registration until they begin losing business. Quality consultant Paul Gladieux says "Businesses in the U.S. have this checkbook mentality. They think . . . 'we'll just write a check . . . have a one-week seminar.' . . . That's where these companies are going to get their heads torn off." ■

SOURCES: Ronald Henkoff, "The Hot New Seal of Quality," *Fortune*, June 28, 1993, 116–120; and Cyndee Miller, "U.S. firms lag in meeting global quality standards," *Marketing News*, February 15, 1993, 1 & 16.

market system, called *Europe '92*. The initiative called for creation of open markets for Europe's 340 million consumers. Europe '92 consisted of 282 directives, most scheduled for implementation by January 1, 1993, proposing dramatic reform and deregulation in areas such as banking, insurance, health, safety standards, airlines, telecommunications, auto sales, social policy, and monetary union.

Initially opposed and later embraced by European industry, the increased competition and economies of scale within Europe will enable companies to grow large and efficient, becoming more competitive in

U.S. and other world markets. Some observers fear that the EU will become a trade barrier, creating a "fortress Europe" that will be difficult to penetrate by companies in other nations.

Implementation of directives regarding the elimination of border controls and deregulations have proceeded on schedule. The deregulation of banking (1993) and insurance (1994) expect to be followed by investment services between 1995 and 1999. New open competition in telecommunications (1993) will lead to deregulation on cross-border calling by mid-decade. The airlines now enjoy free pricing and the licensing of new carriers as a result of deregulation.

Despite the successes, other directives languish amid stiff opposition from member countries:

- *Monetary union*, calling for the establishment of a European central bank and a single currency, met defeat on June 2, 1992, by Danish voters. The approval by other EU members, however, forced a second referendum in Denmark.

- *Social policy*, calling for increased regulations for worker's rights, working hours, subcontracting, and equal benefits for full-time and part-time employees, has been blocked by the British.

- *Automobile legislation* seeks to end the gridlock of antitrust exemptions, exclusive dealer territories, and quotas that force Europeans to pay 25 percent more for automobiles.[15]

These facets of the proposal show the difficulty of building alliances among countries. However, solutions are expected, and the verdict is still out regarding the success of the Europe '92 agenda. Meanwhile, Canada, Mexico, and the United States have established what is expected to be an equally powerful trading alliance.

NORTH AMERICAN FREE TRADE AGREEMENT (NAFTA)

The ratification by the Canadian, Mexican, and U.S. governments of NAFTA opened a $6 trillion megamarket to 363 million consumers. NAFTA is expected to break down as many as 20,000 separate tariffs over a 10- to 15-year period. The treaty builds on the 1989 U.S.–Canada agreement and is expected to spur growth and investment, increase exports, and expand jobs in all three nations.[16]

The 14-month negotiations climaxed August 12, 1992, with agreements in a number of key areas.

- *Agriculture.* Immediate removal on tariffs on half of U.S. farm exports to Mexico with phasing out of remaining tariffs over 15 years.

- *Autos.* Immediate 50 percent cut of Mexican tariffs on autos, reaching zero in 10 years. Mandatory 62.5 percent North American content on cars and trucks to qualify for duty-free status.

- *Transport.* U.S. trucking of international cargo allowed in Mexican border area by mid-1990s and throughout Mexico by the end of the decade.

J.B. Hunt, a diversified transportation company, will reap the benefits of NAFTA, which extends the U.S.-Canadian free trade agreement to Mexico. The largest U.S. carrier in Canada, Hunt recently expanded service into Mexico, joining Transportacion Maritima Mexicana to provide truckline service throughout Mexico and ocean shipping container services from all Mexican ports.

- *Intellectual property.* Mexico's protection for pharmaceutical patents boosted to international standards and North American copyrights safeguarded.

Many groups in the United States opposed the agreement, warning of job loss to Mexico and the potential for industrial "ghost towns." Some environmentalists fear weakened pollution standards and the potential for toxic dumping. Treaty advocates admitted there may be short-term problems but stress the long-term benefits in job creation and heightened standard of living within all three trading partners.[17]

TRADE ALLIANCES: PROMISE OR PITFALL?

The November 1993 U.S. approval of NAFTA, full implementation of most EU agreements, and possible new trade alliances in Central and South America, Southeast Asia, and Eastern Europe point to significant changes in business and industry for the twenty-first century. These developments will provide cheaper Mexican watermelons in the United States, more Israeli shoes in Central Europe, and more Colombian roses in Venezuela. These agreements entail a new future for international companies and pose new questions for international managers.

- Will the creation of multiple trade blocs lead to economic warfare among them?
- Will trade blocs gradually evolve into three powerful trading blocs composed of the American hemisphere, Europe (from Ireland across the former Soviet Union), and the "yen bloc" encompassing the Pacific Rim?
- Will the expansion of global, stateless corporations bypass trading zones and provide economic balance among them?[18]

Only the future will provide answers to these questions. International managers and global corporations will both shape and be shaped by these important trends.

● THE SOCIOCULTURAL ENVIRONMENT

A nation's **culture** includes the shared knowledge, beliefs, and values, as well as the common modes of behavior and ways of thinking, among members of a society. Cultural factors are more perplexing than political and economic factors in foreign countries. Culture is intangible, pervasive, and difficult to learn. It is absolutely imperative that international businesses comprehend the significance of local cultures and deal with them effectively.

culture

The shared knowledge, beliefs, values, behaviors, and ways of thinking among members of a society.

SOCIAL VALUES. Research done by Geert Hofstede on 116,000 IBM employees in 40 countries identified four dimensions of national value systems that influence organizational and employee working relationships.[19]

1 *Power distance.* High **power distance** means that people accept inequality in power among institutions, organizations, and people. Low power distance means that people expect equality in power. Countries that value high power distance are Malaysia, the Philippines, and Panama. Countries that value low power distance are Denmark, Austria, and Israel.

power distance

The degree to which people accept inequality in power among institutions, organizations, and people.

2 *Uncertainty avoidance.* High **uncertainty avoidance** means that members of a society feel uncomfortable with uncertainty and ambiguity and thus support beliefs that promise certainty and conformity. Low uncertainty avoidance means that people have high tolerance for the unstructured, the unclear, and the unpredictable. High uncertainty avoidance countries include Greece, Portugal, and Uruguay. Countries with low uncertainty avoidance values are Singapore and Jamaica.

uncertainty avoidance

A value characterized by people's intolerance for uncertainty and ambiguity and resulting support for beliefs that promise certainty and conformity.

3 *Individualism and collectivism.* **Individualism** reflects a value for a loosely knit social framework in which individuals are expected to take care of themselves. **Collectivism** means a preference for a tightly knit social framework in which individuals look after one another and organizations protect their members' interests. Countries with individualist values include the United States, Canada, Great Britain, and Australia. Countries with collectivist values are Guatemala, Ecuador, and Panama.

individualism

A preference for a loosely knit social framework in which individuals are expected to take care of themselves.

collectivism

A preference for a tightly knit social framework in which individuals look after one another and organizations protect their members' interests.

4 *Masculinity/femininity.* **Masculinity** stands for preference for achievement, heroism, assertiveness, and material success. **Femininity** reflects the values of relationships, modesty, caring for the weak, and quality of life. Societies with strong masculine values are Japan, Austria, Mexico, and Germany. Countries with feminine values are Sweden, Norway, Denmark, and the former Yugoslavia. Both men and women subscribe to the dominant value in masculine and feminine cultures.

masculinity

A cultural preference for achievement, heroism, assertiveness, and material success.

femininity

A cultural preference for modesty, caring for the weak, and quality of life.

Social values influence organizational functioning and management styles. For example, organizations in France and Latin and Mediterranean countries tend to be hierarchical bureaucracies. Germany and other central European countries have organizations that strive to be impersonal, well-oiled machines. In India, Asia, and Africa, organizations are viewed as large families. Effective management styles differ in each country, depending on cultural characteristics.[20]

OTHER CULTURAL CHARACTERISTICS.   Other cultural characteristics that influence international organizations are language, religion, attitudes, social organization, and education. Some countries, such as India, are characterized by *linguistic pluralism*, meaning that several languages exist there. Other countries rely heavily on spoken versus written language. Religion includes sacred objects, philosophical attitudes toward life, taboos, and rituals. Attitudes toward achievement, work, and time can all affect organizational productivity. An attitude called **ethnocentrism** means that people have a tendency to regard their own culture as superior and to downgrade other cultures. Ethnocentrism within a country makes it difficult for foreign firms to operate there. Social organization includes status systems, kinship and families, social institutions, and opportunities for social mobility. Education influences the literacy level, the availability of qualified employees, and the predominance of primary or secondary degrees.

Managers in international companies have found that cultural differences cannot be ignored if international operations are to succeed. For example, Procter & Gamble ran into unanticipated cultural barriers when marketing its Cheer laundry soap in Japan. Cheer initially prospered by discounting its price, but that alienated wholesalers who were not used to having reduced margins.[21] Coke withdrew its 2-liter bottle from the Spanish market after discovering that compartments of Spanish refrigerators were too small for it.[22] Even the powerful Disney organization seriously misjudged per person food and souvenir spending and accommodation needs at EuroDisney in France, forcing the temporary seasonal closing of its 1,100-room Newport Bay Club in the winter of 1992.[23]

On the other hand, organizations that manage cultural differences report major successes. Kellogg introduced breakfast cereals into Brazil, where the traditional breakfast is coffee and a roll. Through carefully chosen advertising, many Brazilians were won over to the American breakfast. Many families now start the day with Kellogg's Sucrilhos (Frosted Flakes) and Crokinhos (Cocoa Krispies).[24]

SUMMARY OF THE INTERNATIONAL ENVIRONMENT

Some of the complexities of operating in diverse countries are illustrated in Exhibit 3.2. The upper portion of the exhibit shows a firm operating in its domestic market and native culture. The lower portion shows how complicated business operations can become when operating in several countries simultaneously. Through its foreign affiliates, the organization must carry on the same basic types of relationships in other countries, but to do so, it must adapt to their cultures and legal-political systems. Moreover, the organization must transcend the boundaries of separate

---

ethnocentrism

A cultural attitude marked by the tendency to regard one's own culture as superior to others.

During construction of the Pan-Pacific Hotel in San Diego, California, Shinto ceremonies were performed at various stages of construction to bless the new building and wish good fortune to the owners.

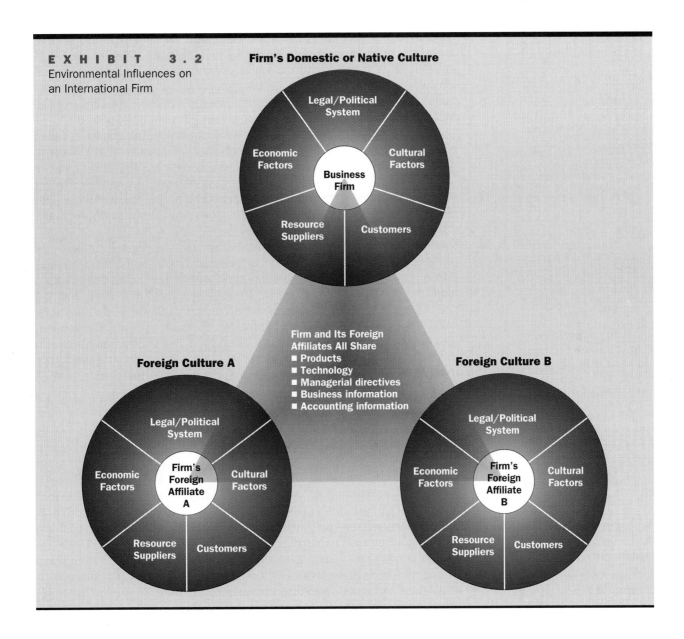

E X H I B I T   3 . 2
Environmental Influences on
an International Firm

Firm and Its Foreign
Affiliates All Share
- Products
- Technology
- Managerial directives
- Business information
- Accounting information

cultures to transfer resources and products between the firm and foreign affiliates. The organization must also coordinate technological know-how, advertising, and managerial directives across cultural boundaries.

One company that is attempting to cross cultural boundaries is Blue Sky Natural Beverage Co.

 **BLUE   SKY   NATURAL   BEVERAGE
COMPANY**

When Robert and Marla Black founded Blue Sky Natural Beverage Company in Santa Fe, New Mexico, sales of the fresh juices and all-natural sodas immediately took off. The company filled a void by marketing the natural beverages in an area where there were no similar products. However, it was not long before Blue Sky had captured all the blue sky a town of 56,000 had to offer. Company president Richard Becker, Marla's brother and an attorney, knew the company did not have the capital required to expand in the $40 billion domestic soft-drink industry. Instead he came up with a novel, albeit somewhat accidental, solution.

A representative from the New Mexico Department of Agriculture called wondering if he could take some samples to the Anuga Trade Show in Cologne, France. Becker agreed, and word came back that the Japanese who attended the show were extremely fond of Blue Sky. Inspired, Becker took more samples to a show in Japan, where one inquiry turned into an order of 1,000 cases. Of the initial overseas venture, Becker said, "We thought of it as a hobby."

However, Becker got serious about this venture when he noted that Seagram, Pepsi-Cola, and Stroh all were debuting soft-drink offerings. Much hard work led to a connection with Cheerio Kansai, an Osaka-based soft drink maker and distributor. They hammered out a deal, and the 20,000-case first order represented 8 percent of Blue Sky's total sales. While overseas sales only account for a small portion of revenues, Becker thinks it is a smart hedge given Blue Sky's lilliputian stature in a land of soda-pop giants. "We're getting all these additional sales," says Becker, "and it's a wonderful way to get our foot in the door."[25] ∎

● GETTING STARTED INTERNATIONALLY

Small- and medium-size companies have a couple of ways of becoming involved internationally. One is to seek cheaper sources of supply offshore, which is called *outsourcing*. Another way is to develop markets for finished products outside their home country, which may include exporting, licensing, and direct investing. These are called **market entry strategies,** because they represent alternative ways to sell products and services in foreign markets. Most firms begin with exporting and work up to direct investment. Exhibit 3.3 shows the strategies companies can use to enter foreign markets.

OUTSOURCING

Global outsourcing, sometimes called *global sourcing,* means engaging in the international division of labor so that manufacturing can be done in countries with the cheapest sources of labor and supplies. A company may take away a contract from a domestic supplier and place it with a company in the Far East, 8,000 miles away. For example, Seagate Technology sells low-cost hard disk drives for personal computers. Its enormous success has been based on using low-cost Asian labor to crank out products cheaply. These products are then finished off and sold in the United States.[26]

A unique variation is the *maquiladora* industry along the Texas-Mexico border. In the beginning, twin plants were set up with the U.S.

market entry strategy

An organizational strategy for entering a foreign market.

global outsourcing

Engaging in the international division of labor so as to obtain the cheapest sources of labor and supplies regardless of country; also called *global sourcing.*

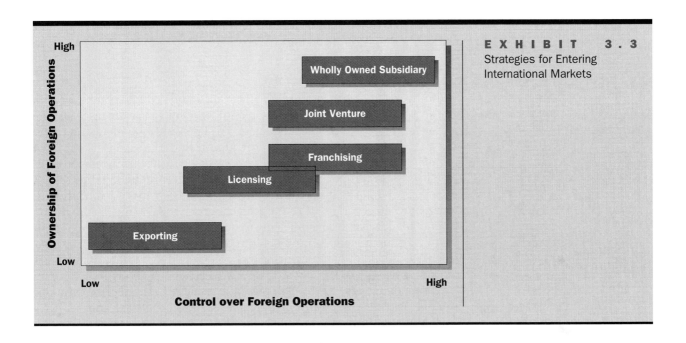

E X H I B I T   3 . 3
Strategies for Entering
International Markets

plant manufacturing components with sophisticated machinery and the Mexican plant assembling components using cheap labor. With increasing sophistication in Mexico, new factories with sophisticated equipment are being built farther south of the border, with assembled products imported into the United States at highly competitive prices.[27] The auto industry took advantage of the *maquiladora* industry throughout the 1980s to combat the Japanese price challenge. By 1992, over 100,000 Mexicans were employed by U.S. auto companies in towns such as Hermosillo, giving the area the nickname "Detroit South." The low-cost, high-quality Mexican workforce has also attracted manufacturers from other countries, such as Nissan, Renault, and Volkswagen.[28]

EXPORTING

With **exporting,** the corporation maintains its production facilities within the home nation and transfers its products for sale in foreign countries.[29] Exporting enables a country to market its products in other countries at small resource cost and with limited risk. Exporting does entail numerous problems based on physical distances, government regulations, foreign currencies, and cultural differences, but it is less expensive than committing the firm's own capital to building plants in host countries. For example, a high-tech equipment supplier called Gerber Scientific Inc. prefers not to get involved directly in foreign country operations. Because machinery and machine tools are hot areas of export, executives are happy to ship overseas. Indeed, more and more small businesses are experiencing great success in international markets.[30]

A form of exporting to less-developed countries is called **countertrade,** which is the barter of products for products rather than the sale of products for currency. Many less-developed countries have products

exporting

An entry strategy in which the organization maintains its production facilities within its home country and transfers its products for sale in foreign markets.

countertrade

The barter of products for other products rather than their sale for currency.

to exchange but have no foreign currency. An estimated 20 percent of world trade is countertrade.

LICENSING

licensing

An entry strategy in which an organization in one country makes certain resources available to companies in another in order to participate in the production and sale of its products abroad.

With **licensing,** a corporation (the licensor) in one country makes certain resources available to companies in another country (the licensee). These resources include technology, managerial skills, and/or patent and trademark rights. They enable the licensee to produce and market a product similar to what the licensor has been producing. This arrangement gives the licensor an opportunity to participate in the production and sale of products outside its home country. Hasbro has licensing agreements with companies in several Latin American countries and Japan. Hasbro builds brand identity and consumer awareness by contracting with toy companies to manufacture products locally. Glidden has licensing arrangements for its paint manufacturing technology with manufacturers in over 25 countries.

franchising

A form of licensing in which an organization provides its foreign franchisees with a complete assortment of materials and services.

Franchising is a form of licensing in which the franchisor provides foreign franchisees with a complete package of material and services, including equipment, products, product ingredients, trademark and trade name rights, managerial advice, and a standardized operating system. Some of the best known international franchisers are the fast-food chains. Kentucky Fried Chicken, Burger King, Wendy's and McDonald's outlets are found in almost every large city in the world. The story is often told of the Japanese child visiting Los Angeles who excitedly pointed out to his parents, "They have McDonald's in America."

Licensing and franchising offer a business firm relatively easy access to international markets, but they limit its participation in and control over the development of those markets.

DIRECT INVESTING

direct investing

An entry strategy in which the organization is involved in managing its production facilities in a foreign country.

joint venture

A variation of direct investment in which an organization shares costs and risks with another firm to build a manufacturing facility, develop new products, or set up a sales and distribution network.

A higher level of involvement in international trade is direct investment in manufacturing facilities in a foreign country. **Direct investing** means that the company is involved in managing the productive assets, which distinguishes it from other entry strategies that permit less managerial control.

Currently, the most popular type of direct investment is to engage in strategic alliances and partnerships. In a **joint venture,** a company shares costs and risks with another firm, typically in the host country, to develop new products, build a manufacturing facility, or set up a sales and distribution network.[31] A partnership is often the fastest, cheapest, and least risky way to get into the global game. Entrepreneurial companies such as Molex, a manufacturer of connectors, and Nypro, a maker of industrial components, both used partnerships to gain overseas access to several countries. Giants such as AT&T and Japan's NEC Corporation joined forces to share design technology and microchip manufacturing. Other giant partnerships include Texas Instruments with Kobe Steel (Japan), Mitsubishi of Japan with Daimler-Benz AG of Germany, and Ford with Volkswagen (in South America) and with Mazda of Japan.[32] International joint ventures are expected to be the hallmark of business in the 1990s.

The other choice is to have a **wholly owned foreign affiliate,** over which the company has complete control. Direct investment provides cost savings over exporting by shortening distribution channels and reducing storage and transportation costs. Local managers also have heightened awareness of economic, cultural, and political conditions. The company must expend capital funds and human resources to acquire productive assets that will be exposed to risks from the host country's economic, legal-political, and sociocultural environments.

For example, companies in the advertising industry have recently become involved in direct investment by buying agencies around the globe to provide advertising services for global companies. Foote Cone & Belding acquired advertising agencies in Europe, South America, and Asia. Saatchi & Saatchi, based in London, has taken over 12 agencies in Europe and the United States. Such mergers create wholly owned subsidiaries that enable advertising agencies to coordinate the advertising for multinational clients. Direct investment gives them complete control over agencies in host countries.[33]

wholly owned foreign affiliate

A foreign subsidiary over which an organization has complete control.

● THE MULTINATIONAL CORPORATION

The size and volume of international business are so large that they are hard to comprehend. The revenue of General Motors ($124 billion) is comparable to the gross domestic product (GDP) of Finland, that of General Electric ($60 billion) is comparable in size to Israel's GDP, Toyota revenues ($78 billion) to Hong Kong's GDP, and those of the Royal Dutch/Shell Group ($104 billion) to the GDP of Norway.[34]

As discussed earlier in this chapter, a large volume of international business is being carried out in a seemingly borderless world by very large international businesses that can be thought of as *global corporations, stateless corporations,* or *transnational corporations.* In the business world, these large international firms typically are called *multinational corporations (MNCs),* which have been the subject of enormous attention and concern. MNCs can move a wealth of assets from country to country and influence national economies, politics, and cultures.

CHARACTERISTICS OF MULTINATIONAL CORPORATIONS

Although there is no precise definition, a **multinational corporation (MNC)** typically receives more than 25 percent of its total sales revenues from operations outside the parent's home country. MNCs also have the following distinctive managerial characteristics:

1 An MNC is managed as an integrated worldwide business system. This means that foreign affiliates act in close alliance and cooperation with one another. Capital, technology, and people are transferred among country affiliates. The MNC can acquire materials and manufacture parts wherever in the world it is most advantageous to do so.

multinational corporation (MNC)

An organization that receives more than 25 percent of its total sales revenues from operations outside the parent company's home country; also called *global corporation* or *transnational corporation.*

2 An MNC is ultimately controlled by a single management authority that makes key, strategic decisions relating to the parent and all affiliates. Although some headquarters are binational, such as the Royal Dutch/Shell Group, some centralization of management is required to maintain worldwide integration and profit maximization for the enterprise as a whole.

3 MNC top managers are presumed to exercise a global perspective. They regard the entire world as one market for strategic decisions, resource acquisition, location of production, advertising, and marketing efficiency.

In few cases, the MNC management philosophy may differ from that described above. For example, some researchers have distinguished among *ethnocentric companies*, which place emphasis on their home countries, *polycentric companies*, which are oriented toward the markets of individual foreign host countries, and *geocentric companies*, which are truly world oriented and favor no specific country.[35] In general, a multinational corporation can be thought of as a business enterprise that is composed of affiliates located in different countries and whose top managers make decisions primarily on the basis of global business opportunities and objectives.

● TAILORING MANAGEMENT STYLE TO INTERNATIONAL CULTURES

Managers in MNCs deal with employees from different cultures. What one culture sees as participative management another sees as incompetence. Before undertaking an assignment in a foreign country, managers must understand the subtleties of culture and how to provide proper leadership, decision making, motivation, and control.[36]

LEADERSHIP

In relationship-oriented societies, leaders should take a strong personal interest in employees. In Asia, the Arab world, and Latin America, managers should use a warm, personalized approach, appearing at soccer games and birthday parties. In Latin America and China, managers should have periodic social visits with workers, inquiring about morale and health.

Leaders should be especially careful about criticizing others. To Asians, Africans, Arabs, and Latin Americans, the loss of self-respect brings dishonor to themselves and their families. Public criticism is intolerable. In a moment of exasperation, an American supervisor on an oil rig in Indonesia shouted at his timekeeper to take the next boat to shore. A mob of outraged Indonesians grabbed fire axes and went after the supervisor. He escaped and barricaded himself in his quarters. The moral: One simply never berates an Indonesian in public.

Because 70 percent of South Korean patients get their medical advice from pharmacists, highly trained company representatives increase respect for the Upjohn Company in the South Korean health care industry. Here, a representative provides information to a pharmacist in Seoul. Drawers in the background contain traditional (herbal) medicine. The Upjohn Company has learned to tailor its management style to local culture as it expands its pharmaceutical business worldwide.

DECISION MAKING

European managers frequently use centralized decision making. American employees might discuss a problem and give the boss a recommendation, but German managers expect the boss to issue specific instructions. East Indian and Latin American employees typically do not understand participatory decision making. Deeply ingrained social customs suggest that a supervisor's effort toward participation signifies ignorance and weakness.

In Arab and African nations, managers are expected to use consultative decision making in the extreme. Arabs prefer one-on-one consultation and make decisions in an informal and unstructured manner.

The Japanese prefer a bottom-up style of decision making, which is consistent with Far Eastern cultures that emphasize group harmony. In Taiwan, Hong Kong, and South Korea, managers are paternalistic figures who guide and help employees.

MOTIVATION

Motivation must fit the incentives within the culture. In Japan, employees are motivated to satisfy the company. A financial bonus for star performance would be humiliating to employees from Japan, China, or the former Yugoslavia. An American executive in Japan offered a holiday trip to the top salesperson, but employees were not interested. After he realized that Japanese are motivated in groups, he changed the reward to a trip for everyone if together they achieved the sales target. They did.

In Latin America, employees work for an individual rather than for a company. Among Turks and Arabs the individual is supreme, and employees are evaluated on their loyalties to superiors more than on job performance.

CONTROL

When things go wrong, managers in foreign countries often are unable to get rid of employees who do not work out. In Europe, Mexico, and Indonesia, to hire and fire on performance seems unnaturally brutal. Workers are protected by strong labor laws and union rules. In Mexico, employees are considered permanent after a 30-day work period. British and Belgian labor laws dramatically favor employees. Managers must find creative ways of dealing with unproductive employees.

In foreign cultures, managers also should not control the wrong things. A Sears manager in Hong Kong insisted that employees come to work on time instead of 15 minutes late. The employees did exactly as they were told, but they also left on time instead of working into the evening as they had previously. A lot of work was left unfinished. The manager eventually told the employees to go back to their old ways. His attempt at control had a negative effect.

In another case a Japanese manager was told to criticize an American employee's performance. It took the manager five tries before he could be direct enough to confront the American on his poor performance. Japanese managers are unused to confrontations.

SUMMARY AND MANAGEMENT SOLUTION

This chapter has stressed the growing importance of an international perspective on management. Successful companies are preparing to expand their business overseas and to withstand domestic competition from foreign competitors. Business in the global arena involves special risks and difficulties because of complicated economic, legal-political, and sociocultural forces. Moreover, the global environment changes rapidly, as illustrated by the emergence of the European Union, the North American Free Trade Agreement (NAFTA), and the shift in Eastern Europe to democratic forms of government.

Rod Waters knew it was the death knell for Florod if he could not improve product quality; that had to be his primary strategy in going up against his new international competitor. After seeing his enterprise undercut because of reliance on one product, Waters decided to look into diversifying his products. Consultants from the Department of Commerce devised a plan to test five new products and markets. However, his best efforts at improving quality failed, and by 1982 sales were only 60 percent of the two years previous. Then, just when Florod seemed near bottoming out, the market research paid off. Plenty of potential business existed for a laser cutter that could fix problems on integrated-circuit chips. Waters came up with a cutter good enough to cut wires at 1/50th the width of a human hair.

Sales of the laser cutter rose steadily, and Waters decided to avoid a repeat of his previous experience through an interesting turnabout. Using an employee fluent in Japanese and knowledgeable about the culture, Waters returned NEC's favor by entering an agreement with the import/export company Hakuto. Florod began selling laser cutters in Japan.

Waters is not delusional about the near death experience of Florod, attributing it to an inability to consistently produce a quality product. He also remains philosophical about NEC. "That wonderful company, NEC, that almost put us out of business, has set us up for spectacular success," he said.[37]

Much of the growth in international business has been carried out by large businesses called *MNCs*. These large companies exist in an almost borderless world, encouraging the free flow of ideas, products, manufacturing, and marketing among countries to achieve the greatest efficiencies. Products sold in any one country may contain parts manufactured and assembled in several countries. Managers in MNCs deal with employees from various countries and can learn to tailor their management style to cultural differences.

DISCUSSION QUESTIONS

1. Why do you think international businesses traditionally prefer to operate in industrialized countries? Discuss.
2. What considerations in recent years have led international businesses to expand their activities into less-developed countries?

3. What policies or actions would you recommend to an entrepreneurial business wanting to do business in Europe?

4. What steps could a company take to avoid making product design and marketing mistakes when introducing new products into a foreign country?

5. Compare the advantages associated with the foreign market entry strategies of exporting, licensing, and wholly owned subsidiaries.

6. Should a multinational corporation operate as an integrated, worldwide business system, or would it be more effective to let each subsidiary operate autonomously?

7. What does it mean to say that the world is becoming "borderless"? That large companies are "stateless"?

8. What might managers do to avoid making mistakes concerning control and decision making when operating in a foreign culture?

9. What is meant by the cultural values of individualism and masculinity/femininity? How might these values affect organization design and management processes?

MANAGEMENT IN PRACTICE: EXPERIENTIAL EXERCISE

A global environment requires that American managers learn to deal effectively with people in other countries. The assumption that foreign business leaders behave and negotiate in the same manner as Americans is false. How well prepared are you to live with globalization? Consider the following.

Are you guilty of:	Definitely No				Definitely Yes
1. Impatience? Do you think "Time is money" or "Let's get straight to the point"?	1	2	3	4	5
2. Having a short attention span, bad listening habits, or being uncomfortable with silence?	1	2	3	4	5
3. Being somewhat argumentative, sometimes to the point of belligerence?	1	2	3	4	5
4. Ignorance about the world beyond your borders?	1	2	3	4	5
5. Weakness in foreign languages?	1	2	3	4	5
6. Placing emphasis on short-term success?	1	2	3	4	5
7. Believing that advance preparations are less important than negotiations themselves?	1	2	3	4	5
8. Being legalistic? Of believing "A deal is a deal," regardless of changing circumstances?	1	2	3	4	5
9. Having little interest in seminars on the subject of globalization, failing to browse through libraries or magazines on international topics, not interacting with foreign students or employees?	1	2	3	4	5
Total Score					_____

If you scored less than 27, congratulations. You have the temperament and interest to do well in a global company. If you scored more than 27, it's time to consider a change. Regardless of your score, go back over each item and make a plan of action to correct deficiencies indicated by answers to any question of 4 or 5.

SOURCE: Reprinted by permission of the publisher from Cynthia Barmun and Netasha Wolninsky, "Why Americans Fail at Overseas Negotiations," *Management Review* (October 1989), 55–57, © 1989 American Management Association, New York. All rights reserved.

CASE FOR ANALYSIS

RUSSIAN KIOSK OWNER

Alexei Grigoriev, the 24-year-old founder of a Moscow-based specialty kiosk chain called Creation, is facing more than the average pitfalls for a start-up entrepreneur. Bribery is virtually a necessary business practice in Moscow, where worries about both extortion attempts and police harassment are everyday occurrences. Getting a handle on costs and deliveries of Creations' eclectic products is also a wholly ad hoc exercise. Because Grigoriev so suspects his inventory to be stolen, smuggled, or some other type of contraband, he has simply stopped asking about the source. He carries a pistol just in case.

Surprisingly, Grigoriev is not involved in organized crime. He is just a trail-blazing businessman trying to make it in the almost anything-goes, free-enterprise environment of Moscow. Even though capitalism is all the rage, few people know much about it. State monopolies still dominate, controlling most aspects of daily life from production to transportation to sales. If the Western way of doing things takes hold, it will clearly begin at the grass roots with people like Grigoriev. He is doing quite well: his five private kiosks sell $500,000 worth of German chocolates, French liqueurs, U.S. cigarettes, and other products annually, a princely income in the former Soviet Union. However, it has not been easy.

"Little old ladies living on a 300-ruble monthly pension look at my prices and call me a thief," he says. He adds, however, that most people understand how business works, and those that do not by now, never will. Grigoriev can at least sympathize with the plight of the average Muscovite. After controls were lifted in 1990, prices have increased 1200 percent. In a classic example of trying to recapture lost market share, Grigoriev has lowered prices 30 to 50 percent. "Many of our middle-class clients have left us," he says. "We're trying to win them back."

Reattracting customers is only one of many problems. He employs around 60 people and personally tracks store inventories on a ledger he keeps with him. Sales and receipts seldom approach even a rough balance, leading him to strongly suspect theft and moonlighting operations arranged by his help. The entire staff changes almost every month.

Grigoriev believes the key to retail success is securing goods in an economy where distribution channels are erratic and products stolen from state factories are commonplace. His vodka supplier secures its product from workers at the Samara Stolichnaya factory. Amaretto comes from Latvia, and cigarettes from a Moscow commodity exchange. Grigoriev buys ham and sausage from a man whose curiously unrelated occupation is working in a Russian–Belgian clothing factory, not far from a Russian–Spanish meat processing plant. Grigoriev pays in cash, and asks no questions. "It's all absolutely aboveboard," the man insists.

The city of Moscow taxes prohibitively, taking 10 percent of profits and another 28 percent on the overall business. But it makes zero-interest loans available and helps expedite new store openings. Grigoriev facilitates this process, not through bribes, but by what are referred to as "presents" of meals, cognac, or other such niceties. Despite all the day-to-day problems, Grigoriev is a happy Russian capitalist who sounds positively American dream-like in his aspirations. "This is my calling," he says, "and I want to be the best of all."

● QUESTIONS

1. What management techniques described in this book could Grigoriev use to address some of his problems?
2. How are Grigoriev's experiences indicative of the obstacles U.S. businesses might face in the former Soviet Union?
3. Do you think an American entrepreneur could successfully expand into the former Soviet Union? Why or why not?

SOURCE: Adi Ignatius, "Moscow Shop Owner Finds He Is Natural at Raw Capitalism," *The Wall Street Journal*, March 25, 1992.

REFERENCES

1. David E. Gumpert, "Turnabout Is Fair Play," *INC.*, September 1987, 120–124.

2. Yao-Su Yu, "Global or Stateless Corporations Are National Firms with International Operations," *California Management Review* 34 (Winter), 107–126; Jonathan P. Hicks, "Foreign Owners Are Shaking Up the Competition," *The New York Times*, May 28, 1989, sec. 3, 9; and Ira C. Magaziner and Mark Patinkin, *The Silent War* (New York: Random House, 1989).

3. William Holstein, Stanley Reed, Jonathan Kapstein, Todd Vogel, and Joseph Weber, "The Stateless Corporation," *Business Week*, May 14, 1990, 98–105.

4. Nancy J. Adler, *International Dimensions of Organizational Behavior* (Boston: PWS-Kent, 1991), 7–8; Holstein et al., "The Stateless Corporation"; and Richard Daft, *Organization Theory and Design* (St Paul, Minn.: West, 1992).

5. Holstein et al., "The Stateless Corporation."

6. William Taylor, "The Logic of Global Business: An Interview with ABB's Percy Barnevik," *Harvard Business Review* (March–April 1991), 91–105; and Holstein et al., "The Stateless Corporation."

7. John S. Hill and Richard R. Still, "Adapting Products to LDC Tastes," *Harvard Business Review* 62 (March–April 1984), 92–101; and David A. Ricks, *Big Business Blunders: Mistakes in Multinational Marketing* (Homewood, Ill.: Dow Jones-Irwin, 1983).

8. Karen Paul and Robert Barbarto, "The Multinational Corporation in the Less Developed Country: The Economic Development Model versus the North-South Model," *Academy of Management Review* 10 (1985), 8–14.

9. Kathleen Deveny, "McWorld?" *Business Week*, October 13, 1986, 78–86.

10. Bruce Kogut, "Designing Global Strategies: Profiting from Operational Flexibility," *Sloan Management Review* 27 (Fall 1985), 27–38.

11. Mark Fitzpatrick, "The Definition and Assessment of Political Risk in International Business: A Review of the Literature," *Academy of Management Review* 8 (1983), 249–254.

12. "Multinational Firms Act to Protect Overseas Workers from Terrorism," *The Wall Street Journal*, April 29, 1986, 31.

13. Patricia Sellers, "Where Killers and Kidnappers Roam," *Fortune*, September 23, 1991, 8.

14. John Templeton, Ken Olsen, David Greising, Jonathan Kapstein, and William Glasgall, "Eastward Ho! The Pioneers Plunge In," *Business Week*, April 15, 1991, 51–53.

15. Shawn Tully, "Europe '92: More Unity Than You Think," *Fortune*, August 24, 1992, 136–142.

16. Barbara Rudolph, "Megamarket," *Time*, August 10, 1992, 43–44.

17. Amy Borrus, "A Free-Trade Milestone, with Many More Miles to Go," *Business Week*, August 24, 1992, 30–31.

18. Keith Bradsher, "As Global Talks Stall, Regional Trade Pacts Multiply," *The New York Times*, August 23, 1992, F5.

19. Geert Hofstede, "The Interaction between National and Organizational Value Systems," *Journal of Management Studies* 22 (1985), 347–357; and Geert Hofstede, "The Cultural Relativity of the Quality of Life Concept," *Academy of Management Review* 9 (1984), 389–398.

20. Ellen F. Jackofsky, John W. Slocum, Jr., and Sara J. McQuaid, "Cultural Values and the CEO: Alluring Companions?" *Academy of Management Executive* 2 (1988), 39–49.

21. Jeffrey A. Trachtenberg, "They Didn't Listen to Anybody," *Forbes*, December 15, 1986, 168–169.

22. Orla Sheehan, "Managing a Multinational Corporation: Tomorrow's Decision Makers Speak Out," *Fortune*, August 24, 1992, 233.

23. Stewart Toy, Patricia Oster, and Ronald Grover, "The Mouse Isn't Roaring," *Business Week*, August 24, 1992, 38.

24. Kenneth Labich, "America's International Winners," *Fortune*, April 14, 1986, 34–46.

25. Paul B. Brown, "Over There," *INC.*, April 1990, 105–106; and Kevin McLaughlin, "Becker Finds It Natural to Sell Sodas in Japan," *World Trade*, February/March 1990, 6.

26. Frank T. Curtin, "Global Sourcing: Is It Right for Your Company?" *Management Review* (August 1987), 47–49; and Richard Brandt, "Seagate Goes East—and Comes Back a Winner," *Business Week*, March 16, 1987, 94.

27. Gary Jacobson, "The Boom on Mexico's Border," *Management Review* (July 1988), 21–25.

28. Stephen Baker, David Woodruff, and Elizabeth Weiner, "Detroit South," *Business Week*, March 16, 1992, 98–103.

29. Jen Kerr, "Export Strategies," *Small Business Reports* (May 1989), 20–25.

30. William J. Holstein and Brian Bremmer, "The Little Guys Are Making It Big Overseas," *Business Week*, February 27, 1989, 94–96; and Iris Lorenz-Fife, "Resource Guide: Small-Business Help from the Government," *Entrepreneur*, December 1989, 168–174.

31. Kathryn Rudie Harrigan, "Managing Joint Ventures," *Management Review* (February 1987), 24–41; and Therese R. Revesz and Mimi Cauley de Da La Sierra, "Competitive Alliances: Forging Ties Abroad," *Management Review* (March 1987), 57–59.

32. Bernard Wysocki, Jr., "Cross-Border Alliances Become Favorite Way to Crack New Markets," *The Wall Street Journal*, March 26, 1990, A1, A12; and Andrew Kupfer, "How to Be a Global Manager," *Fortune*, March 14, 1988, 52–58.

33. Janice Castro, "Heavy-Duty Mergers," *Time*, May 12, 1986, 72–73.

34. "How Revenues of the Top Ten Global Companies Compare with Some National Economies," *Fortune*, July 27, 1992, 16.

35. Howard V. Perlmutter, "The Tortuous Evolution of the Multinational Corporation," *Columbia Journal of World Business* (January/February 1969), 9–18;

and Youram Wind, Susan P. Douglas, and Howard V. Perlmutter, "Guidelines for Developing International Marketing Strategies," *Journal of Marketing* (April 1973), 14–23.

36. The following discussion is based on Lennie Copeland and Lewis Gregg, "Getting the Best from Foreign Employees," *Management Review* (June 1986), 19–26.

37. David Gumpert, "Turnabout Is Fair Play."

THE ENVIRONMENT AND CORPORATE CULTURE

4

CHAPTER OUTLINE ▲

LEARNING OBJECTIVES ▼

After studying this chapter, you should be able to

- Describe the task and general environments and the dimensions of each.

- Explain how organizations adapt to an uncertain environment and identify techniques managers use to influence and control the external environment.

- Define corporate culture and give organizational examples.

- Explain organizational symbols, stories, heroes, slogans, and ceremonies and how they relate to corporate culture.

- Describe how corporate culture relates to the environment.

- Define a symbolic manager and explain the tools a symbolic manager

The worst nightmare for any restaurant chain is a well-publicized food-poisoning scare. That is exactly what happened on January 11, 1993, at a Jack in the Box in Tacoma, Washington. Two-year-old Michael Nole died ten days after eating hamburger meat tainted by the lethal *E. coli* bacteria. By then, however, as many as 300 other people had also been affected, either from eating at Jack in the Box restaurants scattered across three states or coming in contact with those individuals who had. ▪ As the tragedy unfolded, the company faltered badly. An admission of guilt was almost a week in coming. Even then, company president Robert J. Nugent seemed more intent on casting his own net of blame than taking full responsibility. He first chided state health personnel for failing to keep the company apprised about new cooking regulations, and then singled out Vons Companies, the meat supplier. ▪ Not surprisingly, customers avoided the fast-food chain, with many locations reporting as much as a 20 percent decrease in sales. Austin Wallestad, owner of eight Jack in the Box restaurants, said, "This thing is killing us." ▪ Do you think that Jack in the Box executives could have anticipated and avoided the problems with the tainted hamburger meat? If you were Nugent, how would you respond to these problems?[1]

Jack in the Box faced a crisis brought on by seemingly unpredictable events within both the internal and external environment. The environment surprises many companies. Union Carbide faced a crisis when a gas leak killed more than 2,500 people in Bhopal, India. That disaster damaged Carbide's ability to compete for international contracts and by 1992 had reduced the company to half its prior size.[2]

Organizations may be affected by a variety of environmental forces such as strikes, technological advances in the industry, or competitive price wars. Government actions, regulations and red tape can also affect an organization's environment and foment a crisis. Passage of the Americans with Disabilities Act forced companies to evaluate existing conditions that required compliance and make adjustments in a number of areas—from promotion practices to parking and restroom access. Changes in Medicare payments may force many rural hospitals to close.

Although few companies experience a crisis as serious as the one resulting from a gas leak, unexpected events that can seriously harm performance occur in the environment of every organization. During the lingering recession in the early 1990s, companies such as H. J. Heinz, Sears, TRW, and General Electric underwent major internal changes—restructuring, discarding product lines, and trimming work forces. Without these major changes, the companies would no longer fit the reality of the changing external environment.

The study of management traditionally has focused on factors within the organization—a closed systems view—such as leading, motivating, and controlling employees. The classical, behavioral, and management science schools described in Chapter 2 focused on internal aspects of organizations over which managers have direct control. These views are accurate but incomplete. As discussed in Chapter 3, globalization and the trend toward a borderless world affects companies in new ways. Even for those companies that try to operate solely on the domestic stage, events that have greatest impact typically originate in the external environment. To be effective, managers must monitor and respond to the environment—an open systems view.

This chapter explores in detail components of the external environment and how they affect the organization. We will also examine a major part of the organization's internal environment—corporate culture. Corporate culture is shaped by the external environment and is an important part of the context within which managers do their jobs.

● THE EXTERNAL ENVIRONMENT

The world as we know it is undergoing tremendous and far-reaching change. This change can be understood by defining and examining components of the external environment.

The external **organizational environment** includes all elements existing outside the boundary of the organization that have the potential to affect the organization.[3] The environment includes competitors, resources, technology, and economic conditions that influence the organization. It does not include those events so far removed from the organization that their impact is not perceived.

organizational environment

All elements existing outside the organization's boundaries that have the potential to affect the organization.

The organization's external environment can be further conceptualized as having two layers: general and task environments as illustrated in Exhibit 4.1.[4]

The **general environment** is the outer layer that is widely dispersed and affects organizations indirectly. It includes social, demographic, and economic factors that influence all organizations about equally. Increases in the inflation rate or the percentage of dual-career couples in the work force are part of the organization's general environment. These events do not directly change day-to-day operations, but they do affect all organizations eventually. The **task environment** is closer to the organization and includes the sectors that conduct day-to-day transactions with the organization and directly influence its basic operations and performance. It is generally considered to include competitors, suppliers, and customers.

general environment

The layer of the external environment that affects the organization indirectly.

The organization also has an **internal environment,** which includes the elements within the organization's boundaries. The internal environment is composed of current employees, management, and especially corporate culture, which defines employee behavior in the internal environment and how well the organization will adapt to the external environment.

task environment

The layer of the external environment that directly influences the organization's operations and performance.

internal environment

The environment within the organization's boundaries.

Exhibit 4.1 illustrates the relationship among the general, task, and internal environments. As an open system, the organization draws resources from the external environment and releases goods and services back to it. We will now discuss the two layers of the external environment in more detail. Then we will discuss corporate culture, the key element in the internal environment. Other aspects of the internal environment such as structure and technology will be covered in Parts III and IV of this book.

GENERAL ENVIRONMENT

The general environment represents the outer layer of the environment. These dimensions influence the organization over time but often are not involved in day-to-day transactions with it. The dimensions of the general environment include international, technological, sociocultural, economic, and legal-political.

INTERNATIONAL. The **international dimension** of the external environment represents events originating in foreign countries as well as opportunities for American companies in other countries. Note in Exhibit 4.1 that the international dimension represents a context that influences all other aspects of the external environment. The international environment provides new competitors, customers, and suppliers, as well as shaping social, technological, and economic trends.

international dimension

Portion of the external environment that represents events originating in foreign countries as well as opportunities for American companies in other countries.

One study identified 136 U.S. industries—including automobiles, accounting services, entertainment, consumer electronics, and publishing—that will have to compete on a global basis or disappear. The high-quality, low-priced automobiles from Japan and South Korea have permanently changed the American automobile industry. As we discussed in Chapter 3, many companies have parts supplied from countries such as Mexico because of low-priced labor. A drop in the dollar's foreign

Location of the Organization's
General, Task, and Internal
Environments

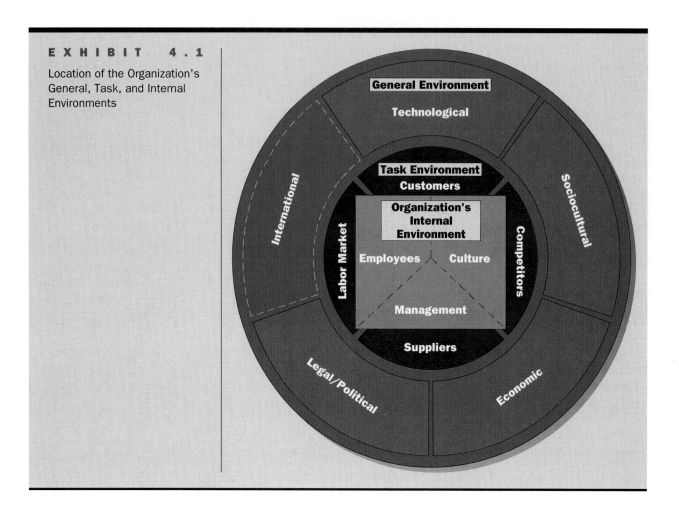

exchange rate lowers the price of U.S. products overseas, increasing export competitiveness.

One example of fierce foreign competition is Toyo Toki, Japan's leading maker of toilets and bathtubs, which has now targeted the U.S. market. Toyo Toki plans to offer initially products not produced by American manufacturers, such as an electronically controlled toilet and bidet combined in one unit. American companies are worried about the competition. The chief executive of American Standard said, "I would rank them as our number-one threat in the future. We have to hurry."[5]

Managers used to working and thinking about the domestic environment must learn new rules to cope with goods, services, and ideas circulating around the globe. For example, products and services exist in a one-world market. A better machine built in Oklahoma City will find buyers from Europe and Asia. Moreover, competitors in a global village come from all over. A company that does not export will still run into competitors in its own marketplace, including some from developing nations. The world is also a source of supply as well as a market. For example, new products such as liquid Tide are composed of materials and ideas from around the world.

Perhaps the hardest lesson for managers in the United States to learn is that they do not know best. U.S. decision makers know little about issues and competition in foreign countries. U.S. arrogance is a shortcut to failure. To counter this, Pall Corporation keeps a team of Ph.D.s traveling around the world gathering current information on markets and issues.[6]

The global environment represents an ever-changing and uneven playing field compared with the domestic environment. Changes in the international domain can abruptly turn the domestic environment upside down. Consider, for example, the "peace dividend" brought on by the end of the Cold War, and the fall of communism. Despite the need for periodic military action in areas such as the Persian Gulf or Somalia, the peace dividend has increased demand for military cuts, pushing smaller defense contractors out of business and forcing large companies such as McDonnell Douglas, General Dynamics, and Martin Marietta to convert a significant portion of their operations into nonmilitary production.[7] Top industry scientists and engineers are switching to civilian developments such as high-definition television and new areas of transportation such as electric cars.[8]

TECHNOLOGICAL. The **technological dimension** includes scientific and technological advancements in a specific industry as well as in society at large. In recent years, the most striking advances have been in the computer industry. Supercomputers have astonishing power, and many companies are utilizing computerized systems such as automated offices, robotics, and computer-controlled machines. High-definition television promises to revolutionize the worldwide electronics industry. Revolutionary discoveries in biomimetics (the use of nature as models) and atomscompics (molecular architecture) are leading to high-performance materials that are lighter, stronger, and more resistant to temperature extremes. Smart composite materials, embedded with sensors that enable them to think for themselves, promise new strides for the space program and the aircraft industry.[9] Aircraft surface materials can be embedded with fiber-optic sensors that can feel the weight of ice or the "touch" of enemy radar.[10] These and other technological advances can change the rules of the game; thus, every organization must be ready to respond.

technological dimension

The dimension of the general environment that includes scientific and technological advancements in the industry and society at large.

SOCIOCULTURAL. The **sociocultural dimension** of the general environment represents the demographic characteristics as well as the norms, customs, and values of the general population. Important sociocultural characteristics are geographical distribution and population density, age, and education levels. Today's demographic profiles are the foundation of tomorrow's work force and consumers. Forecasters see increased globalization of both consumer markets and the labor supply, with increasing diversity both within organizations and consumer markets.[11] For example, the 1990 U.S. census reports the following key demographic trends:

sociocultural dimension

The dimension of the general environment representing the demographic characteristics, norms, customs, and values of the population within which the organization operates.

1 African-Americans are the largest ethnic group with a median age in the 18–35 range.

2 Aging baby-boomers (born between 1946 and 1964) comprise 31 percent of the population.

3 In 1990, the 4.2 million births were the most since 1963, giving credence to the prediction of a "baby-boomlet" as career women race to beat their biological clocks.

4 The United States will continue to receive a flood of immigrants, largely from Asia (35.2 percent) and Mexico (23.7 percent).[12]

Demography also shapes society's norms and values. Recent sociocultural trends that are affecting many companies include the trend toward no smoking, the anti-cholesterol fervor, the greater purchasing power of young children, and the increased diversity of consumers, with specialized markets for groups such as Hispanics and women over 30.

economic dimension

The dimension of the general environment representing the overall economic health of the country or region in which the organization functions.

ECONOMIC.   The **economic dimension** represents the general economic health of the country or region in which the organization operates. Consumer purchasing power, unemployment rate, and interest rates are part of an organization's economic environment. Not-for-profit organizations such as the Red Cross and the Salvation Army find a greater demand for their services during economic decline but receive smaller contributions. They must adapt to these changes in economic conditions. One significant recent trend in the economic environment is the frequency of mergers and acquisitions. The corporate economic landscape is being altered. One of the hottest deals was the merger of Time, the nation's biggest publisher, with Warner Communications, an entertainment conglomerate. In the media industry alone, Sony purchased CBS Records to guarantee control over a supply of music for its Walkman customers. News Corporation acquired both Fox TV and Triangle, publisher of *TV Guide.* Bertelsmann acquired both Doubleday Publishers and RCA Records. The impact of these deals on employees can be overwhelming, creating uncertainty about future job security. The deal is just the beginning of employee uncertainty, because about half of the acquired companies are resold.[13]

legal-political dimension

The dimension of the general environment that includes federal, state, and local government regulations and political activities designed to control company behavior.

LEGAL-POLITICAL.   The **legal-political dimension** includes government regulations at the local, state, and federal levels as well as political activities designed to influence company behavior. The U.S. political system encourages capitalism, and the government tries not to overregulate business. However, government laws do specify rules of the game. The federal government influences organizations through the Occupational Safety and Health Administration (OSHA), Environmental Protection Agency (EPA), fair trade practices, libel statutes allowing lawsuits against business, consumer protection legislation, product safety requirements, import and export restrictions, and information and labeling requirements. Although designed to solve problems, the influx of regulations often creates problems for organizations. For example, OSHA's 1992 mandatory regulations for exposure to blood-borne diseases require a detailed list of all exposed workers, free vaccinations, creation of a detailed exposure-controlled plan, free employee exposure-reduction training, provision of protective garments, and maintenance records for OSHA review. Employers agree to the need for stronger safety measures, but many view the new regulations as "overkill" and a costly intrusion on companies.[14] Many companies are likewise concerned about the

Changes in the legal-political environment have directly affected Bumble Bee tuna and similar industries. The nutritional information and the "dolphin-safe" logo shown on the label are results of new government regulations and environmental pressures.

impact of the Clinton health-care reform package. Small companies, such as V-J Electronics, are especially wary of the financial and personnel "costs" of reform.

 ## V-J ELECTRONICS ASSEMBLIES

Payroll at Melanie Jimmerson-Bradford's V-J Electronics Assemblies totals $25,000 per month, and the company does not offer health insurance. Under proposed federal health-care reforms, V-J would have to start adding in an additional 3.5 percent of its payroll (around $900 a month) to cover insurance costs for its 14 employees. This increase translates only one way to Jimmerson-Bradford: "The only way any small business can cut costs significantly is by cutting employees."

Jimmerson-Bradford and other small, entrepreneurial company owners that currently do not offer health insurance coverage are understandably upset. Their enterprises will suffer. However, the 32 percent of companies with 25 or fewer employees that already have health plans will probably benefit, since they can join pools and have premiums capped at a lower rate.

In the first quarter of 1992, Jimmerson-Bradford was named woman of the month by the *Houston Post*. However, that same day, her bank was shut down by the FDIC. A personal aversion to seeking protection in bankruptcy led her to take out a loan against her $1 million company so she could keep paying her help. She said then that the devil was a banker. She now is beginning to think that the devil's actually a well-intentioned Washington reformer legislating her people out of work.[15]

TASK ENVIRONMENT

As described above, the task environment includes those sectors that have a direct working relationship with the organization, among them customers, competitors, suppliers, and the labor market.

CUSTOMERS.   Those people and organizations in the environment who acquire goods or services from the organization are **customers.** As recipients of the organization's output, customers are important because they determine the organization's success. Patients are the customers of hospitals, students the customers of schools, and travelers the customers of airlines. Companies such as AT&T, General Foods, and Beecham Products have all designed special programs and advertising campaigns to court their older customers, who are, with the aging of baby boomers, becoming a larger percentage of their market.[16] Overbuilding in the hotel industry forced companies such as Hyatt and Marriott to spend additional money on advertising, direct mail, giveaways, and expansion into new markets to improve customer demand.

COMPETITORS.   Other organizations in the same industry or type of business that provide goods or services to the same set of customers are referred to as **competitors.** Each industry is characterized by specific competitive issues. The recording industry differs from the steel industry and the pharmaceutical industry. Competition in the steel industry, especially from international producers, caused some companies to go bankrupt. Companies in the pharmaceutical industry are highly profitable because it is difficult for new firms to enter it. Within some industries, competitors must unite to achieve common objectives. By the 1990s, Apple, IBM, and Compaq were locked in a titanic power struggle to dominate the personal computer hardware industry as well as to break Microsoft Corporation's domination of the software industry. In a flanking action against Microsoft, Apple and IBM entered a joint venture called Taligent, Inc., for the development of new operating systems software.[17]

SUPPLIERS.   The raw materials the organization uses to produce its output are provided by **suppliers.** A steel mill requires iron ore, machines, and financial resources. A small, private university may utilize hundreds of suppliers for paper, pencils, cafeteria food, computers, trucks, fuel, electricity, and textbooks. Large companies such as General Motors, Westinghouse, and Exxon depend on as many as 5,000 suppliers. The Big Three automakers now acquire a larger share of parts from fewer suppliers. They are trying to build a good relationship with these suppliers so that they will receive high-quality parts as well as low prices. With just a few suppliers, a company becomes vulnerable to supplier problems. For example, a UAW walkout at a fabrication plant in Lordstown, Ohio, idled GM's Saturn plant in Tennessee. Organizations also depend on banks for capital with which to finance new equipment and buildings.

LABOR MARKET.   The **labor market** represents people in the environment who can be hired to work for the organization. Every organization

---

customers

People and organizations in the environment who acquire goods or services from the organization.

competitors

Other organizations in the same industry or type of business that provide goods or services to the same set of customers.

suppliers

People and organizations who provide the raw materials the organization uses to produce its output.

labor market

The people available for hire by the organization.

needs a supply of trained, qualified personnel. Unions, employee associations, and the availability of certain classes of employees can influence the organization's labor market. Two labor market factors having an impact on organizations right now are (1) the necessity for continuous investment through education and training in human resources to meet the competitive demands of the borderless world and (2) the effects of international trading blocs, automation, and shifting plant location upon labor dislocations, creating unused labor pools in some areas and labor shortages in others.[18]

Northern Telecom, a Canadian company with U.S. headquarters in Nashville, Tennessee, is an example of a complex environment.

 ## NORTHERN TELECOM LIMITED

The external environment for Northern Telecom Ltd. is illustrated in Exhibit 4.2 on page 108. Once considered only an appendage of powerful AT&T, the Canadian company now challenges the U.S. giant by securing top global accounts such as supplying digital switching equipment for the White House. Most problems from the external environment come from competitors and changes in technology. European rivals such as Siemens and Alcatel attempt to block entry of Northern to European Union public phone contracts, arguing that European companies have no supply access to the lucrative North American markets. At the same time, Northern is attempting to crack the Japanese market dominated by Fujitsu, Oki, NEC, and Hitachi. Northern's efforts to resolve these competitive problems include establishing a $1 billion R&D budget. The company is playing catch-up in both cellular and wireless markets and is pioneering fiber-optic technology for transmission equipment. Globally, Northern may slip past EU problems by purchasing Britain's STC PLC, forming an alliance with France's Matra, and launching joint ventures in Spain and Poland.

Northern Telecom's 57,000 employees also have a strong internal environment, developing the "no-excuses" culture necessary to compete in the tough telecommunications industry. Northern's "Vision 2,000 Leadership" campaign uses rallies, banners, and slogans to reinforce its goal of "one team, one vision." Under a strong team concept, the company's switch factory in North Carolina has been heralded as one of the top manufacturing operations in the world, with workers setting their own pace and charting their own production. Northern Telecom is Canada's most successful multinational and under CEO Paul Stern is clearly headed toward a major role on the world stage.[19] ■

● THE ORGANIZATION-ENVIRONMENT RELATIONSHIP

Why do organizations care so much about factors in the external environment? The reason is that the environment creates uncertainty for organization managers, and they must respond by

EXHIBIT 4.2

The External Environment of Northern Telecom (NT)

Economic
- Sales over $102 billion
- 11 straight quarters of record earnings
- Sales to exceed $200 billion by 2000 with 1/2 outside North America
- Focus is low-cost manufacturing
- Recession in North America

Legal/Political
- Canadian ownership
- Breakup of AT&T in 1984
- Tough EU regulations
- Canada & U.S. trade agreement
- New tax laws
- Protectionist legislation abroad

Competitors
- AT&T, U.S.
- Siemens, Germany
- Alcatel, France
- Ericson, Sweden
- NEC, Japan
- Focus on low-cost manufacturing

Customers
- Want low price and high quality
- Businesses, not-for-profit organizations
- New cellular and wireless markets

Technological
- Pioneer digital switch
- $1.2 billion R&D budget
- Catching up in cellular and wireless developments
- Seeking new telecommunications applications
- Developing fiber optics for transmission equipment

Sociocultural
- New telecommunications applications
- Opening of new markets worldwide
- Cellular phone life-styles

Suppliers
- Components from subcontractors
- Banks, bondholders provide capital
- Obtain quality parts from suppliers worldwide

Labor Market
- U.S.: Texas, North Carolina, Tennessee, and California
- Treat employees well
- Not unionized
- Hire college graduates

NT

International
- Headquarters in Toronto & McLean, Virginia
- Bought Britain's STC PLC
- Won business in China, Turkey, Australia, and Russia
- Largest supplier of telecommunications gear to Japanese market

- Joint ventures in Spain and Poland
- Alliance with Alcatel of France for digital mobile phone equipment
- Hire nationals in host countries

SOURCE: W. C. Symonds, J. B. Levine, N. Gross, and P. Coy, "High-Tech Star: Northern Telecom Is Challenging Even AT&T," *Business Week*, July 27, 1992, 54–58. Used by permission of *Business Week*. © 1992.

designing the organization to adapt to the environment or to influence the environment.

ENVIRONMENTAL UNCERTAINTY

Organizations must manage environmental uncertainty to be effective. *Uncertainty* means that managers do not have sufficient information about environmental factors to understand and predict environmental needs and changes.[20] As indicated in Exhibit 4.3, environmental characteristics that influence uncertainty are the number of factors that affect the organization and the extent to which those factors change. A large multinational like Northern Telecom has thousands of factors in the external environment creating uncertainty for managers. When external factors change rapidly, the organization experiences very high uncertainty; examples are the electronics and aerospace industries. Firms must make efforts to adapt to these changes. When an organization deals with only a few external factors and these factors are relatively stable, such as for soft-drink bottlers or food processors, managers experience low uncertainty and can devote less attention to external issues.

Two basic strategies for coping with high environmental uncertainty are to adapt the organization to changes in the environment and to influence the environment to make it more compatible with organizational needs.

ADAPTING TO THE ENVIRONMENT

If the organization faces increased uncertainty with respect to competition, customers, suppliers, or government regulation, managers can use

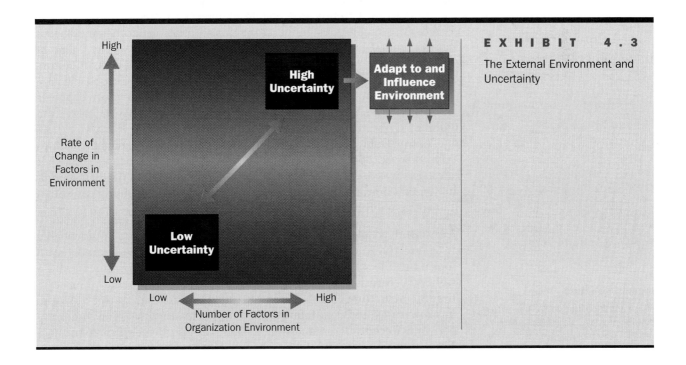

E X H I B I T   4 . 3

The External Environment and Uncertainty

several strategies to adapt to these changes, including boundary-spanning roles, increased planning and forecasting, a flexible structure, and mergers or joint ventures.

boundary-spanning roles

Roles assumed by people and/or departments that link and coordinate the organization with key elements in the external environment.

BOUNDARY-SPANNING ROLES.　　Departments and **boundary-spanning roles** link and coordinate the organization with key elements in the external environment. Boundary spanners serve two purposes for the organization: They detect and process information about changes in the environment, and they represent the organization's interest to the environment.[21] People in departments such as marketing and purchasing span the boundary to work with customers and suppliers, both face to face and through market research. Perhaps the largest growth area in boundary spanning is competitive intelligence, also known as snooping and spying. McDonnell Douglas used competitive intelligence to get the jump on Boeing with its new prop-fan airliner. Coors used competitive intelligence to avoid getting behind in wine coolers. Mary Kay executives cried "foul" after discovering rival Avon had hired Dallas private detectives to dig through its trash.[22] Xerox buys rival copiers for its engineers, who take them apart and design a better product component by component. Eighty percent of the Fortune 1000 companies maintain in-house snoops, also known as *competitor intelligence professionals*. Most of their work is strictly legal, relying on commercial data bases, news clippings, help-wanted advertisements, trade publications, product literature, and personal contacts.[23]

FORECASTING AND PLANNING.　　Forecasting and planning for environmental changes are major activities in many corporations. Planning departments often are created when uncertainty is high.[24] Forecasting is an effort to spot trends that enable managers to predict future events. Forecasting techniques range from quantitative economic models of environmental business activity to newspaper clipping services. One of these services, called Burrelle's Information Services, Inc., monitors 16,000 newspapers and magazines and predicts future trends. Chase investors used information about rapidly multiplying television channels in Western Europe to invest in MCA, Inc., which had a valuable film library.

Control Data, Heinz, United Airlines, and Waste Management, Inc., have devised specific management plans for handling crises. Whether the crisis is a hostile takeover attempt or product tampering, an organization that does not have a plan will make mistakes. Planning can soften the adverse effect of rapid shifts in the environment.

organic structure

An organizational structure that is free flowing, has few rules and regulations, encourages employee teamwork, and decentralizes decision making to employees doing the job.

FLEXIBLE STRUCTURE.　　An organization's structure should enable it to effectively respond to external shifts. Research has found that a loose, flexible structure works best in an uncertain environment and a tight structure is most effective in a certain environment.[25] The term **organic structure** characterizes an organization that is free flowing, has few rules and regulations, encourages teamwork among employees, and decentralizes decision making to employees doing the job. This type of structure works best when the environment changes rapidly. Dow Chemical and Star-Kist Foods set up "SWAT" teams that

Stanley Hardware vice-president of marketing Scott Bannell (seated center) carefully notes responses from a consumer focus group about the Stanley Closet Organizer. Bannell and market researcher Larry Dostal (standing) act as boundary spanners to test reactions to a new product and assess whether it meets customer needs.

can swing into action if an unexpected disaster strikes. These teams include members from multiple departments who can provide the expertise needed for solving an immediate problem, such as a plant explosion. Organic organizations create many teams to handle changes in raw materials, new products, government regulations, or marketing. A **mechanistic structure** is just the opposite, characterized by rigidly defined tasks, many rules and regulations, little teamwork, and centralization of decision making. This is fine for a stable environment.

MERGERS AND JOINT VENTURES. As we discussed, mergers are a major factor in a company's external environment. A merger is also a way to reduce uncertainty. A **merger** occurs when two or more organizations combine to become one. For example, General Host acquired Hickory Farms, a retail chain, to become an outlet for General Host's meat products, thereby reducing uncertainty in the customer sector.

A **joint venture** involves a strategic alliance or program by two or more organizations. This typically occurs when the project is too complex, expensive, or uncertain for one firm to do alone. Oil companies have used joint ventures to explore for oil on the continental shelf or in inaccessible regions of Alaska and Canada. Many small businesses are turning to joint ventures with large firms or with international partners.[26] A larger partner can provide sales staff, distribution channels, financial resources, or a research staff. Small businesses seldom have the expertise to deal internationally, so a company such as Nypro, Inc., a plastic injection-molding manufacturer in Clinton, Massachusetts, joins with overseas experts who are familiar with the local rules. Nypro now does business in four countries.

mechanistic structure

An organizational structure characterized by rigidly defined tasks, many rules and regulations, little teamwork, and centralized decision making.

merger

The combination of two or more organizations into one.

joint venture

A strategic alliance or program by two or more organizations.

INFLUENCING THE ENVIRONMENT

The other major strategy for handling environmental uncertainty is to reach out and change those elements causing problems. Widely used techniques for changing the environment include advertising and public relations, political activity, and trade associations. Exhibit 4.4 summarizes the techniques organizations can use to adapt to and influence the external environment.

ADVERTISING AND PUBLIC RELATIONS.   Advertising has become a highly successful way to manage demand for a company's products. Companies spend large amounts of money to influence consumer tastes. Hospitals have begun to advertise through billboards, newspapers, and radio commercials to promote special services. Increased competitiveness among CPA firms and law firms has caused them to start advertising for clients, a practice unheard of a few years ago. Advertising is an important way to reduce uncertainty about clients.

Public relations is similar to advertising except that its goal is to influence public opinion about the company itself. Most companies care a great deal about their public image. Each year *Fortune* rates over 300 companies to see which are the most and least admired in each of 32 industries. Public relations and a good public image are accomplished through advertising as well as speeches and press reports. In the 1960s and 1970s, Dow Chemical became infamous for supplying napalm and Agent Orange to the military for use in Vietnam. Even when it stopped making these products, the image persisted. Dow Chemical attempts to change this view with an upbeat advertising campaign—"Dow Lets You Do Great Things"—and other external communications emphasizing Dow Chemical research and the humanitarian use of its products. Dow Chemical also has a strong in-house ethics program, a model for the industry.[27]

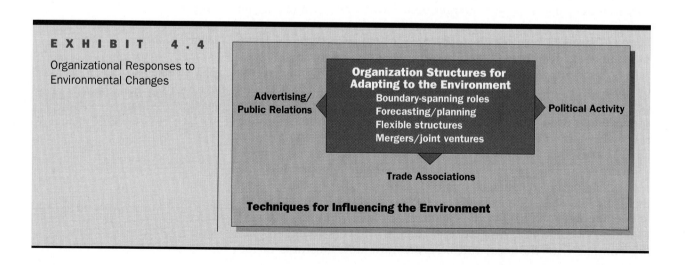

EXHIBIT 4.4

Organizational Responses to Environmental Changes

POLITICAL ACTIVITY.   Political activity represents organizational attempts to influence government legislation and regulation. Corporations pay lobbyists to express their views to federal and state legislators. Foreign companies are becoming increasingly savvy in U.S. political maneuvering. For example, Japanese companies have placed former key U.S. political insiders on their payrolls as Washington lobbyists and advisers. Canada's Northern Telecom benefited from its relationship with a Spanish minister in landing a Spanish joint venture. Under pressure from U.S. companies about government-business collaboration in foreign countries, Washington has warmed to a technology policy that provides government policy support to critical technologies and industry study groups.[28]

political activity

Organizational attempts, such as lobbying, to influence government legislation and regulation.

TRADE ASSOCIATIONS.   Most organizations join with others having similar interests; the result is a **trade association.** In this way, organizations work together to influence the environment, including federal legislation and regulation. Most manufacturing companies are part of the National Association of Manufacturers. The National Rifle Association has thousands of individual and corporate members whose interests are served by the freedom to use guns. One of the most influential trade associations in past years was the U.S. League of Savings Institutions, which virtually controlled government regulations pertaining to the savings and loan industry. Federal Home Loan Bank Board officials admit they took many actions and changed regulations to suit the League. That kind of influence over the years may have contributed to problems during the early 1990s within the savings and loan industry, which were partially caused by lack of close and effective regulation.[29]

trade association

An association made up of organizations with similar interests for the purpose of influencing the environment.

After the 1992 riots in Los Angeles, this group of students from a local high school formed their own company and planted a garden. Now they produce their own salad dressing under the name "Food from the Hood." The proceeds go toward scholarships and salaries for the innovative youths.

THE INTERNAL ENVIRONMENT: CORPORATE CULTURE

The internal environment within which managers work includes corporate culture, production technology, organization structure, and physical facilities. Of these, corporate culture has surfaced as extremely important to competitive advantage. The internal culture must fit the needs of the external environment and company strategy. When this fit occurs, highly committed employees create a high-performance organization that is tough to beat.[30]

Culture can be defined as the set of key values, beliefs, understandings, and norms shared by members of an organization.[31] Culture represents the unwritten, informal norms that bind organization members together. Culture can be analyzed at two organizational levels, as illustrated in Exhibit 4.5.[32] At the surface level are visible artifacts, which include manners of dress, stories, physical symbols, organizational ceremonies, and office layout. The surface level represents the cultural patterns observable within an organization. At a deeper level are the values and norms that govern behavior. Values cannot be observed directly, but they can be interpreted from the stories, language, and symbols that represent them. These values are held by organization members who jointly understand their importance. The giant retailer Wal-Mart is an example of how the elements of culture give competitive advantage.

 WAL·MART

One organization with a strong culture is Wal-Mart, where folksy values continue to reflect its small-town beginnings and the personality and principles of its late founder, Sam Walton. Walton and other senior managers

culture

The set of key values, beliefs, understandings, and norms that members of an organization share.

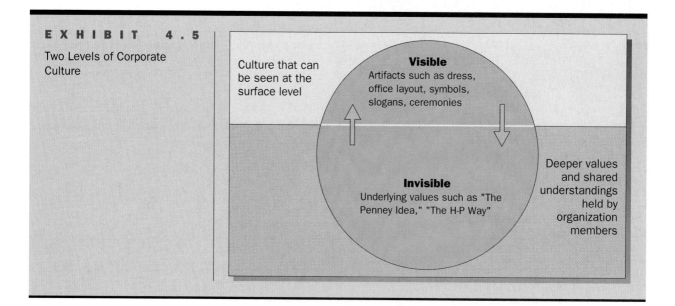

EXHIBIT 4.5

Two Levels of Corporate Culture

Culture that can be seen at the surface level

Visible
Artifacts such as dress, office layout, symbols, slogans, ceremonies

Invisible
Underlying values such as "The Penney Idea," "The H-P Way"

Deeper values and shared understandings held by organization members

used fun-loving motivational tactics that included hog calls, songs, hulas, and the Wal-Mart cheer, "W-A-L-M-A-R-T." These antics, merged with Walton's "break-the-rules" philosophy, formed the cultural core of this unbelievable company. The culture stresses the personal touch, and associates are urged to provide community involvement and individual attention. Department buyers are urged to "get their noses in it" by working with customers on the sales floor once a week. CEO David Glass continues the policy of daily experimentation and change. Individual empowerment, continuous improvement, and profit sharing contribute to that small-town culture of "belonging" that is so easily picked up by Wal-Mart's loyal customers.[33] ■

Some companies put underlying values in writing so they can be passed on to new generations of employees. James Cash Penney believed in the golden rule: Treat employees and customers as you would like to be treated. He wrote down the underlying values in seven guiding principles called "The Penney Idea" that guide employee behavior. One J. C. Penney store manager was reprimanded for making too much profit at customers' expense.[34] Hewlett-Packard created a list of cultural concepts called "The H-P Way." At 3M Company, two fundamental values are the 25 percent rule, which requires that a quarter of sales come from products introduced within the past five years, and the 15 percent rule, which allows any employee to spend up to 15 percent of the workweek on anything he or she prefers, so long as it is product related.[35]

The fundamental underlying values that characterize cultures at J. C. Penney, Wal-Mart, and Hewlett-Packard can be understood through the visible manifestations of symbols, stories, heroes, slogans, and ceremonies. Any company's culture can be interpreted by observing these factors.

SYMBOLS

A **symbol** is an object, act, or event that conveys meaning to others. Symbols associated with corporate culture convey the organization's important values. For example, John Thomas, CEO of a mechanical contractor in Andover, Massachusetts, wanted to imprint the value of allowing mistakes and risk taking. He pulled a $450 mistake out of the Dumpster, mounted it on a plaque, and named it the "No-Nuts Award," for the missing parts. The award is presented annually and symbolizes the freedom to make mistakes but not to make the same mistake twice.[36] Symbolizing his commitment to a true open-door policy, Bill Arnold, president of Nashville's Centennial Medical Center, ripped his office door from its hinges and suspended it from the lobby ceiling for all employees to see.[37] Sequint Computer Systems, Inc., developed the symbol of red buttons worn by people who performed tasks critical to the production of hardware that was behind schedule yet essential to company survival. The red buttons symbolized the gravity of the situation, and all Sequint employees were expected to pitch in and help anybody wearing one.[38]

symbol

An object, act, or event that conveys meaning to others.

Standing in the snow, these First Security Corporation employees are living symbols of company values and employee commitment. The Salt Lake City, Utah-based financial services company is focused on superior customer service and has invested thousands of hours in the training of employees. The result: Giving 110 percent is a way of life, and surveys of 60,000 customers rated First Security performance an astonishing 6.2 overall (on a 7-point scale) in 30 categories.

story

A narrative based on true events that is repeated frequently and shared by organizational employees.

hero

A figure who exemplifies the deeds, character, and attributes of a corporate culture.

STORIES

A **story** is a narrative based on true events that is repeated frequently and shared among organizational employees. Stories are told to new employees to keep the organization's primary values alive. At Nordstrom, Inc., management does not deny the story about a customer who got his money back on a tire. Nordstrom does not sell tires. The story reinforces the store's no-questions-asked return policy. A story at Dayton Hudson about Ken Macke, CEO, tells how he gave a woman a new washing machine because she complained about wanting a broken belt replaced. The story still serves to improve complaint handling at the lowest company levels. A popular story at Hewlett-Packard communicates the values of the founders, David Packard and Bill Hewlett. Bill Hewlett is said to have gone to a plant one Saturday and found a lab stockroom door locked. He cut the padlock and left a note saying, "Don't ever lock this door again. Thanks, Bill." Hewlett wanted engineers to have free access to components—even take them home—to stimulate the creativity that was part of "The H-P Way." Stories in these companies are widely told; every employee knows them and the values they represent.[39]

HEROES

A **hero** is a figure who exemplifies the deeds, character, and attributes of a strong culture. Heroes are role models for employees to follow. Sometimes heroes are real, such as Lee Iacocca, and sometimes they are symbolic, such as the mythical sales representative at Robinson Jewelers who delivered a wedding ring directly to the church because the ring had been ordered late. The deeds of heroes are out of the ordinary but not so far out as to be unattainable by other employees. Heroes show how to do the right thing in the organization. Companies with strong cultures take advantage of achievements to define heroes who uphold key values.

At Minnesota Mining and Manufacturing (3M), top managers keep alive the heroes who developed projects that were killed by top management. One hero was a vice-president who was fired earlier in his career for persisting with a new product even after his boss had told him, "That's a stupid idea. Stop!" After the worker was fired, he would not leave. He stayed in an unused office, working without a salary on the new product idea. Eventually he was rehired, the idea succeeded, and he was promoted to vice-president. The lesson of this hero as a major element in 3M's culture is persist at what you believe in.[40]

SLOGANS

A **slogan** is a phrase or sentence that succinctly expresses a key corporate value. Many companies use a slogan or saying to convey special meaning to employees. H. Ross Perot of Electronic Data Systems established the philosophy of hiring the best people he could find and noted how difficult it was to find them. His motto was "Eagles don't flock. You gather them one at a time." A variation used at PepsiCo to describe the value of turning bright young people into strong managers is "We take eagles and teach them to fly in formation." The slogan chiseled into a 6,000-pound granite slab next to the front door of Stew Leonard's dairy store is "Rule 1—The customer is always right! Rule 2—If the customer is ever wrong, reread Rule 1."[41]

slogan

A phrase or sentence that succinctly expresses a key corporate value.

CEREMONIES

A **ceremony** is a planned activity that makes up a special event and is conducted for the benefit of an audience. Managers hold ceremonies to provide dramatic examples of company values. Ceremonies are special occasions that reinforce valued accomplishments, create a bond among people by allowing them to share an important event, and anoint and celebrate heroes.[42]

The value of a ceremony can be illustrated by the presentation of a major award. For example, Quaker State Minit-Lube, Inc., uses an annual contest and winner's ceremony to signal the importance of speed and quality service for customers. Fourteen jobs associated with an oil change must be performed perfectly in 8 minutes. The award ceremony includes contestants arriving in a white stretch limo, walking on a red carpet through a cheering crowd, and being entertained by a jazz band. This ceremony is consistent with Quaker State's Big Q symbol, which stands for quality. An award can also be bestowed secretly by mailing it to the employee's home or, if a check, by depositing it in a bank. But such procedures would not make the bestowal of rewards a significant organizational event and would be less meaningful to the employee.

ceremony

A planned activity that makes up a special event and is conducted for the benefit of an audience.

In summary, organizational culture represents the values and understandings that employees share, and these values are signified by symbols, stories, heroes, slogans, and ceremonies. Managers help define important symbols, stories, and heroes to shape the culture.

⬤ ENVIRONMENT AND CULTURE

A big influence on internal corporate culture is the external environment. Corporate culture should embody what it takes to succeed in the environment. If the external environment requires extraordinary customer service, the culture should encourage good service; if it calls for careful technical decision making, cultural values should reinforce managerial decision making.

ADAPTIVE CULTURES

Research at Harvard on 207 U.S. firms illustrated the critical relationship between corporate culture and the external environment. The study found that a strong corporate culture alone did not ensure business success unless the culture encouraged healthy adaptation to the external environment. As illustrated in Exhibit 4.6, adaptive corporate cultures have different values and behavior from unadaptive corporate cultures. In adaptive cultures, managers were concerned about customers and those internal people and processes that brought about useful change. In the unadaptive corporate cultures, managers were concerned about themselves, and their values tended to discourage risk taking and

EXHIBIT 4.6 Environmentally Adaptive versus Unadaptive Corporate Cultures		Adaptive Corporate Cultures	Unadaptive Corporate Cultures
	Core Values	Managers care deeply about customers, stockholders, and employees. They also strongly value people and processes that can create useful change (e.g., leadership initiatives up and down the management hierarchy).	Managers care mainly about themselves, their immediate work group, or some product (or technology) associated with that work group. They value the orderly and risk-reducing management process much more highly than leadership initiatives.
SOURCE: John P. Kotter and James L. Heskett, *Corporate Culture and Performance* (New York: The Free Press, 1992) 51.	**Common Behavior**	Managers pay close attention to all their constituencies, especially customers, and initiate change when needed to serve their legitimate interests, even if it that entails taking some risks.	Managers tend to behave somewhat insularly, politically, and bureaucratically. As a result, they do not change their strategies quickly to adjust to or take advantage of changes in their business environments.

change. Thus a strong culture alone is not enough, because an unhealthy culture may encourage the organization to march resolutely in the wrong direction. Healthy cultures help companies adapt to the environment.[43]

TYPES OF CULTURES

One way to think about corporate cultures was suggested by Jeffrey Sonnenfeld and included four types of culture—baseball team, club, academy, and fortress. Each culture has somewhat different potential for supporting a healthy, successful company and has a different impact on the satisfaction and careers of employees.[44]

The *baseball team culture* emerges in an environmental situation with high-risk decision making and fast feedback from the environment. Decision makers quickly learn whether their choice was right or wrong. Talent, innovation, and performance are valued and rewarded. Top performers see themselves as "free agents," and companies scramble for their services. Performers with "low batting averages" are quickly dropped from the line-up. Baseball team cultures are found in fast-paced, high-risk companies involved in areas such as movie production, advertising, and software development where futures are bet on a new product or project.

The *club culture* is characterized by loyalty, commitment, and fitting into the group. This stable, secure environment values age and experience and rewards seniority. As in the case of career military personnel, individuals start young and stay. Club cultures promote from within, and members are expected to progress slowly, proving competence at each level. Individuals tend to be generalists and may have vast experience in a number of organizational functions. Top executives in commercial banks, for example, frequently began as tellers. While many club qualities contribute to flexibility within the organization, they can also contribute to the perception of a closed company, reluctant to change.

The *academy culture* also hires young recruits interested in a long-term association and a slow, steady climb up the organization. Unlike the club culture, however, employees rarely cross from one division to another. Each person enters a specific "track" and gains a high level of expertise in that area. Job and technical mastery are the bases for reward and advancement. Many long-established organizations such as universities, Coca-Cola, Ford, and GM maintain strong academy cultures. While specialization provides job security, this culture may limit broad individual development and interdepartmental collaboration, although it works very well in a stable environment.

The *fortress culture* may emerge in an environmental survival situation. Textile firms and savings and loan organizations are examples of former dominant industries that are now retrenching for survival. The fortress culture offers little job security or opportunity for professional growth while companies restructure and downsize to fit the new environment. This culture is perilous for employees but also offers tremendous turnaround opportunities for individual managers with confidence

LEADING edge   SPARTAN MOTORS

When George W. Sztykiel was 46, he had one son in law school, another in college, and his wife was ill. Then his company, Diamond Reo Trucks Inc., folded. His reaction was to take a second mortgage and, along with three others, build his first truck chassis; Spartan Motors was born. "We had the luxury of having our house burn down at Diamond Reo," he says. "We had the power of poverty."

This novel principle is the guiding force at Spartan, which builds chassis for fire trucks, motor homes, and other types of heavy-duty vehicles. Sztykiel thinks being driven by want forces hard work, which in turn builds value and creates wealth. The complacent die, and so does the company if the hunger ever fades.

Austerity and function also rank high on Sztykiel's priority list. The company's Charlotte, Michigan, headquarters is a threadbare industrial building. The furniture inside is used; "How much production do I get out of a $1,000 desk?" says Sztykiel. In addition, he does not have a secretary because he does not want to worry about keeping her busy. There are no budgets; three department heads have final say on budgetary matters and expenditures are justified by desperate need and how they will improve profitability. Not surprisingly, a 10-member cost-reduction team saved Spartan $500,000 on raw materials in 1991.

Perhaps better than anything else, Spartan's workforce sums up the essence of the company. Only 8 of 380 employees have college or advanced degrees. Most of the company "engineers" began on the assembly line before advancing to the drafting table. Sztykiel is strictly interested in attitude, brains, and people who are not afraid to work. As he says, "Your pedigree means nothing to us."

He likes to hire people right out of high school, believing that the young are better equipped mentally and spiritually to adjust to Spartan's way of doing things. Sztykiel thinks giant manufacturers have lost sight of what they are doing. "Building trucks is not science," he says, "it is art. The old engineers pass on the feeling to the new guys. We produce 10 times faster and cheaper than bigger companies, where they have lost the feeling, so all they can do is apply science."

Sztykiel meets with employees once each quarter to review the company's performance. Mainly for the benefit of new hires, he relates that as the company goes, so go their bonuses. About 10 percent of pre-tax profits are passed out every 90 days. Although Spartan workers earn only about 80 percent of what union counterparts at GM make, Sztykiel tells his workers that Spartan is a good place to be because it is run on the same principles as a family. Hard work is rewarded with profit-sharing, job security, and fair and equal treatment. In an industry fraught with plant closings and layoffs, Spartan has never had a layoff and Sztykiel vows it never will. Disdaining the title of boss, he instead calls himself the number-one servant of the corporation. He makes four times as much as the lowest-paid worker, $78,000. Not surprisingly, Sztykiel thinks his counterparts are outrageously overcompensated.

The past five years have been tough on the heavy-truck industry; many have called it a quasi-depression. During this period, Spartan's revenues have gone up sixfold and earnings increased more than seven times to $5 million. The stock soared 800 percent in 1991 alone.

Spartan's growth has been based on old-fashioned values, but as we will see in Chapter 9, the company has not shied away from innovation and change. GM executives may need to consider trading in some of those high-dollar, non-producing desks, and learn a little about the power of poverty. ■

SOURCE: Edward O. Welles, "The Shape of Things to Come," *INC.*, February 1992, 66–74; and Richard S. Teitelbaum, "Spartan Motors," *Fortune*, December 28, 1992, 55.

and love of challenge. Those who succeed, such as Lee Iaccoca (Chrysler) or William Crouse (president of Ortho Diagnostic Systems, Inc.) earn recognition nationally or within their industry.[45] The Leading Edge box shows how Spartan Motors has created a unique corporate culture.

● CHANGING AND MERGING CORPORATE CULTURES

A corporation's culture may not always be in alignment with its needs and environment. Cultural values may reflect what worked in the past. The difference between desired cultural norms and values and actual norms and values is called the **culture gap**.[46]

Culture gaps can be immense, especially in mergers and acquisitions.[47] Despite the popularity of mergers and acquisitions as a corporate strategy, many fail. Almost one-half of acquired companies are sold within five years, and some experts claim that 90 percent of mergers never live up to expectations.[48] One reason for failure is that although managers are able to integrate the acquired firm's financial systems and production technologies, they typically are unable to integrate the unwritten norms and values that have an even greater impact on a company's success.[49] These problems increase in scope and frequency with global companies and cross-cultural mergers and acquisitions. A merger or acquisition exacts an enormous toll in employee anxiety, fear, and tension. After all, most mergers produce some redefinition of pay, benefits, tasks, and other forms of employee security. Approximately one-third of mergers and acquisitions result in layoffs.[50] These factors create a breakdown in communication, reduced commitment, attempts at self-preservation, and resistance to change. Corporate culture becomes a negative force in which norms and values impede success.

What can managers do to change norms and values toward what is needed for the external environment or for smooth cultural integration during a merger? The answer is symbolic management.

SYMBOLIC MANAGEMENT

To change corporate culture, managers can use cultural artifacts of symbols, stories, slogans, and ceremonies. Managers literally must overcommunicate to ensure that employees understand the new cultural values, and they must signal these values in actions as well as words. A **symbolic manager** defines and uses signals and symbols to influence corporate culture. Symbolic managers influence culture in the following manner:

1 *The symbolic manager articulates a vision for the organizational change that generates excitement and that employees can believe in.* This means the manager defines and communicates central values that employees believe in and will rally around.

2 *The symbolic manager heeds the day-to-day activities that reinforce the vision.* The symbolic manager makes sure that symbols, ceremonies, and slogans match the new values. Even more important, actions speak louder than words. Symbolic managers "walk their talk."[51]

The reason symbolic management works is that executives are watched by employees. Employees attempt to read signals from what executives do, not just from what they say. For example, one senior manager told a story of how employees always knew in advance when

■
culture gap

The difference between an organization's desired cultural norms and values and actual norms and values.

■
symbolic manager

A manager who defines and uses signals and symbols to influence corporate culture.

someone was to be laid off in his company. He finally picked up the pattern. Employees noticed that he always dressed in his favorite pink shirt and matching tie when layoffs were to be announced.

When Les Tiffany, director of production at Physio-Control, Inc., saw falling production and rising employee tension, he developed a vision to increase production levels and to celebrate the achievement of each $500,000 level. Upon attainment of each level, a manager, beginning with Tiffany himself, donned a clown costume and pedaled a tricycle through the plant, towing a siren-screaming red wagon with a banner proclaiming the accomplishment. Employees loved it. A "parade route" developed over the three-month period of the celebrations, and although production was interrupted for several minutes each day, motivation ran high to reach the next level and witness the "clowning" of yet another manager.[52]

Jack Welch transformed General Electric—a huge corporation—by defining a new type of senior manager. His demand was for symbolic managers, which he described as follows: "Somebody who can develop a vision of what he or she wants their . . . activity to do and be. Somebody who is able to articulate what the business is, and gain through a sharing of the discussion—listening and talking—an acceptance of the vision. And someone who then can relentlessly drive implementation of that vision to a successful conclusion."[53]

Symbolic managers search for opportunities. They make public statements, including both oral and written communications, to the organization as a whole. After articulating a vision, managers change corporate culture through hundreds of small deeds, actions, statements, and ceremonies. A strong leader who articulated a clear vision accounted for the extraordinary success of Wal-Mart, Disney, McDonald's, and Levi Strauss. Harold Geneen, former CEO of ITT, captured his corporate value in a few words, "Search for the unshakeable facts."

Scott Kohno, managing director of Chaix & Johnson, shocked and revitalized his 30 employees by hauling his desk from a comfortable executive office with 18-foot ceilings to the middle of the work floor. Kohno compared the move to the "difference between being on the basketball floor instead of the bleachers." The increased contact with staff was soon matched by a supercharged employee energy level.[54]

Another story involving a desk illustrates Mars executives' concern for employees and began when Mr. Mars made a midsummer visit to a chocolate factory:

> He went up to the third floor, where the biggest chocolate machines were placed. It was hotter than the hinges of hell. He asked the factory manager, "How come you don't have air conditioning up here?" The factory manager replied that it wasn't in his budget, and he darn well had to make the budget. While Mr. Mars allowed that was a fact, he nonetheless went over to the nearby phone and dialed the maintenance people downstairs and asked them to come up immediately. He said, "While we (he and the factory manager) stand here, would you please go downstairs and get all (the factory manager's) furniture and other things from his office and bring them up here? Sit them down next to the big chocolate machine up here, if you don't mind." Mr. Mars told him that once the factory had been air conditioned, he could move back to his office any time he wanted.[55]

Stories such as these can be found in most companies and used to enhance the desired culture. The value of stories depends not on whether they are precisely true but whether they are repeated frequently and convey the correct values.

To summarize, symbolic managers can bring about cultural change through the use of public statements, ceremonies, stories, heroes, symbols, and slogans. To change culture, executives must learn ceremonial skills and how to use speech, symbols, and stories to influence company values. Executives do not drive trucks or run machines. To change culture, they must act like evangelists rather than accountants.[56] Symbolic activities provide information about what counts in the company.

SUMMARY AND MANAGEMENT SOLUTION

This chapter discussed several important ideas about internal and external organizational environments. Events in the external environment are considered important influences on organizational behavior and performance. The external environment consists of two layers: the task environment and the general environment. The task environment includes customers, competitors, suppliers, and labor market. The general environment includes technological, sociocultural, economic, legal-political, and international dimensions. Management techniques for helping the organization adapt to the environment include boundary-spanning roles, forecasting and planning, a flexible structure, and mergers and joint ventures. Techniques managers can use to influence the external environment include advertising and public relations, political activities, and trade associations.

Jack in the Box had developed a plan in the mid-1980s to handle just the sort of diasaster that occurred in January 1993. A 12-person crisis team quickly ordered the disposal of 20,000 pounds of hamburger meat that originated from suspect meat-processing plants. It also changed meat suppliers and instructed employees to cook burgers at higher temperatures. A toll-free hotline was established to answer questions and deal with customer complaints.

But even with the crystal clarity of hindsight, the company could and should have done more, both proactively and reactively. Using Johnson & Johnson and the Tylenol poisoning scare of the early 1980s as a model, Jack in the Box might have closed every restaurant for complete inspections. Whether fully warranted or not, such a dramatic gesture might have drastically altered perceptions. The company limited newspaper apologies to the Washington area, ignoring the huge markets to the south in California. In addition, offers to cover victims' medical costs also were late in coming.

Worse still, the crisis team seemed unable to cope with the fast-moving flow of events. San Diego newspapers tied the death of one girl to Jack in the Box despite uncertainty that she had even eaten there. NBC displayed the company logo while reporting the death of another child who had not eaten at a Jack in the Box. Instead of controlling and countering false or misleading stories, the crisis team was steamrolled by them.[57]

Corporate culture, a major element of the internal environment, includes the key values, beliefs, understandings, and norms that organization members share. Organizational activities that illustrate corporate culture include symbols, stories, heroes, slogans, and ceremonies. For the organization to be effective, corporate culture should be aligned with the needs of the external environment.

Four types of culture are baseball team, club, academy, and fortress, each of which suits a specific environment. Jack in the Box currently has something of a fortress mentality as it attempts to retrench and turn around from this controversy. Strong cultures are effective when they enable the organization to adapt to changes in the external environment.

Symbolic managers can change corporate culture by (1) communicating a vision to employees and (2) reinforcing the vision with day-to-day public statements, ceremonies, slogans, symbols, and stories.

DISCUSSION QUESTIONS

1. Some scientists predict major changes in the earth's climate, including a temperature rise of 8°F over the next 60 years. Should any companies be paying attention to this long-range environmental trend? Explain.
2. Would the task environment for a bank contain the same elements as that for a government welfare agency? Discuss.
3. What forces influence organizational uncertainty? Would such forces typically originate in the task environment or the general environment?
4. *In Search of Excellence,* described in Chapter 2, argued that customers were the most important element in the external environment. Are there company situations for which this may not be true?
5. Caterpillar Corporation experienced a period of decline in the 1980s (fueled by low oil prices, high interest rates, a worldwide recession, a soaring U.S. dollar, and Japanese competition) before rebounding in the 1990s. Discuss the type of response Caterpillar's management might have taken to spur the rebound.
6. Define corporate culture and explain its importance for managers.
7. Why are symbols important to a corporate culture? Do stories, heroes, slogans, and ceremonies also have symbolic value? Discuss.
8. Describe the cultural values of a company for which you have worked. Did those values fit the needs of the external environment? Of employees?
9. What type of environmental situation is associated with a baseball team culture? How does this culture differ from the academy culture?
10. Do you think a corporate culture with strong values is better for organizational effectiveness than a culture with weak values? Are there times when a strong culture might reduce effectiveness?

MANAGEMENT IN PRACTICE: ETHICAL DILEMMA

● THE $10,000 LUNCH

Rich has decision responsibility for a $5 million, five-year budget to install a communications network in his company's headquarters building. Suppliers are competitively vying to win contracts for providing the necessary hardware and systems equipment.

Rich is having lunch with his favorite salesperson, Scott. Near the end of lunch, Scott says, "Rich, listen. The end of the quarter is next week, and I am about $100,000 in sales short to get a big $10,000 bonus. If you could sign the purchase agreement on that computer network now instead of in three months, I've got tickets to the Super Bowl. How about it?"

Rich responded, "I've got to think about this. I'll call you tomorrow." Rich wanted desperately to attend the Super Bowl because his favorite team was playing, and his wife wanted to visit family in Pasadena. Back at the office, Rich

thought about the company tradition of purchasing agents and others accepting small favors from suppliers. He also knew that Scott put a lot of effort into bidding for the contract, and his company's bid looked better than any other. Rich also remembered that a newly issued company policy states, "Program managers are prohibited from accepting gifts of any size or form from vendors."

● WHAT DO YOU DO?

1. Sign the contract and accept the tickets. After all, Scott deserved it and would have won the bidding anyway.
2. Ask the support of coworkers. After all, company tradition and cultural values are more important for defining behavior than are written policies.
3. Do not sign the contract or accept the tickets. Breaking company policy is inappropriate.

CASE FOR ANALYSIS

JIM GRALEY'S AUTOBODY SHOP

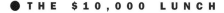

When cousins Jim and Don Graley opened their Chesapeake, Ohio, body shop in the early 1970s, they were a cut above their competition. In an industry with more than its share of sharp practicers, they were honest and hard-working, traits which were instilled in them by an uncle. They advertised frequently and even offered customers a free shuttle service. They soon had a sterling reputation and more work than they could handle. By 1985, however, growth had come to a halt. Competitive interlopers were springing up like weeds. "We were all offering the same thing," Jim said. "Graley's had lost its edge."

But it was not simply the competition. The playing field was changing. While no one was watching, unibody car construction and higher quality finishes completely altered the business. New equipment, at a cost of about $120,000, became a requisite. Despite a lot of advice to the contrary, Jim had abandoned an on-track corporate career for the grit and grime of running his own body shop. He decided he was not going to quit, and he was not going to fail. He would find out the direction the industry was headed, and move toward it.

He did a lot of reading before an obscure statistic provided a blueprint for company turnaround. It seemed 70 percent of new-car-buying decisions were made by women. Without a huge leap of logic, Graley reasoned that many

women would eventually need repairs on their cars. He proceeded from there. Whether he went overboard is still open to speculation.

Graley's Autobody transformed from grimy to gleaming, "a completely different business." Graley hired women to welcome female customers and guide them through the repair process. He redirected advertising to women as well. A computer system was the first step toward his dream of a paperless body shop. A closed-circuit TV was installed in the garage, ostensibly so Graley could give customers a quick status report on their car repairs in progress without leaving his desk. He also laid out some serious money for new equipment: $250,000 for factory-finish paint job ovens, and another $70,000 for frame straighteners and wheel-alignment machines.

As to exactly where the business hit difficulties is not clear; however, it is safe to say that profit-sharing was not favored by the bodymen. In the past, they had always been paid a flat rate based on the job. This system essentially allowed them to control their own fate because the faster they completed their work, the more they earned. Graley's proposal that each take a 34 percent pay cut to share profits fell flat, partly because both Jim and Don complained so often about the company's poor earnings. Some grumbled that the books might get changed before reaching the shop floor.

Although most employees went along with the plan, things got progressively worse from there.

Graley placed another woman (who according to workers didn't know a "taillight from a watermelon") in charge of quality control. Team meetings turned into one-sided lectures by Jim, who avoided the shop for the sanctity of his office. The new equipment often made work harder. Employees complained that Jim's mandated need for speed led to corners being cut and unsafe cars being turned out. At least one bodyman sued the Graleys and won. Overworked men started skipping lunch to meet quotas; Jim started checking his office monitor for loafers. The final straw came when workers convinced themselves that Jim was altering repair time estimates and pocketing the difference.

Like most stories, this situation has at least two sides and maybe more. Jim Graley still has a vision of raising a gritty-by-nature business and running it in a state-of-the-art fashion. His workers, most of whom have eight or more years with the company, are understandably a little set in their ways and fearful of the unknown. Jim Graley says he can understand their resistance. However, he's still not ready to quit, or fail. "If I survive this mess," he says, "this will be a different company."

● **QUESTIONS**

1. Which aspects of the external environment had the greatest impact on Graley's?
2. Do you think Graley went too far in his attempts to adapt to the external environment? Why or why not?
3. What changes could Graley make in the corporate culture that might appease disgruntled workers? If you were Jim Graley, what else would you do?

SOURCE: Elizabeth Conlin, "Collision Course," *INC.*, December 1992, 132–142.

REFERENCES

1. Ronald Grover, Dori Jones Yang, Laura Holson, "Boxed in at Jack in the Box," *Business Week,* February 15, 1993, 40; and Seattle Staff Reports, "Food Poisoning: Killer Hamburgers," *The Economist,* February 13, 1993, 27–28.

2. Scott McMurray, "Wounded Giant: Union Carbide Offers Some Sober Lessons in Crisis Management," *The Wall Street Journal,* January 28, 1991, A1, A9.

3. Richard L. Daft, *Organization, Theory and Design,* 4th ed. (St. Paul, Minn.: West, 1992).

4. L. J. Bourgeois, "Strategy and Environment: A Conceptual Integration," *Academy of Management Review* 5 (1980), 25–39.

5. Based on Marc Beauchamp, "Toilets with Chips," *Forbes,* January 22, 1990, 100–104.

6. Richard I. Kirkland, Jr., "Entering a New Age of Boundless Competition," *Fortune,* March 14, 1988, 40–48; and Kenichin Ohmae, "Managing in a Borderless World," *Harvard Business Review* (May–June 1989), 152–161.

7. Nancy J. Perry, "The Arms Makers' Next Battle," *Fortune,* August 27, 1990, 84–88.

8. Eric Shine, Amy Borrus, John Carey, and Geoffery Smith, "The Defense Whizzies Making It in Civvies," *Business Week,* September 7, 1992, 88–90.

9. Naomi Frundlich, Neil Gross, John Carey, and Robert D. Hof, "The New Alchemy: How Science Is Molding Molecules into Miracle Materials," *Business Week,* July 29, 1991, 48–52.

10. Otis Port, "Materials That Think for Themselves," *Business Week,* December 5, 1988, 166–167.

11. William B. Johnston, "Global Work Force 2000: The New World Labor Market," *Harvard Business Review* (March–April 1991), 115–127.

12. Maria Malloryn and Stephanie Anderson Forest, "Waking Up to a Major Market," *Business Week,* March 23, 1992, 70–73; William Dunn, "Survival by

Numbers," *Nation's Business*, August 1991, 14–21; Joseph Spiers, "The Baby Boomlet Is for Real," *Fortune*, February 10, 1992, 101–104; and Michael Mandel, Christopher Farrell, Dori Jones Yang, Gloria Lau, Christina Del Valle, and S. Lynne Walker, "The Immigrants: How They're Helping to Revitalize the U.S. Economy," *Business Week*, July 13, 1992, 114–122.

13. David Lieverman, "Keeping Up with the Murdochs," *Business Week*, March 20, 1989, 32–34; and Don Lee Bohl, ed., *Tying the Corporate Knot* (New York: American Management Association, 1989).

14. Victoria Reid, "Businesses Upset with OSHA Rules," *The Tennessean*, July 7, 1992, 4E.

15. Sara Collins, "Companies," *U.S. News & World Report*, Oct. 4, 1993, 86.

16. Walecia Konrad and Gail DeGeorge, "U.S. Companies Go for the Gray," *Business Week*, April 3, 1989, 64–67.

17. Peter H. Lewis, "Apple–IBM Venture, with New Leaders, Searchers for a Soul," *The New York Times*, March 8, 1992, F8; and Mark Ivey and Geoff Lewis, "Compaq vs. IBM: Peace Comes to Shove," *Business Week*, May 1, 1989, 132.

18. Michael R. Czinkota and Ilkka A. Ronkines, "Global Marketing 2000: A Marketing Survival Guide," *Marketing Management* (Winter 1992), 37–42.

19. William C. Symonds, Jonathan B. Levine, Neil Gross, and Peter Coy, "High-Tech Star: Northern Telecom Is Challenging Even AT&T," *Business Week*, July 27, 1992, 54–58.

20. Robert B. Duncan, "Characteristics of Organizational Environment and Perceived Environmental Uncertainty," *Administrative Science Quarterly* 17 (1972), 313–327; and Daft, *Organization Theory and Design*.

21. David B. Jemison, "The Importance of Boundary Spanning Roles in Strategic Decision-Making," *Journal of Management Studies* 21 (1984), 131–152; and Marc J. Dollinger, "Environmental Boundary Spanning and Information Processing Effects on Organizational Performance," *Academy of Management Journal* 27 (1984), 351–368.

22. Wendy Zellner and Bruce Hager, "Dumpster Raids? That's Not Very Ladylike, Avon," *Business Week*, April 1, 1991, 32.

23. Brian Dumaine, "Corporate Spies Snoop to Conquer," *Fortune*, November 7, 1988, 68–76; Dodui Tsiantar and John Schwartz, "George Smiley Joins the Firm," *Newsweek*, May 2, 1988, 46–47; and James E. Svatko, "Analyzing the Competition," *Small Business Reports*, January 1989, 21–28.

24. R. T. Lenz and Jack L. Engledow, "Environmental Analysis Units and Strategic Decision-Making: A Field Study of Selected 'Leading Edge' Corporations," *Strategic Management Journal* 7 (1986), 69–89; and Mansour Javidan, "The Impact of Environmental Uncertainty on Long-Range Planning Practices of the U.S. Savings and Loan Industry," *Strategic Management Journal* 5 (1984), 381–392.

25. Tom Burns and G. M. Stalker, *The Management of Innovation* (London: Tavistock, 1961).

26. James E. Svatko, "Joint Ventures," *Small Business Reports*, December 1988, 65–70; and Joshua Hyatt, "The Partnership Route," *INC.*, December 1988, 145–148.

27. John A. Byrne, "The Best-Laid Ethics Program . . . ," *Business Week*, March 9, 1992, 67–69; and "Dow Chemical: From Napalm to Nice Guy," *Fortune*, May 12, 1986, 75–78.

28. Edmund Faltermayer, "The Thaw in Washington," *Fortune* (The New American Century), 1991, 46–51; David B. Yoffie, "How an Industry Builds Political Advantage," *Harvard Business Review* (May–June 1988), 82–89; and Douglas Harbrecht, "How to Win Friends and Influence Lawmakers," *Business Week,* November 7, 1988, 36.

29. Monica Langley, "Thrifts' Trade Group and Their Regulators Get Along Just Fine," *The Wall Street Journal,* July 16, 1986, 1, 14.

30. Yoash Wiener, "Forms of Value Systems: A Focus on Organizational Effectiveness and Culture Change and Maintenance," *Academy of Management Review* 13 (1988), 534–545; V. Lynne Meek, "Organizational Culture: Origins and Weaknesses," *Organization Studies* 9 (1988), 453–473; and John J. Sherwood, "Creating Work Cultures with Competitive Advantage," *Organizational Dynamics* (Winter 1988), 5–27.

31. Ralph H. Kilmann, Mary J. Saxton, and Roy Serpa, "Issues in Understanding and Changing Culture," *California Management Review* 28 (Winter 1986), 87–94; and Linda Smircich, "Concepts of Culture and Organizational Analysis," *Administrative Science Quarterly* 28 (1983), 339–358.

32. Edgar H. Schein, "Coming to a New Awareness of Organizational Culture," *Sloan Management Review* (Winter 1984), 3–16; and Vijay Sathe, "Implications of Corporate Culture: A Manager's Guide to Actions," *Organizational Dynamics* (Autumn 1983), 5–23.

33. Wendy Zellner, "Mr. Sam's Experiment Is Alive and Well," *Business Week,* April 20, 1992, 39; Sam Walton (with John Huey), *Sam Walton: Made in America* (New York: Doubleday, 1992); and John Huey, "America's Most Successful Merchant," *Fortune,* September 23, 1991, 46–59.

34. William Taylor, "The Gray Area," *Harvard Business Review* (May–June 1988), 178–182, and "Corporate Culture," *Business Week,* October 27, 1980, 148–160.

35. Russell Mitchell, "Masters of Innovation," *Business Week,* April 10, 1989, 58–63.

36. "Make No Mistake," *INC.,* June 1989, 115.

37. Nancy K. Austin, "Wacky Management Ideas That Work," *Working Woman,* November 1991, 42–44.

38. Susan Benner, "Culture Shock," *INC.,* August 1985, 73–82.

39. Joan O'C. Hamilton, "Why Rivals Are Quaking as Nordstrom Heads East," *Business Week,* June 15, 1987, 99–100; and Charlotte B. Sutton, "Richness Hierarchy of the Cultural Network: The Communication of Corporate Values" (Unpublished manuscript, Texas A&M University, 1985).

40. Terrence E. Deal and Allan A. Kennedy, *Corporate Cultures: The Rites and Rituals of Corporate Life* (Reading, Mass.: Addison-Wesley, 1982).

41. Brian Dumaine, "Those Highflying PepsiCo Managers," *Fortune,* April 10, 1989, 78–86; and Stew Leonard, "Love That Customer!" *Management Review* (October 1987), 36–39.

42. Harrison M. Trice and Janice M. Beyer, "Studying Organizational Cultures through Rites and Ceremonials," *Academy of Management Review* 9 (1984), 653–669.

43. John P. Kotter and James L. Heskett, *Corporate Culture and Performance* (New York: The Free Press, 1992).

44. Jeffrey Sonnenfeld, *The Hero's Farewell: What Happens When CEO's Retire* (New York: Oxford University Press, 1988).

45. William A. Schiermann, "Organizational Change: Lessons from a Turn-around," *Management Review,* April 1992, 34–37.

46. Ralph H. Kilmann, Mary J. Saxton, Roy Serpa, and Associates, *Gaining Control of the Corporate Culture* (San Francisco: Jossey-Bass, 1985).

47. Ralph Kilmann, "Corporate Culture," *Psychology Today,* April 1985, 62–68.

48. Morty Lefkoe, "Why So Many Mergers Fail," *Fortune,* June 20, 1987, 113–114.

49. Ibid.; and Afsaneh Nahavandi and Ali R. Malekzadeh, "Acculturation in Mergers and Acquisitions," *Academy of Management Review* 13 (1988), 79–90.

50. Bohl, *Tying the Corporate Knot.*

51. Thomas J. Peters and Robert H. Waterman, Jr., *In Search of Excellence* (New York: Warner, 1988).

52. Charles A. Jaffe, "Management by Fun," *Nation's Business,* January 1990, 58–60.

53. Russell Mitchell, "Jack Welch: How Good a Manager?" *Business Week,* December 14, 1987, 92–103.

54. Ellyn E. Spragins, "Motivation: Out of the Frying Pan," *INC.,* December 1991, 157.

55. Tom Peters and Nancy Austin, *A Passion for Excellence: The Leadership Difference* (New York: Random House, 1985), 278.

56. Karl E. Weick, "Cognitive Processes in Organizations," in *Research in Organizations,* vol. 1, ed. B. M. Staw (Greenwich, Conn.: JAI Press, 1979).

57. Grover, "Boxed in at Jack in the Box"; "Killer Hamburgers."

II

PLANNING

In meeting its strategic goals for diversity, IDS took a cooking tip from Trinidad and Tobago. There, the national dish, Callaloo, is a metaphor for ethnic diversity in the area, mixing together a wild assortment of ingredients. IDS's corporate version of Callaloo has been developed through a four-point strategic plan for diversity, called LEAD. This recipe includes Leadership from managers, creating an Environment that is open to diversity, Acquiring new and diverse employees, planners, and clients, and Delivering measurable results. IDS has already seen significant increases in work-force diversity. IDS Callaloo has arrived.

MANAGERIAL ETHICS AND CORPORATE SOCIAL RESPONSIBILITY

5

CHAPTER OUTLINE ▲

LEARNING OBJECTIVES ▼

After studying this chapter, you should be able to

- Define ethics and explain how ethical behavior relates to behavior governed by law and free choice.

- Explain the utilitarian, individualism, moral-rights, and justice approaches for evaluating ethical behavior.

- Describe how both individual and organizational factors shape ethical decision making.

- Define corporate social responsibility and how to evaluate it along economic, legal, ethical, and discretionary criteria.

- Describe four corporate responses to social demands.

- Explain the concept of stakeholder and identify important stakeholders for organizations.

- Describe structures managers can use to improve their organizations' ethics and social responsiveness.

Not long ago, W. Mark Baty Jr. was trying to reconcile conflicting impulses. His metals recycling business, Accredited Business Services of Cleveland, was being suffocated with debt. Baty had already borrowed money from family members. Credit card advances had also been used to finance the enterprise. He was playing a shell game with payables and receivables, delaying the former as long as possible while trying to get paid in as little as ten days. Salvation appeared in the form of a big-ticket customer willing to commit. However, Baty would need $60,000 for a heavy hauler truck. He was sure a banker's evaluation of the true nature of his company's finances would make for a short meeting. But, Baty knew that landing this customer would save his company. He was certain he could pay for the truck. He could grow his business exponentially. He would have to lie, maybe only by omission, if he hoped to get the loan for the truck. What choices does Baty have? If you were Baty, how would you handle this ethical dilemma?[1]

Beyond individual ethical concerns, recent news reports of ethical scandals illustrate the importance of the need to discuss ethics and social responsibility. In the 1990s ethics and social responsibility issues are in the forefront of corporate concerns. Corporations are rushing to adopt codes of ethics. Ethics consultants are doing a land-office business. Unfortunately, the trend is necessary.[2]

The state of California charged that 72 Sears, Roebuck tire and auto centers defrauded customers with unnecessary repairs. The findings followed a two-year undercover investigation and resulted in a public apology by Sears chairman Edward Brennan and abandonment of commission sales for auto service departments.[3] In an even further-reaching scandal, the federal government charged the Bank of Credit and Commerce International (BCCI) with a number of criminal counts, including the laundering of drug money and influence peddling. Exxon faced public anger, enormous fines, and a massive cleanup effort following the *Exxon Valdez* oil spill. These instances of fraud, criminal activity, and pollution illustrate the negative side of ethics issues.

There is also positive news to report. In the wake of the 1992 Los Angeles riots, McDonald's fed burned-out citizens, fire fighters, police, and national guard troops and delivered free lunches to 300 students at a nearby school. Anita Roddick's retail chain of Bodyshops supports a variety of environmental and social causes, such as Amnesty International. H. J. Heinz funded infant nutrition studies in China and Thailand through its Institute of Nutritional Sciences. Companies such as Northrop and Manville, embarrassed by scandals, are working overtime to prevent future ethical problems. Among Northrop's reforms, managers are rated by peers and subordinates through anonymous questionnaires. Manville is overcoming its asbestos-tainted past with a trust fund to compensate asbestos victims, regular audits by an independent health committee, and the installation of scrubbers on its smokestacks.[4]

This chapter expands on the ideas about environment and culture discussed in Chapter 4. We will first focus on specific ethical values that build on the idea of corporate culture. Then we will examine corporate relationships to the external environment as reflected in social responsibility. The topic of ethics is hot in corporate America, but it should be approached as more than a fad. We will discuss fundamental approaches that help managers think through ethical issues. Understanding ethical approaches helps managers build a solid foundation on which to base future decision making.

● WHAT IS MANAGERIAL ETHICS?

Ethics is difficult to define in a precise way. In a general sense, **ethics** is the code of moral principles and values that govern the behaviors of a person or group with respect to what is right or wrong. Ethics sets standards as to what is good or bad in conduct and decision making.[5] Ethics deals with internal values that are a part of cor-

ethics

The code of moral principles and values that govern the behaviors of a person or group with respect to what is right or wrong.

Florida Progress Corporation's efforts to show its commitment to a social responsibility approach to the environment is demonstrated through its employees constructing elevated platforms to encourage birds, such as this osprey, to locate nests away from power line poles. These efforts add to the company's reputation as a socially responsible industry leader.

porate culture and shapes decisions concerning social responsibility with respect to the external environment. An ethical issue is present in a situation when the actions of a person or organization may harm or benefit others.[6]

Ethics can be more clearly understood when compared with behaviors governed by laws and by free choice. Exhibit 5.1 illustrates that human behavior falls into three categories. The first is *codified law,* in which values and standards are written into the legal system and enforceable in the courts. In this area, lawmakers have ruled that people and corporations must behave in a certain way, such as obtaining licenses for cars or paying corporate taxes. The domain of *free choice* is at the opposite end of the scale and pertains to behavior about which law has no say and for which an individual or organization enjoys complete freedom. An individual's choice of a marriage partner or religion or a corporation's choice of the number of dishwashers to manufacture are examples of free choice.

Between these domains lies the area of *ethics.* This domain has no specific laws, yet it does have standards of conduct based on shared principles and values about moral conduct that guide an individual or company. In the domain of free choice, obedience is strictly to oneself. In the domain of codified law, obedience is to laws prescribed by the legal system. In the domain of ethical behavior, obedience is to unenforceable norms and standards about which the individual or company is aware. An ethically acceptable decision is both legally and morally acceptable to the larger community.

Many companies and individuals get into trouble with the simplified view that choices are governed by either law or free choice. It leads people to mistakenly assume that "If it's not illegal, it must be ethical," as if there were no third domain.[7] A better option is to recognize the

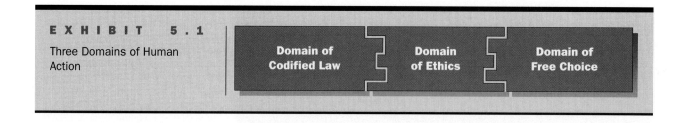

E X H I B I T   5 . 1

Three Domains of Human
Action

Domain of
Codified Law

Domain
of Ethics

Domain of
Free Choice

ethical dilemma

A situation that arises when all alternative choices or behaviors have been deemed undesirable because of potentially negative ethical consequences, making it difficult to distinguish right from wrong.

domain of ethics and accept moral values as a powerful force for good that can regulate behaviors both inside and outside corporations. As principles of ethics and social responsibility are more widely recognized, companies can use codes of ethics and their corporate cultures to govern behavior, thereby eliminating the need for additional laws and avoiding the problems of unfettered choice.

Because ethical standards are not codified, disagreements and dilemmas about proper behavior often occur. An **ethical dilemma** arises in a situation when each alternative choice or behavior is undesirable because of potentially harmful ethical consequences. Right or wrong cannot be clearly identified.

The individual who must make an ethical choice in an organization is the *moral agent*.[8] Consider the dilemmas facing a moral agent in the following situations:

> Shareholders demand that your company pull out of China as a result of the continued repression following the massacre in Tiananmen Square. If you pull out, you withdraw any influence your company may have for change and your Chinese employees will be hurt. If you stay, your company will be indirectly supporting an oppressive government.
>
> You have been asked to fire a marketing supervisor for cheating the company out of $500 on an inflated expense account. You are aware that a manufacturing supervisor allows thousands of dollars of waste because of poor work habits.
>
> Your company has been asked to pay a gratuity in India to speed the processing of an import permit. This is standard procedure, and your company will suffer if you do not pay the gratuity. Is this different from tipping a maitre d' in a nice restaurant?
>
> You are the accounting manager of a division that is $15,000 below profit targets. Approximately $20,000 of office supplies were delivered on December 21. The accounting rule is to pay expenses when incurred. The division general manager asks you not to record the invoice until February.
>
> Your boss says he cannot give you a raise this year because of budget constraints, but he will look the other way if your expense accounts come in a little high because of your good work this past year.

These are the kinds of dilemmas and issues with which managers must deal that fall squarely in the domain of ethics. For a dilemma that really hits home, read the Focus on Ethics box. Now let's turn to approaches to ethical decision making that provide criteria for understanding and resolving these difficult issues.

AIDS IN THE WORKPLACE

As division manager, you take great pride in the accomplishments of your employees. One day, the brightest and best of your employees stops you in the hall and whispers, "Can we talk?" You usher him into your office, close the door, and offer a chair. "What's on your mind?" The division wonder kid closes his eyes, takes a deep breath, and blurts out, "I need some time off. I have a problem. I have AIDS."

This scenario is every employer's nightmare. Unfortunately, it is a scenario being repeated daily in companies around the world, as increasing numbers of employees are infected with the deadly virus. As the disease reaches epidemic proportions, the federal Centers for Disease Control estimate "one in every 250 Americans may be infected by HIV, the virus that causes acquired immune deficiency syndrome." For corporate America, these gloomy statistics mean mounting pressure for implementation of sound AIDS policies, including ongoing education and support.

Efforts of corporate America to deal with the problems surrounding the virus are thus far inadequate.

Many companies can point to a non-discriminatory corporate policy toward victims, including a continuation of benefits. However, the greatest challenges in dealing with AIDS involve carefully honed people skills in the most difficult areas— "dealing with fear, discrimination, and dying in the workplace."

Although the disease cannot be transmitted through casual contact, fear stalks the workplace as non-infected employees cope with irrational worries about using the same restroom facilities or drinking fountain or try to insulate themselves from the pain and suffering of their coworker. Even initial sympathy for the coworker with AIDS can turn to resentment as other employees must increasingly take up the slack caused by the coworker's deteriorating health. In today's team-oriented work environment performance and morale of the entire group may suffer.

Company efforts to deal with the problems of AIDS must be pursued along three fronts. First, the company must develop a policy that protects the right to privacy for all employees and guarantees full benefits for employees with AIDS. The policy must have the full support of the top executives, and allow employees with AIDS to lead a productive work life as long as possible, without fear of isolation.

Second, the company should provide training for management, union officials, supervisors, and all employees. At the management level, training should include professional guidance in addressing worker fears. The company policy should be explained to all employees and include procedures to follow when an employee reports being HIV-positive or having AIDS. All employees should learn the facts about AIDS and should be encouraged through workshops, open discussion, or role-playing exercises, to develop empathy for those who suffer from AIDS.

Third, companies should assist employees with AIDS in coping with the disease, through ongoing counseling, and by helping managers and employees to deal with the special problems and issues involved with AIDS.

By dispelling myths, sensitizing employees, and creating a supportive atmosphere, corporate America will deal more effectively with this tragic disease. ■

SOURCE: Ron Stodghill II, Russell Mitchell, Karen Thurston, and Christina Del Valle, "Why AIDS Policy Must Be a Special Policy," *Business Week* (February 1, 1993), 53–54; and Ron Stodghill II, "Managing AIDS: How One Boss Struggled to Cope," *Business Week* (February 1, 1993), 48–52.

● CRITERIA FOR ETHICAL DECISION MAKING

Most ethical dilemmas involve a conflict between the needs of the part and the whole—the individual versus the organization, or the organization versus society as a whole. For example, should a company install mandatory alcohol and drug testing for employees, which may benefit the organization as a whole but reduce the individual freedom of employees? Or should products that fail to meet tough FDA standards be exported to other countries where government standards are lower, benefiting the company but being potentially harmful to world citizens? Sometimes ethical decisions entail a conflict between two groups. For example, should the potential for local health problems resulting from a company's effluents take precedence over the jobs it creates as the town's leading employer?

Managers faced with these kinds of tough ethical choices often benefit from a normative approach—one based on norms and values—to guide their decision making. Normative ethics uses several approaches to describe values for guiding ethical decision making. Four of these that are relevant to managers are the utilitarian approach, individualism approach, moral-rights approach, and justice approach.[9]

UTILITARIAN APPROACH

utilitarian approach

The ethical concept that moral behaviors produce the greatest good for the greatest number.

The **utilitarian approach,** espoused by the nineteenth-century philosophers Jeremy Bentham and John Stuart Mill, holds that moral behavior produces the greatest good for the greatest number. Under this approach, a decision maker is expected to consider the effect of each decision alternative on all parties and select the one that optimizes the satisfaction for the greatest number of people. Because actual computations can be very complex, simplifying them is considered appropriate. For example, a simple economic frame of reference could be used by calculating dollar costs and dollar benefits. Also, a decision could be made that considers only the people who are directly affected by the decision, not those who are indirectly affected. When GM chose to continue operations at its Arlington, Texas, plant while shutting down its Ypsilanti, Michigan, plant, managers justified the decision as producing the greater good for the corporation as a whole. The utilitarian ethic is cited as the basis for the recent trend among companies to police employee personal habits such as alcohol and tobacco consumption on the job, and in some cases after hours as well, because such behavior affects the entire workplace.[10]

The utilitarian ethic was the basis for the state of Oregon's decision to extend Medicaid to 400,000 previously ineligible recipients by refusing to pay for high-cost, high-risk procedures such as liver transplants and bone-marrow transplants. Although a few people needing these procedures have died because the state would not pay, many people have benefited from medical services they would otherwise have had to go without.[11] Critics of the utilitarian ethic fear a developing tendency toward a "Big Brother" approach and question whether the common good is squeezing the life out of the individual. Critics also claim that the Oregon decision does not fully take into account the concept of justice toward the unfortunate victims of life-threatening diseases.[12]

INDIVIDUALISM APPROACH

The **individualism approach** contends that acts are moral when they promote the individual's best long-term interests. Individual self-direction is paramount, and external forces that restrict self-direction should be severely limited.[13] Individuals calculate the best long-term advantage to themselves as a measure of a decision's goodness. The action that is intended to produce a greater ratio of good to bad for the individual compared with other alternatives is the right one to perform. With everyone pursuing self-direction, the greater good is ultimately served because people learn to accommodate each other in their own long-term interest. Individualism is believed to lead to honesty and integrity because that works best in the long run. Lying and cheating for immediate self-interest just causes business associates to lie and cheat in return. Thus, individualism ultimately leads to behavior toward others that fits standards of behavior people want toward themselves.[14] One value of understanding this approach is to recognize short-term variations if they are proposed. People might argue for short-term self-interest based on individualism, but that misses the point. Because individualism is easily misinterpreted to support immediate self-gain, it is not popular in the highly organized and group-oriented society of today. Individualism is closest to the domain of free choice described in Exhibit 5.1.

individualism approach

The ethical concept that acts are moral when they promote the individual's best long-term interests, which ultimately leads to the greater good.

MORAL-RIGHTS APPROACH

The **moral-rights approach** asserts that human beings have fundamental rights and liberties that cannot be taken away by an individual's decision. Thus an ethically correct decision is one that best maintains the rights of those people affected by it.

Moral rights that could be considered during decision making are

moral-rights approach

The ethical concept that moral decisions are those that best maintain the rights of those people affected by them.

1 The right of free consent—individuals are to be treated only as they knowingly and freely consent to be treated.

2 The right to privacy—individuals can choose to do as they please away from work and have control of information about their private life.

3 The right of freedom of conscience—individuals may refrain from carrying out any order that violates their moral or religious norms.

4 The right of free speech—individuals may criticize truthfully the ethics or legality of actions of others.

5 The right to due process—individuals have a right to an impartial hearing and fair treatment.

6 The right to life and safety—individuals have a right to live without endangerment or violation of their health and safety.

To make ethical decisions, managers need to avoid interfering with the fundamental rights of others. Thus a decision to eavesdrop on employees violates the right to privacy. Sexual harassment is unethical because it violates the right to freedom of conscience. The right of free speech would support whistle-blowers who call attention to illegal or inappropriate action within a company.

JUSTICE APPROACH

justice approach

The ethical concept that moral decisions must be based on standards of equity, fairness, and impartiality.

distributive justice

The concept that different treatment of people should not be based on arbitrary characteristics. In the case of substantive differences, people should be treated differently in proportion to the differences between them.

procedural justice

The concept that rules should be clearly stated and consistently and impartially enforced.

compensatory justice

The concept that individuals should be compensated for the cost of their injuries by the party responsible and also that individuals should not be held responsible for matters over which they have no control.

The **justice approach** holds that moral decisions must be based on standards of equity, fairness, and impartiality. Three types of justice are of concern to managers. **Distributive justice** requires that different treatment of people not be based on arbitrary characteristics. Individuals who are similar in respects relevant to a decision should be treated similarly. Thus men and women should not receive different salaries if they are performing the same job. However, people who differ in a substantive way, such as job skills or job responsibility, can be treated differently in proportion to the differences in skills or responsibility between them. This difference should have a clear relationship to organizational goals and tasks.

Procedural justice requires that rules be administered fairly. Rules should be clearly stated and be consistently and impartially enforced. **Compensatory justice** argues that individuals should be compensated for the cost of their injuries by the party responsible. Moreover, individuals should not be held responsible for matters over which they have no control.

The justice approach is closest to the thinking underlying the domain of law in Exhibit 5.1, because it assumes that justice is applied through rules and regulations. This theory does not require complex calculations such as those demanded by a utilitarian approach, nor does it justify self-interest as the individualism approach does. Managers are expected to define attributes on which different treatment of employees is acceptable. Questions such as how minority workers should be compensated for past discrimination are extremely difficult. However, this approach does justify as ethical behavior efforts to correct past wrongs, playing fair under the rules, and insisting on job-relevant differences as the basis for different levels of pay or promotion opportunities. Most of the laws guiding human resource management (Chapter 10) are based on the justice approach.

The challenge of applying these ethical approaches is illustrated by the decisions facing the rent-to-own industry.

 RENT-TO-OWN INDUSTRY

Sometimes what you don't see is what you get. A Paterson, New Jersey, woman living in public housing found the living room set of her dreams at her friendly rent-to-own store. She contracted to pay $64.29 a month for 18 months, at which time she would own it. That total did not include an extra $14.86 per month for sales tax, liability waivers, and collection fees. Regardless, the woman made $964.35 in payments, or 83 percent of the total, before having to be hospitalized. At that point, the "friendly" rent-to-own merchant came by and took everything back. The original retail price of the furniture: $499.

Ronald Waters, director of government affairs for the Association of Progressive Rental Organization, defends the industry, claiming statistics are on their side. "Only 25 percent or less keep the items to full term," he says. Industry advocates contend they provide a valuable service by offering a short-term alternative to people with bad credit who otherwise would be unable to afford the items. They also point out that repairs through the term of a contract, collection and repossession, and their own costs of funds provide some justification for high pricing. Critics do not believe that these higher costs justify what is termed "price differential," which amounts to more than three times what finance companies charge.

Depending on the particular viewpoint, the rent-to-own industry is either taking advantage of a business opportunity or exploiting a loophole. The Truth in Lending Act and state law govern retail installment sales. However, since, technically, no debt is created and customers do not have to fulfill the terms of the contracts, these statutes are not applicable. It is worthy to note that a large segment of rent-to-own customers are typically among the least advantaged in our society.[15] ■

Consider for a moment how you think the various ethical approaches support and refute the rent-to-own industry's actions.

● FACTORS AFFECTING ETHICAL CHOICES

When managers are accused of lying, cheating, or stealing, the blame is usually placed on the individual or on the company situation. Most people believe that individuals make ethical choices because of individual integrity, which is true, but it is not the whole story. The values held in the larger organization also shape ethical behavior.[16] Let's examine how both the manager and the organization shape ethical decision making.

THE MANAGER

Managers bring specific personality and behavioral traits to the job. Personal needs, family influence, and religious background all shape a manager's value system. Specific personality characteristics, such as ego strength, self-confidence, and a strong sense of independence may enable managers to make ethical decisions.

One important personal trait is the stage of moral development.[17] A simplified version of one model of personal moral development is shown in Exhibit 5.2. At the *preconventional level*, a manager is concerned with the external rewards and punishment and the concrete personal consequences. At level two, called the *conventional level*, people learn to conform to the expectations of good behavior as defined by colleagues, friends, family, and society. People at the conventional level respect external expectations. At level three, called the *principled level*, individuals develop an internal set of standards and values. The individual will even disobey laws that violate these principles. Internal values are more important than expectations of significant others.

	Stage	What Is Considered to Be Right
EXHIBIT 5.2 Three Levels of Personal Moral Development	Level one: Preconventional	Follows rules to avoid physical punishment. Acts in one's immediate interest. Obedience for its own sake.
SOURCE: Based on L. Kohlberg, "Moral Stages and Moralization: The Cognitive– Developmental Approach," in *Moral Development and Behavior: Theory, Research, and Social Issues*, ed. T. Lickona (New York: Holt, Rhinehart, and Winston, 1976).	Level two: Conventional	Good behavior is living up to what is expected by others. Fulfills duties and obligations of social system. Upholds laws.
	Level three: Principled	Aware that people hold different values. Upholds values and rights regardless of majority opinion. Follows self-chosen ethical principles of justice and right.

The great majority of managers operate at level two. A few have not advanced beyond level one. Only about 20 percent of American adults reach the level three stage of moral development. People at level three are able to act in an independent, ethical manner regardless of expectations from others inside or outside the organization. Managers at level three of moral development will make ethical decisions whatever the organizational consequences for them. The Manager's Shoptalk box lists some general guidelines to follow for making ethical decisions.

Higher levels of ethical conduct, especially the principled level, are important because of the impact of globalization on organizational ethics and corporate culture. American managers need to develop sensitivity and openness to other systems. Cross-cultural alliances and mergers create the need to work out differences where ethical values differ. For example, bribery is an accepted way of conducting business in many

Cray Research, Inc.'s supercomputer engineering group takes its social responsibility seriously. Volunteers deliver important extracurricular science and math education opportunities for middle school and high school students in essentially rural areas.

GUIDELINES FOR ETHICAL DECISION MAKING

Alist of guidelines follows that you, the future manager, can apply to difficult social problems and ethical dilemmas you almost surely will face one day. The guidelines will not tell you exactly what to do, but taken in the context of the text discussion, they will help you evaluate the situation more clearly by examining your own values and those of your organization. The answers to these questions will force you to think hard about the social and ethical consequences of your behavior.

1. Is the problem/dilemma really what it appears to be? If you are not sure, *find out*.
2. Is the action you are considering legal? Ethical? If you are not sure, *find out*.
3. Do you understand the position of those who oppose the action you are considering? Is it reasonable?
4. Whom does the action benefit? Harm? How much? How long?
5. Would you be willing to allow everyone to do what you are considering doing?
6. Have you sought the opinion of others who are knowledgeable on the subject and who would be objective?
7. Would your action be embarrassing to you if it were made known to your family, friends, coworkers, or superiors? Would you be comfortable defending your actions to an investigative reporter on the evening news?

There are no correct answers to these questions in an absolute sense. Yet, if you determine that an action is potentially harmful to someone, would be embarrassing to you, or if you do not know the ethical or legal consequences, these guidelines will help you clarify whether the action is socially responsible. ■

SOURCE: Anthony M. Pagano and Jo Ann Verdin, *The External Environment of Business* (New York: Wiley, 1988), Chapter 5.

developing countries. "Grease" payments to customs officials are considered part of their living wage. Failure to play the game could result in loss of outlets, suppliers, and foreign revenues. On the other hand, foreign bribery is illegal under the U.S. Foreign Corrupt Practices Act. Managers must use mature ethical judgment in resolving these difficult international issues.[18]

THE ORGANIZATION

The values adopted within the organization are important, especially when we understand that most people are at the level two stage of moral development, which means they believe their duty is to fulfill obligations and expectations of others. As discussed in Chapter 4, corporate culture can exert a powerful influence on behavior in organizations. For example, an investigation of thefts and kickbacks in the oil business found that the cause was the historical acceptance of thefts and kickbacks. Employees were socialized into those values and adopted them as appropriate. In most companies, employees believe that if they do not go along with the ethical values expressed, their jobs will be in jeopardy or they will not fit in.[19]

Culture can be examined to see the kinds of ethical signals given to employees. Exhibit 5.3 indicates questions to ask to understand the cultural system. Heroes provide role models that can either support or

EXHIBIT 5.3

Questions for Analyzing a
Company's Cultural Impact
on Ethics

SOURCE: Linda Klebe Trevino, "A Cultural Perspective on Changing and Developing Organizational Ethics," in *Research in Organizational Change and Development*, eds. R. Woodman and W. Pasmore (Greenwich, Conn.: JAI Press, 1990), 4.

1. Identify the organization's heroes. What values do they represent? Given an ambiguous ethical dilemma, what decision would they make and why?
2. What are some important organizational rituals? How do they encourage or discourage ethical behavior? Who gets the awards, people of integrity or individuals who use unethical methods to attain success?
3. What are the ethical messages sent to new entrants into the organization— must they obey authority at all costs, or is questioning authority acceptable or even desirable?
4. Does analysis of organizational stories and myths reveal individuals who stand up for what's right, or is conformity the valued characteristic? Do people get fired or promoted in these stories?
5. Does language exist for discussing ethical concerns? Is this language routinely incorporated and encouraged in business decision making?
6. What informal socialization processes exist and what norms for ethical/unethical behavior do they promote?

refute ethical decision making. Founder Tom Watson stood for integrity at IBM and his values are still very much alive. With respect to company rituals, high ethical standards are affirmed and communicated through public awards and ceremonies. Myths and stories can reinforce heroic ethical behavior. For example, a story at Johnson & Johnson describes its reaction to the cyanide poisoning of Tylenol capsule users. After seven people in Chicago died, the capsules were removed from the market voluntarily, costing the company over $100 million. This action was taken against the advice of external agencies—FBI and FDA—but was necessary because of Johnson & Johnson's ethical standards.

Culture is not the only aspect of an organization that influences ethics, but it is a major force because it defines company values. Other aspects of the organization such as explicit rules and policies, the reward system, the extent to which the company cares for its people, the selection system, emphasis on legal and professional standards, and leadership and decision processes can also all have an impact on ethical values and manager decision making.[20]

● WHAT IS SOCIAL RESPONSIBILITY?

Now let's turn to the issue of social responsibility. In one sense, the concept of corporate social responsibility, like ethics, is easy to understand: it means distinguishing right from wrong and doing right. It means being a good corporate citizen. The formal definition of **social responsibility** is management's obligation to make choices and take actions that will contribute to the welfare and interests of society as well as to the organization's.[21]

As straightforward as this definition seems, social responsibility can be a difficult concept to grasp, because different people have different beliefs regarding which actions improve society's welfare.[22] To make matters worse, social responsibility covers a range of issues, many of

social responsibility

The obligation of organization management to make decisions and take actions that will enhance the welfare and interests of society as well as the organization.

which are ambiguous with respect to right or wrong. For example, if a bank deposits the money from a trust fund into a low-interest account for 90 days, from which it makes a substantial profit, has it been unethical? How about two companies' engaging in intense competition, such as that between Cleveland Electric Illuminating Co. and Cleveland Public Power? Is it socially responsible for the stronger corporation to drive the weaker one into bankruptcy? Or consider companies such as A. H. Robins, maker of the Dalkon shield, Manville Corporation, maker of asbestos, Eastern Airlines, or Texaco, the oil company, all of which declared bankruptcy—which is perfectly legal—to avoid mounting financial obligations to suppliers, labor unions, or competitors. These examples contain moral, legal, and economic considerations that make socially responsible behavior hard to define.

● ORGANIZATIONAL STAKEHOLDERS

One reason for the difficulty understanding social responsibility is that managers must confront the question "responsibility to whom?" Recall from Chapter 4 that the organization's environment consists of several sectors in both the task and general environment. From a social responsibility perspective, enlightened organizations view the internal and external environment as a variety of stakeholders.

A **stakeholder** is any group within or outside the organization that has a stake in the organization's performance. Each stakeholder has a different criterion of responsiveness, because it has a different interest in the organization.[23]

stakeholder

Any group within or outside the organization that has a stake in the organization's performance.

Exhibit 5.4 illustrates important stakeholders, including employees, customers, owners, creditors, suppliers, and investors. Investors', owners', and suppliers' interests are served by managerial efficiency, that is, use of resources to achieve profits. Employees expect work satisfaction, pay, and good supervision. Customers are concerned with decisions about the quality and availability of goods and services.

Other important stakeholders are the government and the community. Most corporations exist only under the proper charter and licenses and operate within the limits of safety laws, environmental protection requirements, and other laws and regulations in the government sector. The community includes local government, the natural and physical environments, and the quality of life provided for residents. Special-interest groups, still another stakeholder, may include trade associations, political action committees, professional associations, and consumerists. Socially responsible organizations consider the effects of their actions on all stakeholders. Today, special-interest groups continue to be one of the largest stakeholder concerns that companies face.

Enlightened corporations invest in a number of philanthropic and in-house causes that benefit stakeholders. Cray Research, Inc., invests heavily in science and math education, providing both funding and employee expertise.[24] In New York, Alexander's Department Stores, American

E X H I B I T   5 . 4

Stakeholders Relevant to an
Auto Manufacturer

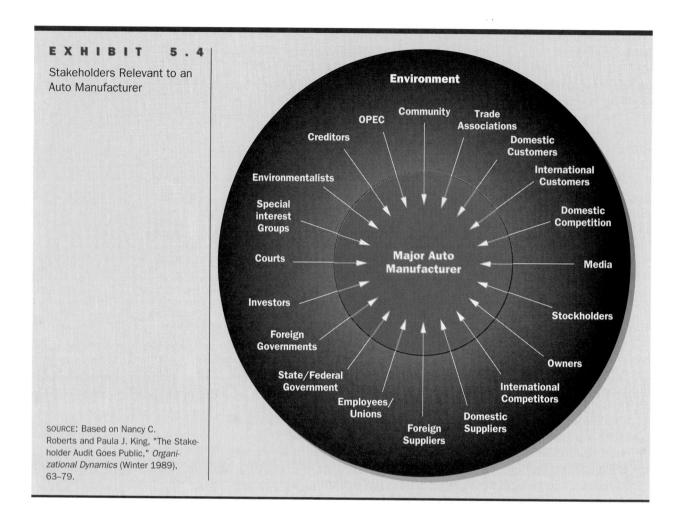

SOURCE: Based on Nancy C.
Roberts and Paula J. King, "The Stakeholder Audit Goes Public," *Organizational Dynamics* (Winter 1989),
63–79.

Express, Citibank, and IBM are all involved with high schools, either
offering courses, providing realistic previews of job demands, or simply
taking teenagers to Yankee Stadium if they have good school attendance
records.[25] DuPont executive Faith Wohl is a corporate pioneer in the area
of work-family coordination—attempting to meet the personal and
social needs of employees. Wohl's division established child care centers,
job sharing for working mothers, and workshops addressing issues such
as rape prevention, racial bias, and sexual harassment.[26]

Well-meaning companies sometimes run afoul of stakeholders anyway. For example, Fina, Inc., established an oil refinery in Port Arthur,
Texas, in 1937. Over the years, subdivisions of attractive ranch-style
homes grew up in the shadow of the Fina plant. Homeowners became
unhappy with the plant in their midst because of its noise and odor. Residents expected the company to purchase their homes at top market
price. Fina made several good faith efforts to resolve problems and then
agreed to purchase the homes because the residents had legitimate
gripes.[27] Companies such as Fina and DuPont are acting in a socially
responsible way by helping stakeholders.

● EVALUATING CORPORATE SOCIAL PERFORMANCE

Once a company is aware of its stakeholders, what criteria can be used to evaluate social performance? One model for evaluating corporate social performance is presented in Exhibit 5.5. The model indicates that total corporate social responsibility can be subdivided into four criteria—economic, legal, ethical, and discretionary responsibilities.[28] The responsibilities are ordered from bottom to top based on their relative magnitude and the frequency with which managers deal with each issue.

Note the similarity between the categories in Exhibit 5.5 and those in Exhibit 5.1. In both cases, ethical issues are located between the areas of legal and freely discretionary responsibilities. Exhibit 5.5 also has an economic category, because profits are a major reason for corporations' existence.

ECONOMIC RESPONSIBILITIES

The first criterion of social responsibility is *economic responsibility.* The business institution is, above all, the basic economic unit of society. Its responsibility is to produce the goods and services that society wants and to maximize profits for its owners and shareholders. Economic responsibility, carried to the extreme, is called the *profit-maximizing view,* advocated by Nobel economist Milton Friedman. This view argues that the corporation should be operated on a profit-oriented basis, with its sole mission to increase its profits so long as it stays within the rules of the game.[29]

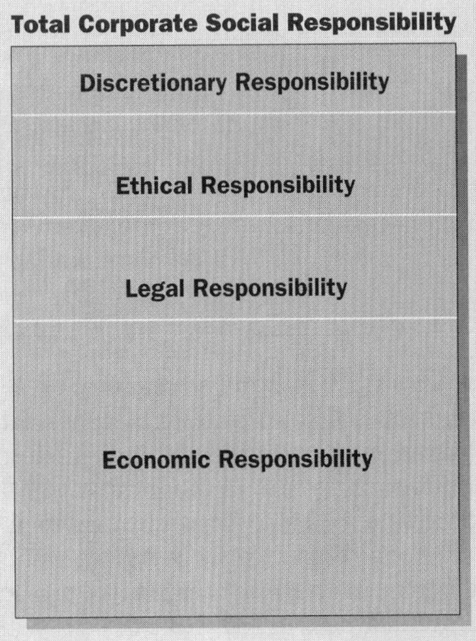

Total Corporate Social Responsibility

- **Discretionary Responsibility**
- **Ethical Responsibility**
- **Legal Responsibility**
- **Economic Responsibility**

EXHIBIT 5.5

Criteria of Corporate Social Performance

SOURCE: Archie B. Carroll, "A Three-Dimensional Conceptual Model of Corporate Performance," *Academy of Management Review* 4 (1979), 499.

The purely profit-maximizing view is no longer considered an adequate criterion of performance in Canada, the United States, and Europe. This approach means that economic gain is the only social responsibility and can lead companies into trouble. A notorious example was Salomon Brothers' attempt to corner the Treasury securities market. Corporate greed, fostered by former chairman John Gutfreund's "win-at-all-costs" culture, resulted in mistakes that led to record penalties of $280 million.[30]

LEGAL RESPONSIBILITIES

All modern societies lay down ground rules, laws, and regulations that businesses are expected to follow. *Legal responsibility* defines what society deems as important with respect to appropriate corporate behavior.[31] Businesses are expected to fulfill their economic goals within the legal framework. Legal requirements are imposed by local town councils, state legislators, and federal regulatory agencies.

Organizations that knowingly break the law are poor performers in this category. Intentionally manufacturing defective goods or billing a client for work not done is illegal. An example of the punishment given to one company that broke the law is shown in Exhibit 5.6.

ETHICAL RESPONSIBILITIES

Ethical responsibility includes behaviors that are not necessarily codified into law and may not serve the corporation's direct economic interests. As described earlier in this chapter, to be *ethical,* organization decision makers should act with equity, fairness, and impartiality, respect the rights of individuals, and provide different treatment of individuals only when relevant to the organization's goals and tasks.[32] *Unethical* behavior occurs when decisions enable an individual or company to gain at the expense of society.

When Control Data took a chance by building a plant in Minneapolis' inner city, it performed an ethical act because top management wanted to provide equal opportunity for the disadvantaged. Other businesses had built in the ghetto and failed. Chairman Norris insisted that the plant attempt to be profitable, but the company also wanted to provide jobs to inner-city residents. In this case, the ethical goals were compatible with the economic goals, and the company achieved both.[33]

DISCRETIONARY RESPONSIBILITIES

discretionary responsibility

Organizational responsibility that is voluntary and guided by the organization's desire to make social contributions not mandated by economics, law, or ethics.

Discretionary responsibility is purely voluntary and guided by a company's desire to make social contributions not mandated by economics, law, or ethics. Discretionary activities include generous philanthropic contributions that offer no payback to the company and are not expected. An example of discretionary behavior occurred when Pittsburgh Brewing Company helped laid-off steelworkers by establishing and contributing to food banks in the Pittsburgh area. It also started a fund-raising program in which people could drink beer with members of the Pittsburgh Steelers for a $5 contribution to their local food bank. Dis-

February 12, 1985

American Caster Corporation

Dear Businesses & Residents of the City & County of Los Angeles

Pollution of our environment has become a crisis.
Intentional clandestine acts of illegal disposal of hazardous waste, or "midnight dumping" are violent crimes against the community.
Over the past 2 years almost a dozen Chief Executive Officers of both large and small corporations have been sent to jail by the L.A. Toxic Waste Strike Force.
They have also been required to pay huge fines; pay for clean-ups; speak in public about their misdeeds; and in some cases place ads publicizing their crime and punishment.

THE RISKS OF BEING CAUGHT ARE TOO HIGH—
AND THE CONSEQUENCES IF CAUGHT ARE NOT WORTH IT!

We are paying the price. *TODAY,* **while you read this ad our President and Vice President are serving time in** *JAIL* **and we were forced to place this ad.**

PLEASE TAKE THE LEGAL ALTERNATIVE AND PROTECT OUR ENVIRONMENT.

Very Truly Yours,

American Caster Corporation
141 WEST AVENUE 34
LOS ANGELES, CA 90031

E X H I B I T   5 . 6

One Company's Punishment for Breaking the Law

SOURCE: Barry C. Groveman and John L. Segal, "Pollution Police Pursue Chemical Criminals," *Business and Society Review* 55 (Fall 1985), 41.

cretionary responsibility is the highest criterion of social responsibility, because it goes beyond societal expectations to contribute to the community's welfare. Another company that carries out discretionary activities is Lady of America Fitness Center.

LADY OF AMERICA FITNESS CENTER

In the tough world of entrepreneurial start-ups, most proprietors are lucky if they get a few hours of sleep each night. Extra time, let alone cash, for charitable donations seems totally out of the question. However, it can be done. And, according to Michelle Wittenberns, it is well worth it.

Wittenberns founded Lady of America Fitness Center Franchises in The Woodlands, Texas. Her biggest motivation for being in business, she says, is to do something positive for the community. She has done this by sponsoring food and clothing drives to benefit battered and abused women. She has also attracted 125,000 clients and is franchising her business. She thinks that with a little imagination anyone can make a contribution. "All small-business owners have something to give that doesn't take working capital out of their pockets," she says.

According to Wittenberns, the key thing charities should be aware of when soliciting small businesses for contributions is that they are unique. Chances are the owners won't have extra cash, but they usually have specialty areas in which they can contribute. For example, Wittenberns' spa seemed a natural for a clothing drive. She was right; when everything was done, contributions totalled 20,000 articles.

Wittenbern also sponsors food drives and gives free workouts to non-members who donate. She views it as a win-win situation. "The way we do it, someone gets a free workout, someone gets some clothing or food, and it helps us in our promotions," she says. "Everybody benefits."[34] ■

● CORPORATE ACTIONS TOWARD SOCIAL DEMANDS

Confronted with a specific social demand, how might a corporation respond? If a stakeholder such as the local government places a demand on the company, what types of corporate action might be taken? Management scholars have developed a scale of response actions that companies use when a social issue confronts them.[35] These actions are obstructive, defensive, accommodative, and proactive and are illustrated on the continuum in Exhibit 5.7.

obstructive response

A response to social demands in which the organization denies responsibility, claims that evidence of misconduct is misleading or distorted, and attempts to obstruct investigation.

OBSTRUCTIVE.   Companies that adopt **obstructive responses** deny all responsibility, claim that evidence of wrongdoing is misleading or distorted, and place obstacles to delay investigation. During the Watergate years, such obstruction was labeled *stonewalling*. A. H. Robins Company reportedly used obstructive actions when it received warnings about its Dalkon shield, an intrauterine device. The company built a wall around itself. It stood against all evidence and insisted to the public that the

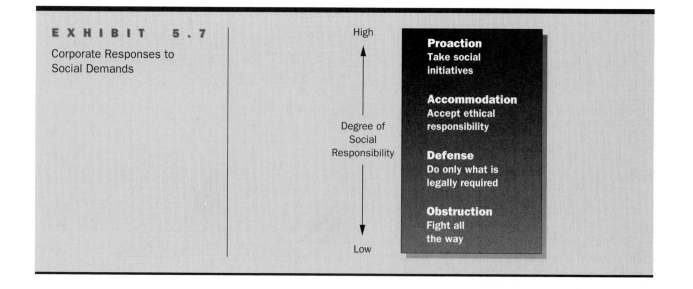

EXHIBIT   5.7

Corporate Responses to Social Demands

High

Degree of Social Responsibility

Low

Proaction
Take social initiatives

Accommodation
Accept ethical responsibility

Defense
Do only what is legally required

Obstruction
Fight all the way

product was safe and effective. The company spared no effort to resist investigation. As word about injuries caused by the Dalkon shield kept pouring in, one attorney was told to search the files and destroy all papers pertaining to the product.[36]

DEFENSIVE.   The **defensive response** means that the company admits to some errors of omission or commission. The company cuts its losses by defending itself but is not obstructive. Defensive managers generally believe that "these things happen, but they are nobody's fault." Goodyear adopted a defensive strategy by deciding to keep its South Africa plants open and provided an intelligent argument for why that was the proper action.

ACCOMMODATIVE.   An **accommodative response** means that the company accepts social responsibility for its actions, although it may do so in response to external pressure. Firms that adopt this action try to meet economic, legal, and ethical responsibilities. If outside forces apply pressure, managers agree to curtail ethically questionable activities. Exxon's decision to clean up the oil spill in Prince William Sound was an accommodative decision based largely on the public's outcry.

PROACTIVE.   The **proactive response** means that firms take the lead in social issues. They seek to learn what is in the public interest and respond without coaxing or pressure from stakeholders. One example of proactive behavior is the Potlatch Corporation. Potlatch makes milk cartons and came up with the idea of printing photographs of missing children on them. The company reported that within days after the Alta-Dena Dairy of Los Angeles placed a missing-kids carton in grocery stores, one of the youngsters returned home.[37] Another proactive response is corporate philanthropy. Many companies, including Miller Brewing, Coca-Cola, and Westinghouse, make generous donations to universities, United Way, and other charitable groups as a way of reaching out and improving society.

These four categories of action are similar to the scale of social performance described in Exhibit 5.5. Obstructiveness tends to occur in firms whose actions are based solely on economic considerations. Defensive organizations are willing to work within the confines of the law. Accommodative organizations respond to ethical pressures. Proactive organizations use discretionary responsibilities to enhance community welfare.

Deja Shoe has taken a proactive approach by doing its part to help preserve the environment.

defensive response

A response to social demands in which the organization admits to some errors of commission or omission but does not act obstructively.

accommodative response

A response to social demands in which the organization accepts—often under pressure—social responsibility for its actions to comply with the public interest.

proactive response

A response to social demands in which the organization seeks to learn what is in its constituencies' interest and to respond without pressure from them.

DEJA SHOE

Deja Shoe wants to get it right. The fledgling shoe manufacturer wants to be profitable, and it wants to be among the vanguard to steer the footwear industry in the direction of environmental awareness. Bob Farentinos, vice president of environmental affairs, calls the company's Eco Sneak "an eclectic array of junk." And, he means it literally.

Stride Rite was the first company to offer on-site day care and one of the first to offer a smoke-free workplace policy. In 1990, Stride Rite opened the first Intergenerational Day Care Center (pictured here). These unique day-care facilities bring together elderly people and children in a loving environment. The Stride Rite Corporation has taken the lead in meeting its social responsibilities.

As much as 70 percent of Deja Shoes are strictly garbage, albeit a specific type. Recycled plastic soda containers, polystyrene cups, magazines, and waste from throwaway diapers all combine to make for solid footing. Not surprisingly, the shoes have a special appeal to customers Farentinos calls "rather green."

The company went public in 1992 and expects to break even by the end of 1994. However, Farentinos is realistic about the nature of business, as well as the challenges ahead. "We can't do what we want to do if we don't make a profit," he says. "And we can't be profitable if we don't have a good product and maintain our standards." It will be a delicate balancing act. The company's decision to forgo some of the standard manufacturing processes that are bad for the environment will increase costs. Research and development expenditures are also above average. The shoe business is no place for the faint of heart. Rumor has it that Nike and Reebok may move into the recycled footwear market themselves. If so, it will be a step in the right direction for the environment. Hopefully, Deja Shoe won't be stepped on in the process.[38] ■

● MANAGING COMPANY ETHICS AND SOCIAL RESPONSIBILITY

Many managers are concerned with improving the ethical climate and social responsiveness of their companies. They do not want to be surprised or be forced into an obstructionist or defensive position. As one expert on the topic of ethics said, "Management is responsible for creating and sustaining conditions in which people are likely to behave themselves."[39] Managers must take active steps to ensure that the company stays on an ethical footing. Management methods for helping organizations be more responsible include leadership by example, codes of ethics, ethical structures, and supporting whistle-blowers.

LEADERSHIP BY EXAMPLE.   The Business Roundtable, an association of chief executives from 250 large corporations, issued a report on ethics policy and practice in companies such as Boeing, Chemical Bank, General Mills, GTE, Xerox, Johnson & Johnson, and Hewlett-Packard.[40] The report concluded that no point emerged more clearly than the crucial role of top management. The chief executive officer and senior managers need to be openly and strongly committed to ethical conduct. They must give constant leadership in renewing the ethical values of the organization. They must be active in communicating that commitment in speeches, directives, company publications, and especially in actions. The same standards should be applied by owners of small businesses. Regardless of the size of the business, top managers must set the tone of the organization by the example of their behavior.

CODE OF ETHICS.   A **code of ethics** is a formal statement of the company's values concerning ethics and social issues; it communicates to employees what the company stands for. Codes of ethics tend to exist in two types: principle-based statements and policy-based statements. *Principle-based statements* are designed to affect corporate culture, define fundamental values, and contain general language about company responsibilities, quality of products, and treatment of employees. General statements of principle are often called *corporate credos*. Examples are GTE's "Vision and Values," Johnson & Johnson's "The Credo," and Hewlett-Packard's "The HP Way."[41]

Policy-based statements generally outline the procedures to be used in specific ethical situations. These situations include marketing practice, conflicts of interest, observance of laws, proprietary information, political gifts, and equal opportunities. Examples of policy-based statements are Boeing's "Business Conduct Guidelines," Chemical Bank's "Code of Ethics," GTE's "Code of Business Ethics" and "Anti-Trust and Conflict of Interest Guidelines," and Norton's "Norton Policy on Business Ethics."[42]

Codes of ethics state the values or behaviors that are expected and those that will not be tolerated, backed up by management's action. Without top management support, there is little insurance that the code will be followed.

ETHICAL STRUCTURES.   Ethical structures represent the various systems, positions, and programs a company can undertake to implement ethical behavior. An **ethics committee** is a group of executives appointed to oversee company ethics. The committee provides rulings on questionable ethical issues. The ethics committee assumes responsibility for disciplining wrongdoers, which is essential if the organization is to directly influence employee behavior. For example, Boeing has an ethics

code of ethics

A formal statement of the organization's values regarding ethics and social issues.

ethics committee

A group of executives assigned to oversee the organization's ethics by ruling on questionable issues and disciplining violators.

ethics ombudsman

An official given the responsibility of corporate conscience who hears and investigates ethics complaints and points out potential ethical failures to top management.

committee of senior managers that reports directly to the board of directors. An **ethics ombudsman** is an official given the responsibility of corporate conscience who hears and investigates ethical complaints and points out potential ethics failures to top management. Pitney Bowes has an ethics ombudsman and offers training seminars and a conduct guide on ethics for employees.

Other structures are ethics training programs and hot lines. For example, Chemical Bank has extensive education programs. All new employees attend an orientation session at which they read and sign off on Chemical's code of ethics. Another part of the program provides vice-presidents with training in ethical decision making.[43] The bank has several other seminars, and the CEO is personally involved by stating his commitment to ethical behavior. A hot line is a toll-free number to which employees can report questionable behavior as well as possible fraud, waste, or abuse. For example, Boeing has a toll-free number for employees to report any kind of ethical violation. LTV Corporation uses a hot line to supplement existing procedures for reporting violations. No reprisals will be taken against anyone using it.

A strong ethics program is important, but it is no guarantee against lapses. Dow Corning, whose faulty silicone breast implants shocked the business community, pioneered an ethics program that was looked on as a model. Established in the mid-1970s, Dow's ambitious ethics program included the Business Conduct committee, training programs, regular reviews and audits to monitor compliance, and reports to the Audit and Social Responsibility committee. What went wrong? The ethics program dealt with the overall environment, but specific programs such as product safety were handled through normal channels—in this case the Medical Device Business Board, which wanted further safety studies.[44] Dow Corning's problems sent a warning to other industries. It is not enough to *have* an impressive ethics program. The ethics program must be merged with day-to-day operations, encouraging ethical decisions to be made throughout the company.

whistle-blowing

The disclosure by an employee of illegal, immoral, or illegitimate practices by the organization.

WHISTLE-BLOWING.   Employee disclosure of illegal, immoral, or illegitimate practices on the employer's part is called **whistle-blowing.**[45] Anyone in the organization can blow the whistle if he or she detects illegal or immoral organizational activities. Whistle-blowers often report wrongdoings to outsiders, such as regulatory agencies, senators, representatives, or newspaper reporters. In enlightened companies, whistle-blowers can also report to an ethics advocate or ethics committee.

Whistle-blowers must be protected if this is to be an effective ethical safeguard; otherwise, they will suffer and the company may continue its unethical or illegal activity. Helen Guercil noticed something peculiar when she went to work as a secretary to the bankruptcy court of Detroit. The multimillion-dollar cases seemed to be heard by the same judge and handled by the same attorneys. She discovered that one lawyer had been awarded $400,000 in bankruptcy fees from this judge. She blew the whistle when she discovered evidence of special favors bought with lavish trips, expensive gifts, and on-the-job sex. An investigation led to the retirement of two judges, the indictment of the chief clerk, and the conviction of the attorney who had been awarded all the money. However, Helen Guercil received a lot of pressure on the job and was eventually fired.[46]

● DO GOOD CITIZENS FINISH FIRST?

The relationship of a corporation's social responsibility to its financial performance concerns both managers and management scholars and has generated a lively debate.[47] One concern of managers is whether good citizenship will hurt performance—after all, ethics programs cost money. A number of studies have been undertaken to determine whether heightened ethical and social responsiveness increases or decreases financial performance. Studies have provided varying results but generally have found that there is a small positive relationship between social responsibility and financial performance.[48] These findings are very encouraging, because they mean that use of resources for the social good does not hurt the company.

A related finding is that firms founded on spiritual values usually perform very well. These firms succeed because they have a clear mission, employees seldom have alcohol and drug problems, and a strong family orientation exists. One of the largest and most successful companies is Chick-fil-A, Inc., which refuses to open on Sunday. The Sunday closing costs some sales and has gotten the chain frozen out of some shopping malls, but the policy helps attract excellent workers, and this offsets any disadvantages.[49]

The important point is that being ethical and socially responsible does not hurt a firm. Enlightened firms can use their discretion to contribute to society's welfare and, in so doing, improve performance.

Rohm & Haas Company believes success can be measured in many categories that do not show in financial statements. An example is the smile on the face of this child, a participant in the company-sponsored Houston Handicapped Kids Day program. The annual event brings together disabled children and their families for a day of supervised play and activities, generating long-lasting positive impact.

SUMMARY AND MANAGEMENT SOLUTION ●

Ethics and social responsibility are hot topics for managers in the 1990s. One study reported that 45 percent of America's 1,000 largest companies entered the 1990s with established ethics programs or workshops, and the percentage was expected to increase.[50] The ethical domain of behavior pertains to values of right and wrong. Ethical decisions and behavior are typically guided by a value system. Four value-based approaches that serve as criteria for ethical decision making are utilitarian, individualism, moral rights, and justice. For an individual manager, the ability to make correct ethical choices will depend on both individual and organizational characteristics. An important individual characteristic is level of moral development. Corporate culture is an organizational characteristic that influences ethical behavior.

Corporate social responsibility concerns a company's values toward society. How can organizations be good corporate citizens? The model for evaluating social performance uses four criteria: economic, legal, ethical, and discretionary. Organizations may use four types of response to specific social pressures: obstructive, defensive, accommodative, and proactive. Evaluating corporate social behavior often requires assessing its impact on organizational stakeholders. Techniques for improving social responsiveness include leadership, codes of ethics, ethical structures, and whistle-blowing. Companies that are socially responsible perform as well as—and often better than—companies that are not socially responsible.

W. Mark Baty's conviction was firm; you don't lie to a banker. However, given his commitment to make his business work, he had another equally solid viewpoint which was to not reveal personal or credit card obligations. He certainly considered his handling of his receivables and payables to be nobody's business but his own. Chicken and egg analogies aside, Baty based his presentation on the moral certainty that he had the customer who would generate enough revenue to pay the debt on the truck. Baty was granted the loan and paid it off. By his perspective, he misled no one and misrepresented nothing in writing. He engaged in something that occurs every day in the business world.[51]

DISCUSSION QUESTIONS

1. Dr. Martin Luther King, Jr., said, "As long as there is poverty in the world, I can never be rich. . . . As long as diseases are rampant, I can never be healthy. . . . I can never be what I ought to be until you are what you ought to be." Discuss this quote with respect to the material in this chapter. Would this be true for corporations, too?

2. Environmentalists are trying to pass laws for oil spills that would remove all liability limits for the oil companies. This would punish corporations financially. Is this the best way to influence companies to be socially responsible?

3. Compare and contrast the utilitarian approach with the moral-rights approach to ethical decision making. Which do you believe is the best for managers to follow? Why?

4. Imagine yourself being encouraged to inflate your expense account. Do you think your choice would be most affected by your individual moral development or by the cultural values of the company for which you worked? Explain.

5. Is it socially responsible for organizations to undertake political activity or join with others in a trade association to influence the government? Discuss.

6. The criteria of corporate social responsibility suggest that economic responsibilities are of the greatest magnitude, followed by legal, ethi-

cal, and discretionary responsibilities. How do these four types of responsibility relate to corporate responses to social demands? Discuss.

7. From where do managers derive ethical values? What can managers do to help define ethical standards for the corporation?

8. Have you ever experienced an ethical dilemma? Evaluate the dilemma with respect to its impact on other people.

9. Lincoln Electric considers customers and employees to be more important stakeholders than shareholders. Is it appropriate for management to define some stakeholders as more important than others? Should all stakeholders be considered equal?

10. Do you think a code of ethics combined with an ethics committee would be more effective than leadership for implementing ethical behavior? Discuss.

MANAGEMENT IN PRACTICE: EXPERIENTIAL EXERCISE

● ETHICAL WORK CLIMATES

Answer the following questions by circling the number that best describes an organization for which you have worked.

	Disagree				Agree
1. What is the best for everyone in the company is the major consideration here.	1	2	3	4	5
2. Our major concern is always what is best for the other person.	1	2	3	4	5
3. People are expected to comply with the law and professional standards over and above other considerations.	1	2	3	4	5
4. In this company, the first consideration is whether a decision violates any law.	1	2	3	4	5
5. It is very important to follow the company's rules and procedures here.	1	2	3	4	5
6. People in this company strictly obey the company policies.	1	2	3	4	5
7. In this company, people are mostly out for themselves.	1	2	3	4	5
8. People are expected to do anything to further the company's interests, regardless of the consequences.	1	2	3	4	5
9. In this company, people are guided by their own personal ethics.	1	2	3	4	5
10. Each person in this company decides for himself or herself what is right and wrong.	1	2	3	4	5

Total Score _____

Add up your score. These questions measure the dimensions of an organization's ethical climate. Questions 1 and 2 measure caring for people, questions 3 and 4 measure lawfulness, questions 5 and 6 measure rules adherence, questions 7 and 8 measure emphasis on financial and company performance, and questions 9 and 10 measure individual independence. Questions 7 and 8 are reverse scored. A total score above 40 indicates a very positive ethical climate. A score from 30 to 40 indicates above-average ethical climate. A score from 20 to 30 indicates a below-average ethical cli-

mate, and a score below 20 indicates a very poor ethical climate.

Go back over the questions and think about changes that you could have made to improve the ethical climate in the organization. Discuss with other students what you could do as a manager to improve ethics in future companies you work for.

SOURCE: Based on Bart Victor and John B. Cullen, "The Organizational Bases of Ethical Work Climates," *Administrative Science Quarterly* 33 (1988), 101–125.

CASE FOR ANALYSIS ●

CLAYTON HOMES, INC.

James Lee Clayton is a swashbuckling entrepreneur who is used to making his own decisions. His company, Clayton Homes, Inc., has been a cash-cow juggernaut for nearly 15 years. Sales and earnings for the Knoxville, Tennessee, mobile-home manufacturing company have increased every year since 1980. Between 1990 and 1993 Clayton Homes stock rose more than 400 percent. However, an incident which at first seemed like an incidental ripple threatened to turn into a tidal wave.

The Tennessee Department of Revenue began to investigate the company's failure to pay certain sales taxes. An internal investigation by a reputable law firm and Arthur Anderson & Company was ordered. The plot thickened two months later when the internal investigation was abruptly suspended. Then, two outside directors tendered identical resignations alluding to problems unrelated to the tax matter about which the company board was already aware. Amidst this backdrop of intrigue and innuendo, a partnership owned by Clayton and his mother sued former Clayton Homes employee Warren Schede in civil court. The action not only blamed Schede for the tax oversights, but also alleged that he was an embezzler. A criminal investigation was launched as a result of this allegation.

Informed observers are convinced that there is no smoking gun anywhere, but they do believe Clayton Homes has problems. James Clayton devotes most of his time to the retail end of his business. "As the company got larger and larger," he says, "I wasn't that close to it." Schede was. As retail division controller he was charged with overseeing 143 sales outlets. He was assisted by a staff of only two other accountants. "Jim Clayton doesn't have a lot of use for accountants," says Michael Heffner, a former company accountant. "He thinks of them as overhead."

Clayton now acknowledges that Schede was given too much operational latitude and not enough supervision. The investigation revealed Schede also directed a good deal of Clayton's personal finances. A former employee, Jerry

Eldridge, described the level of involvement as "so entangled with the payroll and paperwork [of the company] that we couldn't separate it out."

Despite assurances from the company that the situation was well in hand, Wall Street took the news of the suspended investigation badly. In a week's time, Clayton Homes saw 18 percent of its share price lopped off even though earnings remained healthy. Clayton believed the law and accounting firms were setting their sights on executives of the company instead of trying to uncover how Schede allegedly either misdirected, or simply failed to pay, company funds. He griped he had spent hundreds of thousands of dollars and couldn't get the lawyers to deliver a report.

In the final analysis, Clayton fell victim, and as a result victimized shareholders, to a shortcoming common to hard-charging entrepreneurs. As growth mushroomed, he failed to implement the structure and controls necessary to keep account of it. The company has appointed two more outside directors, and quickly voted to begin reinvestigating the tax problems, with yet another law firm. "We can get this behind us," said new director James D. Cockman.

● QUESTIONS

1. What steps could Clayton have taken to ensure that his company maintained an ethical position? Is he ultimately to blame for the company's problems?
2. Do you think the company could benefit from ethical structures? What type?
3. How can Clayton repair the company's tarnished image?

SOURCE: Laurie M. Grossman, "Investigations Jolt Mobile Home Firm Jim Clayton Built," *The Wall Street Journal*, August 30, 1993, A1, A5.

REFERENCES

1. John Case, "Honest Business," *INC.*, January 1990, 65–69.

2. John A. Byrne, "Businesses Are Signing Up for Ethics 101," *Business Week*, February 15, 1988, 56–57.

3. Kevin Kelly and Eric Schine, "How Did Sears Blow This Gasket?" *Business Week*, June 29, 1992, 38; and David Dishneau, "Use of Sales Commissions under Scrutiny," *The State*, Columbia, S.C., July 17, 1992, 12B.

4. Edwin M. Raingold, "America's Hamburger Helper," *Time*, June 29, 1992, 66–67; Laura Zinn, "Whales, Human Rights, Rainforest—and the Heady Smell of Profits," *Business Week*, July 15, 1991, 114–115; Michael Schrofer and Jonathan Kapstein, "Charity Doesn't Begin at Home Anymore," *Business Week*, February 25, 1991, 91; Kenneth Labich, "The New Crisis in Business Ethics," *Fortune*, April 20, 1992, 167–176; and Marge Marjcharlier, "Life after Asbestos: Manville Tries to Build New Identity as a Firm Keen on Environment," *The Wall Street Journal*, May 31, 1990, A1, A9.

5. Gordon F. Shea, *Practical Ethics* (New York: American Management Association, 1988); and Linda K. Trevino, "Ethical Decision Making in Organizations; A Person-Situation Interactionist Model," *Academy of Management Review* 11 (1986), 601–617.

6. Thomas M. Jones, "Ethical Decision Making by Individuals in Organizations: An Issue-Contingent Model," *Academy of Management Review* 16 (1991), 366–395.

7. Rushworth M. Kidder, "The Three Great Domains of Human Action," *Christian Science Monitor*, January 30, 1990.

8. Jones, "Ethical Decision Making."

9. This discussion is based on Gerald F. Cavanagh, Dennis J. Moberg, and Manuel Velasquez, "The Ethics of Organizational Politics," *Academy of Management Review* 6 (1981), 363–374; and Justin G. Longenecker, Joseph A. McKinney, and Carlos W. Moore, "Egoism and Independence: Entrepreneurial Ethics," *Organizational Dynamics* (Winter 1988), 64–72.

10. Zachary Schiller, Walecia Conrad, and Stephanie Anderson Forest, "If You Light Up on Sunday Don't Come in on Monday," *Business Week*, August 26, 1992, 68–72.

11. Ron Winslow, "Rationing Care," *The Wall Street Journal*, November 13, 1989, R24.

12. Alan Wong and Eugene Beckman, "An Applied Ethical Analysis System in Business," *Journal of Business Ethics* 11 (1992), 173–178.

13. John Kekes, "Self-Direction: The Core of Ethical Individualism," *Organizations and Ethical Individualism*, ed. Konstanian Kolenda (New York: Praeger, 1988), 1–18.

14. Tad Tulega, *Beyond the Bottom Line* (New York: Penguin Books, 1987).

15. Suzanne Woolley, "Neither Fish nor Fowl—But Some Call It Foul," *Business Week*, January 25, 1993, 75.

16. This discussion is based on Trevino, "Ethical Decision Making in Organizations."

17. L. Kohlberg, "Moral Stages and Moralization: The Cognitive-Developmental Approach," in *Moral Development and Behavior: Theory, Research, and Social*

Issues, ed. T. Lickona (New York: Holt, Rinehart & Winston, 1976); and L. Kohlberg, "Stage and Sequence: The Cognitive-Developmental Approach to Socialization," in *Handbook of Socialization Theory and Research,* ed. D. A. Goslin (Chicago: Rand McNally, 1969).

18. Alan Wong and Eugene Beckman, "An Applied Ethical Analysis System in Business," *Journal of Business Ethics* 11 (1992), 173–178; and Kent Hodgson, "Adapting Ethical Decisions to a Global Marketplace," *Management Review,* May 1992, 53–57.

19. This discussion is based on Linda Klebe Trevino, "A Cultural Perspective on Changing and Developing Organizational Ethics," in *Research and Organizational Change and Development,* ed. R. Woodman and W. Pasmore (Greenwich, Conn.: JAI Press, 1990), 4.

20. Ibid.; John B. Cullen, Bart Victor, and Carroll Stephens, "An Ethical Weather Report: Assessing the Organization's Ethical Climate," *Organizational Dynamics* (Autumn 1989), 50–62; and Bart Victor and John B. Cullen, "The Organizational Bases of Ethical Work Climates," *Administrative Science Quarterly* 33 (1988), 101–125.

21. Eugene W. Szwajkowski, "The Myths and Realities of Research on Organizational Misconduct," in *Research in Corporate Social Performance and Policy,* ed. James E. Post (Greenwich, Conn.: JAI Press, 1986), 9:103–122; and Keith Davis, William C. Frederick, and Robert L. Blostrom, *Business and Society: Concepts and Policy Issues* (New York: McGraw-Hill, 1979).

22. Douglas S. Sherwin, "The Ethical Roots of the Business System," *Harvard Business Review* 61 (November–December 1983), 183–192.

23. Nancy C. Roberts and Paul J. King, "The Stakeholder Audit Goes Public," *Organizational Dynamics* (Winter 1989), 63–79.

24. Minda Zetlin, "Companies Find Profit in Corporate Giving," *Management Review* (December 1990), 10–15.

25. Jane Salodof, "Public Schools and the Business Community: An Uneasy Marriage," *Management Review* (January 1989), 31–37.

26. Joseph Weber, "Meet DuPont's 'In-house' Conscience," *Business Week,* June 29, 1991, 62–65.

27. Caleb Solomon, "Big Payoff: How a Neighborhood Talked Fina Refinery into Buying It Out," *The Wall Street Journal,* January 10, 1991, A1, A8.

28. Archie B. Carroll, "A Three-Dimensional Conceptual Model of Corporate Performance," *Academy of Management Review* 4 (1979), 497–505.

29. Milton Friedman, *Capitalism and Freedom* (Chicago: University of Chicago Press, 1962), 133; and Milton Friedman and Rose Friedman, *Free to Choose* (New York: Harcourt Brace Jovanovich, 1979).

30. Bruce Hager, "What's behind Business' Sudden Fervor for Ethics?" *Business Week,* September 23, 1991, 65.

31. Eugene W. Szwajkowski, "Organizational Illegality: Theoretical Integration and Illustrative Application," *Academy of Management Review* 10 (1985), 558–567.

32. David J. Fritzsche and Helmut Becker, "Linking Management Behavior to Ethical Philosophy—An Empirical Investigation," *Academy of Management Journal* 27 (1984), 165–175.

33. James J. Chrisman and Archie B. Carroll, "Corporate Responsibility—Reconciling Economic and Social Goals," *Sloan Management Review* 25 (Winter 1984), 59–65.

34. Frances Huffman, "The Gift of Giving," *Entrepreneur*, November 1990, 147–154.

35. Elizabeth Gatewood and Archie B. Carroll, "The Anatomy of Corporate Social Response: The Rely, Firestone 500, and Pinto Cases," *Business Horizons* 24 (September–October 1981), 9–16.

36. John Kenneth Galbraith, "Behind the Wall," *New York Review of Books,* April 10, 1986, 11–13.

37. Milton R. Moskowitz, "Company Performance Roundup," *Business and Society Review* 53 (Spring 1985), 74–77.

38. Janet Falon, "Earth Shoes," *Business Ethics,* November–December 1993, 12.

39. Saul W. Gellerman, "Managing Ethics from the Top Down," *Sloan Management Review* (Winter 1989), 73–79.

40. "Corporate Ethics: A Prime Business Asset," The Business Roundtable, 200 Park Avenue, Suite 2222, New York, N.Y. 10166, February 1988.

41. Ibid.

42. Ibid.

43. Patrick E. Murphy, "Creating Ethical Corporate Structure," *Sloan Management Review* (Winter 1989), 81–87.

44. John A. Byrne, "The Best Laid Ethics Programs . . . ," *Business Week,* March 9, 1992, 67–69.

45. Marcia Parmarlee Miceli and Janet P. Near, "The Relationship among Beliefs, Organizational Positions, and Whistle-Blowing Status: A Discriminant Analysis," *Academy of Management Journal* 27 (1984), 687–705.

46. Clair Safran, "Women Who Blew the Whistle," *Good Housekeeping,* April 1985, 25, 216–219.

47. Philip L. Cochran and Robert A. Wood, "Corporate Social Responsibility and Financial Performance," *Academy of Management Journal* 27 (1984), 42–56.

48. Jean B. McGuire, Alison Sundgren, and Thomas Schneeweis, "Corporate Social Responsibility and Firm Financial Performance," *Academy of Management Journal* 31 (1988), 854–872.

49. Roger Ricklefs, "Christian-Based Firms Find Following Principles Pays," *The Wall Street Journal,* December 8, 1989, B1; and Jo David and Karen File, "Saintly Companies That Make Heavenly Profits," *Working Woman,* October 1989, 122–126, 169–175.

50. Hager, "What's behind Business' Sudden Fervor for Ethics?"

51. John Case, "Honest Business," *INC.,* January 1990, 65–69.

ORGANIZATIONAL GOAL SETTING AND PLANNING

6

CHAPTER OUTLINE

LEARNING OBJECTIVES

After studying this chapter, you should be able to

- Define goals and plans and explain the relationship between them.
- Explain the concept of organizational mission and how it influences goal setting and planning.
- Describe the four essential steps in the MBO process.
- Describe business-level strategies including Porter's competitive forces and product life cycle.
- Explain the major considerations in formulating functional strategies.
- Describe the planning necessary to undertake a new business

Jeffrey Clements was president of Miller Fluid Power, which was worth $45 million when it was bought by a Japanese firm. He left after management styles clashed, and a year and a half later found himself talking with principals of Discovery Zone, a children's fitness center franchiser. Besides the $35,000 for the franchise, as much as $500,000 could be required for equipment, training, and working capital. Clements had several other considerations notwithstanding the significant step of betting his house on the business. He had always been used to making his own decisions. However, with Discovery Zone, he would be buying prearranged business concepts, operations, training methods, and marketing and business systems. He could make suggestions, but he would still have to toe the company line. Clements was also unsure about how this situation would be for a former top executive. If you were Clements would you choose franchising as a means for starting your own business? What factors should he consider in developing his business plan?[1] ■ Clements' situation is not unusual. A growing number of executives are leaving the corporate world to start their own businesses. However, planning is essential even in existing businesses. One of the responsibilities of management is to decide where they want the organization to be in the future and

how to get it there.

In some organizations, typically small ones, planning is informal. In others, managers follow a well-defined planning framework. The company establishes a basic mission and develops formal goals and strategic plans for carrying it out. Shell, Mazda, and United Way undertake a strategic planning exercise each year of reviewing their missions, goals, and plans to meet environmental changes or the expectations of important stake-holders such as the community, owners, or stockholders.

Of the four management functions—planning, organizing, leading, and controlling—described in Chapter 1, planning is considered the most important. Everything else stems from planning. Yet planning is also the most controversial management function. Planning cannot read an uncertain future. Planning cannot tame a turbulent environment.

● OVERVIEW OF GOALS AND PLANS

goal

A desired future state that the organization attempts to realize.

plan

A blueprint specifying the resource allocations, schedules, and other actions necessary for attaining goals.

planning

The act of determining the organization's goals and the means for achieving them.

Goals and plans have become general concepts in our society. A **goal** is a desired future state that the organization attempts to realize.[2] Goals are important because organizations exist for a purpose and goals define and state that purpose. A **plan** is a blueprint for goal achievement and specifies the necessary resource allocations, schedules, tasks, and other actions. Goals specify future ends; plans specify today's means. The word **planning** usually incorporates both ideas; it means determining the organization's goals and defining the means for achieving them. Planning is critical not only to any entrepreneurial venture, but also to established companies. Entrepreneurs will increase the potential for success by adhering to a series of planning steps.

● STARTING AN ENTREPRENEURIAL FIRM

For people who decide that the benefits of entrepreneurship are worth pursuing, the first step is to start with a viable idea for the new venture. With the new idea in mind, a business plan must be drawn and decisions made about legal structure, financing, and basic tactics, such as whether to start the business from scratch and whether to pursue international opportunities from the start.

NEW-BUSINESS IDEA

To some people, the idea for a new business is the easy part. They do not even consider entrepreneurship until they are inspired by an exciting idea. Other people decide they want to run their own business and set about looking for an idea or opportunity. In a 1989 survey of 500 fast-growing firms in the United States, 43 percent of business founders got their idea from work experience in the industry or profession. A few entrepreneurs believed they could do something better, and 11 percent saw an unfilled niche in the marketplace.[3]

The trick for entrepreneurs is to blend their own skills and experience with a need in the marketplace. Acting strictly on one's own skills may produce something no one wants to buy. On the other hand, finding a market niche that you do not have the ability to fill does not work either. Both personal skill and market need typically must be present. For example, single-parent and two-earner households have led some entrepreneurs to use their skills to provide services that meet a need for people short of time. Reunion Time, Inc., arranges high-school reunions, contracting to track down alumni. Moment's Notice Cuisine delivers meals to the homes of its customers who are willing to pay 20 percent over the restaurant price.[4] Jean Griswold, a minister's wife, tried to find volunteers to help elderly parishioners. She had little luck until she realized the old folks would pay for help. She created Special Care, Inc., to hire students to do the work. It is now a $10 million business. She saw the need and had the skill to fill it.[5]

THE BUSINESS PLAN

Once an entrepreneur is inspired by a new-business idea, careful planning is crucial. A **business plan** is a document specifying the business details prepared by an entrepreneur in preparation for opening a new business. Planning forces the entrepreneur to carefully think through all of the issues and problems associated with starting and developing the business. Most entrepreneurs have to borrow money, and a business plan is absolutely critical to persuading lenders and investors to participate in the business.

The details of business plans may vary, but a typical business plan contains much of the following.

■ Mission or vision of the company.

■ Information about the industry and market.

■ Information about suppliers.

■ Information about the number and types of personnel needed.

■ Financial information spelling out the sources and uses of start-up funds and operating funds.

■ Plans for production of the product or service, including layout of the physical plant and production schedules.

■ The business's policy for extending credit to customers.

■ Legal considerations, such as information about licenses, patents, taxes, and compliance with government regulations.

■ Critical risks that may threaten business success.

The business plan should indicate where the product or service fits into the overall industry and should draw on concepts described in other parts of this book. For example, Porter's competitive strategies (page 185) describe the strategies that entrepreneurs can use. Other concepts, such as the breakeven point (Appendix B), income statements, and balance sheets (Chapter 17) are also helpful in developing the business plan. Detailed suggestions for writing a business plan are provided in the Manager's Shoptalk box.

business plan

A document specifying the business details prepared by an entrepreneur in preparation for opening a new business.

HINTS FOR WRITING THE BUSINESS PLAN

THE SUMMARY

■ Should have no more than three pages.
■ Is the most crucial part of your plan because it must capture the reader's interest.
■ Summarize what, how, why, where, etc.
■ Complete this part *after* the final draft of the business plan has been written.

THE BUSINESS DESCRIPTION SEGMENT

■ The name of the business is stated.
■ A background of the industry with history of the company (if any) should be covered here.
■ The potential of the new venture should be described clearly.
■ Any unique or distinctive features of the venture should be spelled out.

THE MARKETING SEGMENT

■ Convince investors that sales projections and competition can be met.
■ Use and disclose market studies.
■ Identify target market, market position, and market share.
■ Evaluate *all* competition and specifically cover "why" and "how" you will be better than the competitors.
■ Identify all market sources and assistance used for this segment.
■ Demonstrate pricing strategy, because your price must penetrate and maintain a market share to *produce profits*. Thus "lowest" price is *not* necessarily the "best" price.
■ Identify your advertising plans with cost estimates to validate the proposed strategy.

THE RESEARCH, DESIGN, AND DEVELOPMENT SEGMENT

■ Cover the *extent* and *costs* involved in needed research, testing, or development.
■ Explain carefully what has been accomplished *already* (prototype, lab testing, early development).
■ Mention any research or technical assistance that has been provided for you.

THE MANUFACTURING SEGMENT

■ Provide the advantages of your location (zoning, tax laws, wage rates).
■ List the production needs in terms of facilities (plant, storage, office space) and equipment (machinery, furnishings, supplies).
■ Describe the access to transportation (for shipping and receiving).
■ Explain proximity to your suppliers.
■ Mention the availability of labor in your location.
■ Provide estimates of manufacturing cost—be careful, too many entrepreneurs "underestimate" their costs.

THE MANAGEMENT SEGMENT

■ Provide resumes of all key people in the management of the venture.
■ Carefully describe the legal structure of the venture (sole proprietorship, partnership, or corporation).
■ Cover the added assistance (if any) of advisers, consultants, and directors.
■ Provide information on how everyone is to be compensated. (How much, also.)

THE CRITICAL RISKS SEGMENT

Point out potential risks *before* investors do:
■ Price cutting by competitors.
■ Potentially unfavorable industrywide trends.
■ Design or manufacturing costs in excess of estimates.
■ Sales projections not achieved.
■ Product development schedule not met.
■ Difficulties or long lead times encountered in the procurement of parts or raw materials.
■ Larger than expected innovation and development costs to stay competitive.
■ Alternative courses of action.

THE FINANCIAL SEGMENT

■ Provide statements.
■ Describe the needed sources for your funds and the uses you intend for the money.
■ Provide a budget.
■ Create stages of financing for purposes of allowing evaluation by investors at various points.

THE MILESTONE SCHEDULE SEGMENT

■ Provide a timetable to show when each phase of the venture is to be completed. This shows the relationship of events and provides a deadline for accomplishment. ■

SOURCE: Donald F. Kuratko and Ray V. Montagno, *The Entrepreneur's Guide to Venture Formation* (Center for Entrepreneurial Resources, Ball State University, 1986), 33–34. Reprinted with permission.

LEGAL FORM

Before entrepreneurs have founded a business, and perhaps again as it expands, they must choose an appropriate legal structure for the company. The three basic choices are proprietorship, partnership, or corporation. A discussion of each type follows.

PROPRIETORSHIP. A **proprietorship** is defined as an unincorporated business owned by an individual for profit. Proprietorships make up 70 percent of the 16 million businesses in the United States. The popularity of this form comes from the fact that it is easy to start and has few legal requirements. A proprietor has total ownership and control of the company and can make all decisions without consulting anyone. However, this type of organization also has drawbacks. The owner has unlimited liability for the business, meaning that if someone sues, the owner's personal as well as business assets are at risk. Also, financing can be harder to obtain because business success rests on one person's shoulders.

proprietorship
An unincorporated business owned by an individual for profit.

PARTNERSHIP. A **partnership** is an unincorporated business owned by two or more people. Partnerships, like proprietorships, are relatively easy to start. Two friends may reach an agreement to start a pet store. To avoid misunderstandings and to make sure the business is well planned, it is wise to draw up and sign a formal partnership agreement with the help of an attorney. The agreement specifies how partners are to share responsibility and resources and how they will contribute their expertise. The disadvantages of partnerships are the unlimited liability of the partners and the disagreements that almost always occur between strong-minded people. A 1992 poll by *INC.* magazine illustrated the volatility of partnerships. Fifty-nine percent of respondents considered partnerships a bad business move, citing reasons such as partner problems and conflicts. Partnerships often dissolve within five years. Respondents who liked partnerships point to the equality of partners (sharing of workload and emotional and financial burdens) as the key to a successful partnership.[6]

partnership
An unincorporated business owned by two or more people.

CORPORATION. A **corporation** is an artificial entity created by the state and existing apart from its owners. As a separate legal entity, the corporation is liable for its actions and must pay taxes on its income. Unlike other forms of ownership, the corporation has a legal life of its own; it continues to exist regardless of whether the owners live or die. And the corporation, not the owners, is sued in the case of liability. Thus continuity and limits on owners' liability are two principal advantages of forming a corporation. For example, a physician can form a corporation so that liability for malpractice will not affect his or her personal assets. The major disadvantage of the corporation is that it is expensive and complex to do the paperwork required to incorporate the business and to keep the records required by law. When proprietorships and partnerships are successful and grow large, they often incorporate to limit liability and to raise funds through the sale of stock to investors.

corporation
An artificial entity created by the state and existing apart from its owners.

FINANCIAL RESOURCES

A crucial concern for entrepreneurs is the financing of the business. An investment is usually required to acquire labor and raw materials and perhaps a building and equipment. The financing decision initially involves two options—whether to obtain loans that must be repaid (debt financing) or whether to share ownership (equity financing). A survey of successful growth businesses asked "How much money was needed to launch the company?" Approximately one-third were started on less than $10,000, one-third needed from $10,000 to $50,000, and one-third needed more than $50,000. The primary source of this money was the entrepreneurs' own resources, but they often had to mortgage their home, borrow money from the bank, or give part of the business to a venture capitalist.[7]

DEBT FINANCING.   Borrowing money that has to be repaid to start a business is **debt financing.** One common source of debt financing for a start-up is to borrow from family and friends. Another common source is a bank loan. Banks provide some 25 percent of all financing for small business. Sometimes entrepreneurs can obtain money from a finance company, wealthy individuals, or potential customers.

Another form of loan financing is provided by the Small Business Administration (SBA). The SBA supplies direct loans to some entrepreneurs who are unable to get bank financing because they are considered high risk. The SBA's guaranteed loan program promises to repay the bank loan if the entrepreneur defaults. Bruce Burdick owns six Computer Land franchises in Kansas City and would not have gotten started without the guaranteed loan program. The SBA is especially helpful for people without substantial assets, providing an opportunity for single parents, minority group members, and others with a good idea. However, as the following example illustrates, qualifying for an SBA-backed loan requires careful preparation.

debt financing

Borrowing money that has to be repaid in order to start a business.

 LAGNIAPPE

After the business plan had been polished and all the financial projections and potential scenarios mapped and rechecked, Margi Showers and Caren Christensen had one more hurdle to clear before launching their new retail venture, Lagniappe. It was an important hurdle, and they were both pretty nervous.

Across the desk at their 10:00 A.M. meeting, West Bank lending officer Michele Gregory turned straight to the numbers in the 71-page bound plan as the two entrepreneurs alternated explaining their retail gift-shop concept. Gregory interrupted frequently with queries, and ended the meeting complimenting the written presentation, and noting, "You'll need more money for advertising, and your sales figures seem too high." Gregory said she would see the entrepreneurs in a week.

At the next meeting, the banker had a list that required clarification. Gregory mentioned that she approves less than half the funding applications she receives. After a long perusal of the newly furnished data she looked up, paused, then said, "Let's do it."

Lagniappe qualified for the SBA-guaranteed loan and began doing business because Showers and Christensen presented not only projected cash flow, but also some what-if scenarios. They kept projections realistic, and consulted the local Small Business Development Center for expert advice. Finally, instead of making a bare-bones request for funds, they presented one that would adequately provide for the needs of the business.[8] ■

EQUITY FINANCING.   Any money invested by owners or by those who purchase stock in a corporation is considered equity funds. **Equity financing** consists of funds that are invested in exchange for ownership in the company. When a corporation's stock is sold only to friends and relatives, this is called a *private stock sale*. When the stock is available for sale to the general public, it is known as a *public sale*. For new businesses, a public sale is not a viable option because the company is not yet profitable. Once the business prospers, the company can sell stock publicly, providing a large financial windfall for the owner.

A **venture capital firm** is a group of companies or individuals that invests money in new or expanding businesses for ownership and potential profits. This is a potential form of capital for businesses with high earning and growth possibilities. Venture capital firms want new businesses with an extremely high rate of return, but in return the venture capitalist will provide assistance, advice, and information to help the entrepreneur prosper. A venture capital firm often has tens or hundreds of millions of dollars available for investment. Venture capitalists learn to spot promising businesses. The strength of the individual entrepreneur should not be underestimated. A survey indicated that venture capital firms bet on the person as well as the business.

equity financing

Financing that consists of funds that are invested in exchange for ownership in the company.

venture capital firm

A group of companies or individuals that invests money in new or expanding businesses for a share of ownership and potential profits.

TACTICS

There are several ways that an aspiring entrepreneur can become a business owner. These include starting a new business from scratch, buying an existing business, or starting a franchise. Other entrepreneurial tactics include participation in a business incubator, being a spin-off of a large corporation, or pursuing international markets from the beginning.

START A NEW BUSINESS.   One of the most common ways to become an entrepreneur is to start a new business from scratch. This is exciting because the entrepreneur sees a need for a product or service that has not been filled before and then sees the idea or dream become a reality. The advantage of this approach is the ability to develop and design the business in the entrepreneur's own way. The entrepreneur is solely responsible for its success. A potential disadvantage is the long time it can take to get the business off the ground and make it profitable. The uphill battle is caused by the lack of established clientele and the many mistakes made by someone new to the business. Moreover, no matter how much planning is done, a start-up is risky; there is no guarantee that the new idea will work.

BUY AN EXISTING BUSINESS.   Because of the long start-up time and the inevitable mistakes, some entrepreneurs prefer to reduce risk by purchasing an existing business. This offers the advantage of a shorter time to get started and an existing track record. The entrepreneur may get a bargain price if the owner wishes to retire or has other family

Entrepreneur Adam Brown found his market niche in 1989, when he *started a new business called* Health Yourself, a fitness equipment retailer. Bolstered by a growing trend toward people working out at home instead of the health club, Health Yourself is experiencing robust sales.

considerations. Moreover, a new business may overwhelm an entrepreneur with the amount of work to be done and procedures to be established. An established business already has filing systems, a payroll tax system, and other operating procedures. Potential disadvantages are the need to pay for goodwill that the owner believes exists and the possible existence of ill will toward the business. In addition, the company may have bad habits and procedures or outdated technology, which may be why the business is for sale.

BUY A FRANCHISE.   Franchising is perhaps the most rapidly growing path to entrepreneurship. Over 500,000 franchisees operate businesses in the United States. **Franchising** is an arrangement by which the owner of a product or service allows others to purchase the right to distribute the product or service with help from the owner. The franchisee invests his or her money and owns the business but does not have to develop a new product, create a new company, or test the market. The franchisee typically pays a flat fee plus a percentage of gross sales. Franchises exist for weight-loss clinics, beauty salons, computer stores, real estate offices, rental cars, and auto tune-up shops.[9] The powerful advantage of a franchise is that management help is provided by the owner. For example, Burger King does not want a franchisee to fail and will provide the studies necessary to find a good location. The franchisor also provides an established name and national advertising to stimulate demand for the product or service. Potential disadvantages are the lack of control that occurs when franchisors want every business managed in exactly the same way. In addition, franchises can be very expensive, running as high as several hundred thousand dollars for a McDonald's restaurant. High costs are followed with monthly payments to the franchisor that can run from 2 to 12 percent of sales.

franchising

An arrangement by which the owner of a product or service allows others to purchase the right to distribute the product or service with help from the owner.

Entrepreneurs who are considering a franchise should investigate the company thoroughly. The entrepreneur is legally entitled to a copy of franchisor disclosure statements, which cover 20 areas, including lawsuits. The entrepreneur should also request information regarding franchisor assistance in selection of location, set-up costs, and securing credit. Entrepreneurs should understand under what circumstances a contract can be terminated and should obtain detailed information in areas such as the management and staff training programs provided (e.g., whether "training" is limited to the distribution of manuals).[10] Answers to such questions improve the chances for choosing a successful franchise.

It is critical to do thorough research *before* signing a franchising contract. Much of the risk in franchising lies in the inability of courts to determine "fault" in failure of the business. For example, 20 failed Florida-based Decorating Den franchises were unsuccessful in lawsuits against the company. Decorating Den, which has grown from 127 franchises to 1,200 in the decade since 1984, appeals to individuals who want to "be their own boss" and who have a "flair for decorating." Part of the appeal also lies in the perception that franchising lowers risk by offering the training, promotional help, and advice of an established company to those with no business or formal decorating training. However, Decorating Den has a 51 percent turnover rate. In the three-year period ending in 1992, 577 of 1,138 franchises were terminated. The company complies with federal guidelines for franchising. The artistic nature of the industry may account for part of the problem. Individuals entering franchises that require special skills should ask themselves additional questions. Most important, perhaps, is whether current skill level, together with training described in the company franchising literature will enable franchisees to compete with skilled decorators and deal with specific client decorating problems. Franchisees should also be aware of the amount of time required in order to turn a profit and the number of hours required. Is it possible to turn a profit while working part-time in order to be home with the kids? Answers to such questions can reduce the risk.[11]

PARTICIPATE IN A BUSINESS INCUBATOR. An attractive innovation for entrepreneurs who want to start a business from scratch is to join a business incubator. Most incubators are sponsored by government organizations to spark job creation and business development. The **business incubator** provides shared office space, management support services, and management advice to entrepreneurs. By sharing office space with other entrepreneurs, managers share information about local business, financial aid, and market opportunities. Although this innovation has been in existence only a few years, the number of business incubators nationwide jumped from 385 in 1990 to approximately 500 by January 1993.[12] What gives incubators an edge is the expertise of the in-house mentor, who serves as adviser, role model, and cheerleader for entrepreneurs. SORRA, Inc., a drug-trial company in Birmingham, Alabama, benefited from the incubation experience. While holding down start-up costs, incubation assisted owner Vally Nance in locating capital as well as a lawyer and an accountant. Nance credits incubation for

business incubator

An innovation that provides shared office space, management support services, and management advice to entrepreneurs.

helping her company to make a "transition of competence and confidence" as it moved from her home basement to the seventh floor offices of a clinic.[13]

BE A SPIN-OFF.   Spin-offs, a unique form of entrepreneurial company, were previously associated with and owe their start-up to another organization. A **spin-off** is an independent company producing a product or service similar to that produced by the entrepreneur's former employer.[14] Spin-offs occur when entrepreneurs quit their employers with a desire to produce a similar product, or in some cases produce a related product that is purchased by the former employer. The former employer may recognize that it can profit from the idea by selling patents to the spin-off and by investing in it. Employer approval is often the basis for a spin-off, although in some cases entrepreneurs start a new business because they disagree with former employers. Disagreement usually revolves around the failure of the employer to try a new idea that the entrepreneur believes in. A frustrated employee should discuss the possibility of starting a spin-off company with the support of his or her current employer. In this way, the spin-off reduces risk and has a source of management advice. The entrepreneur may also have a guaranteed customer for the spin-off's initial output.

CONSIDER GLOBALIZATION.   In today's global marketplace, many new firms start out with the idea of going international immediately. Other countries often provide the best market for American-made products and services. In fact, many businesses fail because the entrepreneur thinks provincially, being unaware of overseas markets. But if the entrepreneur has patience and commitment and is willing to do simple things such as write brochures in the local language, there is an excellent chance for success.

The ability to develop an international business is enhanced by new technology that bypasses former obstacles such as language. AT&T offers a 24-hour phone line with interpreters. Phone hook-ups offered by AT&T, MCI, and Sprint allow direct transmission of electronic mail to distributors' computers worldwide. PC software kits, export computer services, and translation devices such as Seiko's multilanguage translator assist small companies in achieving their export goals. Half of Life Corporation's emergency oxygen kits are shipped overseas. Vita-Mix Corporation, a third generation family-owned business, exports blenders to 20 nations. At the height of the recent recession, Vita-Mix doubled its work force to keep up with orders pouring in to its 800 number. The owner of regional car washes in Portland, Oregon, launched his car wash system as an international business and is now selling in 71 countries and earning $100 million a year.[15]

The United States offers assistance to small companies wishing to enter the global arena. The Trade Information Center offers information on U.S. government export assistance programs and services. Many U.S. government departments offer counseling; research; assistance in finding overseas agents and sales leads; and help with export licensing, loans, export credit insurance, and other services. For example, Fred

---

■
spin-off

An independent company producing a product or service similar to that produced by the entrepreneur's former employer.

Schweser, president of Bird Corporation, received advice on test marketing his popular go-carts overseas. Today, exports account for 10 to 15 percent of Bird's go-cart sales.[16] With the rapid globalization of the U.S. economy, it makes sense for new companies to target foreign markets.

GETTING HELP

The advice given to most entrepreneurs is to find a good accountant and attorney. They can help with the financial and legal aspects of the business. For a business that is incorporated, another great source of help is a board of directors. The entrepreneur can bring together for several meetings a year people who have needed expertise. These people may be recruited from local businesses and universities or be retired executives. Major problems can be discussed with the board. The board receives a small monthly stipend, gets a chance to help a business grow, and in some cases is given part ownership.[17]

Other sources of help are available for new entrepreneurs. For example, the Small Business Administration provides a loan program, described earlier. The government also provides financial assistance for specialized needs:[18]

- Loans for disadvantaged small businesses.
- Loans for physical disasters, such as loss of property due to floods.
- Small-business energy loans for implementing specific energy measures.
- Small-business pollution-control loans to meet pollution-control requirements.

The federal government also provides assistance in exporting. The U.S. Department of Commerce publishes *A Basic Guide to Exporting*, which provides specific information on trade opportunities abroad, foreign markets, financial aid to exporters, tax advantages of exporting, and international trade exhibitions.

In addition, four major management-assistance programs are sponsored by the SBA. The *Service Corps of Retired Executives* (SCORE) provides retired experts to help new businesses. The *Active Corps of Executives* (ACE) is a program in which active executives volunteer service to small business. *Small Business Development Centers* (SBDCs) are typically located on college campuses and keep consulting staff available to provide assistance and research services. The *Small Business Institutes* (SBI) are also operated in conjunction with university business schools and provide student teams to work on planning and analysis with entrepreneurs under a professor's guidance.

● GOALS IN ORGANIZATIONS

Setting goals in businesses of any size starts with top managers. The overall planning process begins with a mission statement and strategic goals for the organization as a whole.

mission

The organization's reason for existence.

mission statement

A broadly stated definition of the organization's basic business scope and operations that distinguish it from similar types of organizations.

ORGANIZATIONAL MISSION

At the top of the goal hierarchy is the **mission**—the organization's reason for existence. The mission describes the organization's values, aspirations, and reason for being. The formal **mission statement** is a broadly stated definition of basic business scope and operations that distinguishes the organization from others of a similar type.[19] The content of a mission statement often focuses on the market and customers and identifies desired fields of endeavor. Some mission statements describe company characteristics such as corporate values, product quality, location of facilities, and attitude toward employees. Mission statements often reveal the company's philosophy as well as purpose. The mission statement for a Vermont-based construction company is presented in Exhibit 6.1. Bread Loaf Construction Company devised its three-sentence mission statement as a way to spur continued growth and to close the communication gap between management and employees. It also helped the company focus on its goals for the future.

 BREAD LOAF CONSTRUCTION COMPANY

According to Mac McLaughlin, CEO of Bread Loaf Construction, setting goals was an annual event. However, the importance of the exercise never quite hit home during the go-go 1980s. Bread Loaf sales increased by a factor of six to $27 million in the five years after 1984. Everyone was so busy just trying to keep up that worrying about the future seemed silly.

But McLaughlin and vice-president John Leehman knew about the cyclical nature of the construction business. They decided that instilling long-term organizational goals was the only way to negotiate the inevitable troughs that lay ahead. They believed the best way to do this was to go right to the Bread Loaf employees themselves.

McLaughlin and Leehman invited 20 representatives from across the company spectrum to a weekend retreat. But before going, each of these representatives solicited input from three other employees on the job. Questions addressed both problems and possible solutions regarding the company's future, and what individuals regarded as roadblocks in their own personal development.

Attendees at the retreat were themselves asked to visualize 10 years hence. "It helped show employees who hadn't thought seriously about Bread Loaf for the long term that there was opportunity to grow here," says McLaughlin. Shifting the focus, the group was then asked to project the company on an international stage, fulfilling both the needs of its employees as well as the communities in which it operated. When agreement was made on these issues, the key question of how to achieve the objectives was posed.

It was decided that Bread Loaf would expand and identify new business opportunities. In keeping with the times, the company changed from a vertical to a horizontal structure. Like the group attending the retreat,

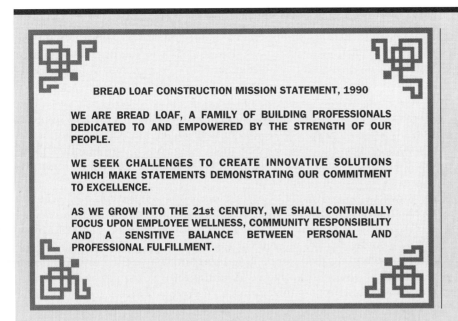

E X H I B I T   6 . 1

Mission Statement for Bread
Loaf Construction Company

> BREAD LOAF CONSTRUCTION MISSION STATEMENT, 1990
>
> WE ARE BREAD LOAF, A FAMILY OF BUILDING PROFESSIONALS DEDICATED TO AND EMPOWERED BY THE STRENGTH OF OUR PEOPLE.
>
> WE SEEK CHALLENGES TO CREATE INNOVATIVE SOLUTIONS WHICH MAKE STATEMENTS DEMONSTRATING OUR COMMITMENT TO EXCELLENCE.
>
> AS WE GROW INTO THE 21st CENTURY, WE SHALL CONTINUALLY FOCUS UPON EMPLOYEE WELLNESS, COMMUNITY RESPONSIBILITY AND A SENSITIVE BALANCE BETWEEN PERSONAL AND PROFESSIONAL FULFILLMENT.

SOURCE: Used with permission of
Bread Loaf Construction Company

cross-sectional teams would formulate and implement programs that clearly defined long-term plans. The three areas of emphasis would be to involve Bread Loaf in the community, to identify business opportunities, and to implement an employee wellness program. Finally, the group summed up the essence of their weekend when they created the company mission statement.[20] ■

The simple statement relays Bread Loaf's vision of who it is to both employees and customers. The mission statement challenges the status quo, demonstrates a commitment to excellence, focuses on day-to-day priorities, reinforces values, and balances priorities.[21]

Such short, straightforward mission statements describe basic business activities and purposes. Another example of this type of mission statement is that of Columbia Gas System, a large gas transmission and distribution company:

> Columbia Gas System, through its subsidiaries, is active in pursuing opportunities in all segments of the natural gas industry and in related energy resource development. Exemplified by Columbia's three-star symbol, the separately managed companies work to benefit: *system stockholders*—through competitive return on their investment; *customers*—through efficient, safe, reliable service; and *employees*—through challenging and rewarding careers.[22]

Because of mission statements such as Bread Loaf's and Columbia's, employees, as well as customers, suppliers, and stockholders, know the company's stated purpose.

GOALS AND PLANS

■
strategic goals

Broad statements of where the organization wants to be in the future; pertain to
the organization as a whole rather than
to specific divisions or departments.

Broad statements describing where the organization wants to be in the future are called **strategic goals.** They pertain to the organization as a whole rather than to specific divisions or departments. Strategic goals are often called *official* goals, because they are the stated intentions of what the organization wants to achieve. Peter Drucker suggests that business organizations' goals encompass more than profits. He suggests that organizations focus on eight content areas: market standing, innovation, productivity, physical and financial resources, profitability, managerial performance and development, worker performance and attitude, and public responsibility.[23]

■
strategic plans

The action steps by which an organization intends to attain its strategic goals.

Strategic plans define the action steps by which the company intends to attain strategic goals. The strategic plan is the blueprint that defines the organizational activities and resource allocations—in the form of cash, personnel, space, and facilities—required for meeting these targets. Strategic planning tends to be long-term and may define organizational action steps from two to five years in the future. The purpose of strategic plans is to turn organizational goals into realities within that time period.

For example, community hospitals face enormous threats as rising health care costs reduce in-patient numbers, forcing many hospital closings or buyouts by huge chains. To achieve strategic goals of quality care at reduced cost, many hospitals are following strategic plans: 1) reallocation of resources for maximum patient benefit for the dollar, 2) restructuring and decentralization to reduce costs and place decision-making closer to the patient level, and 3) diversification for better service with out-patient surgical and cancer-treatment units, the provision of health maintenance centers and nursing homes.[24]

■
tactical goals

Objectives that define the outcomes that
major divisions and departments must
achieve in order for the organization to
reach its overall goals.

Tactical goals are what major divisions and departments within the organization intend to achieve. These objectives apply to middle management and describe what major subunits must do in order for the organization to achieve its overall goals. For example, one tactical goal for Columbia Gas was to "regain a long-term debt rating by the end of 1988." This tactical goal pertains to strategic goal 2 regarding access to reasonable amounts of capital. Achieving this goal will increase the organization's ability to borrow money at a reasonable rate.

■
tactical plans

Plans designed to help execute major
strategic plans and to accomplish a specific part of the company's strategy.

Tactical plans are designed to help execute major strategic plans and to accomplish a specific part of the company's strategy. Tactical plans typically have a shorter time horizon than strategic plans—over the next year or so. For example, Lakeland Regional Medical Center's commitment to "patient focus" resulted in the formation of multiple skill nursing teams working with a small number of patients. Patient comfort is improved by familiarity with staff and the convenience of lab and therapy units located on each floor.[25] Tactical plans define what the major departments and organizational subunits will do to implement the overall strategic plan. Normally, it is the middle manager's job to take the broad strategic plan and identify specific tactical actions.

■
operational goals

Specific, measurable results expected
from departments, work groups, and
individuals within the organization.

Operational goals are the specific results expected from departments, work groups, and individuals. They are precise and measurable.

"Process 150 sales applications each week," "achieve 90 percent of deliveries on time," "reduce overtime by 10 percent next month," and "develop two new elective courses in accounting" are examples of operational objectives.

Operational plans are developed at the lower levels of the organization to specify action steps toward achieving operational goals and to support tactical plans. The operational plan is the department manager's tool for daily and weekly operations. Objectives are stated in quantitative terms, and the department plan describes how objectives will be achieved. Operational planning specifies plans for supervisors, department managers, and individual employees.

Schedules are an important component of operational planning. Schedules define precise time frames for completing each objective required for the organization's tactical and strategic goals. Operational planning also must be coordinated with the budget, because resources must be allocated for desired activities. At Lakeland Regional Medical Center, computers located in patient rooms speeds staff orders for testing and drugs. Lakeland estimates the total cost savings resulting from all efforts at the strategic, tactical, and operational levels will be $20 million per year.[26]

HIERARCHY OF OBJECTIVES

Effectively designed organizational goals and objectives fit into a hierarchy; that is, the achievement of objectives at lower levels permits the attainment of higher-level goals. This is called a *means-ends chain* because lower-level goals lead to accomplishment of higher-level goals. Operational goals lead to the achievement of tactical goals, which in turn lead to the attainment of strategic goals. Strategic goals typically are the responsibility of top management, tactical goals that of middle management, and operational goals that of first-line supervisors and workers.

An example of a goal hierarchy is illustrated in Exhibit 6.2. Note how the strategic goal of "excellent service to customers" translates into "open one new sales office" and "respond to customer inquiries within 2 hours" at lower management levels.

MANAGEMENT BY OBJECTIVES

Management by objectives (MBO) is a method whereby managers and employees define objectives for every department, project, and person and use them to control subsequent performance.[27] MBO can be used at any level—strategical, tactical, or operational. A model of the essential steps of the MBO process is presented in Exhibit 6.3. Four major activities must occur in order for MBO to be successful:[28]

> **1 Setting objectives.** This is the most difficult step in MBO. Setting objectives involves employees at all levels and looks beyond day-to-day activities to answer the question "What are we trying to accomplish?" A good objective should be concrete and realistic, provide a specific target and time frame, and assign responsibility. Objectives may be quantitative or qualitative, depending on

operational plans

Plans developed at the organization's lower levels that specify action steps toward achieving operational goals and support tactical planning activities.

management by objectives

A method of management whereby managers and employees define objectives for every department, project, and person and use them to control subsequent performance.

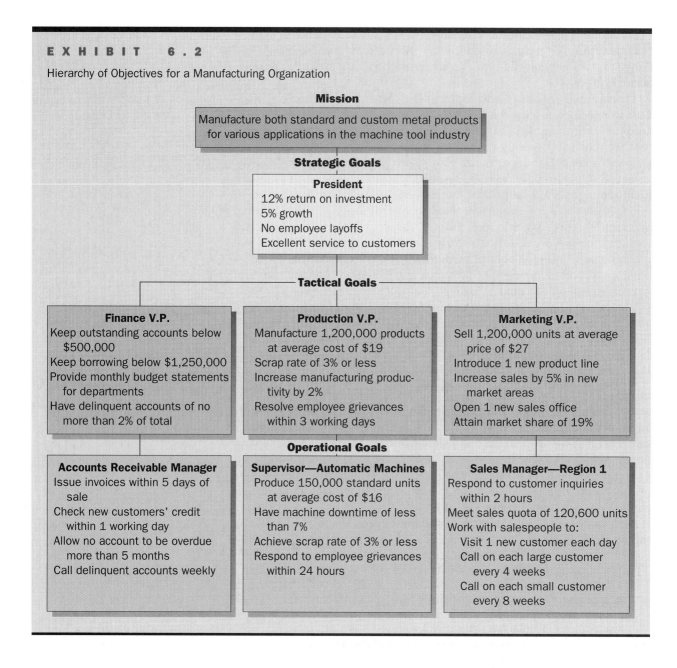

EXHIBIT   6 . 2

Hierarchy of Objectives for a Manufacturing Organization

Mission

Manufacture both standard and custom metal products for various applications in the machine tool industry

Strategic Goals

President
12% return on investment
5% growth
No employee layoffs
Excellent service to customers

Tactical Goals

Finance V.P.	**Production V.P.**	**Marketing V.P.**
Keep outstanding accounts below $500,000	Manufacture 1,200,000 products at average cost of $19	Sell 1,200,000 units at average price of $27
Keep borrowing below $1,250,000	Scrap rate of 3% or less	Introduce 1 new product line
Provide monthly budget statements for departments	Increase manufacturing productivity by 2%	Increase sales by 5% in new market areas
Have delinquent accounts of no more than 2% of total	Resolve employee grievances within 3 working days	Open 1 new sales office
		Attain market share of 19%

Operational Goals

Accounts Receivable Manager	**Supervisor—Automatic Machines**	**Sales Manager—Region 1**
Issue invoices within 5 days of sale	Produce 150,000 standard units at average cost of $16	Respond to customer inquiries within 2 hours
Check new customers' credit within 1 working day	Have machine downtime of less than 7%	Meet sales quota of 120,600 units
Allow no account to be overdue more than 5 months	Achieve scrap rate of 3% or less	Work with salespeople to:
Call delinquent accounts weekly	Respond to employee grievances within 24 hours	Visit 1 new customer each day
		Call on each large customer every 4 weeks
		Call on each small customer every 8 weeks

whether outcomes are measurable. Quantitative objectives are described in numerical terms, such as "Salesperson Jones will obtain 16 new accounts in December." Qualitative objectives use statements such as "Marketing will improve customer service by reducing complaints next year." Objectives should be jointly derived. Mutual agreement between employee and supervisor creates the strongest commitment to achieving objectives. In the case of teams, all team members may participate in setting objectives.

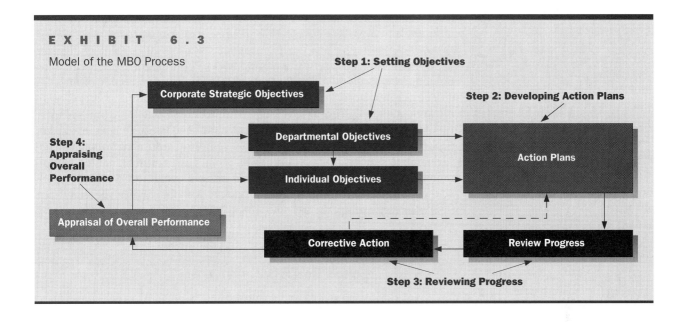

EXHIBIT 6.3

Model of the MBO Process

2 Developing action plans. An *action plan* defines the course of action needed to achieve the stated objectives. Action plans are made for both individuals and departments.

3 Reviewing progress. A periodic progress review is important to ensure that action plans are working. These reviews can occur informally between managers and subordinates, where the organization may wish to conduct three-, six-, or nine-month reviews during the year. This periodic checkup allows managers and employees to see whether they are on target or whether corrective action is necessary. Managers and employees should not be locked into predefined behavior and must be willing to take whatever steps are necessary to produce meaningful results. The point of MBO is to achieve objectives. The action plan can be changed whenever objectives are not being met.

4 Appraising overall performance. The final step in MBO is to carefully evaluate whether annual objectives have been achieved for both individuals and departments. Success or failure to achieve objectives can become part of the performance appraisal system and the designation of salary increases and other rewards. The appraisal of departmental and overall corporate performance shapes objectives for the next year. The MBO cycle repeats itself on an annual basis. The specific application of MBO must fit the needs of each company.

CONTINGENCY PLANS

Contingency plans, also referred to as *scenarios*, define company responses to be taken in the case of emergencies or setbacks. To develop contingency plans, planners identify uncontrollable factors, such as reces-

contingency plans

Plans that define company responses to specific situations such as emergencies or setbacks.

Contingency planning enables crews from British Telecommunications to react quickly to customer needs in times of crisis. A 1992 Irish Republican Army blast in London affected 200 businesses in 30 buildings. But through BT's business recovery program, 400 BT employees, such as the man pictured here, quickly restored service, installing 500 new lines, 420 telephones, and 60 private circuits.

sion, inflation, technological developments, or safety accidents. To minimize the impact of these potential factors, a planning team can forecast the worst-case scenarios. For example, if sales fall 20 percent and prices drop 8 percent, what will the company do? Contingency plans can then be defined for possible layoffs, emergency budgets, and sales efforts.[29]

The Exploration and Development Division of Statoil, a Norwegian oil and gas producer, discovered a number of benefits from scenario planning. Managers were confronted with scenarios such as a market drop in oil prices, a depressed world economy, and a national restructuring that reduced oil dependence. Scenario planning enabled Statoil managers to assess and understand trends, deal more openly with acknowledged uncertainty, learn critical lessons about the need for flexibility and adaptability, and react quickly to obtain a competitive advantage.[30]

● STRATEGIC MANAGEMENT

Strategic management is the set of decisions and actions used to formulate and implement strategies that will provide a competitively superior fit between the organization and its environment so as to achieve organizational objectives.[31] Strategic management is a process used to help managers answer strategic questions such as "Where is the organization now? Where does the organization want to be? What changes and trends are occurring in the competitive environment? What courses of action will help us achieve our goals?" Through strategic management, executives define an overall direction for the organization, which is the firm's grand strategy. The Leading Edge box provides an example of strategic management.

LEVELS OF STRATEGY

Another aspect of strategic management concerns the organizational level to which strategic issues apply. Strategic managers normally think in terms of three levels of strategy—corporate, business, and functional—as illustrated in Exhibit 6.4.[32]

CORPORATE-LEVEL STRATEGY.   The question *What business are we in?* concerns **corporate-level strategy.** Corporate-level strategy pertains to the organization as a whole and the combination of business units and product lines that make up the corporate entity. Strategic actions at this level usually relate to the acquisition of new businesses; additions or divestments of business units, plants, or product lines; and joint ventures with other corporations in new areas. An example of corporate-level strategy was Sears, Roebuck's 1992 decision to drop its "socks and stocks" image and focus again on retailing. This decision reversed a decade-long corporate strategy that saw acquisitions in service areas such as real estate (Coldwell Banker), insurance (Allstate), financial services (Dean Witter), and credit cards (Discover Card). In an attempt to reduce billions in debt and rebound from its number-three industry position behind Wal-Mart and Kmart, Sears is selling much of its financial

■
strategic management

The set of decisions and actions used to formulate and implement strategies that will provide a competitively superior fit between the organization and its environment so as to achieve organizational objectives.

■
corporate-level strategy

The level of strategy concerned with the question: "What business are we in?" Pertains to the organization as a whole and the combination of business units and product lines that make it up.

GRANITE ROCK

Trying to differentiate commodity-type products has always been difficult. However, that is what managers did at Granite Rock, the California producer of crushed stone and other construction materials that we first read about in Chapter 2. The simple, time-honored process is this: a builder sizes up the job and solicits competing bids. The low bid wins because that way the builder makes more money. But Granite Rock routinely charges as much as 6 percent more for material. And business is good.

Granite Rock managers view things a little differently. Where competitors tout price, they talk about quality and value. They back up their argument with customer service, and they do not use scattershot methods in pursuing their differentiation strategy either. Although it might seem obvious, Granite Rock holds the premise that the most important perspective on quality is that of their customers. That is why the company periodically surveys clients to determine their views on a range of quality and service issues. They ask about company performance and how it compares to rivals in the marketplace. This information is then distributed to employees.

Granite Rock has a well-established reputation as a learning and information gathering company. One of the cornerstones of the firm's strategy is that any process worth doing is worth keeping tabs on. That is why all 12 of the company's plants send annual report cards to all customers. The three most active suppliers a customer uses are rated on a venue of product and services. They can be characterized anywhere from the best to terrible. Dave Franceschi, a quality manager and planner thinks the report cards, and as many as 40 other tracking processes, are pivotal in maintaining the company's strategic course. "This is a way for us to sound an alarm if something's not right," he says. Wes Clark also noted the prevalent company pride at Granite Rock as an additional motivator. "Our people are competitive," he says. "They will look at a negative and want to do something about it."

Adaptive is an often-used word to describe Granite Rock's business-level strategy. The company emphasizes education and continually updated information. Unlike most companies, however, Granite Rock translates these processes into a tangible resource. Careful monitoring of competitive forces not only highlights operational flaws but also identifies shifts in the marketplace before competitors are aware of them. This allows Granite Rock to pursue a strategy which is anticipatory as opposed to reactive.

Co-CEO Bruce Woolpert views staying out in front of the competition as a survival issue. "I hope by having everyone involved we're doing more things sooner," says Woolpert. "We may be in certain areas just weeks or months ahead of somebody. Not years. The industry doesn't work that way. These are powerful companies, multibillion-dollar companies, doing business all over the world. We can't stand still." In Chapter 10, we will see how Granite Rock extends the learning process to its employees as well. ■

SOURCES: Edward Welles, "How're We Doing?" *INC.*, May 1991, 80–83; and John Case, "The Change Masters," *INC.*, March 1992, 55–70; company sources.

services divisions to refocus on its core—the retail store.[33] Using the opposite corporate-level strategy, Black & Decker's acquisition of GE's housewares division and then Emhart Corporation redefined it from a power tools producer to a company that also provides household appliances and products for home improvement.[34]

BUSINESS-LEVEL STRATEGY.   The question *How do we compete?* concerns **business-level strategy.** Business-level strategy pertains to each business unit or product line. It focuses on how the business unit competes

business-level strategy

The level of strategy concerned with the question: "How do we compete?" Pertains to each business unit or product line within the organization.

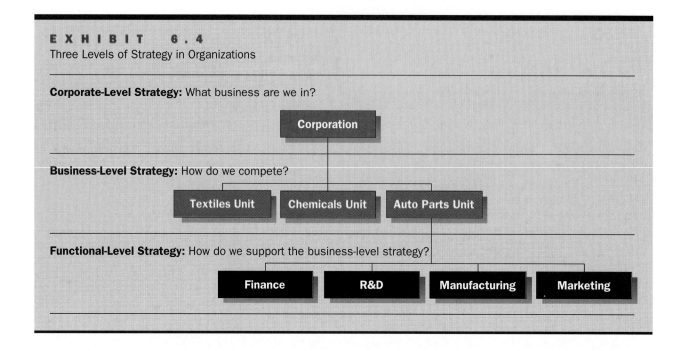

EXHIBIT 6.4
Three Levels of Strategy in Organizations

Corporate-Level Strategy: What business are we in?

Corporation

Business-Level Strategy: How do we compete?

Textiles Unit   Chemicals Unit   Auto Parts Unit

Functional-Level Strategy: How do we support the business-level strategy?

Finance   R&D   Manufacturing   Marketing

within its industry for customers. Strategic decisions at the business level concern amount of advertising, direction and extent of research and development, product changes, new-product development, equipment and facilities, and expansion or contraction of product lines. For example, Food Lion, Inc., one of the fastest-growing grocery chains in the nation, has a business-level strategy of cost reduction. Food Lion's economizing allows it to sell more cheaply than rivals yet maintain a higher profit margin. Jostens, Inc., a Minneapolis producer of high-school rings, has a business-level strategy of competing through product innovation. Although students have become less interested in buying class rings over the years, Jostens now offers 23 different stones and 16,000 ring permutations to fit every student's needs. Salespeople visit high schools personally to beat competitors to the student's door.[35]

functional-level strategy

The level of strategy concerned with the question: "How do we support the business-level strategy?" Pertains to all of the organization's major departments.

FUNCTIONAL-LEVEL STRATEGY.   The question *How do we support the business-level competitive strategy?* concerns **functional-level strategy.** It pertains to the major functional departments within the business unit. Functional strategies involve all of the major functions, including finance, research and development, marketing, manufacturing, and finance. For Hershey to compete on the basis of new-product innovation, its research department adopted a functional strategy for developing new products. The functional strategy for the marketing department of Sherwin-Williams is to develop advertising aimed at specific markets for its paint. For example, its Dutch Boy paint, touted as "the look that gets the looks," is advertised to do-it-yourselfers who shop the discount chains. The "Ask Sherwin-Williams" advertisements target the professional line of paints. This marketing strategy helped the company increase sales when total industry sales fell.[36]

● THE STRATEGIC MANAGEMENT PROCESS

The overall strategic management process is illustrated in Exhibit 6.5. It begins when executives evaluate their current position with respect to mission, goals, and strategies. They then scan the organization's internal and external environments and identify strategic factors that may require change. Internal or external events may indicate a need to redefine the mission or goals or to formulate a new strategy at either the corporate, business, or functional level. Once a new strategy is selected, it is implemented through changes in leadership, structure, human resources, or information and control systems.

SITUATION ANALYSIS

Situation analysis typically includes a search for SWOT—*s*trengths, *w*eaknesses, *o*pportunities, and *t*hreats that affect organizational performance. Situational analysis is important to all companies but is crucial to those considering globalization because of the diverse environments in which they will operate. External information about opportunities and threats may be obtained from a variety of sources, including customers, government reports, professional journals, suppliers, bankers, friends in other organizations, consultants, or association meetings. Many firms hire special scanning organizations to provide them with newspaper clippings and analyses of relevant domestic and global trends. Some firms use more subtle techniques to learn about competitors, such as

situation analysis

Analysis of the strengths, weaknesses, opportunities, and threats (SWOT) that affect organizational performance.

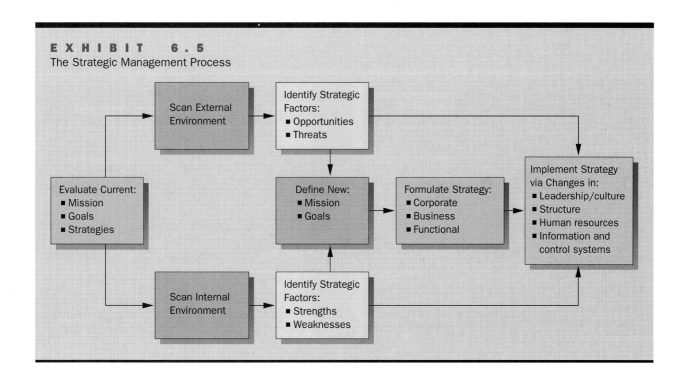

E X H I B I T   6 . 5
The Strategic Management Process

asking potential recruits about their visits to other companies, hiring people away from competitors, debriefing former employees or customers of competitors, taking plant tours posing as "innocent" visitors, and even buying competitors' garbage.[37]

Executives acquire information about internal strengths and weaknesses from a variety of reports, including budgets, financial ratios, profit and loss statements, and surveys of employee attitudes and satisfaction. Managers spend 80 percent of their time giving and receiving information from others. Through frequent face-to-face discussions and meetings with people at all levels of the hierarchy, executives build an understanding of the company's internal strengths and weaknesses.

INTERNAL STRENGTHS AND WEAKNESSES.   *Strengths* are positive internal characteristics that the organization can exploit to achieve its strategic performance goals. *Weaknesses* are internal characteristics that may inhibit or restrict the organization's performance. Some examples of what executives evaluate to interpret strengths and weaknesses are given in Exhibit 6.6. The information sought typically pertains to specific functions such as marketing, finance, production, and R&D. Internal analysis also examines overall organization structure, management competence and quality, and human resource characteristics. Based on their understanding of these areas, managers can determine their strengths or weaknesses vis-à-vis other companies. For example, Marriott Corporation has been able to grow rapidly because of its financial strength. It has a strong financial base, enjoys an excellent reputation with creditors, and has always been able to acquire financing needed to support its strategy of constructing hotels in new locations.[38]

EXTERNAL OPPORTUNITIES AND THREATS.   *Threats* are characteristics of the external environment that may prevent the organization

---

E X H I B I T   6 . 6

Checklist for Analyzing Organizational Strengths and Weaknesses

SOURCE: Based on Howard H. Stevenson, "Defining Corporate Strengths and Weaknesses," *Sloan Management Review* 17 (Spring 1976), 51–68, and M. L. Kastens, *Long-Range Planning for Your Business* (New York: American Management Association, 1976).

Management and Organization	Marketing	Human Resources
Management quality	Distribution channels	Employee age, education
Staff quality	Market share	Union status
Degree of centralization	Advertising efficiency	Turnover, absenteeism
Organization charts	Customer satisfaction	Work satisfaction
Planning, information, control systems	Product quality	Grievances
	Service reputation	
	Sales force turnover	

Finance	Production	Research and Development
Profit margin	Plant location	Basic applied research
Debt-equity ratio	Machinery obsolescence	Laboratory capabilities
Inventory ratio	Purchasing system	Research programs
Return on investment	Quality control	New-product innovations
Credit rating	Productivity/efficiency	Technology innovations

from achieving its strategic goals. *Opportunities* are characteristics of the external environment that have the potential to help the organization achieve or exceed its strategic goals. Executives evaluate the external environment with information about the nine sectors described in Chapter 4. The task environment sectors are the most relevant to strategic behavior and include the behavior of competitors, customers, suppliers, and the labor supply. The general environment contains those sectors that have an indirect influence on the organization but nevertheless must be understood and incorporated into strategic behavior. The general environment includes technological developments, the economy, legal-political and international events, and sociocultural changes. Additional areas that might reveal opportunities or threats include pressure groups, interest groups, creditors, natural resources, and potentially competitive industries.

An example of how external analysis can uncover a threat occurred in the Post cereal business of General Foods in the 1980s. Scanning the environment indicated that Kellogg had increased its market share from 38 to 40 percent while Post's share had dropped from 16 to 14 percent. Information from the competitor and customer sectors indicated that Kellogg had stepped up advertising and new-product introductions. This threat to Post was the basis for a strategic response. The first step was to throw additional dollars into cents-off coupons and discounts to grocery stores. The next step was to develop new cereals, such as the successful Fruit & Fibre.[39]

● BUSINESS-LEVEL STRATEGY

Now we turn to strategy formulation within the strategic business unit, in which the concern is how to compete. Three generic strategies—growth, stability, and retrenchment—apply at the business level, but they are accomplished through competitive actions rather than the acquisition or divestment of business divisions. Two models for formulating strategy are Porter's competitive strategies and the product life cycle. Each provides a framework for business unit competitive action.

PORTER'S COMPETITIVE FORCES AND STRATEGIES

Michael E. Porter studied a number of business organizations and proposed that business-level strategies are the result of five competitive forces in the company's environment.[40]

FIVE COMPETITIVE FORCES.   Exhibit 6.7 illustrates the competitive forces that exist in a company's environment. These forces help determine a company's position vis-à-vis competitors in the industry environment.

1 *Potential new entrants.* Capital requirements and economies of scale are examples of two potential barriers to entry that can keep out

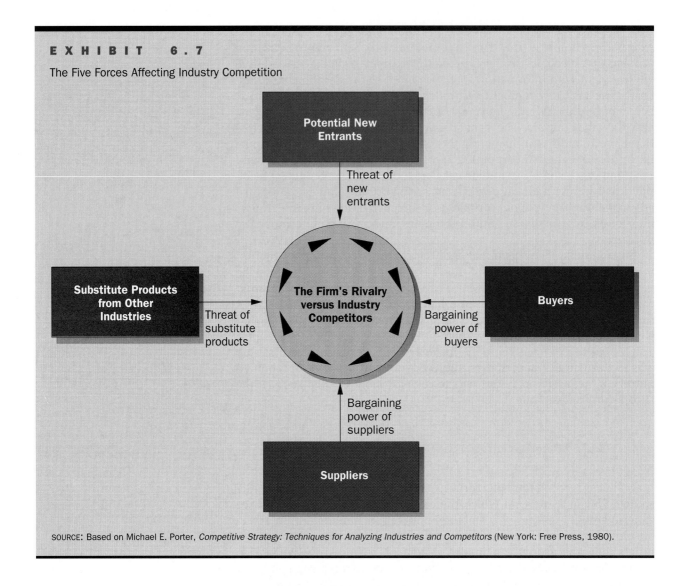

EXHIBIT 6.7

The Five Forces Affecting Industry Competition

SOURCE: Based on Michael E. Porter, *Competitive Strategy: Techniques for Analyzing Industries and Competitors* (New York: Free Press, 1980).

new competitors. It is far more costly to enter the automobile industry, for example, than to start a specialized mail-order business.

2 *Bargaining power of buyers.* Informed customers become empowered customers. As advertising and buyer information educates customers about the full range of price and product options available in the marketplace, their influence over a company increases. This is especially true when a company relies on one or two large, powerful customers for the majority of its sales.

3 *Bargaining power of suppliers.* The concentration of suppliers and the availability of substitute suppliers are significant factors in determining supplier power. The sole supplier of engines to a manufacturer of small airplanes will have great power. Other factors include whether a supplier can survive without a particular purchaser, or whether the purchaser can threaten to self-manufacture the needed supplies.

4 *Threat of substitute products.* The power of alternatives and substitutes for a company's product may be affected by cost changes or trends such as increased health consciousness which will deflect buyer loyalty to companies. Companies in the sugar industry suffered from the growth of sugar substitutes; manufacturers of aerosol spray cans lost business as environmentally conscious consumers chose other products.

5 *Rivalry among competitors.* The scrambling and jockeying for position is often exemplified by what Porter called the "advertising slugfest." As illustrated in Exhibit 6.7, these rivalries are influenced by the preceding four forces as well as cost and product differentiation. A famous example of competitive rivalry is the battle between Pepsi and Coke. In the fountain war, for example, Pepsi used a three-page ad in a 1991 trade journal to report that Coke's pricing policies allowed price breaks to McDonald's, requiring other fast-food chain purchasers of Coke to subsidize the operations of their largest competitor.[41]

COMPETITIVE STRATEGIES.   In finding its competitive edge within these five forces, Porter suggests that a company can adopt one of three strategies: differentiation, cost leadership, and focus. The organizational characteristics typically associated with each strategy are summarized in Exhibit 6.8.

1. Differentiation.   The **differentiation** strategy involves an attempt to distinguish the firm's products or services from others in the industry. The organization may use advertising, distinctive product features, exceptional service, or new technology to achieve a product perceived as unique. The differentiation strategy can be profitable because customers are loyal and will pay high prices for the product. Examples of products that have benefited from a differentiation strategy include

differentiation

A type of competitive strategy with which the organization seeks to distinguish its products or services from competitors'.

Strategy	Commonly Required Skills and Resources
Differentiation	Strong marketing abilities
	Strong coordination among functional departments
	Creative flair
	Strong capability in basic research
	Corporate reputation for quality or technological leadership
Overall cost leadership	Tight cost control
	Process engineering skills
	Intense supervision of labor
	Products designed for ease in manufacture
	Frequent, detailed control reports
Focus	Combination of the above policies directed at the particular strategic target

EXHIBIT   6.8

Organizational Characteristics for Porter's Competitive Strategies

SOURCE: Reprinted with permission of Free Press, a Division of Macmillan, Inc., from *Competitive Strategy: Techniques for Analyzing Industries and Competitors* by Michael E. Porter. Copyright © 1980 by The Free Press.

Mercedes-Benz automobiles, Maytag appliances, and Tylenol, all of which are perceived as distinctive in their markets. Companies that pursue a differentiation strategy typically need strong marketing abilities, a creative flair, and a reputation for leadership.[42]

A differentiation strategy can reduce rivalry with competitors if buyers are loyal to a company's brand. For example, successful differentiation reduces the bargaining power of large buyers because other products are less attractive, and this also helps the firm fight off threats of substitute products. Differentiation also erects entry barriers in the form of customer loyalty that a new entrant into the market would have difficulty overcoming.

cost leadership

A type of competitive strategy with which the organization aggressively seeks efficient facilities, cuts costs, and employs tight cost controls to be more efficient than competitors.

2. Cost Leadership.   With a **cost leadership** strategy, the organization aggressively seeks efficient facilities, pursues cost reductions, and uses tight cost controls to produce products more efficiently than competitors. A low-cost position means that the company can undercut competitors' prices and still offer comparable quality and earn a reasonable profit. Scottish Inns and Motel 6 are low-priced alternatives to Holiday Inn and Ramada Inn. The Food Lion, Inc., grocery chain is a superb example of cost leadership. The company's credo is to do "1,000 things 100% better." Food Lion builds distribution warehouses close to its stores, recycles banana crates as bins for cosmetics, and even uses waste heat from refrigerator units to warm the store. With the lowest costs and lowest prices in the industry, Food Lion is still highly profitable.[43]

Being a low-cost producer provides a successful strategy to defend against the five competitive forces. For example, the most efficient, low-cost company is in the best position to succeed in a price war while still making a profit. Likewise, the low-cost producer is protected from powerful customers and suppliers, because customers cannot find lower prices elsewhere, and other buyers would have less slack for price negotiation with suppliers. If substitute products or potential new entrants occur, the low-cost producer is better positioned than higher-cost rivals to prevent loss of market share. The low price acts as a barrier against new entrants and substitute products.[44]

focus

A type of competitive strategy that emphasizes concentration on a specific regional market or buyer group.

3. Focus.   With a **focus** strategy, the organization concentrates its strategy on a specific regional market or buyer group. The company will use either a differentiation or low-cost approach, but only for a narrow target market. One example of focus strategy is the brokerage firm of Edward D. Jones & Company. It focused on the investment needs of rural America, moving into small towns where Merrill Lynch representatives would not even stop for gas. In this ignored market niche, Jones has opened 1,300 offices and now serves over 1 million customers with its conservative investment philosophy.[45]

Porter found that some businesses did not consciously adopt one of these three strategies and were stuck with no strategic advantage. Without a strategic advantage, businesses earned below-average profits compared with those that used differentiation, cost leadership, or focus strategies.

A *focus and differentiation strategy* gives Dreyer's Grand Ice Cream a competitive edge among premium ice creams. Modern distribution facilities and a second-to-none direct-store delivery system contributed to record sales and earnings despite recession, as well as attracting distribution of "partner brands" such as Ben & Jerry's, Dove brands, and Mars' Snickers and Milky Way ice cream bars.

PRODUCT LIFE CYCLE

The **product life cycle** is a series of stages that a product goes through in its market acceptance, as illustrated in Exhibit 6.9. First, a product is developed within the laboratories of selected companies and then is introduced into the marketplace. If the product succeeds, it enjoys rapid growth as consumers accept it. Next is the maturity stage, in which widespread product acceptance occurs but growth peaks. Gradually the product grows out of favor or fashion and enters the decline stage.[46]

The life cycle concept also applies to services, as the banking example in Exhibit 6.9 shows. In-home banking is a new product, and discount broker services is in the rapid growth stage. Money market accounts have been around for a while and are approaching maturity, which is where drive-in tellers are. Passbook savings accounts are in decline, being replaced by money market accounts and certificates of deposit. The Christmas Club accounts are in serious decline and are available at only a few banks.

Banks and other organizations can tailor strategy to product life cycle stages.[47] During the introduction and growth stages, differentiation strategy is appropriate, because it stresses advertising, attracting new customers, and market growth. After the product reaches maturity, a low-cost strategy is important, because competitors will have developed products that look and perform similarly. Company strategy for a mature product or service should stress efficiency, reduce overhead costs, and seek a price advantage over competitors.

product life cycle

The stages through which a product or service goes: (1) development and introduction into the marketplace, (2) growth, (3) maturity, and (4) decline.

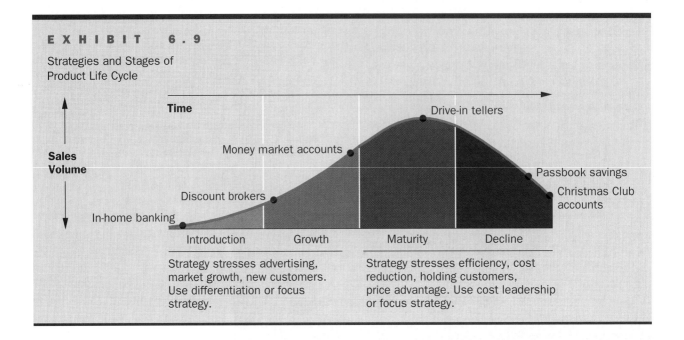

EXHIBIT   6.9

Strategies and Stages of Product Life Cycle

Time

Sales Volume

Drive-in tellers

Money market accounts

Discount brokers

Passbook savings

Christmas Club accounts

In-home banking

Introduction	Growth	Maturity	Decline

Strategy stresses advertising, market growth, new customers. Use differentiation or focus strategy.

Strategy stresses efficiency, cost reduction, holding customers, price advantage. Use cost leadership or focus strategy.

● FUNCTIONAL-LEVEL STRATEGY

Functional-level strategies are the action plans adopted by major departments to support the execution of business-level strategy. Major organizational functions include marketing, production, finance, personnel, and research and development. Senior managers in these departments adopt strategies that are coordinated with the business-level strategy to achieve the organization's strategic goals.[48]

For example, consider a company that has adopted a differentiation strategy and is introducing new products that are expected to experience rapid growth in the early stages of the life cycle. The personnel department should adopt a strategy appropriate for growth, which would mean recruiting additional personnel and training middle managers for movement into new positions. The marketing department should undertake test marketing, aggressive advertising campaigns, and consumer product trials. The finance department should adopt plans to borrow money, handle large cash investments, and authorize construction of new production facilities.

A company with mature products or a low-cost strategy will have different functional strategies. The personnel department should develop strategies for retaining and developing a stable work force, including transfers, advancements, and incentives for efficiency and safety. Marketing should stress brand loyalty and the development of established, reliable distribution channels. Production should maintain long production runs, routinization, and cost reduction. Finance should focus on net cash flows and positive cash balances.

In order to satisfy global demand for Barbies, Nintendos, or Legos, the world's largest children's retail chain, Toys "Я" Us, formulated a *functional-level marketing strategy* that increased the international appeal of toys through advertising (pictured here), high-tech distribution, and price selection.

SUMMARY AND MANAGEMENT SOLUTION

This chapter described several important ideas about organizational goal setting and planning. Organizational planning involves defining goals/objectives and developing a plan with which to achieve them. Goal setting and planning are important to companies of any size, but they are especially crucial to the success of small-business start-ups.

Starting an entrepreneurial firm requires a new-business idea. At that point a comprehensive business plan should be developed and decisions made about legal structure and financing. Tactical decisions for the new venture include whether to start, buy, or franchise, whether to participate in a business incubator, whether to be a company spin-off, and whether to go global.

An organization exists for a single, overriding purpose known as its *mission*—the basis for strategic goals and plans. Goals within the organization are defined in a hierarchical fashion, beginning with strategic goals followed by tactical and operational goals. Plans are defined similarly, with strategic, tactical, and operational plans used to achieve the objectives.

Strategic management begins with an evaluation of the organization's current mission, goals, and strategy. This evaluation is followed by situation analysis (called SWOT analysis), which examines opportunities and threats in the external environment as well as strengths and weaknesses within the organization. Situation analysis leads to the formulation of explicit strategic plans, which then must be implemented.

Strategy formulation takes place at three levels: corporate, business, and functional. Corporate strategies include acquisitions, divestments, and joint ventures. Business-level strategies include Porter's competitive strategies and the product life cycle. Once business strategies have been formulated, functional strategies for supporting them can be developed.

After further research, Jeffrey Clements decided the goal of entrepreneurship was worth pursuing, and that Discovery Zone had some compelling demographics going for it. First, the United States was estimated to have just under 40 million people under the age of 12. By the year 2000 that number was projected to be 47 million. Unfortunately, the majority of them were flabby fixtures in front of the television when they were not in school. The Discovery Zone's premise of getting them in shape was fundamental and made sense. If exercise is fun, you do not have to make kids do it. Clements traded his pinstripes and sedate meeting schedule for a roomful of tunnels, slides, and pyramids, all carefully designed to enhance fitness or coordination. With a weekly gross income of $18,000, he has gotten over his nostalgia for boardroom politics and corporate infighting.[49]

DISCUSSION QUESTIONS

1. Why is purchasing an existing business or franchise less risky than starting a new business?
2. What is the difference between debt financing and equity financing? What are common sources of each type?
3. What types of planning would have helped Exxon respond more quickly to the oil spill from the *Exxon Valdez* near Alaska?
4. Write a brief mission statement for a local business. Can the purpose and values of a small organization be captured in a written statement?
5. If you were a top manager of a medium-size real estate sales agency, would you use MBO? If so, give examples of objectives you might set for managers and sales agents.
6. A new business venture has to develop a comprehensive business plan to borrow money to get started. Companies such as Federal Express, Nike, and Rolm Corporation say they did not follow the orig-

inal plan very closely. Does that mean that developing the plan was a waste of time for these eventually successful companies?

7. Perform a situation (SWOT) analysis for the university you attend. Do you think university administrators consider these factors when devising their strategy?

8. Using Porter's competitive strategies, how would you describe the strategies of Wal-Mart, Bloomingdale's and Kmart?

MANAGEMENT IN PRACTICE: EXPERIENTIAL EXERCISE

● DEVELOPING STRATEGY FOR A SMALL BUSINESS

Instructions: Your instructor may ask you to do this exercise individually or as part of a group. Select a local business with which you (or group members) are familiar. Complete the following activities.

Activity 1   Perform a SWOT analysis for the business.

Strengths: _____
_____
_____
_____
_____

Opportunities: _____
_____
_____
_____
_____

Weaknesses: _____
_____
_____
_____
_____

Threats: _____
_____
_____
_____
_____

Activity 2   Write a statement of the business's current strategy.

Activity 3   Decide on a goal you would like the business to achieve in two years, and write a statement of proposed strategy for achieving that goal.

Activity 4   Write a statement describing how the proposed strategy will be implemented.

Activity 5   What have you learned from this exercise?

CASE FOR ANALYSIS

FRANCHISING

The famous Dickens line—it was the best of times, and the worst of times—certainly sums up the state of available franchises in the United States today.

JoAnne Shaw opened her first specialty coffee shop in 1976 with the idea that she could do things her own way, make money, and retain her independence. Twelve years later she is presiding over the Coffee Beanery Limited and 24 franchises. What seemed like a speculative venture boomed.

Curtis B. Bean knew he could not miss with Checkers of America Inc. The former CEO of Howard Johnson Franchise Systems Inc. had more than 20 years in the business, and all the feedback from franchisees about Car Checkers of New Jersey was positive. He particularly appreciated the mobile inspection policy that protected customers from "lemon" used cars. Unfortunately, it didn't protect Bean from "lemon" franchises, of which he purchased twelve. Almost all of the furnished data and testimonials turned out to be bogus, according to a suit filed by Bean and 15 other would-be franchisees.

Proponents tout the increasing franchise trend as added sinew around the small business backbone of America. Because franchisees purchase refined methods of operation, tested training and development plans, and co-oped advertising, risks of starting a brand new business are also greatly reduced. Critics, and alleged fraud victims like Bean, charge that the $246 billion industry has more than its share of flimflammery and sharp practices. A much bigger problem is the level of control franchisees have over their own operations. And what some consider the worst news of all, Congress appears prepared to regulate the industry, introducing legislation that some observers believe threatens to transform the merely unpalatable into an utter hellbroth.

The results of this may have far-reaching repercussions. Franchises comprise almost 13 percent of retail sales. Corporate layoffs and downsizings have put a number of business people on the streets, and many are anxious to start anew with their own operations. The promised, and purchased, business acumen that comes with a franchise is attractive. However, many franchisors are discovering sins and excesses of their past—bad management decision making, too many locations or too much debt—catching up with them. It has been asserted that when crunch time comes around, many franchisors ignore promises and sometimes end up drawing off customers from franchisees since the number of units in a given area is generally decided by the franchisors.

Not surprisingly, the franchisors have their side of the argument. PepsiCo, Inc., which franchises Taco Bell, Pizza Hut, and Kentucky Fried Chicken, says franchisees are slow to implement necessary changes to keep themselves competitive. Others charge that franchisees expect instant riches without the requisite efforts, and that many do not even bother to study their own businesses thoroughly. Another emerging consensus is that many franchisees (Bean would be a good example), have too much power because of the number of units they can afford to buy. Deep pockets lead to lobbyists, lawyers, and sometimes litigation.

Few would disagree that the deck is stacked decidedly in favor of the franchisors. In a divergence from the past, however, courts have recently handed down rulings in favor of franchisees, particularly in cases where new locations trespassed on existing franchisees' presumed territory. Many are turning to mediation procedures to settle disputes and save legal fees. Fifteen states have disclosure laws governing the sales of franchises; 13 have statutes to define what is permissible between franchisors and franchisees. Many state securities regulators would like to implement uniformity in documentation. And the potential for federal intervention looms.

In the final analysis, those affiliated with both ends of the franchise spectrum will make their own beds. It would be nice if they could come to an equitable reconciliation, particularly because one-eighth of the U.S. retail economy hangs in the balance.

● **Q U E S T I O N S**

1. Can the types of problems faced by franchisees like Curtis Bean be avoided with sufficient planning?
2. What strengths, weaknesses, opportunities and threats do franchisees face?
3. Given the pros and cons of franchising, how can an entrepreneur decide whether it is the best path for going into business?

SOURCE: Michele Galen et al., "Franchise Fracas," *Business Week*, March 22, 1993, 68–72; Meg Whittemore, "Franchising's Appeal to Women," *Nation's Business,* November 1989, 63–64; Meg Whittemore, "An Upbeat Forecast for Franchising," *Nation's Business,* January 1993, 49–56.

REFERENCES

1. Susan Caminiti, "Look Who Likes Franchising Now," *Fortune,* September 23, 1991, 125–131.

2. Amitai Etzioni, *Modern Organizations* (Englewood Cliffs, NJ: Prentice-Hall, 1984), 6.

3. John Case, "The Origins of Entrepreneurship," *INC.,* June 1989, 51–63.

4. Roger Ricklefs, "Pros Dare to Go Where Amateurs No Longer Bother," *The Wall Street Journal,* March 31, 1989, B2.

5. Case, "The Origins of Entrepreneurship."

6. The Inc. Faxpoll, *INC.,* February 1992, 24.

7. "Venture Capitalists' Criteria," *Management Review,* November 1985, 7–8.

8. Louise Washer, "The Business Plan that Gets the Loan, *Working Woman,* January 1990, 37–47.

9. Meg Whittemore, "Four Paths to Franchising," *Nation's Business,* October 1989, 75–85; and Nancy Croft Baker, "Franchising in the 90s," *Nation's Business,* March 1990, 61–68.

10. Charles R. Kuehl and Peggy A. Lambing, *Small Business: Planning and Management,* 3d ed. (Chicago: The Dryden Press, 1994), Chap 5.

11. Louise Washer, "Shattered Dreams: Women Who Lost Almost Everything," *McCalls,* February 1994, 112–121, 170.

12. Alessandra Bianchi, "New Businesses: Incubator Update," *INC.,* January 1993, 49.

13. Bradford McKee, "Managing Your Small Business: Using Incubators as Stepping Stones to Growth," *Nation's Business,* October 1991, 8.

14. Thomas S. Bateman and Carl P. Zeithaml, *Management Function and Strategy* (Homewood, IL: Irwin, 1990).

15. William J. Holstein and Kevin Kelly, "Little Companies, Big Exports," *Business Week,* April 13, 1992, 70–72, and Albert G. Holzinger, "Reach New Markets," *Nation's Business,* December 1990, 18–35.

16. Albert G. Holzinger, "Paving the Way for Small Exporters," *Nation's Business,* June 1992, 42–43.

17. Elizabeth Conlin, "Unlimited Partners," *INC.,* April 1990, 71–79.

18. Kuehl and Lambing, *Small Business.*

19. Mary Klemm, Stuart Sanderson, and George Luffman, "Mission Statements: Selling Corporate Values to Employees," *Long Range Planning* 24, No. 3 (1991), 73–78; John A. Pearce II and Fred David, "Corporate Mission Statements: The

Bottom Line," *Academy of Management Executive,* 1987, 109–116; and Jerome H. Want, "Corporate Mission: The Intangible Contributor to Performance," *Management Review,* August 1986, 46–50.

20. Teri Lammers, "The Effective and Indispensable Mission Statement," *INC.,* August 1992, 75–77; and "Image Builders," *INC.,* November 1992, 112–113.

21. Teri Lammers, "The Effective and Indispensable Mission Statement."

22. "Preparing for the Unexpected," *Columbia Today,* Winter 1985/1986, 2–4.

23. Peter F. Drucker, *The Practice of Management* (New York: Harper's Brothers, 1954), 65–83.

24. Keith H. Hammond, "The Hospital," *Business Week,* January 17, 1994, 48–61.

25. Ibid.

26. Ibid.

27. George S. Odiorne, "MBO: A Backward Glance," *Business Horizons,* 21 (October 1978), 14–24.

28. Jan P. Muczyk and Bernard C. Reimann, "MBO as a Complement to Effective Leadership," *The Academy of Management Executive 3* (1989), 131–138; and W. Giegold, *Objective Setting and the MBO Process,* Vol. 2 (New York: McGraw-Hill 1978).

29. "Corporate Planning: Drafting a Blueprint for Success," *Small Business Report* (August 1987), 40–44.

30. P. R. Stokke, W. K. Ralston, T. A. Boyce, and I. H. Wilson, "Scenario Planning for Norwegian Oil and Gas," *Long-Range Planning* 23 (April 1990), 17–26.

31. John E. Prescott, "Environments as Moderators of the Relationship between Strategy and Performance," *Academy of Management Journal* 29 (1986), 329–346; John A. Pearce II and Richard B. Robinson Jr., *Strategic Management: Strategy, Formulation and Implementation,* 2d ed. (Homewood, IL: Irwin 1985); and David J. Teece, "Economic Analysis and Strategic Management," *California Management Review* 26 (Spring 1984), 87–110.

32. Milton Leontiades, *Strategies for Diversification and Change* (Boston: Little, Brown 1980), 63; and Dan E. Schendel and Charles W. Hofer, eds., *Strategic Management: A New View of Business Policy and Planning* (Boston: Little, Brown, 1979), 11–14.

33. Gregory A. Patterson and Francine Schwadel, "Back in Time: Sears Suddenly Undoes Years of Diversifying Beyond Retail Field," *The Wall Street Journal,* September 30, 1992, A1, A16; and Julia Flynn, David Greising, Kevin Kelly, and Leah Nathans Spiro, "Smaller but Wiser," *Business Week,* October 12, 1992, 28–29.

34. Joseph Weber, "Black & Decker Cuts a Neat Dovetail Joint," *Business Week,* July 31, 1989, 52–53.

35. Richard W. Anderson, "That Roar You Heard Is Food Lion," *Business Week,* August 24, 1987, 65–66; and Jaclyn Fierman, "How to Make Money in Mature Markets," *Fortune,* November 25, 1985, 47–53.

36. Kathleen Madigan, Julia Flynn, and Joseph Walker, "Masters of the Game," *Business Week,* October 12, 1992, 110–118.

37. James E. Svatko, "Analyzing the Competition," *Small Business Reports* (January 1989), 21–28; and Brian Dumaine, "Corporate Spies Snoop to Conquer," *Fortune,* November 7, 1988, 68–76.

38. Steve Swartz, "Basic Bedrooms: How Marriott Changes Hotel Design to Top Mid-Priced Market," *The Wall Street Journal,* September 18, 1985, 1.

39. Pamela Sherrid, "Fighting Back at Breakfast," *Forbes,* October 7, 1985, 126–130.

40. Michael E. Porter, *Competitive Strategy* (New York: Free Press, 1980), 36–46; Danny Miller, "Relating Porter's Business Strategies to Environment and Structure: Analysis and Performance Implementations," *Academy of Management Journal* 31 (1988), 280–308; and Michael E. Porter, "From Competitive Advantage to Corporate Strategy," *Harvard Business Review* (May–June 1987), 43–59.

41. Walecia Konrad and Gail DeGeorge, "Sorry, No Pepsi. How 'Bout a Coke?" *Business Week,* May 27, 1991, 71–72.

42. Thomas L. Wheelen and J. David Hunger, *Strategic Management and Business Policy* (Reading, MA: Addison-Wesley, 1989).

43. Anderson, "That Roar You Heard Is Food Lion,"

44. Arthur A. Thompson, Jr. and A.J. Strickland III, *Strategic Management: Concepts and Cases,* 6th ed. (Homewood, IL: Irwin, 1992).

45. Nathaniel Gilbert, "John W. Bachmann: Securities Well In Hand," *Management Review* (January 1988), 17–19.

46. George W. Potts, "Explode Your Product's Life Cycle," *Harvard Business Review,* (Sept.–Oct. 1988), 32–36; and C. R. Wasson, *Dynamic Competitive Strategy and Product Life Cycles,* 3d ed. (Austin, TX: Austin Press, 1978).

47. Carl R. Anderson and Carl P. Zeithaml, "Stage of the Product Life Cycle, Business Strategy, & Business Performance," *Academy of Management Journal* 27 (1984), 5–24.

48. Harold W. Fox, "A Framework for Functional Coordination," *Atlanta Economic Review* (now *Business Magazine*) (Nov.–Dec. 1973).

49. Susan Caminiti, "Look Who Likes Franchising Now."

MANAGERIAL DECISION MAKING

7

CHAPTER OUTLINE

LEARNING OBJECTIVES

After studying this chapter, you should be able to

- Explain why decision making is an important component of good management.

- Explain the difference between programmed and nonprogrammed decisions and the decision characteristics of risk, uncertainty, and ambiguity.

- Describe the classical and administrative models of decision making and their applications.

- Identify the six steps used in managerial decision making.

- Discuss the advantages and disadvantages of using groups to make decisions.

- Discuss the impact of information technology on operational efficiency and business strategy.

- Describe the importance of information systems for management and the characteristics of useful information.

Ron Berger had a problem. His 385-store National Video chain was the country's biggest video rental franchiser despite what he considered an intolerable operational deficiency. His stores spent an average of $65 for videos. This price meant that 26 rentals were required to recoup the cost. On weekends, however, when locations typically did half their total business, the hot movies were all snapped up and the stores could not afford to buy more copies. The studios were leaving money on the table, the stores were not doing the business they should, and unhappy customers were going home without renting a movie. If you were Berger, what decisions would you consider for remedying the problem? What kind of system could be devised to overcome a situation that no one was happy with?[1] ■ National Video has to find a way to improve on the current system, which is cutting into profits. Ron Berger will have to harness his skills to make decisions that will affect the future of his business. Every organization grows, prospers, or fails as a result of decisions by its managers.

Managers often are referred to as *decision makers*. Although many of their important decisions are strategic, managers also make decisions about every other aspect of an organization, including structure, control systems, responses to the environment, and human resources. Managers scout for problems, make decisions for solving them, and monitor the consequences to see whether additional decisions are required. Good decision making is a vital part of good management, because decisions determine how the organization solves its problems, allocates resources, and accomplishes its objectives.

Decision making is not easy. It must be done amid ever-changing factors, unclear information, and conflicting points of view. For example, when Chairman Patrick Hayes of Waterford Glass tried to cut costs by offering early retirement to the highly paid work force that made Waterford crystal, too many experienced glassblowers opted for retirement. The remaining workers were not able to achieve enough output; hence, crystal operations lost money for two years straight. John Sculley, ex-chairman of Apple Computer, bet on a shortage of memory chips, the personal computer's most common component. Apple acquired a big inventory of high-priced chips, and when the shortage was alleviated a few months later, Apple was forced to lower the price of its expensive Apple products.

Kay Koplovitz worked her way up to CEO of the successful USA Network and recently launched a sci-fi channel. This is a nail-biting gamble as Washington stalks the cable industry with new regulations to cap charges to the public, and an FCC ruling allows phone companies, such as Bell Atlantic, to experiment with "video dial tones," which would bring video movies and other materials into homes by phone rather than cable. Still, Koplovitz and many corporate sponsors believe there are enough fans of ghouls and monsters and Martians to risk the plunge into an area where no network has gone before.[2]

Chapter 6 described strategic planning. This chapter explores the decision process that underlies strategic planning. Plans and strategies are arrived at through decision making; the better the decision making, the better the strategic planning. First we will examine decision characteristics. Then we will look at decision-making models and the steps executives should take when making important decisions. We will also examine how groups of managers make decisions. Finally, we will discuss techniques for improving decision making in organizations.

● TYPES OF DECISIONS AND PROBLEMS

decision

A choice made from available alternatives.

decision making

The process of identifying problems and opportunities and then resolving them.

A **decision** is a choice made from available alternatives. For example, an accounting manager's selection among Bill, Nancy, and Joan for the position of junior auditor is a decision. Many people assume that making a choice is the major part of decision making, but it is only a part.

Decision making is the process of identifying problems and opportunities and then resolving them.[3] Decision making involves effort both prior to and after the actual choice. Thus, the decision as to whether to select Bill, Nancy, or Joan requires the accounting manager to ascertain whether a new junior auditor is needed, determine the availability of potential job candidates, interview candidates to acquire necessary information, select one candidate, and follow up with the socialization of the new employee into the organization to ensure the decision's success.

PROGRAMMED AND NONPROGRAMMED DECISIONS

Management decisions typically fall into one of two categories: programmed and nonprogrammed. **Programmed decisions** involve situations that have occurred often enough to enable decision rules to be developed and applied in the future.[4] Programmed decisions are made in response to recurring organizational problems. The decision to reorder paper and other office supplies when inventories drop to a certain level is a programmed decision. Other programmed decisions concern the types of skills required to fill certain jobs, the reorder point for manufacturing inventory, exception reporting for expenditures 10 percent or more over budget, and selection of freight routes for product deliveries. Once managers formulate decision rules, subordinates and others can make the decision, freeing managers for other tasks.

Nonprogrammed decisions are made in response to situations that are unique, are poorly defined and largely unstructured, and have important consequences for the organization. Nonprogrammed decisions often involve strategic planning, because uncertainty is great and decisions are complex. Nonprogrammed decisions would include decisions to build a new factory, develop a new product or service, enter a new geographical market, or relocate headquarters to a new city. The decision facing National Video's Ron Berger described at the beginning of this chapter is an example of a nonprogrammed decision. Routine decision rules or techniques for solving this problem do not exist. Berger will spend long hours analyzing the problems, developing alternatives, and making a choice about how to increase market share.

CERTAINTY, RISK, UNCERTAINTY, AND AMBIGUITY

In a perfect world, managers would have all the information necessary for making decisions. In reality, however, some things are unknowable; thus, some decisions will fail to solve the problem or attain the desired outcome. Managers try to obtain information about decision alternatives that will reduce decision uncertainty. Every decision situation can be organized on a scale according to the availability of information and the possibility of failure. The four positions on the scale are certainty, risk, uncertainty, and ambiguity, as illustrated in Exhibit 7.1.

CERTAINTY.   **Certainty** means that all the information the decision maker needs is fully available.[5] Managers have information on operating conditions, resource costs or constraints, and each course of action

programmed decision

A decision made in response to a situation that has occurred often enough to enable decision rules to be developed and applied in the future.

nonprogrammed decision

A decision made in response to a situation that is unique, is poorly defined and largely unstructured, and has important consequences for the organization.

certainty

All the information the decision maker needs is fully available.

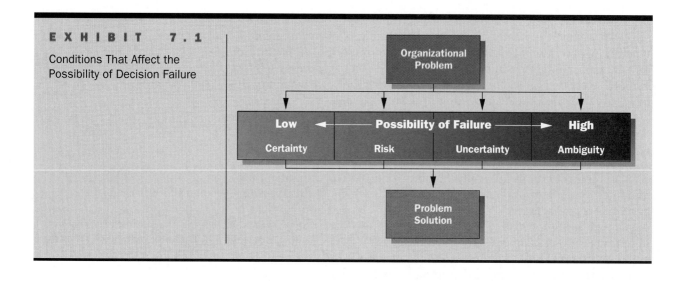

EXHIBIT 7.1

Conditions That Affect the Possibility of Decision Failure

and possible outcome. For example, if a company considers a $10,000 investment in new equipment that it knows for certain will yield $4,000 in cost savings per year over the next five years, managers can calculate a before-tax rate of return of about 40 percent. If managers compare this investment with one that will yield only $3,000 per year in cost savings, they can confidently select the 40 percent return. However, few decisions are certain in the real world. Most contain risk or uncertainty.

RISK. Risk means that a decision has clear-cut objectives and that good information is available, but the future outcomes associated with each alternative are subject to chance. However, enough information is available to allow the probability of a successful outcome for each alternative to be estimated.[6] Statistical analysis might be used to calculate the probabilities of success or failure. The measure of risk captures the possibility that future events will render the alternative unsuccessful. For example, a petroleum executive may bid to sell 10,000 barrels of a petroleum distillate, knowing that there is an 80 percent chance of success with a $5 per barrel price and a 50 percent chance with a $4.20 price. McDonald's took a calculated risk by encouraging franchise experimentation in menus and formats to meet the changing demands of a health-conscious public and increased competition, but with the possible downside risk of harming McDonald's reputation for speed and consistency.[7]

UNCERTAINTY. Uncertainty means that managers know which objectives they wish to achieve but information about alternatives and future events is incomplete.[8] Managers do not have enough information to be clear about alternatives or to estimate their risk. Factors that may affect a decision, such as price, production costs, volume, or future interest rates, are difficult to analyze and predict. Managers may have to make assumptions from which to forge the decision even though it will be wrong if the assumptions are incorrect. Managers may have to come up with creative approaches to alternatives and use personal judgment to determine which alternative is best.

risk

A decision has clear-cut objectives, and good information is available, but the future outcomes associated with each alternative are subject to chance.

uncertainty

Managers know what objective they wish to achieve but information about alternatives and future events is incomplete.

For example, Boeing faces great uncertainty in the decision to build the twenty-first-century airplane. Bypassing the traditional design route of building mock-ups, Boeing will build the new 777 plane, making the radical jump directly from computer image to finished product. Despite the collapse of air carriers such as Eastern and Pan Am, Boeing is gambling that its 777 will secure its future by filling the gap between the 218-passenger 767 and the 419-passenger 747.[9]

Many decisions made under uncertainty do not work out as desired, but sometimes managers must be risk takers. Risk taking is especially important when starting a new business, as illustrated in the Leading Edge box.

AMBIGUITY.   Ambiguity is by far the most difficult decision situation. **Ambiguity** means that the objectives to be achieved or the problem to be solved is unclear, alternatives are difficult to define, and information about outcomes is unavailable.[10] Ambiguity is what students would feel if an instructor created student groups, told each group to write a paper, but gave the groups no topic, direction, or guidelines whatsoever. Ambiguity has been called a "wicked" decision problem. Managers have a difficult time coming to grips with the issues. Wicked problems are associated with manager conflicts over objectives and decision alternatives, rapidly changing circumstances, fuzzy information, and unclear linkages among decision elements.[11] Fortunately, most decisions are not characterized by ambiguity. But when they are, managers must conjure up objectives and develop reasonable scenarios for decision alternatives in the absence of information. One example of an ambiguous decision was the marketing department assignment to develop an advertising campaign for a birth control device. Managers were unclear about advertising norms, to whom the ad should be targeted (men, women, marrieds, singles), ad content, or media. The entire approach had to be worked out without precedent.

ambiguity

The objectives to be achieved or the problem to be solved is unclear, alternatives are difficult to define, and information about outcomes is unavailable.

● DECISION-MAKING MODELS

The approach managers use to make decisions usually falls into one of two types—the classical model or the administrative model. The choice of model depends on the manager's personal preference, whether the decision is programmed or nonprogrammed, and the extent to which the decision is characterized by risk, uncertainty, or ambiguity.

CLASSICAL MODEL

The **classical model** of decision making is based on economic assumptions. This model has arisen within the management literature because managers are expected to make decisions that are economically sensible and in the organization's best economic interests. The assumptions underlying this model are as follows:

classical model

A decision-making model based on the assumption that managers should make logical decisions that will be in the organization's best economic interests.

LEADING edge   GATEWAY 2000

The business plan for Gateway 2000 seemed extraordinarily unextraordinary. In fact, maybe even suicidal. It called for entering a field of about 400 companies selling personal computers. Gateway 2000 would sell by mail order. No special technology or service support would be included. The advertisement campaign was eclectic to say the least. Surely the prognosis would be for a short company history. Incorrect. Gateway 2000, based in North Sioux City, South Dakota, had sales of $1 million in 1986; 1990 sales were $275 million. That compounded growth rate equals a mind-boggling 26,469 percent.

Company co-founder and chief executive Ted Waitt does not see much to get excited about. "People try to make things more complicated than they are," he says. "There's no magic formula. It all revolves around the way we do things." That may be just a bit of an understatement. Waitt has put together a string of risky but well-thought-out decisions. He trusted his intuition to determine what customers wanted. He relied on what appealed to him personally in promoting the products. In perhaps his shrewdest move, he did not let the astronomical growth of the company blur his vision or inflate his ego. That's good, because there are plenty of competitors sharpening their knives and waiting for the day that Waitt missteps, and Gateway takes a dive.

Holding one's breath isn't advisable. Waitt and his partner, Mike Hammond, have built Gateway on sound decision making. In an industry notorious for thin profit margins, they have been flinty-eyed about costs from the outset. "We can't operate on the margins they are operating on," says competitor Arthur Lazere of Northgate Computer Systems. The only high rises in the company's base of operations are windmills or water towers.

Low costs are only part of the story. Waitt relies on what he calls the "value equation." In his view, competitors were missing the real market by selling either stripped-down cheap models or PCs so loaded with the latest technology that they were not affordable. He decided to target the middle of the road, based on the theory that the business was about value, not price. He believed that adding technology made sense only if it adds value for the customer.

From the beginning, Waitt has never veered from his strategy of giving customers more for less. And, he won't incur additional overhead at the expense of profitability either. He decided early on to implement monthly cash bonuses to employees, based on company profits, which eliminated turnover problems.

Waitt knew a corollary key to establishing Gateway 2000 as a low-cost producer was to convince customers that the base was solid. Working from the assumption that mail-order computer buyers would diligently seek out the lowest price, he focused his advertisements on selling the company. In the jungle of PC purveyors, the Gateway advertisement came across as wholesome as a Norman Rockwell painting. Customers could depend on this company.

Ted Waitt has been virtually unerring in his business calls so far, but his biggest decisions may lie ahead. No company can undergo the level of growth Gateway 2000 has without adding management strata. Its problems there will not be any different than any other company: expand, but stay flexible and responsive. In the PC business there will likely never be a shortage of competition.

Gateway 2000 is at a crossroads. Waitt sensed from the beginning that competing on price alone was not the key to success. Logically, the next step would be to enter the corporate market, a different ball game entirely. Becoming a viable player in that market will require increasingly complex decisions relating to marketing, training, and product. Waitt is also pondering potential acquisition candidates. "You reach a plateau where you have to make the right choices," says Tom Quinlan, a hardware editor for *InfoWorld* magazine. "And even if you do, it's difficult to move to the next level." Waitt certainly appears ready for the challenge. ■

SOURCE: Joshua Hyatt, "Betting the Farm," *INC.*, December 1991, 36–45; "Clone King," *Business Week*, January 13, 1992, 134; Kyle Pope, "Gateway to Offer 10.9 Million Shares At $13 to $15 Each," *The Wall Street Journal*, October 22, 1993, A9.

1 The decision maker operates to accomplish objectives that are known and agreed upon. Problems are precisely formulated and defined.

2 The decision maker strives for conditions of certainty, gathering complete information. All alternatives and the potential results of each are calculated.

3 Criteria for evaluating alternatives are known. The decision maker selects the alternative that will maximize the economic return to the organization.

4 The decision maker is rational and uses logic to assign values, order preferences, evaluate alternatives, and make the decision that will maximize the attainment of organizational objectives.

The classical model of decision making is considered to be **normative,** which means it defines how a decision maker *should* make decisions. It does not describe how managers actually make decisions so much as it provides guidelines on how to reach an ideal outcome for the organization. The value of the classical model has been its ability to help decision makers be more rational. For example, many senior managers rely solely on intuition and personal preferences for making decisions.[12] In recent years, the classical approach has been given wider application because of the growth of quantitative decision techniques that use computers. Quantitative techniques (discussed in detail in the appendix) include such things as decision trees, pay-off matrices, breakeven analysis, linear programming, forecasting, and operations research models. The use of computerized information systems and data bases has increased the power of the classical approach.

In many respects, the classical model represents an "ideal" model of decision making that is often unattainable by real people in real organizations. It is most valuable when applied to programmed decisions and to decisions characterized by certainty or risk, because relevant information is available and probabilities can be calculated. One example of the classical approach is the decision model developed by Weyerhaeuser Company for converting a timber harvest into end products. It starts with the description of a tree—size and shape—and evaluates such factors as harvesting costs, hauling, mill location, facility operations, expected end products (plywood, dried trim, fiber, lumber), and customer demand. The model helps managers evaluate hundreds of possibilities for moving lumber through the production process to the consumer and choose the most economically efficient alternatives.[13]

ADMINISTRATIVE MODEL

The **administrative model** of decision making describes how managers actually make decisions in difficult situations, such as those characterized by nonprogrammed decisions, uncertainty, and ambiguity. Many management decisions are not sufficiently programmable to lend themselves to any degree of quantification. Managers are unable to make economically rational decisions even if they want to.[14]

normative

An approach that defines how a decision maker should make decisions and provides guidelines for reaching an ideal outcome for the organization.

administrative model

A decision-making model that describes how managers actually make decisions in situations characterized by nonprogrammed decisions, uncertainty, and ambiguity.

bounded rationality

The concept that people have the time and cognitive ability to process only a limited amount of information on which to base decisions.

satisfice

To choose the first solution alternative that satisfies minimal decision criteria regardless of whether better solutions are presumed to exist.

BOUNDED RATIONALITY AND SATISFICING. The administrative model of decision making is based on the work of Herbert A. Simon. Simon proposed two concepts that were instrumental in shaping the administrative model: bounded rationality and satisficing. **Bounded rationality** means that people have limits, or boundaries, on how rational they can be. The organization is incredibly complex, and managers have the time and ability to process only a limited amount of information with which to make decisions.[15] Because managers do not have the time or cognitive ability to process complete information about complex decisions, they must satisfice. **Satisficing** means that decision makers choose the first solution alternative that satisfies minimal decision criteria. Rather than pursuing all alternatives to identify the single solution that will maximize economic returns, managers will opt for the first solution that appears to solve the problem, even if better solutions are presumed to exist. The decision maker cannot justify the time and expense of obtaining complete information.[16]

An example of both bounded rationality and satisficing occurs when a junior executive on a business trip stains her blouse just prior to an important meeting. She will run to a nearby clothing store and buy the first satisfactory replacement she finds. Having neither the time nor the opportunity to explore all the blouses in town, she satisfices by choosing a blouse that will solve the immediate problem. In a similar fashion, managers generate alternatives for complex problems only until they find one they believe will work. For example, several years ago then-Disney chairman Ray Watson and chief operating officer Ron Miller attempted to thwart takeover attempts, but they had limited options. They satisficed with a quick decision to acquire Arivda Realty and Gibson Court Company. The acquisition of these companies had the potential to solve the problem at hand; thus, they looked no further for possibly better alternatives.[17]

The administrative model relies on assumptions different from those of the classical model and focuses on organizational factors that influence individual decisions. It is more realistic than the classical model for complex, nonprogrammed decisions. According to the administrative model,

1 Decision objectives often are vague, conflicting, and lack consensus among managers. Managers often are unaware of problems or opportunities that exist in the organization.

2 Rational procedures are not always used, and when they are, they are confined to a simplistic view of the problem that does not capture the complexity of real organizational events.

3 Managers' search for alternatives is limited because of human, information, and resource constraints.

4 Most managers settle for a satisficing rather than a maximizing solution. This is partly because they have limited information and partly because they have only vague criteria for what constitutes a maximizing solution.

descriptive

An approach that describes how managers actually make decisions rather than how they should.

The administrative model is considered to be **descriptive,** meaning that it describes how managers actually make decisions in complex situations rather than dictating how they *should* make decisions according to a theoretical ideal. The administrative model recognizes the human and environmental limitations that affect the degree to which managers can pursue a rational decision-making process.

INTUITION. Another aspect of administrative decision making is intuition. **Intuition** represents a quick apprehension of a decision situation based on past experience but without conscious thought.[18] Intuitive decision making is not arbitrary or irrational, because it is based on years of practice and hands-on experience that enable managers to quickly identify solutions without going through painstaking computations. Managers rely on intuition to determine when a problem exists and to synthesize isolated bits of data and experience into an integrated picture. They also use their intuitive understanding to check the results of rational analysis. If the rational analysis does not agree with their intuition, managers may dig further before accepting a proposed alternative.[19]

Intuition helps managers understand situations characterized by uncertainty and ambiguity that have proven impervious to rational analysis. For example, virtually every major studio in Hollywood turned down the *Star Wars* concept except 20th Century Fox. George Lucas, the creator of *Star Wars*, had attempted to sell the concept to 12 major studios before going to Fox. In each case, the concept had been rejected. All 13 studios saw the same numbers, but only Alan Ladd and his associates at Fox had the right "feel" for the decision. Their intuition told them that *Star Wars* would be a success. In addition, George Lucas was told by many experts that the title *Star Wars* would turn away crowds at the box office. His intuition said the title would work. The rest is history.[20]

COALITION BUILDING. The uncertainty of administrative decision making often requires coalition building. A **coalition** is an informal alliance among managers who support a specific goal. *Coalition building* is the process of forming alliances among managers. In other words, a manager who supports a specific alternative, such as increasing the corporation's growth by acquiring another company, talks informally to other executives and tries to persuade them to support the decision. When the outcomes are not predictable, managers gain support through discussion, negotiation, and bargaining. Without a coalition, a powerful individual or group could derail the decision-making process. Coalition building gives several managers an opportunity to contribute to decision making, enhancing their commitment to the alternative that is ultimately adopted.[21]

The successful coalition building of President George Bush in response to Saddam Hussein's invasion of Kuwait in 1990 was an example for both business and political decision makers. Bush successfully built a coalition among the heads of several countries by first having a clear understanding of the need for a coalition, then targeting his message to each coalition member by explaining why Hussein's action threatened each nation's future, and finally by constant communication with the head of each country in the coalition, Congress, and the American public.[22]

Recent research into decision-making procedures has found that the rational, classical procedures are associated with high performance for

intuition

The immediate comprehension of a decision situation based on past experience but without conscious thought.

coalition

An informal alliance among managers who support a specific goal.

Intuition enabled Harry V. Quadracci to pursue a dream, armed with only a handful of employees and one printing press. Today, Quad/Graphics enters its third decade, employs 5,000 people, and is one of the nation's fastest growing printers, serving magazines such as *Time*, *INC.*, and *Business Month*. The company recently topped $500 million in sales.

organizations in stable environments. However, administrative decision-making procedures and intuition have been associated with high performance in unstable environments in which decisions must be made rapidly and under more difficult conditions.[23]

● DECISION-MAKING STEPS

Whether a decision is programmed or nonprogrammed and regardless of the managers' choice of the classical or administrative model of decision making, six steps typically are associated with effective decision processes. These are summarized in Exhibit 7.2.

RECOGNITION OF DECISION REQUIREMENT

problem

A situation in which organizational accomplishments have failed to meet established objectives.

opportunity

A situation in which managers see potential organizational accomplishments that exceed current objectives.

Managers confront a decision requirement in the form of either a problem or an opportunity. A **problem** occurs when organizational accomplishment is less than established objectives. Some aspect of performance is unsatisfactory. An **opportunity** exists when managers see potential accomplishment that exceeds specified current objectives. Managers see the possibility of enhancing performance beyond current levels.

Awareness of a problem or opportunity is the first step in the decision sequence and requires surveillance of the internal and external environment for issues that merit executive attention.[24] This resembles the military concept of gathering intelligence. Managers scan the world around them to determine whether the organization is satisfactorily progressing toward its goals. For example, managers at Wells Fargo & Company in San Francisco survey employees to detect potential human resource problems. The survey covers effectiveness of company advertising, product quality, and responsibility to the community, as well as employee satisfaction and organizational climate.[25]

Some information comes from periodic accounting reports, MIS reports, and other sources that are designed to discover problems before they become too serious. Managers also take advantage of informal sources. They talk to other managers, gather opinions on how things are going, and seek advice on which problems should be tackled or which opportunities embraced.[26]

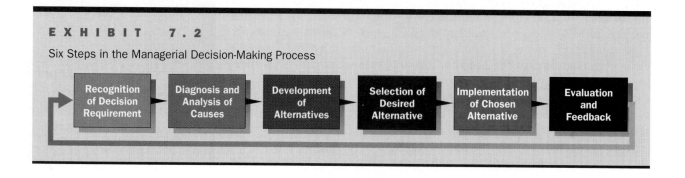

EXHIBIT 7.2

Six Steps in the Managerial Decision-Making Process

Recognition of Decision Requirement → Diagnosis and Analysis of Causes → Development of Alternatives → Selection of Desired Alternative → Implementation of Chosen Alternative → Evaluation and Feedback

Manhattan East Suite Hotels are taking advantage of *technology* to improve their customer service. Upon registering, a new guest is automatically entered into the hotel database; on future visits, the database will give information such as desired room location, requested view, and smoking or nonsmoking preferences.

Recognizing decision requirements is difficult, because it often means integrating bits and pieces of information in novel ways. For example, Worlds of Wonder, Inc., developed the first animated talking toy, called Teddy Ruxpin, and Lazer Tag. The astonishing success of these products was due to the pulse taking of customers. Worlds of Wonder works regularly with 1,000 families chosen at random to learn about problems and opportunities in the marketplace for toys. This early recognition contributed directly to the success of Lazer Tag, a toy geared for the young-adult market.[27]

DIAGNOSIS AND ANALYSIS OF CAUSES

Once a problem or opportunity has come to a manager's attention, the understanding of the situation should be refined. **Diagnosis** is the step in the decision-making process in which managers analyze underlying causal factors associated with the decision situation. Managers make a mistake here if they jump right into generating alternatives without first exploring the cause of the problem more deeply.

Kepner and Tregoe, who have conducted extensive studies of manager decision making, recommend that managers ask a series of questions to specify underlying causes, including the following:

- What is the state of disequilibrium affecting us?
- When did it occur?
- Where did it occur?
- How did it occur?
- To whom did it occur?
- What is the urgency of the problem?
- What is the interconnectedness of events?
- What result came from which activity?

diagnosis

The step in the decision-making process in which managers analyze underlying causal factors associated with the decision situation.

Such questions help specify what actually happened and why. Toyota asked questions like these when diagnosing the need for a new luxury car.

DEVELOPMENT OF ALTERNATIVES

Once the problem or opportunity has been recognized and analyzed, decision makers begin to consider taking action. The next stage is to generate possible alternative solutions that will respond to the needs of the situation and correct the underlying causes.

For a programmed decision, feasible alternatives are easy to identify and in fact usually are already available within the organization's rules and procedures. Nonprogrammed decisions, however, require developing new courses of action that will meet the company's needs. For decisions made under conditions of high uncertainty, managers may develop only one or two custom solutions that will satisfice for handling the problem.

Decision alternatives can be thought of as the tools for reducing the difference between the organization's current and desired performance.

SELECTION OF DESIRED ALTERNATIVE

Once feasible alternatives have been developed, one must be selected. The decision choice is the selection of the most promising of several alternative courses of action. The manager's goal is to make the choice with the least amount of risk and uncertainty. Because some risk is inherent for most nonprogrammed decisions, managers try to gauge prospects for success. Under conditions of uncertainty, they may have to rely on their intuition and experience to estimate whether a given course of action is likely to succeed.

risk propensity

The willingness to undertake risk with the opportunity of gaining an increased payoff.

Making choices depends on managers' personality factors and willingness to accept risk and uncertainty. For example, **risk propensity** is the willingness to undertake risk with the opportunity of gaining an increased payoff. The level of risk a manager is willing to accept will influence the analysis of cost and benefits to be derived from any decision. Consider the situations in Exhibit 7.3. In each situation, which alternative would you choose? A person with a low risk propensity would tend to take assured moderate returns by going for a tie score, building a domestic plant, or pursuing a career as a physician. A risk taker would go for the victory, build a plant in a foreign country, or embark on an acting career.

IMPLEMENTATION OF CHOSEN ALTERNATIVE

implementation

The step in the decision-making process that involves the employment of managerial, administrative, and persuasive abilities to translate the chosen alternative into action.

The **implementation** stage involves the use of managerial, administrative, and persuasive abilities to ensure that the chosen alternative is carried out. The ultimate success of the chosen alternative depends on whether it can be translated into action. Sometimes an alternative never becomes reality because managers lack the resources or energy needed to make things happen. Implementation may require discussion with

For each of the following decisions, which alternative would you choose?

1. In the final seconds of a game with the college's traditional rival, the coach of a college football team may choose a play that has a 95 percent chance of producing a tie score or one with a 30 percent chance of leading to victory or to sure defeat if it fails.

2. The president of a Canadian company must decide whether to build a new plant within Canada that has a 90 percent chance of producing a modest return on investment or to build it in a foreign country with an unstable political history. The latter alternative has a 40 percent chance of failing, but the returns would be enormous if it succeeded.

3. A college senior with considerable acting talent must choose a career. She has the opportunity to go on to medical school and become a physician, a career in which she is 80 percent likely to succeed. She would rather be an actress but realizes that the opportunity for success is only 20 percent.

people affected by the decision. Communication, motivation, and leadership skills must be used to see that the decision is carried out.

One reason Lee Iacocca succeeded in turning Chrysler around was his ability to implement decisions. Iacocca personally hired people from Ford to develop new auto models. He hired people who shared his vision and were eager to carry out his decisions. By contrast, Tandy Corporation's decision to become a major supplier to businesses by setting up 386 computer centers to support a new direct sales force foundered. Tandy has great success selling to consumers through its Radio Shack stores but simply did not know how to sell computers to businesses. The results were disappointing, and many of the computer centers had to be closed. Tandy lacked the ability to implement the decision to go after business customers.[28]

EVALUATION AND FEEDBACK

In the evaluation stage of the decision process, decision makers gather information that tells them how well the decision was implemented and whether it was effective in achieving its objectives. For example, Tandy executives' evaluation of and feedback on the decision to open computer centers revealed poor sales performance. Feedback indicated that implementation was unsuccessful, so computer centers were closed and another approach was tried.

Feedback is important because decision making is a continuous, never-ending process. Decision making is not completed when an executive or board of directors votes yes or no. Feedback provides decision makers with information that can precipitate a new decision cycle. The decision may fail, thus generating a new analysis of the problem, evaluation of alternatives, and selection of a new alternative. Many big problems are solved by trying several alternatives in sequence, each providing modest improvement. Feedback is the part of monitoring that assesses whether a new decision needs to be made.

MDS-Health Ventures, Inc., which provides venture capital for start-up companies, has received positive feedback about its decisions.

MDS HEALTH GROUP LIMITED

Ed Rygiel, senior vice-president of MDS Health Group Limited and CEO of MDS Health Ventures, Inc., the company's Toronto-based venture capital arm, is used to tackling tough decisions. What sets him apart is innovative thinking and a track record that's more than four times better than the average. In just under five years Rygiel has provided venture capital for 20 companies in the infant stage of development. By industry-wide standards, four winners would be normal; Rygiel's selected portfolio boasted 18 successes and two companies that merely performed below his expectations.

Corporate venture capitalists of the past generally limited fundings to businesses that complemented established operations. The symbiosis tended to retard any sort of growth away from the principal company. MDS avoids that pitfall by making rate of return on investments the top priority. Other traditions have also been flouted. Though the importance of management is acknowledged, MDS has underwritten ventures with scientists at the helm. But any company that merits backing can expect support from MDS on everything from scientific matters to administrative and facilities issues. The approach has been working; in 20 years the venture capital arm of the company has failed to increase profits only twice.[29] ∎

⬤ GROUP APPROACHES TO DECISION MAKING

Decision making is something that individual managers often do, but decision makers in the business world also operate as part of a group. Decisions may be made through a committee, a task group, departmental participation, or informal coalitions. The Vroom-Jago model provides ideas for including groups in decision making.

VROOM-JAGO MODEL

Some situations call for group rather than individual decision making. Vroom and Jago developed a model of participation in decision making that provides guidance for practicing managers.[30] The **Vroom-Jago model** helps the manager gauge the appropriate amount of participation for subordinates. It has three major components: leader participation styles, a set of diagnostic questions with which to analyze a decision situation, and a series of decision rules.

LEADER PARTICIPATION STYLES.   The model employs five levels of subordinate participation in decision making ranging from highly autocratic to highly democratic, as illustrated in Exhibit 7.4. Autocratic lead-

Vroom-Jago model

A model designed to help managers gauge the amount of subordinate participation in decision making.

ership styles are represented by AI and AII, consulting style by CI and CII, and a group decision by G. The five styles fall along a continuum, and the manager should select one depending on the situation. If the situation warrants, the manager could make the decision alone (AI), share the problem with subordinates individually (CI), or let group members make the decision (G).

DIAGNOSTIC QUESTIONS.   How does a manager decide which of the five decision styles to use? The appropriate degree of decision participation depends on the responses to eight diagnostic questions. These questions deal with the problem, the required level of decision quality, and the importance of having subordinates commit to the decision.

1 *Quality Requirement* **(QR)**: *How important is the quality of this decision?* If a high-quality decision is important for group performance, the leader has to be actively involved.

2 *Commitment Requirement* **(CR)**: *How important is subordinate commitment to the decision?* If implementation requires that subordinates commit to the decision, leaders should involve the subordinates in the decision process.

3 *Leader's Information* **(LI)**: *Do I have sufficient information to make a high-quality decision?* If the leader does not have sufficient information or expertise, the leader should involve subordinates to obtain that information.

4 *Problem Structure* **(ST)**: *Is the decision problem well structured?* If the problem is ambiguous and poorly structured, the leader will need to interact with subordinates to clarify the problem and identify possible solutions.

E X H I B I T   7 . 4

Five Leader Decision Styles

	Decision Style	Description
Highly Autocratic	**AI**	You solve the problem or make the decision yourself using information available to you at that time.
↑	**AII**	You obtain the necessary information from your subordinates and then decide on the solution to the problem yourself.
	CI	You share the problem with relevant subordinates individually, getting their ideas and suggestions without bringing them together as a group. Then you make the decision.
↓	**CII**	You share the problem with your subordinates as a group, collectively obtaining their ideas and suggestions. Then you make the decision.
Highly Democratic	**G**	You share a problem with your subordinates as a group. Your role is much like that of chairman. You do not try to influence the group to adopt "your" solution, and you are willing to accept and implement any solution that has the support of the entire group.

Note: A = autocratic; C = consultative; G = group.

SOURCE: Reprinted from *The New Leadership: Managing Participation in Organizations* by Victor H. Vroom and Arthur G. Jago, Englewood Cliffs, NJ: Prentice-Hall, 1988. Copyright 1987 by V. H. Vroom and A. G. Jago. Used with permission of the authors.

5 *Commitment Probability* **(CP)**: *If I were to make the decision by myself, is it reasonably certain that my subordinates would be committed to the decision?* If subordinates typically go along with whatever the leader decides, their involvement in the decision process will be less important.

6 *Goal Congruence* **(GC)**: *Do subordinates share the organizational goals to be attained in solving this problem?* If subordinates do not share the goals of the organization, the leader should not allow the group to make the decision alone.

7 *Subordinate Conflict* **(CO)**: *Is conflict over preferred solutions likely to occur among subordinates?* Disagreement among subordinates can be resolved by allowing their participation and discussion.

8 *Subordinate Information* **(SI)**: *Do subordinates have enough information to make a high-quality decision?* If subordinates have good information, then more responsibility for the decision can be delegated to them.

These questions seem detailed, but they quickly narrow the options available to managers and point to the appropriate level of group participation in the decision.

SELECTING A DECISION STYLE. The decision flowchart in Exhibit 7.5 allows a leader to adopt a participation style by answering the questions in sequence. The leader begins at the left side of the chart with question **QR**: How important is the quality of the decision? If the answer is high, then the leader proceeds to question **CR**: How important is subordinate commitment to the decision? If the answer is high, the next question is **LI**: Do I have sufficient information to make a high-quality decision? If the answer is yes, the leader proceeds to answer question **CP** because question **ST** is irrelevant if the leader has sufficient information to make a high-quality decision. Managers can quickly learn to use the basic model to adapt their leadership styles to fit their decision problem and the situation.

Several decision styles are equally acceptable in many situations. When this happens, Vroom and Jago recommend using the most autocratic style because this will save time without reducing decision quality or acceptance.

Although the decision tree model has been criticized as being less than perfect,[31] it is useful to decision makers, and the body of supportive research is growing.[32] Managers make timely, high-quality decisions when following the model. One application of the model occurred at Barouh-Eaton Allen Corporation.

 KO·REC·TYPE

Barouh-Eaton Allen started prospering when owner Vic Barouh noticed that a typist kept a piece of white chalk by her machine. To erase an error, she would lightly rub over it with the chalk. It took several passes, but the correction was neatly made. Barouh's company already made carbon paper, so he tried rubbing chalk on one side of a sheet of paper,

EXHIBIT   7.5

Vroom-Jago Decision Tree for Determining an Appropriate Decision-Making Method—Group Problems

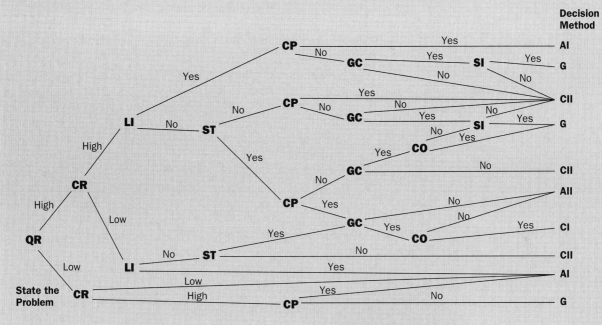

QR How important is the quality of this decision?

CR How important is subordinate commitment to the decision?

LI Do you have sufficient information to make a high-quality decision?

ST Is the problem well structured?

CP If you were to make the decision by yourself, is it reasonably certain that your subordinates would be committed to it?

GC Do subordinates share the organization goals to be attained in solving this problem?

CO Is conflict among subordinates over preferred solutions likely?

SI Do subordinates have sufficient information to make a high-quality decision?

SOURCE: Reprinted from *The New Leadership: Managing Participation in Organizations* by Victor H. Vroom and Arthur G. Jago, Englewood Cliffs, NJ: Prentice-Hall, 1988. Copyright 1987 by V. H. Vroom and A. G. Jago. Used with permission of the authors.

putting the paper between the error and typewriter, and striking the same key. Most of the error disappeared under a thin coating of chalk dust. Thus, Ko-Rec-Type was born. Demand for the product was enormous, and the company prospered.

Then IBM invented the self-correcting typewriter. Within two days after IBM's announcement, nearly 40 people told Barouh that the company was in trouble. Nobody was going to buy Ko-Rec-Type again.

Barouh bought a self-correcting typewriter, took it to the plant, called everybody together, and told them what they had to do. To survive, the company had to learn to make this ribbon. They also had to learn to make the cartridge that held the ribbon, because cartridges could not be purchased on the market. They also had to learn to make the spools that held the tape. They had to learn to make the ink, the machine that puts on ink, injection-molding to make the spools, and so on. It was an enormous challenge. Barouh got everyone involved regardless of position or education.

To everyone's astonishment, Ko-Rec-Type produced the first self-correcting ribbon in only six months. Moreover, it was the only company in the world to produce that product. Barouh later learned that it took IBM six years to make its self-correcting ribbon. With the new product, Ko-Rec-Type's sales remained high and the company avoided disaster.[33] ■

The Vroom-Jago model shows that Vic Barouh used the correct decision style. Moving from left to right in Exhibit 7.5, the questions and answers are as follows. **(QR)** *How important is the quality of this decision?* Definitely high. **(CR)** *How important is subordinate commitment to the decision?* Importance of commitment is probably low, because subordinates had a great deal of respect for Barouh and would do whatever he asked. **(LI)** *Did Barouh have sufficient information to make a high-quality decision?* Definitely no. **(ST)** *Is the problem well structured?* Definitely no. The remaining questions are not relevant because at this point the decision tree leads directly to the CII decision style. Barouh should have used a consultative decision style by having subordinates participate in problem discussions as a group—which he did.

● IMPROVING DECISION-MAKING EFFECTIVENESS

The Vroom-Jago model illustrates that managers can select the amount of group participation in decision making. They can also select decision format. Nominal and Delphi groups normally are convened for the purpose of increasing creativity during group decision making.

NOMINAL GROUPS. Because some participants may talk more and dominate group discussions in interactive groups, the **nominal group** technique was developed to ensure that every group participant has equal input in the decision-making process.[34] The nominal group is structured in a series of steps to equalize participation:

nominal group

A group decision-making format that emphasizes equal participation in the decision process by all group members.

1 Each participant writes down his or her ideas on the problem to be discussed. These ideas usually are suggestions for a solution.

2 A round robin in which each group member presents his or her ideas to the group is set up. The ideas are written down on a blackboard for all members to see. No discussion of the ideas occurs until every person's ideas have been presented and written down for general viewing.

3 After all ideas have been presented, there is an open discussion of the ideas for the purpose of clarification and evaluation. This part of the discussion tends to be spontaneous and unstructured.

4 After the discussion, a secret ballot is taken in which each group member votes for preferred solutions. The adopted decision is the one that receives the most votes.

DELPHI GROUPS. Developed by the Rand Corporation, the **Delphi group** technique is used to combine expert opinions from different perspectives about an ambiguous problem.[35] Unlike interactive and nominal groups, Delphi group participants do not meet face to face—in fact, they never see one another. This technique calls for a group leader to solicit and collate written, expert opinions on a topic through the use of questionnaires. After the answers are received, a summary of the opinions is developed and distributed to participants. Then a new questionnaire on the same problem is circulated. In this second round, participants have the benefit of knowing other people's opinions and can change their suggested answers to reflect this new information. The process of sending out questionnaires and then sharing the results continues until a consensus is reached.

One potential problem in group decision making is groupthink. **Groupthink** is a "mode of thinking that people engage in when they are deeply involved in a cohesive in-group, and when the members' strivings for unanimity override their motivation to realistically appraise alternative courses of action."[36] Groupthink means that people are so committed to the group that they are reluctant to disagree with one another; thus, the group loses the diversity of opinions essential to effective decision making. Another problem—particularly when groups are used for programmed decisions—is decision overkill due to the task's lack of challenge for group members. Finally, there is no clear focus of decision responsibility, because the group rather than any single individual makes the decision.

How can managers overcome groupthink and other disadvantages to avoid costly mistakes? A number of techniques have been developed to help individual managers and groups arrive at better decisions.

A **devil's advocate** is assigned the role of challenging the assumptions and assertions made by the group.[37] The devil's advocate forces the group to rethink its approach to the problem and to avoid reaching premature consensus or making unreasonable assumptions before proceeding with problem solutions.

Multiple advocacy is similar to a devil's advocate except that more advocates and points of view are presented. Minority opinions and unpopular viewpoints are assigned to forceful representatives, who then debate before the decision makers. President Bush was renowned for using multiple advocacy in his decision making. The proposal for clean-air legislation in 1989 was a textbook case, because White House aides staged debates they called "Scheduled Train Wrecks" to help Bush think through the issue. These were live scrimmages with Bush asking questions back and forth during the debate. The result was a decision based on solid argument and understanding of all perspectives.[38]

Brainstorming uses a face-to-face, interactive group to spontaneously suggest ideas for problem solution.[39] Brainstorming is perhaps the best-known decision aid; its primary role is to supply additional, creative solutions. Group members are invited to suggest alternatives regardless of their likelihood of being implemented. No critical comments of any kind are allowed until all suggestions have been listed. Members are encouraged to brainstorm possible solutions out loud, and freewheeling

Delphi group

A group decision-making format that involves the circulation among participants of questionnaires on the selected problem, sharing of answers, and continuous recirculation/refinement of questionnaires until a consensus has been obtained.

groupthink

A phenomenon in which group members are so committed to the group that they are reluctant to express contrary opinions.

devil's advocate

A decision-making technique in which an individual is assigned the role of challenging the assumptions and assertions made by the group to prevent premature consensus.

multiple advocacy

A decision-making technique that involves several advocates and presentation of multiple points of view, including minority and unpopular opinions.

brainstorming

A decision-making technique in which group members present spontaneous suggestions for problem solution, regardless of their likelihood of implementation, in order to promote freer, more creative thinking within the group.

is welcomed. The more novel and unusual the idea, the better. The object of brainstorming is to promote freer, more flexible thinking and to enable group members to build on one another's creativity. The typical session begins with a warmup wherein definitional issues are settled, proceeds through the freewheeling idea-generation stage, and concludes with an evaluation of feasible ideas.[40]

● USING INFORMATION TECHNOLOGY FOR DECISION MAKING

In a very realistic sense, information is the lifeblood of organizations. To appreciate how managers use information in decision making, let us first distinguish data from information and then look at the characteristics of useful information.

DATA VERSUS INFORMATION

data

Raw, unsummarized, and unanalyzed facts.

information

Data that are meaningful and alter the receiver's understanding.

The terms *data* and *information* often are used interchangeably. Yet there is an important difference. **Data** are raw, unsummarized, and unanalyzed facts. **Information** refers to data that are meaningful and alter the receiver's understanding.[41] Information is the data that managers actually use to interpret and understand events in the organization and the environment. For example, Hardee's Restaurants' information systems monitor thousands of data transactions, including food sales, sales tax, water and electricity use, and movement of inventory. However, the raw

Information and computers can be used for more than processing *raw data*. At Boeing, sophisticated digital computer work stations are being used to design and preassemble 100 percent of the Boeing 777 airplane. Customized software will improve accuracy and enhance overall airframe quality.

data are worthless. Data require proper organization to produce meaningful information, such as total sales for all Hardee's Restaurants, sales by store and region, and key efficiency and profitability ratios. By analyzing the data and making comparisons with past performance, planners can both measure results and project future activity. Hardee's successful use of this information system contributed significantly to its rise to number three in the fast-food industry.[42]

CHARACTERISTICS OF USEFUL INFORMATION

What makes information valuable? Information has many attributes, such as verifiability, accessibility, clarity, precision, and cost. Four factors that are especially important for management information are quality, timeliness, completeness, and relevance, as illustrated in Exhibit 7.6.[43]

QUALITY. Information that accurately portrays reality is said to have **quality.** The data are accurate and reliable. If the data say that a valve in a nuclear power plant is open, such quality is important to management decision making. A police officer in San Jose, California, runs a license plate check by tapping into the state license plate records system. If the data were inaccurate, an innocent person could be stopped or a guilty one let go.[44] Quality is what makes any information system work. Once a system is known to have errors, managers will no longer use it, and its value for decision making will disappear.

quality

The degree to which information accurately portrays reality.

TIMELINESS. Information that is available soon after events occur has **timeliness.** Managers work at a fast pace, and things change quickly. The most immediate benefit of computerized management is quick response time. Companies can shorten new-product development time, respond immediately to competitive changes, and shrink the control and feedback cycle within organizations. At Oxford Industries, an Atlanta clothing company, workers' activities are clocked to a thousandth of a minute.

timeliness

The degree to which information is available soon after events occur.

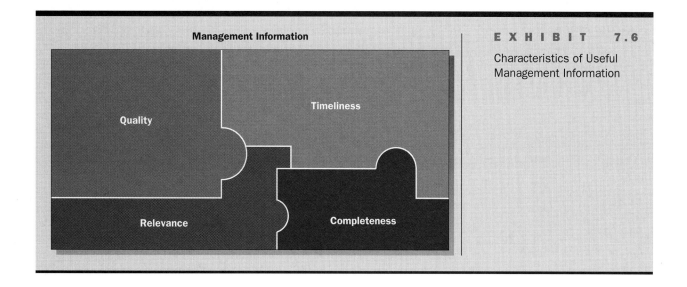

Management Information

Quality

Timeliness

Relevance

Completeness

EXHIBIT 7.6

Characteristics of Useful Management Information

Oxford has figured, for instance, that a stitcher should spend 3.4 seconds on each front pocket and may work on 5,000 pockets a day. The information system gives running updates throughout the day of each worker's pace so that problems can be solved immediately.[45]

completeness

The extent to which information contains the appropriate amount of data.

COMPLETENESS. Information **completeness** refers to the proper quantity of data. Too much data lead to information overload; too little fail to tell the complete story. Managers exercise control by recognizing deviations from targets and instituting necessary changes. Managers often devise *exception reports* that contain only a few pages of deviations from target rather than hundreds of pages of raw data. These reports are complete because they contain key information, but in an amount managers can digest.

relevance

The degree to which information pertains to the problems, decisions, and tasks for which a manager is responsible.

RELEVANCE.   Information **relevance** means that the information must pertain to the problems, decisions, and tasks for which a manager is responsible. Information relevance is a difficult problem for an information system to solve, because every manager's situation is unique. Production managers need data on scrap rates, production volume, and employee productivity. Human resource managers need data on employee background, work experience, insurance programs, employee demographics, and position descriptions. Marketing managers need data on customer accounts, sales forecasts, sales activity, and individual salespeople's commissions.

INFORMATION SYSTEMS

information system

A mechanism for collecting, organizing, and distributing data to organizational employees.

Now that we understand the characteristics of useful information, we will discuss systems for providing information to managers. An **information system** is a mechanism that collects, organizes, and distributes data to organizational personnel. Most information systems are manual, which means that people perform the information activities by hand. For example, Northrop Corporation's manual system generated 400,000 pieces of paper when building each fuselage for the F/A-18 jet fighter. A **computer-based information system (CBIS)** is a system that uses electronic computing technology to create the information system. A CBIS differs from a manual system only in the physical components that perform the functions. Input into a CBIS may be done through a terminal or automatic scanning systems. The computer manipulates data according to defined procedures. Data storage is electronic in the form of magnetic tapes and disks that can store huge volumes of data. Control over the system is provided by a software program that contains specific instructions for organizing data needed by users. Outputs are computer reports of data provided on a terminal screen.

computer-based information system (CBIS)

An information system that uses electronic computing technology to create the information system.

Northrop converted to a computerized information system for building jet fighters. The 10-foot pile of paper (400,000 pieces) for each fuselage was put on one laser disk. Employees now consult a computer for instructions. Supervisors can make instant changes in procedures across the factory, avoiding the inconvenience and confusion of paper changes. Computerizing the information provided a remarkable improvement in timeliness, while maintaining high quality, completeness, and relevance.

The new system helped Northrop save $20 million on the fuselage project.[46]

Connecticut Mutual Life Insurance Company cut average customer query response time from five days to a few hours and increased productivity over 35 percent by phasing out its "paper monster." Information on its 1.2 million policyholders, once housed in football field-size warehouses and requiring fleets of shuttle vans, is now stored on optical disks readily accessed by employees with IBM PCs.[47]

MANAGEMENT INFORMATION SYSTEMS. A **management information system (MIS)** is a mechanism that collects, organizes, and distributes data used by managers in performing their management functions. As information systems evolved, management information systems were the next stage of evolution beyond transaction processing systems. As data bases accumulated, managers began visualizing ways in which the computer could help them make important decisions. Managers needed information in summary form that pertained to specific management problems. The lists of thousands of daily organizational transactions were useless for planning, controlling, or decision making.

MISs provide information reports designed to help managers make decisions. For example, when a production manager needs to make decisions about production scheduling, he or she may need data on the anticipated number of orders in the coming month based on trends, current inventory levels, and availability of equipment and personnel. The MIS can provide these data. At Visible Changes hair salons, for example, managers use the MIS to learn about customer age and sex, repeat business, and productivity by salon and hair stylist."[48]

The MIS requires more complex software that instructs computers to translate data into useful reports. Computer hardware also has become more complex and sophisticated because it needs greater capacity and the ability to integrate diverse data bases. For example, thousands of transactions take place daily in supermarkets. One leader in developing management information systems is Gromer Supermarket, Inc.

management information system (MIS)

A form of CBIS that collects, organizes, and distributes the data managers use in performing their management functions.

 GROMER SUPERMARKET, INC.

Gromer is a huge superstore in Elgin, Illinois. The laser scanners at Gromer's ten checkout counters speed shoppers through the checkout lines, but more important, they provide a great deal of information. Millions of transactions are recorded, and a quarter of a million dollars' worth of computer hardware and software are used to provide management reports on everything from checker efficiency to bagging speed and food turnover. Take cereal, for example. The MIS data showed that Rice Krispies had six size categories, but two were slow movers and thus were eliminated.

In the meat department, MIS reports tell the meat manager how much gross margin a side of beef will produce. The system also describes the cuts from a pork loin that will maximize gross profits. Labor cost decisions are made efficiently because the number of baggers scheduled to work is chosen to fit the number of customers coming through the store and the known rate at which a bagger can bag. The millions of numbers crunched through the MIS system help managers decide how to display products, which products to stock, and how to make storage and delivery more efficient.[49] ■

EXECUTIVE INFORMATION SYSTEMS.   Until recently, information systems have not possessed the sophistication and simplicity that senior executives needed. Executive information systems were developed because managers needed help with unanticipated and unstructured problems that MISs were not flexible enough to provide.

An **executive information system (EIS)** is the use of computer technology to support the information needs of senior managers.[50] EISs were formed from powerful PCs that could shape masses of numbers into simple, colorful charts and from networks that can weave together a company's different hardware and data bases.[51] EISs are also called *decision support systems,* because they allow an executive to interact with the information system to retrieve, manipulate, and display data needed to make specific decisions. For example, the CEO of Duracell asked for data comparing the performance of hourly and salaried work forces in the United States and overseas. Within seconds, he received a table showing that U.S. workers produced more sales. Asking for more data, he discovered that too many overseas salespeople were wasting time calling on small stores. As a result, executives made the decision to sign up distributors to cover small stores, improving foreign profits.[52] EISs give managers access to multiple data bases, depending on their immediate information needs, as illustrated in Exhibit 7.7.

Executive information systems deal with nonprogrammed decisions such as strategic planning. Consequently, the hardware and software technologies are very sophisticated. Indeed, to be accessible to top managers who are not computer experts, up to 75 percent of the computer system's capacity may be used for software that permits managers to "talk" to the system in everyday English. This frees the remaining 25 percent to handle multiple data bases, translate inquiries into simple graphs and charts, and provide an instant answer to almost any ques-

executive information system (EIS)

An interactive CBIS that retrieves, manipulates, and displays information serving the needs of top managers; also called *decision support system.*

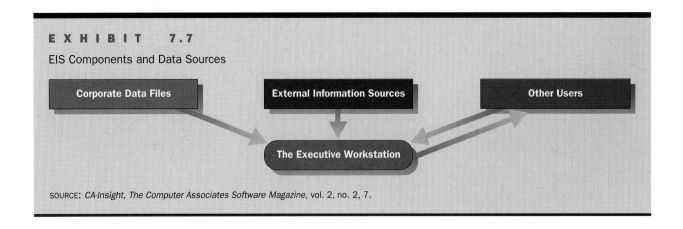

E X H I B I T   7 . 7

EIS Components and Data Sources

Corporate Data Files

External Information Sources

Other Users

The Executive Workstation

SOURCE: *CA-Insight, The Computer Associates Software Magazine,* vol. 2, no. 2, 7.

tion. Initial research indicates that EISs help people make faster and more effective decisions, an important consideration in today's global marketplace.[53]

EISs are being adopted widely. The following are some examples:[54]

- At California Federal, an EIS is used to track CD maturity projections and both consumer and mortgage loan growth to develop a strategy to ensure that managers are on top of opportunities and problems.

- The president of Pratt & Whitney uses an EIS nearly every day to monitor and act on new engine development and manufacturing status information.

- The treasurer of General Motors uses an EIS to get immediate access to international currency information so he can direct currency moves and get instant answers when other GM executives call.

● STRATEGIC USE OF INFORMATION TECHNOLOGY

The adoption of information systems such as MISs, or EISs, has strategic consequences for organizations. One desired consequence is improved operational efficiency, especially in the management functions of decision making and controlling. Operational efficiency enables a company to lower costs, making it more competitive. Another desired consequence is to present new strategic options to

Management efficiency can be greatly improved by the *strategic use of information technology* such as teleconferencing. Employees and managers at diverse locations can be brought together to resolve crises, coordinate projects, and keep communication lines open.

senior managers. Information technology enables the organization to lock in customers and broaden market reach. These options differentiate the firm strategically, giving it advantage in the marketplace.

OPERATIONAL EFFICIENCY AND CONTROL

MANAGEMENT EFFICIENCY. The impact of information technology on management falls primarily on the functions of decision making and control. Information technology is easily adapted to first-line management activities such as production, scheduling, inventory management, and office procedures. At middle management levels, desktop terminals give managers access to more information than ever before, and electronic mail and computer conferencing enable coordination and rapid communication. With electronic mail, managers can avoid telephone tag. Just the reduction in paperwork can improve management efficiency at all levels. Recall how Northrop saved 400,000 pieces of paper on each fuselage it built and how Connecticut Mutual Life Insurance Co. puts its documents on optical disks, giving employees immediate access to documents and saving tons of paperwork.[55]

The efficiency of information technology is realized in many companies by the appointment of a *chief information officer* (CIO) who is responsible for managing organizational data bases and implementing new information technology. Technology can be selected and implemented to fit the strategic needs of the organization. For example, at Primerica, a vice-president of information services spent 75 percent of his time using information technology to cut costs, the key need for Primerica to stay competitive.

A recent phenomenon is the new breed of "wired executives" who can increasingly abandon the confines of corporate offices while staying on top of business through technology. Portable computers, E-mail, cellular phones, voice mail, and faxes have freed executives and allowed them greater productivity. Manville Corp. CEO W. Thomas Stephens sees the computer as mind extension. "It gives you an opportunity to be a lot more powerful and to focus on being creative, rather than spending your time making charts and that sort of thing."[56]

IMPROVED COORDINATION, FLEXIBILITY. Another efficiency of information technology is to break down barriers among departments and across hierarchical levels. Managers who are wired into a computer system communicate with anyone who can help solve a problem. Citicorp managers around the globe seek advice from one another thanks to a computer conferencing system.

cluster organization

An organizational form in which team members from different company locations use CBIS such as electronic mail to solve problems.

A new organizational form is developing called the *cluster organization*. In a **cluster organization,** groups of people work together to solve business problems and then disband when the job is done.[57] At Digital Equipment Corporation, new teams are brought together face-to-face for a week or more to develop closeness and friendship. Then managers return to their regular locations around the world and communicate by electronic mail and group decision support systems. Teams can be clustered together in infinite combinations to solve problems that arise. When a problem is solved, the team disbands and individuals are reformed into new teams.

SMALLER MANAGEMENT STRUCTURE.   The general outcome of information technology has been to reverse the trend of hiring new managers. By speeding up information routing, the number of managers in many organizations has been reduced. This reduction has resulted in an increased span of control and a decrease in the number of levels in the management hierarchy.[58] Technology allows managers to increase their spans of control.

One organization that relies heavily on information technology is cookie retailer Mrs. Fields, Inc., chairman Randy Fields firmly believes in technology as an important management tool to cut paper work, streamline decision making, and provide employees direct access to top managers. Technology has empowered employees at Mrs. Fields and shaved layers of management from the organization chart, creating a flat organization. Fields' commitment to technology is reflected in his day-to-day actions. "If someone comes into my office without their lap-top computer, I tell them, I don't think I can talk to you now. Get your lap-top."[59]

COMPETITIVE STRATEGY

LOCK IN CUSTOMERS.   One of the strengths of computer-based information technology is the competitive advantage with customers. Consider American Hospital Supply Corporation, a health goods manufacturer.

 AMERICAN HOSPITAL SUPPLY CORPORATION

In a smart strategic move, senior executives at American Hospital Supply Corporation decided to give computer terminals free to hospitals around the country. These terminals linked hospital purchasers with American Hospital Supply and enabled them to directly place orders for any of more than 100,000 products. This corporate strategy linked the company directly to its customers, and it was a strategic breakthrough. AHS gained sales and market share at competitors' expense. Hospitals had the advantage of lowered inventory carrying costs, because they were confident that orders with AHS would be processed quickly. AHS was one of the first companies to use information technology in corporate strategy. Customers were locked in because they could not switch to another supplier without losing efficiency and convenience. Interorganizational linkage can link a company with suppliers and bankers as well as customers to gain speedy transactions, providing further competitive advantage.[60] ■

BROADEN MARKET REACH.   Information technology can be used to tap into market intelligence data bases on competitors, demographics, customers, and census factors to spot unused niches and needs for new products. By having salespeople use lap-top computers in the field, a quick call can confirm inventory availability and instantly close a deal. Speed and timely service give an advantage over competitors. For example, Red Lion Inns uses a computer network to target messages to customer groups, give salespeople methods for entering orders directly through portable computers, and stimulate new product features.

SUMMARY AND MANAGEMENT SOLUTION

This chapter made several points about the process of organizational decision making. The study of decision making is important because it describes how managers make successful strategic and operational decisions. Managers must confront many types of decisions, including programmed and nonprogrammed, and decisions differ according to the amount of risk, uncertainty, and ambiguity in the environment.

Two decision-making approaches were described in the classical model and the administrative model. The classical model explains how managers should make decisions so as to maximize economic efficiency. The administrative model describes how managers actually make nonprogrammed, uncertain decisions with skills that include intuition and coalition building.

Decision making should involve six basic steps: problem recognition, diagnosis of causes, development of alternatives, choice of an alternative, implementation of alternative, and feedback and evaluation.

Ron Berger came up with a system he dubbed PPT, or pay-per-transaction. He established a distribution company, Rentrak, which was based on a simple premise that was at first hard to sell. He had to convince movie studios to sell videocassettes to retailers for around $10. For this drastic reduction, the stores would reimburse a kind of royalty back to the studios that ranged from 25 to 55 percent of rental revenue. The sticking point was keeping track of it all; but Berger developed a computerized system that was simple to audit. He eventually took a huge gamble and sold National to concentrate solely on Rentrak. He entered an agreement with a Capital Cities/ABC subsidiary to create a type of scanner that overcomes incompatible software. It could open doors to huge retail outlets that are disinclined to tamper with their existing computer systems. Berger tackled a problem of inefficient operation. Unexpectedly, he is now trying to extend his solution throughout the entire video rental market.[61]

The chapter also described how decisions can be made within organizational groups. The Vroom-Jago model specifies decision characteristics that indicate when groups should participate in decision making. The types of groups may also include nominal groups and Delphi groups. Groups offer a number of advantages and disadvantages compared with individuals. Techniques for improving decision-making quality include devil's advocate, multiple advocacy, and brainstorming. These techniques help managers define problems and develop more creative solutions.

Information systems also process huge amounts of data and transform them into useful information for managers in decision making. Useful information has the characteristics of quality, timeliness, completeness, and relevance. Computer-based information systems provide information for middle managers, and executive information systems help senior executives with strategic questions.

DISCUSSION QUESTIONS

1. You are a busy partner in a legal firm, and an experienced secretary complains of continued headaches, drowsiness, dry throat, and occasional spells of fatigue and flu. She tells you she believes air quality in the building is bad and would like something done. How would you respond?
2. Why is decision making considered a fundamental part of management effectiveness?
3. Explain the difference between risk and ambiguity. How might decision making differ for each situation?
4. Analyze three decisions you made over the past six months. Which of these are programmed, and which are nonprogrammed?
5. The Vroom-Jago model describes five decision styles. How should a manager go about choosing which style to use?
6. What are three types of decision-making groups? How might each be used to help managers make a decision to market a product in a new geographical territory?
7. What is meant by *satisficing* and *bounded rationality*? Why do managers not strive to find the economically best solution for many organizational decisions?
8. What are four characteristics of useful information? How can information systems be designed to include these characteristics?
9. What is an executive information system? How does an EIS differ from an MIS?

MANAGEMENT IN PRACTICE: EXPERIENTIAL EXERCISE

● THE DESERT SURVIVAL SITUATION

The situation described in this exercise is based on over 2,000 actual cases in which men and women lived or died depending on the survival decisions they made. Your "life" or "death" will depend on how well your group can share its present knowledge of a relatively unfamiliar problem so that the team can make decisions that will lead to your survival.

This exercise will challenge your ability to take advantage of a group approach to decision making and to apply decision steps such as developing alternatives and selecting the correct alternative. When instructed, read about the situation and do Step 1 without discussing it with the rest of the group.

The Situation It is approximately 10:00 A.M. in mid-August, and you have just crash landed in the Sonora Desert in the southwestern United States. The light twin-engine plane, containing the bodies of the pilot and the copilot, has completely burned. Only the air frame remains. None of the rest of you has been injured.

The pilot was unable to notify anyone of your position before the crash. However, he had indicated before impact that you were 70 miles south-southwest from a mining camp that is the nearest known habitation and that you were approximately 65 miles off the course that was filed in your VFR Flight Plan.

The immediate area is quite flat and, except for occasional barrel and saguaro cacti, appears to be rather barren. The last weather report indicated the temperature would reach 110° that day, which means that the temperature at ground level will be 130°. You are dressed in lightweight clothing: short-sleeved shirts, pants, socks, and street shoes. Everyone has a handkerchief. Collectively, your pockets contain $2.83 in change, $85.00 in bills, a pack of cigarettes, and a ballpoint pen.

Your Task Before the plane caught fire, your group was able to salvage the 15 items listed in the following table. Your task is to rank these items according to their importance to your survival, starting with "1," the most important, to "15," the least important.

You may assume the following:

1. The number of survivors is the same as the number on your team.
2. You are the actual people in the situation.
3. The team has agreed to stick together.
4. All items are in good condition.

Step 1 Each member of the team is to individually rank each item. Do not discuss the situation or problem until each member has finished the individual ranking.

Step 2 After everyone has finished the individual ranking, rank order the 15 items as a team. Once discussion begins, do not change your individual ranking. Your instructor will inform you how much time you have to complete this step.

Items	Step 1: Your Individual Ranking	Step 2: The Team's Ranking	Step 3: Survival Expert's Ranking	Step 4: Difference between Step 1 and Step 3	Step 5: Difference between Step 2 and Step 3
Flashlight (4-battery size)	_____	_____	_____	_____	_____
Jackknife	_____	_____	_____	_____	_____
Sectional air map of the area	_____	_____	_____	_____	_____
Plastic raincoat (large size)	_____	_____	_____	_____	_____
Magnetic compass	_____	_____	_____	_____	_____
Compress kit with gauze	_____	_____	_____	_____	_____
.45 caliber pistol (loaded)	_____	_____	_____	_____	_____
Parachute (red and white)	_____	_____	_____	_____	_____
Bottle of salt tablets (1,000 tablets)	_____	_____	_____	_____	_____
1 quart of water per person	_____	_____	_____	_____	_____
A book entitled *Edible Animals of the Desert*	_____	_____	_____	_____	_____
A pair of sunglasses per person	_____	_____	_____	_____	_____
2 quarts of 180 proof vodka	_____	_____	_____	_____	_____
1 topcoat per person	_____	_____	_____	_____	_____
A cosmetic mirror	_____	_____	_____	_____	_____
Totals (the lower the score, the better)	_____	_____	_____	_____	_____
				Your Score, Step 4	Team Score, Step 5

Please complete the following steps and insert the scores under your team's number.	Team Number					
	1	2	3	4	5	6
Step 6: Average Individual Score Add up all the individual scores (Step 4) on the team and divide by the number on the team.	_____	_____	_____	_____	_____	_____
Step 7: Team Score	_____	_____	_____	_____	_____	_____
Step 8: Gain Score The difference between the Team Score and the Average Individual Score. If the Team Score is lower than Average Individual Score, then gain is "+." If Team Score is higher than Average Individual Score, then gain is "−."	_____	_____	_____	_____	_____	_____
Step 9: Lowest Individual Score on the Team	_____	_____	_____	_____	_____	_____
Step 10: Number of Individual Scores Lower Than the Team Score	_____	_____	_____	_____	_____	_____

SOURCE: J. Clayton Lafferty, Patrick M. Eady, and Alonzo W. Pond, "The Desert Survival Situation: A Group Decision Making Experience for Examining and Increasing Individual and Team Effectiveness," 8th ed. Copyright © 1974 by Experiential Learning Methods, Inc., 15200 E. Jefferson, Suite 107, Grosse Pointe Park, MI 48230, (313) 823-4400.

CASE FOR ANALYSIS

ARTCALENDAR

ArtCalendar, a monthly publication and company, may be the quintessential definition of a small business. Its 90-square-foot corporate headquarters, situated by the Potomac in old Virginia, is just off the baby's room. However, perhaps that is the entirely appropriate point of origin for a periodical catering to a variety of visual artists. Begun as a part-time endeavor in 1986, the publication's distribution has doubled in size every year for the first five. That left founder Carolyn Blakeslee with the common conundrum confronting most successful start-ups. Could she continue to grow the company without sacrificing in other areas, particularly time with that baby just one door down?

Blakeslee is not prone to knee-jerk reactions, but she built her business largely on guts and guile, not careful planning. The backbone of the publication is 15 pages of listings and forums for artists' work, but she's added topical freelance columns. Upgrading other aspects of the publication is more risky. Adding some color—the majority of subscribers are visual artists and she admits slight embarrassment at the plain Jane appearance of ArtCalendar—and greater editorial content are possibilities. She is also considering soliciting advertising. However, with the

historic growth to date, Blakeslee wonders about changing things that already are working fine.

Whether she wants to or not, Blakeslee may have to expand ArtCalendar for extraneous reasons and because the alternative would ultimately lead to the publication disappearing. The inherent economies of new subscribers would dramatically add to her income from the operation. A corollary to that would be to develop a more valuable entity in the event she decided to sell out. More ominously, and given that the bulk of the periodical is public information, failure to capitalize on her present position could lead to upstart competitors eventually overtaking her.

Blakeslee knows that getting bigger will mean giving up control, at least to some degree. Even delegating clerical duties—Blakeslee now opens her mail while doing her daily 5 miles on a stationary bike—would free up some of her time. And things aren't getting any easier. Mundane details like depending on the post office to consistently deliver second-class postage is bothersome. But increasing the subscription rate to cover first-class, Blakeslee fears, would cost her circulation. These are only the headaches and concerns relating to not expanding her business. Adding new products and personnel to move forward or diversify would definitely upset the current equilibrium she enjoys.

"I have a perfectionist streak, and I can see what the magazine ultimately could be," she says. "Part of me thinks, Don't fool with it if it's working, and part of me can't resist."

Blakeslee did not expect the success that ArtCalendar has experienced. She did not think she would enjoy motherhood with the zest she has either. After she identified her niche, hard work and perseverance were sufficient to sustain what really has been impressive growth. For the future, she will have to determine a direction, define the necessary goals, and adopt plans and strategy requisite to reach her goals. But for now she has to step next door. The baby's crying.

● QUESTIONS

1. Using the decision-making steps outlined in this chapter, describe how Carolyn Blakeslee can decide whether to maintain, expand, or sell ArtCalendar.
2. If Blakeslee decides to remain at the helm, what changes, if any should she make to the product?
3. Are the decisions facing Blakeslee programmed or nonprogrammed? Why?

SOURCE: Leslie Brokaw, "Can Carolyn Blakeslee Have It All?", *INC.*, September 1991, 78–84.

REFERENCES

1. "Redefine the Economics, Ron Berger, Rentrak," *Fortune*, April 5, 1993, 66–67.
2. Mark Maremont, "Waterford Is Showing a Few Cracks," *Business Week*, February 20, 1989, 60–65; John Markoff, "John Sculley's Biggest Test," *The New York Times*, February 26, 1989, section 3, 1, 26: Mark Landler, "People of Earth, We Are a Friendly Channel," *Business Week*, October 5, 1992, 50; and Joseph Weber and Peter Coy, "Look Ma, No Cable: It's Video-By-Phone," *Business Week*, November 14, 1992, 86.
3. Ronald A. Howard, "Decision Analysis: Practice and Promise," *Management Science* 34 (1988), 679–695.
4. Herbert A. Simon, *The New Science of Management* (Englewood Cliffs, NJ: Prentice-Hall, 1977), 47.
5. Samuel Eilon, "Structuring Unstructured Decisions," *Omega* 13 (1985), 369–377; and Max H. Bazerman, *Judgment in Managerial Decision Making* (New York: Wiley, 1986).
6. James G. March and Zur Shapira, "Managerial Perspectives on Risk and Risk Taking," *Management Science* 33 (1987), 1404–1418; and Inga Skromme Baird and Howard Thomas, "Toward a Contingency Model of Strategic Risk Taking," *Academy of Management Review* 10 (1985), 230–243.
7. Lois Therrian, "McRisky," *Business Week*, October 21, 1991, 114–122.
8. Eilon, "Structuring Unstructured Decisions," and Philip A. Roussel, "Cutting Down the Guesswork in R&D," *Harvard Business Review* 61 (September–October 1983), 154–160.
9. Jeremy Main, "Betting on the 21st Century," *Fortune*, April 20, 1992, 102–117.
10. Michael Masuch and Perry LaPotin, "Beyond Garbage Cans: An AI Model of Organizational Choice," *Administrative Science Quarterly* 34 (1989), 38–67; and Richard L. Daft and Robert H. Lengel, "Organizational Information Requirements, Media Richness and Structural Design," *Management Science* 32 (1986), 554–571.
11. David M. Schweiger, William R. Sandberg, and James W. Ragan, "Group Approaches for Improving Strategic Decision Making: A Comparative Analysis of Dialectical Inquiry, Devil's Advocacy, and Consensus," *Academy of Man-*

agement Journal 29 (1986), 51–71; and Richard O. Mason and Ian I. Mitroff, *Challenging Strategic Planning Assumptions* (New York: Wiley Interscience, 1981).

12. Boris Blai, Jr., "Eight Steps to Successful Problem Solving," *Supervisory Management* (January 1986), 7–9; and Earnest R. Acher, "How to Make a Business Decision: An Analysis of Theory and Practice," *Management Review* 69 (February 1980), 54–61.

13. Douglas A. Hay and Paul N. Dahl, "Strategic and Midterm Planning of Forest-to-Product Flows," *Interfaces* 14 (September–October 1984), 33–43.

14. Herbert A. Simon, *The New Science of Management Decision* (New York: Harper & Row, 1960), 5–6; and Amitai Etzioni, "Humble Decision Making," *Harvard Business Review* (July–August 1989), 122–126.

15. James G. March and Herbert A. Simon, *Administrative Behavior,* 2d ed. (New York: Wiley, 1958).

16. Herbert A. Simon, *Models of Man* (New York: Wiley, 1957), 196–205; and Herbert A. Simon, *Administrative Behavior,* 2d ed. (New York: Free Press, 1957).

17. John Taylor, "Project Fantasy: A Behind-the-Scenes Account of Disney's Desperate Battle against the Raiders," *Manhattan* (November 1984).

18. Weston H. Agor, "The Logic of Intuition: How Top Executives Make Important Decisions," *Organizational Dynamics* 14 (Winter 1986), 5–18; and Herbert A. Simon, "Making Management Decisions: The Role of Intuition and Emotion," *Academy of Management Executive* 1 (1987), 57–64.

19. Daniel J. Isenberg, "How Senior Managers Think," *Harvard Business Review* 62 (November–December 1984), 80–90.

20. Annetta Miller and Dody Tsiantar, "A Test for Market Research," *Newsweek,* December 28, 1987, 32–33; and David Frost and Michael Deakin, *David Frost's Book of the World's Worst Decisions* (New York: Crown, 1983), 60–61.

21. William B. Stevenson, Jon L. Pierce, and Lyman W. Porter, "The Concept of 'Coalition' in Organization Theory and Research," *Academy of Management Review,* 10 (1985), 256–268.

22. Ann Reilly Dowd, "George Bush as Crisis Manager," *Fortune,* September 10, 1990, 55–56; and "How Bush Decided," *Fortune,* February 11, 1991, 45–46.

23. James W. Frederickson, "Effects of Decision Motive and Organizational Performance Level on Strategic Decision Processes," *Academy of Management Journal* 28 (1985), 821–843; and James W. Frederickson, "The Comprehensiveness of Strategic Decision Processes: Extension, Observations, Future Directions," *Academy of Management Journal* 27 (1984), 445–466.

24. Marjorie A. Lyles and Howard Thomas, "Strategic Problem Formulation: Biases and Assumptions Embedded in Alternative Decision-Making Models," *Journal of Management Studies* 25 (1988), 131–145; and Susan E. Jackson and Jane E. Dutton, "Discerning Threats and Opportunities," *Administrative Science Quarterly* 33 (1988), 370–387.

25. Larry Reibstein, "A Finger on the Pulse: Companies Expand Use of Employee Surveys," *The Wall Street Journal,* October 27, 1986, 27.

26. Richard L. Daft, Juhani Sormumem, and Don Parks, "Chief Executive Scanning, Environmental Characteristics, and Company Performance: An Empirical Study" (Unpublished manuscript, Texas A&M University, 1988).

27. Jerry Jakuvovics, "Rising Stars in Toys and Togs," *Management Review* (May 1987), 19–20.

28. Todd Mason, "Tandy Finds a Cold, Hard World Outside the Radio Shack," *Business Week,* August 31, 1987, 68–70.

29. John Southerst, "The Start-up Star Who Bets .900," *Canadian Business*, March 1993, 66–72.

30. V. H. Vroom and Arthur G. Jago, *The New Leadership: Managing Participation in Organizations* (Englewood Cliffs, NJ: Prentice-Hall, 1988).

31. R. H. G. Field, "A Test of the Vroom-Yetton Normative Model of Leadership," *Journal of Applied Psychology* (October 1982), 523–532; and R. H. G. Field, "A Critique of the Vroom-Yetton Contingency Model of Leadership Behavior," *Academy of Management Review* 4 (1979), 249–257.

32. Jennifer T. Ettling and Arthur G. Jago, "Participation under Conditions of Conflict: More on the Validity of the Vroom-Yetton Model," *Journal of Management Studies* 25 (1988), 73–83; Madeline E. Heilman, Harvey A. Hornstein, Jack H. Cage, and Judith K. Herschlag, "Reactions to Prescribed Leader Behavior as a Function of Role Perspective: The Case of the Vroom-Yetton Model," *Journal of Applied Psychology* (February 1984), 50–60; and Arthur G. Jago and Victor H. Vroom, "Some Differences in the Incidence and Evaluation of Participative Leader Behavior," *Journal of Applied Psychology* (December 1982), 776–783.

33. Tom Richman, "One Man's Family," *INC.,* November 1983, 151–156.

34. Andre Delbecq, Andrew Van de Ven, and D. Gustafson, *Group Techniques for Program Planning* (Glenview, IL: Scott, Foresman, 1975); and William M. Fox, "Anonymity and Other Keys to Successful Problem-Solving Meetings," *National Productivity Review* 8 (Spring 1989), 145–156.

35. "Group Decision Making: Approaches to Problem Solving," *Small Business Reports* (July 1988), 30–33; and N. Delkey, *The Delphi Method: An Experimental Study of Group Opinion* (Santa Monica, CA: Rand Corporation, 1969).

36. Irving L. Janis, *Group Think,* 2d ed. (Boston: Houghton Mifflin, 1982), 9; and Glen Whyte, "Groupthink Reconsidered," *Academy of Management Review* 14 (1989), 40–56.

37. David M. Schweiger and William R. Sandberg, "The Utilization of Individual Capabilities in Group Approaches to Strategic Decision-Making," *Strategic Management Journal* 10 (1989), 31–43; and "The Devil's Advocate," *Small Business Report* (December 1987), 38–41.

38. Michael Duffy, "Mr. Consensus," *Time,* August 21, 1989, 16–22.

39. "Group Decision-Making," *Small Business Report* (July 1988), 30–33.

40. A. Osborn, *Applied Imagination* (New York: Scribner, 1957).

41. Steven L. Mandell, *Computers and Data Processing* (St. Paul, MN: West, 1985); and Richard L. Daft and Norman B. Macintosh, "A Tentative Exploration into the Amount and Equivocality of Information Processing in Organizational Work Units," *Administrative Science Quarterly* 26 (1981), 207–224.

42. Jeffrey P. Stamen, "Decision Support Systems Help Planners Hit Their Targets," *Journal of Business Strategy* (March–April 1990), 3033; and Craig R. Waters, "Franchise Capital of America," *INC.,* September 1984, 99–108.

43. Charles A. O'Reilly III, "Variations in Decision Makers' Use of Information Sources: The Impact of Quality and Accessibility of Information," *Academy of Management Journal* 25 (1982), 756–771; and Niv Ahituv and Seev Neumann, *Principles of Information Systems for Management,* 2d ed. (Dubuque, IA: Wm. C. Brown, 1986).

44. Bob Davis, "As Government Keeps More Tabs on People, False Accusations Arise," *The Wall Street Journal,* August 20, 1987, 1, 10.

45. Michael W. Miller, "Computers Keep Eye on Workers and See If They Perform Well," *The Wall Street Journal,* June 3, 1985, 1, 12.

46. Frances Seghres, "A Search and Destroy Mission—Against Paper," *Business Week,* February 6, 1989, 91–95.

47. William C. Symonds, "Getting Rid of Paper Is Just the Beginning," *Business Week,* December 21, 1992, 88–89.

48. Bruce G. Posner and Bo Burlingham, "The Hottest Entrepreneur in America," *INC.,* January 1988, 44–58.

49. Gary Geipel, "At Today's Supermarket, the Computer Is Doing It All," *Business Week,* August 11, 1986, 64–65; and Tom Richman, "Supermarket," *INC.,* October 1985, 115–120..

50. Alan Paller, "A Guide to EIS for MIS Directors," CA–Insight: *The Computer Associates Software Magazine* 2 (1989), 5–9.

51. Jeremy Main, "At Last, Software CEOs Can Use," *Fortune,* March 13, 1989, 77–81.

52. Ibid.

53. Ramesh Sharda, Steve H. Barr, and James C. McDonald, "Decision Support System Effectiveness: A Review and an Empirical Test," *Management Science* 34 (1988), 139–159.

54. Paller, "A Guide to EIS for MIS Directors."

55. Pam Carroll, "The Paperless Office Comes True," *Working Woman,* October 1989, 73–76.

56. Gene Bylinsky, "Saving Time with New Technology," *Fortune,* December 30, 1991, 98–104.

57. Lynda M. Applegate, James I. Cash, Jr., and D. Quinn Mills, "Information Technology and Tomorrow's Management," *Harvard Business Review* (November–December 1988), 128–136.

58. E. B. Swanson, "Information in Organization Theory: A Review" (Information Systems Working Paper, UCLA, 1986); John F. Magee, "What Information Technology Has in Store for Managers," *Sloan Management Review* (Winter 1985), 45–49; and John Child, "New Technology and Developments in Management Organization," *Omega* 12 (1984), 211–223.

59. Bylinsky, "Saving Time with New Technology."

60. Rudy Hirschatim and Dennis Adams, "Organizational Connectivity," *Journal of General Managment* 17 (Winter 1990), 65–76; Laton McCartney, "Companies Get a Competitive Edge Using Strategic Computer Systems," *Dun's Business Month,* December 1985, 13–14; and Robert I. Benjamin, John F. Rockart, Michael S. Scott Morton, and John Wyman, "Information Technology: A Strategic Opportunity," *Sloan Management Review* 25 (Spring 1984), 3–10.

61. "Redefine the Economics, Ron Berger, Rentrak," *Fortune,* April 5, 1993, 66–67.

PHOTO PROVIDED COURTESY OF IDS FINANCIAL SERVICES, INC.

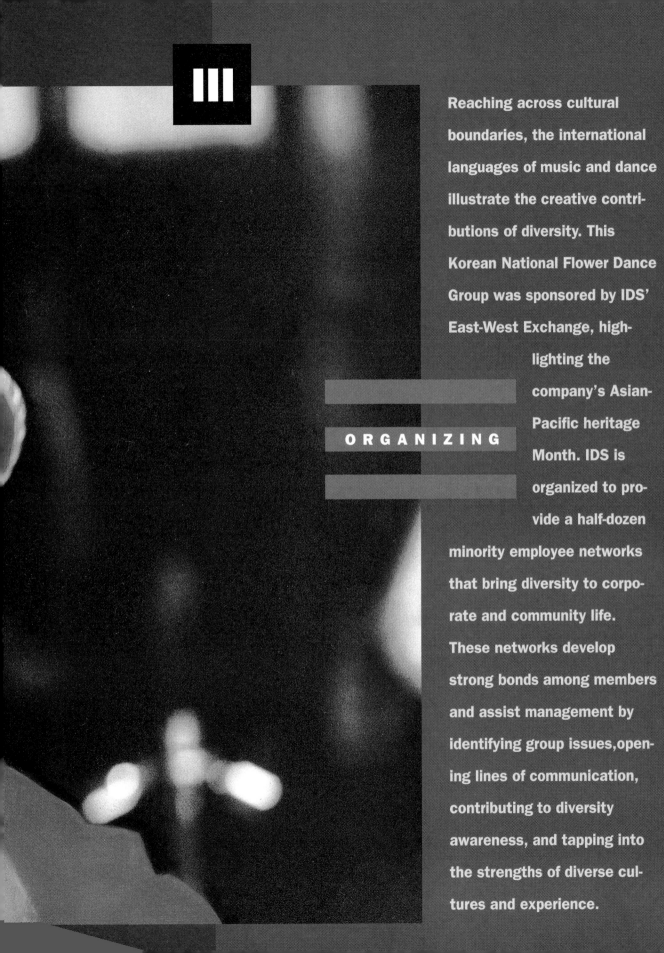

III

ORGANIZING

Reaching across cultural boundaries, the international languages of music and dance illustrate the creative contributions of diversity. This Korean National Flower Dance Group was sponsored by IDS' East-West Exchange, highlighting the company's Asian-Pacific heritage Month. IDS is organized to provide a half-dozen minority employee networks that bring diversity to corporate and community life. These networks develop strong bonds among members and assist management by identifying group issues, opening lines of communication, contributing to diversity awareness, and tapping into the strengths of diverse cultures and experience.

STRUCTURE & FUNDAMENTALS OF ORGANIZING

8

Factors Affecting Structure
Stage of Maturity
The Environment

Organizing the Vertical Structure
Work Specialization
Chain of Command
Authority, Responsibility, and
  Delegation
Span of Management
Centralization and Decentralization
Coordination
Integrating Managers
Task Forces and Teams

Departmentalization
Functional Approach
Divisional Approach
Matrix Approach
Team Approach
Network Approach

CHAPTER OUTLINE ▲

LEARNING OBJECTIVES ▼

After studying this chapter, you should be able to

- Describe how structure can be used to achieve an organization's strategic objectives.

- Describe four stages of the organizational life cycle and explain how size and life cycle influence the correct structure.

- Explain the fundamental characteristics of organizing, including such concepts as work specialization, chain of command, and task forces.

- Explain when specific structural characteristics such as centralization, span of management, and formalization should be used within organizations.

- Compare the functional approach to structure with the divisional approach.

- Explain the matrix approach to structure and its application to both

Max Duncan felt certain he would be successful with Integrity Industries, a specialty chemical blending business. However, there were a few problems. Integrity was about all Duncan had. He had little money, no job, and zero prospects of locating financing for any project remotely having to do with the oil business. In addition, he was in Kingsville, Texas, in the midst of the oil depression. Duncan knew there was still oil-related business to be acquired. He believed that if he put together the operation he had in mind, he would have a cost advantage permitting him to underprice the competition and still make money. Given his limited resources, how could Max Duncan organize the company? How should he go about locating a facility, getting equipment and raw materials, and hiring people who believe in the organization enough to work there?[1]

Every firm wrestles with the problem of how to organize. Reorganization often is necessary to reflect a new strategy, changing market conditions, or innovative production technology. Many companies are restructuring to become leaner, more efficient, and more nimble in a highly competitive global environment.

Under John Akers, IBM decentralized many top-management functions to newly independent divisions.[2] In a major reorganization of Alcoa in 1991, CEO Paul O'Neill ordered work redesign and gave business units greater autonomy.[3] A reorganization of Du Pont Co. reduced management levels from 11 to 7, replaced the traditional executive committee with a new advisory committee representing the company's worldwide organization, and refocused on core industries with spinoffs of several "growth" business.[4]

Each of these organizations is using fundamental concepts of organizing. **Organizing** is the deployment of organizational resources to achieve strategic objectives. The deployment of resources is reflected in the organization's division of labor into specific departments and jobs, formal lines of authority, and mechanisms for coordinating diverse organization tasks.

Organizing is important because it follows from strategy—the topic of Part 2. Strategy defines *what* to do; organizing defines *how* to do it. Organization structure is a tool that managers use to harness resources for getting things done. Part 3 explains the variety of organizing principles and concepts used by managers. This chapter covers fundamental concepts that apply to all organizations and departments and how structural designs are tailored to the organization's situation. Organizations can be structured to facilitate innovation and change.

organizing

The deployment of organizational resources to achieve strategic objectives.

● FACTORS AFFECTING STRUCTURE

How do managers know whether to design a tight or loose structure? The answer lies in the contingency factors that influence organization structure. Recall from Chapter 2 that *contingency* pertains to those factors on which structure depends. Research on organization structure shows that the emphasis given to loose or tight structure depends on the contingency factors such as stage of maturity and environment.

STAGES OF MATURITY

The organization's **size** is its scope or magnitude and frequently is measured by number of employees. A considerable body of research findings has shown that large organizations are structured differently than small ones. Small organizations are informal, have little division of labor, few rules and regulations, ad hoc budgeting and performance systems, and small professional and clerical support staffs. Large organizations such as IBM necessarily have an extensive division of labor, large professional staffs, numerous rules and regulations, and internal systems for control, rewards, and innovation.[5]

size

The organization's scope or magnitude, typically measured by number of employees.

Organizations evolve from small to large by going through stages of a life cycle. Within the **organization life cycle,** organizations follow predictable patterns through major developmental stages that are sequential in nature. This is similar to the product life cycle described in Chapter 6 except that it applies to the organization as a whole. Each stage involves changes in the range of organization activities and overall structure.[6] Every organization progresses through the life cycle at its own pace, but most encounter the four stages defined in Exhibit 8.1: birth, youth, midlife, and maturity.

BIRTH STAGE. In the **birth stage,** the organization is created. The founder is an entrepreneur, who alone or with a handful of employees performs all tasks. The organization is very informal, and tasks are overlapping. There are no professional staff, no rules and regulations, and no internal systems for planning, rewards, or coordination. Decision authority is centralized with the owner. Apple Computer was in the birth stage

organization life cycle

The organization's evolution through major developmental stages.

birth stage

The phase of the organization life cycle in which the company is created.

E X H I B I T   8 . 1

Structural Characteristics during Organization Stages of Maturity

	Birth Stage	**Youth Stage**	**Midlife Stage**	**Maturity Stage**
Size	Small	Medium	Large	Very large
Bureaucracy	Nonbureaucratic	Prebureaucratic	Bureaucratic	Very bureaucratic
Division of labor	Overlapping tasks	Some departments	Many departments, well-defined tasks, organization chart	Extensive—small jobs, written job descriptions
Centralization	One-person rule	Top leaders rule	Decentralization to department heads	Enforced decentralization, top management overloaded
Formalization	No written rules	Few rules	Policy and procedures manuals	Extensive—most activities covered by written manuals
Administrative intensity	Secretary, no professional staff	Increasing clerical and maintenance, little professional staff	Increasing professional support staff	Large—multiple professional and clerical staff departments
Internal systems (information, budget, planning, performance)	Nonexistent	Crude budget and information system	Control systems in place—budget, performance, operational reports	Extensive—planning, financial, and personnel systems added
Lateral teams, task forces for coordination	None	Top leaders only	Some use of integrators and task forces	Frequent at lower levels to break down barriers of bureaucracy

SOURCE: Based on Robert E. Quinn and Kim Cameron, "Organizational Life Cycles and Some Shifting Criteria of Effectiveness: Some Preliminary Evidence," *Management Science* 29 (1983), 31–51; Richard L. Daft and Richard M. Steers, *Organizations: A Micro/Macro Approach* (Glenview, Ill.: Scott, Foresman, 1986).

when it was created by Steven Jobs and Stephen Wozniak in Wozniak's parents' garage. Jobs and Wozniak sold their own belongings to raise money to personally build 200 Apple computers. Kentucky Fried Chicken was in the birth stage when Colonel Harlan Sanders was running a combination gas station/restaurant in Corbin, Kentucky, before the popularity of his restaurant began to spread.

youth stage

The phase of the organization life cycle in which the organization is growing rapidly and has a product enjoying some marketplace success.

YOUTH STAGE.   In the **youth stage,** the organization has more employees and a product that is succeeding in the marketplace. The organization is growing rapidly. The owner no longer has sole possession. A few trusted colleagues share in the decision making, although control is still relatively centralized. A division of labor is emerging, with some designation of task responsibility to newly created departments. Internal systems remain informal. A few formal rules and policies appear, and there are few professional and administrative personnel. Apple Computer was in the youth stage during the years of rapid growth from 1978 to 1981, when the major product line was established and over 2,000 dealers signed on to sell Apple computers. Kentucky Fried Chicken was in the youth stage when Colonel Sanders convinced over 400 franchises in the United States and Canada to use his original recipe. Although both organizations were growing rapidly, they were still being run in a very informal fashion.

midlife stage

The phase of the organization life cycle in which the firm has reached prosperity and grown substantially large.

MIDLIFE STAGE.   By the **midlife stage,** the organization has prospered and grown quite large. At this point, the organization begins to look like a more formalized bureaucracy. An extensive division of labor appears, with statements of policies and responsibilities. Rules, regulations, and job descriptions are used to direct employee activities. Professional and clerical staff are hired to undertake specialized activities in support of manufacturing and marketing. Reward, budget, and accounting control systems are put in place. Top management decentralizes many responsibilities to functional departments, but flexibility and innovation may decline. Apple Computer is now well into the midlife stage because it has adopted a host of procedures, internal systems, and staff departments to provide greater control over the organization. Kentucky Fried Chicken moved into the midlife stage when Colonel Sanders sold his company to John Y. Brown, who took the company through a national promotion and building campaign.

maturity stage

The phase of the organization life cycle in which the organization has become exceedingly large and mechanistic.

MATURITY STAGE.   In the **maturity stage,** the organization is large and mechanistic—indeed, the vertical structure often becomes too strong. Budgets, control systems, rules, policies, large staffs of engineering, accounting, and finance specialists, and a refined division of labor are in place. Decision making is centralized. At this point, the organization is in danger of stagnation. To offset the rigid vertical hierarchy, inspire innovation, and shrink barriers among departments, the organization may reorganize, as IBM did. To regain flexibility and innovation, managers may decentralize and create teams, task forces, and integrator positions. This is especially true for such mature organizations as Procter & Gamble, Sears, and General Motors, which have experienced major changes in the external environment and found that the mature vertical structure inhibited flexible responses.

MOVING THROUGH THE LIFE CYCLE. Organizations do not progress through the four life cycle stages in a logical, orderly fashion. Stages may lead or lag in a given organization. The transition from one stage to the next is difficult and often promotes crises. Employees who were present at the organization's birth often long for the informal atmosphere and resist the formalized procedures, departmentalization, and staff departments required in maturing organizations. Organizations that prematurely emphasize a rigid vertical structure or that stay informal during later stages of the life cycle have the wrong structure for their situation. Performance suffers. The failure of People's Express airline occurred because the firm never grew up. Despite its being the fifth largest airline, top management ran it informally without a strong vertical structure. The structure fit neither People's Express' size nor life cycle stage. Many companies must make changes in their structures as the company life cycle evolves. Consider the developments at Hand Held Products, Inc.

 H A N D   H E L D   P R O D U C T S ,   I N C .

Hand Held Products, Inc., a Charlotte, North Carolina, maker of palm-sized computers that scan and log bar-coded information, always made money. However, the company was not living up to its potential. Inventory costs were too high, and a lot of deliveries did not get out on time. It was as though no one was really paying attention. Founder and chief executive Mike Weaver analyzed the situation, and finally came to a hard decision. Someone had to go, and it was him.

Weaver's instincts and talents fall under the creative and entrepreneurial heading. He admits he was only an average manager and administrator. As a result, he spent his time trying to discover new products while existing operations pretty much moved along on their own. Weaver was sure Hand Held's future held more than the $15 million in annual sales he was wringing out of it.

Weaver became chairman of the board, and Henry W. Bennett was brought on as CEO in 1990. Unlike Weaver, he got a charge out of streamlining day-to-day operations and microscoping budgets. Improvements across the board were almost immediate. Gross margins increased by 10 percent, the time between order and delivery was drastically reduced, and Bennett cut inventory costs by 50 percent. Weaver thinks there comes a time in every company's life when certain decisions determine what the future direction will be. He knows he made the right one for his company.[7] ■

THE ENVIRONMENT

In Chapter 4, we discussed the nature of environmental uncertainty. Environmental uncertainty means that decision makers have difficulty acquiring good information and predicting external changes. Uncertainty occurs when the external environment is rapidly changing and complex. An uncertain environment causes three things to happen within an organization.

1 *Increased differences occur among departments.* In an uncertain environment, each major department—marketing, manufacturing, research and development—focuses on the task and environmental sectors for which it is responsible and hence distinguishes itself from the others with respect to goals, task orientation, and time horizon.[8] Departments work autonomously. These factors create barriers among departments.

2 *The organization needs increased coordination to keep departments working together.* Additional differences require more emphasis on lateral coordination to link departments together and overcome differences in departmental goals and orientations.

3 *The organization must adapt to change.* The organization must maintain a flexible, responsive posture toward the environment. Changes in products and technology require cooperation among departments, which means additional emphasis on coordination through the use of teams, task forces, and lateral information processing.[9]

The contingency relationship between environmental uncertainty and structural approach is illustrated in Exhibit 8.2. Recall from Chapter 4 that when the external environment is more stable, the organization should have a mechanistic structure that emphasizes vertical control. There is little need for change, flexibility, or intense coordination. The structure can emphasize specialization, centralized decision making, wide spans of control, and low administrative overhead. When environmental uncertainty is high, an organic structure that emphasizes lateral relationships such as teams and task forces is appropriate. Vertical structure characteristics such as specialization, centralization, and formalized procedures should be downplayed. In an uncertain environment, the organization figures things out as it goes along, departments must cooperate, and decisions should be decentralized to the teams and task forces working on specific problems.

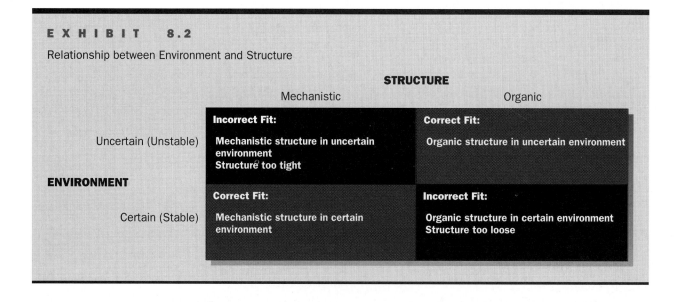

EXHIBIT 8.2

Relationship between Environment and Structure

	STRUCTURE	
	Mechanistic	Organic
ENVIRONMENT		
Uncertain (Unstable)	**Incorrect Fit:** Mechanistic structure in uncertain environment Structure too tight	**Correct Fit:** Organic structure in uncertain environment
Certain (Stable)	**Correct Fit:** Mechanistic structure in certain environment	**Incorrect Fit:** Organic structure in certain environment Structure too loose

When managers use the wrong structure for the environment, reduced performance results. A rigid, mechanistic structure in an uncertain environment prevents the organization from adapting to change. Likewise, a loose, organic structure in a stable environment is inefficient. Too many resources are devoted to meetings and discussions when employees could be more productive focusing on specialized tasks.

● ORGANIZING THE VERTICAL STRUCTURE

The organizing process leads to the creation of organization structure, which defines how tasks are divided and resources deployed. **Organization structure** is defined as (1) the set of formal tasks assigned to individuals and departments; (2) formal reporting relationships, including lines of authority, decision responsibility, number of hierarchical levels, and span of managers' control; and (3) the design of systems to ensure effective coordination of employees across departments.[10]

organization structure
The framework in which the organization defines how tasks are divided, resources are deployed, and departments are coordinated.

The set of formal tasks and formal reporting relationships provides a framework for vertical control of the organization. The characteristics of vertical structure are portrayed in the **organization chart,** which is the visual representation of an organization's structure.

organization chart
The visual representation of an organization's structure.

A sample organization chart for a textile mill is illustrated in Exhibit 8.3. The mill has five major departments—accounting, personnel, manufacturing, marketing, and research and development. The organization chart delineates the chain of command, indicates departmental tasks and how they fit together, and provides order and logic for the organization. Every employee has an appointment task, line of authority, and devision responsibility. The following sections discuss several important features of vertical structure in more detail.

WORK SPECIALIZATION

Organizations perform a wide variety of tasks. A fundamental principle is that work can be performed more efficiently if employees are allowed to specialize.[11] **Work specialization,** sometimes called *division of labor,* is the degree to which organizational tasks are subdivided into separate jobs. Work specialization in Exhibit 8.3 is illustrated by the separation of manufacturing tasks into weaving, yarn, finishing, and needling. Employees within each department perform only the tasks relevant to their specialized function. When work specialization is extensive, employees specialize in a single task. Jobs tend to be small, but they can be performed efficiently. Work specialization is readily visible on an automobile assembly line where each employee performs the same task over and over again. It would not be efficient to have a single employee build the entire automobile or even perform a large number of unrelated jobs.

work specialization
The degree to which organizational tasks are subdivided into individual jobs; also called *division of labor.*

Despite the apparent advantages of specialization, many organizations are moving away from this principle. With too much specialization, employees are isolated and do only a single, tiny, boring job. Many

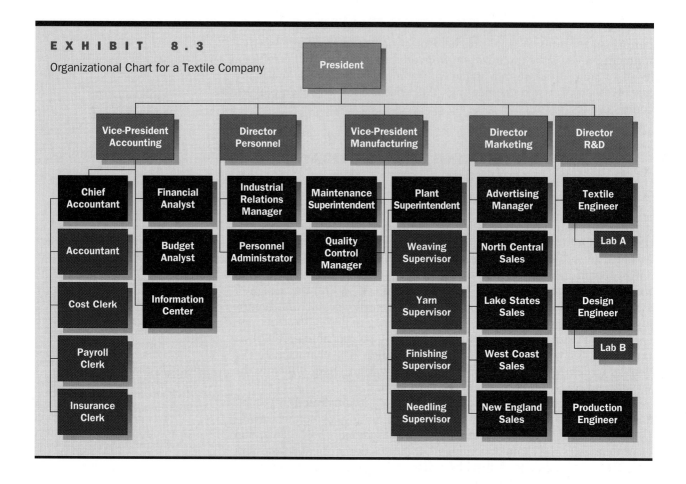

EXHIBIT 8.3

Organizational Chart for a Textile Company

companies are enlarging jobs to provide greater challenges and are even assigning teams to tasks so that employees can rotate among the several jobs performed by the team.

CHAIN OF COMMAND

chain of command

An unbroken line of authority that links all individuals in the organization and specifies who reports to whom.

The **chain of command** is an unbroken line of authority that links all persons in an organization and shows who reports to whom. It is associated with two underlying principles. *Unity of command* means that each employee is held accountable to only one supervisor. The *scalar principle* refers to a clearly defined line of authority in the organization that includes all employees. Authority and responsibility for different tasks should be distinct. All persons in the organization should know to whom they report as well as the successive management levels all the way to the top. In Exhibit 8.3, the payroll clerk reports to the chief accountant, who in turn reports to the vice-president, who in turn reports to the company president.

AUTHORITY, RESPONSIBILITY, AND DELEGATION

authority

The formal and legitimate right of a manager to make decisions, issue orders, and allocate resources to achieve organizationally desired outcomes.

The chain of command illustrates the authority structure of the organization. **Authority** is the formal and legitimate right of a manager to make decisions, issue orders, and allocate resources to achieve organizationally desired outcomes. Authority is distinguished by three characteristics:[12]

1 *Authority is vested in organizational positions, not people.* Managers have authority because of the positions they hold, and other people in the same positions would have the same authority.

2 *Authority is accepted by subordinates.* Although authority flows top down through the organization's hierarchy, subordinates comply because they believe that managers have a legitimate right to issue orders. The acceptance theory of authority argues that a manager has authority only if subordinates choose to accept his or her commands. If subordinates refuse to obey because the order is outside their zone of acceptance, a manager's authority disappears.[13] For example, Richard Ferris, the former chairman of United Airlines, resigned because few people accepted his strategy of acquiring hotels, a car rental company, and other organizations to build a travel empire. When key people refused to accept his direction, his authority was lost, and he resigned.

3 *Authority flows down the vertical hierarchy.* Positions at the top of the hierarchy are vested with more formal authority than are positions at the bottom.

Responsibility is the flip side of the authority coin. **Responsibility** is the duty to perform the task or activity an employee has been assigned. Typically, managers are assigned authority commensurate with responsibility. When managers have responsibility for task outcomes, but little authority, the job is possible but difficult. They rely on persuasion and luck. When managers have authority exceeding responsibility, they may become tyrants, using authority toward frivolous outcomes.[14]

responsibility

The duty to perform the task or activity an employee has been assigned.

The *organizing* effectiveness of the late Sam Walton exemplifies a successful match of leadership style, subordinate characteristics, and situational factors. Walton set high goals for Wal-Mart employees—known at all levels as "associates"—and regularly met with store personnel to express his confidence in their capabilities.

accountability

The fact that the people with authority and responsibility are subject to reporting and justifying task outcomes to those above them in the chain of command.

delegation

The process managers use to transfer authority and responsibility to positions below them in the hierarchy.

span of management

The number of employees who report to a supervisor; also called *span of control*.

Accountability is the mechanism through which authority and responsibility are brought into alignment. **Accountability** means that the people with authority and responsibility are subject to reporting and justifying task outcomes to those above them in the chain of command.[15] Subordinates must be aware that they are accountable for a task and accept the responsibility and authority for performing it. Accountability can be built into the organization structure. For example, at Whirlpool incentive programs provide strict accountability. Performance of all managers is monitored and bonus payments are tied to successful outcomes.

Another concept related to authority is delegation.[16] **Delegation** is the process managers use to transfer authority and responsibility to positions below them in the hierarchy. Most organizations today encourage managers to delegate authority to the lowest possible level to provide maximum flexibility to meet customer needs and adapt to the environment. Managers are encouraged to delegate authority, although they often find it difficult. Techniques for delegation are discussed in the Manager's Shoptalk box. The trend toward increased delegation begins in the chief executive's office in companies such as Johnsonville Foods and General Electric. At Johnsonville, a committee of employees from the shop floor has been delegated authority to formulate the manufacturing budget.

SPAN OF MANAGEMENT

The **span of management** is the number of employees reporting to a supervisor. Sometimes called the *span of control*, this characteristic of structure determines how closely a supervisor can monitor subordinates. Traditional views of organization design recommend a span of management of from four to seven subordinates per manager. However, many organizations have been observed to have larger spans of management and a few smaller. Research on the Lockheed Missile and Space Company and other manufacturing companies has suggested that span of management can vary widely and that several factors influence the span.[17] Generally, when supervisors must be closely involved with subordinates, the span should be small, and when supervisors need little involvement with subordinates, it can be large. The following factors are associated with less supervisor involvement and thus larger spans of control:

1 Work performed by subordinates is stable and routine.

2 Subordinates perform similar work tasks.

3 Subordinates are concentrated in a single location.

4 Subordinates are highly trained and need little direction in performing tasks.

5 Rules and procedures defining task activities are available.

6 Support systems and personnel are available for the manager.

7 Little time is required in nonsupervisory activities such as coordination with other departments or planning.

8 Managers' personal preferences and styles favor a large span.

HOW TO DELEGATE

The attempt by top management to decentralize decision making often gets bogged down because middle managers are unable to delegate. Managers may cling tightly to their decision-making and task responsibilities. Failure to delegate occurs for a number of reasons: Managers are most comfortable making familiar decisions; they feel they will lose personal status by delegating tasks; they believe they can do a better job themselves; or they have an aversion to risk—they will not take a chance on delegating because performance responsibility ultimately rests with them.

Yet decentralization offers an organization many advantages. Decisions are made at the right level, lower-level employees are motivated, and employees have the opportunity to develop decision-making skills. Overcoming barriers to delegation in order to gain these advantages is a major challenge. The following approach can help each manager delegate more effectively:

1. *Delegate the whole task.* A manager should delegate an entire task to one person rather than dividing it among several people. This gives the individual complete responsibility and increases his or her initiative while giving the manager some control over the results.

2. *Select the right person.* Not all employees have the same capabilities and degree of motivation. Managers must match talent to task if delegation is to be effective. They should identify subordinates who have made independent decisions in the past and have shown a desire for more responsibility.

3. *Delegate responsibility and authority.* Merely assigning a task is not effective delegation. The individual must have the responsibility for completing the task and the authority to perform the task as he or she thinks best.

4. *Give thorough instruction.* Successful delegation includes information on what, when, why, where, who, and how. The subordinate must clearly understand the task and the expected results. It is a good idea to write down all provisions discussed, including required resources and when and how the results will be reported.

5. *Maintain feedback.* Feedback means keeping open lines of communication with the subordinate to answer questions and provide advice, but without exerting too much control. Open lines of communication make it easier to trust subordinates. Feedback keeps the subordinate on the right track.

6. *Evaluate and reward performance.* Once the task is completed, the manager should evaluate results, not methods. When results do not meet expectations, the manager must assess the consequences. When they do meet expectations, the manager should reward employees for a job well done with praise, financial rewards when appropriate, and delegation of future assignments.

ARE YOU A POSITIVE DELEGATOR?

Positive delegation is the way an organization implements decentralization. Do you help or hinder the decentralization process? If you answer yes to more than three of the following questions, you may have a problem delegating:

■ I tend to be a perfectionist.
■ My boss expects me to know all the details of my job.
■ I don't have the time to explain clearly and concisely how a task should be accomplished.
■ I often end up doing tasks myself.
■ My subordinates typically are not as committed as I am.
■ I get upset when other people don't do the task right.
■ I really enjoy doing the details of my job to the best of my ability.
■ I like to be in control of task outcomes. ■

SOURCE: Thomas R. Horton, "Delegation and Team Building: No Solo Acts Please," *Management Review*, September 1992, 58–61; Andrew E. Schwartz, "The Why, What, and to Whom of Delegation," *Management Solutions* (June 1987), 31–38; and "Delegation," *Small Business Report* (June 1986), 38–43.

tall structure

A management structure characterized by an overall narrow span of management and a relatively large number of hierarchical levels.

flat structure

A management structure characterized by an overall broad span of control and relatively few hierarchical levels.

centralization

The location of decision authority near top organizational levels.

decentralization

The location of decision authority near lower organizational levels.

TALL VERSUS FLAT STRUCTURE.   The average span of control used in an organization determines whether the structure is tall or flat. A **tall structure** has an overall narrow span and more hierarchical levels. A **flat structure** has a wide span, is horizontally dispersed, and has fewer hierarchical levels.

The trend in the 1980s and 1990s has been toward wider spans of control as a way to facilitate delegation.[18] Exhibit 8.4 illustrates how an international metals company was reorganized. The multilevel set of managers shown in panel (a) was replaced with ten operating managers and nine staff specialists reporting directly to the CEO, as shown in panel (b). The CEO welcomed this wide span of 19 management subordinates because it fit his style, his management team was top quality and needed little supervision, and they were all located on the same floor of an office building.

CENTRALIZATION AND DECENTRALIZATION

Centralization and decentralization pertain to the hierarchical level at which decisions are made. **Centralization** means that decision authority is located near the top of the organization. With **decentralization,** decision authority is pushed downward to lower organization levels. Organizations may have to experiment to find the correct hierarchical level at which to make decisions.

In the United States and Canada, the trend over the last 30 years has been toward greater decentralization of organizations. Decentralization is believed to make greater use of human resources, unburden top managers, ensure that decisions are made close to the action by well-informed people, and permit more rapid response to external changes.

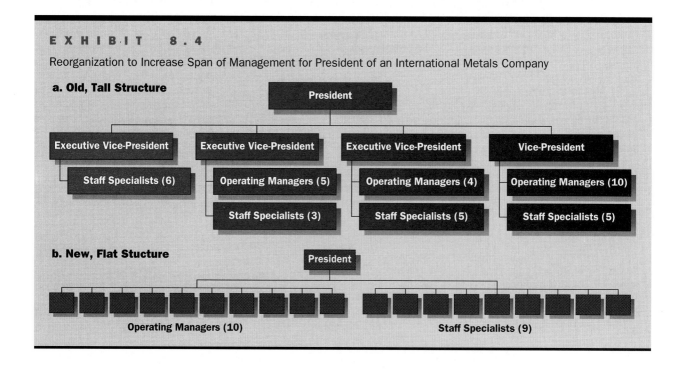

E X H I B I T   8 . 4

Reorganization to Increase Span of Management for President of an International Metals Company

a. Old, Tall Structure

b. New, Flat Stucture

However, this trend does not mean that every organization should decentralize all decisions. Managers should diagnose the organizational situation and select the decision-making level that will best meet the organization's needs. Factors that typically influence centralization versus decentralization are as follows:

1 Greater change and uncertainty in the environment are usually associated with decentralization. Most companies feel greater uncertainty today because of intense global competition; hence, many have decentralized.

2 Corporate history and culture socialize managers into a decision approach, although the approach can be changed. When Alcoa decentralized authority to division managers, it took a long time for them to use their new freedom fully and not expect monitoring from headquarters.

3 In times of crisis or risk of company failure, authority may be centralized at the top. When Honda could not get agreement among divisions about new car models, President Kawamoto made the decision himself.

4 The amount of centralization or decentralization should fit the firm's strategy. For example, Johnson & Johnson gives almost complete authority to its 166 operating companies to develop and market their own products. This decentralization fits the corporate strategy of empowerment that gets each division close to customers so it can speedily adapt to their needs.[19] Decentralization at Alcoa fit the strategy of faster response to customer needs by individual divisions; Honda's move toward centralization achieved standardized decisions for the entire company.[20]

For an example of a company that decentralized its structure in response to a crisis, read the box about the leading edge company, Globe Metallurgical.

Korbel Champagne Cellars recognized a *need for change in their organization* and created the Department of Romance, Weddings, and Entertaining. The department is actively involved in advertising by enhancing and promoting the relationship between champagne and true romance.

● COORDINATION

As organizations grow and evolve, two things happen. First, new positions and departments are added to deal with factors in the external environment or with new strategic needs.[21] For example, Raytheon established a new-products center to facilitate innovation in its various divisions. Korbel Champagne Cellars created a Department of Romance, Weddings, and Entertaining to enhance the linkage between romance and champagne consumption among potential customers. Comerica created a position of corporate quality manager to form a department that would be responsible for Comerica's Managing Total Quality program. Employees in this new department help people understand and implement the quality process within their area. As companies add positions and departments to meet changing needs, they grow more complex, with hundreds of positions and departments performing incredibly diverse activities.

GLOBE METALLURGICAL

Arden C. Sims would be hard-pressed to remember much good about the early days of the labor strife at Globe Metallurgical, the company we first introduced in Chapter 3. The 45 or so managers and salaried employees who stayed on to run the business after the union workers went on strike had their hands full. And they didn't have much use for detailed job descriptions. They worked 12-hour shifts, seven days a week for six months. By doing everything from setting up their own kitchen to producing specialty metals products that would meet customer specifications, everyone got keenly interested in being as efficient as possible. Within a few weeks, the ragtag group had actually improved output by 20 percent.

After metal cooled in eight-foot molds it was removed and slid over a grid where Sims or one of his colleagues got a chain-gang-style workout breaking it into pieces. That sort of labor leads to ingenuity, which came up over dinner one evening. A manager theorized that the impact of simply dumping the metal from the mold directly into a truck would sufficiently fragment it. That suggestion eliminated eight workers and saved $300,000 a year, not to mention a lot of back-aches. It was only one of many organizational changes adopted.

During the first exchange of salvos in Sims' battle with Globe's union, he was negotiating for elimination of 40 full-time jobs. His stint at the furnace made him think he could eliminate five times that many and still improve efficiency. He decided to transform 35 salaried supervisors into hourly employees and hire that same number of additional workers, none with any experience. The new group voted to decertify the union, and after Sims rehired 30 former union workers, the plant returned to full operation of all five furnaces. The work force was pared from 350 before the strike to around 120 after operations returned to normal.

In the midst of the strike, Sims also somehow found time to orchestrate his leveraged buyout of Globe from its parent, Moore McCormack. Wall Street buyers came in for a presentation, but all had variations of the same idea in mind: buying, then busting up Globe, with the pieces being sold off at a profit. Sims finally found Jonathan Lee, who atypically was interested in investing for the long term and directing capital back into R&D. For Sims, the leveraged buyout meant he could restructure the company and put it on a frugal footing for the foreseeable future. He called a meeting and alerted everyone that costs would be scrutinized.

Sims also announced four new policies. Employees would be kept fully apprised of the state of company operations. After all the turmoil the company had gone through, Sims saw this step as the best way to regain trust. He began meeting with groups of 10 to 20 employees on a quarterly basis. Besides give-and-take about operations, Sims made announcements about the current status of another new policy, the company profit-sharing plan. The third policy implementation was bottom-up budgeting. Annual budget data would be based on revenue estimates from sales, and cost and production targets from the plant floor. Savings on quality programs also were monitored. It was only then that projections were sent to accounting for evaluation. Sims' fourth policy was his word and commitment to full employment at the Beverly plant. Employees who ferreted out more efficient methods of doing things did not have to worry about cost-saving themselves out of a job. They simply would be relocated elsewhere. Since then, a lot of jobs have been rendered obsolete, but Sims has kept his word.

Globe Metallurgical underwent the harshest of transformations, but it may be the best illustration of necessity being the mother of invention. The new organization is leaner, more responsive, and efficient, and productive than the old one. The company has organized a structure that enables it to meet the many challenges it faces. ■

SOURCE: Bruce Rayner, "Trial-By-Fire Transformation: An Interview with Globe Metallurgical's Arden C. Sims," *Harvard Business Review*, May–June, 1992, 117–129; Charles E. Lopez, "Globe Metallurgical CEO Arden C. Sims: On Quality and Competition in World Markets," *The Quality Observer*, February 1992, 16–17; and Otis Port et al., "Quality, the Key to Growth for Small Companies and for America," *Business Week*, Nov. 30, 1992, 66–74.

Second, senior managers have to find a way to tie all of these departments together. The formal chain of command and the supervision it provides is effective, but it is not enough. The organization needs systems to process information and enable communication among people in different departments and at different levels. **Coordination** refers to the quality of collaboration across departments. Without coordination, a company's left hand will not act in concert with the right hand, causing problems and conflicts. Coordination is required regardless of whether the organization has a functional, divisional, or team structure. Employees identify with their immediate department or team, taking its interest to heart, and may not want to compromise with other units for the good of the organization as a whole.

In the international arena, coordination is especially important. How can managers ensure that needed coordination will take place in their company? Both domestically and globally? Coordination is the outcome of information and cooperation. Managers can design systems and structures to promote communication. The most important methods for achieving coordination are integrating managers and task forces and teams.

coordination

The quality of collaboration across departments.

INTEGRATING MANAGERS

An **integrating manager** is a person in a full-time position created for the purpose of coordinating the activities of several departments.[22] The distinctive feature of the integrating position is that the person is not a member of one of the departments being coordinated. These positions often have titles such as product manager, project manager, program manager, or branch manager. The coordinator is assigned to coordinate departments on a full-time basis to achieve desired project or product outcomes.

General Mills, Procter & Gamble, and General Foods all use product managers to coordinate their product lines. A manager is assigned to each line, such as Cheerios, Bisquick, and Hamburger Helper. Product managers set budget goals, marketing targets, and strategies and obtain the cooperation from advertising, production, and sales personnel needed for implementing product strategy.

An interesting variation of the integrator role was developed at Florida Power & Light Company. To keep the construction of a nuclear power plant on schedule, several project managers were assigned the role of "Mothers." The philosophy of the person in charge was "If you want something to happen, it has to have a mother." The Mothers could nurture their projects to timely completion. This unusual label worked. Although departmental employees did not report directly to a Mother, the Mothers had a great deal of responsibility, which encouraged departmental managers to listen and cooperate.[23]

integrating manager

An individual responsible for coordinating the activities of several departments on a full-time basis to achieve specific project or product outcomes.

TASK FORCES AND TEAMS

A **task force** is a temporary team or committee designed to solve a short-term problem involving several departments.[24] Task force members represent their departments and share information that enables coordination.

task force

A temporary team or committee formed to solve a specific short-term problem involving several departments.

For example, the Shawmut National Corporation created two task forces in the human resources department to consolidate all employment services into a single area. The task force looked at job banks, referral programs, employment procedures, and applicant tracking systems; found ways to perform these functions for all Shawmut's divisions in one human resource department; and then disbanded.[25] General Motors uses task forces to solve temporary problems in its manufacturing plants. When a shipment of car doors arrived from a fabricating plant with surface imperfections, the plant manager immediately created a task force to solve the problem: "I got the vice president of manufacturing—who is my boss—the plant manager of the stamping plant, the die engineers, the quality engineers, the United Auto Workers representatives from both plants, the Olds guy from Lansing, a Cadillac guy, and the Fisher Body guy from the Tech Center. So I had everybody right out there on the floor looking at the exact part that is giving us the problem, and the problem was resolved in about two hours."[26]

In addition to creating task forces, companies also set up teams. As used for coordination, a **team** is a group of participants from several departments who meet regularly to solve ongoing problems of common interest.[27] The permanent team is similar to a task force except that it works with continuing rather than temporary problems and may exist for several years. For example, PLY GEM, a national manufacturer of home improvement products, has eight operating divisions. To coordinate technology, marketing, and operations skills, an Executive Management Committee consisting of each division president was created. Chemical Bank created a team of consumer banking specialists to devise a unified management system for all of Chemical's suburban branches. The team cuts across departments to develop and implement management techniques that involve customer flow management and teller scheduling that make all branches more efficient.[28]

team

A group of participants from several departments who meet regularly to solve ongoing problems of common interest.

● DEPARTMENTALIZATION

Another fundamental characteristic of organization structure is **departmentalization,** which is the basis for grouping positions into departments and departments into the total organization. Managers make choices about how to use the chain of command to group people together to perform their work. There are five approaches to structural design that reflect different uses of the chain of command in departmentalization. The functional, divisional, and matrix are traditional approaches that rely on the chain of command to define departmental groupings and reporting relationships along the hierarchy. Two contemporary approaches are the use of teams and networks. These newer approaches have emerged to meet organizational needs in a highly competitive global environment. A brief illustration of the five structural alternatives is in Exhibit 8.5 on pages 254–255.

Each approach to structure serves a distinct purpose for the organization, and each has advantages and disadvantages. The basic difference

departmentalization

The basis on which individuals are grouped into departments and departments into total organizations.

among structures is the way in which employees are departmentalized and to whom they report. The differences in structure illustrated in Exhibit 8.5 have major consequences for employee goals and motivation. Let us now turn to each of the five structural designs and examine their implications for managers.[29]

FUNCTIONAL APPROACH

Functional structure is the grouping of positions into departments based on similar skills, expertise, and resource use. A functional structure can be thought of as departmentalization by organizational resources, because each type of functional activity—for example, personnel, accounting, manufacturing—represents specific resources for performing the organization's task. People and facilities representing a common organizational resource are grouped together into a single department.

DIVISIONAL APPROACH

In contrast to the functional approach, in which people are grouped by common skills and resources, the **divisional structure** occurs when departments are grouped together based on organizational outputs. Functional and divisional structures are illustrated in Exhibit 8.5. In the divisional structure, divisions are created as self-contained units for producing a single product. Each functional department resource needed to produce the product is assigned to one division. For example, in a functional structure, all engineers are grouped together and work on all products. In a divisional structure, separate engineering departments are established within each division. Each department is smaller and focuses on a single product line. Departments are duplicated across product lines.

The divisional structure is sometimes called a *product structure, program structure,* or *self-contained unit structure.* Each of these terms means essentially the same thing: Diverse departments are brought together to produce a single organizational output, whether it be a product, a program, or service to a single customer.

In very large companies, a divisional structure is essential. Most large corporations have separate business divisions that perform different tasks, serve different clients, or use different technologies. When a huge organization produces products for different markets, the divisional structure works because each division is an autonomous business.

A major difference between divisional and functional structures is that the chain of command from each function converges lower in the hierarchy. Thus, the divisional structure encourages decentralization. Decision making is pushed down at least one level in the hierarchy, freeing up the president and other top managers for strategic planning.

GEOGRAPHIC-BASED DIVISIONS.   An alternative for assigning divisional responsibility is to group company activities by geographic region. In this structure, all functions in a specific country or region report to the same division manager. This structure focuses company activities on local market conditions. For example, competitive advantage may come

functional structure

An organization structure in which positions are grouped into departments based on similar skills, expertise, and resource use.

divisional structure

An organization structure in which departments are grouped based on similar organizational outputs.

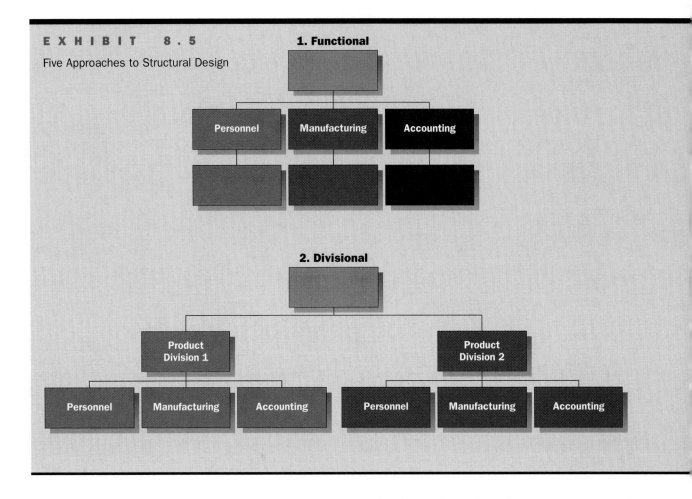

EXHIBIT 8.5

Five Approaches to Structural Design

1. Functional

Personnel   Manufacturing   Accounting

2. Divisional

Product Division 1 — Personnel   Manufacturing   Accounting

Product Division 2 — Personnel   Manufacturing   Accounting

from the production or sale of a product adapted to a given country. For example, at LSI Logic Corporation, management's strategy is to divide the world into three geographic markets—Japan, the United States, and Europe. This way each division has all the resources to focus on the fierce competition in its part of the world.[30] In North America, Sears, Roebuck is organized into five regions, each with its own warehousing, inventory control, distribution system, and stores. This geographic structure enables close coordination of activities to meet the needs of customers within each region.

MATRIX APPROACH

matrix approach

An organization structure that utilizes functional and divisional chains of command simultaneously in the same part of the organization.

The **matrix approach** utilizes functional and divisional chains of command simultaneously in the same part of the organization.[31] The matrix actually has dual lines of authority. In Exhibit 8.6, the functional hierarchy of authority runs vertically and the divisional hierarchy of authority runs laterally. The lateral chain of command formalizes the divisional relationships. Thus, the lateral structure provides coordination across functional departments while the vertical structure provides traditional control within functional departments. The matrix approach to structure

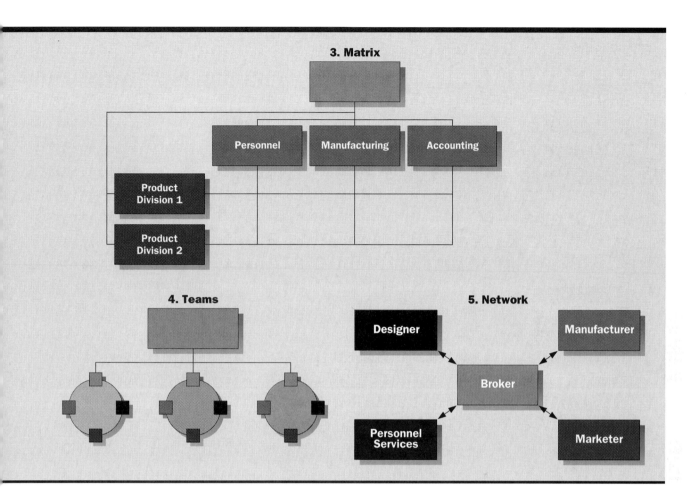

therefore provides a formal chain of command for both the functional and divisional relationships.

The matrix structure often is used by global corporations such as Dow Corning or Asea Brown Boveri. The problem for global companies is to achieve simultaneous coordination of various products within each country or region and for each product line. In a global matrix structure, the two lines of authority may be geographic and product. Managers of local affiliate companies within a country such as Germany report to two superiors. The general manager of a plant producing plastic containers in Germany reports to both the head of the plastics products division and the head of German operations. The German boss coordinates all the affiliates within Germany, and the plastics products boss coordinates the manufacturing and sale of plastics products around the world. The dual authority structure causes confusion, but after managers learn to use it, the matrix provides excellent coordination simultaneously for each geographic region and product line.

KEY RELATIONSHIPS.   The success of the matrix structure depends on the abilities of people in key matrix roles. Exhibit 8.7 provides a close-up of the reporting relationships in the dual chain of command for a

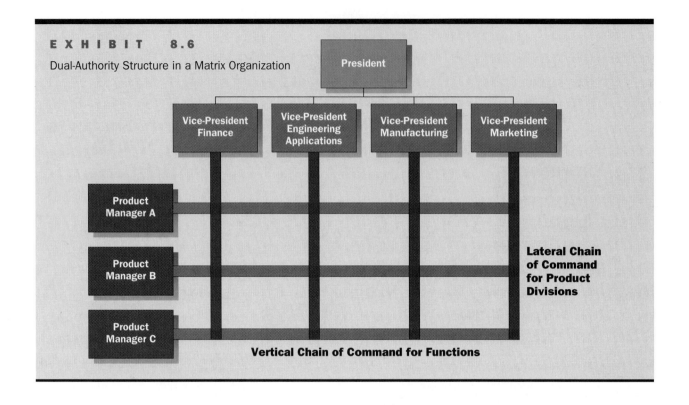

EXHIBIT   8.6

Dual-Authority Structure in a Matrix Organization

domestic company. The senior engineer in the medical products division reports to both the medical products vice-president and the engineering director. This violates the unity of command concept described earlier in this chapter but is necessary to give equal emphasis to both functional and divisional lines of authority. Confusion is reduced by separating responsibilities for each chain of command. The functional boss is responsible for technical and personnel issues, such as quality standards, providing technical training, and assigning technical personnel to projects. The divisional boss is responsible for programwide issues, such as overall design decisions, schedule deadlines, and coordinating technical specialists from several functions.

The senior engineer is called a **two-boss employee** because he or she reports to two supervisors simultaneously. Two-boss employees must resolve conflicting demands from the matrix bosses. They must confront senior managers and reach joint decisions. They need excellent human relations skills with which to confront managers and resolve conflicts. The **matrix boss** is the product or functional boss, who in Exhibit 8.7 is the engineering director and the medical products vice-president. The matrix boss is responsible for one side of the matrix. The top leader is responsible for the entire matrix. The **top leader** oversees both the product and functional chains of command. His or her responsibility is to maintain a power balance between the two sides of the matrix. If disputes arise between them, the problem will be kicked upstairs to the top leader.[32]

two-boss employee

An employee who reports to two supervisors simultaneously.

matrix boss

A product or functional boss, responsible for one side of the matrix.

top leader

The overseer of both the product and the functional chains of command, responsible for the entire matrix.

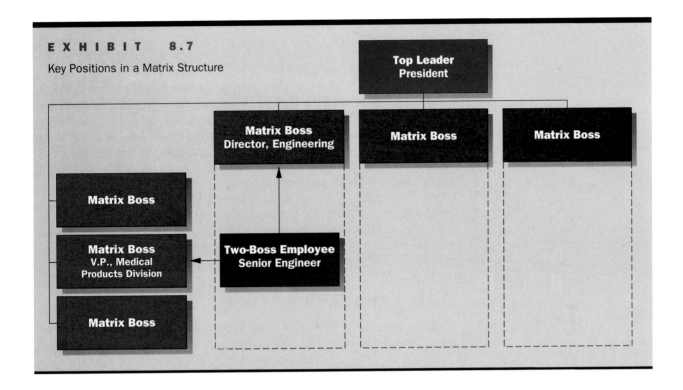

E X H I B I T   8 . 7

Key Positions in a Matrix Structure

Matrix bosses and two-boss employees often find it difficult to adapt to the matrix. The matrix boss has only half of each employee. Without complete control over employees, bosses must consult with their counterparts on the other side of the matrix. This necessitates frequent meetings and discussions to coordinate matrix activities. The two-boss employee experiences problems of conflicting demands and expectations from the two supervisors.

One company in which the matrix structure works very well is Crane Plastics, Inc., in Columbus, Ohio. There is only one matrix boss on the divisional side, but the approach has succeeded because of the skills of Howard Bennett.

 C R A N E   P L A S T I C S ,   I N C .

Gary Fulmer, executive vice-president of Crane Plastics, had not even heard of the matrix structure until he ran across some published articles. The matrix seemed a solution to the intense cooperation needed among departments during a product changeover. "Making the conversion in our large-volume custom products was driving me up a wall," said Fulmer. "Rarely had we done anything that cut across so many departments. It took compounding experts, toolmakers, extrusion people, quality control people—in all, it took about five different disciplines to make this thing work. . . . But it wasn't working." He continued, "People would have a meeting. They'd come back after two or three weeks with all good intentions, but they just didn't get it done, because they had more important things to do in their own functional areas."

Managers resisted the matrix, because team members work for two bosses—product team and function—at the same time. Crane Plastics implemented the matrix with one team boss, and it really began to click when Howard Bennett took that position. Bennett understood lateral relationships. He guarded against interdepartmental friction by having functional department heads sign an agreement allowing their subordinates participation in a product team. His style encouraged cooperation. But Bennett admits it took some practice: "When I assumed this position, I was totally engrossed in manufacturing. . . . I had no sympathy for marketing, accounting, or most of the other functions. This job gave me a broader outlook." Said one team member, "With other companies, matrix management is reduced to shouting matches. . . . It's inevitable any time you have two bosses." But thanks to Howard Bennett, this did not happen at Crane Plastics.[33] ∎

TEAM APPROACH

Probably the most widespread trend in departmentalization has been the effort by companies to implement team concepts. The vertical chain of command is a powerful means of control, but passing all decisions up the hierarchy takes too long and keeps responsibility at the top. Companies in the 1990s are trying to find ways to delegate authority, push responsibility to low levels, and create participative teams that engage the commitment of workers. This approach enables organizations to be more flexible and responsive in the competitive global environment.

Cross-functional teams consist of employees from various functional departments who are responsible to meet as a team and resolve mutual problems. Team members typically still report to their functional departments, but they also report to the team, one member of whom may be the leader. Computer-based companies such as Lanier Technology Corporation, Compaq Computer Corporation, and AST Research are obsessed with creating a team atmosphere using cross-functional teams.[34] At Compaq, lateral groups are called "smart teams," which represent an interdisciplinary approach to management. This structural approach assumes that people from the treasurer's office and engineering have ideas to contribute to decisions about marketing and manufacturing. The Deskpro 286 was created by a smart team in response to IBM's super PC. Kevin Ellington, who was in charge of the project, created his own smart team, drawing members from every department in the company. Team members communicated constantly. Within six months, Compaq was shipping its first models—indeed, it beat IBM to the punch, because IBM was still suffering production problems.[35]

Permanent teams are brought together as a formal department in the organization. Instead of just working together, employees are placed in the same location and report to the same supervisor. In some organizations, such as Ford, permanent teams start at the top with what is called the Office of the Chairman or the Office of the President, in which the two or three top executives work as a team.

cross-functional team
A group of employees assigned to a functional department that meets as a team to resolve mutual problems.

permanent team
A group of participants from several functions who are permanently assigned to solve ongoing problems of common interest.

At lower organization levels, the permanent-team approach resembles the divisional approach described earlier, except that teams are much smaller. Teams may consist of only 20 to 30 members, each bringing a functional specialty to the team. For example, Kollmorgen Corporation, a manufacturer of electronic circuitry and other goods, divided its organization into teams that average 75 employees.[36] Even at this size, employees think of themselves as a team. Performance jumped dramatically after Kollmorgen shifted to this concept.

Kodak has adopted teams for specific products, such as black and white film. Team members—called Zebras—coordinate activities of all departments necessary to produce the film. Hallmark Cards created teams to develop new cards. Previously, artists, designers, and printers were located as much as a block apart although working on the same card. Now they work face-to-face, producing better cards faster.[37]

One dramatic example of reorganizing into permanent teams occurred at an old-line insurance company called Aid Association for Lutherans (AAL).

Kraft USA employees discuss a storyboard for a Kraft Macaroni & Cheese dinner commercial. This is a formal *team*, created by Kraft to achieve a specific goal—develop a commercial for a product.

AID ASSOCIATION FOR LUTHERANS

AAL's traditional organization structure consisted of three functional departments with employees specialized to handle health insurance, life insurance, or support services as illustrated in part (a) of Exhibit 8.8. This structure seemed efficient, but policyholder inquiries often were passed among several departments and then back again. For example, a request to use the cash value of a life policy to pay the premiums for health insurance would bounce through all sections, taking at least 21 days. Coordination across sections took additional time when misunderstandings arose.

Top managers decided to risk everything on a team approach. At precisely 12 noon, nearly 500 clerks, technicians, and managers wheeled their chairs to new locations, becoming part of 25-person teams. The new structure is illustrated in part (b) of Exhibit 8.8. Each section consists of three to four teams that serve a region of the country. Each team has specialists who can do any of the 167 tasks required for policyholder sales and service. The request to pay health insurance premiums with life insurance cash value now is handled in five days. Productivity is up 20 percent and case-processing time has been reduced by as much as 75 percent. Administrative overhead is way down, because teams need little supervision. A total of 55 middle management jobs was eliminated as the teams took over self-management responsibility. AAL now handles 10 percent more transactions of all kinds, with 10 percent fewer employees, thanks to the team concept.[38] ■

NETWORK APPROACH

The newest approach to departmentalization has been called a "dynamic network" organization.[39] The **network structure** means that the organization disaggregates major functions into separate companies that are brokered by a small headquarters organization. Rather than

network structure

An organization structure that disaggregates major functions into separate companies that are brokered by a small headquarters organization.

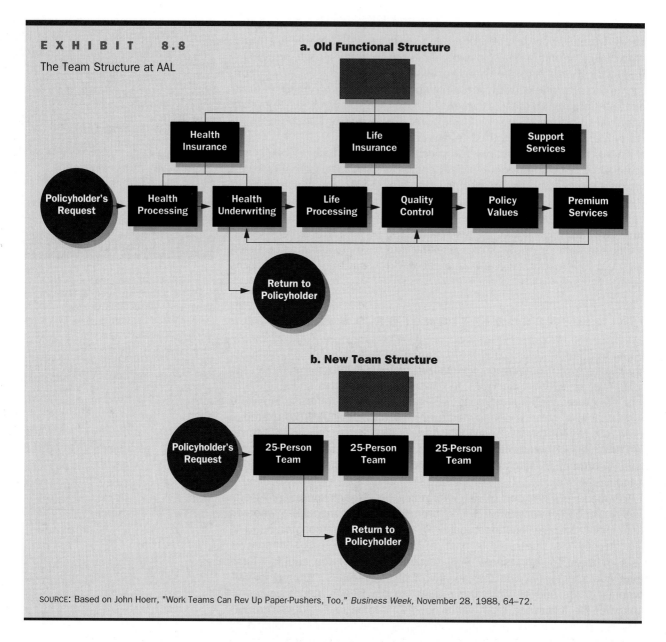

EXHIBIT 8.8

The Team Structure at AAL

a. Old Functional Structure

Health Insurance

Life Insurance

Support Services

Policyholder's Request

Health Processing

Health Underwriting

Life Processing

Quality Control

Policy Values

Premium Services

Return to Policyholder

b. New Team Structure

Policyholder's Request

25-Person Team

25-Person Team

25-Person Team

Return to Policyholder

SOURCE: Based on John Hoerr, "Work Teams Can Rev Up Paper-Pushers, Too," *Business Week*, November 28, 1988, 64–72.

manufacturing, engineering, sales, and accounting being housed under one roof, these services are provided by separate organizations working under contract and connected electronically to the central office.[40]

The network approach is revolutionary, because it is difficult to answer the question, "Where is the organization?" in traditional terms. For example, a firm may contract for expensive services such as training, transportation, legal, and engineering, so these functions are no longer part of the organization. Or consider a piece of ice hockey equipment that is designed in Scandinavia, engineered in the United States, manufactured in South Korea, and distributed in Canada by a Japanese sales organization. These pieces are drawn together contractually and coordinated electronically, creating a new form of organization.

This organizational approach is especially powerful for international operations. For example, Schwinn Bicycle Company went to a network structure, importing bicycles manufactured in Asia and distributing them through independent dealers who are coordinated electronically. Cigna Corporation took over an unused factory in Ireland and hired workers to process medical claims more cheaply and efficiently than could be done in the United States. McGraw-Hill has people working at computer terminals in Ireland also, maintaining worldwide circulation files for its magazines. These departments are tied electronically to the home offices in the United States.[41] High-tech firms such as IBM and Digital Equipment previously did all manufacturing in-house but now are contracting with suppliers around the world.[42] Lewis Galoob Toys, Inc., sold $58 million worth of toys with only 115 employees. Galoob farmed out manufacturing and packaging to contractors in Hong Kong, toy design to independent inventors, and sales to independent distribution representatives. Another name for the network organization is the modular corporation, which is described in the Manager's Shoptalk box.

MANAGER'S shoptalk

THE MODULAR CORPORATION

In the past, companies took great pride in creating a huge, self-sufficient enterprise that did everything for itself from making its own supplies to trucking them to manufacturing facilities sprawled nationwide. As we rush toward the twenty-first century, these monoliths are being replaced by lean structures called the modular corporation. Two industries, apparel and electronics, have championed the modular model with companies such as Nike pioneering the system. But other industries are also catching the modular wave.

The flexible modular structure enables companies to react quickly to the rapidly changing needs of today's marketplace by focusing its personnel, technology, and money on a few core activities while purchasing other activities, such as deliveries, accounting, and even manufacturing, from outside specialists. The modular company is a hub surrounded by a flexible network of top suppliers whose modules can be expanded or cut out in response to changing needs.

The modular system offers two advantages: (1) cost reduction and (2) the opportunity to direct capital to core areas where the company has its greatest competitive edge. Nike and Chrysler offer examples of these advantages.

Nike's corporate offices in Beaverton, Oregon, focus investment on research, design, and technology to meet the changing needs and demands of athletic and fashion-conscious consumers. By outsourcing manufacturing to suppliers in Asia, Nike avoids a huge investment in fixed assets, thereby showing a high return on shareholder equity.

Chrysler Corporation was the first U.S. automaker to adopt the modular approach. Outside suppliers provide 70 percent of Chrysler parts. Cars are built in modules, saving production costs. Four separate interior units, for example, arrive from suppliers in various locations, ready to install on the auto frame.

The keys to success for the modular company are focusing company efforts on the right core specialty, and carefully selecting loyal, dependable suppliers capable of guarding trade secrets and changing and retooling to meet new demands. Strong networks provide a competitive edge, and modular companies may indeed be the wave of the future. ■

SOURCE: Shawn Tully, "The Modular Corporation," *Fortune*, February 8, 1993, 106–116.

SUMMARY AND MANAGEMENT SOLUTION

This chapter introduced a number of important organizing concepts. Fundamental characteristics of organization structure include specialization, chain of command, authority and responsibility, span of management, centralization and decentralization, and coordination. These dimensions of organization represent the vertical hierarchy and indicate how authority and responsibility are distributed along the hierarchy.

The other major concept is departmentalization, which describes how organization employees are grouped. Three traditional approaches are functional, divisional, and matrix; contemporary approaches are team and network structures. The functional approach groups employees by common skills and tasks. The opposite structure is divisional, which groups people by organizational output such that each division has a mix of functional skills and tasks. The matrix structure uses two chains of command simultaneously, and some employees have two bosses. The two chains of command in a domestic organization typically are functional and product division, and for international firms, the two chains of command typically are product and geographic regions. The team approach uses permanent teams and cross-functional teams to achieve better coordination and employee commitment than is possible with a pure functional structure. The network approach, including the modular organization, represents the newest form of organization structure. Departmental tasks are subcontracted to other organizations, so the central organization is simply a broker that coordinates several independent organizations to accomplish its goal. Each organization form has advantages and disadvantages and can be used by managers to meet the needs of the competitive situation.

Contingency factors of stage of maturity and environment influence the correct structural approach. When a firm's strategy is to differentiate the firm's product from a competitor's, a more organic structural approach using teams, decentralization and perhaps a divisional matrix structure is appropriate. When environmental uncertainty is high, lateral coordination is important and the organization should have an organic structure.

Because all Max Duncan had was a vision, he had to start selling pieces of his business before it even existed. In exchange for one year's free use of a vacant building, he gave the owner one-third of Integrity. He used his minuscule capital to pick up bargain-priced equipment, and took advantage of free samples from chemical companies. Instead of one year's salary, he got a top sales manager to take another one-third of the company. To make ends meet, he lived on unemployment benefits. It turned out his projections were correct; his prices were as much as 20 percent lower than competitors'. He reinvested profits, and finally obtained bank financing. In five years since 1987, the company grew 800 percent, and Duncan has never deviated from what got him started and kept him going. He keeps costs and prices low by running the leanest, most efficient operation possible. His work force consists of only 18 people, with two-thirds assigned to production where employees are cross-trained and can easily be moved from one job to another. The only other departments are sales and marketing and accounting, with a combined total of three people. The company also has one secretary. "We have high levels of expertise because all of our people are experienced in our own operation," Duncan says.[43]

DISCUSSION QUESTIONS

1. Sonny Holt, manager of Electronics Assembly, asked Hector Cruz, his senior technician, to handle things in the department while Sonny worked on the budget. Sonny needed peace and quiet for at least a week to complete his figures. After ten days, Sonny discovered that Hector had hired a senior secretary, not realizing that Sonny had promised interviews to two other people. Evaluate Sonny's approach to delegation.
2. Contrast centralization with span of management. Would you expect these characteristics to affect each other in organizations? Why?
3. An organizational consultant was heard to say, "Some aspect of functional structure appears in every organization." Do you agree? Explain.
4. The divisional structure is often considered almost the opposite of a functional structure. Do you agree? Briefly explain the major differences in these two approaches to departmentalization.
5. What are important skills for matrix bosses and two-boss employees in a matrix organization?
6. Some people argue that the matrix structure should be adopted only as a last resort because the dual chains of command can create more problems than they solve. Do you agree or disagree? Why?
7. What is the network approach to structure? Is the use of authority and responsibility different compared with other forms of departmentalization? Explain.
8. Why are divisional structures frequently used in large corporations? Does it make sense for a huge corporation such as American Airlines to stay in a functional structure?
9. An international matrix structure tends to be organized by product divisions and geographic regions. Why would these two chains of command be used rather than product and function as in domestic companies? Explain.
10. What is the difference between a task force and an integrating manager? Which would be more effective in achieving coordination?
11. Discuss why an organization in an uncertain environment requires more horizontal relationship than one in a certain environment.

MANAGEMENT IN PRACTICE: ETHICAL DILEMMA

● QUALITY CONTROL SUPERVISION

Jane was an engineer in the quality control department of a new manufacturing plant. She used to work under Ed, the head of quality control, who in turn reported to the vice-president of manufacturing. Jane is a college graduate and learned a lot from Ed, who has worked in manufacturing for 32 years.

One of Jane's responsibilities was to measure the chemical concentrations in the plant's waste water and sign the monthly reports sent to city officials certifying the concentrations are below dangerous levels. She recently decided to switch to a newer test that is more reliable and less expensive and discovered that the actual concentrations of pollutants are above mandated levels.

Jane showed the new results to Ed, who agreed the situation was serious. However, the vice-president of manufacturing did not agree. After many arguments between Ed and the vice-president, Ed was found overqualified for his job and was transferred to another plant. The vice-president of manufacturing reinstated the old test.

Jane is now head of quality control. The plant just received an exclusive contract that will cause production to double in two years. The chemical concentrations keep rising. The vice-president of manufacturing tells Jane that when concentrations become too high as measured by the old test, they will add more water to dilute the waste.

● W H A T   D O   Y O U   D O ?

1. Obey the vice-president of manufacturing. He has ultimate authority and responsibility for this task.
2. Confront the vice-president of manufacturing and argue the case for better control of pollutants, being prepared to lose your job if necessary.
3. Blow the whistle on the company by taking test results to city officials and the press. This will protect you and force the company to adhere to the tests.

CASE FOR ANALYSIS   ●

PRO FASTENERS, INC.

Pro Fasteners' Alpha was that of a can-do small business. Founded in 1981 by Steve Braccini and his wife Cinde, the minimally capitalized, 24-person operation was basically an outsized industrial hardware store. Its not-quite-yet-arrived-at-Omega is a restructured company that has implemented a host of quality, efficiency, and employee empowerment restructuring programs. The company, which distributes industrial hardware components to the electronics industry, has undergone substantial amounts of angst and pathos.

Like many companies, Pro Fasteners is a mirror of its CEO, Steve Braccini. After giving up drinking in the late 1980s, he resolved to extend his self-improvement to his company. Braccini is a fast-mover, and the shake-up at Pro Fasteners was a blitzkrieg. Business was evolving and economic times were hard. Supplier lists were getting shortened, and only the top servicers were making the cut. Braccini saw a chance to save customers money by efficiently managing their inventories for them. The marketing pitch was simple: customers could eliminate purchasing, receiving, and quality-assurance costs, and with the attendant volume acquisition Pro Fasteners would be doing, per-part prices would actually decrease. Braccini visualized overseeing inventory for lots of large companies, saving them money, and becoming indispensable. All he would need was a huge computer system, and a highly trained and responsive work force that not only could adapt, change, and grow, but that could also assure top-shelf quality standards 100 percent of the time.

To highlight this new emphasis on employee empowerment, Braccini upended the standard pyramid company structure and vested line authority with managers. Employees were assigned into cross-functional teams, with no

management. A lot of people didn't like it. Cinde, Steve's wife, used the metaphor that the chimps were now in charge of the zoo. However, Steve, who was concentrating on long-range planning and absorbing more and more written material about company improvement, figured every company makeover had its rough spots. He ultimately decided to delegate even more authority to lower levels, establishing the Continuous Improvement Council. Its responsibility included anything required to improve quality.

About 12 months into the restructuring, things got rougher, but there were plenty of accomplishments. Teams that ferreted out inefficiencies and corrected them were motivated to press on and find other improvements. Shipping times were reduced, often to a same-day delivery objective. Early shipments that were resulting in a 5 percent rejection rate were eliminated. One group revamped the warehouse and concocted methods to deliver on time all the time with 100 percent correct orders. Consultants gave instruction on total responsibility management and communication skills. Employees went on benchmarking trips to other companies and attended seminars to learn "think quality" procedures aimed at eyeing every product and process from an improvement perspective. Meanwhile, Braccini was talking seriously with IBM about acquiring the AS/400 mini-computer, which would put his company at the top of the industry in efficiency capabilities. Plotting the future had become his obsession, while at the same time more than a few workers wondered if he had thrown away his compass.

Many employees were certain that the time spent on new methods was worth it. Accustomed to an authoritative, hierarchal structure, they noted the hypocrisy of lip-service that supposedly put them in charge. Orders still came from management, and problem solutions had to be submitted for a final okay. Managers, who still had ultimate responsibility for results, were leery of completely relinquishing authority. Communications broke down, and some team members simply abdicated participation. Other key people quit. Cinde often argued with Steve. Her digressing metaphor now had the lunatics in charge of the asylum.

However, growth was marching, and Pro Fasteners' quality and service standards were near perfect. Of 13,000 orders, the company delivered all but 20 on time. Braccini sank a million into the new computer system. Customers were flocking in and salespeople were added. Nevertheless, morale was nonexistent, and team meetings were a thing of the past. Braccini had invested another $4,000 per employee on training. His vision seemed to be coming into focus. However, business was up, yet profits were off by one-half. Steve wondered if he'd been looking at a mirage

all along. He wondered too if Pro Fasteners would have a happy ending or bring down the curtain on a Greek tragedy.

● QUESTIONS

1. How could Pro Fasteners' vertical structure be improved?
2. Does the company need more horizontal coordination? If so, what type would be most beneficial?
3. The improvements in sales and quality indicate the company is headed in the right direction. How do you think the story will end?

SOURCE: John Case, "Quality With Tears," *INC.* June 1992, 83–95; and John Case, "The Best Small Companies To Work For In America," *INC.* November 1992, 89–92.

REFERENCES

1. John Case, "How to Launch an *INC.* 500 Company," *INC.*, October 1992, 91–99.

2. Robert M. Tomasko, "Restructuring: Getting It Right," *Management Review* (April 1992), 10–15.

3. Jacob Rahul, "Thriving In a Lame Economy," *Fortune*, October 5, 1992, 44–54.

4. Joseph Weber, "DuPont's Trailblazer Wants to Get Out of the Woods," *Business Week,* August 31, 1992, 70–71.

5. W. Graham Astley, "Organization Size and Bureaucratic Structure," *Organization Studies* 6 (1985), 201–228; John B. Cullen, Kenneth S. Anderson, and Douglas D. Baker, "Blau's Theory of Structure Differentiation Revisited: A Theory of Structural Change or Scale?" *Academy of Management Journal* 29 (1986), 203–229; and Richard L. Daft, *Organization Theory and Design,* 4th ed. (St. Paul, MN: West, 1992).

6. Robert E. Quinn and Kim Cameron, "Organizational Life Cycles and Shifting Criteria of Effectiveness: Some Preliminary Evidence," *Management Science* 29 (1983), 33–51; and John R. Kimberly, Robert H. Miles, and associates, *The Organizational Life Cycle* (San Francisco: Jossey-Bass, 1980).

7. Mike Weaver, "Steps Aside to Stay Ahead," *Nation's Business*, March 1993, 8.

8. Paul R. Lawrence and Jay W. Lorsch, *Organization and Environment* (Homewood, IL: Irwin, 1969).

9. Robert B. Duncan, "Characteristics of Organizational Environments and Perceived Environmental Uncertainty," *Administrative Science Quarterly* 17 (1972), 313–327; W. Alan Randolph and Gregory G. Dess, "The Congruence Perspective of Organization Design: A Conceptual Model and Multivariate Research Approach," *Academy of Management Review* 9 (1984), 114–127; and Masoud Yasai-Ardekani, "Structural Adaptations to Environments," *Academy of Management Review* 11 (1986), 9–21.

10. John Child, *Organization: A Guide to Problems and Practice,* 2d ed. (London: Harper & Row, 1984).

11. Adam Smith, *The Wealth of Nations* (New York: Modern Library, 1937).

12. This discussion is based on Richard L. Daft, *Organization Theory and Design,* 4th ed. (St. Paul, MN: West, 1992), 387–388.

13. C. I. Barnard, *The Functions of the Executive* (Cambridge, MA: Harvard University Press, 1938).

14. Thomas A. Stewart, "CEOs See Clout Shifting," *Fortune,* November 6, 1989, 66.

15. Michael G. O'Loughlin, "What Is Bureaucratic Accountability and How Can We Measure It?" *Administration & Society* 22, 3 (November 1990), 275–302.

16. Carrie R. Leana, "Predictors and Consequences of Delegation," *Academy of Management Journal* 29 (1986), 754–774.

17. Paul D. Collins and Frank Hull, "Technology and Span of Control: Woodward Revisited," *Journal of Management Studies* 23 (March 1986), 143–164; David D. Van Fleet and Arthur G. Bedeian, "A History of the Span of Management," *Academy of Management Review* 2 (1977), 356–372; and C. W. Barkdull, "Span of Control—A Method of Evaluation," *Michigan Business Review* 15 (May 1963), 25–32.

18. Brian Dumaire, "What the Leaders of Tomorrow See," *Fortune,* July 3, 1989, 48–62.

19. Joseph Weber, "A Big Company That Works," *Business Week,* May 4, 1992, 124–132.

20. Dana Milbank, "Changes at Alcoa Point Up Challenges and Benefits of Decentralized Authority," *The Wall Street Journal,* November 7, 1991, B1; and Clay Chandler and Paul Ingrassia, "Just as U.S. Firms Try Japanese Management, Honda Is Centralizing," *The Wall Street Journal,* April 11, 1991, A1, A10.

21. Richard L. Daft, *Organization Theory and Design,* 4th ed. (St Paul, MN: West, 1992).

22. Paul R. Lawrence and Jay W. Lorsch, "New Managerial Job: The Integrator," *Harvard Business Review* (November–December 1967), 142–151.

23. Ron Winslow, "Utility Cuts Red Tape, Builds Nuclear Plant Almost on Schedule," *The Wall Street Journal,* February 22, 1984, 1, 18.

24. William J. Altier, "Task Forces: An Effective Management Tool," *Management Review* (February 1987), 52–57.

25. "Task Forces Tackle Consolidation of Employment Services," *Shawnut News,* Shawnut National Corporation, May 3, 1989, 2.

26. Michael Brody, "Can GM Manage It All?" *Fortune,* July 8, 1985, 22–28.

27. Henry Mintzberg, *The Structure of Organizations* (Englewood Cliffs, NJ: Prentice-Hall, 1979).

28. Vicki Moss, "BUMP: The Consumer Bank's New Program Helps the Branches Run More Efficiently and Effectively," *Chemical Chronicle,* Chemical Banking Corporation, June–July 1989, 14–15.

29. The following discussion of structural alternatives draws heavily on Jay R. Galbraith, *Designing Complex Organizations* (Reading, MA: Addison-Wesley, 1973); Jay R. Galbraith, *Organization Design* (Reading, MA: Addison-Wesley, 1977); Robert Duncan, "What Is the Right Organization Structure?" *Organizational Dynamics* (Winter 1979), 59–80; and J. McCann and Jay R. Galbraith, "Interdepartmental Relations," in *Handbook of Organizational Design,* P. Nystrom and W. Starbuck, eds. (New York: Oxford University Press, 1981), 60–84.

30. Mike Tharp, "LSI Logic Corp. Does as the Japanese Do," *The Wall Street Journal*, April 17, 1986, 6.

31. Lawton R. Burns, "Matrix Management in Hospitals: Testing Theories of Matrix Structure and Development," *Administrative Science Quarterly* 34 (1989), 349–368.

32. Stanley M. Davis and Paul R. Lawrence, *Matrix* (Reading, MA: Addison-Wesley, 1977).

33. Ellen Kolton, "Team Players," *INC.,* September 1984, 140–144; and personal communication from Howard Bennett, matrix vice-president.

34. Joel Kotkin, "The 'Smart-Team' at Compaq Computer," *INC.,* February 1986, 48–56.

35. Ibid., 56.

36. Lucien Rhodes, "The Passion of Robert Swiggett," *INC.,* April 1984, 121–140.

37. Thomas A. Stewart, "The Search for the Organization of Tomorrow," *Fortune,* May 18, 1992, 92–98.

38. John Hoerr, "Work Teams Can Rev Up Paper-Pushers, Too," *Business Week,* November 28, 1988, 64–72.

39. Charles C. Snow, Raymond E. Miles, and Henry J. Coleman, Jr., "Managing 21st Century Network Organizations," *Organizational Dynamics* 20 (Winter 1992), 5–20, and Miles, "Adapting to Technology and Competition."

40. Raymond E. Miles and Charles C. Snow, "Organizations: New Concepts for New Forms," *California Management Review* 28 (Spring 1986), 62–73; and "Now, The Post-Industrial Corporation," *Business Week*, March 3, 1986, 64–74.

41. Bernard Wysocki, Jr., "American Firms Send Office Work Abroad to Use Cheaper Labor," *The Wall Street Journal*, August 14, 1991, A1, A4.

42. G. Pascal Zachary, "High-Tech Firms Find It's Good to Line Up Outside Contractors," *The Wall Street Journal*, July 29, 1992, A1, A5.

43. John Case, "How to Launch an *INC.* 500 Company," *INC.,* October 1992, 91–99.

INNOVATION AND CHANGE   9

CHAPTER OUTLINE

LEARNING OBJECTIVES ▼

After studying this chapter, you should be able to

- Define organizational change and explain the forces for change.
- Describe the sequence of four change activities that must be performed in order for change to be successful.
- Explain the techniques managers can use to facilitate the initiation of change in organizations, including idea champions and new-venture teams.
- Define sources of resistance to change.
- Explain force field analysis and other implementation tactics that can be used to overcome resistance to change.
- Explain the difference among technology, product, structure, and culture/people changes.
- Explain the change process—bottom up, top down, horizontal—associated with each type of change
- Define organizational development and organizational revitalization.

Just under ten years ago the workers, managers, and owners of Will-Burt Company had little to smile about. The 350-person work force at the manufacturing firm was paid $2 an hour less than similar jobs in the Orrville, Ohio, region. The employees lived up to the vote of no-confidence the low wages implied by maintaining a steady 35 percent rejection rate on all parts produced. Another sign of job dissatisfaction was reflected in the turnover rate; workers quit in droves that approached one-third of the entire work force every year. Meanwhile, the company owners had their own problems. Although profit margins hovered below 5 percent, they were nowhere near the worst news. The collapse of a scaffolding produced by Will-Burt resulted in a settlement of $6 million in damages. A number of other lawsuits were pending, and the owners came to a decision: they would either sell the company or liquidate it. Harry Featherstone, the company's CEO, was instructed to do one or the other within 90 days. However, he thought that Will-Burt could be saved with the right strategy. If you were a manager at Will-Burt, how would you promote innovative behavior in your employees and help the company become more efficient? How would you improve employee attitudes?[1]

Managers at Will-Burt are not alone. Every organization experiences stress and difficulty in coping with change. Innovation from within is widely recognized as one of the critical problems facing business today in the United States and Canada. To be successful, organizations must embrace many types of change. Businesses must develop improved production technologies, create new products desired in the marketplace, implement new administrative systems, and upgrade employees' skills. Companies such as Westinghouse, Black & Decker, and Merck implement all of these changes and more.

How important is organizational change? Consider this: The parents of today's college students grew up without cable television, voice mail, stain-resistant carpet, personal computers, VCRs, electronic games, CDs, cellular phones, video stores, or laser checkout systems in supermarkets. Companies that produce the new products have prospered, but many companies caught with outdated products and technologies have failed. Organizations that change and innovate successfully, such as General Electric, 3M, and Frito-Lay, are both profitable and admired.

Organizational change is defined as the adoption of a new idea or behavior by an organization.[2] In this chapter, we will look at how organizations can be designed to respond to the environment through internal innovation and change. First we will examine the basic forces for organizational change. Then we will look closely at how managers facilitate two change requirements: initiation and implementation. Finally, we will discuss the four major types of change—technology, new product, structure, and culture/people—and how the organization can be designed to facilitate each.

organizational change

The adoption of a new idea or behavior by an organization.

● MANAGING ORGANIZATIONAL CHANGE

Change can be managed. By observing external trends, patterns, and needs, managers use planned change to help the organization adapt to external problems and opportunities.[3] When organizations are caught flat-footed, failing to anticipate or respond to new needs, management is at fault.

An overall model for planned change is presented in Exhibit 9.1. Four events make up the change sequence: (1) internal and external forces for change exist; (2) organization managers monitor these forces and become aware of a need for change; (3) the perceived need triggers the initiation of change; which (4) is then implemented. How each of these activities is handled depends on the organization and managers' styles.

We now turn to a brief discussion of the specific activities associated with the first two events—forces for change and the perceived need for the organization to respond.

FORCES FOR CHANGE

Forces for organizational change exist both in the external environment and within the organization.

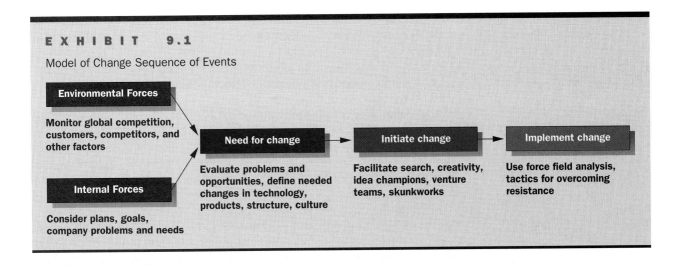

EXHIBIT   9.1

Model of Change Sequence of Events

Environmental Forces

Monitor global competition, customers, competitors, and other factors

Internal Forces

Consider plans, goals, company problems and needs

Need for change

Evaluate problems and opportunities, define needed changes in technology, products, structure, culture

Initiate change

Facilitate search, creativity, idea champions, venture teams, skunkworks

Implement change

Use force field analysis, tactics for overcoming resistance

ENVIRONMENTAL FORCES.   As described in Chapters 3 and 4, external forces originate in all environmental sectors, including customers, competitors, technology, economic forces, and the international arena. For example, many North American companies have been blindsided by global competition. Consider General Electric, which built a new factory to produce microwave ovens. As GE's plans were being made, Yun Soo Chu was working 80 hours per week for Samsung in South Korea to perfect a microwave oven. About the time the GE plant came on stream, Samsung started exporting thousands of microwaves to the United States at one-third the cost of GE microwaves. Today, Samsung has 25 percent of the U.S. market, and GE is one of its best customers. GE closed its microwave plant, preferring to buy the cheaper Samsung ovens to sell under the GE label.[4]

INTERNAL FORCES.   Internal forces for change arise from internal activities and decisions. If top managers select a goal of rapid company growth, internal actions will have to be changed to meet that growth. New departments or technologies will be created. General Motors' senior management, frustrated by poor internal efficiency, designed the Saturn manufacturing plant to solve this internal need. Demands by employees, labor unions, and production inefficiencies can all generate a force to which management must respond with change.

NEED FOR CHANGE

As indicated in Exhibit 9.1, external or internal forces translate into a perceived need for change within the organization.[5] Managers sense a need for change when there is a **performance gap**—a disparity between existing and desired performance levels. The performance gap may occur because current procedures are not up to standard or because a new idea or technology could improve current performance. Recall from Chapter 6 that management's responsibility is to monitor threats and opportunities in the external environment as well as strengths and weaknesses within the organization to determine whether a need for change exists.

performance gap

A disparity between existing and desired performance levels.

A performance gap was perceived by the chief of the Takoma Park Police Department, and he initiated many changes as described in the Leading Edge box.

One striking need for change occurred when executives at Apple Computer realized that they needed to sell in the toughest market of all—Japan's consumer-electronics fortress. In response to this need, Apple has innovated new methods (hiring local management, listing itself on the Japanese stock market), product lines (CD-ROM players and personal digital assistants), and community activism (sponsoring the 1990 Janet Jackson Tokyo concert and the 1992 Japanese Ladies Pro Golf Tournament). Apple not only has penetrated the Japanese fortress but also has achieved a major foothold to become one of the best-selling brands in Japan.[6]

Managers in every company must be alert to problems and opportunities, because the perceived need for change is what sets the stage for subsequent actions that create a new product or technology. Big problems are easy to spot. Sensitive monitoring systems are needed to detect gradual changes that can fool managers into thinking their company is doing fine. An organization may be in greater danger when the environment changes slowly, because managers may fail to trigger an organizational response. Failing to use planned change to meet small needs can place the organization in hot water, as illustrated in the following passage:

> When frogs are placed in a boiling pail of water, they jump out—they don't want to boil to death. However, when frogs are placed in a cold pail of water, and the pail is placed on a stove with the heat turned very low, over time the frogs will boil to death.[7]

● INITIATING CHANGE

After the need for change has been perceived, the next part of the change process is initiating change, a truly critical aspect of change management. This is where the ideas that solve perceived needs are developed. Responses that an organization can make are to search for or create a change to adopt.

SEARCH

search

The process of learning about current developments inside or outside the organization that can be used to meet a perceived need for change.

Search is the process of learning about current developments inside or outside the organization that can be used to meet the perceived need for change. Search typically uncovers existing knowledge that can be applied or adopted within the organization. Managers talk to friends and colleagues, read professional reports, or hire consultants to learn about ideas used elsewhere. For example, an internal consulting program was developed for the Office of Employee Relations for New York State, creating teams of 10 to 20 managers from a cross section of agencies to provide information to managers experiencing problems. The consulting team provided a quick way for managers to search out new ideas used in other departments.

LEADING edge

NOT-FOR-PROFIT INNOVATION IN THE TAKOMA PARK POLICE DEPARTMENT

When the mostly white, middle-class suburb of Takoma Park, Maryland, named A. Tony Fisher, a black man, as police chief, the community considered the appointment itself a dramatic change. It quickly became clear that dramatic change within the police force was just beginning, because Chief Fisher proved a master of innovation.

Abandoning the traditional "us versus them" paramilitary style so often associated with police-community relations, Fisher initiated COP—community oriented policing. Based on the belief that both officers and citizens must respond to each other as individuals, the program establishes police-community partnerships to deal with complex problems. As Chief Fisher

sees it, cold, impersonal "slap on the cuffs, book 'em, and write a report" methods foster only negative relationships. Fisher's critics question the implementation of a "touchy-feely" police style. Is it necessary, they ask, that citizens "like" the officers?

Fisher remains committed to his program, although he makes frequent adjustments and is willing to abandon anything that doesn't work. His programs stress innovative community relations. For example, officer continuing-education programs stress "soft skills" such as persuasion and reasoning in addition to traditional police techniques. Crime prevention programs, press accessibility, and police meetings with neighborhood groups and merchants contribute to a climate of cooperation.

Officers are encouraged to leave their vehicles and use foot patrols. The use of unarmed traffic enforce-

ment assistants relieves the officers of tedious, time-consuming chores. In a much-appreciated program, crime victims are no longer ignored but receive regular reports on the status of investigations.

The jury on COP and similar community-based programs is still out. However, in reaction to the failed policies spotlighted by recent violence in Los Angeles, Miami, and other U.S. cities, more and more police departments are innovating with some form of community-based action.

The days of *Dragnet's* Joe Friday may soon give way to the days of Takoma Park's Tony Fisher. ∎

SOURCE: Joseph N. Boyce, "New Attitude: Softer Style of Policing Takes Hold in Cities Like Takoma Park, Maryland," *The Wall Street Journal*, August 5, 1992, A1, A6.

Many needs, however, cannot be resolved through existing knowledge but require that the organization develop a new response. Initiating a new response means that managers must design the organization so as to facilitate creativity of both individuals and departments, encourage innovative people to initiate new ideas, or create new-venture departments. These techniques have been adopted by such corporations as GE and Apple with great success.

CREATIVITY

Creativity is the development of novel solutions to perceived problems.[8] Creative individuals develop ideas that can be adopted by the organization. People noted for their creativity include Edwin Land, who invented the Polaroid camera; Frederick Smith, who came up with the idea for Federal Express's overnight delivery service during an undergraduate class at Yale; and Swiss engineer George de Mestral, who created Velcro after noticing the tiny hooks on the burrs caught on his wool

creativity
The development of novel solutions to perceived organizational problems.

socks. Each of these people saw unique and creative opportunities in a familiar situation.

One test of creativity is to imagine a block of ice sitting on your desk. What use could you make of it? A creative person might see that it could be used to quench someone's thirst, reduce a patient's fever, crack a victim's skull, or produce steam by boiling.[9] Or consider the person interviewing college graduates for job openings. "Show me a new use for this stapler," the interviewer said. Calmly picking up the scissors on the desk, one creative woman cut the interviewer's tie in half and then stapled it back together. Smiling, she asked, "Now that I've demonstrated my instant mender, how many will you take?"

Each of us has the capacity to be creative. Characteristics of highly creative people are illustrated in the left-hand column of Exhibit 9.2. Creative people often are known for originality, open-mindedness, curiosity, a focused approach to problem solving, persistence, a relaxed and playful attitude, and receptivity to new ideas.[10]

Creativity can also be designed into organizations. Companies or departments within companies can be organized to be creative and initiate changes. The characteristics of creative organizations correspond to those of individuals, as illustrated in the right-hand column of Exhibit 9.2. Creative organizations are loosely structured. People find themselves in a situation of ambiguity, assignments are vague, territories overlap, tasks are poorly defined, and much work is done through teams.[11] Creative organizations have an internal culture of playfulness, freedom, challenge, and grass-roots participation.[12] They harness all potential sources of new ideas from within. Many participative management programs are born out of the desire to enhance creativity for initiating changes. People are not stuck in the rhythm of routine jobs. Managers

EXHIBIT 9.2 Characteristics of Creative People and Organizations	**The Creative Individual**	**The Creative Organization or Department**

	1. Conceptual fluency
	  Openmindedness
		1. Open channels of communication
		  Contact with outside sources
		  Overlapping territories
		  Suggestion systems, brainstorming, nominal group techniques

	2. Originality	2. Assignment of nonspecialists to problems
		  Eccentricity allowed
		  Use of teams

SOURCE: Based on Gary A. Steiner, ed., *The Creative Organization* (Chicago: University of Chicago Press, 1965), 16–18; Rosabeth Moss Kanter, "The Middle Manager as Innovator," *Harvard Business Review* (July–August 1982), 104–105; James Brian Quinn, "Managing Innovation: Controlled Chaos," *Harvard Business Review* 63 (May–June 1985), 73–84.	3. Less authority
	  Independence
		3. Decentralization, loosely defined positions, loose control
		  Acceptance of mistakes
		  Risk-taking norms

	4. Playfulness
	  Undisciplined exploration
	  Curiosity
		4. Freedom to choose and pursue problems
		  Not a tight ship, playful culture
		  Freedom to discuss ideas, long time horizon

	5. Persistence
	  Commitment
	  Focused approach
		5. Resources allocated to creative personnel and projects without immediate payoff
		  Reward system encourages innovation
		  Absolution of peripheral responsibilities

in an insurance company that had been tightly controlled from the top remarked on the changes that enabled them to be more creative:

> We used to run by the book and now I don't even know where the book is.
>
> Yesterday's procedures are outdated today.
>
> If you don't like the organization chart, just wait until next week, we'll have a new one.[13]

The most creative companies encourage employees to make mistakes. Jim Read, president of the Read Corporation, says, "When my employees make mistakes trying to improve something, I give them a round of applause. No mistakes mean no new products. If they ever become afraid to make one, my company is doomed."[14] Ross Perot, who founded EDS, said creative managers could not keep their noses clean: "We teach people that mistakes are like skinned knees for little children. . . . My people are covered with the scars of their mistakes. By the time they get to the top, their noses are pretty well broken."[15]

Open channels of communication, overlapping jobs, discretionary resources, decentralization, and employees' freedom to choose problems and make mistakes can generate unexpected benefits for companies. Creative organizational conditions such as those described in Exhibit 9.2 enable more than 200 new products a year to bubble up from 3M's research labs.

The same creative conditions enabled the solution to the following problem: How do you pack many potato chips into a small space without crushing them? A small company used the analogy in nature of stacking dry leaves and wet leaves. Through the use of such creative thinking, the obvious solution emerged: Mold the chips into uniform, stackable shapes *before* they dry. Armed with this innovation, the company sold its idea to Procter & Gamble, and the canned chip Pringles was born.[16]

IDEA CHAMPIONS

If creative conditions are successful, new ideas will be generated that must be carried forward for acceptance and implementation. This is where idea champions come in. The formal definition of an **idea champion** is a person who sees the need for and champions productive change within the organization. For example, Bonnie McKeever of Federal Express championed the idea of a coalition of companies to combat mounting medical fees. The Memphis Business Group on Health was created, saving its members an estimated tens of millions of dollars through competitive bidding and discounts.[17] Wendy Black of Best Western International championed the idea of coordinating the corporate mailings to the company's 2,800 hoteliers into a single packet every two weeks. Some hotels were receiving three special mailings a day from different departments. Her idea saved $600,000 a year for five years in postage alone.[18]

Remember: Change does not occur by itself. Personal energy and effort are required to successfully promote a new idea. Often a new idea

Creativity is one of two strategic goals implemented by Japan's industry leader in interior design, Takashimaya Company, Ltd. The Takashimaya Relaxation System is designed for improvement of office environments by including a body-sonic chair, LCD screens, and brain-wave controllers, which can be used by office personnel in 15- to 30-minute sessions to reduce stress and open creative channels through increased brain production of alpha waves.

idea champion

A person who sees the need for and champions productive change within the organization.

is rejected by management. Champions are passionately committed to a new product or idea despite rejection by others.

Championing an idea successfully requires roles in organizations, as illustrated in Exhibit 9.3. Sometimes a single person may play two or more of these roles, but successful innovation in most companies involves an interplay of different people, each adopting one role. The *inventor* develops a new idea and understands its technical value but has neither the ability nor the interest to promote it for acceptance within the organization. The *champion* believes in the idea, confronts the organizational realities of costs and benefits, and gains the political and financial support needed to bring it to reality. The *sponsor* is a high-level manager who approves the idea, protects the idea, and removes major organizational barriers to acceptance. The *critic* counterbalances the zeal of the champion by challenging the concept and providing a reality test against hard-nosed criteria. The critic prevents people in the other roles from adopting a bad idea.[19]

Al Marzocchi was both an inventor and a champion at Owens-Corning Fiberglass. He invented ways to strengthen fiberglass, developed the fiberglass-belted tire in conjunction with Armstrong Tire, and pioneered new ways of using asphalt. One reason Marzocchi thrived was that Owens-Corning's president, Harold Boeschenstein, sponsored his activities and held critics at bay. Once Marzocchi violated company rules by going directly to a potential customer, but the president protected him and his idea.[20]

Managers can directly influence whether champions will flourish. When Texas Instruments studied 50 of its new-product introductions, a surprising fact emerged: Without exception, every new product that had failed had lacked a zealous champion. In contrast, most of the new products that succeeded had a champion. Texas Instruments' managers made

EXHIBIT 9.3

Four Roles in Organizational Change

Inventor	Champion	Sponsor	Critic
Develops and understands technical aspects of idea	Believes in idea	High-level manager who removes organizational barriers	Provides reality test
Does not know how to win support for the idea or make a business of it	Visualizes benefits	Approves and protects idea within organization	Looks for shortcomings
	Confronts organizational realities of cost, benefits		Defines hard-nosed criteria that idea must pass
	Obtains financial and political support		
	Overcomes obstacles		

SOURCE: Based on Harold L. Angle and Andrew H. Van De Ven, "Suggestions for Managing the Innovation Journey," in *Research in the Management of Innovation: The Minnesota Studies*, ed. A. H. Van De Ven, H. L. Angle, and M. S. Poole (Cambridge, Mass.: Ballinger/Harper & Row, 1989), and Jay R. Galbraith, "Designing the Innovating Organization," *Organizational Dynamics* (Winter 1982), 5–25.

an immediate decision: No new product would be approved unless someone championed it. At small companies, like Ensoniq Corporation, the roles of inventor, champion, and sponsor are often all rolled into one.

 ## ENSONIQ CORPORATION

The three engineers who had helped develop the Commodore 64 home computer struck out on their own to launch a competing company called Ensoniq Corporation. They were in luck, sort of. The home computer market was at the top of its curve, and very shortly sank like a stone. But fortunately, Robert J. Yannes was a mediocre musician, and Albert J. Charpentier was losing some of his hearing. And, together with partner David B. Crockett, they combined these adversities with a little original thinking, and steered Ensoniq in a different, even more profitable direction.

Yannes, an amateur keyboard player, suspected that there were plenty of other musicians out there whose tones were as unmelodious as his own, and consequently he had designed the sound chip for the Commodore 64. In his search for something that would allow a person of very limited talent to make music, he came up with the Mirage "sampling" keyboard. The sampler, which was actually a computer designed to record and manipulate sounds, could modify a single voice recording into a group harmony, or a single instrument into a symphony. It was also more than $6,000 cheaper than those of competitors. "Overnight, in the musician's world, the keyboard world, we were a known commodity," says company president Crockett. By 1986 the Malvern, Pennsylvania, company earned profits of $2 million on sales of $22.6 million.

Because they custom-designed their microchips, the three engineers regarded Ensoniq as a technologic innovator rather than a musical company. Charpentier's discovery that he had a hearing loss in the high-frequency range gave him another application idea. Building on what they already had, the company came up with Sound Selector. A conventional hearing aid would amplify sound across the spectrum, whether it was audible to the listener or not. Using 13 frequency bands, or more than four times the number then available, the programmable Sound Selector could be precisely adjusted to increase sounds according to the needs of an individual. These idea champions used personal adversity to create new products, and the three partners expect sales of $100 million by 1996.[21] ■

NEW-VENTURE TEAMS

A recent idea for facilitating corporate innovation is known as a new-venture team. A **new-venture team** is a unit separate from the rest of the organization and is responsible for developing and initiating a major innovation.[22] New-venture teams give free reign to members' creativity because their separate facilities and location free them from organizational rules and procedures. These teams typically are small, loosely

new-venture team

A unit separate from the mainstream of the organization that is responsible for developing and initiating innovations.

structured, and organic, reflecting the characteristics of creative organizations described in Exhibit 9.2. Peter Drucker advises organizations that wish to innovate to use a separate team or department:

> For the existing business to be capable of innovation, it has to create a structure that allows people to be entrepreneurial. . . . This means, first, that the entrepreneurial, the new, has to be organized separately from the old and the existing. Whenever we have tried to make an existing unit the carrier of the entrepreneurial project, we have failed.[23]

The new-venture team is quite different from the horizontal relationships or the matrix structure described in Chapter 8. In those structures, employees remain members of their everyday departments and simply work on a project part-time while reporting to their regular boss. Under the new-venture team concept, employees no longer report through the normal structure.[24] The team exists as a separate departmental entity, as illustrated in Exhibit 9.4. New-venture teams are kept small and separate to ensure that no bureaucracy will intrude.

For a giant corporation such as IBM, new-venture teams free people from the constraints of the large organization. IBM's biggest success—the personal computer—was built by a new-venture group. The PC new-venture team was so appealing that 5,000 employees applied for the initial 50 positions.[25] The most recent successful new-venture team at IBM is a small group that built the Power Visualization System, a graphics supercomputer introduced after a mere two years in development. The supercomputer lets scientists and engineers literally "see" the billions of pieces of data their experiments generate.[26]

Other companies that have created new-venture units are Levi Strauss, Dow, and Motorola. 3M uses action teams to create new products. The action team concept allows individuals with product ideas to recruit team members from throughout the company. These people may end up running the newly created division if the idea is successful.[27]

One variation of venture teams used by some companies is called *skunkworks*.[28] **Skunkworks** are small, informal, and sometimes unauthorized groups that create innovations. Companies such as Kollmorgen, Philip Morris, and Macy encourage employees to form informal groups, often working nights and weekends, to develop a new idea. If the new

skunkworks

Small, informal, and sometimes unauthorized groups that create innovations.

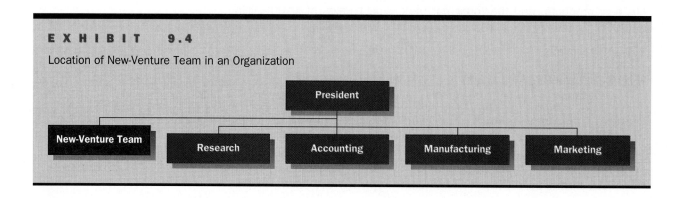

EXHIBIT   9.4

Location of New-Venture Team in an Organization

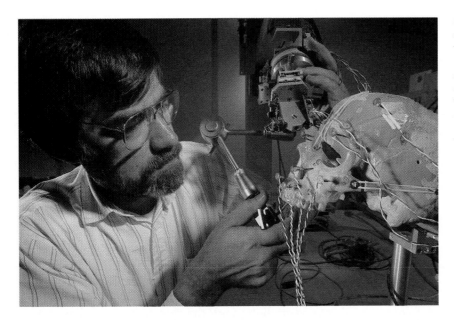

Robosurgeon is an innovative and highly successful surgical device developed through a new venture fund that has proven successful in hip replacement surgery. Acting as a partner and venture capitalist for the project, IBM worked with robotics specialists to develop the system and set up a separate company, Integrated Surgical Systems, to market the technology.

venture is successful, group members are rewarded and encouraged to run the new business.

Another variation of new-venture teams is the **new-venture fund,** which provides resources from which individuals and groups can draw to develop new ideas, products, or businesses. For example, Teleflex, a producer of many technical and consumer products, allocates one-half of 1 percent of sales to a new-venture fund. More than $1 million dollars was allocated to employees in one year to explore new ideas.[29]

new-venture fund

A fund providing resources from which individuals and groups draw to develop new ideas, products, or businesses.

● IMPLEMENTING CHANGE

Creative culture, idea champions, and new-venture teams are ways to facilitate the initiation of new ideas. The other step to be managed in the change process is implementation. A new, creative idea will not benefit the organization until it is in place and being fully utilized. One frustration for managers is that employees often seem to resist change for no apparent reason. To effectively manage the implementation process, managers should be aware of the reasons for employee resistance and be prepared to use techniques for obtaining employee cooperation.

RESISTANCE TO CHANGE

Idea champions often discover that other employees are unenthusiastic about their new ideas. Members of a new-venture group may be surprised when managers in the regular organization do not support or approve their innovations. Managers and employees not involved in an innovation often seem to prefer the status quo. Employees appear to resist change for several reasons, and understanding them helps managers implement change more effectively.

SELF-INTEREST.   Employees typically resist a change they believe will take away something of value. A proposed change in job design, structure, or technology may lead to a perceived loss of power, prestige, pay, or company benefits. The fear of personal loss is perhaps the biggest obstacle to organizational change.[30] When Mesa Oil Corporation tried to buy Phillips Petroleum, Phillips employees started a campaign to prevent the takeover. Employees believed that Mesa would not treat them well and that they would lose financial benefits. Their resistance to change was so effective that the merger failed to take place.

LACK OF UNDERSTANDING AND TRUST.   Employees often do not understand the intended purpose of a change or distrust the intentions behind it. If previous working relationships with an idea champion have been negative, resistance may occur. One manager had a habit of initiating a change in the financial reporting system about every 12 months and then losing interest and not following through. After the third time, employees no longer went along with the change because they did not trust the manager's intention to follow through to their benefit.

UNCERTAINTY.   *Uncertainty* is the lack of information about future events. It represents a fear of the unknown. Uncertainty is especially threatening for employees who have a low tolerance for change and fear the novel and unusual. They do not know how a change will affect them and worry about whether they will be able to meet the demands of a new procedure or technology.[31] Union leaders at General Motors' Steering Gear Division in Saginaw, Michigan, resisted the introduction of employee participation programs. They were uncertain about how the program would affect their status and thus initially opposed it.

DIFFERENT ASSESSMENTS AND GOALS.   Another reason for resistance to change is that people who will be affected by innovation may assess the situation differently than an idea champion or new-venture group. Often critics voice legitimate disagreements over the proposed benefits of a change. Managers in each department pursue different goals, and an innovation may detract from performance and goal achievement for some departments. For example, if marketing gets the new product it wants for its customers, the cost of manufacturing may increase and the manufacturing superintendent thus will resist. Resistance may call attention to problems with the innovation. At a consumer products company in Racine, Wisconsin, middle managers resisted the introduction of a new employee program that turned out to be a bad idea. The managers truly believed that the program would do more harm than good. One manager bluntly told his boss, "I've been here longer than you, and I'll be here after you've gone, so don't tell me what really counts at this company."[32]

These reasons for resistance are legitimate in the eyes of employees affected by the change. The best procedure for managers is not to ignore resistance but to diagnose the reasons and design strategies to gain acceptance by users.[33] Strategies for overcoming resistance to change typically involve two approaches: the analysis of resistance through the force field technique and the use of selective implementation tactics to overcome resistance.

FORCE FIELD ANALYSIS

Force field analysis grew from the work of Kurt Lewin, who proposed that change was a result of the competition between *driving* and *restraining forces.*[34] When a change is introduced, some forces drive it and other forces resist it. To implement a change, management should analyze the change forces. By selectively removing forces that restrain change, the driving forces will be strong enough to enable implementation, as illustrated by the move from A to B in Exhibit 9.5. As restraining forces are reduced or removed, behavior will shift to incorporate the desired changes.

Just-in-time (JIT) inventory control systems schedule materials to arrive at a company just as they are needed on the production line. In an Ohio manufacturing company, management's analysis showed that the driving forces associated with the implementation of JIT were (1) the large cost savings from reduced inventories, (2) savings from needing fewer workers to handle the inventory, and (3) a quicker, more competitive market response for the company. Restraining forces discovered by managers were (1) a freight system that was too slow to deliver inventory on time, (2) a facility layout that emphasized inventory maintenance over new deliveries, (3) worker skills inappropriate for handling rapid inventory deployment, and (4) union resistance to loss of jobs. The driving forces were not sufficient to overcome the restraining forces.

To shift the behavior to JIT, managers attacked the restraining forces. An analysis of the freight system showed that delivery by truck provided

force field analysis

The process of determining which forces drive and which resist a proposed change.

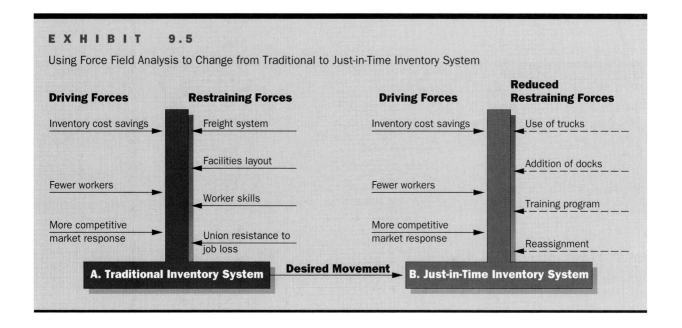

EXHIBIT　9.5

Using Force Field Analysis to Change from Traditional to Just-in-Time Inventory System

the flexibility and quickness needed to schedule inventory arrival at a specific time each day. The problem with facility layout was met by adding four new loading docks. Inappropriate worker skills were attacked with a training program to instruct workers in JIT methods and in assembling products with uninspected parts. Union resistance was overcome by agreeing to reassign workers no longer needed for maintaining inventory to jobs in another plant. With the restraining forces removed, the driving forces were sufficient to allow the JIT system to be implemented.

RESISTANCE REDUCTION TACTICS

The other approach to managing implementation is to adopt specific tactics to overcome employee resistance. For example, resistance to change may be overcome by educating employees or inviting them to participate in implementing the change. Methods for dealing with resistance to change have been studied by researchers. The following five tactics, summarized in Exhibit 9.6, have proven successful.[35]

COMMUNICATION AND EDUCATION.   Communication and education are used when solid information about the change is needed by users and others who may resist implementation. Education is especially important when the change involves new technical knowledge or users are unfamiliar with the idea. Florida Power & Light Company instituted a change in company procedures that initially confused managers. Realizing it had implemented the change too quickly, the company tailored special training sessions to educate managers. The training program resolved the difficulty, and implementation was a success.[36]

PARTICIPATION.   *Participation* involves users and potential resisters in designing the change. This approach is time-consuming, but it pays off because users understand and become committed to the change. When General Motors tried to implement a new management appraisal system

E X H I B I T   9 . 6

Tactics for Overcoming Resistance to Change

SOURCE: Based on J. P. Kotter and L. A. Schlesinger, "Choosing Strategies for Change," *Harvard Business Review* 57 (March–April 1979), 106–114.

Approach	When to Use
Communication, education	■ Change is technical. ■ Users need accurate information and analysis to understand change.
Participation	■ Users need to feel involved. ■ Design requires information from others. ■ Users have power to resist.
Negotiation	■ Group has power over implementation. ■ Group will lose out in the change.
Coercion	■ A crisis exists. ■ Initiators clearly have power. ■ Other implementation techniques have failed.
Top management support	■ Change involves multiple departments or reallocation of resources. ■ Users doubt legitimacy of change.

for supervisors in its Adrian, Michigan, plant, it met with immediate resistance. Rebuffed by the lack of cooperation, top managers proceeded more slowly, involving supervisors in the design of the new appraisal system. Through participation in system design, managers understood what the new approach was all about and dropped their resistance to it. Springfield ReManufacturing Corporation used participation combined with communication to implement much-needed changes at the company.

SPRINGFIELD REMANUFACTURING CORPORATION

Back in the 1970s, a single employee/management meeting at the company now known as Springfield ReManufacturing Corporation provided ample evidence that everything was not as it should be. The workers at what was then International Harvester (IH) Company's ReNew Center division walked in wearing raincoats and galoshes in anticipation of management's latest "snow job." Deciding it was not worth the trouble, IH gave Jack Stack the task of shutting down ReNew.

During a trip through the repair and services plant, Stack sensed the acrimony that inspired employees to wear inclement gear when dealing with their managers. However, he also thought that if the 170-member work force was properly challenged and motivated, the company could succeed. He convinced IH to let him have one last chance with ReNew.

Stack implemented immediate changes in communication and employee participation by asking workers what they thought was needed to improve operations. The company books were opened on a limited basis, and bonuses given for meeting financial projections. The inventory accuracy increased from 48 to 99 percent in a single year. Still, mistrust ran deep. When company financial data were fully disclosed, some employees still simply tossed them into the trash. But eventually, the company culture changed.

Stack and 12 other managers bought the company in 1983 and renamed it Springfield ReManufacturing Corporation. Employee stock ownership amounts to 31 percent, and attitudes have completely changed. "When I came here, I didn't realize that as a worker on the floor you could have a direct impact on the profit," says Candice Smalley. "When we started seeing the financials and hearing about usage and overhead, it made us start trying to improve our quality."

Today, the Springfield, Missouri, engine rebuilder runs 13 plants and has 750 employees. When production problems occur, workers brainstorm to find a solution. Management is seeking to motivate the work force further by directly soliciting new product ideas from employees. Stack, who is company president, is convinced that opening up the books and giving workers a stake in the company saved the day. "The more [employees] learned, the more they could do," he says. "We matched up higher levels of thinking with higher levels of performance."[37] ■

NEGOTIATION. Negotiation is a more formal means of achieving cooperation. *Negotiation* uses formal bargaining to win acceptance and approval of a desired change. For example, if the marketing department fears losing power if a new management structure is implemented, top managers may negotiate with marketing to reach a resolution. General Motors, General Electric, and other companies that have strong unions frequently must formally negotiate change with the unions. The change may become part of the union contract reflecting the agreement of both parties.

COERCION.   *Coercion* means that managers use formal power to force employees to change. Resisters are told to accept the change or lose rewards or even their jobs. Coercion is necessary in crisis situations when a rapid response is urgent. When middle managers at TRW, Inc.'s Valve Division in Cleveland refused to go along with a new employee involvement program, top management reassigned several first-line supervisors and managers. The new jobs did not involve supervisory responsibility. Further, other TRW managers were told that future pay increases depended on their adoption of the new procedures. The coercive techniques were used as a last resort because managers refused to go along with the change any other way.[38]

TOP MANAGEMENT SUPPORT.   The visible support of top management also helps overcome resistance to change. Top management support symbolizes to all employees that the change is important for the organization. Top management support is especially important when a change involves multiple departments or when resources are being reallocated among departments. Without top management support, these changes can get bogged down in squabbling among departments. Moreover, when top managers fail to support a project, they can inadvertently undercut it by issuing contradictory orders. This happened at Flying Tiger Lines before it was acquired by Federal Express. The airborne freight hauler came up with a plan to eliminate excessive paperwork by changing the layout of offices so that two agents rather than four could handle each shipment. No sooner had part of the change been implemented than top management ordered another system; thus, the office layout was changed again. The new layout was not as efficient, but it was the one that top management supported. Had middle managers informed top managers and obtained their support earlier, the initial change would not have been defeated by a new priority.[39]

● TYPES OF PLANNED CHANGE

Now that we have explored how the initiation and implementation of change can be carried out, let us look at the different types of change that occur in organizations. We will address two issues: what parts of the organization can be changed and how managers can apply the initiation and implementation ideas to each type of change.

The four types of organizational change are technology, products, structure, and culture/people, as illustrated in Exhibit 9.7. Organizations may innovate in one or more areas, depending on internal and external

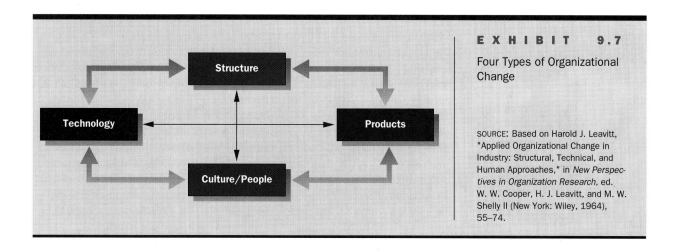

EXHIBIT   9.7

Four Types of Organizational Change

SOURCE: Based on Harold J. Leavitt, "Applied Organizational Change in Industry: Structural, Technical, and Human Approaches," in *New Perspectives in Organization Research,* ed. W. W. Cooper, H. J. Leavitt, and M. W. Shelly II (New York: Wiley, 1964), 55–74.

forces for change. In the rapidly changing toy industry, a manufacturer has to introduce new products frequently. In a mature, competitive industry, production technology changes are adopted to improve efficiency. The arrows connecting the four types of change in Exhibit 9.7 show that a change in one part may affect other parts of the organization: A new product may require changes in technology, and a new technology may require new people skills or a new structure. For example, when Shenandoah Life Insurance Company computerized processing and claims operations, the structure had to be decentralized, employees required intensive training, and a more participative culture was needed.

TECHNOLOGY CHANGES

A **technology change** is related to the organization's production process—how the organization does its work. Technology changes are designed to make the production of a product or service more efficient. For example, the adoption of robotics to improve production efficiency at General Motors and Chrysler is an example of a technology change, as is the adoption of laser-scanning checkout systems at supermarkets. At IBM's manufacturing plant in Charlotte, North Carolina, an automated miniload storage and retrieval system was installed to handle production parts. This change provided an efficient method for handling small-parts inventory and changed the technology of the IBM plant.

How can managers encourage technology change? The general rule is that technology change is bottom up.[40] The *bottom-up approach* means that ideas are initiated at lower organization levels and channeled upward for approval. Lower-level technical experts act as idea champions—they invent and champion technological changes. Employees at lower levels understand the technology and have the expertise needed to propose changes. For example, at Kraft General Foods, employees have proposed several hundred cost-saving projects. One that can save $3.5 million a year is simply to improve the accuracy of machines that weigh product portions.[41]

technology change

A change that pertains to the organization's production process.

Managers can facilitate the bottom-up approach by designing creative departments as described earlier in this chapter. A loose, flexible, decentralized structure provides employees with the freedom and opportunity to initiate continuous improvements. A rigid, centralized, standardized structure stifles technology innovation. Anything managers can do to involve the grass roots of the organization—the people who are experts in their parts of the production process—will increase technology change.

A *top-down approach* to technology change usually does not work.[42] Top managers are not close to the production process and lack expertise in technological developments. Mandating technology change from the top produces fewer rather than more technology innovations. The spark for a creative new idea comes from people close to the technology. The rationale behind Motorola's "participative management program," Data General's "pride teams," and Honeywell's "positive action teams" is to encourage new technology ideas from people at lower levels of the organization.

NEW-PRODUCT CHANGES

product change

A change in the organization's product or service output.

A **product change** is a change in the organization's product or service output. New-product innovations have major implications for an organization, because they often are an outcome of a new strategy and may define a new market.[43] Examples of new products are Frito-Lay's introduction of O'Grady's potato chips, Hewlett-Packard's introduction of a professional computer, and GE's development at its Medical Division of a device for monitoring patients' heart cycles. The Leading Edge box shows how Spartan Motors uses innovation to create new products.

The introduction of a new product is difficult, because it not only involves a new technology but also must meet customers' needs. In most industries, only about one in eight new-product ideas is successful.[44] Companies that successfully develop new products usually have the following characteristics:

1 People in marketing have a good understanding of customer needs.

2 Technical specialists are aware of recent technological developments and make effective use of new technology.

3 Members from key departments—research, manufacturing, marketing—cooperate in the development of the new product.[45]

These findings mean that the ideas for new products typically originate at the lower levels of the organization just as they do for technology changes. The difference is that new-product ideas flow horizontally among departments. Product innovation requires expertise from several departments simultaneously. A new-product failure is often the result of failed cooperation.[46] Puff Pac Inc. is an example of a company that narrowly avoided the pitfalls that can result from failed cooperation and went on to successfully market its new product.

LEADING edge   **SPARTAN MOTORS**

The lean, economical corporate culture George W. Sztykiel implemented at Spartan Motors (which you read about in Chapter 4) is also reflected in the firm's approach to innovation. Through cooperative efforts with suppliers and by constructing chassis from existing parts, Spartan is consistently able to bring its product to the market faster and cheaper than competitors. On average, the company purchases 97 percent of its parts, which leaves the company free to concentrate on design and final assembly. Although the explanation may sound disingenuous, Sztykiel believes in it. "Building trucks is not science," he says, "it is art. We produce 10 times faster and cheaper than big companies, where they have lost the feeling, so all they can do is apply science."

Larry Karkau and Tim Williams are not likely to be mistaken for scientists. Karkau is a 30-year veteran of chassis design; Williams is not easily discouraged once he has set out to do something. Together, they decided to solve an industry enigma that everyone had pretty much given up on. The chassis for a big-ticket motor home cost around $100,000, which limited its market to less than 1,000 a year. It was generally accepted that the market would expand twentyfold if someone could figure out how to reduce the chassis cost by 50 percent.

George Sztykiel has about as much use for corporate plans as he does for budgets, expecially when it comes to designing new products. He let Karkau and Williams chart their own course, but he did not open up his billfold and dump it out on the plant floor. They designed a rear-mounted diesel engine that got better fuel mileage, left more interior room, and ran quieter. By letting suppliers in on what they were doing, the pair managed to get them to manufacture the necessary parts. "The tooling costs were theirs, not ours," says Karkau. John Rouser, sales manager at Cummins Michigan, the diesel engine supplier for the EC-2000 chassis summed up the project, "We take our resources and its resources, and together we go farther than either of us could alone." Sales of the EC-2000 were expected to be $60 million in just its second year of production.

A similar story evolved when Detroit Diesel Corporation began producing its new Series 60 truck engine. Touted for its economic fuel consumption, the engine was regarded as too sluggish for emergency vehicles. Sztykiel got Detroit Diesel to supply him with one, and the Spartan team immediately went to work designing a chassis with two key features for fire engines: a cab that was larger, and could also be protected from heat. The company has put the engine in 40 percent of the fire trucks sold between 1990 and 1992.

The Metrostar was another ad hoc cooperative project Spartan was able to complete in record time. General Motors subsidiary Allison Transmission debuted its electronic World Transmission to be used mostly in buses. Again, Sztykiel persuaded them to send some of the first ones so that his people could build a fire truck chassis around it. Engineers worked side-by-side with assemblers almost round the clock, creating the Metrostar in two and a half months. Typically, a custom chassis costs around $70,000; the price of the Metrostar was $54,000.

Rouser has called the way they do things at Spartan "organized chaos." Sztykiel thinks he has a better way of putting it. "I submit that to achieve unorthodox results you must apply unorthodox methods." ∎

SOURCE: Michael Selz, "Small Manufacturers Display the Nimbleness the Times Require," *The Wall Street Journal,* December 29, 1993, A1–A2; Edward O. Welles, "The Shape of Things to Come," *INC.,* February, 1992, 66–74; Richard S. Teitelbaum, "Spartan Motors," *Fortune,* December 28, 1992, 53; and "In-house Payroll Gives HR More Control," *Personnel Journal,* November 1992, 80L.

PUFF PAC, INC.

Dan Pharo discovered that one way to create an innovative product which is also a hit in the market is to defy logic. Almost everyone has witnessed the frenzy children exhibit ripping the wrapping off Christmas and birthday presents. Pharo created, by accident, an enclosure for gifts so mystifying that many kids are in no hurry to get at the goodies inside.

Pharo visited a friend's sick son in 1983. His cheer-up presents consisted of a small toy and a balloon, the latter of which he promptly exploded during inflation. Luckily, he was at his art studio and had a heat sealing device to repair the blowout. On a whim, he stuck the toy inside before fixing the balloon. The surprise came after arriving at the hospital. "The real thrill for him was the packaging," Pharo says. "Everybody was trying to guess what was in there."

Five years later, Pharo was ready to market the inflatable gift-wrap product. Although it was initially a hit, the Puff Pac really took off after Pharo applied innovation to his original accident. He found a way to suspend a bag inside of a bag through the use of an air exchanger. To fascinated observers, it looked like magic. But besides gift-wrapping, lots of other applications were suddenly a possibility, particularly for product makers constantly at odds with environmentalists over bubble wrap, fabricated foams, and other packaging materials. Financier Don Farrell liked Puff Pac enough to invest $700,000, and he shepherded the company through an initial public offering on the Vancouver Stock Exchange that raised $3 million. Pharo had sense enough to realize his forte was ideas and product development. Keeping that in mind, he brought the best business and marketing heads he could find on board.

Puff Pac had more than its share of start-up troubles. The company entered into a number of unexpected delays with Korean-based Mantae America, Inc. Because of delays and broken promises, Puff Pac lost nearly $2 million in 1990. The failed alliance also forced the company to begin manufacturing its own product, a costly proposition. Failure to meet delivery schedules hurt Puff Pac's reputation badly. But just when the company seemed ready to plunge into the abyss, things began turning around. A Rhode Island firm agreed to sell Puff Pac a state-of-the-art bag-making machine and accept a 15 percent down payment payable in company stock. Foreign licensing deals with two European firms seemed imminent.

Puff Pac will still have to concentrate on inventory controls and just-in-time materials acquisition. However, despite all the adversities associated with taking an innovative idea all the way to a full-fledged business operation, Dan Pharo thinks life is wonderful.[47] ■

horizontal linkage model
An approach to product change that emphasizes shared development of innovations among several departments.

One approach to successful new-product innovation is called the **horizontal linkage model,** which is illustrated in Exhibit 9.8[48] The model shows that research, manufacturing, and marketing must simultaneously develop new products. People from these departments meet frequently in teams and task forces to share ideas and solve problems. Research people inform marketing of new technical developments to learn

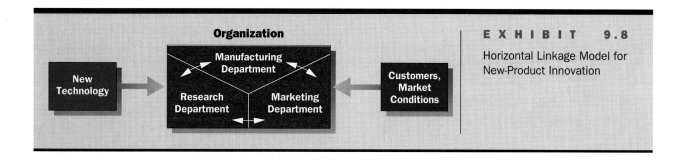

E X H I B I T   9.8

Horizontal Linkage Model for New-Product Innovation

whether they will be useful to customers. Marketing people pass customer complaints to research to use in the design of new products. Manufacturing informs other departments whether a product idea can be manufactured within cost limits. When the horizontal linkage model is used, the decision to develop a new product is a joint one.

Horizontal linkages are being adopted in the computer industry to overcome new-product problems. For example, at Convergent Technologies, Workslate, a portable computer, received accolades when it was introduced. One year later, Workslate was dead. Production problems with the new product had not been worked out. Marketing people had not fully analyzed customer needs. The idea had been pushed through without sufficient consultation among research, manufacturing, and marketing. At Lotus Development Corporation, the delays in new software ran on for months and years, earning the name "vaporware" because they never appeared. New senior vice-president Frank King enforced a regime of daily and weekly meetings involving programmers and code writers, and monthly gatherings of all employees to update one another. These enforced linkages gradually reduced product development time.[49]

Innovation is becoming a major strategic weapon in the global marketplace. One example of innovation is the use of **time-based competition,** which means delivering products and services faster than competitors, giving companies a significant strategic advantage. For example, Hewlett-Packard reduced the time to develop a new printer from 4.5 years to 22 months. Lenscrafters jumped from 3 to 300 stores based on its ability to provide quality eyeglasses in one hour. Dillard's department stores went to an automatic reorder system that replenishes stocks in 12 days rather than 30, providing retail goods to customers more quickly.[50] Sprinting to market with a new product requires a *parallel approach,* or *simultaneous linkage* among departments. This is similar to a rugby match wherein players run together, passing the ball back and forth as they move downfield together. The teamwork required for the horizontal linkage model is a major component of using rapid innovation to beat the competition with speed.[51]

time-based competition

A strategy of competition based on the ability to deliver products and services faster than competitors.

STRUCTURAL CHANGES

Structural changes involve the hierarchy of authority, goals, structural characteristics, administrative procedures, and management systems.[52]

structural change

Any change in the way in which the organization is designed and managed.

Almost any change in how the organization is managed falls under the category of structural change. At General Telephone & Electronics Corporation, structural changes included a structural reorganization, new pay incentives, a revised performance appraisal system, and affirmative action programs. IBM's change from a functional to a product structure was a structural change. The implementation of a no-smoking policy is usually considered a structural or an administrative change.

Successful structural change is accomplished through a top-down approach, which is distinct from technology change (bottom up) and new products (horizontal).[53] Structural change is top down because the expertise for administrative improvements originates at the middle and upper levels of the organization. The champions for structural change are middle and top managers. Lower-level technical specialists have little interest or expertise in administrative procedures. If organization structure causes negative consequences for lower-level employees, complaints and dissatisfaction alert managers to a problem. Employee dissatisfaction is an internal force for change. The need for change is perceived by higher managers, who then take the initiative to propose and implement it.

The top-down process does not mean that coercion is the best implementation tactic. Implementation tactics include education, participation, and negotiation with employees. Unless there is an emergency, managers should not force structural change on employees. They may hit a resistance wall, and the change will fail. This is exactly what happened at the company for which Mary Kay Ash worked before she started her own cosmetics business. The owner learned that even a top-down change in commission rate needs to incorporate education and participation to succeed:

> I worked for a company whose owner decided to revise the commission schedule paid to his sales managers. All brochures and company literature were changed accordingly. He then made plans for personally announcing the changes during a series of regional sales conferences. I accompanied him to the first conference. I'll never forget it.
>
> To an audience of 50 sales managers he announced that the 2 percent override they were presently earning on their units' sales production was to be reduced to 1 percent. "However," he said, "in lieu of that 1 percent, you will receive a very nice gift for each new person you recruit and train."
>
> At that point a sales manager stood up and let him have it with both barrels. She was absolutely furious. "How dare you do this to us? Why, even 2 percent wasn't enough. But cutting our overrides in half and offering us a crummy gift for appeasement insults our intelligence." With that she stormed out of the room. And every other sales manager for that state followed her— all 50 of them. In one fell swoop the owner had lost his entire sales organization in that region—the best in the country. I had never seen such an overwhelming rejection of a change of this kind in my entire life![54]

Top-down change means that initiation of the idea occurs at upper levels and is implemented downward. It does not mean that lower-level employees are not educated about the change or allowed to participate in it.

CULTURE/PEOPLE CHANGES

A **culture/people change** refers to a change in employees' values, norms, attitudes, beliefs, and behavior. Changes in culture and people pertain to how employees think; these are changes in mindset rather than technology, structure, or products. People change pertains to just a few employees, such as when a handful of middle managers is sent to a training course to improve their leadership skills. Culture change pertains to the organization as a whole, such as when Union Pacific Railroad changed its basic mindset by becoming less bureaucratic and focusing employees on customer service and quality through teamwork and employee participation.[55] Training is the most frequently used tool for changing the organization's mindset. A company may offer training programs to large blocks of employees on subjects such as teamwork, listening skills, quality circles, and participative management. At Advanced Network Design, Inc., the company's survival depended on the training that led to a change in the organizational culture.

culture/people change

A change in employees' values, norms, attitudes, beliefs, and behavior.

ADVANCED NETWORK DESIGN, INC.

There was a time when Dave Wiegand did not know an implementer from an initiator. He was pretty certain about something else, however. He had cajoled, threatened, and coerced the 35-member work force at his La Mirada, California, telecommunications company about as much as he could, and production had continued to decline. Barring some sort of last minute heroics, Wiegard would have to shut down Advanced Network Design Inc. In resigned desperation, he sought the help of a turnaround expert.

The first thing Wiegand got educated about was people, that is, the kind he needed, and the kind he did not need. The key to happier employees, higher productivity, and lower turnover was attracting workers with the right skills and attitudes. This objective could be accomplished through testing and specialized interviewing techniques. The next step was to train employees in the areas of the particular job's greatest responsibility. Called result areas, they constituted the majority of what needed to be accomplished. Once a competency level had been achieved, the employee was then permitted the autonomy to carry through on his or her tasks.

That might have been the biggest adjustment for Wiegand. Before this change, he had issued decisional edicts that were half-heartedly applied, at best. That approach was replaced by employee input, discussion, and consensus. Job satisfaction turned out to be the key to higher productivity. "If we don't have satisfied employees, we can't have satisfied customers," Weigand says. "And if you don't have either, you won't be profitable." A number of Wiegand's workers, the so-called implementers, were uncomfortable with the free rein and left. The others, the initiators that remained or were brought in, were the needed ingredient in turning around Advanced Network Design.[56] ■

Another major approach to changing people and culture is organizational development. This has evolved as a separate field that is devoted to large-scale organizational change.

● ORGANIZATIONAL DEVELOPMENT

organizational development (OD)

The application of behavioral science techniques to improve an organization's health and effectiveness through its ability to cope with environmental changes, improve internal relationships, and increase problem-solving capabilities.

Organizational development (OD) is the application of behavioral science knowledge to improve an organization's health and effectiveness through its ability to cope with environmental changes, improve internal relationships, and increase problem-solving capabilities.[57] Organizational development improves working relationships among employees.

The following are three types of current problems that OD can help managers address.[58]

1 *Mergers/Acquisitions.* The disappointing financial results of many mergers and acquisitions are caused by the failure of executives to determine whether the administrative style and corporate culture of the two companies "fit." Executives may concentrate on potential synergies in technology, products, marketing, and control systems but fail to recognize that two firms may have widely different values, beliefs, and practices. These differences create stress and anxiety for employees, and these negative emotions affect future performance. Cultural differences should be evaluated during the acquisition process, and OD experts can be used to smooth the integration of two firms.

2 *Organizational Decline/Revitalization.* Organizations undergoing a period of decline and revitalization experience a variety of problems, including a low level of trust, lack of innovation, high turnover, and high levels of conflict and stress. The period of transition requires opposite behaviors, including confronting stress, creating open communication, and fostering creative innovation to emerge with high levels of productivity. OD techniques can contribute greatly to cultural revitalization by managing conflicts, fostering commitment, and facilitating communication.

3 *Conflict Management.* Conflict can occur at any time and place within a healthy organization. For example, a product team for the introduction of a new software package was formed at a computer company. Made up of strong-willed individuals, the team made little progress because members would not agree on project goals. At a manufacturing firm, salespeople promised delivery dates to customers that were in conflict with shop supervisor priorities for assembling customer orders. In a publishing company, two managers disliked each other intensely. They argued at meetings, lobbied politically against each other, and hurt the achievement of both departments. Organizational development efforts can help solve these kinds of conflicts.

Organizational development can be used to solve the types of problems described above and many others. Specialized OD techniques have been developed for these applications.

OD ACTIVITIES

A number of OD activities have emerged in recent years. Some of the most popular and effective are as follows.

1 *Team-Building Activities.* **Team building** enhances the cohesiveness and success of organizational groups and teams. For example, a series of OD exercises can be used with members of cross-departmental teams to help them learn to act and function as a team. An OD expert can work with team members to increase their communication skills, facilitate their ability to confront one another, and accept common goals.

2 *Survey-Feedback Activities.* **Survey feedback** begins with a questionnaire distributed to employees on values, climate, participation, leadership, and group cohesion within their organization.[59] After the survey is completed, an OD consultant meets with groups of employees to provide feedback about their responses and the problems identified.[60] Employees are engaged in problem solving based on the data.

3 *Intergroup Activities.* These activities include retreats and workshops to improve the effectiveness of groups or departments that must work together. The focus is on helping employees develop the skills to resolve conflicts, increase coordination, and develop better ways of working together.

4 *Process-Consultation Activities.* Organizational development consultants help managers understand the human processes within their organization and how to manage them. Managers learn to think in terms of cultural values, leadership, communication, and intergroup cooperation.

5 *Symbolic Leadership Activities.* This approach helps managers learn to use the techniques for cultural change described in Chapter 4, including public statements, symbols, ceremonies, and slogans. For example, public statements that define a pathfinding vision and cultural values account for the success of such companies as Disney, Dana, and Wal-Mart. Managers can signal appropriate behavior through symbols and ceremonies, such as when Roy Ash had several of AM International's copying machines removed to signal the need for less paperwork. Harold Geneen, president of ITT, captured the new value for his corporation with the slogan: "Search for the Unshakeable Facts," which helped do away with smoke screens and political games.

OD STEPS

Consider the cultural change at Westinghouse Canada's manufacturing facility at Airdrie, Alberta. Cycle time for made-to-order motor-controlled devices was reduced from 17 weeks to 1 week. One major requirement for reducing the time was to change the mindset of both managers and workers to give workers more discretion. Instead of waiting for approval from superiors, production employees now talk directly with customers and suppliers to solve their problems.[61]

team building

A type of OD intervention that enhances the cohesiveness of departments by helping members to learn to function as a team.

survey feedback

A type of OD intervention in which questionnaires on organizational climate and other factors are distributed among employees and the results reported back to them by a change agent.

Videotaped role play, pictured here, allows employees in the Direct Response Group (DRG) of Capital Holding Corp. to simulate real-life customer situations in a *team-oriented environment*. The DRG is undergoing a culture change from mass marketers of insurance products to a customer-driven target marketer. A Lifetime Learning Center helps employees learn new behaviors and skills.

Organizational development experts acknowledge that corporate culture and human behavior are relatively stable and that companywide changes, such as those at Westinghouse Canada, require major effort. The theory underlying organizational development proposes three distinct steps for achieving behavioral and attitudinal change: (1) unfreezing, (2) changing, and (3) refreezing.[62]

In the first step, **unfreezing,** participants must be made aware of problems and be willing to change. This step is often associated with *diagnosis,* which uses an outside expert called a *change agent.* The **change agent** is an OD specialist who performs a systematic diagnosis of the organization and identifies work-related problems. He or she gathers and analyzes data through personal interviews, questionnaires, and observations of meetings. The diagnosis helps determine the extent of organizational problems and helps unfreeze managers by making them aware of problems in their behavior.

The second step, **changing,** occurs when individuals experiment with new behavior and learn new skills to be used in the workplace. This is sometimes known as *intervention,* during which the change agent implements a specific plan for training managers and employees. This plan may include team-building, intergroup, process-consultation, and symbolic leadership activities as described earlier.

The third step, **refreezing,** occurs when individuals acquire new attitudes or values and are rewarded for them by the organization. The impact of new behaviors is evaluated and reinforced. The change agent supplies new data that show positive changes in performance. Senior executives can reward positive behavioral changes by employees. Managers and employees also participate in refresher courses to maintain and reinforce the new behaviors.

unfreezing

A step in the diagnosis stage of organizational development in which participants are made aware of problems in order to increase their willingness to change their behavior.

change agent

An OD specialist who contracts with an organization to facilitate change.

changing

A step in the intervention stage of organizational development in which individuals experiment with new workplace behavior.

refreezing

A step in the reinforcement stage of organizational development in which individuals acquire a desired new skill or attitude and are rewarded for it by the organization.

SUMMARY AND MANAGEMENT SOLUTION

Change is inevitable in organizations. This chapter discussed the techniques available for managing the change process. Managers should think of change as having four elements—the forces for change, the perceived need for change, the initiation of change, and the implementation of change. Forces for change can originate either within or outside the firm, and managers are responsible for monitoring events that may require a planned organizational response. Techniques for initiating changes include designing the organization for creativity, encouraging change agents, and establishing new-venture teams or skunkworks. The final step is implementation. Force field analysis is one technique for diagnosing restraining forces, which often can be removed. Managers also should draw on the implementation tactics of communication, participation, negotiation, coercion, or top management support.

This chapter also discussed specific types of change. Technology changes are accomplished through a bottom-up approach that utilizes experts close to the technology. Successful new-product introduction requires horizontal linkage among marketing, research and development, manufacturing, and perhaps other departments. Structural changes tend to be initiated in a top-down fashion, because upper managers are the administrative experts and champion these ideas for approval and implementation. Culture/people change pertains to the skills, behaviors, and attitudes of employees. Organizational development is an important approach to changes in people's mindset and corporate culture. The OD process entails three steps—unfreezing (diagnosis of the problem), the actual change (intervention), and refreezing (reinforcement of new attitudes and behaviors). Popular OD techniques include team building, survey feedback, intergroup skills, and process consultation.

CEO Harry Featherstone knew that his chances of making the changes necessary to save Will-Burt were slim without commitment and cooperation from his employees. In the hopes that offering them a piece of the company might do it, he worked with the company's lawyer to create an employee stock-ownership plan. The next step was more difficult, but he and the attorney also managed to secure a $2.75 million loan from a local bank for a leveraged buyout.

The odds were against the strategy succeeding. Typically, employee ownership plans require a thorough presentation to make workers comfortable. However, there simply was no time. The pending lawsuits made workers fear that they were being set up, even though the plan was structured so that Featherstone himself was liable if adverse verdicts were returned. To worsen matters, the company debt was such that lay-offs were the only option. However, laying off 80 people did not improve an already dismal morale situation.

For Will-Burt to survive, Featherstone knew quality would have to be improved, and the huge rate of defective output reduced. This meant increased employee education and training. Even though workers initially resisted, and the company was near the fiscal breaking point, Featherstone committed $200,000 for instruction in such areas as reading blueprints and statistical process control. It worked. Time spent remaking parts was reduced by four-fifths in three years, saving nearly the entire budget allocated for education.

Today, Will-Burt's parts rejection rate for repeat customers is as low as two out of every million manufactured. The Department of Labor and the National Association of Manufacturers have studied the company's creative approach to turning things around. Will-Burt has become an example of a small business that used a trained and empowered work force to change the company and propel it toward success.[63]

DISCUSSION QUESTIONS

1. A manager of an international chemical company said that very few new products in her company were successful. What would you advise the manager to do to help increase the company's success rate?

2. What are internal and external forces for change? Which force do you think is the major cause of organizational change?

3. Carefully planned change often is assumed to be effective. Do you think unplanned change can sometimes be beneficial to an organization? Discuss.

4. Why do organizations experience resistance to change? What techniques can managers use to overcome resistance?

5. Explain force field analysis. Analyze the driving and restraining forces for a change with which you have been associated.

6. Define the roles associated with an idea champion. Why are idea champions so essential to the initiation of change?

7. To what extent would changes in technology affect products, and vice versa? Compare the process for changing technology and that for product change.

8. Given that structure change is often made top down, should coercive implementation techniques be used?

9. Do the underlying values of organizational development differ from assumptions associated with other types of change? Discuss.

10. Compare and contrast team-building and survey-feedback techniques for OD intervention.

MANAGEMENT IN PRACTICE: EXPERIENTIAL EXERCISE

● IS YOUR COMPANY CREATIVE?

An effective way to assess the creative climate of an organization for which you have worked is to fill out the questionnaire below. Answer each question based on your work experience in that firm. Discuss the results with members of your group and talk about whether changing the firm along the dimensions in the questions would make it more creative.

Instructions: Answer each of the following questions using the five-point scale. (*Note there is no rating of 4: 0, we never do this; 1, we rarely do this; 2, we sometimes do this; 3, we frequently do this; 5, we always do this.*)

_____ We are encouraged to seek help anywhere inside or outside the organization with new ideas for our work unit.

_____ Assistance is provided to develop ideas into proposals for management review.

_____ Our performance reviews encourage risky, creative efforts, ideas, and actions.

_____ We are encouraged to fill our minds with new information by attending professional meetings, trade fairs, visiting customers, and so on.

_____ Our meetings are designed to allow people to freewheel, brainstorm, and generate ideas.

_____ All members contribute ideas during meetings.

_____ During meetings, there is much spontaneity and humor.

_____ We discuss how company structure and our actions help or spoil creativity within our work unit.

_____ During meetings, the chair is rotated among members.

_____ Everyone in the work unit receives training in creativity techniques and maintaining a creative climate.

To measure how effectively your organization fosters creativity, use the following scale:

Highly effective:	15–20
Moderately effective:	10–14
Moderately ineffective:	5–9
Ineffective:	0–4

SOURCE: Adapted from Edward Glassman, *Creativity Handbook: Idea Triggers and Sparks That Work* (Chapel Hill, N.C.: LCS Press, 1990). Used by permission. (919/967-2015)

CASE FOR ANALYSIS

DESIGN CONTINUUM, INC.

Design Continuum, Inc., (DCI) is no stranger to innovative products. The Boston-based designer has come up with its share of medical and high-tech innovations. The company, which has a staff of about 80 people, did not do badly when it ventured into the realm of sports either. DCI designed the pump sneaker for Reebok International Ltd., and the success of that creation is what attracted the attention of Spalding Sports Worldwide when that company needed development assistance for a new custom baseball glove. It turned out to be a hit, but not without some errors, and more than a few people screaming foul.

DCI formed a project team of a couple of industrial designers and engineers, and the company president to work in tandem with Spalding's liaison Alan Walker, R&D manager of its Diamond Sports Products. Given the long and rich tradition associated with America's pastime, all of them knew that tampering with the design of the baseball glove was like chiseling around on the Statue of Liberty. Even the characteristic shortcomings of a new one, remedied by the breaking-in process of soaking and shaping, had come to be a hallowed undertaking passed from generation to generation.

The designers managed to iron out how their glove fit, folded, and felt. They crossed into uncharted territory when they decided that applying pump technology would not only make a better glove, it would also give the product a uniqueness in marketing. Positioning the air bladder and incorporating the inflation mechanism while maintaining the overall integrity of the glove presented myriad problems. The designers visited Florida with prototypes and gathered data from observing and videotaping year-round softball leaguers who used them. They got players to complete questionnaires about what they liked and did not like about the gloves. More modifications followed. When actual production began other problems had to be solved. But by the summer of 1991, the new glove was ready, in no less than eight different versions.

However, it was not protests from traditionalists that ultimately presented the glove design team its biggest difficulties. It was the somewhat more contemporary pitfall of alleged infringement of proprietary technology. DCI's old collaborator Reebok caught a gander a t the AirFlex globe at the National Sporting Goods of America trade show in Chicago and charged a rip-off of their sneaker technology. Injunctions ensued, with full-blown lawsuits not far behind. The AirFlex had to be pulled from the show until the last day.

Oddly, the Japanese company Mizuno Sports, Inc., introduced an inflation-system glove at the same trade gathering. But since many properties of its AirFit glove were unique, the conclusion was coincidence. Mizuno's offering won a 1991 *Popular Science* award for innovation. Despite the setbacks, DCI/Spalding decided to not only fight Reebok, but continue to market the AirFlex. An undisclosed settlement was reached, but it is generally believed DCI committed no breach in applying pump technology to products other than athletic shoes. Not surprisingly, Reebok later joined the fray and began producing a glove of its own in cooperation with Rawlings, the number-one glove manufacturer in the world.

The portent for the instantly crowded and competitive pump-glove market may be ominous, especially given that top-maker Rawlings grossed only $125 million in glove sales in 1991. Even though both AirFlex and AirFit are selling well, industry insiders point out that the market is small to begin with, and pump gloves will likely never capture more than 5 percent of it anyway. Getting a notable big-leaguer to use AirFlex might be the catalyst to bigger sales, but so far that hasn't happened. Tradition could once again play a part in a baseball saga. It may be that one of tomorrow's superstars, who today is coming up through the pee-wees wearing a pump glove, will have to be the one to bring it to the big leagues.

● QUESTIONS

1. Considering the characteristics required for a company to successfully develop a new product, how would you rate DCI's efforts with the AirFlex? Did the company have a good understanding of customer needs, make effective use of new technology and exhibit a spirit of cooperation among employees?

2. Spalding perceived a need to change the design of the baseball glove despite the product's rich history. Cri-

tique the path Spalding took in initiating and implementing the change.

3. Was it a good idea for Spalding and DCI to tamper with something that obviously wasn't broken? Why or why not?

SOURCE: Justin Martin, "What Fits Better Than a Glove?" *Across the Board,* September 1992, 41–46.

REFERENCES

1. Donna Brown Hogarty, "A Little Education Goes a Long Way," *Management Review,* June 1993, 24–28.

2. Richard L. Daft, "Bureaucratic vs. Nonbureaucratic Structure in the Process of Innovation and Change," in *Perspectives in Organizational Sociology: Theory and Research,* ed. Samuel B. Bacharach (Greenwich, Conn.: JAI Press, 1982), 129–166.

3. Andre L. Delbecq and Peter K. Mills, "Managerial Practices That Enhance Innovation," *Organizational Dynamics* 14 (Summer 1985), 24–34.

4. Ira Magaziner and Mark Tatinkin, *The Silent War: Inside the Global Business Battles Shaping America's Future* (New York: Random House, 1989).

5. Andrew H. Van de Ven, Harold Angle, and Marshall Scott Poole, *Research on the Management of Innovation* (Cambridge, Mass.: Ballinger, 1989).

6. Edward W. Desmond, "Byting Japan," *Time,* October 5, 1992, 68–69.

7. Attributed to Gregory Bateson in Andrew H. Van de Ven, "Central Problems in the Management of Innovation," *Management Science* 32 (1986), 595.

8. Charles Pearlman, "A Theoretical Model for Creativity," *Education* 103 (1983), 294–305; and Robert R. Godfrey, "Tapping Employees' Creativity," *Supervisory Management* (February 1986), 16–20.

9. Craig R. Hickman and Michael A. Silva, "How to Tap Your Creative Powers," *Working Woman,* September 1985, 26–30.

10. Gordon Vessels, "The Creative Process: An Open-Systems Conceptualization," *Journal of Creative Behavior* 16 (1982), 185–196; and Pearlman, "A Theoretical Model."

11. James Brian Quinn, "Managing Innovation: Controlled Chaos," *Harvard Business Review* 63 (May–June 1985), 73–84; Howard H. Stevenson and David E. Gumpert, "The Heart of Entrepreneurship," *Harvard Business Review* 63 (March–April 1985), 85–94; and Marsha Sinetar, "Entrepreneurs, Chaos, and Creativity—Can Creative People Really Survive Large Company Structure?" *Sloan Management Review* 6 (Winter 1985), 57–62.

12. Cynthia Browne, "Jest for Success," *Moonbeams,* August 1989, 3–5; and Rosabeth Moss Kanter, *The Change Masters* (New York: Simon and Schuster, 1983).

13. Kanter, *The Change Masters.*

14. "Hands On: A Manager's Notebook," *INC.,* January 1989, 106.

15. Bo Burlingham and Curtis Hartman, "Cowboy Capitalist," *INC.*, January 1989, 60.

16. Magaly Olivero, "Some Wacko Ideas That Worked," *Working Woman*, September 1990, 147–148.

17. Bonnie McKeever, "How I Did It: Teaming Up to Cut Medical Costs," *Working Woman*, July 1992, 23–24.

18. Katy Koontz, "How to Stand Out from the Crowd," *Working Woman*, January 1988, 74–76.

19. Harold L. Angle and Andrew H. Van de Ven, "Suggestions for Managing the Innovation Journey," in *Research in the Management of Innovation: The Minnesota Studies*, ed. A. H. Van de Ven, H. L. Angle, and Mabel S. Poole (Cambridge, Mass.: Ballinger/Harper & Row, 1989).

20. Gifford Pinchot III, *Intrapreneuring* (New York: Harper & Row, 1985).

21. Sharon Nelton, "How a Pennsylvania Company Makes the Sweet Sounds of Innovation," *Nation's Business*, December 1991, 16.

22. Christopher K. Bart, "New Venture Units: Use Them Wisely to Manage Innovation," *Sloan Management Review* (Summer 1988), 35–43.

23. Peter F. Drucker, *Innovation and Entrepreneurship* (New York: Harper & Row, 1985).

24. Michael Tushman and David Nadler, "Organizing for Innovation," *California Management Review* 28 (Spring 1986), 74–92.

25. Carl E. Larson and Frank M. J. LaFasto, *TeamWork* (Newbury Park, Calif.: Sage, 1989); and "How the PC Changed the Way IBM Thinks," *Business Week*, October 3, 1983, 86–90.

26. John Markoff, "Abe Peled's Secret Start-Up at IBM," *The New York Times*, December 8, 1991, 3–1, 6.

27. Russell Mitchell, "Masters of Innovation: How 3M Keeps Its New Products Coming," *Business Week*, April 10, 1989, 58–63.

28. Tom Peters and Nancy Austin, *A Passion for Excellence: The Leadership Difference* (New York: Random House, 1985).

29. "Teleflex Incorporated Annual Report," 1988, Limerick, Penn.

30. John P. Kotter and Leonard A. Schlesinger, "Choosing Strategies for Change," *Harvard Business Review* 57 (March–April 1979), 106–114.

31. G. Zaltman and R. Duncan, *Strategies for Planned Change* (New York: Wiley Interscience, 1977).

32. Leonard M. Apcar, "Middle Managers and Supervisors Resist Moves to More Participatory Management," *The Wall Street Journal*, September 16, 1985, 25.

33. Dorothy Leonard-Barton and Isabelle Deschamps, "Managerial Influence in the Implementation of New Technology," *Management Science* 34 (1988), 1252–1265.

34. Kurt Lewin, *Field Theory in Social Science: Selected Theoretical Papers* (New York: Harper & Brothers, 1951).

35. Paul C. Nutt, "Tactics of Implementation," *Academy of Management Journal* 29 (1986), 230–261; Kotter and Schlesinger, "Choosing Strategies"; Richard L. Daft and Selwyn Becker, *Innovation in Organizations: Innovation Adoption in School Organizations* (New York: Elsevier, 1978); and Richard Beckhard, *Organization Development: Strategies and Models* (Reading, Mass.: Addison-Wesley, 1969).

36. Patricia J. Paden-Bost, "Making Money Control a Management Issue," *Management Accounting* (November 1982), 48–56; and Apcar, "Middle Managers."

37. Timothy L. O'Brien, "Company Wins Workers' Loyalty by Opening Its Books," *The Wall Street Journal,* December 20, 1993, B1–B2.

38. Apcar, "Middle Managers."

39. Jeremy Main, "The Trouble with Managing Japanese-Style," *Fortune,* April 2, 1984, 50–56.

40. Richard L. Daft, *Organization Theory and Design* (St. Paul, Minn.: West, 1989); and Tom Burns and G. M. Stalker, *The Management of Innovation* (London: Tavistock Publications, 1961).

41. Stratford P. Sherman, "How Philip Morris Diversified Right," *Fortune,* October 23, 1989, 120–129.

42. Richard L. Daft, "A Dual-Core Model of Organizational Innovation," *Academy of Management Journal* 21 (1978), 193–210; and Kanter, *The Change Masters.*

43. Harold J. Leavitt, "Applied Organizational Change in Industry: Structural, Technical, and Human Approaches," in *New Perspectives in Organization Research,* ed. W. W. Cooper, H. J. Leavitt, and M. W. Shelly II (New York: Wiley, 1964), 55–74.

44. Edwin Mansfield, J. Rapoport, J. Schnee, S. Wagner, and M. Hamburger, *Research and Innovation in Modern Corporations* (New York: Norton, 1971).

45. Andrew H. Van de Ven, "Central Problems in the Management of Innovation," *Management Science* 32 (1986), 590–607; Daft, *Organization Theory;* and Science Policy Research Unit, University of Sussex, *Success and Failure in Industrial Innovation* (London: Centre for the Study of Industrial Innovation, 1972).

46. William L. Shanklin and John K. Ryans, Jr., "Organizing for High-Tech Marketing," *Harvard Business Review* 62 (November–December 1984), 164–171; and Arnold O. Putnam, "A Redesign for Engineering," *Harvard Business Review* 63 (May–June 1985), 139–144.

47. Jay Finegan, "Packing Them In," *INC.,* February 1992, 90–97.

48. Daft, *Organization Theory.*

49. Keith H. Hammonds, "Teaching Discipline to Six-Year-Old Lotus," *Business Week,* July 4, 1988, 100–102.

50 Susan Caminiti, "A Quiet Superstar Rises in Retailing," *Fortune,* October 23, 1989, 167–74.

51. Brian Dumaine, "How Managers Can Succeed through Speed," *Fortune,* February 13, 1989, 54–59; and George Stalk, Jr., "Time—The Next Source of Competitive Advantage," *Harvard Business Review* (July–August 1988), 41–51.

52. Fariborz Damanpour, "The Adoption of Technological, Administrative, and Ancillary Innovations: Impact of Organizational Factors," *Journal of Management* 13 (1987), 675–688.

53. Daft, "Bureaucratic vs. Nonbureaucratic Structure."

54. Mary Kay Ash, *Mary Kay on People Management* (New York: Warner, 1984), 75.

55. Edgar H. Schein, "Organizational Culture," *American Psychologist* 45 (February 1990), 109–119; and Andrew Kupfer, "An Outsider Fires Up a Railroad," *Fortune,* December 18, 1989, 133–146.

56. Jay Finegan, "People Power," *INC.,* July 1993, 62–63.

57. Marshall Sashkin and W. Warner Burke, "Organization Development in the 1980s," *General Management* 13 (1987), 393–417; and Edgar F. Huse and Thomas G. Cummings, *Organization Development and Change,* 3d ed. (St. Paul, Minn.: West, 1985).

58. Paul F. Buller, "For Successful Strategic Change: Blend OD Practices with Strategic Management," *Organizational Dynamics* (Winter 1988), 42–55; and Robert M. Fulmer and Roderick Gilkey, "Blending Corporate Families: Management and Organization Development in a Postmerger Environment," *The Academy of Management Executive* 2 (1988), 275–283.

59. David A. Nadler, *Feedback and Organizational Development: Using Data-Based Methods* (Reading, Mass.: Addison-Wesley, 1977).

60. Wendell L. French and Cecil H. Bell, Jr., *Organization Development: Behavioral Science Interventions for Organization Improvement,* 3d ed. (Englewood Cliffs, N.J.: Prentice-Hall, 1984).

61. Buller, "For Successful Strategic Change."

62. Kurt Lewin, "Frontiers in Group Dynamics: Concepts, Method, and Reality in Social Science," *Human Relations* 1 (1947), 5–41; and Huse and Cummings, *Organization Development.*

63. Donna Brown Hogarty, "A Little Education Goes a Long Way," *Management Review,* June 1993, 24–28.

HUMAN RESOURCE MANAGEMENT

10

CHAPTER OUTLINE ▲

LEARNING OBJECTIVES ▼

After studying this chapter, you should be able to

- Explain the role of human resource management in organizational strategic planning.

- Describe federal legislation and societal trends that influence human resource management.

- Describe how human resource professionals work with line managers to attract, develop, and maintain human resources in the organization.

- Explain how organizations determine their future staffing needs through human resource planning.

- Describe the tools managers use to recruit and select employees.

- Describe how organizations develop an effective work force through training and performance appraisal.

- Explain how organizations maintain a work force through the administration of wages and salaries, benefits, and terminations.

When Thomas Melohn acquired North American Tool & Die, Inc., the company was in trouble. The metal-stamping and subassembly small business used older, labor-intensive machines, whereas its well-heeled, offshore competitors used highly automated technology to achieve efficiency and quality. Other domestic job-shops were going out of business left and right, so Melohn needed a strategy to regain his company's competitiveness. North American's profits were marginal, its work force unenthusiastic, and its prospects dim. Employee turnover was 27 percent annually. A full 7 percent of production output was rejected. CEO Melohn agonized over his top priority—how to find and keep good people.[1] ■ What should Thomas Melohn do to meet the need for high-quality employees? Can human resources be part of the strategy to restore North American's competitiveness?

human resource management (HRM)

Activities undertaken to attract, develop, and maintain an effective work force within an organization.

North American Tool & Die's past performance illustrates the need for managing human resources. Thomas Melohn and his management team must develop the company's ability to recruit, train, and keep first-quality employees; otherwise, company growth will be restricted and performance will continue to suffer. The term **human resource management (HRM)** refers to activities undertaken to attract, develop, and maintain an effective work force within an organization. Companies such as General Electric and Hewlett-Packard have become famous for their philosophy about human resource management, which is the foundation of their success. HRM is equally important for not-for-profit organizations. For example, the Catholic church must address the crisis of the sharply declining number of priests. Unless the church can find ways to attract and keep priests, a mere 17,000 priests will be serving 75 million U.S. Catholics by the year 2005.[2]

Over the past decade, human resource management has shed its old "personnel" image and gained recognition as a vital player in corporate strategy. Despite its importance, company employees often do not understand HRM functions. For example, at Transamerica surveys indicated employees were unaware of the full range of human resource services or their access to those services. Effective education about HRM functions is essential.[3]

Human resource management consists of three parts. First, all managers are human resource managers. For example, at IBM every manager is expected to pay attention to the development and satisfaction of subordinates. Line managers use surveys, career planning, performance appraisal, and compensation to encourage commitment to IBM.[4] Second, employees are viewed as assets. Employees, not buildings and machinery, give a company a competitive advantage, such as Tom Melohn is trying to accomplish with North American Tool & Die. Third, human resource management is a matching process, integrating the organization's goals with employees' needs. Employees should receive satisfaction equal to that of the company.

At MagneTek's Blytheville, Arkansas, plant, employees enjoy a daily aerobic class as part of a Total Excellence at MagneTek (TEAM) program, which is one of the HRM "tools" to develop and maintain an effective work force. This program stresses promotion of health and stress reduction as part of overall human resource management.

● GOALS OF HRM

In this chapter, we will examine the three primary goals of HRM as illustrated in Exhibit 10.1. These goals, which take place within the organizational environment, include competitive strategy, federal legislation, and societal trends. The three goals are to attract an effective work force to the organization, develop the work force to its potential, and maintain the work force over the long term.[5] Achieving these goals requires skills in planning, forecasting, training, performance appraisal, wage and salary administration, benefit programs, and even termination. Each of the activities in Exhibit 10.1 will be discussed in this chapter. Most organizations employ human resource professionals to perform these functions. *Human resource specialists* focus on one of the HRM areas, such as recruitment of employees or administration of wage or benefit programs. *Human resource generalists* have responsibility in more than one HRM area.

● ENVIRONMENTAL INFLUENCES ON HRM

"Our strength is the quality of our people."
"Our people are our most important resource."

These often-repeated statements by executives emphasize the importance of HRM. Human resource managers must find, recruit, train, nurture, and retain the best people. Human resource programs are designed to fit organizational needs, core values, and strategic goals. Without the proper personnel, the brightest idea or management fad—whether

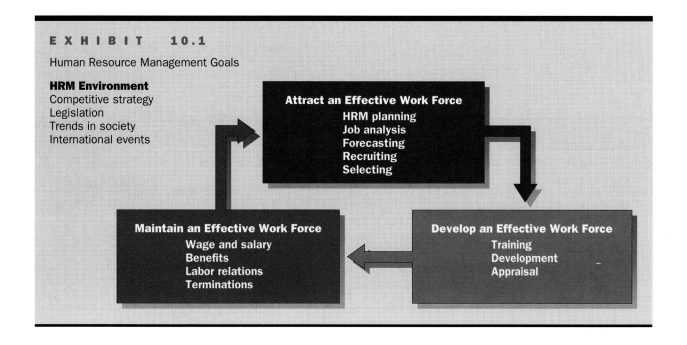

EXHIBIT   10.1

Human Resource Management Goals

HRM Environment
Competitive strategy
Legislation
Trends in society
International events

Attract an Effective Work Force
HRM planning
Job analysis
Forecasting
Recruiting
Selecting

Maintain an Effective Work Force
Wage and salary
Benefits
Labor relations
Terminations

Develop an Effective Work Force
Training
Development
Appraisal

teams, quality circles, or flexible compensation—is doomed to failure. For these reasons, it is important that human resource executives be involved in competitive strategy. Human resource executives also interpret federal legislation and help detect issues and trends both in society and internationally.[6]

COMPETITIVE STRATEGY

The human resource management function has changed enormously over the years. In the 1920s, HRM was a low-level position charged with ensuring that procedures were developed for hiring and firing employees and with implementing benefit plans. By the 1950s unions were a major force, and the HRM manager was elevated to a senior position as chief negotiator. During the 1980s, unions began to decline, and top HRM managers became directly involved in corporate strategic management.[7]

Exhibit 10.2 illustrates the interdependence between company and human resource strategy. The organization's competitive strategy may include mergers and acquisitions, downsizing to increase efficiency, international operations, or the acquisition of automated production technology. These strategic decisions determine the demand for skills and employees. The human resource strategy, in turn, must include the correct employee makeup to implement the organization's strategy. In the 1990s strategic decisions more than ever have to be based on human resource considerations. For example, **downsizing** is the systematic reduction in the number of managers and employees to make a company more cost efficient and competitive.[8] When Boeing CEO Frank Shrontz predicted 1993 price wars and increased competition, the company targeted 25 to 30 percent cost reduction goals. Shrontz focused on the Defense & Space Group, eliminating 16,000 of 53,000 workers through attrition and transfers to other units, making effective use of human resource strategy.[9]

As another example, the introduction of flexible manufacturing systems, which use computers to automate and integrate manufacturing components such as robots, product design, and engineering analysis, have dramatically changed the need for work-force skill. These new

downsizing

The systematic reduction in the number of managers and employees to make a company more cost efficient and competitive.

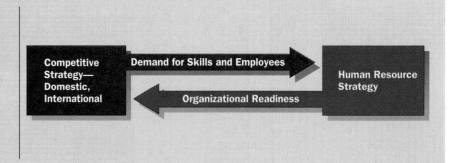

E X H I B I T   1 0 . 2

Interdependence of Organizational and Human Resource Strategy

SOURCE: Adapted from Cynthia A. Lengnick-Hall and Mark L. Lengnick-Hall, "Strategic Human Resources Management: A Review of the Literature and a Proposed Typology," *Academy of Management Review* 13 (1988), 454–470.

machines require a highly skilled work force, including interpersonal skills and the ability to work as a team. To make the strategic change to automated technology, the HRM department must upgrade the skills of shop machine operators and recruit new employees who have human skills as well as technical skills.[10]

FEDERAL LEGISLATION

Over the last 30 years, several federal laws have been passed to ensure equal employment opportunity (EEO). Key legislation and executive orders are summarized in Exhibit 10.3. The point of the laws is to stop discriminatory practices that are unfair to specific groups and to define enforcement agencies for these laws. EEO legislation attempts to balance the pay given to men and women; provide employment opportunities without regard to race, religion, national origin, and sex; ensure fair treatment for employees of all ages; and avoid discrimination against handicapped individuals. More recent legislation pertains to illegal aliens and people with disabilities.

The Equal Employment Opportunity Commission (EEOC) created by the Civil Rights Act of 1964 initiates investigations in response to complaints concerning discrimination. The EEOC is the major agency involved with employment discrimination. **Discrimination** occurs when some applicants are hired or promoted based on criteria that are not job relevant. For example, refusing to hire black people for jobs they could readily handle or paying a woman a lower wage than a man for the same work are discriminatory acts. When discrimination is found, remedies include providing back pay and taking affirmative action. **Affirmative action** requires that an employer take positive steps to guarantee equal employment opportunities for people within protected groups. An affirmative action plan is a formal document that can be reviewed by

discrimination

The hiring or promoting of applicants based on criteria that are not job relevant.

affirmative action

A policy requiring employers to take positive steps to guarantee equal employment opportunities for people within protected groups.

As a winner of the Katherine G. Peden award for corporate excellence in the promotion of women, Louisville Gas & Electric Company prides itself on its strong *affirmative action program.* LG&E's Career Woman of the '90s seminars help women balance their personal and professional lives.

	Federal Law	Year	Provisions
EXHIBIT 10.3 Major Federal Laws Related to Human Resource Management	Equal Pay Act	1963	Prohibits sex differences in pay for substantially equal work.
	Civil Rights Act, Title VII	1964 1967	Prohibits discrimination in employment on basis of race, religion, color, sex, or national origin.
	Executive Orders 11246 and 11375	1965	Requires federal contractors to eliminate employment discrimination through affirmative actions.
	Age Discrimination in Employment Act (amended 1978 and 1986)	1967	Prohibits age discrimination against those between the ages of 40 and 65 years and restricts mandatory retirement.
	Executive Order 11478	1969	Prohibits discrimination in the U.S. Postal Service and various government agencies.
	Occupational Safety and Health Act (OSHA)	1970	Establishes mandatory safety and health standards in organizations.
	Vocational Rehabilitation Act	1973	Prohibits discrimination based on physical or mental handicap and requires that employees be informed about affirmative action plans.
	Vietnam-Era Veterans Readjustment Act	1974	Prohibits discrimination against disabled veterans and Vietnam-era veterans and requires affirmative action.
	Pregnancy Discrimination Act	1978	Requires that women affected by pregnancy, childbirth, or related medical conditions be treated as all other employees for employment-related purposes, including benefits.
	Immigration Reform and Control Act	1986	Prohibits employers from knowingly hiring illegal aliens and prohibits employment on the basis of national origin or citizenship.
	Americans with Disabilities Act	1990	Prohibits discrimination of qualified individuals by employers on the basis of disability, and demands that "reasonable accommodations" be provided for the disabled to allow performance of duties.
	Civil Rights Act	1991	Provides for possible compensatory and punitive damages plus traditional back pay for cases of intentional discrimination brought under Title VII of the 1964 Civil Rights Act. Shifts the burden of proof to the employer.

employees and enforcement agencies. Organizational affirmative action reduces or eliminates internal inequities among affected employee groups.

Failure to comply with equal employment opportunity legislation can result in substantial fines and penalties for employers. For example, Shoney's was accused of discrimination against black employees and job applicants. The class-action suit charged that company policy conspired to limit the number of black employees working in public areas of the restaurant. In 1992 the company agreed to pay $105 million to victims of its hiring, promotion, and firing policies, dating back to 1985.[11] AT&T agreed to pay over $15 million in back wages to women and other minority groups whose pay was deemed to be arbitrarily low because of discriminatory practices. In another case, a policewoman was found to have been sexually harassed and then retaliated against by management for filing a discrimination complaint. She was awarded over $22,000 in back pay and $24,000 in lieu of being reinstated as a police officer.[12]

One thing concerning human resource legislation is clear: The scope of equal employment opportunity legislation is increasing at federal, state, and municipal levels. The working rights and conditions of women, minorities, older employees, and the handicapped will receive increasing legislative attention in the future. Also, most cases in the past have concerned lower-level jobs, but the 1990s will see more attention given to equal employment opportunity in upper-level management positions.

TRENDS IN SOCIETY

The complexity of demands on human resource executives often seems overwhelming. Just as human resource managers learn to insert themselves into corporate strategy making and learn the subtleties of such federal regulations as the Americans with Disabilities Act, other trends that surface raise new problems for staffing the firm. These trends include everything from court decisions that rule against companies that fire employees to dramatic changes in the makeup of the labor force. A few of the important current trends are as follows.

WORK-FORCE DIVERSITY. The ethnic and gender makeup of the people filling jobs in the year 2000 will be different than that of current employees. The implications of this trend are so important that Chapter 11 is devoted to them.

LABOR SUPPLY FLUCTUATIONS. Changing demographics and economic conditions affect labor supply. In the late 1980s, predictions of severe labor shortages proved untrue because of the persistent recession in the early 1990s and the end of the Cold War. The massive reduction in the nation's defense needs and widespread corporate downsizing reversed the labor "shortage" as millions of white-collar and blue-collar Americans joined the ranks of the unemployed. The future labor supply may fluctuate further between shortage and oversupply as economic or demographic conditions change, such as the beginning of baby-boomer retirement in the year 2000.

EMPLOYMENT AT WILL. Employers no longer enjoy the undisputed right to fire employees. Many discharged employees are filing lawsuits with almost 80 percent of the verdicts favoring the employee and damage awards exceeding $100,000. The *employment-at-will* rule traditionally permitted an employer to fire an employee for just cause, or even no cause. Now 40 states have written employment laws to severely limit the "at will" doctrine and to protect against wrongful firing of employees who refuse to violate a law or expose an illegal action by their employers. Although termination is generally accepted by the courts when employers can show employee incompetence or changing business requirements, many employers remain confused about their rights regarding termination. Employers now avoid terms such as *permanent employment,* and many employers are now spelling out their termination policy to employees, asking them to acknowledge that the employment agreement can be terminated at any time, thereby avoiding an implied long-term employment contract.[13]

EMPLOYEE FLEXIBILITY.   One of the clearest trends is the increased effort to obtain quality employees and at the same time reduce excess employee costs so that firms can remain competitive in the global marketplace. This means that employers will be making greater use of part-time employees, work schedules that allow employees to work other than the traditional hours during the day, employee leasing and temporary employees, and employees who work under contract only for specific hours and tasks, thereby allowing employers to get exactly what they need and avoiding the necessity of providing offices and benefits on a full-time basis. Companies such as Bowater, Digital Equipment, Hallmark, Pacific Bell, and Worthington Industries have turned to employee flexibility to reduce costs without having to lay off valued employees. Banc One Wisconsin Corporation has devised a system for utilizing temporary workers that makes them an integral part of the work force.

BANC ONE WISCONSIN CORPORATION

Banc One Wisconsin Corporation left few areas of operations unaffected in its commitment to deliver the highest quality service. The bank's Quality Improvement Program led to some unexpected economies. A redesigned approach to how the bank uses temporary workers has saved the institution as much as $140,000 annually, and improved quality and efficiency in the process.

One of the key concerns of any company using temporaries is how cost-effective the workers can be given the fact that many require some level of instruction and training. Banc One solved this problem by using temporaries who work exclusively for the bank. Those temporaries show up for work already familiar with policies and procedures. This in turn greatly reduces administrative work by bank human resource personnel because the workers know what is expected of them. This also makes them much more productive.

The bank got to the heart of its own needs by surveying where temporaries were most frequently used. The selection process was simplified by finding out where and what type of temporaries were most often required. Software skills were a principal concern; getting temporaries familiarized with the bank's computer language was time consuming. An alternative considered was to negotiate with placement firms for reduced rates, but ultimately it became clear that the work quality could best be maximized by using an exclusive pool of returning temporary employees. Loyalty was enhanced as well.

At first, the bank tried administering the program in-house, but later decided that the best course was to locate a temporary help firm willing to manage the workers. That approach shifted the bulk of administrative duties to the contracting firm and freed up a considerable amount of the bank's human resource department's time for other responsibilities.[14] ■

UNIONIZATION. The general trend in North America is away from unionization, but many employees belong to unions, and labor continues to unionize new companies. The National Labor Relations Act of 1935 provides that employees may elect to be represented by unions in negotiations with employers over wages, hours, and other terms and conditions of employment. Currently, about one-fourth of all workers are covered by collective bargaining agreements. In companies where unions represent workers, union officials research the needs of members, the elements of the pay package, and the employers' financial condition. When a contract expires, union officials negotiate on behalf of the members of the bargaining unit for desired pay components and other issues relevant to workers.[15]

Some companies find unionization a benefit; others try to avoid unionization. Indeed, just the threat of a union may cause an employer to adjust pay and benefits. At Cannon Mills Company, three mills had to be closed and as a result, some employees tried to unionize. Cannon's management responded by persuading workers that the union would not improve benefits and would simply take part of the employees' paychecks in the form of union dues. The most promising trend in recent years has been the responsiveness of unions to new competitive conditions. The need for cross-training, employee participation, and new compensation systems to meet global competition have brought unions into closer collaboration with management.

Within this context of trends in society, human resource managers must achieve the three primary goals described earlier in this chapter: attracting, developing, and maintaining an effective work force for the organization. Let us now review some of the established techniques for accomplishing these goals.

● ATTRACTING AN EFFECTIVE WORK FORCE

The first goal of HRM is to attract individuals who show signs of becoming valued, productive, and satisfied employees. The first step in attracting an effective work force involves human resource planning, in which managers or HRM professionals predict the need for new employees based on the types of vacancies that exist, as illustrated in Exhibit 10.4. The second step is to use recruiting procedures

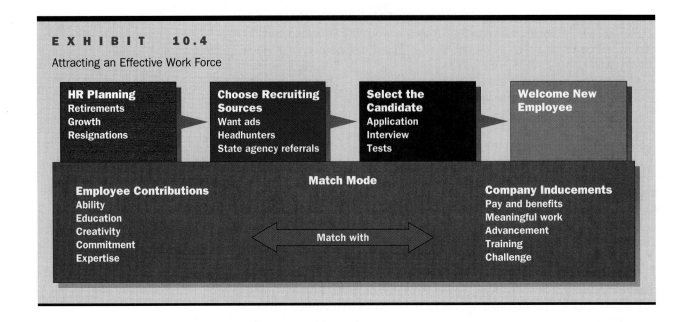

EXHIBIT   10.4

Attracting an Effective Work Force

HR Planning
Retirements
Growth
Resignations

Choose Recruiting Sources
Want ads
Headhunters
State agency referrals

Select the Candidate
Application
Interview
Tests

Welcome New Employee

Match Mode

Employee Contributions
Ability
Education
Creativity
Commitment
Expertise

Match with

Company Inducements
Pay and benefits
Meaningful work
Advancement
Training
Challenge

---

matching model

An employee selection approach in which the organization and the applicant attempt to match each other's needs, interests, and values.

to communicate with potential applicants. The third step is to select from the applicants those persons believed to be the best potential contributors to the organization. Finally, the new employee is welcomed into the organization.

Underlying the organization's effort to attract employees is a matching model. With the **matching model,** the organization and the individual attempt to match the needs, interests, and values that they offer each other. The organization offers "inducements," and the employee offers "contributions."[16] HRM professionals attempt to identify a correct match. For example, a small software developer may require long hours from creative, technically skilled employees. In return, it can offer freedom from bureaucracy, tolerance of idiosyncrasies, and potentially high pay. A large manufacturer can offer employment security and stability, but it may have more rules and regulations and require greater skills for "getting approval from the higher-ups." The individual who would thrive working for the software developer might feel stymied and unhappy working for a large manufacturer. Both the company and the employee are interested in finding a good match.

HUMAN RESOURCE PLANNING

human resource planning

The forecasting of human resource needs and the projected matching of individuals with expected job vacancies.

Human resource planning is the forecasting of human resource needs and the projected matching of individuals with expected vacancies. Human resource planning begins with several questions:

- What new technologies are emerging, and how will these affect the work system?
- What is the volume of the business likely to be in the next five to ten years?
- What is the turnover rate, and how much, if any, is avoidable?

The responses to these questions are used to formulate specific questions pertaining to HRM activities, such as the following:

- How many senior managers will we need during this period?
- What types of engineers will we need, and how many?
- Are persons with adequate computer skills available for meeting our projected needs?
- How many administrative personnel—technicians, secretaries—will we need to support the additional managers and engineers?[17]

Answers to these questions help define the direction for the organization's HRM strategy. For example, if forecasting suggests that there will be a strong need for more technically trained individuals, the organization can (1) define the jobs and skills needed in some detail, (2) hire and train recruiters to look for the specified skills, and/or (3) provide new training for existing employees. By anticipating future HRM needs, the organization can prepare itself to meet competitive challenges more effectively than organizations that react to problems only as they arise.

HRM FORECASTING TECHNIQUES.   A variety of HRM forecasting techniques is in use today. These can be classified as short range and long range.

Short-range forecasting frequently uses the following steps:

- The demand for the organization's product or service is predicted. Major expected external changes (such as increased demand for a new line of products) are accounted for in this estimation.
- The overall sales forecast is estimated; anticipated internal changes (for example, the conversion to word processors from typewriters) are considered.
- Working budgets to reflect the expected work loads of every department are estimated.
- Personnel requirements are determined through conversion of dollars or units into numbers of people.
- Forecasts of labor market conditions or internal organization factors (such as turnover rate) that may affect the future labor supply are considered.

An example of short-range forecasting is USAir's introduction of the first Boeing 737-300 into scheduled service. Introducing a new aircraft into an airline operation required careful planning and coordination, beginning with a forecast of the number of pilots needed. Then 737-300 flight simulators had to be obtained and set up in a classroom. Pilots had to be trained before the new aircraft was introduced. New pilots with qualifications fitting the 737-300 also had to be hired.

Long-range forecasting ranges from the intuitive to the sophisticated. As described in Chapter 7, some forecasting techniques are based on mathematical extrapolation from past trends. Others involve group decision-making techniques, such as the Delphi method, wherein groups of top managers or other experts use their judgment to make forecasts. Statistical data are also used to project the impact of future employment levels, sales activity, employee turnover, and other variables on the organization's future labor needs.

The need for long-range planning was illustrated by General Electric when top executives realized that corporate human resources did not fit new products and technologies. General Electric's chairman said, "We were a company with 30,000 electromechanical engineers becoming a company that needed electronics engineers. We didn't plan for this change . . . and it caused us big problems. . . ." Without planning, a company such as GE could be forced to drain engineers and managers from a stable division to support a growing division, which would propel people into positions above their competence and necessitate a costly rapid-hiring effort.[18]

RECRUITING

recruiting

The activities or practices that define the desired characteristics of applicants for specific jobs.

Recruiting is defined as "activities or practices that define the characteristics of applicants to whom selection procedures are ultimately applied."[19] Although we frequently think of campus recruiting as a typical recruiting activity, many organizations use *internal recruiting*, or "promote-from-within" policies, to fill their higher-level positions.[20] At Mellon Bank, for example, current employees are given preference when a position opens. Open positions are listed in Mellon's career opportunity bulletins, which are distributed to employees. Internal recruiting has several advantages: It is less costly than an external search, and it generates higher employee commitment, development, and satisfaction, because it offers opportunities for career advancement to employees rather than outsiders.

Frequently, however, *external recruiting*—recruiting newcomers from outside the organization—is advantageous. Applicants are provided by a variety of outside sources including newspaper advertising, state employment services, private employment agencies ("headhunters"), job fairs, and employee referrals. Some employers even provide cash awards for employees who submit names of people who subsequently accept employment, because referral is one of the cheapest and most reliable methods for external recruiting.[21]

realistic job preview (RJP)

A recruiting approach that gives applicants all pertinent and realistic information about the job and the organization.

REALISTIC JOB PREVIEWS.   One approach to enhancing recruiting effectiveness is called a *realistic job preview*. A **realistic job preview (RJP)** gives applicants all pertinent and realistic information—positive and negative—about the job and the organization.[22] RJPs enhance employee satisfaction and reduce turnover, because they facilitate matching individuals, jobs, and organizations. Individuals have a better basis on which to determine their suitability to the organization and "self-select" into or out of positions based on full information. When employees choose positions without RJPs, unmet expectations may cause initial job dissatisfaction and increased turnover. For example, Linda McDermott left a good position in an accounting firm to become an executive vice-president of a new management consulting company. She was told she would have a major role in helping the business grow. As it turned out, her boss relegated her to administrative duties so she quit after a few months, causing the company to initiate another lengthy search and sidetracking her career for a year or two.[23]

LEGAL CONSIDERATIONS. Organizations must ensure that their recruiting practices conform to the law. As discussed earlier in this chapter, equal employment opportunity (EEO) laws stipulate that recruiting and hiring decisions cannot discriminate on the basis of race, national origin, religion, or sex. *Affirmative action* refers to the use of goals, timetables, or other methods in recruiting to promote the hiring, development, and retention of "protected groups"—persons historically underrepresented in the workplace. For example, companies adopting an affirmative action policy may recruit at colleges with large enrollments of black students. A city may establish a goal of recruiting one black firefighter for every white firefighter until the proportion of black firefighters is commensurate with that in the community.

Most large companies try to comply with affirmative action and EEO guidelines. Prudential Insurance Company's policy is presented in Exhibit 10.5. Prudential actively recruits employees and takes affirmative action steps to recruit individuals from all walks of life.

SELECTING

The next step for managers is to select desired employees from the pool of recruited applicants. In the **selection** process, employers attempt to determine the skills, abilities, and other attributes a person needs to perform a particular job. Then they assess applicants' characteristics in an attempt to determine the "fit" between the job and applicant characteristics.

selection
The process of determining the skills, abilities, and other attributes a person needs to perform a particular job.

JOB DESCRIPTIONS. A good place to start in making a selection decision is the job description. Human resource professionals or line managers who make selection decisions may have little direct experience with the job to be filled. If these persons are to make a good match between job and candidate, they should read the job description before they review applications.

E X H I B I T   10.5

Prudential's Corporate Recruiting Policy

An Equal Opportunity Employer

Prudential recruits, hires, trains, promotes, and compensates individuals without regard to race, color, religion or creed, age, sex, marital status, national origin, ancestry, liability for service in the armed forces of the United States, status as a special disabled veteran or veteran of the Vietnam era, or physical or mental handicap.

This is official company policy because: ■ we believe it is right
■ it makes good business sense
■ it is the law

We are also committed to an ongoing program of affirmative action in which members of under-represented groups are actively sought out and employed for opportunities in all parts and at all levels of the company. In employing people from all walks of life, Prudential gains access to the full experience of our diverse society.

SOURCE: Prudential Insurance Company.

job description

A listing of duties as well as desirable qualifications for a particular job.

validity

The relationship between an applicant's score on a selection device and his or her future job performance.

application form

A device for collecting information about an applicant's education, previous job experience, and other background characteristics.

A **job description** typically lists job duties as well as desirable qualifications for a particular job. An example of a job description for American Airlines appears in Exhibit 10.6.

SELECTION DEVICES.   Several devices are used for assessing applicant qualifications. The most frequently used are the application form, interview, paper-and-pencil test, and assessment center. Human resource professionals may use a combination of these devices to obtain a valid prediction of employee job performance. **Validity** refers to the relationship between one's score on a selection device and one's future job performance. A valid selection procedure will provide high scores that correspond to subsequent high job performance.

Application Form.   The **application form** is used to collect information about the applicant's education, previous job experience, and other background characteristics. Research in the life insurance industry shows that biographical information inventories can validly predict future job success.[24]

One pitfall to be avoided is the inclusion of questions that are irrelevant to job success. In line with affirmative action, the application form

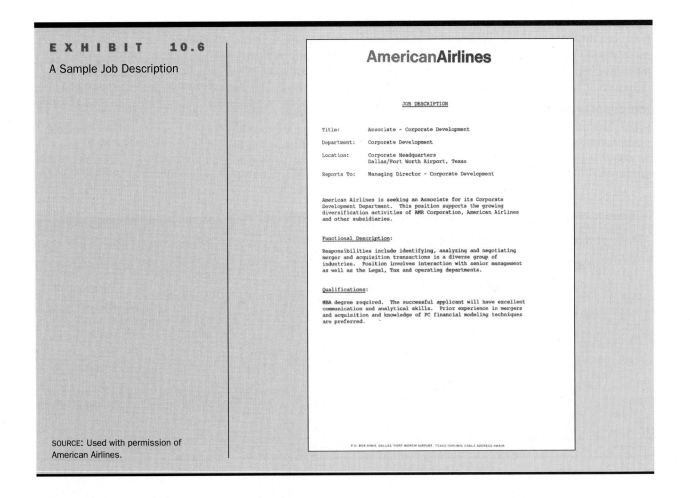

E X H I B I T   10.6

A Sample Job Description

SOURCE: Used with permission of American Airlines.

should not ask questions that will create an adverse impact on "protected groups" unless the questions are clearly related to the job.[25] For example, employers should not ask whether the applicant rents or owns his or her own home because (1) an applicant's response might adversely affect his or her chances at the job, (2) minorities and women may be less likely to own a home, and (3) homeownership is probably unrelated to job performance. On the other hand, the CPA exam is relevant to job performance in a CPA firm; thus, it is appropriate to ask whether an applicant for employment has passed the CPA exam even if only one-half of all women or minority applicants have done so versus nine-tenths of men applicants.

Interview.[26]   The interview is used in the hiring process in almost every job category in virtually every organization. The *interview* serves as a two-way communication channel that allows both the organization and the applicant to collect information that would otherwise be difficult to obtain.

Although widely used, the interview as generally practiced is not a valid predictor of later job performance. Researchers have identified many reasons for this. Interviewers frequently are unfamiliar with the job. They tend to make decisions in the first few minutes of the interview before all relevant information has been gathered. They also may base decisions on personal biases (such as against minority groups or physically unattractive persons and in favor of those similar to themselves). The interviewer may talk too much and spend time discussing matters irrelevant to the job.[27]

Organizations will continue to use interviews despite the pitfalls. Thus, researchers have identified methods for increasing their validity. Advice for effective interviewing—as well as some unusual interview experiences—is summarized in the Manager's Shoptalk box.

Paper-and-Pencil Test.   Many companies use **paper-and-pencil tests** such as intelligence tests, aptitude and ability tests, and personality inventories, particularly those shown to be valid predictors.[28] For example, a 109-question personality test has been used by independent insurance agents to hire clerical and customer service employees. The test is designed to measure such traits as "motivation to please others" and "people orientation." The insurance agencies believe they need something to accurately gauge applicants' strengths and weaknesses. The test has been successful, because candidates hired have displayed strong tendencies to provide service to customers.[29] In France, companies also use a type of paper-and-pencil test to evaluate applicants in a controversial technique that has engendered plenty of praise and criticism.

paper-and-pencil test
A written test designed to measure a particular attribute such as intelligence or aptitude.

 TESTING IN FRANCE

When the list has been reduced, and the final candidates interviewed, and assessed, a final decision has to be made. Who could blame human resource managers for wishing they could look inside an applicant's head to find out exactly what was there? Some believe there is a way.

MANAGER'S shop talk

THE RIGHT WAY TO INTERVIEW A JOB APPLICANT

A so-so interview usually nets a so-so employee. Many hiring mistakes can be prevented during the interview. The following techniques will ensure a successful interview:

1. Know what you want. Before the interview, prepare questions based on your knowledge of the job to be filled. If you do not have a thorough knowledge of the job, read a job description. If possible, call one or more jobholders and ask them about the job duties and what is required to succeed. Another idea is to make up a list of traits and qualifications for the ideal candidate. Be specific about what it will take to get the job done.

2. Prepare a road map. Develop questions that will reveal whether the candidate has the correct background and qualifications. The questions should focus on previous experiences that are relevant to the current job. If the job requires creativity and innovation, ask a question such as "What do you do differently from other sales reps?"

3. Use open-ended questions in which the right answer is not obvious. Ask the applicant to give specific examples of previous work experiences. For example, don't ask, "Are you a hard worker?" or "Tell me about yourself." Instead ask, "Can you give me examples from your previous work history that reflect your level of motivation?" or "How did you go about getting your current job?"

4. Do not ask questions that are *irrelevant to the job.* This is particularly important when the irrelevant questions might adversely affect minorities or women. Questions that are considered objectionable are the same as those considered objectionable on application forms.

5. Listen, don't talk. You should spend most of the interview listening. If you talk too much, the focus will shift to you and you may miss important cues. Listen carefully to tone of voice as well as content. Body language also can be revealing; for example, failure to make eye contact can be a danger signal.

6. Allow enough time so that the interview will not be rushed. Leave time for the candidate to ask questions about the job. The types of questions the candidate asks can be an important clue to his or her interest in the job. Try to delay forming an opinion about the applicant until after the entire interview has been completed.

7. Avoid reliance on your memory. Request the applicant's permission to take notes; then do so unobtrusively during the interview or immediately after. If several applicants are interviewed, notes are essential for remembering what they said and the impressions they made.

Even a well-planned interview may be disrupted by the unexpected. Robert Half asked vice-presidents and personnel directors at 100 major American corporations to describe the most unusual thing that they were aware of ever happening during a job interview. Various applicants reportedly:

- "Wore a Walkman and said she could listen to me and the music at the same time."
- "Announced she hadn't had lunch and proceeded to eat a hamburger and french fries in the interviewer's office."
- "Wore a jogging suit to interview for a position as a vice-president."
- "He said he was so well-qualified that if he didn't get the job, it would prove that the company's management was incompetent."
- "A balding candidate abruptly excused himself. He returned to the office a few minutes later wearing a hairpiece."
- "Not only did he ignore the 'No Smoking' sign in my office, he lit up the wrong ends of several filter-tip cigarettes."
- "She chewed bubble gum and constantly blew bubbles."
- "Job applicant challenged the interviewer to arm wrestle."
- "He stretched out on the floor to fill out the job application."
- "He interrupted to telephone his therapist for advice on answering specific interview questions."
- "He dozed off and started snoring during the interview."
- "He said that if he were hired, he would demonstrate his loyalty by having the corporate logo tattooed on his forearm." ■

SOURCE: James M. Jenks and Brian L. P. Zevnik, "ABCs of Job Interviewing," *Harvard Business Review* (July–August 1989), 38–42; and Martha H. Peak, "What Color Is Your Bumbershoot?" Reprinted by permission of publisher from *Management Review* (October 1989), 63, © 1989. American Management Association, New York. All rights reserved.

Handwriting analysis is a standard hiring tool in France. Called graphology, it is used by an estimated three-quarters of the country's firms. Few firms make it the deciding factor, interviews still do that, but writing often confirms, or allays, suspicions about a particular candidate. Serge Vandaele, director of recruitment at the French bank Credit Lyonnais believes handwriting analysis is a useful complement. "Nine out of 10 times," he says, "my independent appraisal of a candidate coincides with the graphologist's."

There is more to it than mere penmanship. According to graphologists, the amount of top margin an applicant uses yields insight into a person's order, ambition, and idealism. Selecting a minimal right-hand margin may indicate spontaneity and a penchant for action. How the left side of the page sets up indicates personal discipline, or lack of it. Then, the writer can begin worrying about whether the pen strokes are inadvertently revealing a need for approval or some sinister fixation on the past.

Graphology is inexpensive and quick. Although viewed as a sham by dissenters, experts in the field claim they can help companies avoid bad hiring decisions. Many experts refund their fees if the analysis turns out to be faulty. However, that would be small consolation to an applicant wrongly disqualified by the procedure. For now, U.S. job seekers need not brush-up their pen strokes. France is still the only place where graphology is widely used.[30] ■

Assessment Center.   First developed by psychologists at AT&T, assessment centers are used to select individuals with high potential for managerial careers by such organizations as AT&T, IBM, General Electric, and JCPenney.[31] **Assessment centers** present a series of managerial situations to groups of applicants over, say, a two- or three-day period. One technique is the "in-basket" simulation, which requires the applicant to play the role of a manager who must decide how to respond to ten memos in his or her in-basket within a two-hour period. Panels of two or three trained judges observe the applicant's decisions and assess the extent to which they reflect interpersonal, communication, and problem-solving skills.

assessment center

A technique for selecting individuals with high managerial potential based on their performance on a series of simulated managerial tasks.

Assessment centers have proven to be valid predictors of managerial success,[32] and some organizations now use them for hiring technical workers. At Kimberly-Clark's newest plants, for example, applicants for machine operator jobs are put through a simulation in which they are asked to play the role of a supervisor. The idea is to see whether candidates have sufficient "people skills" to fit into the participative work atmosphere. Assessment centers are important because they provide a more valid measure of interpersonal skills than do paper-and-pencil tests.

● DEVELOPING AN EFFECTIVE WORK FORCE

Following selection, the major goal of HRM is to develop employees into an effective work force. Development includes training and performance appraisal.

TRAINING AND DEVELOPMENT

Training and development represent a planned effort by an organization to facilitate employees' learning of job-related behaviors.[33] Some authors distinguish the two forms of intervention by noting that the term *training* usually refers to teaching lower-level or technical employees how to do their present jobs, whereas *development* refers to teaching managers and professionals the skills needed for both present and future jobs. For simplicity, we will refer to both interventions as *training*.

Organizations spend nearly $100 billion each year on training. In 1987 IBM reported spending more than $750 million a year on corporate schooling, more than the entire budget of Harvard University.[34] Training may occur in a variety of forms. The most common method is on-the-job training. In **on-the-job training (OJT),** an experienced employee is asked to take a new employee "under his or her wing" and show the newcomer how to perform job duties. OJT has many advantages, such as few out-of-pocket costs for training facilities, materials, or instructor fees and easy transfer of learning back to the job. The learning site is the work site.

Other frequently used training methods include

- *Orientation training,* in which newcomers are introduced to the organization's "culture," its standards, and goals.

- *Classroom training,* including lectures, films, audiovisual techniques, and simulations.

- *Programmed and computer-assisted instruction,* in which the employee works at his or her own pace to learn material from a text that includes exercises and quizzes to enhance learning.

- *Conference and case discussion groups,* in which participants analyze cases or discuss topics assisted by a training leader.

Companies such as Toyota that spend heavily on selection also invest in employee training. The 10 percent of employees selected undergo several weeks of training for their specific jobs, often at the employees' own expense. At General Motors' truck plant, each assembly line worker received 400 to 500 hours of paid training. Each skilled worker got training of 1,000 hours—the equivalent to almost six months. Motorola, Macy's, and Texas Instruments are examples of companies that appreciate the importance of thorough training to remain competitive in the global marketplace. However, large companies are not the only ones to recognize the benefits of training. Though still a relatively new trend, workplace education in basic skills by small companies also is on the rise. According to the Southport Institute for Policy Analysis, 3 to 5 percent of small businesses have basic skills programs, but 20 percent have such aspirations. The Print & Copy Factory of San Francisco is among those leading the way.

on-the-job training (OJT)

A type of training in which an experienced employee "adopts" a new employee to teach him or her how to perform job duties.

PRINT & COPY FACTORY

It may not take a genius to operate a copy machine, but Print & Copy Factory owner Ray Tom believes that even workers hired for the most mundane of tasks can benefit from a comprehensive training program. He has introduced a system that provides clear objectives for employees to progress, and a number of identifiable and gratifying achievement milestones along the way.

Tom has made training integral to the workplace. It begins immediately after an employee is hired, and progresses through five levels of operation and maintenance, with commensurate pay and promotion increases. Because Print & Copy does not have a big educational budget, the company maintains an available library of tapes and instructional books. Compliance is ensured by having employees provide a brief synopsis of what they learned from each issue. Company classes are formed on a need basis, and workers can progress to the management level at their own pace. A checklist outlines the skills required for each job level, and employees are tested before being promoted.

Currently, almost three-fourths of Tom's managers are workers who entered at the bottom and pursued just such a path. The Print & Copy Factory has a stable work force of 180 and annual revenues of $8 million, due in large part to the cost-effective training and educational investment by its owner.[35] ■

Many companies are increasing training budgets and experimenting with a variety of new training methods. The popularity of manufacturing teams, for example, has led to new ideas in training. "Cross-discipline" training enables employees to understand the relationship of their job to others so that everyone works toward the common corporate goal. "Integrative learning" uses team exercises to establish and reinforce effective teamwork habits.[36]

PROMOTION FROM WITHIN.   Promotion from within helps companies retain and develop productive employees. It provides challenging assignments, prescribes new responsibilities, and helps employees grow by developing their abilities.

One approach to promotion from within is *job posting*, which means that positions are announced on bulletin boards or in company publications as openings occur. Interested employees notify the human resource department, which then helps make the fit between employees and positions.

Another approach is the *employee resource chart*, which is designed to identify likely successors for each management position. The chart looks like a typical organization chart with every employee listed. Every key position includes the names of top candidates to move into that position when it becomes vacant. Candidates are rated on a five-point scale reflecting whether they are ready for immediate promotion or need additional experience. These charts show the potential flow of employees up through the hierarchy and provide motivation to employees who have an opportunity for promotion.

Training and development of new employees is important at the Tattered Covered Book Store. Managers discuss store policies and procedures as well as store layout and goals with new employees.

PERFORMANCE APPRAISAL

Performance appraisal is another important technique for developing an effective work force. **Performance appraisal** comprises the steps of observing and assessing employee performance, recording the assessment, and providing feedback to the employee. Managers use performance appraisal to describe and evaluate the employees' performances. During performance appraisal, skillful managers give feedback and praise concerning the acceptable elements of the employee's performance. They also describe performance areas that need improvement. Employees can use this information to change their job performance. Performance appraisal can also reward high performers with merit pay, recognition, and other rewards.

For example, PepsiCo uses performance appraisal to weed out the weak and nurture the strong. First, each boss is required to sit down with subordinates once a year and discuss performance. This appraisal pertains to what the manager did to make a big difference in the business, not whether he or she is a nice person. Second, managers then are divided into four categories. Those at the top are promoted. Those in the second group get challenging jobs. Those in the third category continue to be evaluated and rotated. Those in the bottom category are out.[37]

Generally, HRM professionals concentrate on two things to make performance appraisal a positive force in their organization: (1) the accurate assessment of performance through the development and application of assessment systems such as rating scales and (2) training managers to effectively use the performance appraisal interview so managers can provide feedback that will reinforce good performance and motivate employee development.

ASSESSING PERFORMANCE ACCURATELY.   To obtain an accurate performance rating, managers must acknowledge that jobs are multidimensional and performance thus may be multidimensional as well. For example, a sports broadcaster may perform well on the job-knowledge dimension; that is, she or he may be able to report facts and figures about the players and describe which rule applies when there is a questionable play on the field. But the same sports broadcaster may not perform as well on another dimension, such as communication. She or he may be unable to express the information in a colorful way that interests the audience or may interrupt the other broadcasters.

If performance is to be rated accurately, the performance appraisal form should require the rater—usually the supervisor—to assess each relevant performance dimension. A multidimensional form increases the usefulness of the performance appraisal for giving rewards and facilitates employee growth and development.

Although we would like to believe that every manager carefully assesses employees' performances, researchers have identified several rating problems.[38] For example, **halo error** occurs when an employee receives the same rating on all dimensions even if his or her performance is good on some dimensions and poor on others. **Homogeneity** occurs when a rater gives all employees a similar rating even if their performances are not equally good.

performance appraisal

The process of observing and evaluating an employee's performance, recording the assessment, and providing feedback to the employee.

halo error

A type of rating error that occurs when an employee receives the same rating on all dimensions regardless of his or her performance on individual ones.

homogeneity

A type of rating error that occurs when a rater gives all employees a similar rating regardless of their individual performances.

One approach to overcome management performance evaluation errors is to use a behavior-based rating technique, such as the behaviorally anchored rating scale. The **behaviorally anchored rating scale (BARS)** is developed from critical incidents pertaining to job performance. Each job performance scale is anchored with specific behavioral statements that describe varying degrees of performance. By relating employee performance to specific incidents, raters can more accurately evaluate an employee's performance.[39]

Exhibit 10.7 illustrates the BARS method for evaluating a production line supervisor. The production supervisor's job can be broken down into several dimensions, such as equipment maintenance, employee training, or work scheduling. A behaviorally anchored rating scale should be developed for each dimension. The dimension in Exhibit 10.7 is work scheduling. Good performance is represented by a 7, 8, or 9 on the scale and unacceptable performance as a 1, 2, or 3. If a production

behaviorally anchored rating scale (BARS)

A rating technique that relates an employee's performance to specific job-related incidents.

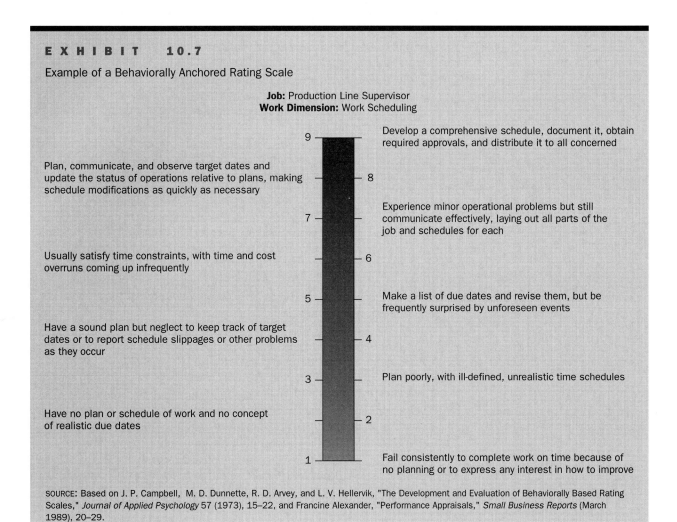

E X H I B I T   10.7

Example of a Behaviorally Anchored Rating Scale

Job: Production Line Supervisor
Work Dimension: Work Scheduling

9 — Develop a comprehensive schedule, document it, obtain required approvals, and distribute it to all concerned

Plan, communicate, and observe target dates and update the status of operations relative to plans, making schedule modifications as quickly as necessary — 8

7 — Experience minor operational problems but still communicate effectively, laying out all parts of the job and schedules for each

Usually satisfy time constraints, with time and cost overruns coming up infrequently — 6

5 — Make a list of due dates and revise them, but be frequently surprised by unforeseen events

Have a sound plan but neglect to keep track of target dates or to report schedule slippages or other problems as they occur — 4

3 — Plan poorly, with ill-defined, unrealistic time schedules

Have no plan or schedule of work and no concept of realistic due dates — 2

1 — Fail consistently to complete work on time because of no planning or to express any interest in how to improve

SOURCE: Based on J. P. Campbell, M. D. Dunnette, R. D. Arvey, and L. V. Hellervik, "The Development and Evaluation of Behaviorally Based Rating Scales," *Journal of Applied Psychology* 57 (1973), 15–22, and Francine Alexander, "Performance Appraisals," *Small Business Reports* (March 1989), 20–29.

supervisor's job has eight dimensions, the total performance evaluation will be the sum of the scores for each of eight scales.[40]

PERFORMANCE APPRAISAL INTERVIEW.   Most corporations provide formal feedback in the form of an annual **performance appraisal interview** with the employee. Too often, however, this meeting between boss and subordinate does not stimulate better job performance.[41] Managers may be unaware of the true causes of performance problems, because they have not carefully observed employee job activities. They may have a number of useful ideas for subordinates but present them in a threatening manner. As a result, employees may feel defensive and reject suggestions for improvement.

Research into the performance appraisal interview suggests a number of steps that will increase its effectiveness.[42]

1 Raters (usually supervisors) should be knowledgeable about the subordinates' jobs and performance levels.

2 Raters should welcome employee participation during the interview rather than "tell and sell" their views by lecturing to subordinates. This is particularly true when the employee is knowledgeable and accustomed to participating with the supervisor.

3 A flexible approach to feedback based on the characteristics of the subordinate, the job, and his or her performance level is useful. For example, newer employees need more frequent feedback than other employees do.

4 Training is used to help supervisors devise interview strategies for different situations. Role-playing that involves practice appraisal interviews is helpful for this purpose.

Performance feedback is more effective when it includes specific examples of good and bad performance. For example, "Your attendance record shows that you were here on time nearly every day this month, and this is a great improvement over last month" is more specific and helpful than "You seem to have a much better attitude these days about your work." Some experts suggest that managers keep diaries of employee performance so they will not have to rely on their memories to generate specific examples.

One of the most recent appraisal innovations is to involve peers in performance review. Companies such as General Electric, Public Service of New Mexico, and Raritan Steel have found that this *peer review* process dramatically increases openness, commitment, and trust within the organization and prevents problems that sometimes occur with a one-on-one interview. Managers learn that employees have good opinions about performance, and soliciting opinions from other employees provides a group approach to problem solving around important performance issues.[43] A few forward-looking companies are even experimenting with a bottom-up performance appraisal process in which subordinates provide a performance appraisal of their boss.

If done correctly, the appraisal process can lead to better performance. For example, Granite Rock uses its performance appraisal system as a springboard for comprehensive employee training and development, as the Leading Edge Box on p. 325 illustrates.

---

performance appraisal interview

A formal review of an employee's performance conducted between the superior and the subordinate.

GRANITE ROCK COMPANY

We know from Chapter 6 that Bruce Woolpert implemented a management system and strategy at Granite Rock to cope with evolving changes in the market. He also transformed the company into a learning organization to gain a competitive advantage. By implementing such a strategy, Woolpert brought back a single raw material: the company's human resources.

At Granite Rock, the Individual Professional Development Plan takes the place of standard job descriptions and performance reviews. Workers meet annually with supervisors and plot goals. These can include everything from skill development to job advancement. Both the company and employees gain an enhanced perspective from these exchanges. Managers get a clear picture of employee aspirations. The input from superiors, as well as advice and assistance about goal achievement, helps engender loyalty from subordinates. The appraisals are not just idle talk. Managers follow up by holding round-table sessions to discuss the best education

and training that will help workers achieve their goals.

This process has led to the establishment of the so-called Granite-rock University. Employees can sign up on company time for leadership instruction, statistical process controls, or a venue of some 50 different industry training courses. In a typical year, employees can attend speaking presentations on subjects ranging from improving quality and team effectiveness, to enhanced managerial methods and basic legal questions. Programs conducted by outside consultants, as well as technical presentations by company suppliers, are well-attended affairs. If a local college is the only place a particular course is offered, the company will pay for the tuition fees.

Two of the most important benefits of such company-wide training are improved responsiveness at the customer level, and a core competency that encourages initiative in the area of problem solving. Despite the fact that the company is unionized, many of the 400 employees at Granite Rock perform more than one job. Most are also members of one or more than 100 quality teams. In Woolpert's view, the time and place to correct problems is immediately,

and at the source. Automatic and systematic response mechanisms provide the method, and well-trained employees the means.

Woolpert has always taken training seriously. Workers spend 37 hours a year in training at an average cost of $1,697 per employee. This investment in work force training is substantial for a company the size of Granite Rock, but it may represent a bargain considering that poor quality workmanship, refunds, and lost customers can cost companies as much as 30 percent of sales.

Woolpert has instituted revolutionary changes across the board at Granite Rock. Transforming the company into a high-tech commodity manufacturer in a price-driven industry was a risky proposition. However, he recognized that fundamental changes must begin with a committed, educated work force. ■

SOURCE: "Staying a Stone's Throw Ahead of Competition," *Personnel Journal*, January 1994, 56; "The Change Masters," *INC.*, March 1992, 58–70; Edward O. Welles, "How're We Doing?" *INC.*, May 1991, 80–83; Bruce Nussbaum et al., "Corporate Refugees," *Business Week*, April 12, 1993, 58–65; company sources.

● MAINTAINING AN EFFECTIVE WORK FORCE

Now we turn to the topic of how managers and HRM professionals maintain a work force that has been recruited and developed. Maintenance of the current work force involves compensation, wage and salary structure, benefits, and occasional terminations.

COMPENSATION

The term **compensation** refers to (1) all monetary payments and (2) all goods or commodities used in lieu of money to reward employees.[44] An organization's compensation structure includes wages and/or salaries and benefits such as health insurance, paid vacations, or employee fitness centers. A company's compensation structure does not just happen. It is designed to fit company strategy and to provide compensation equity.

COMPENSATION STRATEGY.   Ideally, management's strategy for the organization should be a critical determinant of the features and operations of the pay system.[45] For example, managers may have the goal of maintaining or improving profitability or market share by stimulating employee performance. Thus, they should design and use a merit pay system rather than a system based on other criteria such as seniority. As another example, managers may have the goal of attracting and retaining desirable employees. Here they can use a pay survey to determine competitive wages in comparable companies and adjust pay rates to meet or exceed the going rates.

Pay-for-performance systems are becoming extremely popular in both large and small businesses, including Caterpillar, Aluminum Company of America, and au Bon Pain. These systems are usually designed as a form of profit sharing to reward employees when profitability goals are met. At Alcoa, payouts to employees equal 7 percent of each worker's salary. Caterpillar employees each received an $800 bonus, and Ford employees received an average $3,700 per employee. Employees have an incentive to make the company more efficient and profitable, because if goals are not met, no bonuses are paid. Jim Bernstein, CEO of General Health, Inc., a small business, promised all 30 employees they would get an extra month's pay if the company hit the sales target. Sales shot up, going far beyond the target, showing how powerful the correct incentive can be.[46]

COMPENSATION EQUITY.   Managers often wish to maintain a sense of fairness and equity within the pay structure and thereby fortify employee morale. **Job evaluation** refers to the process of determining the value or worth of jobs within an organization through an examination of job content. Job evaluation techniques enable managers to compare similar and dissimilar jobs and to determine internally equitable pay rates—that is, pay rates that employees believe are fair compared with those for other jobs in the organization. Managers also may want to provide income security so that their employees need not be overly concerned with the financial consequences of disability or retirement.

WAGE AND SALARY STRUCTURE

Large organizations typically employ HRM compensation specialists to establish and maintain a pay structure. They may also hire outside consultants, such as the Hay Group or PAQ (Position Analysis Questionnaire) Associates, whose pay systems have been adopted by many companies

---

■
compensation

Monetary payments (wages, salaries) and nonmonetary goods/commodities (fringe benefits, vacations) used to reward employees.

■
job evaluation

The process of determining the values of jobs within an organization through an examination of job content.

and government organizations. The majority of large public- and private-sector U.S. employers use some formal process of job evaluation.[47]

The most commonly used job evaluation system is the **point system.**[48] First, compensation specialists must ensure that job descriptions are complete, up to date, and accurate. Next, top managers select compensable job factors (such as skill, effort, and responsibility) and decide how each factor will be weighed in establishing job worth. These factors are described in a point manual, which is used to assign point values to each job. For example, the characteristic of "responsibility" could receive from 0 to 5 points depending on whether job responsibility is "routine work performed under close supervision" (0 points) or "complete discretion with errors having extreme consequences to the organization and public safety" (5 points).

The compensation specialist then compares each job factor in a given job description to that specified in the point manual. This process is repeated until the job has been evaluated on all factors. Then the compensation specialist evaluates a second job and repeats the process until all jobs have been evaluated.

The job evaluation process can establish an internal hierarchy of job worth. However, to determine competitive market pay rates, most organizations obtain one or more pay surveys. **Pay surveys** show what other organizations pay incumbents in jobs that match a sample of "key" jobs selected by the organization. Pay surveys are available from many sources, including consulting firms and the U.S. Bureau of Labor Statistics.

The compensation specialist then compares the survey pay rates for key jobs with their job evaluation points by plotting them on a graph as illustrated in Exhibit 10.8. The **pay-trend line** shows the relationship

point system

A job evaluation system that assigns a predetermined point value to each compensable job factor in order to determine the worth of a given job.

pay survey

A study of what other companies pay employees in jobs that correspond to a sample of key positions selected by the organization.

pay-trend line

A graph that shows the relationship between pay and total job point values for determining the worth of a given job.

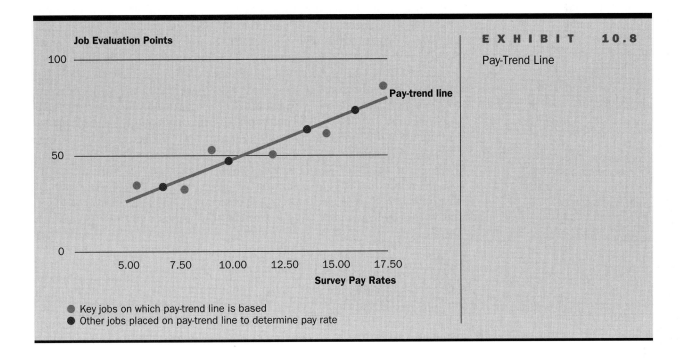

EXHIBIT 10.8

Pay-Trend Line

between pay and total point values. The compensation specialist can use the pay-trend line to determine the pay values of all jobs for which point values have been calculated. Ranges of pay for each job class are established, enabling a newcomer or lower performer to be paid less than other people in the same job class. The organization must then specify how individuals in the same job class can advance from the low to the high end of the range. For example, the organization can reward merit, seniority, or a combination of both.

BENEFITS

The wage and salary structure is an important part of the compensation package that maintains a productive work force, but equally important are the benefits offered by the organization. Benefits were once called "fringe" benefits, but this term is no longer accurate because they are now a central rather than peripheral part of the pay structure. A U.S. Chamber of Commerce survey has revealed that benefits in general compose more than one-third of labor costs and in some industries, nearly two-thirds.[49]

A major reason that benefits make up such a large portion of the compensation package is that health care costs have been increasing so quickly. Because employers frequently provide health care insurance as an employee benefit, these costs are important in the management of benefits. Between 1983 and 1993, annual corporate spending on health care tripled, to $225 billion.[50] Health benefit packages may change again during health care reform under President Clinton. As a result, many companies are reviewing health plans.

Organizations that want to provide cost-effective benefits should be sensitive to changes in employee life-styles. Several years ago, benefits were based on the assumption that the typical worker was a married man with a dependent wife and two school-age children. The benefits packages provided life insurance coverage for the worker, health insurance coverage for all family members, and no assistance with child care expenses. But today fewer than 10 percent of American workers fit the description of the so-called typical worker.[51] Increased work-force diversity means that far more workers are single; in addition, both spouses in most families are working. These workers are not likely to value the traditional benefits package. In response, some companies are establishing *cafeteria-plan benefits packages* that allow employees to select the benefits of greatest value to them.[52] Other companies use surveys to determine which combination of fixed benefits is most desirable. At Wabash National, executives decided employees could benefit most if a pay-for-performance system was applied to the company's retirement plan.

 WABASH NATIONAL

At the risk of trying to fix something that was not really broken, Lafayette, Indiana, trailer manufacturer Wabash National decided to improve on its employee 401(k) plan. Typically, an employer matches a percentage of what a worker elects to contribute to such a plan, at some fixed arbitrary rate. Wabash decided there was a better way.

Under its 401(k), if the company makes any gross profit, it matches workers' contributions up to 5 percent of their total salary at a rate of 30 cents on the dollar. Each one-quarter profit percentage increase beyond 5 percent earns a 1 percent increase in what the company will match for individual retirement funds. For example, if Wabash earns a 6 percent pre-tax profit, employees earn a 34 percent matching figure.

One obvious result of the Wabash approach is enhanced motivation for workers. The company also does a good job of making sure they understand the advantages of its plan. After becoming eligible, employees can expect a thorough briefing by the manager of the company fund. Family members can also attend. On average, just under six out of every ten employees participate in their company 401(k) plan. The story is different at Wabash, where more than 90 percent of employees are enrolled.[53] ■

TERMINATION

Despite the best efforts of line managers and HRM professionals, the organization will lose employees. Some will retire, others will depart voluntarily for other jobs, and still others will be forced out through mergers and cutbacks or for poor performance. The value of termination for maintaining an effective work force is twofold. First, employees who are poor performers can be dismissed. Productive employees often resent disruptive, low-performing employees who are allowed to stay with the company and receive pay and benefits comparable to theirs. Second, employers can use exit interviews. An **exit interview** is an interview conducted with departing employees to determine why they are leaving.[54] The value of the exit interview is to provide an excellent and inexpensive tool for learning about pockets of dissatisfaction within the organization and hence for reducing future turnover.

With so many companies experiencing downsizing through mergers or because of global competition, often a large number of managers and workers are terminated at the same time. In these cases, enlightened companies try to find a smooth transition for departing employees. For example, General Electric laid off 900 employees in three gradual steps. It also set up a reemployment center to assist employees in finding new jobs or in learning new skills. It provided counseling in how to write a resume and conduct a job search. An additional step General Electric took was to place an advertisement in local newspapers saying that these employees were available. By showing genuine concern in helping place laid-off employees, a company communicates the value of human resources and helps maintain a positive corporate culture.[55]

exit interview

An interview conducted with departing employees to determine the reasons for their termination.

SUMMARY AND MANAGEMENT SOLUTION

This chapter described several important points about human resource management in organizations. All managers are responsible for human resources, and most organizations have a human resource department that works with line managers to ensure a productive work force. The human resource department is responsible for interpreting and responding to the large human resource environment. The HR department must be part of the organization's competitive strategy, implement procedures to reflect federal and state legislation, and respond to trends in society. Within this context, the HR department tries to achieve three goals for the organization. The first goal of the human resource department is to attract an effective work force through human resource planning, recruiting, and employee selection. The second is to develop an effective work force. Newcomers are introduced to the organization and to their jobs through orientation and training programs. Moreover, employees are appraised through performance appraisal programs. The third goal is to maintain an effective work force. Human resource managers retain employees with wage and salary systems, benefits packages, and termination procedures.

Thomas Melohn, president of North American Tool & Die, used these ideas when he was faced with low profits, an unenthusiastic work force, a 7 percent customer reject rate of production, and 27 percent employee turnover. He attacked this problem by setting up systems to recruit and hire the best possible employees. First, he got the word out to generate a large pool of applicants, only 10 percent of whom made it to a formal interview. The interviews focused on finding people with the right values who could do quality work and fit the culture and strategy of North American. References were carefully checked, and a trial work period was used to see if the employee was compatible. These procedures took a great deal of time, but acquiring the right human resources has produced impressive results: employee turnover plummeted to less than 4 percent, the customer reject rate dropped below 0.1 percent, employees became enthusiastic, and profits increased 100 percent a year for seven years. Human resources have enabled this small company to beat well-heeled foreign competitors at price, quality, and delivery.[56]

DISCUSSION QUESTIONS

1. It is the year 2010. In your company, central planning has given way to front-line decision making and bureaucracy has given way to teamwork. Shop floor workers use computers and robots. There is a labor shortage for many job openings, and the few applicants lack skills to work in teams, make decisions, or use sophisticated technology. As vice-president of human resource management since 1990, what did you do to prepare for this problem?

2. If you were asked to advise a private company about its equal employment opportunity responsibilities, what two points would you emphasize as most important?

3. How can the human resource activities of planning, recruiting, performance appraisal, and compensation be related to corporate strategy?

4. Think back to your own job experience. What human resource management activities described in this chapter were performed for the job you filled? Which ones were absent?

5. Why are planning and forecasting necessary for human resource management? Discuss.
6. How "valid" do you think the information obtained from a personal interview versus a paper-and-pencil test versus an assessment center would be for predicting effective job performance for a college professor? An assembly-line worker in a team-oriented plant? Discuss.
7. What techniques can managers adopt to improve their recruiting and interviewing practices?
8. How does affirmative action differ from equal employment opportunity in recruiting and selection?
9. How can exit interviews be used to maintain an effective work force?
10. Describe the procedure used to build a wage and salary structure for an organization.

MANAGEMENT IN PRACTICE: ETHICAL DILEMMA

● FRATERNIZATION POLICY

Previous complications prompted Aeronautical Associates to write a human resource policy prohibiting married couples from working in the company, even in different departments.

Tom and Ginny were secretly married two years after Ginny was hired by the company. Although they worked in separate departments, cross-functional projects sometimes required professional cooperation between them. Tom and Ginny always maintained a professional relationship at work, making sure their performance was not hampered by their personal life.

After completion of an especially important project, Tom and Ginny's departments met informally to celebrate at a local restaurant. During the gathering, one of Tom and Ginny's friends from outside the company entered the restaurant by chance and unknowingly revealed their secret in front of several coworkers.

Monday morning, Tom came to see you, his supervisor, about an appropriate course of action.

● WHAT DO YOU DO?

1. Do nothing. Things have worked out okay, so do not make an issue of it.
2. Work toward keeping Tom and Ginny with the company but also seek mild punishment for them. Unpunished disregard of company policy would send a negative message to other employees.
3. Insist one of them leave the company. Tom and Ginny caused the problem by not being forthright.
4. Fight the policy. Champion Tom and Ginny's cause with upper management, because the company has no right to limit personal relationships.

CASE FOR ANALYSIS

CUNNINGHAM COMMUNICATION, INC.

Andrea Cunningham had reached the summit only to fall into the standard entrepreneurial trap. Her Santa Clara-based public relations firm had acquired some of Silicon Valley's best clients including Motorola, Hewlett-Packard, as well as formidable software manufacturers such as Borland International and Aldus Corporation. This business helped push revenues at Cunningham Communication, Inc., to $3 million annually. However, despite a staff of 24, Cunningham ran the operation virtually single-handedly. She had not delegated effectively, esprit de corps was nonexistent, and internecine warfare among her managers was rampant. The final quarter of 1989 threatened to be the first money-loser in company history, and Cunningham seriously considered throwing in the towel.

Since going out on her own, Cunningham's philosophy, by industry standards anyway, had been unique. Any PR firm could package and disseminate information; she thought it was just as important to keep clients apprised of how they were perceived by the market. This meant keeping tabs on the financial community, the press, consultants, customers, and even employees within the firm. It also placed a premium on selecting the right kind of employees, because the next step was by far the hardest. Clients had to have extreme confidence in the PR people in charge of their account because oftentimes those people were the bearers of unhappy tidings about operations, or at least how the general public regarded them. Not surprisingly, client turnover is high at most PR agencies. Employee job-hopping also is common, as PR representatives go from agency to agency in search of higher pay and new challenges.

Cunningham wanted to avoid the common pitfalls by maximizing customer satisfaction and employee output. However, her initial efforts were undercut by inherent human foibles. She tried assigning clients to individual teams, and giving bonuses on profitability. But, competition in the firm quickly turned ugly. Turf wars erupted, employees refused to share information, and cooperation disappeared. Cunningham Communications was in danger of imploding.

Working with her human resource manager and a host of others, Cunningham set out to devise a way to attract and keep the type of employees that would make up the firm she envisioned. They defined a career path within the company that helped eliminate turnover and elevated associates to a level of competence that inspired the confidence of clients. A goal-driven salary/bonus system was adopted, along with a cooperative management program called input teams, and a comprehensive training program. To the casual observer, the program got off to an uneven start at best. In the next six months all but three members of the senior staff were gone. "It was hard," says Cunningham, "but they weren't right for the company."

The goal-driven salary/bonus system allowed associates to select both their own salaries and the slate of responsibilities and objectives that accompanied it. Each associate met monthly with his or her own adviser to work out problems. According to Cunningham, employees rarely requested compensation out of line with their worth, and because of the frequent advisory sessions, most knew when they had failed to meet expectations and did not complain about withheld compensation. The feedback process also sharpened focus in situations that changed quickly, and was inherently cost-effective because associates could earn additional money only by generating more revenue.

The next part of Cunningham's plan was to establish input teams so that she could set company goals at the top and let everyone else execute them. Each team was presented with yearly objectives and assigned to devise the necessary plans and budgets to achieve them. Every employee was a member of at least one team, meeting five hours per week. Cunnigham believed the time was well spent. Everyone learned the tough trade-offs managers have to make, and what it takes to follow through. Team members knew they could influence company direction thereby engendering an egalitarian company spirit.

Cunningham decided no organizational makeover would succeed without training. New employees were taught everything from the company history to the 401(k) plan to what is called the Cunningham Culture. They were familiarized with the input teams, as well as the various company departments, and nearly everyone became a time-management adherent before they were through. Within six months new hires underwent a three-day, formal training session at what was known as CCI University. Less structured "town meeting" get-togethers allowed associates to air problems and devise solutions with fellow workers every other month.

Andrea Cunningham knew a lot about the PR business. But she finally realized she could not continue to do everything herself if she wanted her company to grow. The really hard part turned out to be defining a vision, and then giving her employees the method, means, and incentives to make it happen. Change was not easy, and she admits the company, which now has a work force of 59, is still feeling its way. At one of the company's annual update meetings, Cunningham summed up her views to employees: "Basically the management team of this company is just five regular people who know nothing more about running a company than any of you do. It's just that we spend more of our time doing it. We make a lot of mistakes; we do our experiments; we change things. We're not perfect," she said, adding that even more change will be necessary for the company to continue growing. "But, " she concludes, "it will be OK."

● Q U E S T I O N S

1. As Cunningham told her employees, the management team is not perfect. Evaluate the effectiveness of the firm's goal-driven salary/bonus system, input teams and training program. What are the strengths and weaknesses of the plan?
2. What else could Cunningham do to attract, develop, and maintain an effective work force?
3. Are the problems Cunningham faces typical of the challenges of human resource management? Why or why not?

SOURCE: Leslie Brokaw, "Playing for Keeps," *INC.*, May 1992, 30–41.

REFERENCES

1. Thomas Melohn, "Screening for the Best Employees," *INC.*, January 1987, 104–106.

2. R. Gustav Niebuhr, "Mass Shortage: Catholic Church Faces Crisis as Priests Quit and Recruiting Falls," *The Wall Street Journal*, November 13, 1990, A1, A13.

3. David E. Bowen and Edward E. Lawler III, "Total Quality-Oriented Human Resource Management," *Organizational Dynamics* (Spring 1992), 29–41.

4. D. Kneale, "Working at IBM: Intense Loyalty in a Rigid Culture," *The Wall Street Journal*, April 7, 1986, 17.

5. Cynthia D. Fisher, "Current and Recurrent Challenges in HRM," *Journal of Management* 15 (1989), 157–180.

6. Lloyd Baird and Iian Meshoulam, "Getting Payoff from Investment in Human Resource Management," *Business Horizons* (January–February 1992), 60–75; and Donna Brown, "HR: Survival Tool for the 1990s," *Management Review* (March 1991), 10–14.

7. Cynthia A. Lengnick-Hall and Mark L. Lengnick-Hall, "Strategic Human Resources Management: A Review of the Literature and a Proposed Typology," *Academy of Management Review* 13 (1988), 454–470; and "Human Resources Managers Aren't Corporate Nobodies Any More," *Business Week*, December 2, 1985, 58–59.

8. Steven H. Appelbaun, Roger Simpson, and Barbara T. Shapiro, "The Tough Test of Downsizing," *Organizational Dynamics* (Autumn 1987), 68–79.

9. Shawn Tully, "Can Boeing Reinvent Itself?" *Fortune*, March 8, 1993, 66–73.

10. Richard E. Walton and Gerald I. Susman, "People Policies for the New Machines," *Harvard Business Review* 87 (March–April 1987), 98–106; and Randall S. Schuler and Susan E. Jackson, "Linking Competitive Strategies with Human Resource Management Practices," *The Academy of Management Executive* 1 (1987), 207–219.

11. Deidre A. Depke, "Picking Up the Tab for Bias at Shoney's," *Business Week*, November 6, 1992, 50.

12. Robert L. Mathis and John H. Jackson, *Personnel/Human Resource Management* (St. Paul, Minn.: West, 1988); and Terry L. Leap and Michael D. Crino, *Personnel/Human Resource Management* (New York: Macmillan, 1989).

13. William E. Fulmer and Ann Wallace Casey, "Employment at Will: Options for Managers," *Academy of Management Executive* 4 (May 1990), 102–107; Aaron Bernstein, "More Dismissed Workers Are Telling It to the Judge," *Business Week*, October 17, 1988, 68–69; and Michael Goldblatt, "Preserving the Right to Fire," *Small Business Report* (December 1986), 87.

14. Jeffery E. Struve, "Making the Most of Temporary Workers," *Personnel Journal*, November 1991, 43–46.

15. Rod Willis, "Can American Unions Transform Themselves?" *Management Review* (February 1988), 12–21.

16. James G. March and Herbert A. Simon, *Organizations* (New York: Wiley, 1958).

17. Dennis J. Kravetz, *The Human Resources Revolution* (San Francisco, Calif.: Jossey-Bass, 1989).

18. D. Quinn Mills, "Planning with People in Mind," *Harvard Business Review* 63 (July–August 1985), 97–105; and USAir, *1985 Annual Report*, 5.

19. J. W. Boudreau and S. L. Rynes, "Role of Recruitment in Staffing Utility Analysis," *Journal of Applied Psychology* 70 (1985), 354–366.

20. Brian Dumaine, "The New Art of Hiring Smart," *Fortune,* August 17, 1987, 78–81.

21. P. Farish, "HRM Update: Referral Results," *Personnel Administrator* 31 (1986), 22.

22. J. P. Wanous, *Organizational Entry* (Reading, Mass.: Addison-Wesley, 1980).

23. Larry Reibstein, "Crushed Hopes: When a New Job Proves to Be Something Different," *The Wall Street Journal,* June 10, 1987, 25.

24. P. W. Thayer, "Somethings Old, Somethings New," *Personnel Psychology* 30 (1977), 513–524.

25. J. Ledvinka, *Federal Regulation of Personnel and Human Resource Management* (Boston: Kent, 1982); and Civil Rights Act, Title VII, 42 U.S.C. Section 2000e *et seq.* (1964).

26. The material in this section is largely drawn from R. D. Arvey and J. E. Campion, "The Employment Interview: A Summary and Review of Recent Research," *Personnel Psychology* 35 (1982), 281–322.

27. James M. Jenks and Brian L. B. Zevnik, "ABCs of Job Interviewing," *Harvard Business Review* (July–August 1989), 38–42.

28. A. Brown, "Employment Tests: Issues without Clear Answers," *Personnel Administrator* 30 (1985), 43–56.

29. Larry Reibstein, "More Firms Use Personality Tests for Entry-Level, Blue-Collar Jobs," *The Wall Street Journal,* January 16, 1986, 25.

30. Judson Gooding, "By Hand, By Jove," *Across the Board,* December 1991, 43–47.

31. "Assessment Centers: Identifying Leadership through Testing," *Small Business Report* (June 1987), 22–24; and W. C. Byham, "Assessment Centers for Spotting Future Managers," *Harvard Business Review* (July–August 1970), 150–167.

32. G. F. Dreher and P. R. Sackett, "Commentary: A Critical Look at Some Beliefs about Assessment Centers," in *Perspectives on Employee Staffing and Selection,* ed. G. F. Dreher and P. R. Sackett (Homewood, Ill.: Irwin, 1983), 258–265.

33. Bernard Keys and Joseph Wolfe, "Management Education and Development: Current Issues and Emerging Trends," *Journal of Management* 14 (1988), 205–229.

34. Michael Brody, "Helping Workers to Work Smarter," *Fortune,* June 8, 1987, 86–88.

35. Martha E. Mangelsdorf, "Ground-Zero Training," *INC.,* February 1993, 82–93.

36. Max Messmar, "Cross-Discipline Training: A Strategic Method to Do More with Less," *Management Review* (May 1992), 26–28; Robert Cournoyer, "Integrative Learning Speeds Teamwork," *Management Review* (December 1991), 43–44; and Christopher Power, "Coffee, Tea, and the Power of Positive Thinking," *Business Week,* July 31, 1989, 36.

37. Brian Dumaine, "Those Highflying PepsiCo Managers," *Fortune,* April 10, 1989, 78–86.

38. V. R. Buzzotta, "Improve Your Performance Appraisals," *Management Review* (August 1988), 40–43; and H. J. Bernardin and R. W. Beatty, *Performance Appraisal: Assessing Human Behavior at Work* (Boston: Kent, 1984).

39. Ibid.

40. Francine Alexander, "Performance Appraisals," *Small Business Reports* (March 1989), 20–29.

41. D. Cederblom, "The Performance Appraisal Interview: A Review, Implications, and Suggestions," *Academy of Management Review* 7 (1982), 219–227.

42. Buzzotta, "Improve Your Performance Appraisals," and Alexander, "Performance Appraisals."

43. Andrea Gabor, "Take This Job and Love It," *The New York Times,* January 26, 1992, F1, F6; and Steve Ventura and Eric Harvey, "Peer Review: Trusting Employees to Solve Problems," *Management Review* (January 1988), 48–51.

44. Henderson, *Compensation Management.*

45. Renée F. Broderick and George T. Milkovich, "Pay Planning, Organization Strategy, Structure and 'Fit': A Prescriptive Model of Pay" (Paper presented at the 45th Annual Meeting of the Academy of Management, San Diego, August 1985).

46. Michael Schroeder, "Watching the Bottom Line Instead of the Clock," *Business Week,* November 7, 1988, 134–136; and Bruce G. Posner, "You Get What You Pay For," *INC.,* September 1988, 91–92.

47. L. R. Burgess, *Wage and Salary Administration* (Columbus, Ohio: Merrill, 1984); and E. J. McCormick, *Job Analysis: Methods and Applications* (New York: AMACOM, 1979).

48. B. M. Bass and G. V. Barrett, *People, Work, and Organizations: An Introduction to Industrial and Organizational Psychology,* 2d ed. (Boston: Allyn & Bacon, 1981); and D. Doverspike, A. M. Carlisi, G. V. Barrett, and R. A. Alexander, "Generalizability Analysis of a Point-Method Job Evaluation Instrument," *Journal of Applied Psychology* 68 (1983), 476–483.

49. U.S. Chamber of Commerce, *Employee Benefits 1983* (Washington, D.C.: U.S. Chamber of Commerce, 1984).

50. Christopher Farrell, Paul Magnusson, and Wendy Zellner, "The Scary Math of New Hires," *Business Week,* February 22, 1993, 70–71.

51. J. A. Haslinger, "Flexible Compensation: Getting a Return on Benefit Dollars," *Personnel Administrator* 30 (1985), 39–46, 224.

52. Robert S. Catapano-Friedman, "Cafeteria Plans: New Menu for the '90s," *Management Review* (November 1991), 25–29.

53. "Not Just Your Ordinary 401(k)," *INC.,* November 1993, 128.

54. "Exit Interviews: An Overlooked Information Source," *Small Business Report* (July 1986), 52–55.

55. Rod Willis, "What's Happening to America's Middle Managers," *Management Review* (January 1987), 23–26; and Yvette Debow, "GE: Easing the Pain of Layoffs," *Management Review* (September 1987), 15–18.

56. Melohn, "Screening for the Best Employees."

MANAGING DIVERSE EMPLOYEES

11

CHAPTER OUTLINE

LEARNING OBJECTIVES

After studying this chapter, you should be able to

- Explain the dimensions of employee diversity and why ethnorelativism is the appropriate attitude for today's corporations.

- Discuss the changing workplace and the management activities required for a culturally diverse work force.

- Explain affirmative action and why factors such as the glass ceiling have kept it from being more successful.

- Describe how to change the corporate culture, structure, and policies and how to use diversity awareness training to meet the needs of diverse employees.

- Explain what people expect in organizations, including the addressing of issues such as invisible minorities and sexual harassment.

- Describe benefits that accrue to companies that value diversity and the cost to companies that ignore it.

The Kentucky Fried Chicken unit of PepsiCo, Inc., established its Designate program to attract seasoned executives from other companies, with special attention given to attracting and keeping female and minority-group members. The Designate philosophy is to bring in the best people but to choose diversity when two people are equally qualified. One such executive is Larry Drake, recruited from archrival Coca-Cola Co. While being recruited, Drake had genuine reservations about the program. He did not want to be hired as a "token." He did not want to generate resentment among white colleagues who wanted the job, and he did not want the affirmative action stigma of being hired because of race rather than talent. KFC executives had similar concerns and wanted to prevent a backlash from white employees seeking promotions for themselves.[1]

■ How do you feel about KFC's Designate program for recruiting minorities? Do you agree with Drake's concerns about accepting a job through the program? If you were a senior manager at KFC, how would you resolve the concerns of Drake and KFC executives?

KFC's Designate program represents the type of program many companies are undertaking to promote diversity in the workplace, including top management ranks. While KFC actively recruits women and minorities, backlash among white workers seeking promotions is reduced by hiring candidates who already have established solid careers and have a positive chemistry with the company. Drake, for example, was interviewed by many people at KFC to head off any problems.

The management of employee diversity entails recruiting, training, and fully utilizing workers who reflect the broad spectrum of society in all areas—gender, race, age, ethnicity, religion, disability, sexual orientation, education, and economic level.

Companies such as Honeywell, Procter & Gamble, and Mobil Oil all have established programs for increasing diversity. These programs teach current employees to value ethnic, racial, and gender differences, direct their recruiting efforts, and provide development training for females and minorities. These companies value diversity and are enforcing this value in day-to-day recruitment and promotion decisions.

Companies are beginning to reflect the U.S. image as a melting pot, but with a difference. In the past, the United States was a place where people of different national origins, ethnicities, races, and religions came together and blended to resemble one another. The U.S. melting pot attracted immigrants from Ireland following the famine in the mid-1800s, and immigrants came later from Poland, Russia, and Italy to work in railroads, mines, and factories. Opportunities for advancement were limited to those workers who fit easily into the mainstream of the larger culture. Some immigrants chose desperate measures to fit in, such as abandoning their native language, changing their last name, and sacrificing their own unique cultures. In essence, everyone in workplace organizations was encouraged to share similar beliefs, values, and life-styles despite differences in gender, race, and ethnicity.[2]

Now organizations such as KFC recognize that everyone is not the same and that the differences people bring to the workplace are valuable.[3] Rather than expecting all employees to adopt similar attitudes and values, companies are learning that these differences enable them to compete globally and to acquire rich sources of new talent. Although diversity in North America has been a reality for many years, genuine efforts to accept and *manage* diverse people are a phenomenon of the 1990s.

This chapter introduces the topic of diversity, its causes and consequences. Ways to deal with work-force diversity are discussed, and organizational responses to diversity are explored. The negative consequences of ignoring diversity in today's world are identified, and the benefits of successfully maintaining a diverse work force are discussed.

● VALUING DIVERSITY

A Digital Equipment Corporation factory near Boston produces keyboards for Digital's computers. The factory employs 350 people, who come from 44 countries and speak 19 languages. When plant managers issue written announcements, they are printed in English, French, Spanish, Chinese, Portuguese, Vietnamese, and Haitian Creole.[4] This astonishing diversity is becoming typical in many companies.

Most managers, from any ethnic background, are ill-prepared to handle these multicultural differences. Many Americans attended segregated schools, lived in racially unmixed neighborhoods, and were unexposed to people substantially different from themselves.[5] A typical manager, schooled in traditional management training, easily could make the following mistakes.[6]

- Delighted with the new technique developed by a Native American employee, a manager rewarded her with great fanfare and congratulations in front of her peers. The employee was humiliated and didn't return to work for three weeks.

- A manager, having learned that a friendly pat on the arm or back would make workers feel good, took every chance to touch his subordinates. His Asian employees hated being touched, and thus started avoiding him, and several asked for transfers.

- A manager declined a gift offered by a new employee, an immigrant who wanted to show gratitude for her job. He was concerned about ethics and explained the company's policy about not accepting gifts. The employee was so insulted she quit.

- Hoping to head off problems with new equipment, a production supervisor asked his Filipino staff to alert him to difficulties with new equipment. They responded by using masking tape and other makeshift remedies to get the machines working without telling him.

These issues related to cultural diversity are difficult and real. But before discussing how companies handle them, let's define *diversity* and explore people's attitudes toward it.

Consumers Gas, Canada's largest natural gas distribution utility, is committed to diversity, and it is demonstrated by a long-term program that includes in-house surveys to determine cultural diversity, and efforts to attract a diverse work force through an aggressive ad campaign. Here, some of the CG employees representing 22 countries celebrate cultural diversity at CG's 1992 Consumers Caravan.

work-force diversity

Hiring people with different human qualities who belong to various cultural groups.

DIMENSIONS OF DIVERSITY

Work-force diversity means the hiring and inclusion of people with different human qualities or who belong to various cultural groups. From the perspective of individuals, diversity means including people different from themselves along dimensions such as age, ethnicity, gender, or race.

Several important dimensions of diversity are illustrated in Exhibit 11.1. The inner circle represents primary dimensions of diversity, which include inborn differences or differences that have ongoing impact throughout one's life.[7] These are age, ethnicity, gender, physical abilities, race, and sexual orientation. These dimensions are core elements through which people shape their self-image and world view.

Secondary dimensions of diversity, illustrated in the outer ring of Exhibit 11.1, can be acquired or changed throughout one's lifetime. These dimensions tend to have less impact than those of the core but nevertheless have impact on a person's self-definition and world view. For example, Vietnam veterans may be perceived differently from other people and may have been profoundly affected by their military experience.

E X H I B I T   11.1

Primary and Secondary Dimensions of Diversity

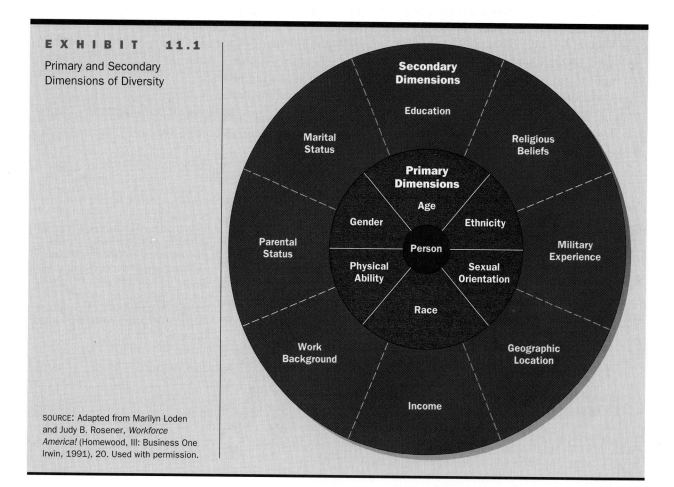

SOURCE: Adapted from Marilyn Loden and Judy B. Rosener, *Workforce America!* (Homewood, Ill: Business One Irwin, 1991), 20. Used with permission.

Married people may be perceived differently and have somewhat different attitudes from people who are single. Likewise, work experience, education, and geographic location add dimensions to the way people define themselves and are defined by others.

A 55-year-old white male, an M.B.A. from Harvard and the father of two grown children, who is vice-president of a Fortune 500 company, may be perceived very differently from a female clerical worker, age 25, who is a single mother of two children and is attending evening classes to earn a college degree. Based on this information, can you predict the personal priorities and career expectations each person may have of the organization? The challenge for companies today is to recognize these differences and to value and use the unique strengths each person brings to the workplace.[8]

ATTITUDES TOWARD DIVERSITY

Valuing diversity by welcoming, recognizing, and cultivating differences among people so they can develop their unique talents and be effective organizational members is difficult to achieve. **Ethnocentrism** is the belief that one's own group and subculture are inherently superior to other groups and cultures. Ethnocentrism makes it difficult to value diversity. Viewing one's own culture as the best culture is a natural tendency among most people.[9] Moreover, the business world tends to reflect the values, behaviors, and assumptions based on the experiences of a rather homogeneous, white, middle-class, male work force.[10] Indeed, most theories of management presume that workers share similar values, beliefs, motivations, and attitudes about work and life in general. These theories presume there is one set of behaviors that best help an organization to be productive and effective and therefore should be adopted by all employees.[11] This one-best-way approach explains why a male manager may cause a problem by touching Asian employees or not knowing how to handle a gift from an immigrant.

Ethnocentric viewpoints and a standard set of cultural practices produce a **monoculture,** a culture that accepts only one way of doing things and one set of values and beliefs. Exhibit 11.2 illustrates the assumptions that produce a monoculture and the type of monoculture that exists in many U.S. organizations. The assumption that people who are different are somehow deficient hampers efforts to take advantage of unique talents and abilities. Assumptions that diversity threatens smooth organizational functioning, that people who complain are oversensitive, or that people should not call attention to differences all support the status quo. These assumptions discourage analysis of organizational subcultures and allow managers to ignore the changes occurring in the workplace. These assumptions create a dilemma for women, blacks, gays, immigrants, physically disabled, and other culturally diverse people who are expected to behave like members of the dominant group.

These assumptions of equality as sameness typically produce an "ideal" employee, qualities of which are listed in the center of Exhibit 11.2. When qualities such as being married, competitive, and Protestant become the norm for everyone, many people feel as if they do not fit

ethnocentrism

The belief that one's own group or subculture is inherently superior to other groups or cultures.

monoculture

A culture that accepts only one way of doing things and one set of values and beliefs.

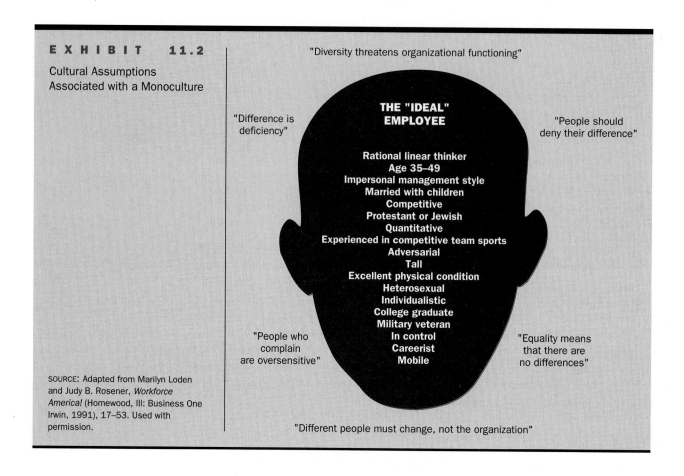

"Diversity threatens organizational functioning"

"Difference is
deficiency"

**THE "IDEAL"
EMPLOYEE**

"People should
deny their difference"

Rational linear thinker
Age 35–49
Impersonal management style
Married with children
Competitive
Protestant or Jewish
Quantitative
Experienced in competitive team sports
Adversarial
Tall
Excellent physical condition
Heterosexual
Individualistic
College graduate
Military veteran
In control
Careerist
Mobile

"People who
complain
are oversensitive"

"Equality means
that there are
no differences"

"Different people must change, not the organization"

SOURCE: Adapted from Marilyn Loden
and Judy B. Rosener, *Workforce
America!* (Homewood, III: Business One
Irwin, 1991), 17–53. Used with
permission.

ethnorelativism

The belief that groups and subcultures
are inherently equal.

pluralism

The organization accommodates several
subcultures, including employees who
would otherwise feel isolated and
ignored.

into the organization. Diverse employees may feel undue pressure to conform, may be the victims of stereotyping attitudes, and may be presumed guilty because they are deficient. White males who typically fit the notions of an ideal employee often see themselves as quite diverse but are perceived by others to be homogeneous; such stereotyped ideas leave little room for people of color, gay men, women, the elderly, and others who do not fit the image of the ideal employee.

The goal for organizations seeking cultural diversity is pluralism rather than a monoculture, ethnorelativism rather than ethnocentrism. **Ethnorelativism** is the belief that groups and subcultures are inherently equal. **Pluralism** means that an organization accommodates several subcultures. Movement toward pluralism seeks to fully integrate into the organization the employees who otherwise would feel isolated and ignored. As the work force changes, organizations will come to resemble a global village.

Most organizations must undertake conscious efforts to shift from a monoculture perspective to one of pluralism. Employees in a monoculture may not be aware of culture differences, or they may have acquired negative stereotypes toward other cultural values and assume that their own culture is superior. Through effective training, employees can be helped to accept different ways of thinking and behaving, the first step away from narrow, ethnocentric thinking. Ultimately, employees are able to integrate diverse cultures, which means that judgments of appropriateness, goodness, badness, and morality are no longer applied to cultural differences. Cultural differences are experienced as essential, natural, and joyful, enabling an organization to enjoy true pluralism and take advantage of diverse human resources.[12]

For example, Avon has the expressed goal of breaking out of its monoculture thinking about appropriate salespeople and customers in order to accept employees from multiple cultures. Avon has implemented training courses through which top management and other employees learn how to make this transition. By helping employees develop greater sensitivity and acceptance of cultural difference, Avon moves away from an ethnocentric attitude and is able to accept and integrate people from diverse cultural backgrounds.

● THE CHANGING WORKPLACE

The importance of cultural diversity and employee attitudes that welcome cultural differences will result from the inevitable changes taking place in the workplace, in our society, and in the economic environment. These changes include globalization and the changing work force.[13] Earlier chapters described the impact of global competition on business in North America. Competition is intense. About 70 percent of all U.S. businesses are engaged directly in competition with companies overseas. Companies that succeed in this environment need to adopt radical new ways of doing business, with sensitivity toward the needs of different cultural practices. For example, approximately 18 car companies, especially those from Japan and Germany, have established

Umanoff & Parsons, a New York bakery and catering firm, has created a diverse management team of loyal, dedicated workers such as the group pictured here. Umanoff & Parsons illustrates ethnorelativism and pluralism by going beyond the traditional job pool of white male candidates and embracing women, minorities, and immigrants.

design centers in Los Angeles. Southern California is viewed as a melting pot, an Anglo-Afro-Latino-Asian ethnic mix. Companies that need to sell cars all over the world love the diverse values in this multicultural proving ground.[14]

Other companies such as 3M and Hewlett-Packard built plants overseas in places such as Bangalore, India, or Guadalajara, Mexico, not only to obtain inexpensive labor but also to develop a presence in rapidly growing markets. The international diversity must be integrated into the overall company to allow it to work effectively.[15]

The single biggest challenge facing companies is the changing composition of the work force. The average worker is older now, and many more women, people of color, and immigrants are entering the work force. Indeed, white males, the majority of workers in the past, compose less than half of the work force, and white, native-born males are expected to contribute only 15 percent of new entrants to the work force through the year 2000.[16]

Exhibit 11.3 illustrates the management activities required for dealing with a culturally diverse work force. For example, consider the increased career involvement of women. By the year 2000, it is estimated that 61 percent of the women in the United States will be employed, constituting 47 percent of the work force, almost equaling the percentage of male workers.[17] This change represents an enormous opportunity to organizations, but it also means that organizations must deal with issues such as work-family conflicts, dual-career couples, and sexual harassment. Since seven of ten women in the labor force have children, organizations should prepare to take more of the responsibility for child care.

Moreover, can human resource management systems operate bias-free, dropping the perception of a middle-age white male as the ideal employee? People of African, Asian, and Hispanic descent make up 21 percent of the American population today, and that figure will grow to 25 percent in ten years. Already more than 30 percent of New York City's residents are foreign born. Miami is two-thirds Hispanic-American; Detroit is two-thirds African-American; San Francisco is one-third Asian-American.[18] Organizations must face the issues of dealing with race, ethnicity, and nationality without bias in order to provide a prejudice-free workplace.

Top managers can help shape organizational values and employee mindsets about cultural differences. Moreover, educational programs can promote knowledge and acceptance of diverse cultures and educate management on valuing these differences. As yet another example of the urgent need for valuing and managing diversity, an increasing number of immigrants are entering North America. In previous generations, most foreign-born immigrants came from Western Europe. Now more than 84 percent come from Asia and Latin America.[19] Immigrants come to the United States with a wide range of backgrounds, often without adequate skill in using English. They need sufficient educational programs to acquire the technical and customer service skills required in a service economy. Much of this training will be provided by corporations.

Companies that recognize these management requirements not only are accepting diversity but also are teaching employees to value it. Kinney Shoes is one leader in this area.

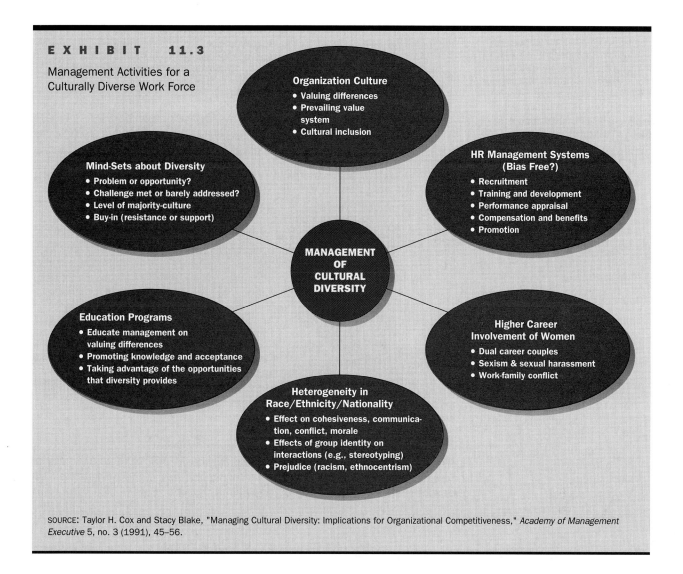

EXHIBIT 11.3

Management Activities for a Culturally Diverse Work Force

Organization Culture
- Valuing differences
- Prevailing value system
- Cultural inclusion

HR Management Systems (Bias Free?)
- Recruitment
- Training and development
- Performance appraisal
- Compensation and benefits
- Promotion

Mind-Sets about Diversity
- Problem or opportunity?
- Challenge met or barely addressed?
- Level of majority-culture
- Buy-in (resistance or support)

MANAGEMENT OF CULTURAL DIVERSITY

Education Programs
- Educate management on valuing differences
- Promoting knowledge and acceptance
- Taking advantage of the opportunities that diversity provides

Higher Career Involvement of Women
- Dual career couples
- Sexism & sexual harassment
- Work-family conflict

Heterogeneity in Race/Ethnicity/Nationality
- Effect on cohesiveness, communication, conflict, morale
- Effects of group identity on interactions (e.g., stereotyping)
- Prejudice (racism, ethnocentrism)

SOURCE: Taylor H. Cox and Stacy Blake, "Managing Cultural Diversity: Implications for Organizational Competitiveness," *Academy of Management Executive* 5, no. 3 (1991), 45–56.

 KINNEY SHOES

Top managers at Kinney Shoes recognize that the company's customer base is diverse and that its retail employees should reflect that diversity. An education program has been implemented to ensure that the hiring practices of store managers will enable women and minorities to enter the corporation in numbers that reflect the customer base. John Kozlouski, senior vice-president of human resources, says this is not a question of numbers but of teaching people to value ethnic, racial, and gender differences as the right thing to do. Executives and store managers attend a diversity training program that encourages people to face their own stereotypes and prejudices and to recognize that many assumptions they make about groups of people are erroneous.

As one example, some store managers mistakenly interpreted an accent, in particular a Spanish accent, as evidence of low intelligence.

Stockton Record president Orage Quarles III (second from right) shaped organizational values for the California newspaper. Believing the work force should reflect the community composed of 57 percent white and 43 percent minorities, Quarles recruits diverse employees and insists that diversity extend to the top leadership of the company.

Indeed, accents are not reflections of ability or lack of it, and Kinney's program helped store managers to recognize that limited English skills do not mean a person cannot sell shoes.[20] ∎

● AFFIRMATIVE ACTION

Since 1964, civil legislation has prohibited discrimination in hiring based on race, religion, sex, or national origin. As described in Chapter 10 of the text, these policies were designed to facilitate recruitment, retention, and promotion of minorities and women. To some extent, these policies have been successful, opening organization doors to women and minorities. However, despite the job opportunities, women and minorities have not succeeded in getting into top management posts. The reasons are associated with shortcomings in the affirmative action approach.

AFFIRMATIVE ACTION—LIMITED SUCCESS

Affirmative action was developed in response to conditions 30 years ago. Adult white males dominated the work force, and economic conditions were stable and improving. Because of widespread prejudice and discrimination, legal and social coercion were necessary to allow women, people of color, immigrants, and other minorities to become part of the economic system.[21]

Today, the situation has changed. More than half the U.S. work force consists of women and minorities; the economic situation is changing rapidly, as a result of international competition.

Within this fluid situation, many companies actively recruited women and minorities to comply with affirmative action guidelines. Companies often succeeded in identifying a few select individuals who were recruited, trained, and given special consideration. These people carried great expectations and pressure. They were highly visible role models for the newly recruited groups. It was generally expected that these individuals would march right to the top of the corporate ladder.

Within a few years, it became clear that few of these people would reach the top. Management typically was frustrated and upset because of the money poured into the affirmative action programs. The individuals were disillusioned about how difficult it was to achieve and felt frustrated and alienated. Managers were unhappy with the program failures and may have doubted the qualifications of people they recruited. Did they deserve the jobs at all? Were women and minority candidates to blame for the failure of the affirmative action program?

The cycle may begin again with additional women, people of color, and immigrants brought into the system dominated by white, male, native-born individuals who compose a homogeneous culture. The burden of adaptation once again is placed on the candidates coming through the system rather than on the organization itself. The affirmative action cycle may fail repeatedly, with part of the reason attributed to what is called the *glass ceiling*.

THE GLASS CEILING

The **glass ceiling** is an invisible barrier that separates women and minorities from top management positions. They can look up through the ceiling and see top management, but prevailing attitudes are invisible obstacles to their own advancement. A recent study suggested the additional existence of "glass walls," which serve as invisible barriers to important lateral movement within the organization. Glass walls bar experience in areas such as line supervisor positions that would enable women and minorities to advance vertically.[22]

Evidence of the glass ceiling is the distribution of women and minorities where they are clustered at the bottom levels of the corporate hierarchy. Only 2 percent of top executives in the United States are women, and only 9 percent of all managers are minorities.[23] Women and minorities also earn substantially less. Black employees earn only 10 to 26 percent of what their white counterparts earn, even when educational backgrounds are similar. Women earn considerably less than their male peers, and the gap widens as they move up the corporate hierarchy. At the level of vice-president, a woman's average salary is 42 percent less than her male counterpart.

Why does the glass ceiling persist? The monoculture at top levels is the most frequent explanation. Top-level corporate culture evolves

glass ceiling

Invisible barrier that separates women and minorities from top management positions.

around white American males, who tend to hire and promote people who look, act, and think like them. Compatibility in thought and behavior plays an important role at higher levels of organizations.[24] Of the people moving up the corporate ladder, white men tend to be more compatible with those already at the top.

Another reason for the persistent glass ceiling is the relegation of women and minorities to less visible positions and projects so that their work fails to come to the attention of top executives. Stereotyping by male middle managers may lead to the assumption that a woman's family life will interfere with her work or that minorities lack competence for important assignments. Women and minorities often believe that they must work harder and perform at higher levels than their white male counterparts in order to be noticed, recognized, fully accepted, and promoted. Women and minorities also may believe that they, not the culture of the organization, carry the burden of change.

CURRENT DEBATES ABOUT AFFIRMATIVE ACTION

In recent years, Washington has sent mixed messages to women and minorities. President Bush's firm "no quotas" position stood in sharp contrast to the passage of the 1990 Americans with Disabilities Act, or the 1991 Civil Rights Act. Each issue stirred debate about cultural bias versus increasing government interference with business.

A hotly debated diversity issue at present is homosexuals in the workplace. Recent debate has focused upon the inclusion of gays in the military. The Supreme Court ordered the return of an admitted gay naval petty officer to his military duties, and President Clinton voiced support for a policy that would allow gays to serve in the military. Incidents of "gay bashing" have been reported, indicating the extreme responses of some people to this issue.[25]

Most gay men and lesbians believe that they are asked to check their private lives at the door of their company. Thus, they feel isolated and afraid, believing they will be victims of hostility and discrimination on the basis of sexual orientation. Many gays fabricate heterosexual identities. One man, a successful manager at a direct-marketing company, lost his mentor when his own homosexuality was revealed. Another man, who makes several hundred thousand dollars a year buying and selling commodities, says that his fellow traders would destroy him if they knew he is gay. Apple and Digital Equipment were among the first companies to encourage gay employee groups to form support networks. Homosexual employees at AT&T, Coors, and Sun Microsystems have formed groups to lobby top management on issues important to them. Slowly these companies are learning to accept diversity that includes sexual orientation.[26]

Ultimately, the problem with affirmative action boils down to an unspoken and often unintended sexism and racism in organizations. Top managers find it hard to understand just how white and male their corporate culture is, and how forbidding it seems to those who obviously are different.[27] Racism and sexism often take the form of subtle exclusiveness whereby women and minorities are not able to establish relationships that enable them to learn, move up, and succeed in an organization. Their ideas may not be taken as seriously as those of a white man. A typical situation is that of a committee meeting, with several white male managers and one white woman manager sitting around a conference table. The woman offers a suggestion that is ignored. Ten minutes later a man makes the same suggestion and it readily is discussed and accepted. Typically, the men are not even aware that they have discriminated.

● NEW RESPONSES TO CULTURAL DIVERSITY

Affirmative action opened the doors of organizations in this country to women and minorities. However, the path toward promotion to top ranks has remained closed for the most part, with many women and minorities hitting the glass ceiling.[28] Recognizing this, the federal government responded with the Civil Rights Act of 1991 to amend and strengthen the Civil Rights Act of 1964 and to strengthen and improve federal civil rights laws. In particular, the 1991 act is designed "to provide appropriate remedies for intentional discrimination and unlawful harassment in the workplace," and "to expand the scope of relevant civil rights statutes in order to provide adequate protection of victims of discrimination." Affirmative action helps, but it is not enough. Companies are finding new ways to deal with the obstacles that prevent women and minorities from advancing to senior management positions in the future.

How can managers prepare their organizations to accommodate diversity in the future? One approach involves evaluating the value of diversity to an organization.[29] Questions such as those in Exhibit 11.4 can be used to examine beliefs and values about a diverse work force and should clarify a vision of the new workplace. Organization leaders and managers must come to terms with their own definitions of diversity and should be encouraged to think beyond race and gender issues to consider factors such as education, background, and personality differences.

Once a vision for a diverse workplace has been created and defined, the organization can analyze and assess the current culture and systems within the organization. This assessment is followed by a willingness to change the status quo in order to modify current systems and ways of thinking. Throughout this process, people need support in dealing with the many challenges and inevitable conflicts they will face. Training and support are important for the people in pioneering roles. Finally, managers should not de-emphasize affirmative action programs, because these are critical for giving minorities and women access to jobs in the organization.

Once managers truly accept the need for a program to develop a truly diverse workplace, action can begin. A program to implement such a change involves three major steps: (1) building a corporate culture that

EXHIBIT   11.4

Organizational Steps to Valuing Diversity

Why is valuing diversity good for this organization?

Compliance with the law
Community relations, social/ethical responsibility
Valuing diversity=competitive edge

What is my vision of a diverse work force?

Values women and minorities at all levels
Keeps people's identities intact
Is diverse and offers opportunity

What is my definition of diversity?

Race, gender, religion, ethnicity, age
Sexual orientation, background, education
"Differences" among people

What is the corporate culture in my organization?

Values (Who is important here?)
Myths (Who are the "heroes"?)
Norms (How should one act to get ahead?)
Can differences be accommodated?

What modifications do we make?

Change recruitment and promotion patterns
Develop new systems (mentoring, sponsorship, promotion)
Change the models of acceptable managerial behavior

What kind of support will people need?

Recognition that people are "pioneers"
Dealing constructively with conflict
Training and helping as people change

What can we do to help us value diversity?

Keep affirmative action programs, but move beyond
Keep the doors of the organization open
Open doors at higher levels in the organization

SOURCE: Adapted from Roosevelt Thomas, Jr., "From Affirmative Action to Affirming Diversity," *Harvard Business Review* 68, no. 2 (1990), 107–117.

values diversity; (2) changing structures, policies, and systems to support diversity; and (3) providing diversity awareness training. For each of these efforts to succeed, top management support is critical, as well as holding all managerial ranks accountable for increasing diversity. Stein & Company president Julia Stasch has shown just what a difference it can make if top management supports a high level of diversity.

STEIN & COMPANY

In America, all a businessperson has to do is produce high-quality goods at the lowest cost possible, stand behind the product, and stay on top of what customers want. Everyone has the same shot at success, or so the theory goes. In the construction business, however, that is not exactly true. Statistically, women make up only 2 percent of the industry, which does not sit well with Julia M. Stasch, president of Chicago's Stein & Company.

Using three times as many women as the industry average, Stein has completed $775 million worth of construction since 1990. Stasch made subcontractors meet her affirmative action standards. As a result, women received 7 percent of the workload at the Metcalfe Federal Building; 6 percent of the workers at the USG Building were women. "She does it because she believes it's fair and moral and right," says Chairman Richard Stein. "It's also good business."

Indeed it has been. Warranted or not, segments of the construction industry have a reputation for cynicism regarding minority hiring practices. At Stein & Company, word has equalled deed, and in the process, the company has become something of a standard bearer. It has also garnered some of the Windy City's prime building jobs. Stein will manage construction of Chicago's $750 million light-rail system and will oversee the $675 million addition to the city's McCormick Place convention center. Carmen P. Caldero was one of the officials who awarded the McCormick job to Stein. "We looked at what the developers had actually done versus what they were promising to do," Caldero says. "Stein & Company developed the model that others are emulating."[30] ∎

CHANGING THE CORPORATE CULTURE

For the most part, today's corporate cultures reflect the white male model of doing business. These cultures are not conducive to including women and minorities in important decision-making processes or enabling them to go high in the corporate hierarchy. The end result of this mismatch between the dominant culture and the growing employee population of minorities and women is that many employees' talents will be underutilized, and the corporation will be less competitive.

Chapters 4 and 9 describe approaches for changing corporate culture. Managers can start by actively using symbols for the new values, such as encouraging and celebrating the promotion of minorities. To promote positive change, executives must change their own assumptions and recognize that employee diversity is real, is good, and must be valued. Executives must lead the way in changing from a white male monoculture to a multiculture in which differences among people are valued.

To accomplish this, managers must be willing to examine the unwritten rules and assumptions. What are the myths about minorities? What are the values that exemplify the existing culture? Are unwritten rules communicated from one person to another in a way that excludes women and minorities? For example, many men may not discuss unwritten rules with women and minorities because they assume everyone is aware of them and they do not want to seem patronizing.[31]

Companies are addressing the issue of changing culture in a variety of ways. Some are using surveys, interviews, and focus groups to identify how the cultural values affect minorities and women. Others have set up structured networks of people of color, women, and other minority groups to explore the issues they face in the workplace, and to recommend changes to senior management.

Many companies have discovered that people will choose companies that are accepting, inviting, friendly, and that help them meet personal goals.[32] Successful companies carefully assess their cultures and make changes from the top down because the key to productivity is a loyal, trained, capable work force. New cultural values mean that the exclusionary practices of the past must come to an end.

CHANGING STRUCTURES AND POLICIES

Many policies within organizations originally were designed to fit the stereotypical male employee. Now leading companies are changing structures and policies to facilitate the recruitment and career advancement of diverse employee groups.

RECRUITMENT.   A good way to revitalize the recruiting process is for the company to examine employee demographics, the composition of the labor pool in the area, and the composition of the customer base. Managers then can work toward a work force composition that reflects the labor pool and the customer base. Moreover, the company can look at dimensions of diversity other than race and gender, including age, ethnicity, physical abilities, and sexual orientation.[33]

For many organizations, a new approach to recruitment will mean recruiting more effectively than today. This could mean making better use of formal recruiting strategies, internship programs to give people opportunities, and developing creative ways to draw upon previously unused labor markets.

CAREER ADVANCEMENT.   The successful advancement of diverse group members means that the organizations must find ways to eliminate the glass ceiling. One of the most successful structures to accomplish this is the mentoring relationship. A mentor is a higher ranking, senior organizational member who is committed to providing upward mobility and support to a protégé's professional career.[34] Mentoring provides minorities and women with direct training and inside information on the norms and expectations of the organization. A mentor also acts as a friend or counselor, enabling the employee to feel more confident and capable.

Research indicates that women and minorities are less likely than men to develop mentoring relationships.[35] In the workplace where people's backgrounds are diverse, forging these relationships may be more difficult. Women often do not seek mentors because they feel job competency is enough to succeed, or they may fear that initiating a mentoring relationship could be misunderstood as a romantic overture. Male mentors may feel uncomfortable with minority male protégés. Their backgrounds and interests may differ, leaving them with nothing but work in common. Male mentors may stereotype women as mothers, wives, or sisters rather than as executive material. The few minorities and women who have reached the upper ranks often are overwhelmed with mentoring requests from people like themselves, and they may feel uncomfortable in highly visible minority-minority or female-female mentoring relationships, which isolate them from the white male status quo.

The solution is for organizations to overcome some of the barriers to mentor relationships between white males and minorities. When organizations can institutionalize the value of white males actively seeking women and minority protégés, the benefits will mean that women and minorities will be steered into pivotal jobs and positions critical to advancement. Mentoring programs also are consistent with the Civil Rights Act of 1991 that requires the diversification of middle and upper management.

ACCOMMODATING SPECIAL NEEDS.   Many people have special needs of which male top managers are unaware. For example, if a number of people entering the organization at the lower level are single parents, the company can reassess job scheduling and opportunities for child care. If a substantial labor pool is non-English-speaking, training materials and information packets can be provided in another language. Trader Publications discovered that accommodating its multiethnic workers' special needs allowed it to better serve a diverse customer base.

 TRADER PUBLICATIONS

The skills required for managing a diverse workforce are not acquired overnight, and they usually do not come without commitment. Managers who overlook this requirement, never mind moral and legal pitfalls, will probably pay a big price in lost business.

Debi Kelly knows that better than anyone else. As human resource director for Trader Publications, she has two main objectives in overseeing the company's 230-person, multiethnic work force. First, she must see that everyone gets along and functions as a cohesive unit. Then she has to ensure that workers are prepared to relate to the needs of the company's San Diego customer base, which itself is growing more diverse each day. She has managed to handle problems and misunderstandings at Trader's through give-and-take meetings, or remedies as simple as hiring bilingual interpreters to serve as liaisons between management and ethnic groups.

With Hispanics, Asians, and African-Americans making up a large portion of Trader's clientele, it is only sensible to elevate ethnic employees to decision-making levels in order to identify niches and create new customers for the company's magazines, which feature classified ads for everything from cars to houses. This process means the elimination of the so-called "glass ceiling," or the artificial barriers that in the past have impeded nonwhite, female, or other minority workers from advancement to mid- or senior-level positions.[36] ■

Companies must also address changing family needs. The modern family may be a single parent home or one in which both parents work, which means that the company may provide structures to deal with child care, maternity or paternity leave, flexible work schedules, home-based employment, and perhaps part-time employment or seasonal hours that reflect the school year. The key to attracting and keeping elderly or disabled workers may include long-term care insurance and special health or life benefits. Alternative work scheduling also may be important for these groups of workers.

In the United States, racioethnic minorities and immigrants have fewer educational opportunities than most other groups. Many companies have started working with high schools to provide fundamental skills in literacy and arithmetic, or they provide these skills within the company to upgrade employees to appropriate educational levels. The movement toward increasing educational services for employees can be expected to increase for immigrants and the economically disadvantaged in the years to come.

DIVERSITY AWARENESS TRAINING

diversity awareness training

Special training designed to make people aware of their own prejudices and stereotypes.

Many organizations, including Monsanto, Xerox, and Mobil Oil, provide special training, called **diversity awareness training,** to help people become aware of their own cultural boundaries, their prejudices and stereotypes, so they can learn to work and live together. Working or living within a multicultural context requires a person to use interaction skills that transcend the skills typically effective when dealing with others from one's own in-group.[37] Diversity awareness programs help people learn how to handle conflict in a constructive manner, which tends to reduce stress and negative energy in diverse work teams.

A basic aim of awareness training is to help people recognize that hidden and overt biases direct their thinking about specific individuals and groups. If people can come away from a training session recognizing that they prejudge people and that this needs to be consciously addressed in communications with and treatment of others, an important goal of diversity awareness training has been reached.

Many diversity awareness programs used today are designed to help people of varying backgrounds communicate effectively with one another and to understand the language and context used in dealing with people from other groups. The point of this training is to help people be more flexible in their communications with others, to treat each person as an individual, and not to rely on stereotypes. Effective programs move people toward being open in their relationships with others. For example, if you were a part of such a program, it would help you develop an explicit awareness of your own cultural values, your own cultural boundaries, and your own cultural behaviors. Then you would be provided the same information about other groups, and you would be given the opportunity to learn about and communicate with people from other groups. One of the most important elements in diversity training is to bring together people of differing perspectives so that they can engage in learning new interpersonal communication skills with one another.

● DEFINING NEW RELATIONSHIPS IN ORGANIZATIONS

Men, women, people of color, whites, older people, younger people, the physically able, the physically disabled, and others are all struggling to define new ways of relating in the workplace. In the past, ways of relating to other groups were defined outside the workplace, in the family or community. The stereotypes and role expectations that define traditional ways of relating often did not allow these groups to develop their unique strengths at work. Diverse organizations have the potential to meet the wants of all groups, including "invisible" minorities, while fostering balanced priorities and psychological intimacy, and preventing sexual harassment.

WHAT PEOPLE WANT

People in all groups are struggling to identify how to relate to people who are different from themselves. Most employees genuinely want to learn how to handle work relationships without being affected by stereotypes and prejudices, and they are becoming more sensitive to what others need and want in work relationships.

Questions for understanding what people want and for avoiding stereotypes are illustrated in Exhibit 11.5. Men have needs as well as women, whites as well as blacks.[38] Exhibit 11.5 illustrates factors that would increase comfort levels in organizations and decrease tension among people of diverse backgrounds. Understanding what people want enables them to relate to one another with authenticity and acceptance. Understanding these needs helps managers respect and accept others on their own terms. Everyone, not just minorities, has needs and wants that can be met in a workplace that acknowledges and values diversity.

INVISIBLE MINORITIES

Considerable focus has been placed on the problems, rights, and working conditions of visible minorities—women, blacks, Asians, Hispanics, the aged, the disabled—but members of "invisible minorities" continue suffering prejudice, alienation, and isolation. **Invisible minorities** include individuals who share a social stigma that is not visibly recognizable.[39] Concerns about unmasking the stigma so that it becomes visible become the major social dynamic for these groups. We all have so-called skeletons in our closets, but the potential social stigma toward invisible minorities dominates their working and social relationships. For example, gays and lesbians, unwed parents, atheists, children of gays, family members of people with AIDS, and members of 12-step recovery programs for alcohol, drugs, or eating disorders often feel they must carefully guard their "real" lives. Members of invisible minorities wonder: "Should I tell?" "Whom should I tell?" "Will they find out?" "How will they react?"

As companies increasingly focus on diversity issues and establish programs dealing with various groups and subcultures, management can also develop an awareness of, and sensitivity to, the experiences of people in less visible minority groups.

invisible minorities

Individuals who share a social stigma that is not visibly recognizable.

BALANCING FAMILY PRIORITIES

With 8.7 million single moms and 1.4 million single dads in the work force, managers are discovering that family programs are no longer a luxury, but a necessity, for competitive companies. Many companies

EXHIBIT 11.5

Building a Multiculture: What Do People Want?

SOURCE: Adapted from Marilyn Loden and Judy B. Rosener, *Workforce America!* (Homewood, Ill: Business One Irwin, 1991), 76–78. Used with permission.

Younger and Older Employees Want

To have more respect for their life experiences
To be taken seriously
To be challenged by their organizations, not patronized

Women Want

To be recognized as equal contributors
To have active support of male colleagues
To have work and family issues actively addressed by organizations

Men Want

To have the same freedom to grow/feel that women have
To be perceived as allies, not the enemy
To bridge the gap with women at home and at work

People of Color Want

To be valued as unique individuals, as members of ethnically
   diverse groups, as people of different races, and as equal contributors
To establish more open, honest, working relationships with people of other races and
   ethnic groups
To have the active support of white people in fighting racism

White People Want

To have their ethnicity acknowledged
To reduce discomfort, confusion, and dishonesty in dealing with people of color
To build relationships with people of color based on common goals, concerns, and
   mutual respect for differences

Disabled People Want

To have greater acknowledgment of and focus on abilities, rather than on disabilities
To be challenged by colleagues and organizations to be the best
To be included, not isolated

Able-Bodied People Want

To develop more ease in dealing with physically disabled people
To give honest feedback and appropriate support without being patronizing or
   overprotective

Gay Men and Lesbians Want

To be recognized as whole human beings, not just sexual beings
To have equal employment protection
To have increased awareness among people regarding the impact of heterosexism in the
   workplace

Heterosexuals Want

To become more aware of lesbian and gay issues
To have a better understanding of the legal consequences of being gay in America
To increase dialogue about heterosexist issues with lesbians and gay men

have come to believe that successful family policies will increasingly attract and retain the most talented workers.[40]

Family-friendly companies such as Johnson & Johnson, Aetna, and AT&T have established a variety of programs—family-care leave, on-site day-care centers, health care for part-timers, flexible schedules, job-sharing, subsidies and grants for child care, work at home, and children's after-school or summer programs—to meet changing family needs and values. Despite the programs and policies of some companies, however, business in general has been unable to respond to family needs or to assist employees trying to balance work and family responsibilities. Family issues have become a topical corporate issue, but only a small percentage of businesses actually have strong family programs to address them. The pressure for developing these programs is mounting, but companies attempting to implement them should avoid acting precipitously. They must carefully analyze employee needs as well as company resources in responding to this pressure. One expert on work and family issues states that to be successful, family programs must be seen as a central part of the company's business mission.[41] As the Leading Edge box on Harbor Sweets, Inc., illustrates, even small businesses can find ways to successfully promote diversity while helping workers balance family priorities and their desire for job satisfaction.

EMOTIONAL INTIMACY

Another outcome of diversity is a greater incidence of close friendships between men and women in the workplace. Close relationships between men and women often have been discouraged in companies for fear that they would disrupt the balance of power and threaten organizational stability.[42] This opinion grew out of the assumption that organizations are designed for rationality and efficiency, which were best achieved in a nonemotional environment. Close relationships between men and women could become romantic or sexual in nature, upsetting the stable working relationships. The Focus on Ethics box discusses some ethical problems with office romances.

A recent study of friendships in organizations sheds interesting light on this issue.[43] Managers and workers responded to a survey about emotionally intimate relationships with both male and female coworkers. Many men and women reported having close relationships with an opposite-sex coworker. Called "nonromantic love relationships," the friendships resulted in trust, respect, constructive feedback, and support in achieving work goals. Intimate friendships did not necessarily become romantic, and they affected each person's job and career in a positive way. Rather than causing problems, nonromantic love relationships, according to the study, affected work teams in a positive manner because conflict was reduced. Indeed, men reported somewhat greater benefit than women from these relationships, perhaps because the men had fewer close relationships outside the workplace upon which to depend.

In any event, the evidence suggests that close psychological and emotional relationships between men and women at work are healthy and helpful. The challenge is for people to learn to cultivate these relationships and thus benefit themselves and their organizations.

SEXUAL HARASSMENT

While psychological closeness between men and women in the workplace may be a positive experience, sexual harassment is not. Sexual

LEADING edge   HARBOR SWEETS, INC.

Harbor Sweets seems to have defied all odds in becoming a $2.5 million company. As you read in Chapter 1, it did so by making the needs of its employees a company priority. At Harbor, diversity only begins to describe the work force. An employee might be a high school student trying to earn extra money, or one of the many immigrants from as far away as Laos, Turkey, or the Dominican Republic. Over half of the workers are physically or mentally challenged, elderly, students, mothers, or persons who speak English as a second language.

Diversity at Harbor is not limited to worker nationalities or physical capabilities. Company founder Benneville Strohecker is cognizant of the fact that candy making can become tedious even in the best of settings. To keep things interesting, employees are urged to perform different jobs. Most have performed a range of production functions, from combining ingredients and cooking the product, to wrapping and packaging it for delivery to the customer. Employees usually manage to work out scheduling among themselves. This form of on-the-job cross-training has the additional benefit of ensuring that necessary expertise will be on hand when needed. This can be critical since demand at Harbor Sweets is seasonal and layoffs frequent.

Another benefit of encouraging flexible schedules and part-time workers is the loyalty it engenders. Workers are eager to go the extra mile for a company that does the same for them, and in the process Strohecker enjoys the talents of employees who would otherwise be laid off if they were forced to adhere to conventional routines. To Strohecker's workers, their job is more than a mere paycheck. It is a family, and an ongoing commitment. "What I've learned is that these weird management ideas turned out to be damned good business," Strohecker says.

Strohecker's example of a diversified work force has impacted other U.S. companies. He has not only demonstrated that it can work, but has been at the forefront in urging companies to go even further, principally in dealing with AIDS in the work place. In 1988 he took one year off from Harbor to devote all his attention to making other CEOs aware of the issue of AIDS. With characteristic self-effacement, he says it might just take an old, heterosexual, white CEO to get the point across that AIDS is not just a gay or IV drug user problem. "It's our problem," Strohecker says, "and we need to provide leadership."

Strohecker certainly seems more altruistic than the average chief executive, but he's still a businessman. In the beginning, his company could not have taken off without allowing workers more than typical flexibility. He's stuck with it for more self-serving reasons: It's working.

■

SOURCE: Anne Driscoll, "Candy Man of the People," *The Boston Globe*, March 29, 1992, 1; Tracy E. Benson, "In Trust We Manage," *Industry Week*, March 4, 1991, 26–27; and Martha E. Mangelsdorf, "Managing the New Work Force," *INC.*, January 1990, 78–83; and company sources.

harassment is illegal. As a form of sexual discrimination, sexual harassment in the workplace is a violation of Title VII of the 1964 Civil Rights Act. Sexual harassment in the classroom is a violation of Title VIII of the Education Amendment of 1972. The following categorize various forms of sexual harassment:

■ *Generalized.* This form involves sexual remarks and actions that are not intended to lead to sexual activity but that are directed toward a coworker based solely on gender and reflect on the entire group.

■ *Inappropriate/Offensive.* Though not sexually threatening, it causes discomfort in a coworker, whose reaction in avoiding the harasser may limit his or her freedom and ability to function in the workplace.

OFFICE ROMANCE

These days when Cupid strikes a pose, arrow at the ready, many office workers run for cover. Whether it's a reaction to memories of the Clarence Thomas confirmation hearings, or lessons learned from infamous office liaisons reported in the press, many employees are thinking twice about answering love's call, and management is especially "arrow-shy."

Why? Office romance is an increasingly risky business. Although most companies have no policy forbidding employee dating, in today's changing business environment there is increased concern about conflicts of interest, sexual harassment, employee morale, and public perception. These concerns mean that while the majority of companies accept coworker dating among peers, an increasing number are reevaluating and formulating policies regarding boss-subordinate romantic relationships.

How should supervisor-subordinate affairs be handled? The romance seldom escapes the suspicions and gossip of other employees. More important, knowledge of an affair often undermines the business environment, monopolizes conversations, invites controversy and potential embarrassment, and damages company morale. Employees scrutinize the behavior and judgment of the supervisor, whose leadership and credibility may suffer irreparable damage. In today's business climate, a supervisor is more likely than in previous eras to suffer the consequences of an office affair.

An example is Standley H. Hoch, CEO of General Public Utilities Corp. of New Jersey. G.P.U. board members received an anonymous letter charging Hoch with conflict of interest, resulting from a long affair with Susan Schepman, G.P.U.'s recently hired vice-president of communications. The letter claimed Hoch awarded Schepman's previous employer, Fleishman-Hillard, Inc., a public relations contract without competitive bidding, and later hired Schepman and awarded her with a vice-presidency based on their relationship. A confrontation between Hoch and the board resulted in the CEO's resignation.

While such scenarios involving the supervisor are becoming more frequent, the subordinate generally suffers most from office affairs. The reasons vary, but the main reason stems from the fact that women are still more likely to be the subordinate in a supervisor-subordinate relationship. The bottom line is that women face a social double standard that more often punishes the woman involved in an affair. In addition, women who are attempting to break through the glass ceiling find that if they get involved in an office romance they face the age-old inference of office romance as a contributing factor in their success.

In addressing the issue of employee dating, only a few companies, such as Apple Computer and DuPont, have rules pertaining to boss-subordinate relationships. When such relationships develop, the typical solution is to transfer one of the parties involved. But as ethics issues take on greater significance in the corporate world, new policies can be expected to evolve. ■

SOURCE: Ellen Rapp, "Dangerous Liaisons," *Working Woman*, February 1992, 56–61; and Marilyn Moats Kennedy, "Romance in the Office," *Across the Board*, March 1992, 23–27.

- *Solicitation with Promise of Reward.* This action treads a fine line as an attempt to "purchase" sex, with the potential for criminal prosecution.
- *Coercion with Threat of Punishment.* The harasser coerces a coworker into sexual activity by using the threat of power (through recommendations, grades, promotions and so on) to jeopardize the victim's career.
- *Sexual Crimes and Misdemeanors.* The highest level of sexual harassment, these acts would, if reported to the police, be considered felony crimes and misdemeanors.[44]

The Anita Hill–Clarence Thomas hearings focused national attention on the problem of sexual harassment. Sexual harassment claims increased 50 percent in the months following the 1991 hearings.[45] Perhaps this focus on sexual harassment is responsible for the recent court cases that shifted the focus away from the harasser's *intentions* toward the *feelings* of the alleged victim.[46]

Women who are moving up the corporate hierarchy by entering male-dominated industries report a high frequency of harassment. Surveys report an increase in sexual harassment programs, but female employees also report a lack of prompt and just action by executives to incidents of sexual harassment. However, companies are discovering that "an ounce of prevention really is worth a pound of cure." Top executives are seeking to address problems of harassment through company diversity programs, revised complaint systems and grievance procedures, written policy statements, workshops, lectures, and role-playing exercises to increase employee sensitivity and awareness to the issue.[47]

● GLOBAL DIVERSITY

One of the most rapidly increasing sources of diversity in North American companies is globalization, which means hiring employees in many countries. Some estimate that by the year 2000, half of the world's assets will be controlled by multinational corporations.[48] Globalization means that companies must apply diversity management across a broader stage than North America. This means that managers must develop new skills and awareness to handle the unique challenges of global diversity: cross-cultural understanding, the ability to build networks, and the understanding of geopolitical forces. Two significant aspects of global diversity programs involve employee selection and training and the understanding of the communication context.

SELECTION AND TRAINING

expatriates

Employees who live and work in a country other than their own.

Expatriates are employees who live and work in a country other than their own. Careful screening, selection, and training of employees to serve overseas increase the potential for corporate global success. Human resource managers consider global skills in the selection process. In addition, expatriates receive cross-cultural training that develops language skills and cultural and historical orientation. Career-path counseling is often available.[49]

Equally important, however, is honest self-analysis by overseas candidates and their families. Before seeking or accepting an assignment in another country, a candidate should ask himself or herself questions such as the following:

- Is your spouse interrupting his or her own career path to support your career? Is that acceptable to both of you?

- Is family separation for long periods involved?

- Can you initiate social contacts in a foreign culture?

- Can you adjust well to different environments and changes in personal comfort or quality of living, such as the lack of television, gasoline at $5 per gallon, limited hot water, varied cuisine, national phone strikes, and *warm* beer?
- Can you manage your future reentry into the job market by networking and maintaining contacts in your home country?[50]

Employees working overseas must adjust to all of these conditions. Managers going global may find that their own management "style" needs adjustment to succeed in a foreign country. One aspect of this adjustment is learning the communication context of a foreign location.

COMMUNICATION CONTEXT

People from some cultures tend to pay more attention to the social context (social setting, nonverbal behavior, social status) of their verbal communication than Americans do. For example, General Norman Schwarzkopf soon realized that social context was of considerable importance to leaders of Saudi Arabia. During the initial buildup for the Persian Gulf War, he suppressed his own tendency toward impatience and devoted hours to "philosophizing" with members of the Saudi royal family. Schwarzkopf realized it was *their* way of making decisions.[51]

Exhibit 11.6 indicates how the emphasis on social context varies among countries. In a **high-context culture,** people are sensitive to circumstances surrounding social exchanges. People use communication primarily to build personal social relationships; meaning is derived from context—setting, status, nonverbal behavior—more than from explicit words; relationships and trust are more important than business; and the welfare and harmony of the group are valued. In a **low-context culture,** people use communication primarily to exchange facts and information, meaning is derived primarily from words, business transactions are more important than building relationships and trust, and individual welfare and achievement are more important than the group.[52]

To understand how differences in cultural context affect communications, consider the U.S. expression, "The squeaky wheel gets the oil." It

high-context culture

A culture in which communication is used to enhance personal relationships.

low-context culture

A culture in which communication is used to exchange facts and information.

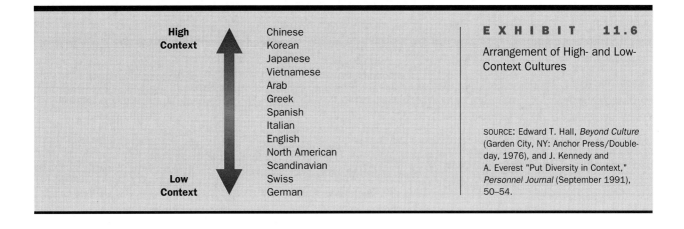

High Context	Chinese
Low Context	Korean
	Japanese
	Vietnamese
	Arab
	Greek
	Spanish
	Italian
	English
	North American
	Scandinavian
	Swiss
	German

E X H I B I T   11.6

Arrangement of High- and Low-Context Cultures

SOURCE: Edward T. Hall, *Beyond Culture* (Garden City, NY: Anchor Press/Doubleday, 1976), and J. Kennedy and A. Everest "Put Diversity in Context," *Personnel Journal* (September 1991), 50–54.

means that the loudest person will get the most attention, and attention is assumed to be favorable. Equivalent sayings in China and Japan are "Quacking ducks get shot" and "The nail that sticks up gets hammered down," respectively. Standing out as an individual in these cultures clearly merits unfavorable attention.

High-context cultures include Asian and Arab countries. Low-context cultures tend to be American and Northern European. Even within North America, cultural subgroups vary in the extent to which context counts, explaining why differences between groups make successful communication difficult. White females, Native Americans, and African-Americans all tend to prefer higher context communication than do white males. A high-context interaction requires more time because a relationship has to be developed, and trust and friendship must be established. Furthermore, most male managers and most people doing the hiring in organizations are from low-context cultures, which conflicts with people entering the organization from a background in a higher context culture. Overcoming these differences in communication is a major goal of diversity awareness training.

● BENEFITS AND COSTS OF DIVERSITY

As a general rule, organizations have not been highly successful in managing women and minorities, as evidenced by higher turnover rates, higher absenteeism, lower job satisfaction, and general frustration over career development for these groups. Moreover, the fact that women and minorities are clustered at lower organization levels indicates they are not progressing as far as they might and are not developing their full potential.[53] Thus, valuing diversity provides distinct benefits to organizations and ignoring diversity has specific costs, which are summarized in Exhibit 11.7.

BENEFITS OF VALUING DIVERSITY

Hal Burlingham, AT&T senior vice-president for human resources, said, "Valuing diversity is not only the right thing to do, it's the right busi-

EXHIBIT 11.7 Benefits and Costs from Diversity Issues	BENEFITS of Valuing Diversity	COSTS of Ignoring Diversity
	1. Increased opportunity to develop employee and organizational potential	1. Reduced individual and organizational productivity
	2. Enhanced recruiting and retention	2. Tarnished corporate image
	3. Successful interaction with clients/ marketplace	3. Substantial monetary cost
	4. Increased creativity and adaptation	

ness thing to do. Companies that do a good job of valuing and effectively managing diversity in the 1990s will have a competitive advantage over the ones that don't."[54] Paying attention to the diverse work force has become an economic imperative. There is no question that the work force is changing and that U.S. organizations have to change to reflect the new work force composition.

The first benefit of valuing diversity is the opportunity to develop employee and organizational potential. This means higher morale, because people feel valued for what they bring to the organization. It also produces better relationships at work, because people acquire the skills to recognize, understand, and accept cultural differences. Developing employee skills and valuing diversity have become a bottom-line business issue. If organizations do not welcome people who look and act differently from white males, then the organizations will not have enough people to do the job. As David Charms, president of Xerox Corporation, said, "American business will not be able to survive if we do not have a large, diverse work force, because those are the demographics, no choice. The company that gets out in front of managing diversity, in my opinion, will have a competitive edge."[55]

Second, companies that treat women and racioethnic minorities well will be able to recruit the best employees, both those new to the work force and experienced employees from other organizations. Retaining these employees means a qualified, trained work force for the future. Demographics tell us that the labor market is slowly tightening, and those organizations that boast a healthy environment for women and minorities will be in the best competitive position to attract and retain scarce employees.

Successful interaction between the client and the marketplace is the third benefit from diversity. A representational work force enables a company to understand better the needs of its clients. Culture plays an important part in determining the goods, entertainment, social services, and household products that people buy and use. Understanding how people live and what they need will help organizations adapt to changing consumer populations. This understanding comes in part from including representatives from that population in the work force.

Finally, organizations can expect enhanced creativity and adaptability from a diverse work force. Research has shown that diverse groups tend to be more creative than homogeneous groups, in part because people with diverse backgrounds bring different perspectives to problem solving. The presence of cultural and gender diversity in a group reduces the risk of "groupthink" when people contribute freely to a discussion.

Research also indicates that women and racioethnic minorities tend to have more flexible cognitive styles, thereby helping establish norms of flexible thinking. Moreover, the simple act of learning about other cultural practices enables organizations to expand their thinking about the world. Once employees increase flexibility in cultural thinking, it becomes easier for them to be flexible in their thinking about other things as well.

COSTS OF IGNORING DIVERSITY

The costs associated with high turnover and absenteeism are well understood. When organizations can adapt to the needs of a diverse work force, rather than expect the work force to adapt to the organization, absenteeism and turnover can be turned around and satisfaction increased.[56] The consequences of not valuing diversity include loss of productivity, a poor image for the organization, and the monetary cost of unhappy employees.

Reduced individual and organizational productivity occurs when women and minorities experience prejudice and nonacceptance. They feel unappreciated, do not expect to advance, and feel resentment that saps energy and productivity for the organization. People who feel excluded do not take risks for the organization, are less innovative, and are less aggressive in pressing their ideas or in assuming leadership. They will not voice disagreement, because they want to be accepted and included.

Second, a less obvious cost is the tarnished corporate image and reputation developed around employee dissatisfaction. If a corporation becomes known as one that alienates nontraditional employees, that corporation will have a hard time finding qualified workers and managers in a period of limited labor supply. Organizational reputation spreads quickly through informal networks in minority and female groups. Networks even can cause students to avoid certain organizations in campus interviews.

The third important cost is financial. A company loses all the money invested in recruiting and training when a dissatisfied employee leaves. One formula to help compute how much money is wasted when minorities and females are dissatisfied includes the fees for Equal Employment Opportunity disputes, costs of recruiting replacement employees, the wasted training for those who left, and the cost of additional training for those who stay.[57] The sum of these items indicates the amount of money a company wastes each year when diversity is not valued. For example, legal experts estimate that $25,000 is the minimum cost to open an EEO case, increasing to $100,000 if the case goes to trial, before damages or rewards. Or consider an organization with 10,000 employees, 35 percent of whom are likely to be women and minorities. If the turnover rate for these employees is double that of white males, and it costs $25,000 to recruit and train each person, an average annual savings of $3.5 million accrues from reducing their turnover rates to that of white males.

With the anticipated tight job market, corporations that want to be successful must embrace diversity. A number of innovative companies are already responding. Apple Computer appointed a multicultural and affirmative action manager, Avon established a cultural network, and Corning provides minority job rotation for expanded job experience and better promotion opportunities. DuPont and Hewlett-Packard provide diversity awareness workshops, seminars, and training, and Honeywell, Procter & Gamble, and Security Pacific Bank have established mentoring programs, adversary counsels, and minority networks.[58]

As one senior executive said, "In a country seeking competitive advantage in a global economy, the goal of managing diversity is to develop our capacity to accept, incorporate, and empower the diverse human talents of the most diverse nation on earth. It is our reality. We need to make it our strength."[59]

SUMMARY AND MANAGEMENT SOLUTION

Several important ideas pertain to work-force diversity, which is the inclusion of people with different human qualities and from different cultural groups. Dimensions of diversity are both primary, such as age, gender, and race, and secondary, such as education, marital status, and income. Ethnocentric attitudes generally produce a monoculture that accepts only one way of doing things and one set of values and beliefs, thereby excluding nontraditional employees from full participation.

Acceptance of work-force diversity is becoming especially important because of sociocultural changes and the changing work force. Diversity in the workplace reflects diversity in the larger environment. Innovative companies are initiating a variety of programs to take advantage of the diverse work force.

Consider Larry Drake at KFC, who was described in the chapter opening management problem. Upon entering KFC's Designate program, his anticipation of a new challenge was tempered by genuine concerns that he and other minority participants might become mere "tokens" in another high-sounding program with good intentions but little substance. These fears seemed legitimate during his first months with KFC as he breaded onion rings and scrubbed floors in the middle of the night. However, during its first two years, KFC's Designate program raised the number of KFC women and minority top-level managers from zero to seven. Among them, Drake has now risen to the position of vice-president and general manager in charge of more than 1,000 KFC restaurants, making him the most senior black executive. This diversity program works.[60]

Affirmative action programs have been successful in gaining employment for women and minorities, but the glass ceiling has kept many women and minorities from obtaining top management positions. The Civil Rights Act of 1991 amends and strengthens the Civil Rights Act of 1964.

Breaking down the glass ceiling ultimately means changing the corporate culture within organizations, changing internal structures and policies toward employees, including accommodating special needs, and providing diversity awareness training to help people become aware of their own cultural boundaries and prejudices. This training also helps employees learn to communicate with people from other cultural contexts.

The increased diversity in organizations has produced unexpected benefits, such as enabling all groups to define what they want from the company; it has enabled women who use an interactive leadership style to succeed and has provided opportunities for emotional intimacy and friendship between men and women that are beneficial to all parties. Increasing diversity also means that organizations must develop programs to deal with global as well as domestic diversity and with potential conflicts, such as sexual harassment, that arise.

Valuing diversity has many benefits, such as developing employees to their full potential and allowing successful interaction with diverse clients in the marketplace. Organizations that ignore diversity reduce productivity, suffer tarnished corporate images, and suffer substantial financial costs associated with turnover, training, and EEO disputes.

DISCUSSION QUESTIONS

1. If you were a senior manager at a company such as KFC, how would you resolve the concerns of everyone involved when female or minority senior managers are hired from outside?
2. Some people argue that social class is a major source of cultural differences, yet social class is not listed as a primary or secondary dimension in Exhibit 11.1. Discuss reasons for this.
3. Have you been associated with an organization that made assumptions associated with a monoculture? Describe the culture.
4. Do you think any organization successfully can resist diversity today? Discuss.
5. What is the glass ceiling, and why do you think it has proved to be such a barrier to women and minorities?
6. In preparing an organization to accept diversity, do you think it is more important to change the corporate culture or to change structures and policies? Explain.
7. If a North American corporation could choose either high-context or low-context communications, which do you think would be best for the company's long-term health? Discuss.
8. What do you think the impact on an organization would be for diversity within its own country versus international diversity? Discuss.
9. Many single people meet and date people from their work organization because the organization provides a context within which to know and trust another person. How do you think this practice affects the potential for emotional intimacy? Sexual harassment?

MANAGEMENT IN PRACTICE: ETHICAL DILEMMA

● PROMOTION OR NOT?

You are the president of CrownCutters, Inc. You have worked closely with Bill Smith for several years now. In many situations, he has served as your *de facto* right-hand person.

Due to a retirement, you have an opening in the position of executive vice-president. Bill is the natural choice—and this is obvious to the other mid- and senior-level managers at CrownCutters. Bill is popular with most of the managers in the company. Of course, he also has his share of detractors.

Prior to announcing the appointment of Bill Smith, you receive a memo from Jane Jones, your controller. Jane's memo indicates that she was subjected to sporadic sexual harassment by Bill starting ten years ago when she first joined the company and was working for him. Her memo indicates that the harassment essentially stopped six years ago when she moved to a position in which Bill was no longer her superior. She requests that this information be kept totally confidential.

You have never heard of any allegations like this about Bill before.

● WHAT DO YOU DO?

1. Move ahead with the promotion because even if true, this is an isolated incident that is a part of Bill's past and is not his current behavior.
2. Stop the promotion because Bill is not the type of person who should help lead the company and shape its values.
3. Put the promotion on hold until you can discuss the situation extensively with Bill and Jane, although this means the accusation probably will become public knowledge.

SOURCE: This case was provided by Professor David Scheffman, Owen Graduate School of Management, Vanderbilt University, Nashville, Tennessee.

CASE FOR ANALYSIS

FLAGSTAR COMPANIES

Flagstar Companies' CEO Jerry Richardson was always one to stand for his principles. He left the Baltimore Colts in 1961 because the team wouldn't pay him what he thought he was worth. He headed back to Spartanburg, South Carolina, even though the money separating the two sides was a grand total of $250, or 2.5 percent of the total contract.

The problems in Baltimore did not compare to what came later. Richardson was a fast-food pioneer in the southeast, beginning with a Hardee's franchise. Little more than 30 years later his dining empire employed 120,000 people and included Hardee's, Denny's, and a number of other eateries. It was then that Richardson was socked with a crisis that must have reminded him of a blindside from his old NFL days.

In the beginning, Richardson thought the problems were a misunderstanding that could be logically explained. His managers had reported an outbreak of "dine and dash" at several locations. They didn't think it imprudent to require prepayment. However, the news got worse. The prepayment policy was allegedly applied disproportionately to blacks. The problem gained momentum as other black customers surfaced charging they were ignored altogether by waitpersons.

With the Justice Department investigating, Richardson fired or transferred guilty employees and invited civil rights groups to meet with him. He apologized to the customers. He assembled a cultural diversity team to heighten awareness about racism. "It makes no sense that we would condone racism," he says. "We're $2 billion in debt. Denny's needs all the customers it can get." Ultimately, a deal with the Justice Department called for random checks for signs of discrimination. This agreement did not stop plaintiff's attorneys from establishing a toll-free line which former Denny's customers were encouraged to call if they felt they had been unfairly treated. Several customers already planned to sue and a sufficient number would qualify the case for a class-action lawsuit.

Two months after reaching the deal with the Justice Department, things worsened for Flagstar. In May 1993, six black members of the Secret Service who went to a Denny's in Annapolis, Maryland, complained that they were denied service while their white co-workers were served promptly. The six agents filed suit against Flagstar even though Richardson had moved quickly to terminate the manager for failing to report the incident. Similar allegations were raised by 125 black choir members who stopped at a restaurant in Virginia. "It was 11:30 P.M. on a Sunday, and our manager told this bus group it would take a while to service them," says Flagstar vice-president of communications Coleman Sullivan. "There was no discrimination."

Despite Richardson's best efforts at mending fences, Flagstar fell short in several key areas. The company had no blacks among the ranks of its senior managers, officers, or directors. And, only one of the 163 Denny's franchise owners was black. Richardson began working with the NAACP to boost the minority presence in the company, but critics charged that his efforts were too little, too late. As Flagstar board member Gus Oliver said, "I thought we were doing everything we could."

● QUESTIONS

1. Which of the following terms best decribes Flagstar's attitude toward diversity: ethnocentrism, monoculture, ethnorelativism, or pluralism? Explain your answer.

2. Richardson is undoubtedly making efforts to change the corporate culture at Flagstar by being more sensitive to concerns of minorities. What else could he do in the area of recruitment, career advancement and accommodating special needs?

3. Describe the costs of ignoring diversity in terms of what happened at Flagstar.

SOURCE: Andrew E. Serwer, "What to Do When Race Charges Fly," *Fortune,* July 12, 1993, 95–96; and Chuck Hawkins, "Denny's: The Stain That Isn't Coming Out," *Business Week,* June 28, 1993, 98–99.

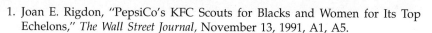

REFERENCES

1. Joan E. Rigdon, "PepsiCo's KFC Scouts for Blacks and Women for Its Top Echelons," *The Wall Street Journal,* November 13, 1991, A1, A5.

2. M. Fine, F. Johnson, and M. S. Ryan, "Cultural Diversity in the Workforce," *Public Personnel Management* 19 (1990), 305–319.

3. Taylor Cox, Jr., "Managing Cultural Diversity: Implications for Organizational Competitiveness," *Academy of Management Executive* 5, no. 3 (1991), 45–56.

4. Joel Dreyfuss, "Get Ready for the New Workforce," *Fortune,* April 29, 1990, 165–181.

5. Lennie Copeland, "Valuing Diversity, Part I: Making the Most of Cultural Differences at the Workplace," *Personnel,* June 1988, 52–60.

6. Lennie Copeland, "Learning to Manage a Multicultural Workforce," *Training,* May 25, 1988, 48–56.

7. Marilyn Loden and Judy B. Rosener, *Workforce America!* (Homewood, Ill.: Business One Irwin, 1991).

8. N. Songer, "Workforce Diversity," *B & E Review,* April–June 1991, 3–6.

9. G. Haight, "Managing Diversity," *Across the Board* 27, no. 3 (1990), 22–29.

10. Songer, "Workforce Diversity."

11. Robert Doktor, Rosalie Tung, and Maryann Von Glinow, "Future Directions for Management Theory Development," *Academy of Management Review* 16 (1991), 362–365.

12. M. Bennett, "A Developmental Approach to Training for Intercultural Sensitivity," *International Journal of Intercultural Relations* 10 (1986), 179–196.

13. C. Keen, "Human Resource Management Issues in the '90s," *Vital Speeches* 56, no. 24 (1990), 752–754.

14. Kurt Anderson, "California Dreamin'," *Time*, September 23, 1991, 38–42.

15. Brian O'Reilly, "Your New Global Workforce," *Fortune*, December 14, 1992, 52–66.

16. W. B. Johnston and A. H. Packer, *Workforce 2000* (Indianapolis, Ind.: Hudson Institute, 1987).

17. United States Department of Labor, *Opportunity 2000: Creative Affirmative Action Strategies for a Changing Workforce* (Indianapolis, Ind.: Hudson Institute, 1988).

18. Copeland, "Valuing Diversity, Part I: Making the Most of Cultural Differences at the Workplace."

19. S. Hutchins, Jr., "Preparing for Diversity: The Year 2000," *Quality Process* 22, no. 10 (1989), 66–68.

20. J. Santoro, "Kinney Shoes Steps into Diversity," *Personnel Journal* 70, no. 9 (1991), 72–77.

21. Roosevelt Thomas, Jr., "From Affirmative Action to Affirming Diversity," *Harvard Business Review* (March–April 1990), 107–117.

22. Julie Amparano Lopez, "Study Says Women Face Glass Walls as Well as Ceilings," *The Wall Street Journal*, March 3, 1992, B1, B2.

23. C. Soloman, "Careers under Glass," *Personnel Journal* 69, no. 4 (1990), 96–105.

24. Ibid.

25. William A. Henry III, "A Mind-set Under Siege," *Time*, November 30, 1992, 40–42.

26. Thomas A. Stewart, "Gay in Corporate America," *Fortune*, December 16, 1991, 42–56.

27. B. Geber, "Managing Diversity," *Training* 27, no. 7 (1990), 23–30.

28. Anne B. Fisher, "When Will Women Get to the Top?" *Fortune*, September 21, 1992, 44–56.

29. Thomas, "From Affirmative Action to Affirming Diversity."

30. Julia Flynn, "Julia Stasch Raises the Roof for Feminism," *Business Week*, January 25, 1993, 102.

31. Copeland, "Learning to Manage a Multicultural Workforce."

32. Geber, "Managing Diversity."

33. Loden and Rosener, *Workforce America!*

34. B. Ragins, "Barriers to Mentoring: The Female Manager's Dilemma," *Human Relations* 42, no. 1 (1989), 1–22.

35. Mary Zey, "A Mentor for All," *Personnel Journal*, January 1988, 46–51.

36. Sharon Nelton, "Winning with Diversity," *Nation's Business*, September 1992, 18–23.

37. J. Black and M. Mendenhall, "Cross-Cultural Training Effectiveness: A Review and a Theoretical Framework for Future Research," *Academy of Management Review* 15 (1990), 113–136.

38. Loden and Rosener, *Workforce America!*

39. David Shallenberger, "Invisible Minorities: Coming Out of the Classroom Closet," *Journal of Management Education* (August 1991), 325–334.

40. Aaron Bernstein, "When the Only Parent Is Daddy," *Business Week,* November 23, 1992, 122–127; Keith H. Hammonds and William C. Symonds, "Taking Baby Steps toward a Daddy Track," *Business Week,* April 15, 1991, 90–92; and Sue Shellenbarger, "More Job Seekers Put Family Needs First," *The Wall Street Journal,* November 15, 1991, B1, B12.

41. Aaron Bernstein, Joseph Weber, Lisa Driscoll, and Alice Cuneo, "Corporate America Is Still No Place for Kids," *Business Week,* November 21, 1991, 234–238.

42. E. G. Collins, "Managers and Lovers," *Harvard Business Review* 61 (1983), 142–153.

43. S. A. Lobel, R. E. Quinn, and A. Warfield, "Between Men and Women: An Exploration of Psychological Intimacy in Relationships at Work." Working paper, University of Michigan, 1991.

44. "Sexual Harassment: Vanderbilt University Policy" (Nashville: Vanderbilt University, 1993).

45. Troy Segal, Kevin Kelly, and Alisa Solomon, "Getting Serious about Sexual Harassment," *Business Week,* November 9, 1992, 78–82.

46. "The *INC.* FaxPoll: What Are You Doing about Sexual Harassment?" *INC.,* August 1992, 16.

47. Segal et al., "Getting Serious"; "The *INC.* FaxPoll"; and Gary Baseman, "Sexual Harassment: The Inside Story," *Working Woman,* June 1992, 47–51, 78.

48. Joel Dreyfuss, "Get Ready for the New Work Force," *Fortune,* April 23, 1990, 165–181; and Ronald E. Dulek, John S. Fielden, and John S. Hill, "International Communication: An Executive Primer," *Business Horizons,* January–February 1991, 20–25.

49. Joanne S. Lublin, "Companies Use Cross-Cultural Training to Help Their Employees Adjust Abroad," *The Wall Street Journal,* August 4, 1992, B1, B9.

50. Gilbert Fuchsberg, "As Costs of Overseas Assignments Climb, Firms Select Expatriates More Carefully," *The Wall Street Journal,* January 9, 1992, B3, B4.

51. Brian Dumaine, "Management Lessons from the General," *Fortune,* November 2, 1992, 143.

52. J. Kennedy and A. Everest, "Put Diversity in Context," *Personnel Journal,* September 1991, 50–54.

53. Cox, "Managing Cultural Diversity."

54. J. Castelli, "Education Forms Common Bond," *HRMagazine* 35, no. 6 (1990), 46–49.

55. Copeland, "Valuing Diversity, Part 1: Making the Most of Cultural Differences at the Workplace."

56. Cox, "Managing Cultural Diversity."

57. S. Caudron, "Monsanto Response to Diversity," *Personnel Journal* 69, no. 11 (1990), 72–80.

58. Suzanne B. Laporte, "12 Companies That Do the Right Thing," *Working Woman*, January 1991, 57–59.

59. Thomas, "From Affirmative Action to Affirming Diversity."

60. Rigdon, "PepsiCo's KFC Scouts."

PHOTO PROVIDED COURTESY OF IDS FINANCIAL SERVICES, INC.

IV

Rollerblades? Safari hat? Crazy T-shirts? Who are these guys racing through the corporate hallways of downtown Minneapolis? It's part of IDS' approach to leadership, motivation, and teamwork. President and CEO Jeff Stiefler (center) and Gary Lumpkin from the TV show "Good Company" recognize winners of the annual Premier Performers Award. This prestigious award recognizes employees who personify IDS values, provide superior customer service, contribute to team spirit, and appreciate the diversity of other employees. The winners, such as Anne Green of TransAction Services (second from left), are proven leaders who reflect the values of senior management.

LEADERSHIP

CHAPTER OUTLINE

LEARNING OBJECTIVES ▼

After studying this chapter, you should be able to

- Define leadership and explain its importance for organizations.

- Identify personal characteristics associated with effective leadership.

- Explain the five sources of leader influence and how each causes different subordinate behavior.

- Describe the leader behaviors of initiating structure and consideration and when they should be used.

- Describe Hersey and Blanchard's situational theory and its application to subordinate participation.

- Explain how leadership fits the organizational situation and how organizational characteristics can substitute for leadership behaviors.

It would be difficult to find a more impressive leadership résumé than that of Roger Staubach. From the 1963 Heisman Trophy to a combat tour in Vietnam to a record 23 come-from-behind victories in the NFL that earned him the nickname Captain Comeback, Roger Staubach not only performed feats that became legendary, but also inspired those around him to performances they never dreamed possible. After retiring from football, Staubach had to tailor those leadership qualities to fit his second career in real estate. ■ Only time would tell if Staubach would be like so many other ex-athletes who tried to wring business success out of past gridiron heroics. Could he translate the same leadership principles used on the football field into success in the highly competitive real estate industry? Will Roger Staubach's charismatic leadership be useful in his new career? What leadership style would you recommend that he adopt for his real estate company?[1]

Fred Cain and his "Bull Gang" of maintenance workers at Asarco's Tennessee mines have accumulated 350,000 hours over a 15-year period without a single lost-time injury, earning them Tennessee's 1990 Excellence at Work Award. Cain is an example of a leader with legitimate, expert, and referent power sources.

leadership

The ability to influence people toward the attainment of organizational goals.

power

The potential ability to influence others' behavior.

Roger Staubach is a proven leader in many areas who has developed his own unique style. Many styles of leadership can be successful in organizations depending on the leader and the situation. For example, Compaq Computer Corporation recently lapsed into recession doldrums, but the aggressive, "can-do" leadership style of new president Eckhard Pfeiffer fired up the company's vision for producing lower-priced computers. Under this leadership style, Compaq turned around in a year and is now going after the competition with a vengeance. In another case, Steve Chen inspired 40 people to leave Cray Research with him because of his dream to build a super computer that Cray decided not to build. Consider the leadership style of Irish pop star Bob Geldof, who mobilized aid for Ethiopia's famine-stricken population in the 1980s. Geldof threaded together diverse international forces to create historical music events, Band Aid and Live Aid. Alternatively stroking, coaxing, and prodding, Geldof successfully coordinated communication technology and delicate star egos into a "collective individualism." Today, executives for global companies study Geldof's multinational coordination techniques.[2]

This chapter explores one of the most widely discussed and researched topics in management—leadership. Here we will define leadership and explore the sources of leadership influence. We will discuss trait, behavioral, and contingency theories of leadership effectiveness. We will also explore the *charismatic leader*, who creates a vision, inspires loyalty, and leads corporate transformation. Chapters 13 through 15 deal with many of the functions of leadership, including employee motivation, communication, and leading groups.

● THE NATURE OF LEADERSHIP

Among all the ideas and writings about leadership, three aspects stand out—people, influence, and goals. Leadership occurs between people, involves the use of influence, and is used to attain goals.[3] *Influence* means that the relationship among people is not passive. Moreover, influence is designed to achieve some end or goal. Thus, **leadership** as defined here is the ability to influence people toward the attainment of goals. This definition captures the idea that leaders are involved with other people in the achievement of objectives.

Leadership is reciprocal, occurring *between* people.[4] Leadership is a "people" activity, distinct from administrative paper shuffling or problem-solving activities. Leadership is dynamic and involves the use of power. Power is important for influencing others, because it determines whether a leader is able to command compliance from followers.

SOURCES OF LEADER INFLUENCE

Power is the potential ability to influence the behavior of others.[5] Power represents the resources with which a leader effects changes in employee behavior. Leadership is the actual use of that power. Within organizations, leaders typically have five sources of power: legitimate, reward, coercive, expert, and referent.[6]

LEGITIMATE POWER. Power coming from a formal management position in an organization and the authority granted to it is called **legitimate power.** For example, once a person has been selected as a supervisor, most workers understand that they are obligated to follow his or her direction with respect to work activities. Subordinates accept this source of power as legitimate, which is why they comply.

REWARD POWER. Another kind of power, **reward power,** stems from the leader's authority to bestow rewards on other people. Leaders may have access to formal rewards, such as pay increases or promotions. They also have at their disposal rewards such as praise, attention, and recognition. Leaders can use rewards to influence subordinates' behavior.

COERCIVE POWER. The opposite of reward power is **coercive power:** It refers to the leader's authority to punish or recommend punishment. Leaders have coercive power when they have the right to fire or demote employees, criticize, or withdraw pay increases. For example, if Paul, a salesman, does not perform as expected, his supervisor has the coercive power to criticize him, reprimand him, put a negative letter in his file, and hurt his chance for a raise.

EXPERT POWER. Power resulting from a leader's special knowledge or skill regarding the tasks performed by followers is referred to as **expert power.** When the leader is a true expert, subordinates go along with recommendations because of his or her superior knowledge. Leaders at supervisory levels often have experience in the production process that gains them promotion. At top management levels, however, leaders may lack expert power because subordinates know more about technical details than they do.

REFERENT POWER. The last kind of power, **referent power,** comes from leader personality characteristics that command subordinates' identification, respect, and admiration so they wish to emulate the leader. When workers admire a supervisor because of the way she deals with them, the influence is based on referent power. Referent power depends on the leader's personal characteristics rather than formal title or position and is most visible in the area of charismatic leadership, which will be discussed later in this chapter.

THE USE OF POWER

Leaders use the above five sources of power to affect the behavior and performance of followers. But how do followers react to each source? Three reactions that have been studied are commitment, compliance, and resistance by followers.[7] *Commitment* means that workers will share the leader's point of view and enthusiastically carry out instructions. Expert power and referent power are the sources most likely to generate follower commitment. *Compliance* means that workers will obey orders and carry out instructions, although they may personally disagree with the instructions and will not necessarily be enthusiastic. Legitimate power and reward power are most likely to generate follower compliance. *Resistance* means that workers will deliberately try to avoid carrying out

legitimate power

Power that stems from a formal management position in an organization and the authority granted to it.

reward power

Power that results from the leader's authority to reward others.

coercive power

Power that stems from the leader's authority to punish or recommend punishment.

expert power

Power that stems from the leader's special knowledge of or skill in the tasks performed by subordinates.

referent power

Power that results from leader characteristics that command subordinates' identification with, respect and admiration for, and desire to emulate the leader.

instructions and attempt to disobey orders. Coercive power most often generates resistance.

For example, Glenn Van Pelt, production supervisor at a steel fabrication plant, was respected by everyone for his knowledge of production and for his pleasant attitude. Glenn asked John Simmons, one of his line managers, to reassign one of his people to help finish a project under way in another department. Although John's own people were stretched to the max, he appreciated his boss's good judgment and trusted his expertise. John agreed to lend an employee to Glenn, and thus committed himself to the success of the project. If Glenn's leadership style had been more coercive, John would likely have resisted and found a reason why he could not spare an employee. Glenn's referent and expert leadership style inspired support and cooperation.

A significant recent trend in corporate America is for top executives to *empower* lower employees. Fully 74 percent of executives in a survey claimed that they are more participatory, more concerned with consensus building, and rely more on communication than on command compared with the past. Executives no longer hoard power. For example, at Johnsonville Foods, the real power of top executives comes from giving it up to others who are in a better position to get things done. Empowering employees works because total power in the organization seems to increase. Everyone has more say and hence contributes more to organizational goals. The goal of senior executives in many corporations today is not simply to wield power but also to give it away to people who can get jobs done.[8]

● LEADERSHIP TRAITS

traits

The distinguishing personal characteristics of a leader, such as intelligence, values, and appearance.

Early efforts to understand leadership success focused on the leader's personal characteristics or traits. **Traits** are the distinguishing personal characteristics of a leader, such as intelligence, values, and appearance. The early research focused on leaders who had achieved a level of greatness and hence was referred to as the *great man* approach. The idea was relatively simple: Find out what made these people great and select future leaders who already exhibited the same traits or could be trained to develop them. Generally, research found only a weak relationship between personal traits and leader success.[9] For example, three football coaches—Tom Osborne at Nebraska, Lou Holtz at Notre Dame, and Joe Paterno at Penn State—have different personality traits, but all are successful leaders of their football programs.

In addition to personality traits, physical, social, and work-related characteristics of leaders have been studied. Exhibit 12.1 summarizes the physical, social, and personal leadership characteristics that have received the greatest research support.[10] However, these characteristics do not stand alone. The appropriateness of a trait or set of traits depends on the leadership situation. The same traits do not apply to every organization.

For example, Sarah Brown is the manager of Far Eastern imports for a major steel corporation. There is an opening for a subordinate man-

E X H I B I T   12.1

Personal Characteristics of Leaders

Physical characteristics	**Personality**	**Social characteristics**
Activity	Alertness	Ability to enlist cooperation
Energy	Originality, creativity	Cooperativeness
	Personal integrity, ethical conduct	Popularity, prestige
Social background	Self-confidence	Sociability, interpersonal skills
Mobility		Social participation
	Work-related characteristics	Tact, diplomacy
Intelligence and ability	Achievement drive, desire to excel	
Judgment, decisiveness	Drive for responsibility	
Knowledge	Responsibility in pursuit of objectives	
Fluency of speech	Task orientation	

SOURCE: Adapted from Bernard M. Bass, *Stogdill's Handbook of Leadership*, rev. ed. (New York: Free Press, 1981), 75–76. This adaptation appeared in R. Albanese and D. D. Van Fleet, *Organizational Behavior: A Managerial Viewpoint* (Hinsdale, Ill.: Dryden Press, 1983).

ager in her department who will supervise the field sales personnel. For this position, the personal characteristic of intelligence and a working knowledge of steel product marketing are important, as are desire for responsibility, a task orientation, and supervisory skills. Sarah Brown's ability to understand the situation and the type of leader who will succeed in it will help her select the appropriate person for the job.

● AUTOCRATIC VERSUS DEMOCRATIC LEADERS

One way to approach leader characteristics is to examine autocratic and democratic leaders. An **autocratic leader** is one who tends to centralize authority and rely on legitimate, reward, and coercive power. A **democratic leader** delegates authority to others, encourages participation, and relies on expert and referent power to influence subordinates.

The first studies on these leadership characteristics were conducted at Iowa State University by Kurt Lewin and his associates.[11] These studies compared autocratic and democratic leaders and produced some interesting findings. The groups with autocratic leaders performed highly so long as the leader was present to supervise them. However, group members were displeased with the close, autocratic style of leadership, and feelings of hostility frequently arose. The performance of groups who were assigned democratic leaders was almost as good, and these were characterized by positive feelings rather than hostility. In addition, under the democratic style of leadership, group members performed well even when the leader was absent and left the group on its own.[12] The participative techniques and majority rule decision making used by the democratic leader trained and involved group members such that they performed well with or without the leader present. These characteristics of

autocratic leader

A leader who tends to centralize authority and rely on legitimate, reward, and coercive power to manage subordinates.

democratic leader

A leader who delegates authority to others, encourages participation, and relies on expert and referent power to manage subordinates.

These Army recruits learn about auto-cratic leadership very early in their ser-vice career. The military has a well-defined authority structure, and leaders are able to use legitimate, reward, and coercive power on subordinates.

democratic leadership explain why the empowerment of lower employ-ees is a popular trend in companies today.

This early work suggested that leaders were either autocratic or democratic in their approach. However, further work by Tannenbaum and Schmidt indicated that leadership could be a continuum reflecting different amounts of employee participation.[13] Thus, one leader might be autocratic (boss centered), another democratic (subordinate centered), and a third a mix of the two styles. The leadership continuum is illus-trated in Exhibit 12.2.

Tannenbaum and Schmidt suggested that the extent to which leader-ship is boss centered or subordinate centered depends on organizational circumstances. For example, if there is time pressure on a leader or if it takes too long for subordinates to learn how to make decisions, the leader will tend to use an autocratic style. When subordinates are able to learn decision-making skills readily, a participative style can be used. Another situational factor is the skill difference between subordinates and leader. The greater the skill difference, the more autocratic the leader approach, because it is difficult to bring subordinates up to the leader's expertise level.[14]

For example, Stephen Fleming uses an autocratic style as a marketing manager in an oil products company. He is being groomed for a higher position because his marketing department has performed so well. How-ever, this has meant time spent at meetings away from his group, and their performance has declined because the subordinates have not learned to function independently. In contrast, Dorothy Roberts, CEO of Echo Scarves, believes that people are managed best by showing them respect and courtesy. Decision making is shared by representatives of design, sales, marketing, and operations. In the traditionally tough fash-ion industry, her nice-guy leadership style permeates the entire company, creating a unique corporate culture that is open, honest, and supportive

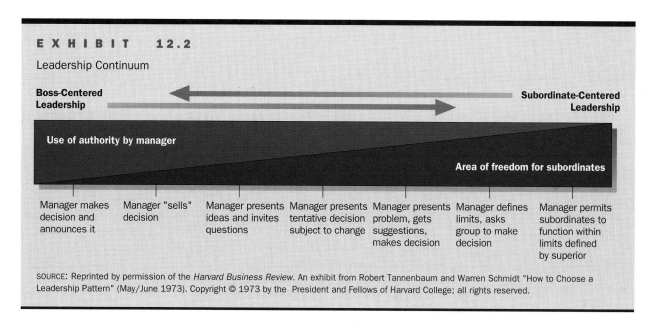

E X H I B I T   1 2 . 2

Leadership Continuum

Boss-Centered Leadership ← → **Subordinate-Centered Leadership**

Use of authority by manager

Area of freedom for subordinates

| Manager makes decision and announces it | Manager "sells" decision | Manager presents ideas and invites questions | Manager presents tentative decision subject to change | Manager presents problem, gets suggestions, makes decision | Manager defines limits, asks group to make decision | Manager permits subordinates to function within limits defined by superior |

SOURCE: Reprinted by permission of the *Harvard Business Review*. An exhibit from Robert Tannenbaum and Warren Schmidt "How to Choose a Leadership Pattern" (May/June 1973). Copyright © 1973 by the President and Fellows of Harvard College; all rights reserved.

of employees. Company prosperity is centered on treating people well. Roberts' leadership style creates satisfied employees who in turn create satisfied customers, which may be more difficult with an autocratic leadership style.[15] The founder of SBT Corporation, Robert Davies, evolved from an autocratic leader to a democratic leader after finding that his employees were more effective if they were encouraged to play a greater role in running the company.

S B T   C O R P O R A T I O N

Robert Davies used a forceful, authoritarian management style. A background with six corporations and the U.S. Navy will do that to you. But after starting SBT, which was originally a systems integrator company but now an accounting-software company, he discovered he could still learn some new tricks.

In building his company from a 10-person operation to an 80-employee, $10-million-a-year company, Davies found that flexibility was not only imperative with customers, but was also the way to get the most from employees. To give them input into company decisions, and at the same time create an atmosphere that encouraged it, Davies tapped a group of 15 line managers to meet weekly. Two employees could also sign up. Ideas and discussion about operations were presented at these gatherings, enhancing understanding in all areas of the company.

Davies took things one step further. Getting people together, in his view, does not do much good if they are fearful about voicing criticisms. Davies implemented an E-mail system linking over 100 stations in the company network to assuage fear about voicing criticisms. Anything could be input, anonymously if the sender wished. SBT has evolved into a management-by-consensus business. Davies reserves some decisions, as well as the right to overrule, but he found that if the majority of the

people carrying out a plan did not agree with it, it usually did not succeed. He also found out that involving everyone has turned SBT into an
idea factory. "I never know who will give us the next great suggestion,"
he says.[16] ■

● TWO-DIMENSIONAL APPROACHES

The autocratic and democratic styles suggest that it
is the "behavior" of the leader rather than a personality trait that determines leadership effectiveness. Perhaps any leader can adopt the correct
behavior with appropriate training. The focus of recent research has
shifted from leader personality traits toward the behaviors successful
leaders display. Important research programs on leadership behavior
were conducted at Ohio State University, the University of Michigan,
and the University of Texas.

OHIO STATE STUDIES

Researchers at Ohio State University surveyed leaders to study hundreds
of dimensions of leader behavior.[17] They identified two major behaviors,
called *consideration* and *initiating structure*.

Consideration is the extent to which the leader is mindful of subordinates, respects their ideas and feelings, and establishes mutual trust.
Considerate leaders are friendly, provide open communication, develop
teamwork, and are oriented toward their subordinates' welfare.

Initiating structure is the extent to which the leader is task oriented
and directs subordinate work activities toward goal attainment. Leaders
with this style typically give instructions, spend time planning, emphasize deadlines, and provide explicit schedules of work activities.

Consideration and initiating structure are independent of each other,
which means that a leader with a high degree of consideration may be
either high or low on initiating structure. A leader may have any of four
styles: high initiating structure–low consideration, high initiating structure–high consideration, low initiating structure–low consideration, or
low initiating structure–high consideration. The Ohio State research
found that the high consideration–high initiating structure style
achieved better performance and greater satisfaction than the other
leader styles. However, new research has found that effective leaders
may be high on consideration and low on initiating structure or low on
consideration and high on initiating structure, depending on the situation. Thus, the "high-high" style is not always the best.[18]

MICHIGAN STUDIES

Studies at the University of Michigan at about the same time took a different approach by comparing the behavior of effective and ineffective
supervisors.[19] The most effective supervisors were those who focused on
the subordinates' human needs in order to "build effective work groups
with high performance goals." The Michigan researchers used the term
employee-centered leaders for leaders who established high performance

---

consideration

A type of leader behavior that describes
the extent to which a leader is sensitive
to subordinates, respects their ideas
and feelings, and establishes mutual
trust.

initiating structure

A type of leader behavior that describes
the extent to which a leader is task oriented and directs subordinates' work
activities toward goal achievement.

goals and displayed supportive behavior toward subordinates. The less effective leaders were called *job-centered leaders;* these tended to be less concerned with goal achievement and human needs in favor of meeting schedules, keeping costs low, and achieving production efficiency.

THE LEADERSHIP GRID

Blake and Mouton of the University of Texas proposed a three-dimensional leadership theory called **leadership grid** that builds on the work of the Ohio State and Michigan studies.[20] The three-dimensional model and five of its seven major management styles are depicted in Exhibit 12.3. Each axis on the grid is a 9-point scale, with 1 meaning low concern and 9 high concern.

Team management (9,9) often is considered the most effective style and is recommended for managers because organization members work together to accomplish tasks. *Country club management* (1,9) occurs when primary emphasis is given to people rather than to work outputs. *Authority-obedience management* (9,1) occurs when efficiency in operations is the dominant orientation. *Middle of the Road management* (5,5) reflects a moderate amount of concern for both people and production. *Impoverished management* (1,1) means the absence of a management philosophy; managers exert little effort toward interpersonal relationships or work accomplishment.

leadership grid

A three-dimensional leadership theory that measures a leader's concern for people and concern for production.

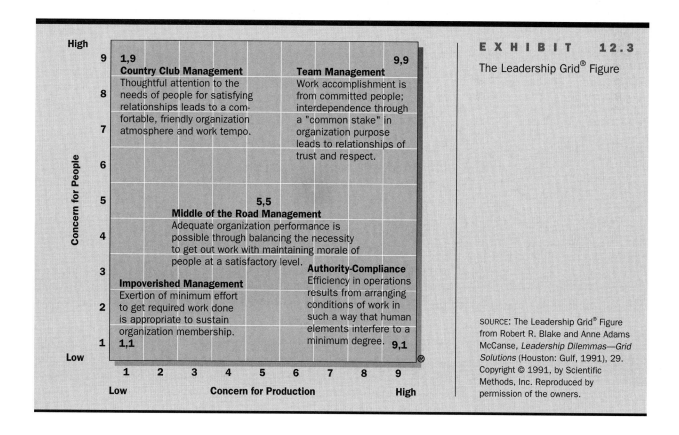

SOURCE: The Leadership Grid® Figure from Robert R. Blake and Anne Adams McCanse, *Leadership Dilemmas—Grid Solutions* (Houston: Gulf, 1991), 29. Copyright © 1991, by Scientific Methods, Inc. Reproduced by permission of the owners.

E X H I B I T   12.3

The Leadership Grid® Figure

● CONTINGENCY APPROACHES

Several models of leadership that explain the relationship between leadership styles and specific situations have been developed. These are termed **contingency approaches** and include the leadership model developed by Fiedler and his associates, the situational theory of Hersey and Blanchard, and the substitutes-for-leadership concept.

contingency approach

A model of leadership that describes the relationship between leadership styles and specific organizational situations.

FIEDLER'S CONTINGENCY THEORY

An early, extensive effort to combine leadership style and organizational situation into a comprehensive theory of leadership was made by Fiedler and his associates.[21] The basic idea is simple: Match the leader's style with the situation most favorable for his or her success. By diagnosing leadership style and the organizational situation, the correct fit can be arranged.

LEADERSHIP STYLE. The cornerstone of Fiedler's contingency theory is the extent to which the leader's style is relationship oriented or task oriented. A *relationship-oriented leader* is concerned with people, as in the consideration style described earlier. A *task-oriented leader* is primarily motivated by task accomplishment, which is similar to the initiating structure style described earlier.

Leadership style was measured with a questionnaire known as the least preferred coworker (LPC) scale. The **LPC scale** has a set of 16 bipolar adjectives along an 8-point scale. Examples of the bipolar adjectives used by Fiedler on the LPC scale are as follows:

LPC scale

A questionnaire designed to measure relationship-oriented versus task-oriented leadership style according to the leader's choice of adjectives for describing the "least preferred coworker."

open	—	—	—	—	—	—	—	—	guarded
quarrelsome	—	—	—	—	—	—	—	—	harmonious
efficient	—	—	—	—	—	—	—	—	inefficient
self-assured	—	—	—	—	—	—	—	—	hesitant
gloomy	—	—	—	—	—	—	—	—	cheerful

If the leader describes the least preferred coworker using positive concepts, he or she is considered relationship oriented, that is, cares about and is sensitive to other people's feelings. Conversely, if a leader uses negative concepts to describe the least preferred coworker, he or she is considered task oriented, that is, sees other people in negative terms and places greater value on task activities than on people.

SITUATION. Leadership situations can be analyzed in terms of three elements: the quality of leader-member relationships, task structure, and position power.[22] Each of these elements can be described as either favorable or unfavorable for the leader.

1 *Leader-member relations* refers to group atmosphere and members' attitude toward and acceptance of the leader. When subordinates trust, respect, and have confidence in the leader, leader-member relations are considered good. When subordinates distrust, do not respect, and have little confidence in the leader, leader-member relations are poor.

2 *Task structure* refers to the extent to which tasks performed by the group are defined, involve specific procedures, and have clear, explicit goals. Routine, well-defined tasks, such as those of assembly line workers, have a high degree of structure. Creative, ill-defined tasks, such as research and development or strategic planning, have a low degree of task structure. When task structure is high, the situation is considered favorable to the leader; when low, the situation is less favorable.

3 *Position power* is the extent to which the leader has formal authority over subordinates. Position power is high when the leader has the power to plan and direct the work of subordinates, evaluate it, and reward or punish them. Position power is low when the leader has little authority over subordinates and cannot evaluate their work or reward them. When position power is high, the situation is considered favorable for the leader; when low, the situation is unfavorable.

Combining the three situational characteristics yields a list of eight leadership situations, which are illustrated in Exhibit 12.4. Situation I is most favorable to the leader because leader-member relations are good, task structure is high, and leader position power is strong. Situation VIII is most unfavorable to the leader because leader-member relations are poor, task structure is low, and leader position power is weak. All other octants represent intermediate degrees of favorableness for the leader.

CONTINGENCY THEORY.   When Fiedler examined the relationships among leadership style, situational favorability, and group task performance, he found the pattern shown in Exhibit 12.5. Task-oriented leaders are more effective when the situation is either highly favorable or highly unfavorable. Relationship-oriented leaders are more effective in situations of moderate favorability.

The reason the task-oriented leader excels in the favorable situation is that when everyone gets along, the task is clear and the leader has power; all that is needed is for someone to take charge and provide direction. Similarly, if the situation is highly unfavorable to the leader, a

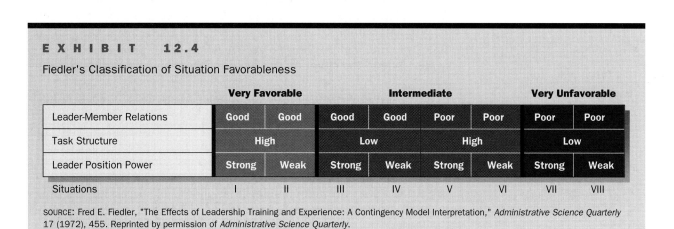

EXHIBIT   12.4

Fiedler's Classification of Situation Favorableness

	Very Favorable		Intermediate				Very Unfavorable	
Leader-Member Relations	Good	Good	Good	Good	Poor	Poor	Poor	Poor
Task Structure	High		Low		High		Low	
Leader Position Power	Strong	Weak	Strong	Weak	Strong	Weak	Strong	Weak
Situations	I	II	III	IV	V	VI	VII	VIII

SOURCE: Fred E. Fiedler, "The Effects of Leadership Training and Experience: A Contingency Model Interpretation," *Administrative Science Quarterly* 17 (1972), 455. Reprinted by permission of *Administrative Science Quarterly*.

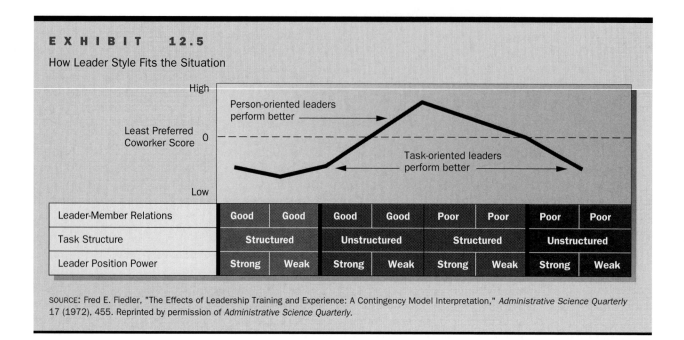

EXHIBIT   12.5

How Leader Style Fits the Situation

Leader-Member Relations	Good	Good	Good	Good	Poor	Poor	Poor	Poor
Task Structure	Structured		Unstructured		Structured		Unstructured	
Leader Position Power	Strong	Weak	Strong	Weak	Strong	Weak	Strong	Weak

SOURCE: Fred E. Fiedler, "The Effects of Leadership Training and Experience: A Contingency Model Interpretation," *Administrative Science Quarterly* 17 (1972), 455. Reprinted by permission of *Administrative Science Quarterly*.

great deal of structure and task direction is needed. A strong leader defines task structure and can establish authority over subordinates. Because leader-member relations are poor anyway, a strong task orientation will make no difference in the leader's popularity.

The reason the relationship-oriented leader performs better in situations of intermediate favorability is that human relations skills are important in achieving high group performance. In these situations, the leader may be moderately well liked, have some power, and supervise jobs that contain some ambiguity. A leader with good interpersonal skills can create a positive group atmosphere that will improve relationships, clarify task structure, and establish position power.

A leader, then, needs to know two things in order to use Fiedler's contingency theory. First, the leader should know whether he or she has a relationship- or task-oriented style. Second, the leader should diagnose the situation and determine whether leader-member relations, task structure, and position power are favorable or unfavorable. Fitting leader style to the situation can yield big dividends in profits and efficiency.[23]

An important contribution of Fiedler's research is that it goes beyond the notion of leadership styles to show how styles fit the situation to improve organizational effectiveness. On the other hand, the model has also been criticized.[24] Using the LPC score as a measure of relationship- or task-oriented behavior seems simplistic, and how the model works over time is unclear. For example, if a task-oriented leader is matched with an unfavorable situation and is successful, the organizational situation is likely to improve and become more favorable to the leader.

HERSEY AND BLANCHARD'S SITUATIONAL THEORY

The **situational theory** of leadership is an interesting extension of the two-dimensional theories described earlier and summarized in the managerial grid (Exhibit 12.3). The point of Hersey and Blanchard is that subordinates vary in maturity level. People low in task maturity, because of little ability or training, or insecurity, need a different leadership style than those who are highly mature and have good ability, skills, confidence, and willingness to work.[25]

The relationships between leader style and task maturity are summarized in Exhibit 12.6. The upper part of the exhibit indicates style of leader, which is based on a combination of relationship behavior and task behavior. The bell-shaped curve is called a prescriptive curve, because it indicates when each leader style should be used. The four styles—telling (S1), selling (S2), participating (S3), and delegating (S4)—depend on the maturity of followers, indicated in the lower part of Exhibit 12.6. M1 is low maturity and M4 represents high maturity. The

situational theory

A contingency approach to leadership that links the leader's two-dimensional style with the task maturity of subordinates.

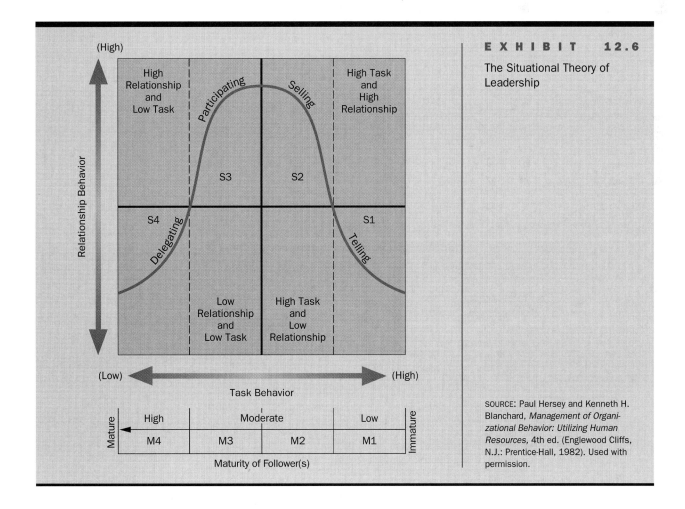

E X H I B I T   1 2 . 6

The Situational Theory of Leadership

SOURCE: Paul Hersey and Kenneth H. Blanchard, *Management of Organizational Behavior: Utilizing Human Resources*, 4th ed. (Englewood Cliffs, N.J.: Prentice-Hall, 1982). Used with permission.

telling style is for low-maturity subordinates, because people are unable and unwilling to take responsibility for their own task behavior. The selling and participating styles work for followers with moderate maturity, and delegating is appropriate for employees with high maturity.

This contingency model is easier to understand than Fiedler's model, but it incorporates only the characteristics of followers, not those of the situation. The leader should evaluate subordinates and adopt whichever style is needed. If one or more followers are immature, the leader must be very specific, telling them exactly what to do, how to do it, and when. For followers high in maturity, the leader provides a general goal and sufficient authority to do the task as they see fit. Leaders must carefully diagnose the maturity level of followers and then tell, sell, participate, or delegate.

A public example of the wrong leadership style occurred at the Department of Housing and Urban Development (HUD). Samuel Pierce, Jr., the secretary of HUD during the Reagan administration, used a hands-off, delegating style. Yet employees within HUD were not mature, reportedly using their positions to provide favors and contracts to friends and political supporters. The net result has been a charge of mismanagement against the leader of HUD, because the leadership style did not fit the situation.[26]

SUBSTITUTES FOR LEADERSHIP

The contingency leadership approaches considered so far have focused on the leaders' style, and the subordinates' nature. The final contingency approach suggests that situational variables can be so powerful that they actually substitute for or neutralize the need for leadership.[27] This approach outlines those organizational settings in which a leadership style is unimportant or unnecessary.

Exhibit 12.7 shows the situational variables that tend to substitute for or neutralize leadership characteristics. A **substitute** for leadership makes the leadership style unnecessary or redundant. For example,

substitute

A situational variable that makes a leadership style redundant or unnecessary.

EXHIBIT 12.7
Substitutes and Neutralizers for Leadership

Variable	Task-Oriented Leadership	People-Oriented Leadership
Organizational variables: Group cohesiveness	Substitutes for	Substitutes for
Formalization	Substitutes for	No effect on
Inflexibility	Neutralizes	No effect on
Low positional power	Neutralizes	Neutralizes
Physical separation	Neutralizes	Neutralizes
Task characteristics: Highly structured task	Substitutes for	No effect on
Automatic feedback	Substitutes for	No effect on
Intrinsic satisfaction	No effect on	Substitutes for
Group characteristics: Professionalism	Substitutes for	Substitutes for
Training/Experience	Substitutes for	No effect on
Low value of rewards	Neutralizes	Neutralizes

highly professional subordinates who know how to do their tasks do not need a leader who initiates structure for them and tells them what to do. A **neutralizer** counteracts the leadership style and prevents the leader from displaying certain behaviors. For example, if a leader has absolutely no position power or is physically removed from subordinates, the leader's ability to give directions to subordinates is greatly reduced.

Situational variables in Exhibit 12.7 include characteristics of the group, the task, and the organization itself. For example, when subordinates are highly professional and experienced, both leadership styles are less important. The employees do not need much direction or consideration. With respect to task characteristics, highly structured tasks substitute for a task-oriented style and a satisfying task substitutes for a people-oriented style. With respect to the organization itself, group cohesiveness substitutes for both leader styles. Formalized rules and procedures substitute for leader task orientation. Physical separation of leader and subordinate neutralizes both leadership styles.

The value of the situations described in Exhibit 12.7 is that they help leaders avoid leadership overkill. Leaders should adopt a style with which to complement the organizational situation. For example, the work situation for bank tellers provides a high level of formalization, little flexibility, and a highly structured task. The head teller should not adopt a task-oriented style, because the organization already provides structure and direction. The head teller should concentrate on a people-oriented style. In other organizations, if group cohesiveness or previous training meet employees' social needs, the leader is free to concentrate on task-oriented behaviors. The leader can adopt a style complementary to the organizational situation to ensure that both task needs and people needs of the work group will be met.

neutralizer

A situational variable that counteracts a leadership style and prevents the leader from displaying certain behaviors.

● CHARISMATIC LEADERSHIP

In Chapter 1, we defined management to include the management functions of leading, planning, organizing, and controlling. But recent work on leadership has begun to distinguish leadership as something more: a quality that inspires and motivates people beyond their normal levels of performance.

TRANSACTIONAL LEADERS

The traditional management function of leading has been called *transactional leadership*.[28] **Transactional leaders** clarify the role and task requirements of subordinates, initiate structure, provide appropriate rewards, and try to be considerate to and meet the social needs of subordinates. The transactional leader's ability to satisfy subordinates may improve productivity. Transactional leaders excel at management functions. They are hardworking, tolerant, and fair minded. They take pride in keeping things running smoothly and efficiently. Transactional leaders often stress the impersonal aspects of performance, such as plans, schedules, and budgets. They have a sense of commitment to the organization and conform to organizational norms and values.

transactional leader

A leader who clarifies subordinates' role and task requirements, initiates structure, provides rewards, and displays consideration for subordinates.

The phenomenal growth of Microsoft Corporation is directly linked to Bill Gates' dedication to innovation and hard work. While known as a demanding boss, Gates encourages creativity and recognizes his employees' achievements.

CHARISMATIC LEADERS

charismatic leader

A leader who has the ability to motivate subordinates to transcend their expected performance.

Charismatic leadership goes beyond transactional leadership techniques. The **charismatic leader** has the capacity to motivate people to do more than normally expected. The impact of charismatic leaders is normally from (1) stating a lofty vision of an imagined future that employees identify with, (2) shaping a corporate value system for which everyone stands, and (3) trusting subordinates and earning their complete trust in return.[29] Charismatic leaders raise subordinates' consciousness about new outcomes and motivate them to transcend their own interests for the sake of the department or organization. Charismatic leaders tend to be less predictable than transactional leaders. They create an atmosphere of change, and they may be obsessed by visionary ideas that excite, stimulate, and drive other people to work hard. Charismatic leaders have an emotional impact on subordinates. They stand for something, have a vision of the future, are able to communicate that vision to subordinates, and motivate them to realize it.[30] The Manager's Shoptalk box provides a short quiz to help you determine whether you have the potential to be a charismatic leader.

Charismatic leaders include Mother Theresa, Martin Luther King, Jr., and Adolf Hitler. The true charismatic leader often does not fit within a traditional organization and may lead a social movement rather than a formal organization.

Charismatic leaders like Dr. King would applaud the corporate viewpoint expressed in Exhibit 12.8, and agree with critics who charge that today's typical U.S. company has a tendency to be "overmanaged and underled." Managers cope with "organizational complexity"; leaders initiate "productive change."[31] Transformational leaders balance the demands of both. **Transformational leaders** are similar to charismatic leaders but are distinguished by their special ability to bring about innovation and change.[32]

transformational leader

A leader distinguished by a special ability to bring about innovation and change.

ARE YOU A LEADER?

If you were the head of a major department in a corporation, how important would each of the following activities be to you? Answer yes or no to indicate whether you would strive to perform each activity.

1. Help subordinates clarify goals and how to reach them.
2. Give people a sense of mission and overall purpose.
3. Help get jobs out on time.
4. Look for the new product or service opportunities.
5. Use policies and procedures as guides for problem solving.
6. Promote unconventional beliefs and values.
7. Give monetary rewards in exchange for high performance from subordinates.
8. Command respect from everyone in the department.
9. Work alone to accomplish important tasks.
10. Suggest new and unique ways of doing things.
11. Give credit to people who do their jobs well.
12. Inspire loyalty to yourself and to the organization.
13. Establish procedures to help the department operate smoothly.
14. Use ideas to motivate others.
15. Set reasonable limits on new approaches.
16. Demonstrate social nonconformity.

The even-numbered items represent behaviors and activities of charismatic leaders. Charismatic leaders are personally involved in shaping ideas, goals, and direction of change. They use an intuitive approach to develop fresh ideas for old problems and seek new directions for the department or organization. The odd-numbered items are considered more traditional management activities, or what would be called *transactional leadership*. Managers respond to organizational problems in an impersonal way, make rational decisions, and coordinate and facilitate the work of others. If you answered yes to more even-numbered than odd-numbered items, you may be a potential charismatic leader. ∎

SOURCE: Based on Bernard M. Bass, *Leadership and Performance beyond Expectations* (New York: Free Press, 1985); and Lawton R. Burns and Selwyn W. Becker, "Leadership and Managership," in *Health Care Management*, ed. S. Shortell and A. Kaluzny (New York: Wiley, 1986).

Transformational leaders emerge to take an organization through a major strategic change, such as revitalization. They have the ability to make the necessary changes in the organization's mission, structure, and human resource management. Employees are persuaded to go along. In recent years, a number of firms, such as Compaq Computer, Campbell Soup, and Tenneco, have undergone transformation after appointing a new chief to act in the leadership role. Eckhard Pfeiffer of Compaq, David Johnson of Campbell Soup, and Mike Walsh of Tenneco helped invigorate and revitalize their firms.

● FEMALE LEADERSHIP

As women move into higher positions in organizations, changes in management style and corporate culture can be expected. One of the first changes to be perceived is that women bring a different leadership style to organizations, a style that is very effective in today's turbulent corporate environment.

EXHIBIT   12.8

Leaders versus Managers

**Let's Get
Rid of
Management**

People
don't want
to be
managed.
They want
to be led.
Whoever heard
of a world
manager?
World leader,
yes.
Educational leader.
Political leader.
Religious leader.
Scout leader.
Community leader.
Labor leader.
Business leader.
They lead.
They don't manage.
The carrot
always wins
over the stick.
Ask your horse.
You can *lead* your
horse to water,
but you can't
manage him
to drink.
If you want to
manage somebody,
manage yourself.
Do that well
and you'll
be ready to
stop managing.
And start
leading.

SOURCE: Courtesy of United Technologies Corporation, Hartford, CT 06101.

Leadership qualities for white American males have included aggressiveness, initiative, individual assertiveness, and presenting oneself as a take-charge kind of person. Men tend to be competitive, individualistic, and like working in a vertical hierarchy. Many men describe their leadership behavior as transactional, that is, as a series of transactions with subordinates. Employees do things for the manager in exchange for rewards. When engaging in transactional leadership, white males are likely to use legitimate power, reward power, and formal authority.

Although women also possess assertiveness, initiative, and aggressiveness, they tend to stress and engage in leadership behaviors that can be called *interactive*. An **interactive leader** is concerned with consensus building, is open and inclusive, encourages participation by others, and is more caring than the leadership style of many males.[33] Interactive leadership helps subordinates see that their self-interest and the organization's interest are the same—striving to reach organizational goals enables employees to reach personal goals. Female leaders such as Anita Roddick of the Body Shop (featured in the Leading Edge box), or Linda Wachner of Warnaco, are often more willing to empower people, enhance people's self-worth, and to share power and information.

The interactive leadership style is not limited to women. Anyone can develop these qualities, and both men and women engage in this style

interactive leader

A leader who is concerned with consensus building, is open and inclusive, and encourages participation.

LEADING edge   THE BODY SHOP INTERNATIONAL

In the beginning, most experts would probably have bet Body Shop founder Anita Roddick's fervor about environmental issues would ultimately be her downfall, if she stuck with it. However, the opposite has been true. As you read in Chapter 5, she has been the Body Shop's driving force and guiding inspiration for almost 20 years. She combined the right amount of sound business acumen and charismatic leadership to accomplish a rare feat. She convinced customers that her company was truly concerned about the collective good: theirs, hers, everyone's. There are currently Body Shops in 37 countries and many believe the big growth is yet to come. Because of Roddick, the company's original mission and company culture has never wavered.

Besides being a committed environmentalist herself, Roddick knew that selling consumers on the fact that a business was truly concerned with more than sales revenue and profits made trust integral to every transaction. She also knew that in an age of cynicism, a company that failed to live up to its half of such a bargain did not usually get

a second chance. That's why, as the Body Shop has rapidly expanded around the globe, Roddick has pressed for more environmentally conscious operations, not less.

How Roddick has inspired her employees is perhaps the most telling aspect of her leadership abilities. Most corporate employees have endured managerial directives emphasizing the importance of meeting sales or production projections, no matter what. It is almost impossible to get people like that to believe that a business considers anything but the bottom line.

Yet, Body Shop employees who have seen Roddick's environmental commitments gain momentum, using stores to champion various causes and even establishing an in-house Environmental Projects department that keeps track of the company's own compliance. What's amazing about employees of the Body Shop is they seem to have adopted Roddick's insouciance about company profits, even though the company offers equity participation and incentive programs. Most seem to have embraced Roddick's attitude. "The idea of business, I'd agree, is not to lose money," she says. "But to focus all the time on profits, profits, profits, I have to say I think it's deeply boring."

Roddick reconciles this seeming incongruity by educating employees

about both products and the environment, and in turn makes them as committed as she is about what a constructive force the Body Shop can be. She doesn't find the actual business boring in the least. She knows that convincing employees is the first and most important step in getting word out on issues she considers ciritical. "You educate people by their passions," she says. "You find ways to grab their imagination. You want them to feel they are doing something important, that they're not a lone voice, that they are the most powerful, potent people on the planet."

Profits boring? Committed employees who do not look at every sale as do-or-die, and who actually believe the pitch they are delivering to customers? Sounds like business heresy. However, it does sound somehow oddly reminiscent of someone who wanted to found a cosmetic company that could do business, and at the same time do something good for everyone. ∎

SOURCE: Bo Burlingham, "This Woman Has Changed Business Forever," *INC.*, June 1990, 34–46; and "The Body Shop: Marketer with a Message," *Focus Japan*, July 1991, 8.

of leadership if they so choose. Interactive leadership is consistent with the recent trend toward participation and empowerment taking place in our society, and it is especially appropriate in fast-changing organizations. Many male managers are learning to develop an interactive leadership style that includes empathy, attention to nonverbal behavior, cooperation, collaboration, and listening.[34]

SUMMARY AND MANAGEMENT SOLUTION

This chapter covered several important ideas about leadership. The early research on leadership focused on personal traits such as intelligence, energy, and appearance. Later, research attention shifted to leadership behaviors that are appropriate to the organizational situation. Two-dimensional approaches dominated the early work in this area; consideration and initiating structure were suggested as behaviors that lead work groups toward high performance. The Ohio State and Michigan approaches and the managerial grid are in this category. Contingency approaches include Fiedler's theory, Hersey and Blanchard's situational theory, and the substitutes-for-leadership concept.

Recent leadership concepts include charismatic leadership and interactive leadership. Charismatic leadership is the ability to articulate a vision and motivate employees to make it a reality. Charismatic leaders are especially important during organizational transformation. Interactive leadership is typical of many females; it involves consensus building, empowerment, and information and power sharing.

Ironically, one of the greatest hurdles Staubach had to overcome in his second career was avoiding discussions about his last one. "You'd go to a meeting [with prospective clients], and most of the time they wanted to talk about sports," says Ka Cotter, an executive vice-president with the Staubach Company. Staubach had referent power and a rock-solid reputation for integrity. However, it took some work to prove he had the leadership qualities to do business.

He had created a service specialty real estate firm aimed at a unique industry niche. The company would represent businesses needing to build, purchase, or lease all types of commercial space. By representing only users, the company would not have to worry about conflicts of interest, a common industry problem. In order to achieve the high standards of total quality management he wanted to emphasize in his firm, Staubach adopted the same democratic style of leadership that had made him so successful as a football player. He divided employees into teams, giving each full responsibility for meeting the needs of their customers. Although the pay structure included a salary, employee bonuses were based mainly on client satisfaction as measured through a formal survey. By providing this type of achievement-oriented leadership, Staubach avoided fights over commissions and got satisfied customers. He also made sure he practiced what he preached by being as supportive of his employees as he expected them to be with customers. "You have to treat your people with integrity if you expect them to treat customers the same way," he says.

The company's guarantee of quality is proof that Staubach's leadership skills have been effective. If a customer believes the services provided do not live up to the contracted fee, they can have it reduced to what they think the value added for the services was. The Staubach Company record? After over 11 years of operation, it stands at 139-1.

Only one client asked for a reduction. Such a lofty guarantee might be a risky proposition for most firms. However, it's all in a day's work for Captain Comeback.[35]

DISCUSSION QUESTIONS

1. Rob Martin became manager of a forklift assembly plant and believed in participative management, even when one supervisor used Rob's delegation to replace two competent line managers with his own friends. What would you say to Rob about his leadership style in this situation?
2. Suggest some personal traits that you believe would be useful to a leader. Are these traits more valuable in some situations than in others?
3. What is the difference between trait theories and behavioral theories of leadership?
4. Suggest the sources of power that would be available to a leader of a student government organization. To be effective, should student leaders keep power to themselves or delegate power to other students?
5. Would you prefer working for a leader who has a consideration or an initiating structure leadership style? Discuss the reasons for your answer.
6. What similarities do you see between the following contingency leadership theories: Hersey-Blanchard and Fiedler.
7. What is charismatic leadership? Differentiate between charismatic leadership and transactional leadership. Give an example of each.
8. One critic argued that women should not be stereotyped as having a leadership style different from that of men. Do you agree? Do you think that women, on average, have a more interactive style of leadership than men? Discuss.
9. Do you think leadership style is fixed and unchangeable for a leader or flexible and adaptable? Discuss.
10. Consider the leadership position of a senior partner in a law firm. What task, subordinate, and organizational factors might serve as substitutes for leadership in this situation?

MANAGEMENT IN PRACTICE: EXPERIENTIAL EXERCISE

● T – P   L E A D E R S H I P   Q U E S T I O N N A I R E :   A N   A S S E S S M E N T   O F   S T Y L E

Some leaders deal with general directions, leaving details to subordinates. Other leaders focus on specific details with the expectation that subordinates will carry out orders. Depending on the situation, both approaches may be effective. The important issue is the ability to identify relevant dimensions of the situation and behave accordingly. Through this questionnaire, you can identify your relative emphasis on two leadership dimensions: task orientation and people orientation. These are not opposite approaches, and an individual can rate high or low on either or both.

Directions: The following items describe aspects of leadership behavior. Respond to each item according to the way you would most likely act if you were the leader of a work group. Circle whether you would most likely behave in the described way: always (A), frequently (F), occasionally (O), seldom (S), or never (N).

A F O S N   1. I would most likely act as the spokesperson of the group.

A F O S N   2. I would encourage overtime work.

A F O S N   3. I would allow members complete freedom in their work.

A F O S N   4. I would encourage the use of uniform procedures.

A F O S N   5. I would permit members to use their own judgment in solving problems.

A F O S N   6. I would stress being ahead of competing groups.

A F O S N   7. I would speak as a representative of the group.

A F O S N   8. I would needle members for greater effort.

A F O S N   9. I would try out my ideas in the group.

A F O S N   10. I would let members do their work the way they think best.

A F O S N   11. I would be working hard for a promotion.

A F O S N   12. I would tolerate postponement and uncertainty.

A F O S N   13. I would speak for the group if there were visitors present.

A F O S N   14. I would keep the work moving at a rapid pace.

A F O S N   15. I would turn the members loose on a job and let them go to it.

A F O S N   16. I would settle conflicts when they occur in the group.

A F O S N   17. I would get swamped by details.

A F O S N   18. I would represent the group at outside meetings.

A F O S N   19. I would be reluctant to allow the members any freedom of action.

A F O S N   20. I would decide what should be done and how it should be done.

A F O S N   21. I would push for increased production.

A F O S N   22. I would let some members have authority which I could keep.

A F O S N   23. Things would usually turn out as I had predicted.

A F O S N   24. I would allow the group a high degree of initiative.

A F O S N   25. I would assign group members to particular tasks.

A F O S N   26. I would be willing to make changes.

A F O S N   27. I would ask the members to work harder.

A F O S N   28. I would trust the group members to exercise good judgment.

A F O S N   29. I would schedule the work to be done.

A F O S N   30. I would refuse to explain my actions.

A F O S N   31. I would persuade others that my ideas are to their advantage.

A F O S N   32. I would permit the group to set its own pace.

A F O S N   33. I would urge the group to beat its previous record.

A F O S N   34. I would act without consulting the group.

A F O S N   35. I would ask that group members follow standard rules and regulations.

T _____ P _____

SOURCE: The T–P Leadership Questionnaire was adapted by J. B. Ritchie and P. Thompson in *Organization and People* (New York: West, 1984). Copyright 1969 by the American Educational Research Association. Adapted by permission of the publisher.

The T–P Leadership Questionnaire is scored as follows:

a. Circle the item number for items 8, 12, 17, 18, 19, 30, 34, and 35.

b. Write the number 1 in front of a *circled item number* if you responded S (seldom) or N (never) to that item.

c. Also write a number 1 in front of *item numbers not circled* if you responded A (always) or F (frequently).

d. Circle the number 1s that you have written in front of the following items: 3, 5, 8, 10, 15, 18, 19, 22, 24, 26, 28, 30, 32, 34, and 35.

e. *Count the circled number 1s.* This is your score for concern for people. Record the score in the blank following the letter P at the end of the questionnaire.

f. *Count uncircled number 1s.* This is your score for concern for task. Record this number in the blank following the letter T.

CASE FOR ANALYSIS

YOUNG MANAGERS

Young managers who are eager to make their mark at new positions of leadership should beware. There are prerequisites to implementing changes, even good ones. Academic credentials and the assumption of a title do not automatically guarantee respect from subordinates. In the beginning, directive leadership can be a disaster. If a new manager, particularly a young one, does not take the time to get to know staffers, seek their input, and establish effective lines of communication, employee resentment and resistance will ensure an adverse outcome. After all, no strategy is brilliant enough to implement itself.

Andrea David is a 24-year-old manager of payment service for Manufacturers and Traders Trust in New York. Her seven-person staff includes people older than her parents. She learned quickly that workplace values and goals often differ greatly depending on an employee's age. Older workers attach importance to the security, camaraderie, and sense of belonging that comes with years on the job. Young managers' priorities focus on status, success, competition, power, and money. David learned early that being open-minded and flexible in her thinking paid off. She instructed a subordinate to change the layout of a spreadsheet, not the actual numbers on it. The employee, wondering aloud what possible difference the position of the numbers could make, brought David to a realization. "Some people don't do things exactly the way you do," she says, "but as long as the job is well done, you can't criticize."

James T. "Ty" Anderson became NatWest USA's Loan Management Division's youngest senior vice president in 1990. This distinction made him aware of the tendency of peers to compare their career progress with his. To get around the problem, he takes an achievement-oriented leadership approach and actively assists his 20 staff members plan and chart their own paths. "They should be made aware that their careers haven't been forestalled and that there's some career development planned for them."

Judy Magnus-Long, vice president and manager of human resources at a New York-based advertising firm, experienced another problem that sometimes cannot be overcome. She was promoted to a position many thought would go to another older employee. "I tried to do the things one says you should do," Magnus-Long says. "I asked her advice, let her know she was valued, that I needed the benefit of her experience. And I did get it, but it was not done overzealously." Or, for very long, either. The employee quit about 30 days later.

Tom Adams, vice president of business planning for Xerox Corporation, assumed his first managerial position at age 25. He believes showing employees that you genuinely care about them as individuals is one of the most important components of success. Adams views what happened to Magnus-Long as inevitable. He thinks keeping managers with coinciding career tracks at close quarters is inviting disaster. "One of the first rules of business is, get candid, confident, and challenging. I have never done it before. I have never failed at anything I've tried. We will get it done together. Can I count on your support?"

● QUESTIONS

1. What sources of power should young managers rely on, and how are followers likely to react?
2. Based on Fiedler's contingency theory, what leadership style should young managers adopt?
3. Have you ever been placed in a position of leadership? What approach did you take?

SOURCE: Minda Zetlin, "Young Managers Face a Generation Gap," *Management Review,* January 1992, 10–15.

REFERENCES

1. Albert G. Holzinger, "How to Succeed by Really Trying," *Nation's Business,* August 1992, 50–51.

2. Catherine Arnst and Stephanie Anderson Forest, "Compaq: How It Made Its Impressive Move Out of the Doldrums," *Business Week,* November 2, 1992, 146–151; "The Newsmakers," *Business Week,* April 18, 1986, 194; and David C. Limerick, "Managers of Meaning: From Bob Geldof's Band Aid to Australian CEOs," *Organizational Dynamics,* Spring 1990, 22–23.

3. Gary Yukl, "Managerial Leadership: A Review of Theory and Research," *Journal of Management* 15 (1989), 251–289.

4. James M. Kouzes and Barry Z. Posner, "The Credibility Factor: What Followers Expect from Their Leaders," *Management Review,* January 1990, 29–33.

5. Henry Mintzberg, *Power in and around Organizations* (Englewood Cliffs, N.J.: Prentice-Hall, 1983); and Jeffrey Pfeffer, *Power in Organizations* (Marshfield, Mass.: Pitman, 1981).

6. J. R. P. French, Jr., and B. Raven, "The Bases of Social Power," in *Group Dynamics,* ed. D. Cartwright and A. F. Zander (Evanston, Ill.: Row, Peterson, 1960), 607–623.

7. G. A. Yukl and T. Taber, "The Effective Use of Managerial Power," *Personnel* (March–April 1983), 37–44.

8. Ralph Stayer, "How I Learned to Let My Workers Lead," *Harvard Business Review* (November–December 1990), 66–83; Thomas A. Stewart, "New Ways to Exercise Power," *Fortune,* November 6, 1989, 52–64; and Thomas A. Stewart, "CEOs See Clout Shifting," *Fortune,* November 6, 1989, 66.

9. G. A. Yukl, *Leadership in Organizations* (Englewood Cliffs, N.J.: Prentice-Hall, 1981); and S. C. Kohs and K. W. Irle, "Prophesying Army Promotion," *Journal of Applied Psychology* 4 (1920), 73–87.

10. R. Albanese and D. D. Van Fleet, *Organizational Behavior: A Managerial Viewpoint* (Hinsdale, Ill.: Dryden Press, 1983).

11. K. Lewin, "Field Theory and Experiment in Social Psychology: Concepts and Methods," *American Journal of Sociology* 44 (1939), 868–896; K. Lewin and R. Lippitt, "An Experimental Approach to the Study of Autocracy and Democracy: A Preliminary Note," *Sociometry* 1 (1938), 292–300; K. Lewin, R. Lippitt, and R. K. White, "Patterns of Aggressive Behavior in Experimentally Created Social Climates," *Journal of Social Psychology* 10 (1939), 271–301.

12. R. K. White and R. Lippitt, *Autocracy and Democracy: An Experimental Inquiry* (New York: Harper, 1960).

13. R. Tannenbaum and W. H. Schmidt, "How to Choose a Leadership Pattern," *Harvard Business Review* 36 (1958), 95–101.

14. F. A. Heller and G. A. Yukl, "Participation, Managerial Decision-Making and Situational Variables," *Organizational Behavior and Human Performance* 4 (1969), 227–241.

15. Patricia O'Toole, "How Do You Build a $44 Million Company? By Saying 'Please,'" *Working Woman,* April 1990, 88–92.

16. Robert Davies, "Managing by Listening," *Nation's Business,* September 1993, 6.

17. C. A. Schriesheim and B. J. Bird, "Contributions of the Ohio State Studies to the Field of Leadership," *Journal of Management* 5 (1979), 135–145; and C. L. Shartle, "Early Years of the Ohio State University Leadership Studies," *Journal of Management* 5 (1979), 126–134.

18. P. C. Nystrom, "Managers and the High-High Leader Myth," *Academy of Management Journal* 21 (1978), 325–331; and L. L. Larson, J. G. Hunt, and R. N. Osborn, "The Great High-High Leader Behavior Myth: A Lesson from Occam's Razor," *Academy of Management Journal* 19 (1976), 628–641.

19. R. Likert, "From Production- and Employee-Centeredness to Systems 1–4," *Journal of Management* 5 (1979), 147–156.

20. Robert R. Blake and Jane S. Mouton, *The Managerial Grid III* (Houston: Gulf, 1985).

21. F. E. Fiedler, "Assumed Similarity Measures as Predictors of Team Effectiveness," *Journal of Abnormal and Social Psychology* 49 (1954), 381–388; F. E. Fiedler, *Leader Attitudes and Group Effectiveness* (Urbana, Ill.: University of Illi-

nois Press, 1958); and F. E. Fiedler, *A Theory of Leadership Effectiveness* (New York: McGraw-Hill, 1967).

22. F. E. Fiedler and M. M. Chemers, *Leadership and Effective Management* (Glenview, Ill.: Scott, Foresman, 1974).

23. F. E. Fiedler, "Engineer the Job to Fit the Manager," *Harvard Business Review* 43 (1965), 115–122; and F. E. Fiedler, M. M. Chemers, and L. Mahar, *Improving Leadership Effectiveness: The Leader Match Concept* (New York: Wiley, 1976).

24. R. Singh, "Leadership Style and Reward Allocation: Does Least Preferred Coworker Scale Measure Tasks and Relation Orientation?" *Organizational Behavior and Human Performance* 27 (1983), 178–197; and D. Hosking, "A Critical Evaluation of Fiedler's Contingency Hypotheses," *Progress in Applied Psychology* 1 (1981), 103–154.

25. Paul Hersey and Kenneth H. Blanchard, *Management of Organizational Behavior: Utilizing Human Resources*, 4th ed. (Englewood Cliffs, N.J.: Prentice-Hall, 1982).

26. E. J. Dionne, Jr., "Pierce at H.U.D.: Eight Years of Hands-Off Management," *The New York Times*, June 18, 1989, 1.

27. S. Kerr and J. M. Jermier, "Substitutes for Leadership: Their Meaning and Measurement," *Organizational Behavior and Human Performance* 22 (1978), 375–403; and Jon P. Howell and Peter W. Dorfman, "Leadership and Substitutes for Leadership among Professional and Nonprofessional Workers," *Journal of Applied Behavioral Science* 22 (1986), 29–46.

28. The terms *transactional* and *transformational* come from James M. Burns, *Leadership* (New York: Harper & Row, 1978); and Bernard M. Bass, "Leadership: Good, Better, Best," *Organizational Dynamics* 13 (Winter 1985), 26–40.

29. Jay A. Conger and Rabindra N. Kanungo, "Toward a Behavioral Theory of Charismatic Leadership in Organizational Settings," *Academy of Management Review* 12 (1987), 637–647; Walter Kiechel III, "A Hard Look at Executive Vision," *Fortune*, October 23, 1989, 207–211; and Allan Cox, "Focus on Teamwork, Vision, and Values," *The New York Times*, February 26, 1989, F3.

30. Robert J. House, "Research Contrasting the Behavior and Effects of Reputed Charismatic vs. Reputed Non-Charismatic Leaders" (Paper presented as part of a symposium, "Charismatic Leadership: Theory and Evidence," Academy of Management, San Diego, 1985).

31. John P. Kotter, "What Leaders Really Do," *Harvard Business Review* (May–June 1990), 103–111.

32. Noel M. Tichy and David O. Ulrich, "The Leadership Challenge—A Call for the Transformational Leader," *Sloan Management Review* 26 (Fall 1984), 59–68.

33. Judy Rosener, "Ways Women Lead," *Harvard Business Review* (November–December 1990), 119–125; and Nelton, "Men, Women, & Leadership."

34. M. Fine, F. Johnson, and M. S. Ryan, "Cultural Diversity in the Workforce," *Public Personnel Management* 19 (1990), 305–319.

35. Albert G. Holzinger, "How to Succeed by Really Trying."

MOTIVATION IN ORGANIZATIONS   13

CHAPTER OUTLINE ▲

LEARNING OBJECTIVES ▼

After studying this chapter, you should be able to

- Define *motivation* and explain the difference between current approaches and traditional approaches to motivation.

- Identify and describe content theories of motivation based on employee needs.

- Identify and explain process theories of motivation.

- Describe reinforcement theory and how it can be used to motivate employees.

- Explain the path-goal theory.

- Discuss major approaches to job design and how job design influences motivation.

- Discuss new management applications of motivation theories.

At 30, Gary Aronson was frustrated, bored, and wondering why he was in the gourmet fast-food business. As manager of an Au Bon Pain store, he made a meager $26,000 a year and was known as a whiner and complainer. His heart was not in what he considered a dead-end job, and many of his employees seemed to feel the same. The best he could hope for after five more years was another $3,000 in annual income, so he put in his time trying to figure out what he was going to do next. Unfortunately, Gary Aronson was typical of managers in all 40 Au Bon Pain stores.[1] ■ If you were the president of Au Bon Pain, how would you motivate managers like Gary Aronson to give their all to the company? Is high motivation even possible in this kind of service business? What sparks improved performance?

The problem for Au Bon Pain is that unmotivated managers mean unmotivated employees, all doing minimum work and causing the chain to lose its competitive edge. One secret of success for small- and medium-size businesses is motivated and enthusiastic employees. The challenge facing Au Bon Pain and other companies is to keep employee motivation consistent with organizational objectives. Motivation is a challenge for managers because motivation arises from within employees and typically differs for each employee. For example, Janice Rennie makes a staggering $350,000 a year selling residential real estate in Toronto; she attributes her success to the fact that she likes to listen carefully to clients and then find a house to meet their needs. Greg Storey is a skilled machinist who is challenged by writing programs for numerically controlled machines. After dropping out of college, he swept floors in a machine shop and was motivated to learn to run the machines. Frances Blais sells *World Book Encyclopedia*. She is a top salesperson, but she does not care about the $50,000-plus commissions: "I'm not even thinking money when I'm selling. I'm really on a crusade to help children read well." In stark contrast, Rob Michaels gets sick to his stomach before he goes to work. Rob is a telephone salesperson who spends all day trying to get people to buy products they do not need, and the rejections are painful. His motivation is money; he earned $120,000 in the past year and cannot make nearly that much doing anything else.[2]

Rob is motivated by money, Janice by her love of listening and problem solving, Frances by the desire to help children read, and Greg by the challenge of mastering numerically controlled machinery. Each person is motivated to perform, yet each has different reasons for performing. With such diverse motivations, it is a challenge for managers to motivate employees toward common organizational goals.

This chapter reviews theories and models of employee motivation. First we will review traditional approaches to motivation. Then we will cover models that describe the employee needs and processes associated with motivation. Finally, we will discuss the designing of jobs to increase employee motivation.

● THE CONCEPT OF MOTIVATION

motivation

The arousal, direction, and persistence of behavior.

Most of us get up in the morning, go to school or work, and behave in ways that are predictably our own. We respond to our environment and the people in it with little thought as to why we work hard, enjoy certain classes, or find some recreational activities so much fun. Yet all of these behaviors are motivated by something. **Motivation** generally is defined as the arousal, direction, and persistence of behavior.[3] The study of motivation concerns what prompts people to initiate action, what influences their choice of action, and why they persist in that action over time.

A simple model of human motivation is illustrated in Exhibit 13.1. People have basic *needs,* such as for food, achievement, or monetary gain, that translate into an internal tension that motivates specific behaviors with which to fulfill the need. To the extent that the behavior is suc-

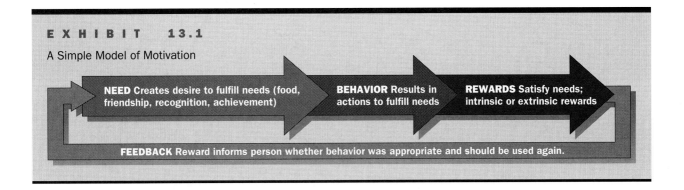

EXHIBIT   13.1

A Simple Model of Motivation

NEED Creates desire to fulfill needs (food, friendship, recognition, achievement)

BEHAVIOR Results in actions to fulfill needs

REWARDS Satisfy needs; intrinsic or extrinsic rewards

FEEDBACK Reward informs person whether behavior was appropriate and should be used again.

cessful, the person is rewarded in the sense that the need is satisfied. The reward also informs the person that the behavior was appropriate and can be used again in the future.

Rewards are of two types: intrinsic and extrinsic. **Intrinsic rewards** are received as a direct consequence of a person's actions. The completion of a complex task may bestow a pleasant feeling of accomplishment. **Extrinsic rewards** are given by another person, typically a manager, and include promotions and pay increases. For example, Frances Blais sells encyclopedias for the intrinsic reward of helping children read well. Rob Michaels, who hates his sales job, nevertheless is motivated by the extrinsic reward of high pay.

The importance of motivation as illustrated in Exhibit 13.1 is that it can lead to behaviors that reflect high performance within organizations.[4] Managers can use motivation theory to help satisfy employees' needs and simultaneously encourage high work performance.

intrinsic reward

A reward received as a direct consequence of a person's actions.

extrinsic reward

A reward given by another person.

● FOUNDATIONS OF MOTIVATION

A manager's assumptions about employee motivation and use of rewards depend on his or her perspective on motivation. Three distinct perspectives on employee motivation that have evolved are the traditional approach, the human relations approach, and the human resources approach.[5] The most recent theories about motivation represent a fourth perspective called *contemporary approaches.*

TRADITIONAL APPROACH

The study of employee motivation really began with the work of Frederick W. Taylor on scientific management. Recall from Chapter 2 that scientific management pertains to the systematic analysis of an employee's job for the purpose of increasing efficiency. Economic rewards are provided to employees for high performance. The emphasis on pay evolved into the perception of workers as *economic people*—people who would work harder for higher pay. This approach led to the development of incentive pay systems, in which people were paid strictly on the quantity and quality of their work outputs.

HUMAN RELATIONS APPROACH

The economic man was gradually replaced by a more sociable employee in managers' minds. Beginning with the landmark Hawthorne studies at a Western Electric plant, noneconomic rewards, such as congenial work groups who met social needs, seemed more important than money as a motivator of work behavior.[6] For the first time, workers were studied as people, and the concept of *social man* was born. Further study led researchers to conclude that simply paying attention to workers could change their behavior for the better, this was called the *Hawthorne effect*.

HUMAN RESOURCE APPROACH

The human resource approach carries the concepts of economic man and social man further to introduce the concept of the *whole person*. Human resource theory suggests that employees are complex and motivated by many factors. For example, the work by McGregor on Theory X and Theory Y described in Chapter 2 argued that people want to do a good job and that work is as natural and healthy as play. Proponents of the human resource approach believed that earlier approaches had tried to manipulate employees through economic or social rewards. By assuming that employees are competent and able to make major contributions, managers can enhance organizational performance. The human resource approach laid the groundwork for contemporary perspectives on employee motivation.

CONTEMPORARY APPROACHES

Contemporary approaches to employee motivation are dominated by three types of theories, each of which will be discussed in the remaining sections of this chapter. The first are *content theories,* which stress the analysis of underlying human needs. Content theories provide insight into the needs of people in organizations and help managers understand how needs can be satisfied in the workplace. *Process theories* concern the thought processes that influence behavior. They focus on how employees seek rewards in work circumstances. *Reinforcement theories* focus on employee learning of desired work behaviors. In Exhibit 13.1, content theories focus on the concepts in the first box, process theories on those in the second, and reinforcement theories on those in the third.

● CONTENT PERSPECTIVES ON MOTIVATION

content theories

A group of theories that emphasize the needs that motivate people.

Content theories emphasize the needs that motivate people. At any point in time, people have basic needs such as those for food, achievement, or monetary reward. These needs translate into an internal drive that motivates specific behaviors in an attempt to fulfill the needs. An individual's needs are like a hidden catalog of the things he or she wants and will work to get. To the extent that managers understand worker needs, the organization's reward systems can be designed to meet them and reinforce employees for directing energies and priorities toward attainment of organizational goals.

HIERARCHY OF NEEDS THEORY

Probably the most famous content theory was developed by Abraham Maslow.[7] Maslow's **hierarchy of needs theory** proposes that humans are motivated by multiple needs and that these needs exist in a hierarchical order as illustrated in Exhibit 13.2. Maslow identified five general types of motivating needs in order of ascendance:

1 *Physiological needs.* These are the most basic human physical needs, including food, water, and sex. In the organizational setting, these are reflected in the needs for adequate heat, air, and base salary to ensure survival.

2 *Safety needs.* These are the needs for a safe and secure physical and emotional environment and freedom from threats, that is, for freedom from violence and for an orderly society. In an organizational workplace, safety needs reflect the needs for safe jobs, fringe benefits, and job security.

3 *Belongingness needs.* These needs reflect the desire to be accepted by one's peers, have friendships, be part of a group, and be loved. In the organization, these needs influence the desire for good relationships with coworkers, participation in a work group, and a positive relationship with supervisors.

4 *Esteem needs.* These needs relate to the desire for a positive self-image and to receive attention, recognition, and appreciation from others. Within organizations, esteem needs reflect a motivation for

hierarchy of needs theory

A content theory that proposes that people are motivated by five categories of needs—physiological, safety, belongingness, esteem, and self-actualization—that exist in a hierarchical order.

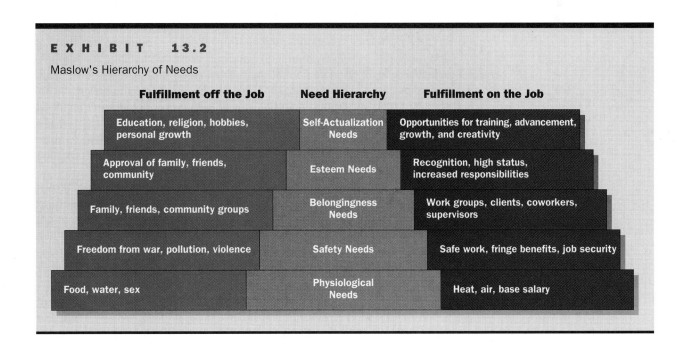

E X H I B I T   13.2

Maslow's Hierarchy of Needs

Fulfillment off the Job	Need Hierarchy	Fulfillment on the Job
Education, religion, hobbies, personal growth	Self-Actualization Needs	Opportunities for training, advancement, growth, and creativity
Approval of family, friends, community	Esteem Needs	Recognition, high status, increased responsibilities
Family, friends, community groups	Belongingness Needs	Work groups, clients, coworkers, supervisors
Freedom from war, pollution, violence	Safety Needs	Safe work, fringe benefits, job security
Food, water, sex	Physiological Needs	Heat, air, base salary

recognition, an increase in responsibility, high status, and credit for contributions to the organization.

5 *Self-actualization needs.* These represent the need for self-fulfillment, which is the highest need category. They concern developing one's full potential, increasing one's competence, and becoming a better person. Self-actualization needs can be met in the organization by providing people with opportunities to grow, be creative, and acquire training for challenging assignments and advancement.

According to Maslow's theory, lower-order needs take priority—they must be satisfied before higher-order needs are activated. The needs are satisfied in sequence: Physiological needs come before safety needs, safety needs before social needs, and so on. A person desiring physical safety will devote his or her efforts to securing a safer environment and will not be concerned with esteem needs or self-actualization needs. Once a need is satisfied, it declines in importance and the next higher need is activated. When a union wins good pay and working conditions for its members, basic needs are met; union members may then desire to have belongingness and esteem needs met in the workplace.

One example of meeting employee needs is the Super Vision program sponsored by Domino's Pizza Distribution.

 DOMINO'S PIZZA DISTRIBUTION

Domino's Pizza Distribution is the subsidiary that provides the makings for the millions of "diet busters" delivered daily by Domino's Pizza. And, it does quite well. Over a 12-year period, DPD's revenues have increased 120-fold. The meteoric increase is in large part attributable to a management approach called Super Vision, which both challenges and rewards employees.

DPD performs functions ranging from dough production to shipping and receiving. However, management does not think fulfilling its company objectives is likely if it cannot help employees realize their own goals and aspirations. To do that, DPD assists employees in achieving a balance in five basic areas: spiritual, physical, mental, social, and financial. Employees also undergo job planning and review about every six weeks. One-on-one sessions with team leaders permit individuals to talk about future aspirations, and provide a forum for reviewing job performance, analyzing problems, and commending outstanding work.

Under Super Vision, outstanding performances by team members in any category earn special recognition from management. Employees are afforded an avenue for registering complaints or offering suggestions through monthly surveys. Workers also gain exposure to communications channels at monthly meetings directed by outside facilitators. Peer recognition is a big part of Super Vision. But personal growth plays an equally important role.

Super Vision can be time-consuming, but Domino's views it as an investment. Being cognizant of the needs of employees, nurturing personal growth, and rewarding exceptional performance cannot help but lead to a better, more motivated work force. That, in turn, translates to a better company.[8] ■

TWO-FACTOR THEORY

Frederick Herzberg developed another popular theory of motivation called the *two-factor theory.*[9] Herzberg interviewed hundreds of workers about times when they were highly motivated to work and other times when they were dissatisfied and unmotivated at work. His findings suggested that the work characteristics associated with dissatisfaction were quite different from those pertaining to satisfaction, which prompted the notion that two factors influence work motivation.

The two-factor theory is illustrated in Exhibit 13.3. The center of the scale is neutral, meaning that workers are neither satisfied nor dissatisfied. Herzberg believed that two entirely separate dimensions contribute to an employee's behavior at work. The first, called **hygiene factors,** involves the presence or absence of job dissatisfiers, such as working conditions, pay, company policies, and interpersonal relationships. When hygiene factors are poor, work is dissatisfying. However, good hygiene factors simply remove the dissatisfaction; they do not in themselves cause people to become highly satisfied and motivated in their work.

The second set of factors does influence job satisfaction. **Motivators** are higher-level needs and include achievement, recognition, responsibility, and opportunity for growth. Herzberg believed that when

hygiene factors

Factors that involve the presence or absence of job dissatisfiers, including working conditions, pay, company policies, and interpersonal relationships.

motivators

Factors that influence job satisfaction based on fulfillment of higher-level needs such as achievement, recognition, responsibility, and opportunity for growth.

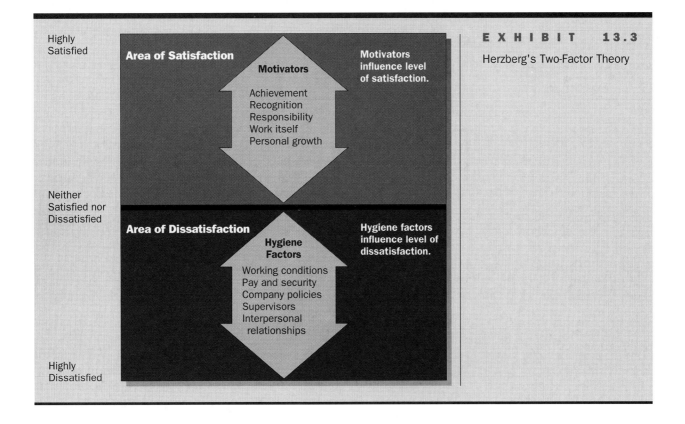

E X H I B I T   1 3 . 3

Herzberg's Two-Factor Theory

motivators are absent, workers are neutral toward work, but when motivators are present, workers are highly motivated and satisfied. Thus, hygiene factors and motivators represent two distinct factors that influence motivation. Hygiene factors work only in the area of dissatisfaction. Unsafe working conditions or a noisy work environment will cause people to be dissatisfied; their correction will not lead to a high level of motivation and satisfaction. Motivators such as challenge, responsibility, and recognition must be in place before employees will be highly motivated to excel at their work.

The implication of the two-factor theory for managers is clear. Providing hygiene factors will eliminate employee dissatisfaction but will not motivate workers to high achievement levels. On the other hand, recognition, challenge, and opportunities for personal growth are powerful motivators and will promote high satisfaction and performance. The manager's role is to remove dissatisfiers—that is, provide hygiene factors sufficient to meet basic needs—and then use motivators to meet higher-level needs and propel employees toward greater achievement and satisfaction. Consider the manager's role at YSI, Inc.

 YSI, INC.

Malte Von Matthiessen, president of YSI, Inc., knows about motivation. When he took the reins of YSI, the company was overstaffed, quality was low, and both growth and profits were stagnant. Relations between management and workers were good, but Matthiessen could ill afford to fail either to provide adequate hygiene factors or to meet higher-level needs of employees as he attempted to turn around YSI.

Matthiessen solved the overstaffing situation by allowing employee reduction through natural attrition rather than firings, and he placed new emphasis on higher-quality and new, advanced product lines. Perhaps his greatest change involved the use of a motivational tool: empowerment of employees. Shop-floor units were reorganized into work centers, each responsible for its own hiring, problem solving, and quality. Increased employee training and employee access to management information about customer needs, inventories, budgets, and manufacturing procedures motivated employees to think creatively and use their newfound authority to improve the company.

Has Matthiessen's motivational approach worked? Within its first two years, YSI, Inc., saved roughly $1 million in manufacturing costs. YSI employees have renewed pride in company profitability and in their own increased knowledge as they discuss yield rates, new methods of problem solving, or performance-to-schedule ratios.[10] ■

ACQUIRED NEEDS THEORY

The final content theory was developed by David McClelland. The *acquired needs theory* proposes that certain types of needs are acquired during the individual's lifetime. In other words, people are not born with these needs but may learn them through their life experiences.[11] The three needs most frequently studied are these:

1 *Need for achievement:* the desire to accomplish something difficult, attain a high standard of success, master complex tasks, and surpass others.

2 *Need for affiliation:* the desire to form close personal relationships, avoid conflict, and establish warm friendships.

3 *Need for power:* the desire to influence or control others, be responsible for others, and have authority over others.

Early life experiences determine whether people acquire these needs. If children are encouraged to do things for themselves and receive reinforcement, they will acquire a need to achieve. If they are reinforced for forming warm human relationships, they will develop a need for affiliation. If they get satisfaction from controlling others, they will acquire a need for power.

For over 20 years, McClelland studied human needs and their implication for management. People with a high need for achievement tend to be entrepreneurs. They like to do something better than competitors and take sensible business risks. On the other hand, people who have a high need for affiliation are successful "integrators," whose job is to coordinate the work of several departments in an organization.[12] Integrators include brand managers and project managers who must have excellent people skills. People high in need for affiliation are able to establish positive working relationships with others.

A high need for power often is associated with successful attainment of top levels in the organizational hierarchy. For example, McClelland studied managers at AT&T for 16 years and found that those with a high need for power were more likely to follow a path of continued promotion over time. Over half of the employees at the top levels had a high need for power. In contrast, managers with a high need for achievement but a low need for power tended to peak earlier in their careers and at a lower level. The reason is that achievement needs can be met through the task itself, but power needs can be met only by ascending to a level at which a person has power over others.

In summary, content theories focus on people's underlying needs and label those that motivate people to behave. The hierarchy of needs

Tammy Ackers, Taco Bell store manager in Ashland, Kentucky, enjoys her new Trans Am, first prize in a contest among store teams. Tammy possesses both the need for achievement and affiliation, which account for her store's astonishing success, with 45 percent real growth in an area with 30 percent unemployment, an outstanding store quality rating, and increases of over 30 percent in profitability.

theory, the two-factor theory, and the acquired needs theory all help managers understand what motivates people. In this way, managers can design work to meet needs and hence elicit appropriate and successful work behaviors.

● PROCESS PERSPECTIVES ON MOTIVATION

Process theories explain how workers select behavioral actions to meet their needs and determine whether their choices were successful. There are three basic process theories: equity theory, path-goal theory, and expectancy theory.

EQUITY THEORY

Equity theory focuses on individuals' perceptions of how fairly they are treated compared with others. Developed by J. Stacy Adams, equity theory proposes that people are motivated to seek social equity in the rewards they expect for performance.[13]

According to equity theory, if people perceive their compensation as equal to what others receive for similar contributions, they will believe that their treatment is fair and equitable. People evaluate equity by a ratio of inputs to outcomes. Inputs to a job include education, experience, effort, and ability. Outcomes from a job include pay, recognition, benefits, and promotions. The input to outcome ratio may be compared to another person in the work group or to a perceived group average. A state of **equity** exists whenever the ratio of one person's outcomes to inputs equals the ratio of another's outcomes to inputs.

Inequity occurs when the input-outcome ratios are out of balance, such as when a person with a high level of education or experience receives the same salary as a new, less educated employee. Perceived inequity also occurs in the other direction. Thus, if an employee discovers she is making more money than other people who contribute the same inputs to the company, she may feel the need to correct the inequity by working harder, getting more education, or considering lower pay. Perceived inequity creates tensions within individuals that motivate them to bring equity into balance.[14]

The most common methods for reducing a perceived inequity are these:

- *Change inputs.* A person may choose to increase or decrease his or her inputs to the organization. For example, underpaid individuals may reduce their level of effort or increase their absenteeism. Overpaid people may increase effort on the job.
- *Change outcomes.* A person may change his or her outcomes. An underpaid person may request a salary increase or a bigger office. A union may try to improve wages and working conditions in order to be consistent with a comparable union whose members make more money.
- *Distort perceptions.* Research suggests that people may distort perceptions of equity if they are unable to change inputs or outcomes.

process theories
A group of theories that explain how employees select behaviors with which to meet their needs and determine whether their choices were successful.

equity theory
A process theory that focuses on individuals' perceptions of how fairly they are treated relative to others.

equity
A situation that exists when the ratio of one person's outcomes to inputs equals that of another's.

They may artificially increase the status attached to their jobs or distort others' perceived rewards to bring equity into balance.

- *Leave the job.* People who feel inequitably treated may decide to leave their jobs rather than suffer the inequity of being under- or overpaid. In their new jobs, they expect to find a more favorable balance of rewards.

The implication of equity theory for managers is that employees indeed evaluate the perceived equity of their rewards compared to others'. An increase in salary or a promotion will have no motivational effect if it is perceived as inequitable relative to that of other employees. Some organizations, for example, have created a two-tier wage system to reduce wage rates. New employees make far less than experienced ones, which creates a basis for inequity. Flight attendants at American Airlines are determined to topple the two-tier structure under which they are paid. Chris Boschert, who sorts packages for United Parcel Service, was hired after the two-tier wage system took effect. "It makes me mad," Boschert said. "I get $9.68 an hour, and the guy working next to me makes $13.99 doing exactly the same job."[15] Inequitable pay puts pressure on employees that is sometimes almost too great to bear. They attempt to change their work habits, try to change the system, or leave the job.[16]

PATH-GOAL THEORY

Another process theory, called the **path-goal theory,** proposes that individual motivation depends on the leader's ability to clarify the behavior necessary for task accomplishments and rewards.[17] As illustrated in Exhibit 13.4, employee motivation may be increased by either (1) clarifying the subordinates' path to the rewards that are available or (2) increasing the rewards that they value and desire. Path clarification means that the leader works with individuals to help them identify and learn the behaviors that will lead to successful task accomplishment and organizational rewards. Increasing rewards means that the leader talks with subordinates to learn which rewards are important to them—that is, whether they desire intrinsic rewards from the work itself or extrinsic rewards such as raises or promotions. The leader's job is to increase personal payoffs to subordinates for goal attainment and to make the paths to these payoffs clear and easy to travel.[18]

This model consists of three sets of contingencies—leader behavior and style, situational contingencies, and the use of rewards to meet subordinates' needs.[19]

LEADER BEHAVIOR.   The path-goal theory suggests a fourfold classification of leader behaviors.[20] These classifications are the types of leader behavior the leader can adopt to impact employee motivation and include supportive, directive, achievement-oriented, and participative styles.

Supportive leadership involves leader behavior that shows concern for subordinates' well-being and personal needs. Leadership behavior is open, friendly, and approachable, and the leader creates a team climate and treats subordinates as equals. Supportive leadership is similar to the consideration leadership described in Chapter 12.

path-goal theory

A process theory that proposes that individual motivation depends on the leader's ability to clarify the behavior necessary for task accomplishments and rewards.

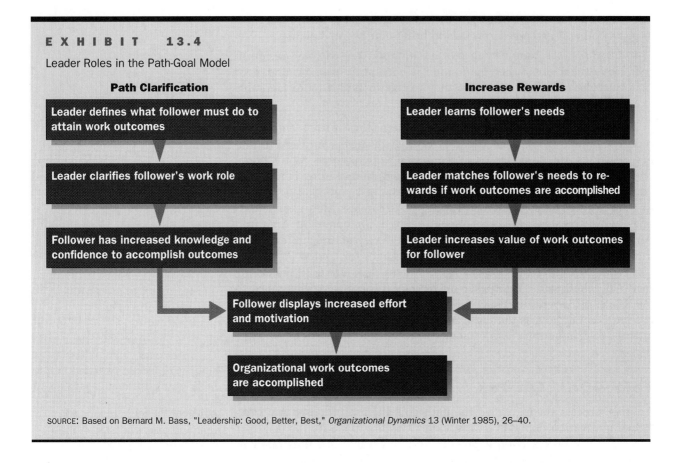

EXHIBIT   13.4

Leader Roles in the Path-Goal Model

Path Clarification

Leader defines what follower must do to attain work outcomes

Leader clarifies follower's work role

Follower has increased knowledge and confidence to accomplish outcomes

Increase Rewards

Leader learns follower's needs

Leader matches follower's needs to rewards if work outcomes are accomplished

Leader increases value of work outcomes for follower

Follower displays increased effort and motivation

Organizational work outcomes are accomplished

SOURCE: Based on Bernard M. Bass, "Leadership: Good, Better, Best," *Organizational Dynamics* 13 (Winter 1985), 26–40.

Directive leadership occurs when the leader tells subordinates exactly what they are supposed to do. Leader behavior includes planning, making schedules, setting performance goals and behavior standards, and stressing adherence to rules and regulations. Directive leadership behavior is similar to the initiating structure leadership style described in Chapter 12.

Participative leadership means that the leader consults with his or her subordinates about decisions. Leader behavior includes asking for opinions and suggestions, encouraging participation in decision making, and meeting with subordinates in their workplaces. The participative leader encourages group discussion and written suggestions.

Achievement-oriented leadership occurs when the leader sets clear and challenging objectives for subordinates. Leader behavior stresses high-quality performance and improvement over current performance. Achievement-oriented leaders also show confidence in subordinates and assist them in learning how to achieve high goals.

The four types of leader behavior are not considered ingrained personality traits; rather, they reflect types of behavior that every leader is able to adopt to meet employee motivational needs.

SITUATIONAL CONTINGENCIES. The two important situational contingencies in the path-goal theory are (1) the personal characteristics of group members and (2) the work environment. Personal characteristics of subordinates are similar to Hersey and Blanchard's maturity level

(Chapter 12) and include such factors as ability, skills, needs, and motivations. For example, if an employee has a low level of ability or skill, additional training or coaching may need to be provided in order for the worker to improve performance. If a subordinate is self-centered, rewards must be manipulated to motivate him or her. Subordinates who want clear direction and authority require a directive leader who will tell them exactly what to do. Craftworkers and professionals, however, may want more freedom and autonomy and work best under a participative leadership style.

The work environment contingencies include the degree of task structure, the nature of the formal authority system, and the work group itself. The task structure is similar to the same concept described in Fiedler's contingency theory (Chapter 12); it includes the extent to which tasks are defined and have explicit job descriptions and work procedures. The formal authority system includes the amount of legitimate power used by managers and the extent to which policies and rules constrain employees' behavior. Work group characteristics are the educational level of subordinates and the quality of relationships among them.

USE OF REWARDS. Recall that the leader's responsibility is to clarify the path to rewards for subordinates or to increase the amount of rewards to enhance satisfaction and job performance. In some situations, the leader works with subordinates to help them acquire the skills and confidence needed to perform tasks and achieve rewards already available. In others, the leader may develop new rewards to meet the specific needs of a subordinate.

Exhibit 13.5 illustrates how leadership behavior is tailored to meet the motivational needs of followers. In situation 1, the subordinate lacks

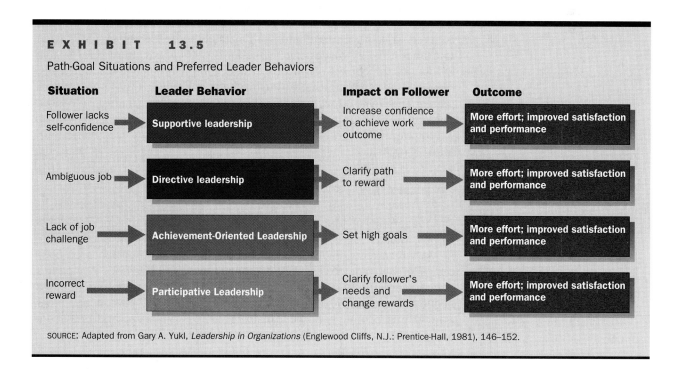

E X H I B I T   1 3 . 5

Path-Goal Situations and Preferred Leader Behaviors

Situation	Leader Behavior	Impact on Follower	Outcome
Follower lacks self-confidence	Supportive leadership	Increase confidence to achieve work outcome	More effort; improved satisfaction and performance
Ambiguous job	Directive leadership	Clarify path to reward	More effort; improved satisfaction and performance
Lack of job challenge	Achievement-Oriented Leadership	Set high goals	More effort; improved satisfaction and performance
Incorrect reward	Participative Leadership	Clarify follower's needs and change rewards	More effort; improved satisfaction and performance

SOURCE: Adapted from Gary A. Yukl, *Leadership in Organizations* (Englewood Cliffs, N.J.: Prentice-Hall, 1981), 146–152.

Mary Kay Cosmetics is known for its elaborate reward system. At the annual seminar, beauty consultants are recognized for their achievements in sales.

confidence; thus, the supportive leadership style provides the social support with which to encourage the subordinate to undertake the behavior needed to do the work and receive the rewards. In situation 2, the job is ambiguous and the employee is not performing effectively. Directive leadership behavior is used to give instructions and clarify the task so that the follower will know how to accomplish it and receive rewards. In situation 3, the subordinate is unchallenged by the task; thus, an achievement-oriented behavior is used to set higher goals. This clarifies the path to rewards for the employee. In situation 4, an incorrect reward is given to a subordinate and the participative leadership style is used to change this. By discussing the subordinate's needs, the leader is able to identify the correct reward for task accomplishment. In all four cases, the outcome of fitting the leadership behavior to the situation produces greater employee effort by either clarifying how subordinates can receive rewards or changing the rewards to fit their needs.

No one understands the value of motivation and rewards better than Mary Kay Ash.

 MARY KAY COSMETICS

The leadership of Mary Kay Ash, chairman emeritus of Mary Kay Cosmetics, makes full use of equal measures of enthusiasm and rewards. At Mary Kay, recognition occupies the same level of importance as compensation for most of the beauty consultants. The cosmetic company's annual seminar in Dallas comes complete with coronations, bauble bequests, and kissy-face, and participants would not have it any other way. At this company, nothing matters but performance, and producers enjoy plaudits not only from peers, but from Mary Kay herself.

She crowns four women at the seminar, recognizing employees who have distinguished themselves in sales or recruiting. She then repeats a trademark story of a saleswoman for Stanley Home Products who was so impoverished she had to borrow $12 to get to her company convention in 1937. She saw the company's top saleswoman crowned queen, and vowed she would be the one to be recognized the following year. Of course she was, and of course it was Mary Kay. The poignancy of the story is hammered home when the riveted employees groan at the retelling that their chairman didn't receive the elegant handbag her predecessor had been awarded, getting something called a flounder light instead.

Such disappointments don't occur at the Mary Kay get-together in Dallas. The woman who calls her beauty consultants "daughters" and generously recognizes their achievements and improvements would not hear of it. And, her leadership and motivational skills have placed such an indelible stamp on her company that it's difficult to tell where one ends and the other begins.[21] ■

Path-goal theorizing can be complex, but much of the research on it has been encouraging.[22] Using the model to specify precise relationships and make exact predictions about employee outcomes may be difficult, but the four types of leader behavior and the ideas for fitting them to situational contingencies provide a useful way for leaders to think about motivating subordinates.

EXPECTANCY THEORY

Expectancy theory suggests that motivation depends on individuals' expectations about their ability to perform tasks and receive desired rewards. Expectancy theory is associated with the work of Victor Vroom, although a number of scholars have made contributions in this area.[23] Expectancy theory is concerned not with identifying types of needs but with the thinking process that individuals use to achieve rewards. Consider Bill Bradley, a university student with a strong desire for a B in his accounting course. Bill has a C+ average and one more exam to take. Bill's motivation to study for that last exam will be influenced by (1) the expectation that hard study will lead to an A on the exam and (2) the expectation that an A on the exam will result in a B for the course. If Bill believes he cannot get an A on the exam or that receiving an A will not lead to a B for the course, he will not be motivated to study exceptionally hard.

Expectancy theory is based on the relationship among the individual's *effort,* the individual's *performance,* and the desirability of *outcomes* associated with high performance. These elements and the relationships among them are illustrated in Exhibit 13.6. The keys to expectancy theory are the expectancies for the relationships among effort, performance, and outcomes with the value of the outcomes to the individual.

E → P expectancy involves whether putting effort into a task will lead to high performance. For this expectancy to be high, the individual must have the ability, previous experience, and necessary machinery, tools,

expectancy theory

A process theory that proposes that motivation depends on individuals' expectations about their ability to perform tasks and receive desired rewards.

E → P expectancy

Expectancy that putting effort into a given task will lead to high performance.

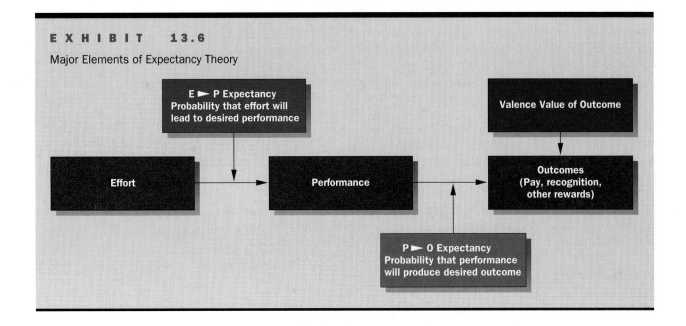

E X H I B I T   1 3 . 6

Major Elements of Expectancy Theory

P → O expectancy

Expectancy that successful performance of a task will lead to the desired outcome.

valence

The value or attraction an individual has for an outcome.

and opportunity to perform. For Bill Bradley to get a B in the accounting course, the E → P expectancy is high if Bill truly believes that with hard work, he can get an A on the final exam. If Bill believes he has neither the ability nor the opportunity to achieve high performance, the expectancy will be low, and so will be his motivation.

P → O expectancy involves whether successful performance will lead to the desired outcome. In the case of a person who is motivated to win a job-related award, this expectancy concerns the belief that high performance will truly lead to the award. If the P → O expectancy is high, the individual will be more highly motivated. If the expectancy is that high performance will not produce the desired outcome, motivation will be lower. If an A on the final exam is likely to produce a B in the accounting course, Bill Bradley's P → O expectancy will be high. Bill may talk to the professor to see whether an A will be sufficient to earn him the B in the course. If not, he will be less motivated to study hard for the final exam.

Valence is the value of outcomes, or attraction for outcomes, for the individual. If the outcomes that are available from high effort and good performance are not valued by employees, motivation will be low. Likewise, if outcomes have a high value, motivation will be higher.

Expectancy theory attempts not to define specific types of needs or rewards but only to establish that they exist and may be different for every individual. One employee may want to be promoted to a position of increased responsibility, and another may have high valence for good relationships with peers. Consequently, the first person will be motivated to work hard for a promotion and the second for the opportunity for a team position that will keep him or her associated with a group.

A simple sales department example will explain how the expectancy model in Exhibit 13.6 works. If Jane Anderson, a salesperson at the Diamond Gift Shop, believes that increased selling effort will lead to higher personal sales, we can say that she has a high E → P expectancy. Moreover, if Jane also believes that higher personal sales will lead to a bonus or pay raise, we can say that she has a high P → O expectancy. Finally, if Jane places a high value on the bonus or pay raise, valence is high and Jane will have a high motivational force. On the other hand, if either the E → P or P → O expectancy is low, or if the money or promotion has low valence for Jane, the overall motivational force will be low. For an employee to be highly motivated, all three factors in the expectancy model must be high.[24]

IMPLICATIONS FOR MANAGERS.   The expectancy theory of motivation is similar to the path-goal theory. Both theories are personalized to subordinates' needs and goals. The managers' responsibility is to help subordinates meet their needs and at the same time attain organizational goals. Managers must try to find a match between a subordinate's skills and abilities and the job demands. To increase motivation, managers can clarify individuals' needs, define the outcomes available from the organization, and ensure that each individual has the ability and support (namely, time and equipment) needed to attain outcomes.

Some companies use expectancy theory principles by designing incentive systems that identify desired organizational outcomes and give everyone the same shot at getting the rewards. The trick is to design a system that fits with employees' abilities and needs. Consider the changes made by Solar Press, Inc.

 S O L A R   P R E S S ,   I N C .

Back in the 1970s, when Solar Press was a small family-owned business, owner John Hudetz passed out checks most months for $20 to $60. Everybody got the same amount, but no one understood why they received it.

To tie bonuses more clearly to productivity, this direct-mail company next divided employees into teams, giving each team a bonus based on whether it produced more than other teams. Production immediately jumped, but teams started competing with one another in an unhealthy way. Teams would not perform regular maintenance on equipment, for example, and hoarded ideas from fellow employees for fear of not winning their bonus. This competitiveness within Solar Press caused more problems than it solved.

In 1987 Solar Press adopted another system. When individual employees did a good job, they were given a pay increase. Moreover, all employees were given bonuses from a pool based on company profits. Thus employees cooperated to help the company make more money. When the company did well, employees got a share.

In 1989, management went one step further by increasing employee participation in yearly planning. In a one-day planning session called "brain day," employees reviewed sales, production goals, equipment needs, and so on for the next year. The sessions allowed workers to see where they fit in the overall plan and how their contribution affected over-all performance. The system now in place works well. By 1990 sales had increased 18 percent and the company had added 100 workers and opened another plant.[25] ∎

In the initial system at Solar Press, the connections among effort, per-formance, and outcomes were unclear. In the group system, employees had the ability to keep the E → P expectancy high, and the P → O expectancy was also high, although it threw groups into competition. Expectancies under the most recent system are also high, and to achieve desired outcomes, employees are motivated to cooperate for the benefit of the company.

● REINFORCEMENT PERSPECTIVE ON MOTIVATION

The reinforcement approach to employee motivation sidesteps the issues of employee needs and thinking processes described in the content and process theories. **Reinforcement theory** simply looks at the relationship between behavior and its consequences. It focuses on changing or modifying the employees' on-the-job behavior through the appropriate use of immediate rewards and punishments.

REINFORCEMENT TOOLS

Behavior modification is the name given to the set of techniques by which reinforcement theory is used to modify human behavior. The basic assumption underlying behavior modification is the **law of effect,** which states that behavior that is positively reinforced tends to be repeated, and behavior that is not reinforced tends not to be repeated. **Reinforcement** is defined as anything that causes a certain behavior to be repeated or inhibited. The four reinforcement tools are positive reinforcement, avoid-ance learning, punishment, and extinction.[26] Each type of reinforcement is a consequence of either a pleasant or unpleasant event being applied or withdrawn following a person's behavior. The four types of rein-forcement are summarized in Exhibit 13.7.

POSITIVE REINFORCEMENT.   *Positive reinforcement* is the administra-tion of a pleasant and rewarding consequence following a desired behav-ior. A good example of positive reinforcement is immediate praise for an employee who arrives on time or does a little extra in his or her work. The pleasant consequence will increase the likelihood of the excellent work behavior occurring again.

AVOIDANCE LEARNING.   *Avoidance learning* is the removal of an unpleasant consequence following a desired behavior. Avoidance learn-ing is sometimes called *negative reinforcement.* Employees learn to do the right thing by avoiding unpleasant situations. Avoidance learning occurs

---

■
reinforcement theory

A motivation theory based on the rela-tionship between a given behavior and its consequences.

■
behavior modification

The set of techniques by which reinforce-ment theory is used to modify human behavior.

law of effect

The assumption that positively reinforced behavior tends to be repeated and unreinforced or negatively reinforced behavior tends to be inhibited.

reinforcement

Anything that causes a given behavior to be repeated or inhibited.

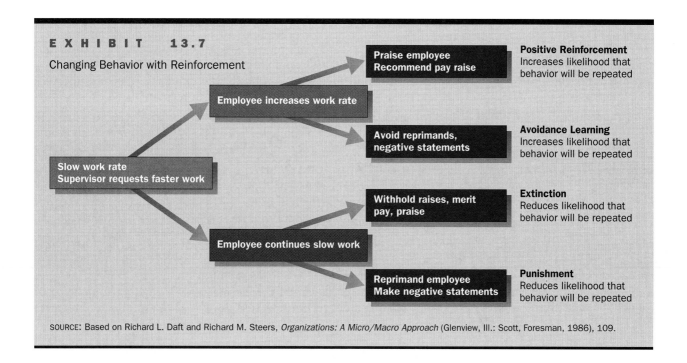

EXHIBIT 13.7

Changing Behavior with Reinforcement

SOURCE: Based on Richard L. Daft and Richard M. Steers, *Organizations: A Micro/Macro Approach* (Glenview, Ill.: Scott, Foresman, 1986), 109.

when a supervisor stops harassing or reprimanding an employee once the incorrect behavior has stopped.

PUNISHMENT.   *Punishment* is the imposition of unpleasant outcomes on an employee. Punishment typically occurs following undesirable behavior. For example, a supervisor may berate an employee for performing a task incorrectly. The supervisor expects that the negative outcome will serve as a punishment and reduce the likelihood of the behavior recurring. The use of punishment in organizations is controversial and often criticized because it fails to indicate the correct behavior.

EXTINCTION.   *Extinction* is the withdrawal of a positive reward, meaning that behavior is no longer reinforced and hence is less likely to occur in the future. If a perpetually tardy employee fails to receive praise and pay raises, he or she will begin to realize that the behavior is not producing desired outcomes. The behavior will gradually disappear if it is continually nonreinforced.

Some executives use reinforcement theory very effectively to shape employees' behavior. Jack Welch, chairman of General Electric, always made it a point to reinforce behavior. As an up-and-coming group executive, Welch reinforced purchasing agents by having someone telephone him whenever an agent got a price concession from a vendor. Welch would stop whatever he was doing and call the agent to say, "That's wonderful news; you just knocked a nickel a ton off the price of steel." He would also sit down and scribble out a congratulatory note to the agent. The effective use of positive reinforcement and the heightened motivation of purchasing employees marked Jack Welch as executive material in the organization.[27]

SCHEDULES OF REINFORCEMENT

A great deal of research into reinforcement theory suggests that the timing of reinforcement has an impact on the speed of employee learning. **Schedules of reinforcement** pertain to the frequency with and intervals over which reinforcement occurs. A reinforcement schedule can be selected to have maximum impact on employees' job behavior. There are five basic types of reinforcement schedules, which include continuous and four types of partial reinforcement.

CONTINUOUS REINFORCEMENT.   With a **continuous reinforcement schedule,** every occurrence of the desired behavior is reinforced. This schedule can be very effective in the early stages of learning new types of behavior, because every attempt has a pleasant consequence.

PARTIAL REINFORCEMENT.   However, in the real world of organizations, it is often impossible to reinforce every correct behavior. With a **partial reinforcement schedule,** the reinforcement is administered only after some occurrences of the correct behavior. There are four types of partial reinforcement schedules: fixed interval, fixed ratio, variable interval, and variable ratio.

Fixed-Interval Schedule.   The *fixed-interval schedule* rewards employees at specified time intervals. If an employee displays the correct behavior each day, reinforcement may occur every week. Regular paychecks or quarterly bonuses are examples of a fixed-interval reinforcement.

Fixed-Ratio Schedule.   With a *fixed-ratio schedule,* reinforcement occurs after a specified number of desired responses, say, after every fifth. For example, paying a field hand $1.50 for picking 10 pounds of peppers is a fixed-ratio schedule. Most piece-rate pay systems are considered fixed-ratio schedules.

Variable-Interval Schedule.   With a *variable-interval schedule,* reinforcement is administered at random times that cannot be predicted by the employee. An example would be a random inspection by the manufacturing superintendent of the production floor, at which time he or she commends employees on their good behavior.

Variable-Ratio Schedule.   The *variable-ratio schedule* is based on a random number of desired behaviors rather than on variable time periods. Reinforcement may occur sometimes after 5, 10, 15, or 20 displays of behavior. One example is the attraction of slot machines for gamblers. People anticipate that the machine will pay a jackpot after a certain number of plays, but the exact number of plays is variable.

The schedules of reinforcement available to managers are illustrated in Exhibit 13.8. Continuous reinforcement is most effective for establishing new learning, but behavior is vulnerable to extinction. Partial reinforcement schedules are more effective for maintaining behavior over extended time periods. The most powerful is the variable-ratio schedule, because employee behavior will persist for a long time due to the administration of reinforcement only after a long interval.[28]

---

schedule of reinforcement

The frequency with and intervals over which reinforcement occurs.

continuous reinforcement schedule

A schedule in which every occurrence of the desired behavior is reinforced.

partial reinforcement schedule

A schedule in which only some occurrences of the desired behavior are reinforced.

E X H I B I T   1 3 . 8

Schedules of Reinforcement

Schedule of Reinforcement	Nature of Reinforcement	Effect on Behavior When Applied	Effect on Behavior When Withdrawn	Example
Continuous	Reward given after each desired behavior	Leads to fast learning of new behavior	Rapid extinction	Praise
Fixed-interval	Reward given at fixed time intervals	Leads to average and irregular performance	Rapid extinction	Weekly paycheck
Fixed-ratio	Reward given at fixed amounts of output	Quickly leads to very high and stable performance	Rapid extinction	Piece-rate pay system
Variable-interval	Reward given at variable times	Leads to moderately high and stable performance	Slow extinction	Performance appraisal and awards given at random times each month
Variable-ratio	Reward given at variable amounts of output	Leads to very high performance	Slow extinction	Sales bonus tied to number of sales calls, with random checks

Reinforcement works at such organizations as Campbell Soup Co., Michigan Bell, and General Electric, because managers reward appropriate behavior. They tell employees what they can do to receive reinforcement, tell them what they are doing wrong, distribute rewards equitably, tailor rewards to behaviors, and keep in mind that failure to reward deserving behavior has an equally powerful impact on employees.

● JOB DESIGN FOR MOTIVATION

A *job* in an organization is a unit of work that a single employee is responsible for performing. A job could include writing tickets for parking violators in New York City or doing long-range planning for ABC television. Jobs are important because performance of their components may provide rewards that meet employees' needs. An assembly line worker may install the same bolt over and over, whereas an emergency room physician may provide each trauma victim with a unique treatment package. Managers need to know what aspects of a job provide motivation as well as how to compensate for routine tasks that have little inherent satisfaction. **Job design** is the application of motivational theories to the structure of work for improving productivity and satisfaction. Approaches to job design are generally classified as job simplification, job rotation, job enlargement, and job enrichment.

JOB SIMPLIFICATION

Job simplification pursues task efficiency by reducing the number of tasks one person must do. Job simplification is based on principles

job design

The application of motivational theories to the structure of work for improving productivity and satisfaction.

job simplification

A job design whose purpose is to improve task efficiency by reducing the number of tasks a single person must perform.

drawn from scientific management and industrial engineering. Tasks are designed to be simple, repetitive, and standardized. As complexity is stripped from a job, the worker has more time to concentrate on doing more of the same routine task. Workers with low skill requirements can perform the job, and the organization achieves a high level of efficiency. Indeed, workers are interchangeable, because they need little training or skill and exercise little judgment. As a motivational technique, however, job simplification has failed. People dislike routine and boring jobs and react in a number of negative ways, including sabotage, absenteeism, and unionization. Job simplification is compared with job rotation and job enlargement in Exhibit 13.9.

JOB ROTATION

job rotation

A job design that systematically moves employees from one job to another to provide them with variety and stimulation.

Job rotation systematically moves employees from one job to another, thereby increasing the number of different tasks an employee performs without increasing the complexity of any one job. For example, an autoworker may install windshields one week and front bumpers the next. Job rotation still takes advantage of engineering efficiencies, but it provides variety and stimulation for employees. Although employees may find the new job interesting at first, the novelty soon wears off as the repetitive work is mastered.

Companies such as National Steel, Motorola, and Dayton Hudson have built on the notion of job rotation to train a flexible work force. As companies break away from ossified job categories, workers can perform several jobs, thereby reducing labor costs. One employee might shift between the jobs of drill operator, punch operator, and assembler, depending on the company's need at the moment. Some unions have resisted the idea, but many now go along, realizing that it helps the company be more competitive.[29]

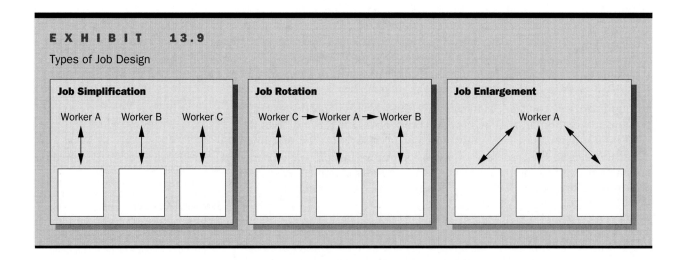

E X H I B I T   13.9

Types of Job Design

Job Simplification	Job Rotation	Job Enlargement
Worker A Worker B Worker C	Worker C → Worker A → Worker B	Worker A

JOB ENLARGEMENT

Job enlargement combines a series of tasks into one new, broader job. This is a response to the dissatisfaction of employees with oversimplified jobs. Instead of only one job, an employee may be responsible for three or four and will have more time to do them. Job enlargement provides job variety and a greater challenge for employees. At Maytag, jobs were enlarged when work was redesigned such that workers assembled an entire water pump rather than doing each part as it reached them on the assembly line. In General Motors' new assembly plants, the assembly line is gone. In its place is a motorized carrier that transports a car through the assembly process. The carrier allows a vehicle to stop, and a group of workers performs logical blocks of work, such as installing an engine and its accessories. The workers get to perform an enlarged job on a stationary automobile rather than a single task on a large number of automobiles.

job enlargement

A job design that combines a series of tasks into one new, broader job to give employees variety and challenge.

JOB ENRICHMENT

Recall the discussion of Maslow's need hierarchy and Herzberg's two-factor theory. Rather than just changing the number and frequency of tasks a worker performs, **job enrichment** incorporates high-level motivators into the work, including job responsibility, recognition, and opportunities for growth, learning, and achievement. In an enriched job, employees have control over the resources necessary for performing it, make decisions on how to do the work, experience personal growth, and set their own work pace. Many companies, including AT&T, IBM, and General Foods, have undertaken job enrichment programs to increase employees' motivation and job satisfaction. But perhaps no

job enrichment

A job design that incorporates achievement, recognition, and other high-level motivators into the work.

Employee autonomy is an important concept at Creative Learning Systems. Here, several employees test a unique room built for computer-assisted learning.

other company has successfully taken the concepts to the extremes described in the following example.

 SEMCO

Once, at a mythical company in a faraway and chaotic land, most employees set their salaries and divided bonuses from profits any way they chose. Everyone worked when they wanted and established their own sales and production goals. They also picked their own supervisors, and periodically rated their performances. Some workers earned more than their boss; everyone knew what everyone else earned. No restrictions for travel or business expenses existed. The company ledger was open for inspection at any time. Big decisions affecting the company, things like diversification or acquisitions, were made by all employees.

If this sounds like a perfect recipe for corporate suicide, consider that the scenario contains only one inaccuracy. The company isn't imaginary. It's Semco, a Brazilian manufacturer of various types of industrial equipment, and it earned $3 million on revenues of $30 million in fiscal 1993. The firm has 300 employees, and 200 others who perform complementary functions as independent subcontractors.

Semco's owner, Ricardo Semler, believes in treating his workers like adults. He also is tight-fisted with a buck, or Brazilian new cruzado, as the case may be. The company has no debt, and budget controls are tight. Semler expects worker performance to translate into a company dividend. Since employee bonuses are also tied to earnings, workers police themselves. Few risk taking advantage of the system because it amounts to lightening the paychecks of peers. In this case, job enrichment combined with prudent monetary controls has meant success at a company that sounds like a worker's utopian dream.[30] ■

JOB CHARACTERISTICS MODEL

■

work redesign

The altering of jobs to increase both the quality of employees' work experience and their productivity.

job characteristics model

A model of job design that comprises core job dimensions, critical psychological states, and employee growth-need strength.

The most recent work on job design is the job characteristics model developed by Richard Hackman and Greg Oldham.[31] Hackman and Oldham's research concerned **work redesign,** which is defined as altering jobs to increase both the quality of employees' work experience and their productivity. Hackman and Oldham's research into the design of hundreds of jobs yielded the **job characteristics model,** which is illustrated in Exhibit 13.10. The model consists of three major parts: core job dimensions, critical psychological states, and employee growth-need strength.

CORE JOB DIMENSIONS.   Hackman and Oldham identified five dimensions that determine a job's motivational potential:

1 *Skill variety* is the number of diverse activities that compose a job and the number of skills used to perform it. A routine, repetitious assembly line job is low in variety, whereas an applied research position that entails working on new problems every day is high in variety.

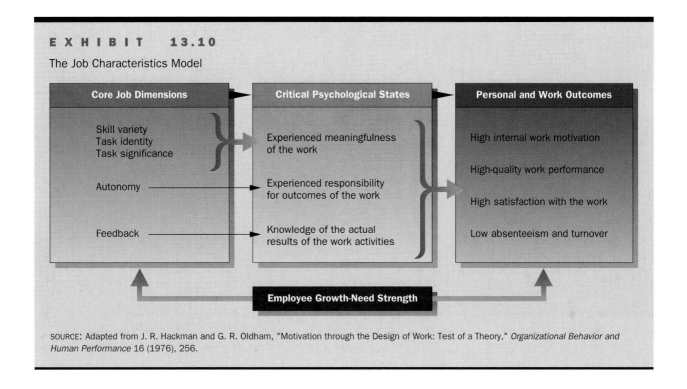

E X H I B I T   1 3.10

The Job Characteristics Model

Core Job Dimensions	Critical Psychological States	Personal and Work Outcomes
Skill variety Task identity Task significance	Experienced meaningfulness of the work	High internal work motivation
Autonomy	Experienced responsibility for outcomes of the work	High-quality work performance High satisfaction with the work
Feedback	Knowledge of the actual results of the work activities	Low absenteeism and turnover

Employee Growth-Need Strength

SOURCE: Adapted from J. R. Hackman and G. R. Oldham, "Motivation through the Design of Work: Test of a Theory," *Organizational Behavior and Human Performance* 16 (1976), 256.

2 *Task identity* is the degree to which an employee performs a total job with a recognizable beginning and ending. A chef who prepares an entire meal has more task identity than a worker on a cafeteria line who ladles mashed potatoes.

3 *Task significance* is the degree to which the job is perceived as important and having impact on the company or consumers. People who distribute penicillin and other medical supplies during times of emergencies would feel they have significant jobs.

4 *Autonomy* is the degree to which the worker has freedom, discretion, and self-determination in planning and carrying out tasks. A house painter can determine how to paint the house; a paint sprayer on an assembly line has little autonomy.

5 *Feedback* is the extent to which doing the job provides information back to the employee about his or her performance. Jobs vary in their ability to let workers see the outcomes of their efforts. A football coach knows whether the team won or lost, but a basic research scientist may have to wait years to learn whether a research project was successful.

The job characteristics model says that the more these five core characteristics can be designed into the job, the more the employees will be motivated and the higher will be performance quality and satisfaction. Read the box on the next page to see how Harbor Sweets, the leading edge company described in chapters 1 and 11, has designed jobs to incorporate several of the characteristics previously described.

We already know about founder Benneville Strohecker's innovative idea of making trust the foundation of managing his Harbor Sweets candy company. And we know he's attracted a diverse work force composed of immigrants from around the globe, the handicapped, and age groups that span from high-schoolers to senior citizens. But how does he keep them motivated? After all, we also know the pay scale at Harbor is not exceptional, and the seasonal nature of the business makes layoffs a fact of life. Conventional wisdom would probably hold that relying too heavily on employee integrity is asking for trouble. In addition, effectively motivating such a disparate work force also might be a tall order. But Strohecker has some-how combined unconventional management methods with his own personal touch, and turned factors that might be detrimental in other companies into key motivators at Harbor Sweets.

Strohecker's very first employees set the tone for almost everyone that followed. Because he badly needed the help, neighbors stopped by his basement at their convenience, not his. He could not even promise when they would be paid. The situation also meant he had little choice but to take worker empowerment to the limit as well. His small staff not only handled purchasing, cooking, wrapping, and shipping, they also maintained receivables and kept track of the payroll. But instead of taking advantage, the employees took ownership and responsibility for product quality and output that they might never have assumed otherwise. One carry-over that remains today is the prerogative of any worker to withdraw candy that he or she feels might not meet customer expectations. Essentially, every employee is in charge of quality control.

The self-motivating atmosphere of the company's earliest days carried over as Harbor began to grow. Increased volume led to more complexity, and more problems. With very limited management oversight, workers devised the best available solutions on their own. They also balanced production on an ad hoc basis. Coworkers requiring assistance needed only to ask, and the favor was reciprocated later. Strohecker's single expectation of his employees was that they produced the best candy possible. Permitting them to do so almost completely on their own maximized initiative and efficiency. Companies can seldom expect a work force earning minimum wages to accomplish much more than minimum output. Strohecker's approach has upended that kind of thinking. His employees are a lot more interested in what they produce than what they receive.

Time will tell whether relying on trust and a diverse work force free to schedule itself around other needs will continue to meet company needs. Strohecker admits that as the popularity of Harbor Sweets increases, it becomes harder to maintain the flexibility that has become a hallmark of the candy-maker. And, new sources of business have led to changes that are a departure from the past.

When USAir Group Inc. began regularly ordering chocolate mints for passengers, Harbor was forced into something of a metamorphosis. The steady demand of a single product made a deviation from the company's 16-year variable pro-duction routine mandatory. For the first time ever, Harbor began using a regular, fixed shift five days a week. Workers that committed to the schedule could earn a nice premium over colleagues who required flexible hours. Veteran employees with years of service found themselves earning less than other workers, some of them newly hired. There were grumblings that Harbor Sweets was in danger of becoming just another factory interested only in the bottom line.

For Strohecker and Harbor Sweets, the year-round source of income that the USAir account represents is not something that could be passed up because of worries it might upset the company culture. The challenge will be to maintain the level of employee motivation and dedication as the scope and complexity of operations increases. One alternative would be to spin off production runs for the company's biggest customers. Such a move might lead to direct competition with much larger candy companies, and Strohecker has always feared that those kinds of battles invariably lead to diminished quality. From the beginning, Strohecker's employees and the motivation he inspired in them were what set his company and product apart from the competition. Though his summation of what he hopes for the future is ambiguous, he doesn't sound willing to depart from the people who got him where he is. "I don't want to get small and I don't want to get big," he says. "What I want to do is stay conscious of the consumer need for our type of product." ■

SOURCE: Martha E. Mangelsdorf, "Managing The New Work Force," *INC.*, January 1990, 78–83; Tracy E. Benson, "In Trust We Manage, *Industry Week,* March 4, 1991, 26–27; and Anne Driscoll, "Candy Man of the People," *The Boston Globe,* March 29, 1992, 1.

CRITICAL PSYCHOLOGICAL STATES.   The model posits that core job dimensions are more rewarding when individuals experience three psychological states in response to job design. In Exhibit 13.10, skill variety, task identity, and task significance tend to influence the employee's psychological state of *experienced meaningfulness of work.* The work itself is satisfying and provides intrinsic rewards for the worker. The job characteristic of autonomy influences the worker's *experienced responsibility.* The job characteristic of feedback provides the worker with *knowledge of actual results.* The employee thus knows how he or she is doing and can change work performance to increase desired outcomes.

PERSONAL AND WORK OUTCOMES.   The impact of the five job characteristics on the psychological states of experienced meaningfulness, responsibility, and knowledge of actual results leads to the personal and work outcomes of high work motivation, high work performance, high satisfaction, and low absenteeism and turnover.

EMPLOYEE GROWTH-NEED STRENGTH.   The final component of the job characteristics model is called *employee growth-need strength,* which means that people have different needs for growth and development. If a person wants to satisfy lower-level needs, such as safety and belongingness, the job characteristics model has less effect. When a person has a high need for growth and development, including the desire for personal challenge, achievement, and challenging work, the model is especially effective. People with a high need to grow and expand their abilities respond very favorably to the application of the model and to improvements in core job dimensions.

● NEW MOTIVATIONAL PROGRAMS

Organizations have adopted a number of new programs in recent years that apply motivational theory to improve employees' satisfaction and performance. These new forms of incentive pay and employee involvement include pay for performance, gain sharing, ESOPs, lump-sum bonuses, pay for knowledge, and flexible work schedules. Although money may not be the prime motivator, companies can combine these ideas with other ideas from this chapter to create their own motivational program.

PAY FOR PERFORMANCE

Pay for performance means that employees are rewarded in proportion to their performance contributions. Typically called *merit pay,* this is a logical outgrowth of such motivational concepts as expectancy theory and reinforcement theory because pay raises are tied to work behavior. In many organizations, pay raises had become automatic and merit pay had no meaning.

This trend is illustrated at General Motors, which dropped annual cost-of-living raises for salaried employees and established a pay-for-performance system. A merit increase is something employees have to earn. Bosses have to pick the top 10 percent of performers, the next 25

pay for performance

A motivational compensation program that rewards employees in proportion to their performance contributions.

percent, the next 55 percent, and the bottom 10 percent and enforce pay differences among the groups.[32]

GAIN SHARING

gain sharing

A motivational compensation program that rewards employees and managers when predetermined performance targets are met.

Gain sharing is an incentive program in which employees and managers within a designated unit receive bonuses when unit performance beats a predetermined performance target. These targets may specify productivity, costs, quality, customer service, or profits. Unlike pay for performance, gain sharing encourages coordination and teamwork because all employees are contributing to the benefit of the business unit. Most companies develop a precise formula that is calculated for, say, a six-month period, after which bonuses may be paid.[33]

An example of successful gain sharing is the experience of Carrier, a subsidiary of United Technologies. Carrier's six plants in Syracuse, New York, adopted a gain-sharing program called *Improshare*. Under the program, the savings in labor cost resulting from increased productivity and quality are split 50-50 between the company and all employees (from management to line workers). Carrier workers enthusiastically embraced the new program. When a water main broke, flooding one shop floor, all employees pitched in, making repairs throughout the day and night, so that production could be met and no one would miss the weekly bonus. In the first year, Carrier employees in Syracuse shared in a total of $3 million in bonuses from savings due to increased productivity and quality.[34]

ESOPs

employee stock ownership plan (ESOP)

A motivational compensation program that gives employees part ownership of the organization.

Employee stock ownership plans (ESOPs) give employees partial ownership of the business, thereby allowing them to share in improved profit performance. ESOPs have been popular with small businesses, although a few large businesses such as Avis, Procter & Gamble, and JCPenney have also adopted ESOPs. The ESOP allows a company to boost productivity at the cost of ownership, which most business executives are finding to be a good trade. Employees work harder because they are owners and share in gains and losses. For ESOPs to work, managers must provide complete financial information to employees, give employees the right to participate in major decisions, and give employees voting rights, which include voting for the board of directors.

At Avis, employees take their ownership seriously. Each class of line worker, from mechanics to rental agents, meets in employee participation groups in which they suggest ways of improving customer service and running the business more efficiently. Since start of the ESOP, Avis has recorded higher profit-sales ratios than Hertz and now aims to overtake Hertz in market share.[35] The Leading Edge box on Springfield ReManufacturing shows how an ESOP plan, in combination with job enrichment, helped initiate a dramatic turnaround in the firm's success.

LUMP-SUM BONUSES

lump-sum bonus

A motivational compensation program that rewards employees with a one-time cash payment based on performance.

Often salary increases do not seem very large when spread over an entire year. **Lump-sum bonuses** are one-time cash payments based on perfor-

LEADING **edge**

SPRINGFIELD REMANUFACTURING EMPLOYEES ARE OWNERS TOO

In 1983, Springfield ReManufacturing Corporation was a poorly performing division of International Harvester. By 1990, it was a phenomenally successful independent corporation that serviced clients such as Mercedes-Benz and General Motors. With sales of over $58 million a year, SRC grew 35 to 40 percent annually during the seven years since its management team bought it. When asked about this remarkable turnaround, the corporation's director of human resources says, "It's pretty simple. We make sure every employee understands how their work adds to or subtracts from every line on the financial statement. . . ." Through strong job enrichment programs, as well as an ESOP plan, Springfield ReManufacturing motivates its workers to be full participants.

CEO Jack Stack credits his approach to problems he saw at International Harvester. "There was a tremendous distinction between the working class and management. The only way we communicated was through a contract." So when he took over SRC, Stack was determined to make a strong investment in human capital. Motivating employ-

ees was his first priority. The foundation of his approach is perhaps best expressed by director of human resources, Gary Brown: "We're trying to create a working environment that involves ordinary, blue-collar workers in more than just day-to-day routines. We firmly believe employees are capable of more than coming to work just to grind crankcases."

The most important part of Stack's program is the employee stock ownership plan. Like many ESOPs, it is designed to reinforce full participation and instill a sense of pride in the corporation's success. SRC wants its employees to feel like business partners who will see increased financial benefits from improving performance.

In fact, when an SRC employee is first hired, he or she is told that 70 percent of the job is rebuilding engines and 30 percent is learning how to make profits. As part of their basic training, all employees must learn how to evaluate weekly income statements, cash flow projections, debt-to-equity ratios, balance sheets, after-tax profits, and net earnings. Everyone is expected to understand the bottom line effect of his or her job and to help SRC achieve maximum profitability.

This involvement in the corporation's financial standing is carried out through information meetings

held twice each month. Senior managers and supervisors begin each meeting with a status discussion that leads to a revised financial forecast. Supervisors then hold meetings on the shop floor. They pass out the revised forecast and conduct a question-and-answer session. In this way the entire work force, from telephone operators to top management, knows exactly how the company is doing.

As part of SRC's job enrichment policy, the company also offers regularly scheduled courses in topics such as accounting, warehousing, and remedial reading for those who need it. Many well-prepared employees go on to manage one of SRC's many branches and have the opportunity to buy out a large percent of the particular company they run.

Stack claims the difference that makes SRC so successful is that employees "understand performance and productivity as equity." SRC has given its people the tools to improve their careers and a piece of the profits that their efforts build. Given the fact that the stock has gone from 10 cents to $13.80 a share, this is some of the best motivation possible. ∎

SOURCE: Based on Frank T. Adams, "Motivation and the Bottom Line," *Human Capital*, July 1990, 19–26.

mance. The single payment is designed to increase motivational value of a pay increase. For example, a 10 percent raise for an employee earning $20,000 would be a one-time $2,000 payment. This plan works when employees have a sense that their bonus truly mirrors the company's prosperity. It also lets the company control wage costs by not building increases into the permanent wage structure unless company performance is good.

PAY FOR KNOWLEDGE

pay for knowledge

A motivational compensation program that links employee's salary with the number of tasks performed.

Pay for knowledge means that an employee's salary is increased with the number of tasks he or she can do. This is linked to the ideas of job rotation and job enrichment, because employees learn the skills for many jobs. Pay for knowledge increases company flexibility and efficiency, because fewer employees are needed to perform all tasks. Workers achieve a broader perspective, making them more adept at problem solving. To implement this plan, a company must have a well-developed employee-assessment procedure, and jobs must be well identified so that pay can be increased as new job skills are acquired.

FLEXIBLE WORK SCHEDULES

Flexible work schedules drop the restriction that employees work the normal eight-hour workday from 8 AM to 5 PM. These modifications include the four-day workweek, flex time, and job sharing.

With the *four-day workweek* employees work four days for ten hours each instead of five days for eight hours. The motivational factor is that of meeting the needs of a diverse work force.

Flex time allows employees to determine their workday schedules. People can choose starting and quitting times. For example, a company may have core hours during which employees must be present, perhaps from 9 AM to 4 PM. Employees then are free to start work anywhere from 7 AM to 9 AM and to finish anywhere from 4 PM to 6 PM, depending on their own needs and desires. A number of companies, including DuPont, IBM, and Avon have implemented flexible scheduling. Small companies like Hemmings Motor News also have discovered the benefits of flex time.

HEMMINGS MOTOR NEWS

Hemmings Motor News of Bennington, Vermont, keeps employees happy and turnover to a minimum by permitting employees to work virtually any schedule they choose. The company operates from 7 AM to 10 PM some days, enabling workers to fit work around day care and other needs. Other options include working for two-week periods, followed by two weeks off. And, regardless of the types of schedule an employee selects, it doesn't affect the medical benefits offered. Part-time workers receive the same coverage as full-time staffers. The company also picks up the whole tab on workers' health and dental premiums too.

After the birth or adoption of a child, both male and female employees can continue drawing two-thirds of their pay for six weeks. If necessary, they can take an additional six months unpaid. After that, part-time work is an option. Through the use of flex time, variable scheduling and generous benefits, Hemmings has been able to keep motivated and talented employees around that otherwise would have been lost.[36] ■

Job sharing involves two or more persons jointly covering one job over a 40-hour week. Job sharing allows part-time workers, such as a mother with small children, to work only part of a day without having to create a special job. Job sharing also relieves job fatigue if work is routine or monotonous.

SUMMARY AND MANAGEMENT SOLUTION

This chapter introduced a number of important ideas about the motivation of people in organizations. The content theories of motivation focus on the nature of underlying employee needs. Maslow's hierarchy of needs, Herzberg's two-factory theory, and McClelland's acquired needs theory all suggest that people are motivated to meet a range of needs. Process theories examine how people go about selecting rewards with which to meet needs. Equity theory says that people compare their contributions and outcomes with others' and are motivated to maintain a feeling of equity. The path-goal theory specifies that individual motivation depends on the leader's ability to clarify the behaviors necessary for task accomplishment and rewards. Expectancy theory suggests that people calculate the probability of achieving certain outcomes. Managers can increase motivation by treating employees fairly and by clarifying employee paths toward meeting their needs. Still another motivational approach is reinforcement theory, which says that employees learn to behave in certain ways based on the availability of reinforcements.

The application of motivational ideas is illustrated in job design and other motivational programs. Job design approaches include job enrichment and work redesign, which provide an opportunity for employees to meet higher-level needs. Other motivational programs include pay for performance, gain sharing, ESOPs, lump-sum bonuses, pay for knowledge, and flexible work schedules. A highly successful application of motivational ideas occurred for store managers at Au Bon Pain.

Recall from the chapter opening case that Gary Aronson was an unmotivated store manager at Au Bon Pain, making a mere $26,000 a year. Thanks to a new incentive system, Aronson will make at least $80,000 this year, and he throws his heart and soul into his work, putting in a minimum of 65 hours a week and loving it. The dramatic motivation began when top executives devised a plan to split controllable profits on a 50-50 basis with store managers. Controllable profits are ones store managers can do something about. Aronson got rid of one assistant manager to save on overhead, reorganized the store to increase seating capacity, and motivated his own staff more effectively to ensure prompt service. Aronson and other store managers solved problems they had previously dumped on the company. Under the new system, stores ran 40 percent ahead of their profit goals, showing that incentives and a sense of ownership work.[37] Perhaps the best explanation for the sharply improved performance is expectancy theory, because managers saw how to link effort and performance to the outcomes they desired. They also received positive reinforcement, and their job responsibilities were enriched, thereby satisfying higher-level needs.

DISCUSSION QUESTIONS

1. Low-paid service workers represent a motivational problem for many companies. Consider the ill-trained and poorly motivated X-ray machine operators trying to detect weapons in airports. How might these people be motivated to reduce boredom and increase their vigilance?

2. One small company recognizes an employee of the month, who is given a parking spot next to the president's space near the front door. What theories would explain the positive motivation associated with this policy?

3. Campbell Soup Company reduces accidents with a lottery. Each worker who works 30 days or more without losing a day for a job-related accident is eligible to win prizes in a raffle drawing. Why has this program been successful?

4. One executive argues that managers have too much safety because of benefit and retirement plans. He rewards his managers for taking risks and has removed many guaranteed benefits. Would this approach motivate managers? Why?

5. If an experienced secretary discovered that she made less money than a newly hired janitor, how would she react? What inputs and outcomes might she evaluate to make this comparison?

6. Would you rather work for a supervisor high in need for achievement, need for affiliation, or need for power? Why? What are the advantages and disadvantages of each?

7. A survey of teachers found that two of the most important rewards were the belief that their work was important and a feeling of accomplishment. Is this consistent with Hackman and Oldham's job characteristics model?

8. The teachers in question 7 also reported that pay and fringe benefits were poor; yet they continued to teach. Use Herzberg's two-factor theory to explain this finding.

9. Many organizations use sales contests and motivational speakers to motivate salespeople to overcome frequent rejections and turndowns. How would these devices help motivate salespeople?

10. What characteristics of individuals determine the extent to which work redesign will have a positive impact on work satisfaction and work effectiveness?

11. Which of the new motivational programs would you be most comfortable with as a manager? Why?

MANAGEMENT IN PRACTICE: EXPERIENTIAL EXERCISE

● MOTIVATION QUESTIONNAIRE

You are to indicate how important each characteristic is to you. Answer according to your feelings about the most recent job you had or about the job you currently hold. Circle the number on the scale that represents your feeling—1 (very unimportant) to 7 (very important).

When you have completed the questionnaire, score it as follows:

Rating for question 5 = ___ . Divide by 1 = ___ security.
Rating for questions 9 and 13 = ___ . Divide by 2 = ___ social.

Rating for questions 1, 3, and 7 = ___ . Divide by 3 = ___ esteem.
Rating for questions 4, 10, 11, and 12 = ___ . Divide by 4 = ___ autonomy.
Rating for questions 2, 6, and 8 = ___ . Divide by 3 = self-actualization.

The instructor has national norm scores for presidents, vice-presidents, and upper middle-level, lower middle-level, and lower-level managers with which you can compare your *mean* importance scores. How do your scores compare with the scores of managers working in organizations?

1.	The feeling of self-esteem a person gets from being in that job	1	2	3	4	5	6	7
2.	The opportunity for personal growth and development in that job	1	2	3	4	5	6	7
3.	The prestige of the job inside the company (that is, regard received from others in the company)	1	2	3	4	5	6	7
4.	The opportunity for independent thought and action in that job	1	2	3	4	5	6	7
5.	The feeling of security in that job	1	2	3	4	5	6	7
6.	The feeling of self-fulfillment a person gets from being in that position (that is, the feeling of being able to use one's own unique capabilities, realizing one's potential)	1	2	3	4	5	6	7
7.	The prestige of the job outside the company (that is, the regard received from others not in the company)	1	2	3	4	5	6	7
8.	The feeling of worthwhile accomplishment in that job	1	2	3	4	5	6	7
9.	The opportunity in that job to give help to other people	1	2	3	4	5	6	7
10.	The opportunity in that job for participation in the setting of goals	1	2	3	4	5	6	7
11.	The opportunity in that job for participation in the determination of methods and procedures	1	2	3	4	5	6	7
12.	The authority connected with the job	1	2	3	4	5	6	7
13.	The opportunity to develop close friendships in the job	1	2	3	4	5	6	7

SOURCE: Lyman W. Porter, *Organizational Patterns of Managerial Job Attitudes* (New York: American Foundation for Management Research, 1964), 17, 19.

CASE FOR ANALYSIS

MOTIVATING TRUCK DRIVERS

CRST Inc., a long-haul trucking firm, worked hard to increase market share through cost-cutting and improved service. However, expansion has been stymied by an unexpected development. With business better than ever, the company finds itself with parked trucks and undelivered freight either languishing on loading docks or being snapped up by the trucking industry's arch-competitor, the railroads. The reason: CRST has been unable to recruit, train, or re-train a sufficient number of drivers to haul the loads.

It is not because of lack of trying. CRST's recruiting department is bigger than its sales force. The problem in attracting and motivating drivers is the general sentiment among truckers that they are overworked and underpaid.

Throw in long periods away from the family and paychecks that are notoriously unpredictable, and the results aren't surprising. At some companies, the annual turnover rate among drivers tops 100 percent. Working drivers like John Rose of Roland Transport Inc. are quitting, and to find a potential replacement for him is hard. Rose earned around $32,000 annually, but he reckons that between driving, sleeping, or waiting to load or unload, that figure computes to less than minimum wage.

Most insiders say the culprit is deregulation and cost-cutting. Rate decreases made it necessary to squeeze every segment of the industry, including driver pay. Service improvements largely entailed adopting greater flexibility. In the past, drivers usually had predictable routes. That was better for them, but it didn't get the most out of the truck. Today truckers on call go anywhere and everywhere, based upon the customer's needs and the best use of equipment. It's a marvelous improvement in efficiency, but it's difficult on anyone trying to raise a family, or even let them know for certain when they might return home.

Scanning the horizon doesn't reveal much in the way of encouraging portents. The number of people in the predominant driver age group of 21 to 30 is declining. Federal licensing and drug-testing have eliminated another 5 percent from the pool. In addition, governmental cutbacks on federally guaranteed loans to drivers in training pared that number by half. Ironically, an improving economy is only worsening the situation.

One firm that has had good success in overcoming drivers' discontent, and has managed to improve customer satisfaction in the process, is American Freightways Corp. Sheridan Garrison sold his Harrison, Arkansas-based family trucking business in 1979, shortly before the start of deregulation. After biding his time and watching a number of other small, unionized over-the-road companies go out of business, he opened Arkansas Freightways in 1982. From the beginning he has made service everyone's principal priority, even if it cost the company money. And, his capital investments in technology made life a lot easier for his drivers.

Arkansas Freightways, which became American Freightways after expanding into 11 states, was one of the first trucking firms to publish its schedules. To help drivers chart their courses and minimize inventory costs, every truck was equipped with a computer. Knowing that his drivers were a primary contact point with customers, Garrison invested in their long-term well-being by providing incentives.

Unions made four swipes at American in a two-year period in an effort to enlist the 5,000-member work force. Each time they were overwhelmingly voted down. "American Freightways treats us with respect," says driver Jefferson Jackson, who formerly had nine years at a unionized freight hauler. "There's none of that running you off to a grievance hearing or some union [policy]."

For the near term, American Freightways will likely be the exception instead of the rule. Former drivers are increasingly opting for jobs in the construction industry. Many have pulled up stakes and migrated to parts of the country that enjoy the highest number of warm weather months. Carriers have taken note and reacted. They are making efforts to revamp operations that will improve working conditions to either lure them back or attract first-time drivers to the industry. M.S. Carriers of Memphis, Tennessee, developed four regional hubs to shorten runs and permit a quarter of its drivers to get home every night. J.B. Hunt of Lowell, Arkansas, now ships more of its long-haul freight by rail. Turnover for drivers delivering to trains is more than four times less than those making long-haul, over-the-road runs.

Trucking companies are trying everything to attract new drivers. CRST has begun paying for drivers' training. Many are offering $1,000 signing bonuses. Company recruiters routinely visit geographic regions experiencing plant shutdowns in other industries. The theory is that recently laid-off workers will jump at any offer of employment. In reality, it doesn't always work that way. Auto workers, or anyone else who has been employed in a factory environment for a number of years, often experience great difficulty adjusting to the demands of long-haul trucking.

Truck drivers are not the first casualty of a U.S. industry shake-up, and they will not be the last. If nothing else, however, the loss of revenue and freight business will inspire company owners like Sheridan Garrison to devise even more ingenious incentives to attract long-haul truck drivers back to the road. All that remains to be seen is what form these incentives ultimately take, and how they can be shoe-horned into the overall economies of the freight business.

● QUESTIONS

1. What techniques described in this chapter could trucking companies use to better satisfy drivers' hierarchy of needs? Is there anything they could learn from American Freightways' approach?
2. Do you think new motivational programs such as employee stock ownership plans and lump sum bonuses would be sufficient to keep drivers motivated? Why or why not?
3. How could the truck driver's job be redesigned to include the five dimensions that Hackman and Oldham identified as key to a job's motivational potential?

SOURCE: William Stern, "A Lesson Learned Early," *Forbes*, Nov. 8, 1993, 220–221; James Aley et al., "The Outlook For 22 Industries," *Fortune*, Jan. 10, 1994, 48; and Daniel Machalaba, "Long Haul, Trucking Firms Find It Is a Struggle to Hire and Retain Drivers," *The Wall Street Journal*, December 28, 1993, 1.

REFERENCES

1. Bruce G. Posner, "May the Force Be with You," *INC.*, July 1987, 70–75; and Carolyn Walkup, "Commissary, New Outlets Boost Au Bon Pain's Net," *Nation's Restaurant News*, December 2, 1991, 14.

2. David Silburt, "Secrets of the Super Sellers," *Canadian Business*, January 1987, 54–59; "Meet the Savvy Supersalesmen," *Fortune*, February 4, 1985, 56–62; Michael Brody, "Meet Today's Young American Worker," *Fortune*, November 11, 1985, 90–98; and Tom Richman, "Meet the Masters. They Could Sell You Anything . . . ," *INC.*, March 1985, 79–86.

3. Richard M. Steers and Lyman W. Porter, eds., *Motivation and Work Behavior*, 3d ed. (New York: McGraw-Hill, 1983).

4. Kenneth A. Kovach, "What Motivates Employees? Workers and Supervisors Give Different Answers," *Business Horizon* 30 (September–October), 58–65.

5. Steers and Porter, *Motivation*.

6. J. F. Rothlisberger and W. J. Dickson, *Management and the Worker* (Cambridge, Mass.: Harvard University Press, 1939).

7. Abraham F. Maslow, "A Theory of Human Motivation," *Psychological Review* 50 (1943), 370–396.

8. Donald J. Vlcek, Jr., and Jeffrey P. Davidson, "The Domino Effect," *Small Business Reports*, September 1992, 68–71.

9. Frederick Herzberg, "One More Time: How Do You Motivate Employees?" *Harvard Business Review* (January–February 1968), 53–62.

10. John Case, "The Open-Book Managers," *INC.*, September 1990, 104–113.

11. David C. McClelland, *Human Motivation* (Glenview, Ill.: Scott, Foresman, 1985).

12. David C. McClelland, "The Two Faces of Power," in *Organizational Psychology*, ed. D. A. Colb, I. M. Rubin, and J. M. McIntyre (Englewood Cliffs, N.J.: Prentice-Hall, 1971), 73–86.

13. J. Stacy Adams, "Injustice in Social Exchange," in *Advances in Experimental Social Psychology*, 2d ed., ed. L. Berkowitz (New York: Academic Press, 1965); and J. Stacy Adams, "Toward an Understanding of Inequity," *Journal of Abnormal and Social Psychology* (November 1963), 422–436.

14. Ray V. Montagno, "The Effects of Comparison to Others and Primary Experience on Responses to Task Design," *Academy of Management Journal* 28 (1985), 491–498; and Robert P. Vecchio, "Predicting Worker Performance in Inequitable Settings," *Academy of Management Review* 7 (1982), 103–110.

15. "The Double Standard That's Setting Worker Against Worker," *Business Week*, April 8, 1985, 70–71.

16. James E. Martin and Melanie M. Peterson, "Two-Tier Wage Structures: Implications for Equity Theory," *Academy of Management Journal* 30 (1987), 297–315.

17. M. G. Evans, "The Effects of Supervisory Behavior on the Path-Goal Relationship," *Organizational Behavior and Human Performance* 5 (1970), 277–298; M. G. Evans, "Leadership and Motivation: A Core Concept," *Academy of Management Journal* 13 (1970), 91–102; and B. S. Georopoulos, G. M. Mahoney, and N. W. Jones, "A Path-Goal Approach to Productivity," *Journal of Applied Psychology* 41 (1957), 345–353.

18. Robert J. House, "A Path-Goal Theory of Leader Effectiveness," *Administrative Science Quarterly* 16 (1971), 321–338.

19. M. G. Evans, "Leadership" in *Organizational Behavior,* ed. S. Kerr (Columbus, Ohio: Grid, 1974), 230–233.

20. Robert J. House and Terrence R. Mitchell, "Path-Goal Theory of Leadership," *Journal of Contemporary Business* (Autumn 1974), 81–97.

21. Alan Farnham, "Mary Kay's Lessons in Leadership," *Fortune,* September 20, 1993, 68–77.

22. Charles Greene, "Questions of Causation in the Path-Goal Theory and Leadership," *Academy of Management Journal* 22 (March 1979), 22–41; and C. A. Schriesheim and M. A. von Glinow, "The Path-Goal Theory of Leadership: A Theoretical and Empirical Analysis," *Academy of Management Journal* 20 (1977), 398–405.

23. Victor H. Vroom, *Work and Motivation* (New York: Wiley, 1964); B. S. Gorgopoulos, G. M. Mahoney, and N. Jones, "A Path-Goal Approach to Productivity," *Journal of Applied Psychology* 41 (1957), 345–353; and E. E. Lawler III, *Pay and Organizational Effectiveness: A Psychological View* (New York: McGraw-Hill, 1981).

24. Richard L. Daft and Richard M. Steers, *Organizations: A Micro/Macro Approach* (Glenview, Ill.: Scott, Foresman, 1986).

25. Anne Murphy, "Outline for an Open-Book Company," *INC.,* September 1990, 112–113; and Bruce G. Posner, "If at First You Don't Succeed," *INC.,* May 1989, 132–184.

26. H. Richlin, *Modern Behaviorism* (San Francisco: Freeman, 1970); and B. F. Skinner, *Science and Human Behavior* (New York: Macmillan, 1953).

27. Tom Peters and Nancy Austin, *A Passion for Excellence: The Leadership Difference* (New York: Random House, 1985), 267.

28. L. M. Sarri and G. P. Latham, "Employee Reaction to Continuous and Variable Ratio Reinforcement Schedules Involving a Monetary Incentive," *Journal of Applied Psychology* 67 (1982), 506–508; and R. D. Pritchard, J. Hollenback, and P. J. DeLeo, "The Effects of Continuous and Partial Schedules of Reinforcement on Effort, Performance, and Satisfaction," *Organizational Behavior and Human Performance* 25 (1980), 336–353.

29. Norm Alster, "What Flexible Workers Can Do," *Fortune,* February 13, 1989, 62–66.

30. "Diary of an Anarchist," *The Economist,* June 26, 1993, 66.

31. J. Richard Hackman and Greg R. Oldham, *Work Redesign* (Reading, Mass.: Addison-Wesley, 1980); and J. Richard Hackman and Greg Oldham, "Motivation through the Design of Work: Test of a Theory," *Organizational Behavior and Human Performance* 16 (1976), 250–279.

32. Jacob M. Schleslinger, "GM's New Compensation Plan Reflects General Trend Tying Pay to Performance," *The Wall Street Journal,* January 26, 1988, 31.

33. Timothy L. Ross, Larry Hatcher, and Ruth Ann Ross, "From Piecework to Companywide Gainsharing," *Management Review* (May 1989), 22–26; and Nancy J. Perry, "Here Come Richer, Riskier Pay Plans," *Fortune,* December 19, 1988, 50–58.

34. Perry, "Here Come Richer, Riskier Pay Plans."

35. Christopher Farrell and John Hoerr, "ESOPs: Are They Good for You?" *Business Week,* May 15, 1989, 116–123; and John Case, "ESOPs: Dead or Alive?" *INC.,* June 1988, 94–100.

36. Michael P. Cronin, "One Life to Live," *INC.,* July 1993, 56–57.

37. "Expansion Boosts Au Bon Pain," *Nation's Restaurant News,* August 3, 1991, 14; and Posner, "May the Force Be with You."

COMMUNICATION IN ORGANIZATIONS   14

CHAPTER OUTLINE ▲

LEARNING OBJECTIVES ▼

After studying this chapter, you should be able to

- Explain why communication is essential for effective management.
- Define the basic elements of the communication process.
- Describe how perception, nonverbal behavior, and listening affect communication among people.
- Describe the concept of channel richness and explain how communication channels influence the quality of communication among managers.
- Explain the difference between formal and informal organizational communications and the importance of each for organization management.
- Describe team communications and how structure influences communication outcomes.
- Describe barriers to organizational communications and suggest ways

When Libby Cook, Michael Gilliland, and Randy Clapp started the first Wild Oats Market in Boulder, Colorado, keeping up with customers and employees was easy. But four years and 11 stores later, the demands of running a company had eclipsed the threesome's ability to monitor the pulse of individual stores. Employee training had become hit-or-miss, and performance evaluations were drifting in chronically late. They knew the best way to ensure customers were satisfied was to make sure their staff was happy. However, with stores in over three states, it simply was impossible to regularly visit them all. They had to devise a method whereby Wild Oats employees could let them know what they liked and did not like about their jobs. If the founders could reconnect with what was going on inside every store, they could head off potential problems before they caused customers to look for other places to shop. If you were in charge at Wild Oats, what methods would you use to reestablish the lines of communications with employees? In your opinion, can the barriers to communication be overcome?[1]

The founders of Wild Oats Market believed in communication but faced problems in breaking down communication barriers. In today's intensely competitive environment, senior executives at most companies are trying to improve communication. The president of Syntex Corporation, a pharmaceuticals maker, eats breakfast at 7:30 each morning in the employee cafeteria exchanging information with workers. The president and CEO of Windham Hill Records holds weekly one-hour meetings with rank-and-file employees, giving each the opportunity to discuss the week ahead. This formula keeps all employees informed about activities and problems in other departments. John Scully, former CEO of Apple Computer, insisted that top executives listen to customer complaints on the toll-free number. Although Apple executives often lacked the technical expertise to solve customers' problems, they quickly learned customers' concerns about Apple computers.[2]

These executives are interested in staying connected with employees and customers and with shaping company direction. To do so, they must be in touch; hence they excel at personal communications. Nonmanagers often are amazed at how much energy successful executives put into communication. Consider the comment about Robert Strauss, former chairman of the Democratic National Committee and former ambassador to Russia:

> One of his friends says, "His network is everywhere. It ranges from bookies to bank presidents. . . ."
>
>   He seems to find time to make innumerable phone calls to "keep in touch"; he cultivates secretaries as well as senators; he will befriend a middle-level White House aide whom other important officials won't bother with. Every few months, he sends candy to the White House switchboard operators.[3]

This chapter explains why executives such as Robert Strauss, John Scully, and the presidents of Windham Hill Records and Syntex Corporation are effective communicators. First we will see how managers' jobs require communication. Next, we will define *communication* and describe a model of the communication process. Then we will consider the interpersonal aspects of communication, including perception, channels, and listening skills, that affect managers' ability to communicate. Next, we will look at the organization as a whole and consider formal upward and downward communications as well as informal communications. Finally, we will examine barriers to communication and how managers can overcome them.

● COMMUNICATION AND THE MANAGER'S JOB

How important is communication? Consider this: Managers spend at least 80 percent of every working day in direct communication with others. In other words, 48 minutes of every hour is spent in meetings, on the telephone, or talking informally while walking around. The other 20 percent of a typical manager's time is spent doing desk work, most of which is also communication in the form of reading and writing.[4]

Communication permeates every management function described in Chapter 1.[5] For example, when managers perform the planning function, they gather information; write letters, memos, and reports; and then meet with other managers to explain the plan. When managers lead, they communicate with subordinates to motivate them. When managers organize, they gather information about the state of the organization and communicate a new structure to others. Communication skills are a fundamental part of every managerial activity.

WHAT IS COMMUNICATION?

Before going further, let us determine what communication is. A professor at Harvard once asked a class to define communication by drawing pictures. Most students drew a manager speaking or writing. Some placed "speech balloons" next to their characters; others showed pages flying from a typewriter. "No," the professor told the class, "none of you have captured the essence of communication." He went on to explain that communication means to "share"—not "to speak" or "to write."

Communication thus can be defined as the process by which information is exchanged and understood by two or more people, usually with the intent to motivate or influence behavior. Communication is not just sending information. This distinction between *sharing* and *proclaiming* is crucial for successful management. A manager who does not listen is like a used-car salesperson who claims, "I sold a car—they just did not buy it." Management communication is a two-way street that includes listening and other forms of feedback. Effective communication, in the words of one expert, is as follows:

> When two people interact, they put themselves into each other's shoes, try to perceive the world as the other person perceives it, try to predict how the other will respond. Interaction involves reciprocal role-taking, the mutual employment of empathetic skills. The goal of interaction is the merger of self and other, a complete ability to anticipate, predict, and behave in accordance with the joint needs of self and other.[6]

It is the desire to share understanding that motivates executives to visit employees on the shop floor or eat breakfast with them. The things managers learn from direct communication with employees shape their understanding of the corporation.

THE COMMUNICATION PROCESS

Many people think communication is simple because they communicate without conscious thought or effort. However, communication is usually complex, and the opportunities for sending or receiving the wrong messages are innumerable. How often have you heard someone say, "But that's not what I meant"? Have you ever received directions you thought were clear and yet still got lost? How often have you wasted time on misunderstood instructions?

communication

The process by which information is exchanged and understood by two or more people, usually with the intent to motivate or influence behavior.

encode

To select symbols with which to compose a message.

message

The tangible formulation of an idea to be sent to a receiver.

channel

The carrier of a communication.

decode

To translate the symbols used in a message for the purpose of interpreting its meaning.

feedback

A response by the receiver to the sender's communication.

To more fully understand the complexity of the communication process, note the key elements outlined in Exhibit 14.1. Two common elements in every communication situation are the sender and the receiver. The *sender* is anyone who wishes to convey an idea or concept to others, to seek information, or to express a thought or emotion. The *receiver* is the person to whom the message is sent. The sender **encodes** the idea by selecting symbols with which to compose a message. The **message** is the tangible formulation of the idea that is sent to the receiver. The message is sent through a **channel,** which is the communication carrier. The channel can be a formal report, a telephone call, or a face-to-face meeting. The receiver **decodes** the symbols to interpret the meaning of the message. Encoding and decoding are potential sources for communication errors, because knowledge, attitudes, and background act as filters and create "noise" when translating from symbols to meaning. Finally, **feedback** occurs when the receiver responds to the sender's communication with a return message. Without feedback, the communication is *one-way;* with feedback, it is *two-way.* Feedback is a powerful aid to communication effectiveness, because it enables the sender to determine whether the receiver correctly interpreted the message.

Managers who are effective communicators understand and use the circular nature of communication. For example, James Treybig of Tandem Computers, Inc., widened the open-door policy in order to communicate with employees. Treybig appears on a monthly television program broadcast over the company's in-house television station. Employees around the world watch the show and call in their questions and comments. The television is the channel through which Treybig sends his encoded message. Employees decode and interpret the message and encode their feedback, which is sent through the channel of the telephone hookup. The communication circuit is complete. Similarly, Tom Monaghan, president of Domino's Pizza, maintains communication

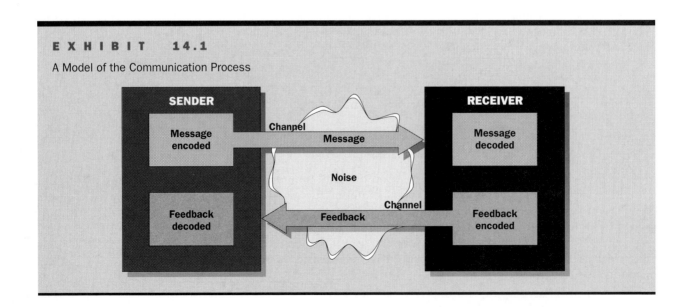

E X H I B I T   14.1

A Model of the Communication Process

channels with employees when he fields complaints for two hours during a monthly "call-in." Monaghan also maintains toll-free numbers on which employees call him directly. Treybig and Monaghan understand the elements of communication and have developed systems that work.[7]

● COMMUNICATING AMONG PEOPLE

The communication model in Exhibit 14.1 illustrates the components that must be mastered for effective communication. Communications can break down if sender and receiver do not encode or decode language in the same way.[8] The selection of communication channels can determine whether the message is distorted by noise and interference. The listening skills of both parties can determine whether a message is truly shared. Thus, for managers to be effective communicators, they must understand how interpersonal factors such as perception, communication channels, nonverbal behavior, and listening all work to enhance or detract from communication.

PERCEPTION AND COMMUNICATION

The way we perceive people is the starting point for how we communicate. When one person wishes to share an idea with another, the message is formulated based on references constructed from past events, experiences, expectations, and current motivations. When a receiver hears a message, he or she relies on a particular frame of reference for decoding and understanding it. The more similar the frames of reference between people, the more easily they can communicate.

Perception is the process people use to make sense out of the environment. However, perception in itself does not always lead to an accurate picture of the environment.[9] **Perceptual selectivity** is the process by which individuals screen and select the various objects and stimuli that vie for their attention. Certain stimuli catch their attention, and others do not. Once a stimulus is recognized, individuals organize or categorize it according to their frame of reference, that is, **perceptual organization.** Only a partial cue is needed to enable perceptual organization to take place. For example, all of us have spotted an old friend from a long distance and, without seeing the face or other features, recognized the person from the body movement.

The most common form of perceptual organization is stereotyping. A **stereotype** is a widely held generalization about a group of people that assigns attributes to them solely on the basis of one or a few categories, such as age, race, or occupation. For example, young people may assume that older people are old-fashioned or conservative. Students may stereotype professors as absent-minded or as political liberals.

How do perceptual selectivity and organization affect manager behavior? Consider the following comment from Joe, a staff supervisor, on his expectations about the annual budget meeting with his boss, Charlie:

> About a month before the meetings are to begin, I find myself waking up around 4:00 A.M., thinking about Charlie and the arguments I'm going to have

perception

The process of making sense out of one's environment.

perceptual selectivity

The screening and selection of objects and stimuli that compete for one's attention.

perceptual organization

The categorization of an object or stimulus according to one's frame of reference.

stereotype

A widely held generalization about a group of people that assigns attributes to them solely on the basis of a limited number of categories.

with him. I know he'll accuse me of trying to "pad" my requests and, in turn, I'll accuse him of failing to understand the nature of my department's needs. I'll be trying to anticipate every little snide remark he can generate and every argument that he's likely to propose, and I'll be getting ready with snide remarks and arguments of my own. This year, as always, I've got to be sure to get him before he gets me.[10]

Joe's selective perception will cause him to immediately recognize any cues that resemble snide remarks. He will also organize these remarks to fit his belief that Charlie's motivation is to reduce his budget. No matter what frame of mind Charlie brings to the communication, Joe is set to perceive in his own way, which will surely prevent open and honest communication.

Perceptual differences and perceptual mistakes also occur when people perceive simple objects in dissimilar ways. Typical examples are illustrated in Exhibit 14.2. In panel (a), many people see a sad old woman, but others see a beautiful young lady with a large head covering. In panel (b), the top airplane looks larger to most people because of perceptual organization. The background lines provide a frame of reference that distorts the actual size of the airplanes.

An important point for managers to understand is that perceptual differences are natural but can distort messages and create noise and interference for communications. Each person has a distinct personality and perceptual style; hence each interprets messages in a personal way. Managers should remember that words can mean different things to different people and should not assume that they already know what the other person or the communication is about.

COMMUNICATION CHANNELS

Managers have a choice of many channels through which to communicate to other managers or employees. A manager may discuss a problem face-to-face, use the telephone, write a memo or letter, or put an item in a newsletter, depending on the nature of the message. Recent research

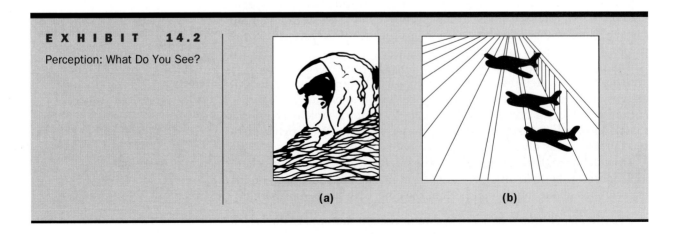

EXHIBIT 14.2

Perception: What Do You See?

(a)   (b)

has attempted to explain how managers select communication channels to enhance communication effectiveness.[11] The research has found that channels differ in their capacity to convey information. Just as a pipeline's physical characteristics limit the kind and amount of liquid that can be pumped through it, a communication channel's physical characteristics limit the kind and amount of information that can be conveyed among managers. The channels available to managers can be classified into a hierarchy based on information richness. **Channel richness** is the amount of information that can be transmitted during a communication episode. The hierarchy of channel richness is illustrated in Exhibit 14.3.

The capacity of an information channel is influenced by three characteristics: (1) the ability to handle multiple cues simultaneously; (2) the ability to facilitate rapid, two-way feedback; and (3) the ability to establish a personal focus for the communication. Face-to-face discussion is the richest medium, because it permits direct experience, multiple information cues, immediate feedback, and personal focus. Face-to-face discussions facilitate the assimilation of broad cues and deep, emotional understanding of the situation. For example, Tony Burns, CEO of Rider Systems, Inc., likes to handle things face-to-face: "You can look someone in the eyes, and you can tell by the look in his eyes or the inflection in his voice what the real problem or question or answer is."[12] Telephone conversations and interactive electronic media, such as video conferencing and electronic mail, lack the element of "being there." Eye contact, gaze, blush, posture, and body language cues are eliminated. Written media that are personalized, such as memos, notes, and letters, can be personally focused, but they convey only the cues written on paper and are slow to provide feedback. Impersonal written media, including fliers, bulletins, and standard computer reports, are the lowest in richness. These channels are not focused on a single receiver, use limited information cues, and do not permit feedback.

Channel selection depends on whether the message is routine or nonroutine. *Nonroutine messages* typically are ambiguous, concern novel events, and impose great potential for misunderstanding. Nonroutine

Direct, face-to-face communication is the key to unity within the Ito-Yokado Co., Ltd., culture. Here, a weekly meeting of management and store personnel provides face-to-face communication regarding marketing strategies, innovative ideas, and improved retail knowledge.

channel richness

The amount of information that can be transmitted during a communication episode.

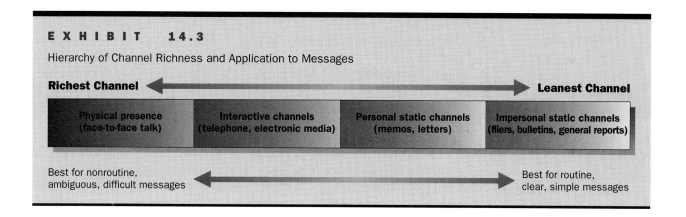

E X H I B I T   14.3

Hierarchy of Channel Richness and Application to Messages

Richest Channel ⬅————————————————➡ **Leanest Channel**

| Physical presence (face-to-face talk) | Interactive channels (telephone, electronic media) | Personal static channels (memos, letters) | Impersonal static channels (fliers, bulletins, general reports) |

Best for nonroutine, ambiguous, difficult messages ⬅————————————————➡ Best for routine, clear, simple messages

messages often are characterized by time pressure and surprise. Managers can communicate nonroutine messages effectively only by selecting rich channels. On the other hand, routine communications are simple and straightforward. *Routine messages* convey data or statistics or simply put into words what managers already agree on and understand. Routine messages can be efficiently communicated through a channel lower in richness. Written communications also should be used when the audience is widely dispersed or when the communication is "official" and a permanent record is required.[13]

Consider a CEO trying to work out a press release with public relations people about a plant explosion that injured 15 employees. If the press release must be ready in three hours, the communication is truly nonroutine and forces a rich information exchange. The group will meet face-to-face, brainstorm ideas, and provide rapid feedback to resolve disagreement and convey the correct information. If the CEO has three days to prepare the release, less information capacity is needed. The CEO and public relations people might begin developing the press release with an exchange of memos and telephone calls.

The key is to select a channel to fit the message. One CEO who understood the importance of channel selection was Jim Balkcom.

 # TECHSONIC INDUSTRIES INC.

Techsonic Industries Inc. CEO Jim Balkcom learned that one of life's hardest realities goes double for business. Through the late 1980s the sonar-device maker for sport fishermen was the second biggest employer in tiny Eufaula, Alabama. Sales tripled to $70 million over five years and the payroll peaked at 440 people. However, then the boom turned to bust, and the work force had to be slashed by more than half. Balkcom knew the thing he wanted most to avoid was exactly what he had to do.

Facing workers fearful of losing their source of livelihood was not an attractive prospect, but that's what Balkcom did. In addition to weekly executive gatherings, he began holding monthly company meetings with employees. He issued assurances that Techsonic was not going out of business. He was equally forthright in admitting that he did not know when things might improve, or if they might get worse in the near term. Balkcom also convened two meetings a year to deliver up-to-date reports of the company's condition. Other gatherings were more difficult. "We had a special meeting after each of the reductions in the work force to tell people what was going on," he says.

At each assembly, he faced tough questioning. His responses were always candid, and if he did not have an answer, he was upfront about that too. His belief was that employee morale would suffer far more if workers were left in the dark. Balkcom decided that making the best of a bad situation meant laying it on the line with his workers. He selected the most straightforward channel of communication and avoided any sort of posturing. Although it was the most difficult course, it was the right thing to do.[14] ■

NONVERBAL COMMUNICATION

Nonverbal communication refers to messages sent through human actions and behaviors rather than through words.[15] Although most nonverbal communication is unconscious or subconscious on our part, it represents a major portion of the messages we send and receive. Most managers are astonished to learn that words themselves carry little meaning. Major parts of the shared understanding from communication come from the nonverbal messages of facial expression, voice, mannerisms, posture, and dress.

Nonverbal communication occurs mostly face-to-face. One researcher found three sources of communication cues during face-to-face communication: the verbal, which are the actual spoken words; the vocal, which include the pitch, tone, and timber of a person's voice; and facial expressions. According to this study, the relative weights of these three factors in message interpretation are as follows: verbal impact, 7 percent; vocal impact, 38 percent; and facial impact, 55 percent.[16]

This research strongly implies that "it's not what you say, but how you say it." Nonverbal messages convey thoughts and feelings with greater force than do our most carefully selected words. Body language often communicates our real feelings eloquently. Thus, while the conscious mind may be formulating vocal messages such as "I'm happy" or "Congratulations on your promotion," the body language may be signaling true feelings through blushing, perspiring, glancing, crying, or avoiding eye contact. When the verbal and nonverbal messages are contradictory, the receiver may be confused and usually will give more weight to behavioral actions than to verbal messages.[17]

A manager's office also sends powerful nonverbal cues. For example, what do the following seating arrangements mean if used by your supervisor: (1) She stays behind her desk and you sit in a straight chair on the opposite side. (2) The two of you sit in straight chairs away from her desk, perhaps at a table. (3) The two of you sit in a seating arrangement consisting of a sofa and easy chair. To most people, the first arrangement indicates "I'm the boss here" or "I'm in authority." The second arrangement indicates "This is serious business." The third indicates a more casual and friendly, "Let's get to know each other."[18] Nonverbal messages can be a powerful asset to communication if they complement and support verbal messages. Managers should pay close attention to nonverbal behavior when communicating. They must learn to coordinate their verbal and nonverbal messages and at the same time be sensitive to what their peers, subordinates, and supervisors are saying nonverbally.

LISTENING

Managers who believe that giving orders is the important communication requirement are in for a surprise. The new skill is *listening*, both to customers and to employees. Most executives believe that important information flows from the bottom up, not the top down, and managers had better be tuned in.[19] In the communication model at the beginning

nonverbal communication

A communication transmitted through actions and behaviors rather than through words.

listening

The skill of receiving messages to accurately grasp facts and feelings to interpret the genuine meaning.

of the chapter in Exhibit 14.1, the listener is responsible for message reception, which is a vital link in the communication process. **Listening** involves the skill of receiving messages to accurately grasp facts and feelings to interpret the message's genuine meaning. Only then can the receiver provide the feedback with which to complete the communication circuit. Listening requires attention, energy, and skill.

Many people do not listen effectively. They concentrate on formulating what they are going to say next rather than on what is being said to them. Our listening efficiency, as measured by the amount of material understood and remembered by subjects 48 hours after listening to a 10-minute message, is, on average, no better than 25 percent.[20]

What constitutes good listening? Exhibit 14.4 gives ten keys to effective listening and illustrates a number of ways to distinguish a bad listener from a good listener. A good listener finds areas of interest, is flexible, works hard at listening, and uses thought speed to mentally summarize, weigh, and anticipate what the speaker says.

Norman Brinker, chairman of Chili's, Inc., has a bedrock belief in listening. He says it is important to hear what employees have to say. They are not to be bullied. Tom Peters, the famous management author and consultant, says that executives can become good listeners by observing the following: Effective listening is engaged listening; ask dumb questions, break down barriers by participating with employees in casual get-togethers, force yourself to get out and about, provide listening forums, take notes, promise feedback—and deliver.[21]

EXHIBIT 14.4

Ten Keys to Effective Listening

Keys	Poor Listener	Good Listener
1. Listen actively	Is passive, laid back	Asks questions, paraphrases what is said
2. Find areas of interest	Tunes out dry subjects	Looks for opportunities, new learning
3. Resist distractions	Is easily distracted	Fights or avoids distractions; tolerates bad habits; knows how to concentrate
4. Capitalize on the fact that thought is faster than speech	Tends to daydream with slow speakers	Challenges, anticipates, mentally summarizes; weighs the evidence; listens between the lines to tone of voice
5. Be responsive	Is minimally involved	Nods; shows interest, give and take, positive feedback
6. Judge content, not delivery	Tunes out if delivery is poor	Judges content; skips over delivery errors
7. Hold one's fire	Has preconceptions, starts to argue	Does not judge until comprehension is complete
8. Listen for ideas	Listens for facts	Listens to central themes
9. Work at listening	Shows no energy output; faked attention	Works hard, exhibits active body state, eye contact
10. Exercise one's mind	Resists difficult material in favor of light, recreational material	Uses heavier material as exercise for the mind

SOURCE: Adapted from Sherman K. Okum, "How to Be a Better Listener," *Nation's Business* (August 1975), 62; and Philip Morgan and Kent Baker, "Building a Professional Image: Improving Listening Behavior," *Supervisory Management* (November 1985), 34–38.

● ORGANIZATIONAL COMMUNICATION

Another aspect of management communication concerns the organization as a whole. Organizationwide communications typically flow in three directions—downward, upward, and horizontally. Managers are responsible for establishing and maintaining formal channels of communication in these three directions. Managers also use informal channels, which means they get out of their offices and mingle with employees.

FORMAL COMMUNICATION CHANNELS

Formal communication channels are those that flow within the chain of command or task responsibility defined by the organization. The three formal channels and the types of information conveyed in each are illustrated in Exhibit 14.5.[22]

DOWNWARD COMMUNICATION.   The most familiar and obvious flow of formal communication, **downward communication,** refers to the messages and information sent from top management to subordinates in a downward direction. For example, management at Trans-Matic (makers

formal communication channel

A communication channel that flows within the chain of command or task responsibility defined by the organization.

downward communication

Messages sent from top management down to subordinates.

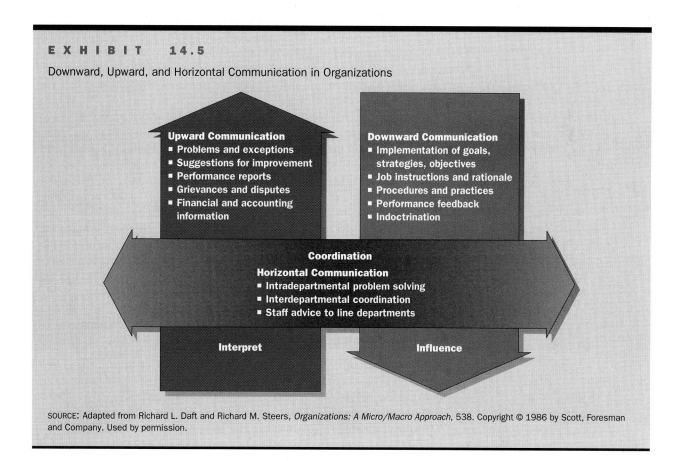

EXHIBIT   14.5

Downward, Upward, and Horizontal Communication in Organizations

Upward Communication
- Problems and exceptions
- Suggestions for improvement
- Performance reports
- Grievances and disputes
- Financial and accounting information

Downward Communication
- Implementation of goals, strategies, objectives
- Job instructions and rationale
- Procedures and practices
- Performance feedback
- Indoctrination

Coordination

Horizontal Communication
- Intradepartmental problem solving
- Interdepartmental coordination
- Staff advice to line departments

Interpret

Influence

SOURCE: Adapted from Richard L. Daft and Richard M. Steers, *Organizations: A Micro/Macro Approach*, 538. Copyright © 1986 by Scott, Foresman and Company. Used by permission.

Downward communication is important to managers at Reflexite Corporation. Financial information is distributed to the employees, who are shareholders in the corporation.

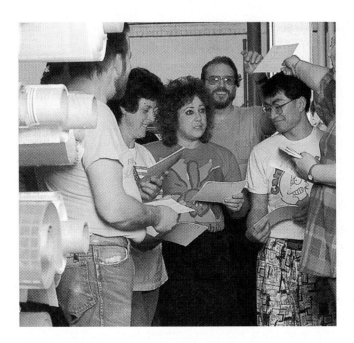

of stamped metal parts) distributes monthly reports to all employees, detailing financial data and performance analyses. The honest, up-front approach provides employees advance warning of potential downturns and keeps employees abreast of management strategies for cost cutting, retooling, and other necessary changes. The communication builds empathy for management and creates a climate of working *together* for solutions during tough times.[23]

Managers can communicate downward to employees through speeches, messages in company publications, electronic mail, information leaflets tucked into pay envelopes, material on bulletin boards, and policy and procedure manuals. When Gerald M. Lieberman, senior human resources officer at Citicorp, launched the company's Choices '91 flexible benefits plan, he communicated options to 56,000 employees using several information channels: workbooks, videos, seminars, software, and a hot line. Lieberman understands that different employees are responsive to different kinds of communication. A computer whiz likes information software better than reading a benefits booklet. A secretary may enjoy the give-and-take of an information seminar. Lieberman's communication strategy enabled individual employees to study their options and make wise choices.[24]

Downward communication in an organization usually encompasses the following topics:

1 *Implementation of goals, strategies, and objectives.* Communicating new strategies and goals provides information about specific targets and expected behaviors. It gives direction for lower levels of the organization. Example: "The new quality campaign is for real. We must improve product quality if we are to survive."

2 *Job instructions and rationale.* These are directives on how to do a specific task and how the job relates to other organizational activities. Example: "Purchasing should order the bricks now so the work crew can begin construction of the building in two weeks."

3 *Procedures and practices.* These are messages defining the organization's policies, rules, regulations, benefits, and structural arrangements. Example: "After your first 90 days of employment, you are eligible to enroll in our company-sponsored savings plan."

4 *Performance feedback.* These messages appraise how well individuals and departments are doing their jobs. Example: "Joe, your work on the computer network has greatly improved the efficiency of our ordering process."

5 *Indoctrination.* These messages are designed to motivate employees to adopt the company's mission and cultural values and to participate in special ceremonies, such as picnics and United Way campaigns. Example: "The company thinks of its employees as family and would like to invite everyone to attend the annual picnic and fair on March 3."

The major problem with downward communication is *drop off*, the distortion or loss of message content. Although formal communications are a powerful way to reach all employees, much information gets lost—25 percent or so each time a message is passed from one person to the next. In addition, the message can be distorted if it travels a great distance from its originating source to the ultimate receiver. A tragic example is the following:

> A reporter was present at a hamlet burned down by the U.S. Army 1st Air Cavalry Division in 1967. Investigations showed that the order from the Division headquarters to the brigade was: "On no occasion must hamlets be burned down."
>
> The brigade radioed the battalion: "Do not burn down any hamlets unless you are absolutely convinced that the Viet Cong are in them."
>
> The battalion radioed the infantry company at the scene: "If you think there are any Viet Cong in the hamlet, burn it down."
>
> The company commander ordered his troops: "Burn down that hamlet."[25]

Information drop off cannot be completely avoided, but the techniques described in the previous sections can reduce it substantially. Using the right communication channel, consistency between verbal and nonverbal messages, active listening, and aligning messages with the perception of users can maintain communication accuracy as it moves down the organization.

UPWARD COMMUNICATION. Formal **upward communication** includes messages that flow from the lower to the higher levels in the organization's hierarchy. Most organizations take pains to build in healthy channels for upward communication. Employees need to air grievances, report progress, and provide feedback on management initiatives. Coupling the flow of upward and downward communication

upward communication

Messages transmitted from the lower to the higher level in the organization's hierarchy.

ensures that the communication circuit between managers and employees is complete.[26] Five types of information communicated upward are the following:

1 *Problems and exceptions.* These messages describe serious problems with and exceptions to routine performance in order to make senior managers aware of difficulties. Example: "The printer has been out of operation for two days, and it will be at least a week before a new one arrives."

2 *Suggestions for improvement.* These messages are ideas for improving task-related procedures to increase quality or efficiency. Example: "I think we should eliminate step 2 in the audit procedure because it takes a lot of time and produces no results."

3 *Performance reports.* These messages include periodic reports that inform management how individuals and departments are performing. Example: "We completed the audit report for Smith & Smith on schedule but are one week behind on the Jackson report."

4 *Grievances and disputes.* These messages are employee complaints and conflicts that travel up the hierarchy for a hearing and possible resolution. Example: "The manager of operations research cannot get the cooperation of the Lincoln plant for the study of machine utilization."

5 *Financial and accounting information.* These messages pertain to costs, accounts receivable, sales volume, anticipated profits, return on investment, and other matters of interest to senior managers. Example: "Costs are 2 percent over budget, but sales are 10 percent ahead of target, so the profit picture for the third quarter is excellent."

Many organizations make a great effort to facilitate upward communication. Mechanisms include suggestion boxes, employee surveys, open-door policies, management information system reports, and face-to-face conversations between workers and executives.

William J. O'Brien, CEO of Hanover Insurance Company, points out: "The fundamental movement in business in the next 25 years will be in the dispersing of power, to give meaning and fulfillment to employees in a way that avoids chaos and disorder." Power sharing means inviting upward communication. At Pacific Gas & Electric, CEO Richard A. Clark keeps employee communication lines open with employee surveys, biannual video presentations, and monthly brown-bag lunches to hear questions and complaints.[27]

Despite these efforts, however, barriers to accurate upward communication exist. Managers may resist hearing about employee problems, or employees may not trust managers sufficiently to push information upward.[28] One of the most innovative programs ensuring that information gets to top managers without distortion was developed by Hyatt Hotels.

HYATT HOTELS

Honest communication is so important that Hyatt Hotels developed unique ways to keep information flowing upward from employees. Myrna Hellerman, vice-president of human resources, developed a communication strategy that includes several programs:

1 *Confidential surveys* allow employees to comment freely and confidentially on any aspect of Hyatt.

2 *Employee forums* provide an annual opportunity for employees to drop by and talk to their general manager in the relaxed atmosphere of a hotel suite. Discussions can be about anything during this personal-level communication.

3 *Hyattalks* are monthly gab sessions between managers and a select group of employees, focusing on employee needs and methods of improving service.

4 *In-Touch Day* is the most innovative of the programs. In-Touch Day gives management an opportunity to spend time in the trenches— folding napkins, making pastry, cleaning tubs and toilets—to better understand both employees and customers. As top executives acquaint themselves with the daily routines and problems of bellhops, waiters, housekeepers, and chefs, they increase their own awareness of how management actions affect others.

Hellerman sees Hyatt's many communication efforts as a bonding experience between management and employees. These innovative upward-communication techniques put the responsibility for the company's success with lower-level employees, and managers act on what they hear.[29] ∎

HORIZONTAL COMMUNICATION. Horizontal communication is the lateral or diagonal exchange of messages among peers or coworkers. It may occur within or across departments. The purpose of horizontal communication is not only to inform but also to request support and coordinate activities. Horizontal communication falls into one of three categories:

horizontal communication
The lateral or diagonal exchange of messages among peers or coworkers.

1 *Intradepartmental problem solving.* These messages take place between members of the same department and concern task accomplishment. Example: "Betty, can you help us figure out how to complete this medical expense report form?"

2 *Interdepartmental coordination.* Interdepartmental messages facilitate the accomplishment of joint projects or tasks. Example: "Bob, please contact marketing and production and arrange a meeting to discuss the specifications for the new subassembly. It looks like we may not be able to meet their requirements."

3 *Staff advice to line departments.* These messages often go from specialists in operations research, finance, or computer services to line managers seeking help in these areas. Example: "Let's go talk to the manufacturing supervisor about the problem he's having interpreting the computer reports."

Recall from Chapter 8 that many organizations build in horizontal communications in the form of task forces, committees, or even a matrix structure to encourage coordination. For example, Carol Taber, publisher of *Working Woman,* was bothered by the separation of departments at her magazine. She instituted frequent meetings among department heads and a monthly report to keep everyone informed and involved on a horizontal basis.[30] The Leading Edge box shows how Reflexite Corporation devised a formal communication channel that encouraged horizontal, downward, and upward communication.

INFORMAL COMMUNICATION CHANNELS

informal communication channel

A communication channel that exists outside formally authorized channels without regard for the organization's hierarchy of authority.

Informal communication channels exist outside the formally authorized channels and do not adhere to the organization's hierarchy of authority. Informal communications coexist with formal communications but may skip hierarchical levels, cutting across vertical chains of command to connect virtually anyone in the organization. For example, Jim Treybig of Tandem Computer uses informal channels by letting any employee reach him through his computer terminal. Treybig also holds a Friday afternoon beer bust at each of Tandem's 132 offices worldwide. The idea is to create an informal communication channel for employees. Treybig says, "Over beer and popcorn, employees are more willing to talk openly." [31] An illustration of both formal and informal communications is given in Exhibit 14.6. Note how formal communications can be vertical or horizontal, depending on task assignments and coordination responsibilities.

Two types of informal channels used in many organizations are "management by wandering around" and the "grapevine."

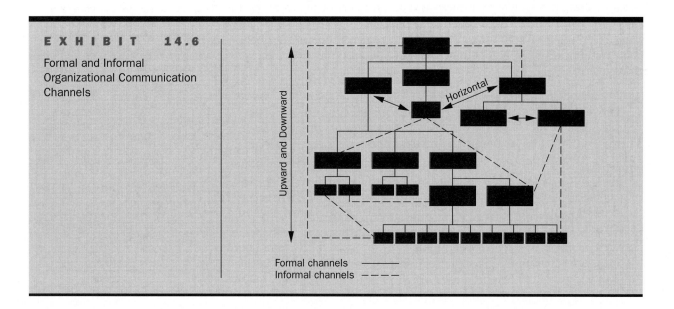

EXHIBIT 14.6

Formal and Informal Organizational Communication Channels

Formal channels ———
Informal channels - - - - -

LEADING edge   **REFLEXITE CORPORATION**

Cecil Ursprung, CEO of Reflexite Corporation, a $31-million-a-year manufacturer of reflective plastics, has always had definite, if somewhat unusual, ideas about what employees want from a company. He believes they want to be committed, and have the power to influence decisions that affect their work lives. Take care of those things, and the motivational and output payback will be a thousand times greater than the cost.

Ursprung assigned manufacturing manager Matt Guyer the formidable task of devising a system whereby employees had an effective communication channel. Ursprung did not want workers' ideas or suggestions funneled into a black hole, never to be seen again. He also did not want a replica of some company structure that already existed. On the other hand, he wanted to see something more than suggestion boxes bolted to the walls.

Guyer, a disciple of total quality management approach, created the Employee Assistance Request form, aptly dubbed EARS. Under the system, employees get a formal communication channel to register problems. They also learn how to correctly and systematically solve their problems. Instead of an ad hoc approach, the EARS program involves documenting, plotting, and graphing possible root causes of a problem to determine the amount of delay

and waste it is actually causing. This is a critical aspect of the program. "EARS works," says Guyer, "by making people who identify problems step back and quantify the magnitude of the problem and its impact on the entire company before offering a solution. That allows them not only to offer better solutions but also to understand why some problems are given a higher priority than others."

When an employee identifies a problem, an action leader joins him or her to study the situation and begin the form. This happens within 24 hours. If the difficulty spans departmental lines or is particularly difficult, a team may be assembled. Posting progress reports throughout the company ensures that the employee who brings a problem to light carries through with its solution. It also allows the entire work force access to work being done in other parts of the company. If employees recognize a difficulty they have experienced before, they can lend assistance. Ursprung also stays apprised of developments through a weekly check of the EARS system.

The EARS program does not terminate when a particular problem is eliminated. Every EARS form includes a follow-up date. That's when the person who originally identified the problem is contacted again to make certain there has been no recurrence. If so, the originator, action leader, and EARS coordinator all sign off.

The last step in the EARS program goes a long way toward achieving Ursprung's original vision.

Two weeks after the follow-up date, top managers are given an EARS form. They find the person who originated it, meet them and then thank them. Reflexite has come up with a certificate of appreciation handed out at company meetings. Employees annual-review folders now also include EARS contributions.

Every company would like to come up with a system that taps the problem-solving skills of all employees. The difficulty is to create a formal communication structure that can accomplish it without upending operations. Reflexite Corporation's EARS program does more than solve problems. It enables employees to determine what the problem is costing and therefore what priority it should be assigned. It also provides systematic methods of finding solutions. The additional benefit of employees who know their voices are heard may approach Ursprung's original estimate. In five years beginning in 1986, Reflexite sales quadrupled. The work force grew by a factor of three and profits rose nearly 600 percent. It is successfully taking on much larger 3M Corporation, and has moved into Mexico, Canada, and Europe. If projections are correct, Reflexite will be a $100 million worldwide company by the year 2000. ■

SOURCE: John Case, "Collective Effort," *Inc.,* January 1992, 32–43; and Teri Lammers, "The Effective Employee-Feedback System," *INC.,* February 1993, 109–111.

management by wandering around (MBWA)

A communication technique in which managers interact directly with workers to exchange information.

MANAGEMENT BY WANDERING AROUND. The communication technique known as **management by wandering around (MBWA)** was made famous by the books *In Search of Excellence* and *A Passion for Excellence*.[32] These books describe executives who talk directly with employees to learn what is going on. MBWA works for managers at all levels. They mingle and develop positive relationships with employees, and learn directly from them about their department, division, or organization. For example, the president of ARCO had a habit of visiting a district field office. Rather than schedule a big strategic meeting with the district supervisor, he would come in unannounced and chat with the lowest-level employees. Andy Pearson of PepsiCo started his tours from the bottom up: He went directly to a junior assistant brand manager and asked, "What's up?" In any organization, both upward and downward communication are enhanced with MBWA. Managers have a chance to describe key ideas and values to employees and in turn learn about the problems and issues confronting employees.

When managers fail to take advantage of MBWA, they become aloof and isolated from employees. For example, Peter Anderson, president of Ztel, Inc., a maker of television switching systems, preferred not to personally communicate with employees. He managed at arm's length. As one manager said, "I don't know how many times I asked Peter to come to the lab, but he stayed in his office. He wasn't that visible to the troops." This formal management style contributed to Ztel's troubles and eventual bankruptcy.[33]

In contrast, Bob Crawford, founder of Brook Furniture Rental has learned how MBWA can work to a company's advantage.

 BROOK FURNITURE RENTAL

More and more managers believe that seeking employee input is one of the best ways to solve business problems. Bob Crawford, founder and CEO of Brook Furniture Rental, thinks uninhibited two-way communication is also a key to growth. "People will put every effort into advancing the business if they can communicate their ideas freely," he says. Crawford makes sure they get plenty of opportunities.

Crawford greets employees by first name on his frequent trips through the company's cavernous warehouses. He directs training sessions, and solicits ideas for improving the business from everyone, even newly hired employees. He occasionally goes along on sales calls. "In this impersonal society, people want a personal touch," he says.

The personal touch is not the only thing that's gotten lost, at least in Crawford's view. He calls listening the most potent communications tool, and he does not think enough people know how to do it. He emphasizes this to his salespeople. "The secret of good human dynamics is a balance between talking and listening," he says. "You need to absorb data before imparting information."

It's a secret Crawford is using to good success. His company sales are around $50 million. Managing by wandering around, greeting employ-

At Flowers Industries, Inc., a leader in the baked foods industry, Chairman Amos McMullian (left) encourages information communication channels to address the concerns of employees and the community. Flowers' employees are committed to a better society and seek involvement with government through the Chairman's Council for Better Government, a voluntary, nonprofit organization.

ees by name, and maintaining an atmosphere where communication in both directions is encouraged provides a lot of benefits. And, the key has been just learning how to listen.[34] ■

THE GRAPEVINE. The **grapevine** is an informal, person-to-person communication network of employees that is not officially sanctioned by the organization.[35] The grapevine links employees in all directions, ranging from the president through middle management, support staff, and line employees. The grapevine will always exist in an organization, but it can become a dominant force when formal channels are closed. In such cases, the grapevine is actually a service because the information it provides helps makes sense of an unclear or uncertain situation. Employees use grapevine rumors to fill in information gaps and clarify management decisions. The grapevine tends to be more active during periods of change, excitement, anxiety, and sagging economic conditions. For example, when Jel, Inc., an auto supply firm, was under great pressure from Ford and GM to increase quality, rumors circulated on the shop floor about the company's possible demise. Management changes to improve quality—learning statistical process control, introducing a new compensation system, buying a fancy new screw machine from Germany—all started out as rumors, circulating days ahead of the actual announcements, and were generally accurate.[36]

Research suggests that a few people are primarily responsible for the grapevine's success. Exhibit 14.7 illustrates the two most typical grapevines.[37] In the *gossip chain,* a single individual conveys a piece of news to many other people. In a *cluster chain,* a few individuals each convey information to several others. Having only a few people conveying information may account for the accuracy of grapevines. If every person told one other person in sequence, distortions would be greater.

grapevine

An informal, person-to-person communication network of employees that is not officially sanctioned by the organization.

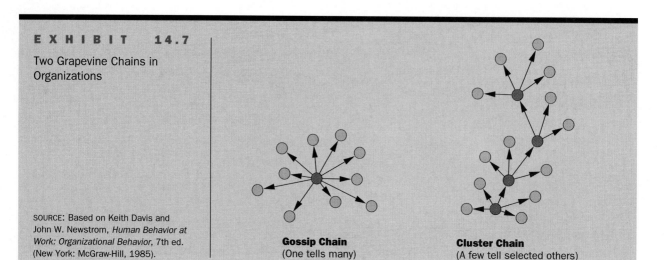

EXHIBIT 14.7

Two Grapevine Chains in Organizations

SOURCE: Based on Keith Davis and John W. Newstrom, *Human Behavior at Work: Organizational Behavior*, 7th ed. (New York: McGraw-Hill, 1985).

Gossip Chain
(One tells many)

Cluster Chain
(A few tell selected others)

Surprising aspects of the grapevine are its accuracy and its relevance to the organization. About 80 percent of grapevine communications pertain to business-related topics rather than personal, vicious gossip. Moreover, from 70 to 90 percent of the details passed through a grapevine are accurate.[38] Many managers would like the grapevine to be destroyed because they consider its rumors to be untrue, malicious, and harmful to personnel. Typically this is not the case; however, managers should be aware that almost five of every six important messages are carried to some extent by the grapevine rather than through official channels. When official communication channels are closed, destructive rumors can occur.

● COMMUNICATING IN TEAMS

The importance of teamwork in organizations, discussed in more detail in Chapter 15, emphasizes the need for team communication. Team members work together to accomplish tasks, and the team's communication structure influences both team performance and employee satisfaction. Research into team communication has focused on two characteristics: the extent to which team communications are centralized and the nature of the team's task.[39] The relationship between these characteristics is illustrated in Exhibit 14.8. In a **centralized network,** team members must communicate through one individual to solve problems or make decisions. In a **decentralized network,** individuals can communicate freely with other team members. Members process information equally among themselves until all agree on a decision.[40]

In laboratory experiments, centralized communication networks achieved faster solutions for simple problems. Members could simply pass relevant information to a central person for a decision. Decentralized communications were slower for simple problems because information was passed among individuals until someone finally put the

centralized network

A team communication structure in which team members communicate through a single individual to solve problems or make decisions.

decentralized network

A team communication structure in which team members freely communicate with one another and arrive at decisions together.

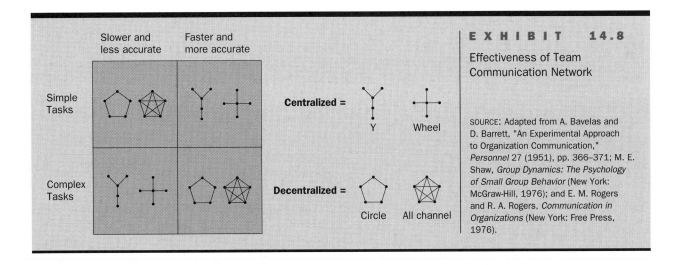

EXHIBIT   14.8

Effectiveness of Team
Communication Network

SOURCE: Adapted from A. Bavelas and
D. Barrett, "An Experimental Approach
to Organization Communication,"
Personnel 27 (1951), pp. 366–371; M. E.
Shaw, *Group Dynamics: The Psychology
of Small Group Behavior* (New York:
McGraw-Hill, 1976); and E. M. Rogers
and R. A. Rogers, *Communication in
Organizations* (New York: Free Press,
1976).

pieces together and solved the problem. However, for more complex problems, the decentralized communication network was faster. Because all necessary information was not restricted to one person, a pooling of information through widespread communications provided greater input into the decision. Similarly, the accuracy of problem solving was related to problem complexity. The centralized networks made fewer errors on simple problems but more errors on complex ones. Decentralized networks were less accurate for simple problems but more accurate for complex ones.[41]

The implication for organizations is as follows: In a highly competitive global environment, organizations use groups and teams to deal with complex problems. When team activities are complex and difficult, all members should share information in a decentralized structure to

An open communication channel between members of a team is critical to the success of a project. Here, employees on the work team iron out details for solving a production problem.

solve problems. Teams need a free flow of communication in all directions.[42] Members should be encouraged to discuss problems with one another, and a large percentage of employee time should be devoted to information processing. However, groups who perform routine tasks spend less time processing information, and thus communications can be centralized. Data can be channeled to a supervisor for decisions, freeing workers to spend a greater percentage of time on task activities.

● MANAGING ORGANIZATIONAL COMMUNICATION

Many of the ideas described in this chapter pertain to barriers to communication and how to overcome them. Barriers can be categorized as those that exist at the individual level and those that exist at the organizational level. First we will examine communication barriers; then we will look at techniques for overcoming them. These barriers and techniques are summarized in Exhibit 14.9.

BARRIERS TO COMMUNICATION

Barriers to communication can exist within the individual or as part of the organization.

INDIVIDUAL BARRIERS.   First, there are interpersonal barriers; these include problems with emotions and perceptions held by employees. For example, rigid perceptual labeling or categorizing of others prevents modification or alteration of opinions. If a person's mind is made up before the communication starts, communication will fail. Moreover, people with different backgrounds or knowledge may interpret a communication in different ways.

Second, selecting the wrong channel or medium for sending a communication can be a problem. For example, when a message is emo-

---

EXHIBIT   14.9

Communication Barriers and Ways to Overcome Them

Barriers	How to Overcome
Individual	
Interpersonal dynamics	Active listening
Channels and media	Selection of appropriate channel
Semantics	Knowledge of other's perspective
Inconsistent cues	MBWA
Organizational	
Status and power differences	Climate of trust
Departmental needs and goals	Development and use of formal channels
Communication network unsuited to task	Changing organization or group structure to fit communication needs
Lack of formal channels	Encouragement of multiple channels, formal and informal

tional, it is better to transmit it face-to-face rather than in writing. On the other hand, writing works best for routine messages but lacks the capacity for rapid feedback and multiple cues needed for difficult messages.

Third, semantics often causes communication problems. **Semantics** pertains to the meaning of words and the way they are used. A word such as "effectiveness" may mean achieving high production to a factory superintendent and employee satisfaction to a personnel staff specialist. Many common words have an average of 28 definitions; thus, communicators must take care to select the words that will accurately encode ideas.[43]

Fourth, sending inconsistent cues between verbal and nonverbal communications will confuse the receiver. If one's facial expression does not match one's words, the communication will contain noise and uncertainty. The tone of voice and body language should be consistent with the words, and actions should not contradict words.

ORGANIZATIONAL BARRIERS. Organizational barriers pertain to factors for the organization as a whole. First is the problem of status and power differences. Low-power people may be reluctant to pass bad news up the hierarchy, thus giving the wrong impression to upper levels.[44] High-power people may not pay attention or may feel that low-status people have little to contribute.

Second, differences across departments in terms of needs and goals interfere with communications. Each department perceives problems in its own terms. The production department is concerned with production efficiency and may not fully understand the marketing department's need to get the product to the customer in a hurry.

Third, the communication flow may not fit the group's or organization's task. If a centralized communication structure is used for nonroutine tasks, there will not be enough information circulated to solve problems. The organization, department, or group is most efficient when the amount of communication flowing among employees fits the task.

Fourth, the absence of formal channels reduces communication effectiveness. Organizations must provide adequate upward, downward, and horizontal communication in the form of employee surveys, open-door policies, newsletters, memos, task forces, and liaison personnel. Without these formal channels, the organization cannot communicate as a whole.

OVERCOMING COMMUNICATION BARRIERS

Managers can design the organization so as to encourage positive, effective communication. Designing involves both individual skills and organizational actions.

INDIVIDUAL SKILLS. Perhaps the most important individual skill is active listening. Active listening means asking questions, showing interest, and occasionally paraphrasing what the speaker has said to ensure that one is interpreting accurately. Active listening also means providing feedback to the sender to complete the communication loop.

Second, individuals should select the appropriate channel for the message. A complicated message should be sent through a rich channel, such

semantics

The meaning of words and the way they are used.

as face-to-face discussion or telephone. Routine messages and data can be sent through memos, letters, or electronic mail, because there is little chance of misunderstanding.

Third, senders and receivers should make a special effort to understand each other's perspective. Managers can sensitize themselves to the information receiver so that they will be better able to target the message, detect bias, and clarify missed interpretations. By understanding others' perspectives, semantics can be clarified, perceptions understood, and objectivity maintained.

The fourth individual skill is management by wandering around. Managers must be willing to get out of the office and check communications with others. For example, John McDonnell of McDonnell Douglas always eats in the employee cafeteria when he visits far-flung facilities. Through direct observation and face-to-face meetings, managers develop an understanding of the organization and are able to communicate important ideas and values directly to others. The Leading Edge Box describes one manager who has mastered the individual skills necessary for effective communication.

ORGANIZATIONAL ACTIONS.   Perhaps the most important thing managers can do for the organization is to create a climate of trust and openness. This will encourage people to communicate honestly with each other. Subordinates will feel free to transmit negative as well as positive messages without fear of retribution. Efforts to develop interpersonal skills among employees can be made to foster openness, honesty, and trust.

Second, managers should develop and use formal information channels in all directions. Scandinavian Design uses two newsletters to reach employees. GM's Packard Electric plant is designed to share all pertinent information—financial, future plans, quality, performance—with employees. Bank of America uses programs called Innovate and Idea Tap to get ideas and feedback from employees. Other techniques include direct mail, bulletin boards, and employee surveys.

Third, managers should encourage the use of multiple channels, including both formal and informal communications. Multiple communication channels include written directives, face-to-face discussions, MBWA, and the grapevine. For example, managers at GM's Packard Electric plant use multimedia, including a monthly newspaper, frequent meetings of employee teams, and an electronic news display in the cafeteria. Sending messages through multiple channels increases the likelihood that they will be properly received.

Fourth, the structure should fit communication needs. For example, Harrah's created the Communication Team as part of its structure at the Casino/Holiday Inn in Las Vegas. The team includes one member from each department. It deals with urgent company problems and helps people think beyond the scope of their own departments to communicate with anyone and everyone to solve those problems. An organization can be designed to use teams, task forces, integrating managers, or a matrix structure as needed to facilitate the horizontal flow of information for

LEADING edge   **BODY SHOP**

Communication has never been a problem for Anita Roddick, whom we read about in Chapters 5 and 12. From the rostrum of her 1,100 Body Shop stores in some 45 countries, she has advocated for environmental and social concerns, ethical business operations, and a host of other causes. The quality of business, according to Roddick, is far more important than what is made or how much of it gets sold. As for actually promoting products, well, that too is anathema. Roddick's business heresies are endless. She has recently discovered that, despite wisdom to the contrary, people still often do take shots at the messenger.

Roddick had to spend most of 1993 fighting fires. After cooperating with Fulcrum Productions in making a company documentary, Roddick was dismayed when the film leveled accusations of hypocrisy in the Body Shop's use of ingredients that had been tested on animals and insinuated that the company was in shaky financial condition. Roddick and her husband, Gordon, sued for libel. A jury found in favor of the Roddicks and awarded damages of almost $412,000, but Anita Roddick tearfully admitted it was an experience she never wanted to repeat. She compared the court fight to a month and a half in a mahogany coffin.

Roddick learned that making the transition from small to super-large business is difficult, and that more than losing track of every employee's name is involved. The process is even more complicated for a company that must safeguard the pristine image that comprises the biggest part of its competitive advantage, at least in many consumers' minds.

Critics were quick to pounce when Roddick had to announce the previous fiscal year's results in the spring of 1993. Profits were down 15 percent, and analysts and shareholders alike were wondering if the natural fad had finally fizzled. Roddick ridiculed investors, calling them greedy speculators trying to make money off buying and selling. As for the Body Shop earnings not meeting expectations, Roddick seemed unconcerned. "They expected us to make $36 million," she asked rhetorically. "Tough—we made $33 million."

Body Shop skeptics were quieted further when the first half-year 1993 earnings results were made public. Profits exceeded analysts' projections, and almost 65 percent of the jump came from Body Shops outside of Britain.

Roddick's role as chief company spokesperson once again was of paramount importance, especially in the United States. Americans tend to be more price-conscious than European consumers, and much less brand loyal. And the natural cosmetics industry is already overpopulated. Initial curiosity will bring in customers. However, Roddick will have to consistently communicate every bit of her environmental and socially conscious fervor to maintain market share.

Roddick admits that from the day she founded her first store she has been trying to change the language of business. Ironically, she had to use the press to get her message across even back then. When two nearby funeral homes objected to the Body Shop name so close to their establishments, she turned to the newspaper to publicize the plight of a struggling female entrepreneur about to be put out of business because of threatened lawsuits. The public rallied to her aid, and customers flocked into her store.

She also has had to respond to publicity that's been neither kind nor helpful. Founding a company that holds itself up to be on the cutting edge of ethical and environmental business practices invites a hard look from the press, and other segments of the public as well. Roddick expects the criticisms and periodic investigations will continue. She also knows that judgments for her company will likely be less lenient than any others. But, she also thinks if she can continue to communicate the company message, she will have achieved her original goal of operating a solid worldwide business that earns a profit while doing no environmental harm. ■

SOURCE: Jennifer Conlin, "Survival of the Fittest," *Working Woman,* February 1994, 29–73; Bo Burlingham, "This Woman Has Changed Business Forever," *INC.,* June 1990, 34–46; and "The Body Shop: Marketer with a Message," *Focus Japan,* July 1991, 8.

coordination and problem solving. Structure should also reflect group information needs. When group tasks are difficult, a decentralized structure should be implemented to encourage discussion and participation.

SUMMARY AND MANAGEMENT SOLUTION

This chapter described several important points about communicating in organizations. Communication takes up 80 percent of a manager's time. Communication is a process of encoding an idea into a message, which is sent through a channel and decoded by a receiver. Communication among people can be affected by perceptions, communication channels, nonverbal communication, and listening skills.

At the organizational level, managers are concerned with managing formal communications in a downward, upward, and horizontal direction. Informal communications also are important, especially management by wandering around and the grapevine. Moreover, research shows that communication structures in groups and departments should reflect the underlying tasks.

Finally, several barriers to communication were described. These barriers can be overcome by active listening, selecting appropriate channels, engaging in MBWA, developing a climate of trust, using formal channels, and designing the correct structure to fit communication needs. A good example of overcoming barriers to communication occurred at Wild Oats, which was described in the chapter's opening management problem.

Wild Oats staffers were known for their free-spirited attitudes. Cook, Gilliland, and Clapp kept that in mind when they came up with a questionnaire designed to gauge employee morale and job satisfaction. The evaluation spectrum ranged from "awful" or "remarkably bad" to "wonderful" or "terrific." The so-called Happiness Index pegged respondents' sentiments anywhere from "giddy" to "suicidal." Gilliland soon discovered that his store managers were taking criticisms hard, even if responses ran as high as six to one positive. To avoid this, he began reviewing the questionnaires and eliminating gratuitous or nonconstructive carping before sitting down to personally go over the surveys with his managers. The feedback has not only given a clear idea of work force morale in the various stores, but has also resulted in employee solutions to specific problems. Wild Oats has adopted an employee stock ownership plan and set aside $200 for every worker to participate in a wellness program of their choice. Both of the policy changes were the result of feedback from the surveys. Turnover has tracked downward since the questionnaire was introduced. Gilliland thinks the biannual surveys not only have enhanced communication and motivation with front-line employees, they have resulted in at least 20 useful suggestions being implemented every time workers return them.[45]

DISCUSSION QUESTIONS

1. ATI Medical, Inc., has a "no-memo" policy. The 300 employees must interact directly for all communications. What impact do you think this policy would have on the organization?
2. Describe the elements of the communication process. Give an example of each part of the model as it exists in the classroom during communication between teacher and students.
3. How might perception influence communication accuracy? Is perception more important for ambiguous or unambiguous messages? Explain.
4. Should the grapevine be eliminated? How might managers control information that is processed through the grapevine?
5. What do you think are the major barriers to upward communication in organizations? Discuss.
6. What is the relationship between group communication and group task? For example, how should communications differ in a strategic planning group and a group of employees who stack shelves in a grocery store?
7. Some senior managers believe they should rely on written information and computer reports because these yield more accurate data than do face-to-face communications. Do you agree?
8. Why is management by wandering around considered effective communication? Consider channel richness and nonverbal communications in formulating your answer.
9. Is speaking accurately or listening actively the more important communication skill for managers? Discuss.
10. Assume that you have been asked to design a training program to help managers become better communicators. What would you include in the program?

MANAGEMENT IN PRACTICE: EXPERIENTIAL EXERCISE

● LISTENING SELF-INVENTORY

Instructions: Go through the following questions, checking yes or no next to each question. Mark it as truthfully as you can in the light of your behavior in the last few meetings or gatherings you attended.

	Yes	No
1. I frequently attempt to listen to several conversations at the same time.	____	____
2. I like people to give me only the facts, then let me make my own interpretation.	____	____
3. I sometimes pretend to pay attention to people.	____	____

	Yes	No
4. I consider myself a good judge of nonverbal communications.	____	____
5. I usually know what another person is going to say before he or she says it.	____	____
6. I usually end conversations that don't interest me by diverting my attention from the speaker.	____	____
7. I frequently nod, frown, or whatever to let the speaker know how I feel about what he or she is saying.	____	____

	Yes	**No**
8. I usually respond immediately when someone has finished talking.	___	___
9. I evaluate what is being said while it is being said.	___	___
10. I usually formulate a response while the other person is still talking.	___	___
11. The speaker's "delivery" style frequently keeps me from listening to content.	___	___
12. I usually ask people to clarify what they have said rather than guess at the meaning.	___	___
13. I make a concerted effort to understand other people's points of view.	___	___
14. I frequently hear what I expect to hear rather than what is said.	___	___
15. Most people feel that I have understood their point of view when we disagree.	___	___

The correct answers according to communication theory are as follows: No for questions 1, 2, 3, 5, 6, 7, 8, 9, 10, 11, 14. Yes for questions 4, 12, 13, 15. If you missed only one or two questions, you strongly approve of your own listening habits, and you are on the right track to becoming an effective listener in your role as manager. If you missed three or four questions, you have uncovered some doubts about your listening effectiveness, and your knowledge of how to listen has some gaps. If you missed five or more questions, you probably are not satisfied with the way you listen, and your friends and coworkers may not feel you are a good listener either. Work on improving your active listening skills.

SOURCE: Ethel C. Glenn and Elliott A. Pood, "Listening Self-Inventory." Reprinted by permission of the publisher from *Supervisory Management* (January 1989), 12–15. © 1989, American Management Association, New York. All rights reserved.

CASE FOR ANALYSIS

CARTER AUTO PARTS

For Fred Carter, owner of four Carter Auto Parts stores, competing with the likes of Gateway and Auto Zone was not easy. However, he managed to grow his business and eventually employed 40 people equally divided at each location. Carter recognized early that volume buying by the big chain stores would afford them a price advantage on many products. Although he couldn't always compete on discounts, Carter thought he could make up the difference in other areas. If he could get the message across to employees that service and customer satisfaction were the number one priority at Carter's Auto Parts, he thought customers would be willing to overlook prices that were slightly higher than his big competitors'.

Because he was always good at fixing cars, Carter found it natural to work part-time at Jim's Auto Parts all the way through high school. The way Jim had handled employees seemed natural too. Even though Carter was by far the youngest person on the payroll, Jim treated him and everyone equally. He trusted them enough to be honest and straightforward, and he expected the same treatment in return. By the time Jim decided to retire, Carter had been made manager. Thinking he might never get a better opportunity, he combined a family loan with a small amount of bank financing and owner credit Jim was willing to extend, and bought the business.

Carter knew his work force could be a tremendous asset if he could continue what the former owner had started, as well as communicating the vision he had in mind of where the company was going. He started meeting informally with employees on the first Monday morning of every month. The get-togethers were brief. At that point, Carter's burgeoning empire consisted of only the original store and six employees. But instead of allowing his pint-sized staff to develop an inferiority complex about their number, he turned it into a strength. They could react faster to problems that might occur, he told them, because there were so few of them. All they had to do was communicate effectively with each other. He encouraged them to make decisions on their own and assured them there would be no repercussions if it turned out badly. And, he listened carefully to them for suggestions he could implement from the top.

Carter's policies translated to success and growth in a hurry. Increased responsibilities in hiring, bookkeeping, and scouting the competition eventually meant the monthly meetings fell by the wayside, but the owner never felt out of touch. After all, he spent some part of every week working side-by-side with employees in one of four stores. He thought he had promoted three good managers. Because he had a lot of faith in their abilities, he did not think it was necessary to stay on top of operations to the extent he once had. Besides, he was working on an employee idea of adding service bays to the existing locations. Car repairs would complement the business already in place, and add to profits that were already bigger than he ever dreamed possible.

However, Carter found himself reassessing everything after reviewing an annual inventory count. It showed substantial losses in two stores, and the conclusion was inescapable. His employees or customers were stealing. Whatever the case, he felt it was his fault. He'd either hired personnel that wasn't paying attention—a bad situation—or his staff included outright thieves, a worse scenario. Either way, it was bad decision making on his part.

Without consulting his managers or employees, Carter implemented new company policies. Security cameras were installed in all of his stores. He also requested that all employees undergo voluntary polygraph examinations, with the implied threat that those who refused might just as well seek a career elsewhere. A lot of work had gone into building his business, and Carter considered most of his employees friends. But, at the same time, he was determined to find out where the merchandise had gone. He included a memo outlining the new policies and the reasons for them with everyone's next paycheck.

It turned out the reasons did not matter much. Carter's memo might not have done much to affect the conscience of the guilty parties, if in fact there were any on the staff, but it was hugely successful in shattering the morale of everyone else. Rumors sprang up and took on a life of their own. Older workers seemed to direct their suspicions at younger colleagues based on some perceived generational shortcomings. Cooperation virtually disappeared, and along with it went Carter Auto Parts stores' customer service advantage. When Carter realized what the internecine squab-

bling was doing to his business and called a company-wide meeting, monthly sales figures were already reflecting a 15 percent decline.

Fred Carter had been the inspirational leader of his business. By the time he called the company meeting to order, his presence had become a divisive influence. His explanations for bringing everyone under scrutiny did little to assuage the bad feelings. When the results of the polygraphs came back inconclusive, he realized his knee-jerk reaction to a symptom came close to bankrupting the business. Restoring employee morale in the aftermath of the debacle would be tough. Restoring monthly meetings was a possibility, spending more time working alongside employees in the stores was another. He would have plenty of time to think it all over, while monitoring his new security cameras and deciding if removing them might be the best idea of all.

● **Q U E S T I O N S**

1. Describe some formal and informal communication channels that Carter might be able to establish in order to improve morale at the stores.
2. When did the first signs of communication problems surface at Carter's? What caused them?
3. Do you think the communication barriers can be overcome without leaving permanent scars?

SOURCE: This case was provided by Sean Lanham.

REFERENCES

1. Phaedra Hise, "The Motivational Employee-Satisfaction Questionnaire," *INC.*, February 1994, 73–75.
2. "Hands On: Tell Us about It," *INC.*, June 1990, 101; and Thomas F. O'Boyle and Carol Hymowitz, "More Corporate Chiefs Seek Direct Contact with Staff, Customers," *The Wall Street Journal*, February 27, 1985, 1, 12.
3. Elizabeth B. Drew, "Profile: Robert Strauss," *The New Yorker*, May 7, 1979, 55–70.
4. Henry Mintzberg, *The Nature of Managerial Work* (New York: Harper & Row, 1973).
5. Fred Luthans and Janet K. Larsen, "How Managers Really Communicate," *Human Relations* 39 (1986), 161–178; and Larry E. Penley and Brian Hawkins, "Studying Interpersonal Communication in Organizations: A Leadership Application," *Academy of Management Journal* 28 (1985), 309–326.
6. D. K. Berlo, *The Process of Communication* (New York: Holt, Rinehart and Winston, 1960), 24.
7. Nelson W. Aldrich, Jr., "Lines of Communication," *INC.*, June 1986, 140–144.
8. Bruce K. Blaylock, "Cognitive Style and the Usefulness of Information," *Decision Sciences* 15 (Winter 1984), 74–91.

9. Richard L. Daft and Richard M. Steers, *Organizations: A Micro/Macro Approach* (Glenview, Ill.: Scott, Foresman, 1986).

10. James R. Wilcox, Ethel M. Wilcox, and Karen M. Cowan, "Communicating Creatively in Conflict Situations," *Management Solutions* (October 1986), 18–24.

11. Robert H. Lengel and Richard L. Daft, "The Selection of Communication Media as an Executive Skill," *Academy of Management Executive* 2 (August 1988), 225–232; and Richard L. Daft and Robert H. Lengel, "Organizational Information Requirements, Media Richness and Structural Design," *Managerial Science* 32 (May 1986), 554–572.

12. Ford S. Worthy, "How CEOs Manage Their Time," *Fortune,* January 18, 1988, 88–97.

13. Richard L. Daft, Robert H. Lengel, and Linda Klebe Trevino, "Message Equivocality, Media Selection and Manager Performance: Implication for Information Systems," *MIS Quarterly* 11 (1987), 355–368.

14. Edward O. Welles, "Bad News," *INC.,* April 1991, 45–49.

15. I. Thomas Sheppard, "Silent Signals," *Supervisory Management* (March 1986), 31–33.

16. Albert Mehrabian, *Silent Messages* (Belmont, Calif.: Wadsworth, 1971); and Albert Mehrabian, "Communicating without Words," *Psychology Today,* September 1968, 53–55.

17. Sheppard, "Silent Signals."

18. Arthur H. Bell, *The Complete Manager's Guide to Interviewing* (Homewood, Ill.: Richard D. Irwin, 1989).

19. C. Glenn Pearce, "Doing Something about Your Listening Ability," *Supervisory Management* (March 1989), 29–34; and Tom Peters, "Learning to Listen," *Hyatt Magazine* (Spring 1988), 16–21.

20. Gerald M. Goldhaber, *Organizational Communication,* 4th ed. (Dubuque, Iowa: Wm. C. Brown, 1980), 189.

21. Peters, "Learning to Listen."

22. Daft and Steers, *Organizations;* and Daniel Katz and Robert Kahn, *The Social Psychology of Organizations,* 2d ed. (New York: Wiley, 1978).

23. Edward O. Welles, "Bad News," *INC.,* April 1991, 45–49.

24. Claudia H. Deutsch, "Managing: The Multimedia Benefits Kit," *The New York Times,* October 14, 1990, Sec. 3, 25.

25. J. G. Miller, "Living Systems: The Organization," *Behavioral Science* 17 (1972), 69.

26. Michael J. Glauser, "Upward Information Flow in Organizations: Review and Conceptual Analysis," *Human Relations* 37 (1984), 613–643; and "Upward/Downward Communication: Critical Information Channels," *Small Business Report* (October 1985), 85–88.

27. Anne B. Fisher, "CEO's Think That Morale Is Dandy," *Fortune,* November 18, 1991, 83–84.

28. Mary P. Rowe and Michael Baker, "Are You Hearing Enough Employee Concerns?" *Harvard Business Review* 62 (May–June 1984), 127–135; W. H. Read, "Upward Communication in Industrial Hierarchies," *Human Relations* 15 (February 1962), 3–15; and Daft and Steers, *Organizations.*

29. Myrna Hellerman, "How I Did It: Giving Executives a Field Day," *Working Woman,* March 1992, 37–40.

30. Jacqueline Kaufman, "Carol Taber, Working Woman," *Management Review* (October 1986), 60–61.

31. O'Boyle and Hymowitz, "More Corporate Chiefs Seek Direct Contact with Staff, Customers."

32. Thomas J. Peters and Robert H. Waterman, *In Search of Excellence* (New York: Harper & Row, 1982); and Tom Peters and Nancy Austin, *A Passion for Excellence: The Leadership Difference* (New York: Random House, 1985).

33. Lois Therrien, "How Ztel Went from Riches to Rags," *Business Week,* June 17, 1985, 97–100.

34. Faye Rice, "Champions of Communication," *Fortune,* June 3, 1991, 112–116.

35. Keith Davis and John W. Newstrom, *Human Behavior at Work: Organizational Behavior,* 7th ed. (New York: McGraw-Hill, 1985).

36. Joshua Hyatt, "The Last Shift," *INC.,* February 1989, 74–80.

37. Goldhaber, *Organizational Communication;* and Philip V. Louis, *Organizational Communication,* 3d ed. (New York: Wiley, 1987).

38. Donald B. Simmons, "The Nature of the Organizational Grapevine," *Supervisory Management* (November 1985), 39–42; and Davis and Newstrom, *Human Behavior.*

39. E. M. Rogers and R. A. Rogers, *Communication in Organizations* (New York: Free Press, 1976); and A. Bavelas and D. Barrett, "An Experimental Approach to Organization Communication," *Personnel* 27 (1951), 366–371.

40. This discussion is based on Daft and Steers, *Organizations.*

41. Bavelas and Barrett, "An Experimental Approach"; and M. E. Shaw, *Group Dynamics: The Psychology of Small Group Behavior* (New York: McGraw-Hill, 1976).

42. Richard L. Daft and Norman B. Macintosh, "A Tentative Exploration into the Amount and Equivocality of Information Processing in Organizational Work Units," *Administrative Science Quarterly* 26 (1981), 207–224.

43. James A. F. Stoner and R. Edward Freeman, *Management,* 4th ed. (Englewood Cliffs, N.J.: Prentice-Hall, 1989).

44. Janet Fulk and Sirish Mani, "Distortion of Communication in Hierarchical Relationships," in *Communication Yearbook,* vol. 9, ed. M. L. McLaughlin (Beverly Hills, Calif.: Sage, 1986), 483–510.

45. Hise, "The Motivational Employee-Satisfaction Questionnaire."

TEAMWORK IN ORGANIZATIONS 15

CHAPTER OUTLINE ▲

LEARNING OBJECTIVES ▼

After studying this chapter, you should be able to

- Identify the types of teams in organizations.

- Discuss new applications of teams to facilitate employee involvement.

- Identify roles within teams and the type of role you could play to help a team be effective.

- Explain the general stages of team development.

- Explain the concepts of team cohesiveness and team norms and their relationship to team performance.

- Understand the causes of conflict within and among teams and how to reduce conflict.

- Discuss the assets and liabilities of organizational teams.

om Huber, president of Hearing Technology, Inc., founded his hearing-aid company to provide a flexible response to dealers. His six employees could provide a rapid three-day response to dealers for custom hearing aids. The sales, production, and credit people had the right attitude to make things happen. But when the company quickly grew to 80 employees, response times for orders stretched to eight days, enough to cause dealers to try other manufacturers. Moreover, the dealers complained about the sluggish credit department, its poor coordination with production and sales, and the slowness with which suggestions were implemented. Huber tried to refocus everyone's efforts by one-on-one sessions and speeches, but sluggishness remained. Huber started to wonder if his company, at 80 employees, had grown so inflexible and unresponsive that it could not be competitive.[1] ■ What would you recommend to Tom Huber to recapture flexibility and responsiveness in his growing company? How might the formation of teams help solve this problem?

The problems facing a small business like Hearing Technology also confront large companies. How can they be more flexible and responsive in an increasingly competitive global environment? A quiet revolution is taking place in corporate America as more companies try using teams as a solution. The notion of teamwork is changing the look of organizations. Teams are replacing individuals as the basic building block of organizations. The significance of teamwork is reflected by the results of a *Wall Street Journal* survey of 200 Fortune 500 companies that found that teamwork was the most frequent topic to be taught in company training programs.[2] In an article called "The Team as Hero," the authors argue that

> If we are to compete in today's world, we must begin to celebrate collective entrepreneurship, endeavors in which the whole of the effort is greater than the sum of individual contributions. We need to honor our teams more, our aggressive leaders and maverick geniuses less.[3]

Teams are popping up in the most unexpected places. At AT&T, teams rather than individuals are used to create new telephones. Volvo uses teams of hourly workers to assemble a complete car, abandoning the assembly line. Hecla Mining Company uses teams for company goal setting; a major telecommunications company uses teams of salespeople to deal with big customers with complex purchasing requirements; and

Teams are emerging as a powerful management tool and are popping up in the most unexpected places, such as the Zoological Society of San Diego, which is using a new team concept to remodel animal displays according to bioclimatic zones. The new team concept replaces 50 functional departments and focuses group attention on quality and goal achievement.

Lassiter Middle School in Jefferson County, Kentucky, uses teams of teachers to prepare daily schedules and handle student discipline problems. Multinational corporations are now using international teams composed of managers from different countries. Ford uses teams to spot quality problems and improve efficiency, and other manufacturers use teams to master sophisticated new production technologies.[4] As we saw in Chapter 7, teams are often used to make important decisions, and many organizations are now run by top management teams under the title of Office of the CEO.

As we will see in this chapter, teams have emerged as a powerful management tool, because they involve and empower employees. Teams can cut across organizations in unusual ways. Hence workers are more satisfied, and higher productivity and product quality typically result. Moreover, managers discover a more flexible organization in which workers are not stuck in narrow jobs.

This chapter focuses on teams and their new applications within organizations. We will define various types of teams, explore their stages of development, and examine such characteristics as size, cohesiveness, and norms. We will discuss how individuals can make contributions to teams and review the benefits and costs associated with teamwork. Teams are an important aspect of organizational life, and the ability to manage them is an important component of manager and organization success.

● TEAMS AT WORK

In this section, we will first define teams and then discuss a model of team effectiveness that summarizes the important concepts.

WHAT IS A TEAM?

A **team** is a unit of two or more people who interact and coordinate their work to accomplish a specific objective.[5] This definition has three components. First, two or more people are required. Teams can be quite large, running to as many as 75 people, although most have fewer than 15 people. Second, people in a team have regular interaction. People who do not interact, such as when standing in line at a lunch counter or riding in an elevator, do not compose a team. Third, people in a team share a performance objective, whether it be to design a new type of hand calculator or write a textbook. Students often are assigned to teams to do classwork assignments, in which case the purpose is to perform the assignment and receive an acceptable grade. A "team" is similar to what is usually called a "group" in organizations, but "team" has become the popular word in the business community. The team concept implies a greater sense of mission and contest, although the words can be used interchangeably. For an illustration of the various forms teams can take within an organization, read about leading edge company Gateway 2000 in the box.

team

A unit of two or more people who interact and coordinate their work to accomplish a specific objective.

LEADING edge   GATEWAY 2000

For Gateway 2000, the leading edge company introduced in Chapter 7, the honeymoon may not be over quite yet. But, what's left of it cannot possibly be as heady and blissful as what came before. Even cofounder Ted Waitt admits that much of Gateway's success is attributable to being overlooked by competitors. "We were unknown before, and that was an advantage," he says. "Nobody knew who we were, so we snuck up on the competition."

Stepping up to the next level, attracting corporate customers, and expanding on the base of technically knowledgeable computer buyers, the company has established promises to be a challenge. Waitt has always relied on a "real value" core philosophy of business, providing better products at lower prices than competitors can offer. This means Gateway will increasingly look to cellular manufacturing and worker teams to further streamline production already regarded as among the leanest and most efficient in the industry.

Gateway uses the team approach in most phases of its operations. Groups of 20 are in charge of technology. Waitt meets twice a month with 10 principal lieutenants called the Action Committee. The company

marketing director uses a team of four to canvass customers about pricing and how product features and capabilities meet consumer needs.

The computer industry is infamous for brutal competition and low margins. Because of that fact, Waitt has avoided entanglements that would lead Gateway too far afield from its core competencies: marketing and service. The company subcontracts manufacturing. Inventory is kept to a minimum, and any costs that do not add to customer satisfaction or service are eliminated. Finished computers are nowhere to be found at Gateway. However, all the necessary components are on hand. When orders come in, teams of technicians quickly assemble the needed products. Using this system, the company has managed to keep its profit margins scintillatingly high, often approaching 20 percent.

Waitt may find such hefty earnings harder and harder to come by with the likes of Dell, IBM, and Compaq all fighting for a greater share of the direct marketing computer business. But he will stick with what he thinks differentiates Gateway from the rest of the pack. "The PC business is not about price," he says, "it's about value, or what you can give the customer for his or her money." Waitt insists that this so-called real value credo is what he falls back on when coming

to the right decision is difficult. And, it's why his company's culture is one of lean, efficient operations. Resting on past laurels or complacency is not likely to be one of Gateway's problems. "Companies get caught up in themselves and what they want to accomplish versus what their customers really want," he says. "We can't lose sight of what got us to where we are."

To most employees, Waitt has already ascended to legendary status, but he acknowledges he's a better leader than manager. However, that will come in handy. Inspiring team leaders in sales, service, and assembly has been integral to the success Gateway has enjoyed. Attracting new corporate customers and staying out in front of big competitors will require a lot more of the same. In Chapter 17, we will see how Gateway uses strict management control systems to keep the company on the right track. ∎

SOURCE: Joshua Hyatt, "Betting The Farm," *INC.,* December 1991, 36–45; Jon Holten, "Head 'Em Up," *Sunday World Herald,* January 23, 1994, 14A; Lois Therrien, "Why Gateway Is Racing to Answer on the First Ring," *Business Week,* September 13, 1993, 92–94; Michael Noer, "New Kid on the Block," *Forbes,* February 14, 1994, 178; and Kyle Pope, "Gateway to Offer 10.9 Million Shares At $13 to $15 Each," *The Wall Street Journal,* October 22, 1993, A9.

MODEL OF WORK TEAM EFFECTIVENESS

Some of the factors associated with team effectiveness are illustrated in Exhibit 15.1. Work team effectiveness is based on two outcomes—productive output and personal satisfaction.[6] *Satisfaction* pertains to the

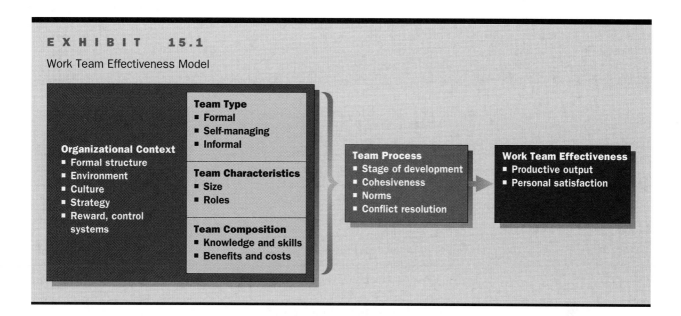

EXHIBIT   15.1

Work Team Effectiveness Model

Organizational Context
- Formal structure
- Environment
- Culture
- Strategy
- Reward, control systems

Team Type
- Formal
- Self-managing
- Informal

Team Characteristics
- Size
- Roles

Team Composition
- Knowledge and skills
- Benefits and costs

Team Process
- Stage of development
- Cohesiveness
- Norms
- Conflict resolution

Work Team Effectiveness
- Productive output
- Personal satisfaction

team's ability to meet the personal needs of its members and hence maintain their membership and commitment. *Productive output* pertains to the quality and quantity of task outputs as defined by team goals.

The factors that influence team effectiveness begin with the organizational context.[7] The organizational context in which the group operates is described in other chapters and includes such factors as structure, strategy, environment, culture, and reward systems. Within that context, managers define teams. Important team characteristics are the type of team, the team structure, and team composition. Managers must decide when to create permanent teams within the formal structure and when to use a temporary task team. Team size and roles also are important. Managers must also consider whether a team is the best way to do a task. If costs outweigh benefits, managers may wish to assign an individual employee to the task.

These team characteristics influence processes internal to the team, which in turn affect output and satisfaction. Leaders must understand and manage stages of development, cohesiveness, norms, and conflict in order to establish an effective team. These processes are influenced by team and organizational characteristics and by the ability of members and leaders to direct these processes in a positive manner.

The model of team performance in Exhibit 15.1 is the basis for this chapter. In the following sections, we will examine types of organizational teams, team structure, internal processes, and team benefits and costs.

● TYPES OF TEAMS

Many types of teams can exist within organizations. The easiest way to classify teams is in terms of those created as part of the organization's formal structure and those created to increase employee participation.

FORMAL TEAMS

formal team

A team created by the organization as part of the formal organization structure.

vertical team

A formal team composed of a manager and his or her subordinates in the organization's formal chain of command.

horizontal team

A formal team composed of employees from about the same hierarchical level but from different areas of expertise.

Formal teams are created by the organization as part of the formal organization structure. Two common types of formal teams are vertical and horizontal, which typically represent vertical and horizontal structural relationships, as described in Chapter 8. These two types of teams are illustrated in Exhibit 15.2. A third type of formal team is the special-purpose team.

VERTICAL TEAM. A **vertical team** is composed of a manager and his or her subordinates in the formal chain of command. Sometimes called a *functional team* or a *command team*, the vertical team may in some cases include three or four levels of hierarchy within a functional department. Typically, the vertical team includes a single department in an organization. The third-shift nursing team on the second floor of St. Luke's Hospital is a vertical team that includes nurses and a supervisor. A financial analysis department, a quality control department, an accounting department, and a human resource department are all command teams. Each is created by the organization to attain specific goals through members' joint activities and interactions.

HORIZONTAL TEAM. A **horizontal team** is composed of employees from about the same hierarchical level but from different areas of expertise.[8] A horizontal team is drawn from several departments, is given a specific task, and may be disbanded after the task is completed. The two most common types of horizontal teams are task forces and committees.

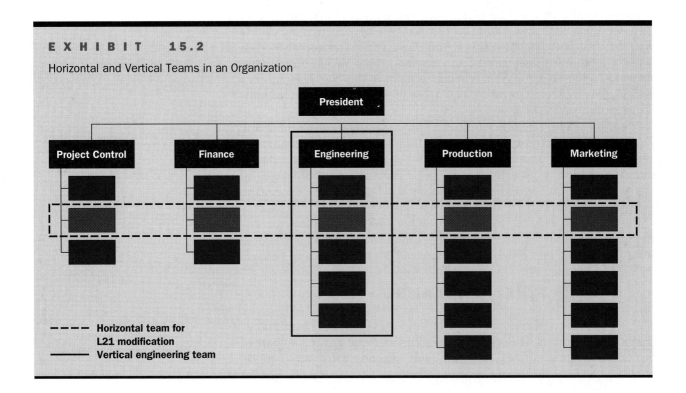

EXHIBIT 15.2

Horizontal and Vertical Teams in an Organization

- - - - Horizontal team for L21 modification
———— Vertical engineering team

As described in Chapter 8, a *task force* is a group of employees from different departments formed to deal with a specific activity and existing only until the task is completed. Sometimes called a *cross-functional team*, the task force might be used to create a new product in a manufacturing organization or a new history curriculum in a university. Several departments are involved and many views have to be considered, so these tasks are best served with a horizontal team. IBM used a large task force to develop the System 360. Contact among team members was intense, and principal players met every day.

A **committee** is generally long-lived and may be a permanent part of the organization's structure. Membership on a committee is usually decided by a person's title or position rather than by personal expertise. A committee often needs official representation, compared with selection for a task force, which is based on personal qualifications for solving a problem. Committees typically are formed to deal with tasks that recur regularly. For example, a grievance committee handles employee grievances; an advisory committee makes recommendations in the areas of employee compensation and work practices; a worker-management committee may be concerned with work rules, job design changes, and suggestions for work improvement.[9]

As part of the horizontal structure of the organization, task forces and committees offer several advantages: (1) They allow organization members to exchange information; (2) they generate suggestions for coordinating the organizational units that are represented; (3) they develop new ideas and solutions for existing organizational problems; and (4) they assist in the development of new organizational practices and policies.

committee

A long-lasting, sometimes permanent team in the organization structure created to deal with tasks that recur regularly.

SPECIAL-PURPOSE TEAM.   Special-purpose teams are created outside the formal organization structure to undertake a project of special importance or creativity. McDonald's created a special team to create the Chicken McNugget. E. J. (Bud) Sweeney was asked to head up a team to bring bits of batter-covered chicken to the marketplace. The McNugget team needed breathing room and was separated from the formal corporate structure to give it the autonomy to perform successfully. A special-purpose team is still part of the formal organization and has its own reporting structure, but members perceive themselves as a separate entity.[10]

The formal teams described above must be skillfully managed to accomplish their purpose. One important skill, knowing how to run a team meeting, is described in the Manager's Shoptalk box.

special-purpose team

A team created outside the formal organization to undertake a project of special importance or creativity.

SELF-MANAGING TEAMS

Employee involvement through teams is designed to increase the participation of lower-level workers in decision making and the conduct of their jobs, with the goal of improving performance. Employee involvement represents a revolution in business prompted by the success of teamwork in Japanese companies. Hundreds of companies, large and small, are jumping aboard the bandwagon, including Boeing, Caterpillar, LTV Steel, Cummins Engine, and Tektronix. Employee involvement

MANAGER'S shop talk

HOW TO RUN A GREAT MEETING

Many executives believe that meetings are a waste of time. Busy executives may spend up to 70 percent of their time in meetings at which participants doodle, drink coffee, and think about what they could be doing back in their offices.

Meetings need not be unproductive. Most meetings are called to process important information or to solve a problem. The key to success is what the chairperson does. Most of the chairperson's contributions are made before the meeting begins. He or she should make sure discussion flows freely and follow up the meeting with agreed-upon actions. The success of a meeting depends on what is done in advance of, during, and after it.

Prepare in Advance. Advance preparation is the single most important tool for running an efficient, productive meeting. Advance preparation should include the following:

1. Define the objective. Is the objective to communicate critical information? To discuss a difficult problem? To reach a final decision? If the purpose of the meeting is to "discuss the reduction of the 1994 research and development budget," then say so explicitly in the memo sent out to members.

2. Circulate background papers. Any reading materials relevant to the discussion should be given to each member in advance. These can be circulated with the agenda or with the minutes of the previous meeting. Members as well as the chairperson must be prepared, so make sure members know their assignments and have background materials.

3. Prepare an agenda. The agenda is a simple list of the topics to be discussed. It is important because it keeps the meeting on track. The agenda provides order and logic and gives the chairperson a means of control during the meeting if the discussion starts to wander.

4. Issue invitations selectively. If the group gets too big, the meeting will not be productive. If members with little to learn or contribute are invited, they will be bored. If everyone is expected to participate, membership between four and seven is ideal. Twelve is the outside limit; above 12, many people will just sit and listen.

5. Set a time limit. A formal meeting should have a specified amount of time. The ending time should be announced in advance, and the agenda should require the meeting to move along at a reasonable pace. Unexpected issues can be handled if they will take little time; otherwise, they should be postponed until another meeting.

During the Meeting. If the chairperson is prepared in advance, the meeting will go smoothly. Moreover, certain techniques will bring out the

---

problem-solving team

Typically 5 to 12 hourly employees from the same department who meet to discuss ways of improving quality, efficiency, and the work environment.

started out simply with techniques such as information sharing with employees or asking employees for suggestions about improving the work. Gradually, companies moved toward greater autonomy for employees, which led first to problem-solving teams and then to self-managing teams.[11]

Problem-solving teams typically consist of 5 to 12 hourly employees from the same department who voluntarily meet two hours a week to discuss ways of improving quality, efficiency, and the work environment. Recommendations are proposed to management for approval. Problem-solving teams are usually the first step in a company's move toward greater employee participation. The most widely known application is quality circles, initiated by the Japanese, in which employees focus on ways to improve quality in the production process. USX has adopted this approach in several of its steel mills, recognizing that quality takes a team effort. Under the title All Product Excellence program (APEX), USX

best in people and make the meeting even more productive:

6. Start on time. This sounds obvious—but do not keep busy people waiting. Some companies have a norm of waiting five minutes for everyone to arrive and then beginning the meeting even if some people are absent. Starting on time also has symbolic value, because it tells people that the topic is important.

7. State the purpose. The chairperson should start the meeting by stating the explicit purpose and clarifying what should be accomplished by the time the meeting is over. Members should already know the purpose, but this restatement helps refocus everyone's attention on the matter at hand.

8. Encourage participation. Good meetings contain lots of discussion. If the chairperson merely wants to present one-way information to members, he or she should send a memo. A few subtle techniques go a long way toward increasing participation:

a. Draw out the silent. This means saying, "Bob, what do you think of Nancy's idea?"

b. Control the talkative. Some people overdo it and dominate the discussion. The chairperson's job is to redirect the discussion toward other people. This is more effectively done by drawing other people into the discussion than by trying to quiet the talkative people.

c. Encourage the clash of ideas. A good meeting is not a series of dialogues but a cross-current of discussion and debate. The chairperson guides, mediates, stimulates, and summarizes this discussion. Many effective chairpeople refuse to participate in the debate, preferring to orchestrate it instead.

d. Call on the most senior people last. Sometimes junior people are reluctant to disagree with senior people, so it is best to get the junior people's ideas on the table first. This will provide wider views and ideas.

e. Give credit. Make sure that people who suggest ideas get the credit, because people often make someone else's ideas their own. Giving due credit encourages continued participation.

f. Listen. The chairperson should not preach or engage in one-on-one dialogue with group members. The point is to listen and to facilitate discussion. If the chairperson really listens, he or she will be able to lead the meeting to a timely conclusion and summarize what has been accomplished.

After the meeting. The actions following the meeting are designed to summarize and implement agreed-upon points. Postmeeting activities are set in motion by a call to action.

9. End with a call to action. The last item of the meeting's agenda is to summarize the main points and make sure everyone understands his or her assignments. Deadlines should be prescribed. The chairperson should also commit to sending out minutes, organizing the next meeting, and mailing other materials that participants may need.

10. Follow-up. Mail minutes of the meeting to members. Use this memorandum to summarize the key accomplishments of the meeting, suggest schedules for agreed-upon activities, and start the ball rolling in preparation for the next meeting. ∎

SOURCE: Based on Edward Michaels, "Business Meetings," *Small Business Reports* (February 1989), 82–88; Daniel Stoffman, "Waking Up to Great Meetings," *Canadian Business*, November 1986, 75–79; and Antoney Jay, "How to Run a Meeting," *Harvard Business Review* (March–April 1976), 120–134.

has set up 40 APEX teams of up to 12 employees at its plant in West Mifflin, Pennsylvania. These teams meet several times a month to solve quality problems. The APEX teams have since spread to mills in Indiana, Ohio, and California.[12]

As a company matures, problem-solving teams can gradually evolve into self-managing teams, which represent a fundamental change in how employee work is organized. **Self-managing teams** consist of 5 to 20 multiskilled workers who rotate jobs and produce an entire product or service. Self-managing teams are permanent teams that typically include the following elements:

self-managing team
A team consisting of 5 to 20 multiskilled workers who rotate jobs to produce an entire product or service, often supervised by an elected member.

- The team includes employees with several skills and functions, and the combined skills are sufficient to perform a major organizational task. A team may include members from the foundry, machining, grinding, fabrication, and sales departments, with each member cross-trained to perform one another's jobs. The team eliminates barriers between departments, enabling excellent coordination to produce a product or service.

■ The team is given access to resources such as information, equipment, machinery, and supplies needed to perform the complete task.

■ The team is empowered with decision-making authority, which means that members have the freedom to select new members, solve problems, spend money, monitor results, and plan for the future.[13]

In a self-managing team, team members take over managerial duties such as scheduling work or vacations or ordering materials. They work with minimum supervision, perhaps electing one of their own as supervisor, who may change each year. Volvo uses self-managing teams of seven to ten hourly workers to assemble four cars per shift. At a General Mills cereal plant, manufacturing teams of hourly workers purchased the shop-floor machinery, and they now schedule, operate, and maintain the machinery. They do it so well that the factory runs without managers during the night shift.[14] The Leading Edge box provides an example of a small company, Whole Foods Market, that successfully uses self-managing teams.

AT&T Credit Corporation set up teams of 10 to 15 workers that are responsible for dealing with all customer requests. The credit teams establish a personal relationship with AT&T salespeople and customers and take responsibility for solving customers' problems. The teams are largely self-managing, making their own decisions about how to deal with customers, schedule their time off, reassign work when people are absent, and interview prospective employees. The result is that teams process up to 800 credit applications a day versus 400 previously, and they often reach a final answer within 24 hours, compared with several days previously.[15] Small companies also are trying to integrate team approaches into their production plants, as the experience of Stevens Point Brewery illustrates.

 STEVENS POINT BREWERY, INC.

Back in 1989, Ken Shibilski's Stevens Point Brewery, Inc., was a small business in imminent danger of being tapped out. In seven years, sales had fallen by one-third, and the prospects of regaining market share from giants like Miller and Anheuser Busch weren't good. As Shibilski saw things, the only hope for Stevens Point was to remake itself as a specialty brewer. Raising prices while cutting costs and expanding distribution would be risky, and he would need a lot of help from employees, but he decided he had little choice.

Shibilski decided to gently implement a team concept at the brewery. He put his brewmaster and superintendent in charge of weekly meetings, diminishing the feeling that radical changes were coming down from Shibilski at the top. In the past, employees had either packaged beer or

LEADING edge

TEAMWORK AT WHOLE FOODS MARKET

Why would a wealthy Houston lawyer and his wife drive out of their way on a Sunday morning to shop at John Mackey's Whole Foods Market? Like many people, they have discovered that despite the higher prices, they prefer the quality and healthfulness of the foods his store offers. They recognize that the service is outstanding too. Mackey's first store started with a mission to get people to eat in a more healthy way. By 1992 Mackey's health-food chain stretched from coast to coast, continuing a policy of adding new regions and stores each year. Sales in 1992 doubled the 1989 figures to reach nearly $100 million.

A typical Whole Foods Market can be 20,000 square feet and carry over 10,000 items. Although many customers start out shopping at Whole Foods for gourmet products such as balsamic vinegar or radicchio, Mackey believes that they return because they become interested in healthier eating. In fact,

the stores are geared toward providing educational information about the products. Organic produce is clearly marked, as are high fiber, low sodium, and low fat items. Each store has an information booth, and clerks frequently lead shoppers on a tour of the store. A monthly newsletter keeps patrons up to date on new products. Mackey attributes a large measure of his success to the spirit of teamwork that is found throughout the organization.

John Mackey compares his Austin-based company to the United Federation of Planets in "Star Trek." He uses this analogy because the key to his management style is teams. Each store department such as dairy, meats, or produce, has its own team of workers. Unlike the centralized buying of big food chains, each team at Whole Foods makes its own purchasing decisions. Mackey's belief is that team members will know their own customers best. He awards the team a bonus based on their gross margin, so they have an incentive to purchase exactly the right amount of stock. To boost productivity, he sets a labor budget for each team but

allows members to keep any savings as an additional bonus. While this scheme does not save wages, it does save on benefits that would be paid to additional workers and encourages strong team unity. Teams are even responsible for voting on whether a new employee may stay on the job after a six-week probation period.

Mackey's team system motivates employees to feel good about their work, serve their customers well, and help bring in profits. Compared to the average supermarket chain's operating margin of 2.6 percent, Whole Foods maintains an impressive 3.7 percent.

Some may balk when Mackey says, "We're trying to build a company on trust and love," but as a successful entrepreneur with plans to keep growing, he has created the organization to do it. ■

SOURCE: Based on Wendy Zellner, "Moving Tofu into the Mainstream," *Business Week*, May 25, 1992, 94; and Toni March, "Good Food, Great Margins," *Forbes*, October 17, 1988, 112–115.

brewed it. The new realities that union workers would have to live with were that henceforth everyone would be cross trained to perform more than one job. Because of their background, workers were understandably slow on the uptake, but eventually the 12-member work force began pulling together and even offering ideas on how operations could be improved. Shibilski expedited the process when he upgraded plant equipment and allowed employees input on how it should best be organized.

Shibilski took note of even small details. During meetings, managers sat at the table with the rank-and-file. This avoided the connotation of a superior presiding over subordinates. Gestures like that, along with being straightforward with workers and appealing to them to pull together, made the difference at Stevens Point Brewery.[16] ■

● WORK TEAM CHARACTERISTICS

Teams in organizations take on characteristics that are important to internal processes and team performance. Two characteristics of concern to managers are team size and member roles.

SIZE

The ideal size of work teams is often thought to be seven, although variations of from five to 12 are typically associated with good team performance. These teams are large enough to take advantage of diverse skills, enable members to express good and bad feelings, and aggressively solve problems. They are also small enough to permit members to feel an intimate part of the group.

In general, as a team increases in size, it becomes harder for each member to interact with and influence the others. A summary of research on group size suggests the following:

1 Small teams (two to four members) show more agreement, ask more questions, and exchange more opinions. Members want to get along with one another. Small teams report more satisfaction and enter into more personal discussions. They tend to be informal and make few demands on team leaders.

2 Large teams (12 or more) tend to have more disagreements and differences of opinion. Subgroups often form, and conflicts among them occur. Demands on leaders are greater because there is more centralized decision making and less member participation. Large teams also tend to be less friendly. Turnover and absenteeism are higher in a large team, especially for blue-collar workers. Because less satisfaction is associated with specialized tasks and poor communication, team members have fewer opportunities to participate and feel an intimate part of the group.[17]

As a general rule, large teams make need satisfaction for individuals more difficult; thus, there is less reason for people to remain committed to their goals. Teams of from five to 12 seem to work best. If a team grows larger than 20, managers should divide it into subgroups, each with its own members and goals.

MEMBER ROLES

For a team to be successful over the long run, it must be structured so as to both maintain its members' social well-being and accomplish its task. In successful teams, the requirements for task performance and social satisfaction are met by the emergence of two types of roles: task specialist and socioemotional.[18]

People who play the **task specialist role** spend time and energy helping the team reach its goal. They often display the following behaviors:

■ *Initiation:* Propose new solutions to team problems.

■ *Give opinions:* Offer opinions on task solutions; give candid feedback on others' suggestions.

task specialist role

A role in which the individual devotes personal time and energy to helping the team accomplish its task.

- *Seek information:* Ask for task-relevant facts.
- *Summarize:* Relate various ideas to the problem at hand; pull ideas together into a summary perspective.
- *Energize:* Stimulate the team into action when interest drops.[19]

People who adopt a **socioemotional role** support team members' emotional needs and help strengthen the social entity. They display the following behaviors:

- *Encourage:* Are warm and receptive to others' ideas; praise and encourage others to draw forth their contributions.
- *Harmonize:* Reconcile group conflicts; help disagreeing parties reach agreement.
- *Reduce tension:* May tell jokes or in other ways draw off emotions when group atmosphere is tense.
- *Follow:* Go along with the team; agree to other team members' ideas.
- *Compromise:* Will shift own opinions to maintain team harmony.[20]

Exhibit 15.3 illustrates task specialist and socioemotional roles in teams. When most individuals in a team play a social role, the team is socially oriented. Members do not criticize or disagree with one another and do not forcefully offer opinions or try to accomplish team tasks, because their primary interest is to keep the team happy. Teams with mostly socioemotional roles can be very satisfying, but they also can be unproductive. At the other extreme, a team made up primarily of task specialists will tend to have a singular concern for task accomplishment. This team will be effective for a short period of time but will not be

socioemotional role

A role in which the individual provides support for team members' emotional needs and social unity.

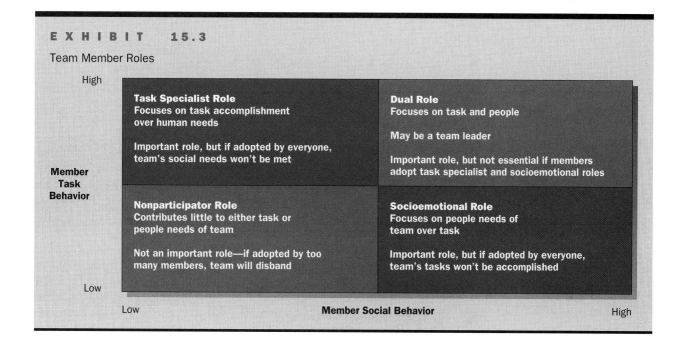

EXHIBIT 15.3

Team Member Roles

High

Member Task Behavior

Task Specialist Role
Focuses on task accomplishment over human needs

Important role, but if adopted by everyone, team's social needs won't be met

Dual Role
Focuses on task and people

May be a team leader

Important role, but not essential if members adopt task specialist and socioemotional roles

Nonparticipator Role
Contributes little to either task or people needs of team

Not an important role—if adopted by too many members, team will disband

Socioemotional Role
Focuses on people needs of team over task

Important role, but if adopted by everyone, team's tasks won't be accomplished

Low

Low   **Member Social Behavior**   High

dual role

A role in which the individual both contributes to the team's task and supports members' emotional needs.

nonparticipator role

A role in which the individual contributes little to either the task or members' socioemotional needs.

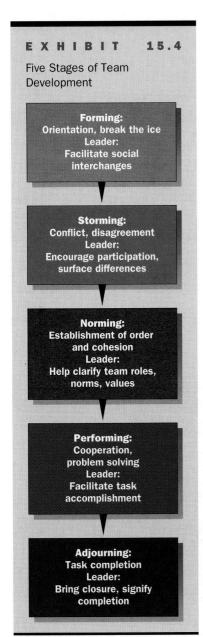

EXHIBIT   15.4

Five Stages of Team Development

Forming:
Orientation, break the ice
Leader:
Facilitate social interchanges

Storming:
Conflict, disagreement
Leader:
Encourage participation, surface differences

Norming:
Establishment of order and cohesion
Leader:
Help clarify team roles, norms, values

Performing:
Cooperation, problem solving
Leader:
Facilitate task accomplishment

Adjourning:
Task completion
Leader:
Bring closure, signify completion

satisfying for members over the long run. Task specialists convey little emotional concern for one another, are unsupportive, and ignore team members' social and emotional needs. The task-oriented team can be humorless and unsatisfying.

As Exhibit 15.3 illustrates, some team members may play a dual role. People with **dual roles** both contribute to the task and meet members' emotional needs. Such people may become team leaders because they satisfy both types of needs and are looked up to by other members. Exhibit 15.3 also shows the final type of role, called the *nonparticipator role*. People in the **nonparticipator role** contribute little to either the task or the social needs of team members. They typically are held in low esteem by the team.

The important thing for managers to remember is that effective teams must have people in both task specialist and socioemotional roles. Humor and social concern are as important to team effectiveness as are facts and problem solving. Managers also should remember that some people perform better in one type of role; some are inclined toward social concerns and others toward task concerns. A well-balanced team will do best over the long term because it will be personally satisfying for team members and permit the accomplishment of team tasks.

● TEAM PROCESSES

Now we turn our attention to internal team processes. Team processes pertain to those dynamics that change over time and can be influenced by team leaders. In this section, we will discuss the team processes of stages of development, cohesiveness, and norms. The fourth type of team process, conflict, will be covered in the next section.

STAGES OF TEAM DEVELOPMENT

After a team has been created, there are distinct stages through which it develops.[21] New teams are different from mature teams. Recall a time when you were a member of a new team, such as a fraternity or sorority pledge class, a committee, or a small team formed to do a class assignment. Over time the team changed. In the beginning, team members had to get to know one another, establish roles and norms, divide the labor, and clarify the team's task. In this way, members became parts of a smoothly operating team. The challenge for leaders is to understand the stage of the team's development and take action that will help the group improve its functioning.

Research findings suggest that team development is not random but evolves over definitive stages. Several models describing these stages exist; one useful model is shown in Exhibit 15.4. The five stages typically occur in sequence. In teams that are under time pressure or that will exist for only a few days, the stages may occur rapidly. Each stage confronts team leaders and members with unique problems and challenges.[22]

FORMING.   The **forming** stage of development is a period of orientation and getting acquainted. Members break the ice and test one another for friendship possibilities and task orientation. Team members find which behaviors are acceptable to others. Uncertainty is high during this stage, and members usually accept whatever power or authority is offered by either formal or informal leaders. Members are dependent on the team until they find out what the ground rules are and what is expected of them. During this initial stage, members are concerned about such things as "What is expected of me?" "What is acceptable?" "Will I fit in?" During the forming stage, the team leader should provide time for members to get acquainted with one another and encourage them to engage in informal social discussions.

STORMING.   During the **storming** stage, individual personalities emerge. People become more assertive in clarifying their roles and what is expected of them. This stage is marked by conflict and disagreement. People may disagree over their perceptions of the team's mission. Members may jockey for positions, and coalitions or subgroups based on common interests may form. One subgroup may disagree with another over the total team's goals or how to achieve them. The team is not yet cohesive and may be characterized by a general lack of unity. Unless teams can successfully move beyond this stage, they may get bogged down and never achieve high performance. During the storming stage, the team leader should encourage participation by each team member. Members should propose ideas, disagree with one another, and work through the uncertainties and conflicting perceptions about team tasks and goals.

NORMING.   During the **norming** stage, conflict is resolved and team harmony and unity emerge. Consensus develops on who has the power, who is the leader, and members' roles. Members come to accept and understand one another. Differences are resolved, and members develop a sense of team cohesion. This stage typically is of short duration. During the norming stage, the team leader should emphasize oneness within the team and help clarify team norms and values.

PERFORMING.   During the **performing** stage, the major emphasis is on problem solving and accomplishing the assigned task. Members are committed to the team's mission. They are coordinated with one another and handle disagreements in a mature way. They confront and resolve problems in the interest of task accomplishment. They interact frequently and direct discussion and influence toward achieving team goals. During this stage, the leader should concentrate on managing high task performance. Both socioemotional and task specialists should contribute.

ADJOURNING.   The **adjourning** stage occurs in committees, task forces, and teams that have a limited task to perform and are disbanded afterward. During this stage, the emphasis is on wrapping up and gearing down. Task performance is no longer a top priority. Members may feel heightened emotionality, strong cohesiveness, and depression or even regret over the team's disbandment. They may feel happy about mission accomplishment and sad about the loss of friendship and associations. At this point, the leader may wish to signify the team's disbanding with a

forming
The stage of team development characterized by orientation and acquaintance.

storming
The stage of team development in which individual personalities and roles, and resulting conflicts, emerge.

norming
The stage of team development in which conflicts developed during the storming stage are resolved and team harmony and unity emerge.

performing
The stage of team development in which members focus on problem solving and accomplishing the team's assigned task.

adjourning
The stage of team development in which members prepare for the team's disbandment.

ritual or ceremony, perhaps giving out plaques and awards to signify closure and completeness. One team that successfully moved through the various stages of development is described in the following example.

 ASEA BROWN BOVERI CANADA INC.

When Toronto-based electrical manufacturer Asea Brown Boveri Canada Inc. told a group of employees to come up with a team-based factory, the company had some specific objectives in mind. All that was required was halving production time while increasing production by 30 percent and reducing the work force from 150 to 120 employees. And, the design needed to be in place and working within seven months. The seven-member team assembled to design the new factory covered the entire spectrum in age, gender, race, company rank, and length of service.

The work demands were great, particularly in the beginning. After training, the team began process mapping to determine the time required to manufacture the product from order entry to billing. Benchmarking trips proved to be the area where the greatest team bonding occurred. Dining out or spending time around the hotel was an opportunity for members to get to know each other on a deeper personal level. The benchmarking phase was also the point when the team began to solidify its ideas together. The strongest of these carried through to the design phase. By then, all the members were extremely confident in what they had collectively formulated.

The team came up with what it called a Master Plan, using flow charts to depict proposals and what they were designed to achieve. Everyone believed the plan exceeded the team's original goals. After it was presented, the design team was disbanded. Some former members joined the implementation team; some were moved to other positions or promoted; others returned to their old jobs. The general sentiment was that the experience had been uplifting.[23] ∎

TEAM COHESIVENESS

■
team cohesiveness

The extent to which team members are attracted to the team and motivated to remain in it.

Another important aspect of the team process is cohesiveness. **Team cohesiveness** is defined as the extent to which members are attracted to the team and motivated to remain in it.[24] Members of highly cohesive teams are committed to team activities, attend meetings, and are happy when the team succeeds. Members of less cohesive teams are less concerned about the team's welfare. High cohesiveness is normally considered an attractive feature of teams.

DETERMINANTS OF TEAM COHESIVENESS.   Characteristics of team structure and context influence cohesiveness. First is *team interaction*. The greater the amount of contact among team members and the more time spent together, the more cohesive the team. Through frequent interactions, members get to know one another and become more devoted to the team.[25] Second is the concept of *shared goals*. If team members agree on goals, they will be more cohesive. Agreeing on purpose and direction binds the team together. Third is *personal attraction to the team,* meaning that members have similar attitudes and values and enjoy being together.

Two factors in the team's context also influence group cohesiveness. The first is the presence of competition. When a team is in moderate competition with other teams, its cohesiveness increases as it strives to win. Whether competition is among sales teams to attain the top sales volume or among manufacturing departments to reduce rejects, competition increases team solidarity and cohesiveness.[26] Finally, team success and the favorable evaluation of the team by outsiders add to cohesiveness. When a team succeeds in its task and others in the organization recognize the success, members feel good, and their commitment to the team will be high.

Chaparral Steel, an amazingly successful steel company in Midlothian, Texas, encourages team cohesiveness through promotion of the "Chaparral Process." The steel maker strives to create super teams in which each member sees his or her job in relation to the entire organization and its goals. Commitment to cohesiveness and efficiency enables Chaparral teams to perform amazing tasks. The purchase and installation of new mill equipment is a highly complicated task for any steel company, and calibrating and fine-tuning the steel-making process can take years. However, a Chaparral team of four completed the worldwide search, purchase negotiations, shipment, and installation in one year.[27]

CONSEQUENCES OF TEAM COHESIVENESS.   The outcome of team cohesiveness can fall into two categories—morale and productivity. As a general rule, morale is higher in cohesive teams because of increased communication among members, a friendly team climate, maintenance of membership because of commitment to the team, loyalty, and member participation in team decisions and activities. High cohesiveness has almost uniformly good effects on the satisfaction and morale of team members.[28]

With respect to team performance, research findings are mixed,[29] but cohesiveness may have several effects. First, in a cohesive team, members' productivity tends to be more uniform. Productivity differences among members is small because the team exerts pressure toward conformity. Noncohesive teams do not have this control over member behavior and therefore tend to have wider variation in member productivity.

With respect to the productivity of the team as a whole, research findings suggest that cohesive teams have the potential to be productive, but the degree of productivity depends on the relationship between management and the working team. Thus, team cohesiveness does not necessarily lead to higher team productivity. One study surveyed over 200 work teams and correlated job performance with their cohesiveness.[30] Highly cohesive teams were more productive when team members felt management support and less productive when they sensed management hostility and negativism. Management hostility led to team norms and goals of low performance, and the highly cohesive teams performed poorly, in accordance with their norms and goals.

The relationship between performance outcomes and cohesiveness is illustrated in Exhibit 15.5. The highest productivity occurs when the

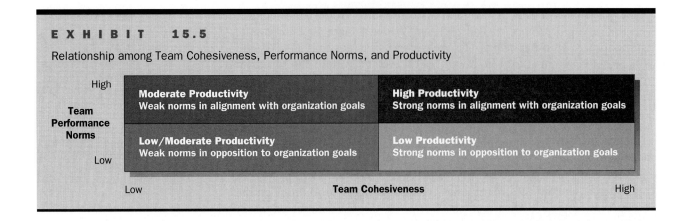

EXHIBIT 15.5

Relationship among Team Cohesiveness, Performance Norms, and Productivity

Team Performance Norms		
High	**Moderate Productivity** Weak norms in alignment with organization goals	**High Productivity** Strong norms in alignment with organization goals
Low	**Low/Moderate Productivity** Weak norms in opposition to organization goals	**Low Productivity** Strong norms in opposition to organization goals
	Low Team Cohesiveness High	

team is cohesive and also has a high performance norm, which is a result of its positive relationship with management. Moderate productivity occurs when cohesiveness is low, because team members are less committed to performance norms. The lowest productivity occurs when cohesiveness is high and the team's performance norm is low. Thus, cohesive teams are able to attain their goals and enforce their norms, which can lead to either very high or very low productivity.

TEAM NORMS

norm

A standard of conduct that is shared by team members and that guides their behavior.

A team **norm** is a standard of conduct that is shared by team members and guides their behavior.[31] Norms are informal. They are not written down as are rules and procedures. Norms are valuable because they define boundaries of acceptable behavior. They make life easier for team members by providing a frame of reference for what is right and wrong. Norms identify key values, clarify role expectations, and facilitate team survival. For example, union members may develop a norm of not cooperating with management because they do not trust management's motives. In this way, norms protect the group and express key values.

Norms begin to develop in the first interactions among members of a new team.[32] Norms that apply to both day-to-day behavior and employee output and performance gradually evolve. Norms thus tell members what is acceptable and direct members' actions toward acceptable productivity or performance. Four common ways in which norms develop for controlling and directing behavior are illustrated in Exhibit 15.6.[33]

CRITICAL EVENTS.   Often *critical events* in a team's history establish an important precedent. One example occurred when Arthur Schlesinger, despite his serious reservations about the Bay of Pigs invasion, was pressured by Attorney General Robert Kennedy not to raise his objections to President Kennedy. This critical incident helped create a norm in which team members refrained from expressing disagreement with the president.

Any critical event can lead to the creation of a norm. In one organization, a department head invited the entire staff to his house for din-

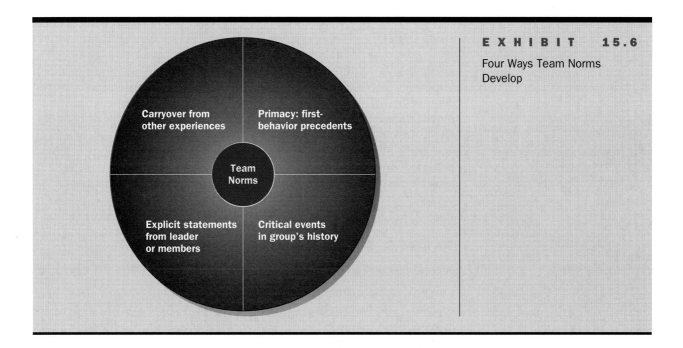

EXHIBIT   15.6

Four Ways Team Norms
Develop

ner. The next day people discovered that no one had attended, and this resulted in a norm prohibiting outside entertaining.[34]

PRIMACY.   *Primacy* means that the first behaviors that occur in a team often set a precedent for later team expectations. For example, when the president of Sun Company set up teams in the Dallas-based exploration division, top managers made sure the initial meetings involved solving genuine company problems. The initial success created a norm that team members carried into other work. "Suddenly we had two hundred evangelists," said James E. McCormick, president of Sun Explorations and Production.[35]

CARRYOVER BEHAVIORS.   *Carryover behaviors* bring norms into the team from outside. One current example is the strong norm against smoking in many management teams. Some team members sneak around, gargling with mouthwash, and fear expulsion because the team culture believes everyone should kick the habit. At such companies as Johnson & Johnson, Dow Chemical, and Aetna Life & Casualty, the norm is, "If you want to advance, don't smoke."[36] Carryover behavior also influences small teams of college students assigned by instructors to do class work. Norms brought into the team from outside suggest that students should participate equally and help members get a reasonable grade.

EXPLICIT STATEMENTS.   With *explicit statements*, leaders or team members can initiate norms by articulating them to the team. Explicit statements symbolize what counts and thus have considerable impact. Making explicit statements is probably the most effective way for managers to change norms in an established team.

● MANAGING TEAM CONFLICT

The final characteristic of team process is conflict. Of all the skills required for effective team management, none is more important than handling the conflicts that inevitably arise among members. Whenever people work together in teams, some conflict is inevitable. Conflict can arise among members within a team or between one team and another. **Conflict** refers to antagonistic interaction in which one party attempts to block the intentions or goals of another.[37] Competition, which is rivalry between individuals or teams, can have a healthy impact because it energizes people toward higher performance.[38] However, too much conflict can be destructive, tear relationships apart, and interfere with the exchange of ideas and information.[39]

CAUSES OF CONFLICT

Several factors can cause people to engage in conflict:[40]

SCARCE RESOURCES.   Resources include money, information, and supplies. In their desire to achieve goals, individuals may wish to increase their resources, which throws them into conflict. Whenever individuals or teams must compete for scarce or declining resources, conflict is almost inevitable.

JURISDICTIONAL AMBIGUITIES.   Conflicts also emerge when job boundaries and responsibilities are unclear. When task responsibilities are well defined and predictable, people know where they stand. When they are unclear, people may disagree about who has responsibility for specific tasks or who has a claim on resources. The conflict between owners' and players' associations in both professional football and baseball is often a struggle to see which organization has jurisdiction over such things as drug testing.[41]

COMMUNICATION BREAKDOWN.   Communication, as described in Chapter 14, is sometimes faulty. Poor communications result in misperceptions and misunderstandings of other people and teams. In some cases, information may be intentionally withheld, which can jeopardize trust among teams and lead to long-lasting conflict.

PERSONALITY CLASHES.   A personality clash occurs when people simply do not get along with one another and do not see eye to eye on any issue. Personality clashes are caused by basic differences in personality, values, and attitudes. Often it's a good idea to simply separate the parties so that they need not interact with one another.

POWER AND STATUS DIFFERENCES.   Power and status differences occur when one party has disputable influence over another. Low-prestige individuals or departments may resist their low status. People may engage in conflict to increase their power and influence in the team or organization.

GOAL DIFFERENCES.   Conflict often occurs simply because people are pursuing conflicting goals. Goal differences are natural in organizations. Individual salespeople's targets may put them in conflict with one

---

■
conflict

Antagonistic interaction in which one party attempts to thwart the intentions or goals of another.

The trust being developed here is an example of team-building and project partnering, a major component in Gilbane Building Company's culture. Gilbane is now extending the team concept to include clients, customers, and subcontractors.

another or with the sales manager. Moreover, the sales department may have goals that conflict with those of manufacturing. One conflict emerged within the United Auto Workers (UAW) because one subgroup is against teamwork, believing that it exploits workers and does nothing but make them work harder. Other factions in the UAW believe it is beneficial for both workers and the organization. These opposing goals are causing major clashes between these UAW subgroups.[42]

An interesting example of conflict occurred within a product marketing team at Salvo, a designer of computer software programs.

 SALVO, INC.

Product marketing teams at Salvo develop demonstration tapes of its new games and programs for use in dealer stores. The tapes are filled with sound, color, and clever graphics that are successful sales tools. The marketing person on the team works up an outline for a tape based on product content. The outline is then submitted to the team member from the information systems department to work out the displays and graphics.

Larry from marketing is energetic, has a good sense of humor, and has a high standard for excellence. He knows what a computer can do, but he is not a programmer. Larry submitted an outline of a new video-tape to Eric in information systems for development. Eric, a new member of the team, is serious and somewhat introverted. He sent a highly technical memo to Larry explaining why the project wouldn't work as requested. Larry was upset, because he didn't understand the memo or why Eric had written a memo instead of talking to him face-to-face.

Larry and Eric had a blowup at their first meeting because of their different goals and personalities. Miscommunication further aggravated the situation. Also, it was unclear who was responsible for each task in the development of the demonstration tapes, because Eric was new and unaccustomed to taking orders from another team member. Although both Eric and Larry supposedly had the same team goal, the problems with personality, communication, jurisdictional ambiguity, and individual goals caused an almost explosive conflict between them.[43] ■

STYLES TO HANDLE CONFLICT

Teams as well as individuals develop specific styles for dealing with conflict, based on the desire to satisfy their own concern versus the other party's concern. A model that describes five styles of handling conflict is in Exhibit 15.7. The two major dimensions are the extent to which an individual is assertive versus cooperative in his or her approach to conflict.

Effective team members vary their style of handling conflict to fit a specific situation. Each style is appropriate in certain cases.

1 The *competing style*, which reflects assertiveness to get one's way, should be used when quick, decisive action is vital on important

EXHIBIT   15.7

A Model of Styles to Handle
Conflict

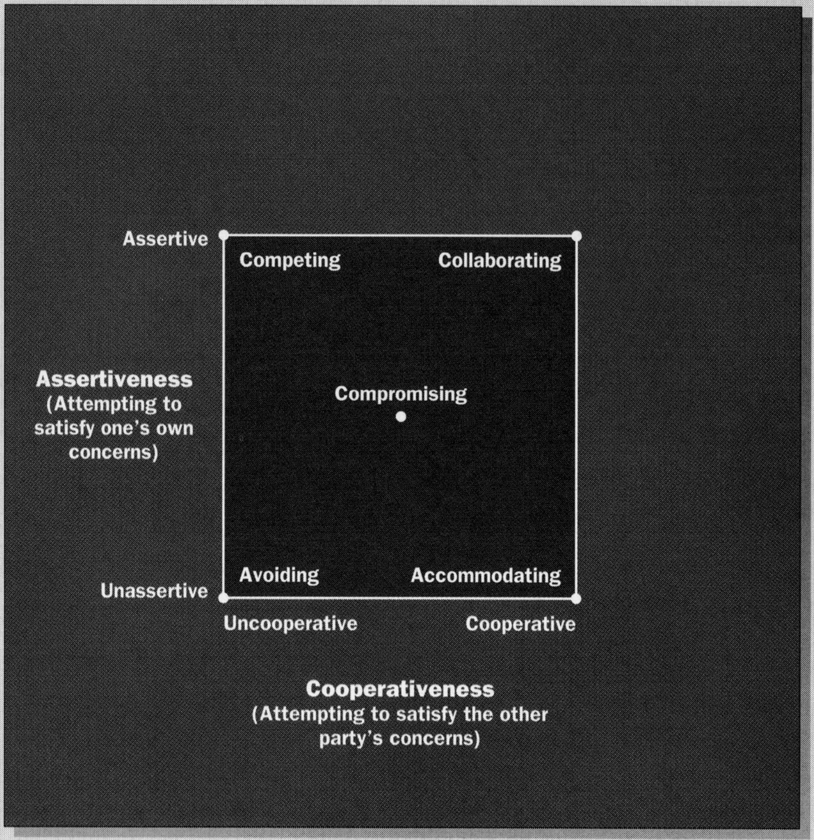

SOURCE: Adapted from Kenneth Thomas,
"Conflict and Conflict Management," in
*Handbook of Industrial and Organiza-
tional Behavior*, ed. M. D. Dunnette
(New York: John Wiley, 1976), 900.

issues or unpopular actions, such as during emergencies or urgent
cost cutting.

2 The *avoiding style,* which reflects neither assertiveness nor cooperativeness, is appropriate when an issue is trivial, when there is no
chance of winning, when a delay to gather more information is
needed, or when a disruption would be very costly.

3 The *compromising style* reflects a moderate amount of both assertiveness and cooperativeness. It is appropriate when the goals on both
sides are equally important, when opponents have equal power and
both sides want to split the difference, or when people need to
arrive at temporary or expedient solutions under time pressure.

4 The *accommodating style* reflects a high degree of cooperativeness,
which works best when people realize that they are wrong, when
an issue is more important to others than to oneself, when building
social credits for use in later discussions, and when maintaining
harmony is especially important.

5 The *collaborating style* reflects both a high degree of assertiveness
and cooperativeness. The collaborating style enables both parties to

win, although it may require substantial bargaining and negotiation. The collaborating style is important when both sets of concerns are too important to be compromised, when insights from different people need to be merged into an overall solution, and when the commitment of both sides is needed for a consensus.[44]

The various styles of handling conflict can be used when an individual disagrees with others. But what does a manager or team member do when a conflict erupts among others within a team or among teams for which the manager is responsible? Research suggests that several techniques can be used as strategies for resolving conflicts among people or departments. These techniques might also be used when conflict is formalized, such as between a union and management.

SUPERORDINATE GOALS.   The larger mission that cannot be attained by a single party is identified as a **superordinate goal.**[45] A superordinate goal requires the cooperation of the conflicting parties for achievement. People must pull together. To the extent that employees can be focused on team or organization goals, the conflict will decrease because they see the big picture and realize they must work together to achieve it.

superordinate goal
A goal that cannot be reached by a single party.

BARGAINING/NEGOTIATION.   Bargaining and negotiation mean that the parties engage one another in an attempt to systematically reach a solution. They attempt logical problem solving to identify and correct the conflict. This approach works well if the individuals can set aside personal animosities and deal with the conflict in a businesslike way.

MEDIATION.   Using a third party to settle a dispute involves **mediation.** A mediator could be a supervisor, higher-level manager, or someone from the human resource department. The mediator can discuss the conflict with each party and work toward a solution. If a solution satisfactory to both sides cannot be reached, the parties may be willing to turn the conflict over to the mediator and abide by his or her solution.

mediation
The process of using a third party to settle a dispute.

PROVIDING WELL-DEFINED TASKS.   When conflict is a result of ambiguity, managers can reduce it by clarifying responsibilities and tasks. In this way, all parties will know the tasks for which they are responsible and the limits of their authority.

FACILITATING COMMUNICATION.   Managers can facilitate communication to ensure that conflicting parties hold accurate perceptions. Providing opportunities for the disputants to get together and exchange information reduces conflict. As they learn more about one another, suspicions diminish and improved teamwork becomes possible.

For example, the conflict between Larry and Eric at Salvo, Inc., over the demonstration tape was eventually resolved by improved communication, clear definition of their respective tasks, and stronger commitment to the superordinate goal of finishing the tape. Part of the problem was that Larry was using a competing style and Eric an avoiding style in dealing with this issue. Larry went to see Eric and discussed the problem with him. The discussion revealed that they were pursuing different goals because Larry wanted the tape right away and Eric wanted to keep it until he could perfect it. Discussing each point of view was a

Like a football team trying to move the ball downfield to score, Marshall Industries' superordinate goals are based on shared principles, including quality and customer service. This electronics distributor uses superordinate goals to work toward alignment of all departments and reduction of conflict and competition.

collaborative style that was a key to their solution. Debbie, another team member, agreed to help them so that the tape could be of high quality and still be finished in two weeks. Larry and Eric also worked out a clear schedule that specified their respective responsibilities and tasks.

● BENEFITS AND COSTS OF TEAMS

In deciding whether to use teams to perform specific tasks, managers must consider both benefits and costs. Teams may have positive impact on both the output productivity and satisfaction of members. On the other hand, teams may also create a situation in which motivation and performance are actually decreased.

POTENTIAL BENEFITS OF TEAMS

Teams come closest to achieving their full potential when they enhance individual productivity through increased member effort, members' personal satisfaction, integration of diverse abilities and skills, and increased organizational flexibility.

LEVEL OF EFFORT.   Employee teams often unleash enormous energy and creativity from workers who like the idea of using their brains as well as their bodies on the job. Companies such as Kimberly-Clark have noticed this change in effort among employees as they switched to team approaches.[46] One explanation for this motivation is the research finding that working in a team increases an individual's motivation and performance. **Social facilitation** refers to the tendency for the presence of others to enhance an individual's motivation and performance. Simply being in the presence of other people has an energizing effect.[47]

SATISFACTION OF MEMBERS. As described in Chapter 13, employees have needs for belongingness and affiliation. Working in teams can help meet these needs. Participative teams reduce boredom and often increase employees' feeling of dignity and self-worth because the whole person is employed. People who have a satisfying team environment cope better with stress and enjoy their jobs.

EXPANDED JOB KNOWLEDGE AND SKILLS. The third major benefit of using teams is that employees bring greater knowledge and ability to the task. For one thing, multiskilled employees learn all of the jobs that the team performs. Teams also have the intellectual resources of several members who can suggest shortcuts and offer alternative points of view for team decisions.

ORGANIZATIONAL FLEXIBILITY. Traditional organizations are structured so that each worker does only one specific job. But when employee teams are used, from five to 15 people work next to one another and are able to exchange jobs. Work can be reorganized and workers reallocated as needed to produce products and services with great flexibility. The organization is able to be responsive to rapidly changing customer needs. Teams have proven to be effective for a number of technically sophisticated manufacturers, from car makers to computer builders. But the benefits of teams may soon show up in more mundane, everyday undertakings. It's already happening at Hannaford Bros. distribution center in Schodack Landing, New York.

social facilitation

The tendency for the presence of others to influence an individual's motivation and performance.

HANNAFORD BROS.

Hannaford Bros.' 120-member warehouse work force is applying team concepts, and a few high-tech applications, to what has generally been regarded as labor intensive: order filling. However, not at Hannaford. Its workers move fast, produce big, and are continually in the process of upgrading their skills. They also seem to get a kick out of doing their jobs better. The happy punch line is that they are helping to reduce the last number on many people's supermarket receipts.

Teams at Hannaford take care of their own scheduling, sanitation, and safety and inspections. All of that is easier since members receive training in these and other areas on a rotating basis. Almost 20 percent of each employee's time is spent in training and development. Teams also hire new members and have big input into terminations, which are about as frequent as the 1 percent rate of absenteeism. "We have more to say in what we do," says team member Tyler Towne. "It's amazing how much we get done." Adds fellow worker Andrew Kopczyski, "It would be hard for me to go back to a traditional workplace."

At Hannaford, motivated employees can make learning pay. Team contributions are recognized and rewarded, but expanding skills in budgeting, communications, or other technical areas garners additional pay increases. However, there is more behind the employee commitment at Hannaford than bigger paychecks. Most admit that it takes the right kind of person to adapt to the system at their company. But the ones who do adapt have taken ownership responsibility for themselves and their company. Says Hannaford's vice-president of warehousing, Andrew Westlund, "I have not seen a place [in food distribution] that has higher productivity."[48] ∎

POTENTIAL COSTS OF TEAMS

When managers decide whether to use teams, they must assess certain costs or liabilities associated with teamwork. When teams do not work very well, the major reasons usually are power realignment, free riding, coordination costs, or legal hassles.

POWER REALIGNMENT. When companies form shop workers into teams, the major losers are lower- and middle-level managers. These managers are reluctant to give up power. Indeed, when teams are successful, fewer supervisors are needed. This is especially true for self-managing teams, because workers take over supervisory responsibility. The adjustment is difficult for managers who fear the loss of status or even their job and who have to learn new, people-oriented skills to survive.[49]

free rider

A person who benefits from team membership but does not make a proportionate contribution to the team's work.

FREE RIDING. The term **free rider** refers to a team member who attains benefit from team membership but does not do a proportionate share of the work.[50] Free riding is sometimes called *social loafing,* because members do not exert equal effort. In large teams, some people are likely to work less. For example, research found that the pull exerted on a rope was greater by individuals working alone than by individuals in a group. Similarly, people who were asked to clap and make noise made more noise on a per person basis when working alone or in small groups than they did in a large group.[51] The problem of free riding has been experienced by people who have participated in student project groups. Some students put more effort into the group project than others, and often it seems that no members work as hard for the group as they do for their individual grades.

coordination costs

The time and energy needed to coordinate the activities of a team to enable it to perform its task.

COORDINATION COSTS. The time and energy required to coordinate the activities of a group to enable it to perform its task are called **coordination costs.** Groups must spend time getting ready to do work and lose productive time in deciding who is to do what and when.[52] Once again, student project groups illustrate coordination costs. Members must meet after class just to decide when they can meet to perform the task. Schedules must be checked, telephone calls made, and meeting times arranged in order to get down to business. Hours may be devoted to the administration and coordination of the group. Students often feel they could do the same project by themselves in less time.

LEGAL HASSLES. As more companies use teams, new questions of legality surface. A 1990 National Labor Relations Board judgment against management's use of union-member teams at Electromation, Inc., has set a confusing precedent. The Wagner Act of 1935 was enacted to prevent companies from forming organizations or employee committees to undercut legitimate unions. Union leaders today support the formation of problem-solving teams but may balk when management takes an active role in the formation and direction of such teams. As union membership and power decline, increasingly vocal critics charge that the team concept is a management ploy to kill unions. Auto workers especially are challenging team approaches because union jobs continue to disappear despite repeated concessions. Although few experts expect the courts to halt teams altogether, most believe that strict new guidelines will be implemented to control the formation and use of teams.[53]

SUMMARY AND MANAGEMENT SOLUTION

Several important concepts about teams were described in this chapter. Organizations use teams both to achieve coordination as part of the formal structure and to encourage employee involvement. Formal teams include vertical teams along the chain of command and horizontal teams such as cross-functional task forces and committees. Special-purpose teams are used for special, large-scale, creative organization projects. Employee involvement via teams is designed to bring lower-level employees into decision processes to improve quality, efficiency, and satisfaction. Companies typically start with problem-solving teams, which may evolve into self-managing teams that take on responsibility for management activities.

For example, Hearing Technology, Inc., described at the beginning of this chapter, grew rapidly to 80 employees and became sluggish in its response to hearing-aid dealers. President Tom Huber was frustrated because the three-day response time increased to eight days, provoking complaints from dealers. Huber's attempt to reenergize the company failed, and he tried a drastic restructuring into employee teams. Huber implemented three things that made the team approach work: Regular meetings of employee teams were held, usually every week; departments were encouraged to talk with one another and work together through cross-functional teams; and power was shared with employees. Four longtime employees supervised manufacturing as a team, reinforcing the team approach. With teams, the response time for custom orders was halved to four days, and dealers were happy again. Employees began enjoying themselves, too.[54]

Most teams go through systematic stages of development: forming, storming, norming, performing, and adjourning. Team characteristics that can influence organizational effectiveness are size, cohesiveness, norms, and members' roles. All teams experience some conflict because of scarce resources, ambiguous responsibility, communication breakdown, personality clashes, power and status differences, and goal conflicts. Techniques for resolving these conflicts include superordinate goals, bargaining, clear definition of task responsibilities, mediation, and communication. Advantages of using teams include increased motivation, diverse knowledge and skills, satisfaction of team members, and organizational flexibility. Potential costs of using teams are power realignment, free riding, coordination costs, and legal hassles.

DISCUSSION QUESTIONS

1. Volvo went to self-managed teams to assemble cars because of the need to attract and keep workers in Sweden, where pay raises are not a motivator (high taxes) and many other jobs are available. Is this a good reason for using a team approach? Discuss.
2. During your own work experience, have you been part of a formal vertical team? A task force? A committee? An employee involvement team? How did your work experience differ in each type of team?
3. What are the five stages of team development? What happens during each stage?
4. How would you explain the emergence of problem-solving and self-managing teams in companies throughout North America? Do you think implementation of the team concept is difficult in these companies? Discuss.
5. Assume that you are part of a student project team and one member is not doing his or her share. Which conflict resolution strategy would you use? Why?
6. Do you think a moderate level of conflict might be healthy for an organization? Discuss.
7. When you are a member of a team, do you adopt a task specialist or socioemotional role? Which role is more important for a team's effectiveness? Discuss.
8. What is the relationship between team cohesiveness and team performance?
9. Describe the advantages and disadvantages of teams. In what situations might the disadvantages outweigh the advantages?
10. What is a team norm? What norms have developed in teams to which you have belonged?

MANAGEMENT IN PRACTICE: ETHICAL DILEMMA

Nancy was part of a pharmaceutical team developing a product called loperamide, a liquid treatment for diarrhea for people unable to take solid medicine, namely infants, children, and the elderly. Loperamide contained 44 times the amount of saccharin allowed by the FDA in a 12-ounce soft drink, but there were no regulations governing saccharin content in medication.

Nancy was the only medical member of the seven-person project team. The team made a unanimous decision to reduce the saccharin content before marketing loperamide, so the team initiated a three-month effort for reformulation. In the meantime, management was pressuring the team to allow human testing with the original formula until the new formula became available. After a heated team debate, all the team members except Nancy voted to begin testing with the current formula.

Nancy believed it was unethical to test a drug she considered potentially dangerous on old people and children. As the only medical member of the team, she had to sign the forms allowing testing. She refused and was told that unless she signed, she would be removed from the project, demoted, and seen as a poor team player, nonpromotable, lacking in judgment, and unable to work with marketing people. Nancy was aware that no proof existed that high saccharin would be directly harmful to potential users of loperamide.

● **W H A T   D O   Y O U   D O ?**

1. Refuse to sign. As a medical doctor, Nancy must stand up for what she believes is right.
2. Resign. There is no reason to stay in this company and be punished for ethically correct behavior. Testing the drug will become someone else's responsibility.
3. Sign the form. The judgment of other team members cannot be all wrong. The loperamide testing is not illegal and will move ahead anyway, so it would preserve team unity and company effectiveness to sign.

SOURCE: Based on Tom L. Beauchamp, *Ethical Theory and Business*, 2d ed. (Englewood Cliffs, N.J.: Prentice-Hall, 1983).

CASE FOR ANALYSIS

XEL COMMUNICATIONS INC.

When Bill Sanko and some partners put together the buyout of XEL Communications Inc. from GTE Corporation, things were not bad. But Sanko knew they could be much better. He decided the fastest way to get the new telecommunications-equipment company up to speed was to get everyone actively contributing to customer satisfaction, product quality, and lower costs.

Sanko issued a vision statement, urged all 180 employees to become self-managing, and finally redesigned the entire company around self-managed work teams. The teams performed wonderfully, so well that the Association for Manufacturing Excellence selected the Aurora, Colorado-based company to be featured in a video on team-based management. Along with the drastically reduced cycle times, lowered cost of assembly, halved inventory expenses, and increased quality levels, there were problems, however. And some of them were lulus.

"Staffing up is probably five times harder with self-directed work teams," says Julie Rich, XEL human-resource director and one of Sanko's partners. The obvious solution to this problem is to involve existing team members in the hiring process. But those teams were created to increase quality and production. Sanko even made sure teams were evaluated on the basis of output. Because of that fact, no one wants to take the time required to help choose new people. And they create other problems too.

"I feel sorry for new people," says Teri Mantooth. "Your first instinct is, 'Oh, no, we've got a new person and we're going to get throttled; we're not going to make our numbers.'" Because team members, not supervisors, are held accountable for meeting production goals, they take an understandably dim view of anyone viewed as an obstacle to

achieving the desired objectives. When the company tried using temporary help, they got an even chillier reception. The use of a training team did not work either. The company now is experimenting with pairing new hires with experienced team members.

Production line workers probably never dreamed the day would come when they would welcome the sight of a supervisor approaching. But that has been the case when squabbling breaks out on the factory floor. "If one team is fighting, other teams will eat on it," says Mantooth. "You know, like, 'Guess what so-and-so said?'" Within teams, unresolved acrimony can place a drag on productivity, and often produces a cycle of discontent. At XEL, veteran workers or team leaders usually step into the fray and isolate the disputants. They then attempt to referee a solution between the disagreeing factions. Still, the problem illustrates that one or two unhappy members can wreak considerable havoc among self-managed teams, for themselves and the company.

XEL discovered all teams are not created equally. Some required almost no oversight. Others had more difficulty in attaining what is called "maturity" around the company, and one had to be dissolved entirely. But almost any intervention by management can be tricky. Autonomy, once granted, is not easily given up. Conflicting complaints from different teams has resulted in managers having to sit down and sort things out. But generally, XEL management leaves teams with the resources and gives them the latitude to solve their own problems.

A number of other requirements go hand-in-hand with implementing self-managed teams. XEL now offers training in everything from English to cost accounting. Stress management is also part of the curriculum. Traditional compensation systems have been rendered obsolete. To be effective, pay must be structured to encourage a team's collective performance. Workers accustomed to standing out individually can find this adjustment difficult. XEL uses skill-based pay, which encourages workers to acquire more than one skill. In addition, the company offers merit pay upgrades contingent on both team output and review by coworkers. Profit sharing is also disbursed every quarter dependent upon company performance. Plenty of employees have problems with this compensation framework. Sometimes workers cannot control or do not like the team on which they end up working. Peer reviews can fall prey to all manner of vagaries. And company output is subject to external variables that no employee can begin to control.

Sanko envisioned a company of self-managed workers, and by implementing teams, that is exactly what he got. It's hard to argue with the results. XEL's cost of assembly was cut by 25 percent; inventory reduced by 50 percent; quality is up nearly one-third; cycle times have been dramatically reduced from eight weeks to four days. Sales have increased almost 50 percent. Despite the remarkable improvements, making teams effective has not been easy, and the necessary adjustments are continuing to evolve. Sanko admits that giving up control and throwing away traditional management axioms was difficult. But continued healthy earnings cannot help but ease the transition process.

● QUESTIONS

1. If you were a team leader at XEL, how would you go about playing the task specialist and socioemotional roles described in the chapter?
2. Describe the causes of team conflict at XEL. What style would you recommend for handling the conflict?
3. In light of the tremendous benefits that have resulted from implementation of self-managed teams at XEL, how essential is it for management to address the problems outlined in this case? Should they consider just leaving well enough alone?

SOURCE: John Case, "What the Experts Forgot to Mention," *INC.,* September 1993, 66–77.

REFERENCES

1. Bruce G. Posner, "Divided We Fall," *INC.,* July 1989, 105–106.
2. "Training in the 1990s," *The Wall Street Journal,* March 1, 1990, B1.
3. Robert B. Reich, "Entrepreneurship Reconsidered: The Team as Hero," *Harvard Business Review* (May–June 1987), 77–83.
4. Frank V. Cespedes, Stephen X. Dole, and Robert J. Freedman, "Teamwork for Today's Selling," *Harvard Business Review* (March–April 1989), 44–55; Victoria J. Marsick, Ernie Turner, and Lars Cederholm, "International Managers as Team Leaders," *Management Review* (March 1989), 46–49; and "Team Goal-Setting," *Small Business Report* (January 1988), 76–77.
5. Carl E. Larson and Frank M. J. LaFasto, *TeamWork* (Newbury Park, Calif.: Sage, 1989).
6. Eric Sundstrom, Kenneth P. De Meuse, and David Futrell, "Work Teams," *American Psychologist* 45 (February 1990), 120–133.
7. Deborah L. Gladstein, "Groups in Context: A Model of Task Group Effectiveness," *Administrative Science Quarterly* 29 (1984), 499–517.
8. Thomas Owens, "Business Teams," *Small Business Report* (January 1989), 50–58.
9. "Participation Teams," *Small Business Report* (September 1987), 38–41.
10. Larson and LaFasto, *TeamWork.*

11. James H. Shonk, *Team-Based Organizations* (Homewood, Ill.: Business One Irwin, 1992); and John Hoerr, "The Payoff from Teamwork," *Business Week,* July 10, 1989, 56–62.

12. Gregory L. Miles, "Suddenly, USX Is Playing Mr. Nice Guy," *Business Week,* June 26, 1989, 151–152.

13. Thomas Owens, "The Self-Managing Work Team," *Small Business Reports,* February 1991, 53–65.

14. Brian Dumaine, "Who Needs a Boss?" *Fortune,* May 7, 1990, 52–60.

15. John Hoerr, "Benefits for the Back Office, Too," *Business Week,* July 10, 1989, 59.

16. Michael Barrier, "Doing Well What Comes Naturally," *Nation's Business,* September 1992, 25–26.

17. For research findings on group size, see M. E. Shaw, *Group Dynamics,* 3d ed. (New York: McGraw-Hill, 1981), and G. Manners, "Another Look at Group Size, Group Problem-Solving and Member Consensus," *Academy of Management Journal* 18 (1975), 715–724.

18. George Prince, "Recognizing Genuine Teamwork," *Supervisory Management* (April 1989), 25–36; K. D. Benne and P. Sheats, "Functional Roles of Group Members," *Journal of Social Issues* 4 (1948), 41–49; and R. F. Bales, *SYMOLOG Case Study Kit* (New York: Free Press, 1980).

19. Robert A. Baron, *Behavior in Organizations,* 2d ed. (Boston: Allyn & Bacon, 1986).

20. Ibid.

21. Kenneth G. Koehler, "Effective Team Management," *Small Business Report,* July 19, 1989, 14–16; and Connie J. G. Gersick, "Time and Transition in Work Teams: Toward a New Model of Group Development," *Academy of Management Journal* 31 (1988), 9–41.

22. Bruce W. Tuckman and Mary Ann C. Jensen, "Stages of Small-Group Development Revisited," *Group and Organizational Studies* 2 (1977), 419–427; and Bruce W. Tuckman, "Developmental Sequences in Small Groups," *Psychological Bulletin* 63 (1965), 384–399. See also Linda N. Jewell and H. Joseph Reitz, *Group Effectiveness in Organizations* (Glenview, Ill.: Scott, Foresman, 1981).

23. B. Randall Palef, "The Team and Me: Reflections of a Design Group," *Personnel Journal,* February 1994, 48.

24. Shaw, *Group Dynamics.*

25. Daniel C. Feldman and Hugh J. Arnold, *Managing Individual and Group Behavior in Organizations* (New York: McGraw-Hill, 1983).

26. Ricky W. Griffin, *Management* (Boston: Houghton Mifflin, 1990).

27. Dumaine, "Who Needs a Boss?"

28. Dorwin Cartwright and Alvin Zander, *Group Dynamics: Research and Theory,* 3d ed. (New York: Harper & Row, 1968); and Elliot Aronson, *The Social Animal* (San Francisco: W. H. Freeman, 1976).

29. Peter E. Mudrack, "Group Cohesiveness and Productivity: A Closer Look," *Human Relations* 42 (1989), 771–785.

30. Stanley E. Seashore, *Group Cohesiveness in the Industrial Work Group* (Ann Arbor, Mich.: Institute for Social Research, 1954).

31. J. Richard Hackman, "Group Influences on Individuals," in *Handbook of Industrial and Organizational Psychology*, ed. M. Dunnette (Chicago: Rand McNally, 1976).

32. Kenneth Bettenhausen and J. Keith Murnighan, "The Emergence of Norms in Competitive Decision-Making Groups," *Administrative Science Quarterly* 30 (1985), 350–372.

33. The following discussion is based on Daniel C. Feldman, "The Development and Enforcement of Group Norms," *Academy of Management Review* 9 (1984), 47–53.

34. Hugh J. Arnold and Daniel C. Feldman, *Organizational Behavior* (New York: McGraw-Hill, 1986).

35. Kenneth Libich, "Making over Middle Managers," *Fortune*, May 8, 1989, 58–64.

36. Alix M. Freedman, "Cigarette Smoking Is Growing Hazardous to Career in Business," *The Wall Street Journal*, April 23, 1987, 1, 14.

37. Stephen P. Robbins, *Managing Organizational Conflict: A Nontraditional Approach* (Englewood Cliffs, N.J.: Prentice-Hall, 1974).

38. Daniel Robey, Dana L. Farrow, and Charles R. Franz, "Group Process and Conflict in System Development," *Management Science* 35 (1989), 1172–1191.

39. Koehler, "Effective Team Management"; and Dean Tjosvold, "Making Conflict Productive," *Personnel Administrator* 29 (June 1984), 121.

40. This discussion is based in part on Richard L. Daft, *Organization Theory and Design* (St. Paul, Minn.: West, 1992), Chapter 13.

41. Brian Bremner, "That Head-Banging You Hear Is the NFL Owners," *Business Week*, September 4, 1989, 36.

42. Wendy Zeller, "The UAW Rebels Teaming Up against Teamwork," *Business Week*, March 27, 1989, 110–114; and Wendy Zeller, "Suddenly, the UAW Is Raising Its Voice at GM," *Business Week*, November 6, 1989, 96–100.

43. Based on Mary Jean Parson, "The Peer Conflict," *Supervisory Management* (May 1986), 25–31.

44. This discussion was based on K. W. Thomas, "Towards Multidimensional Values in Teaching: The Example of Conflict Behaviors," *Academy of Management Review* 2 (1977), 487.

45. Robbins, *Managing Organizational Conflict*.

46. Gary Jacobson, "A Teamwork Ultimatum Puts Kimberly-Clark's Mill Back on the Map," *Management Review* (July 1989), 28–31.

47. R. B. Zajonc, "Social Facilitation," *Science* 149 (1965), 269–274.

48. Steve Weinstein, "Teams Without Managers," *Progressive Grocer*, September 1992, 101–106.

49. Aaron Bernstein, "Detroit vs. the UAW: At Odds over Teamwork," *Business Week*, August 24, 1987, 54–55.

50. Robert Albanese and David D. Van Fleet, "Rational Behavior in Groups: The Free-Riding Tendency," *Academy of Management Review* 10 (1985), 244–255.

51. Baron, *Behavior in Organizations.*

52. Harvey J. Brightman, *Group Problem Solving: An Improved Managerial Approach* (Atlanta: Georgia State University, 1988).

53. Aaron Bernstein, "Putting a Damper on That Old Team Spirit," *Business Week,* May 4, 1992, 60; and Hoerr, "Is Teamwork a Management Plot? Mostly Not," 70.

54. Posner, "Divided We Fall."

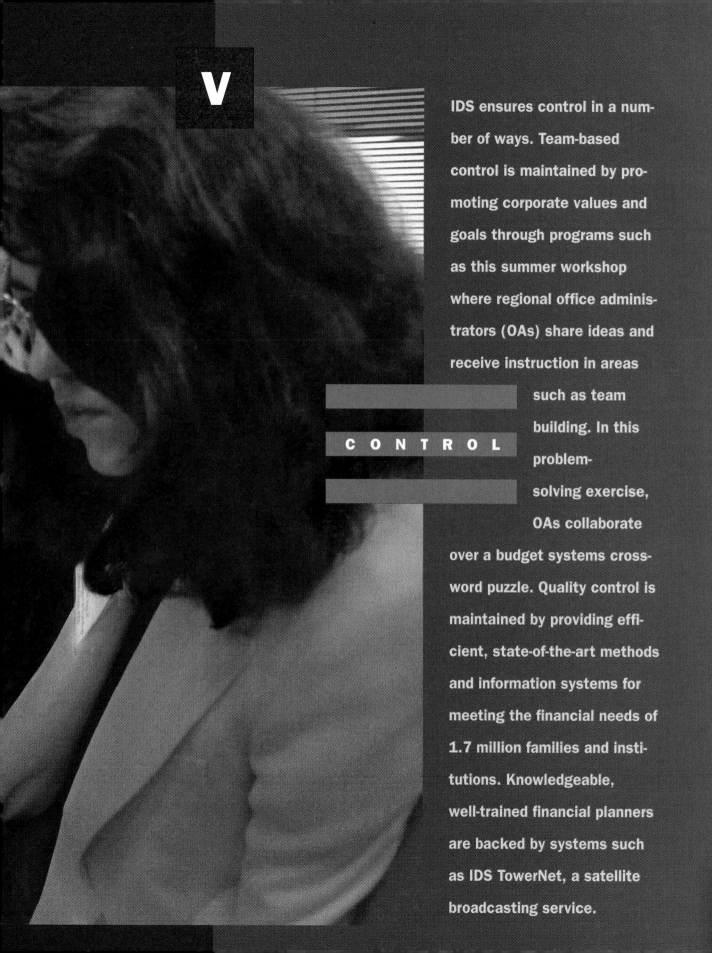

V

CONTROL

IDS ensures control in a number of ways. Team-based control is maintained by promoting corporate values and goals through programs such as this summer workshop where regional office administrators (OAs) share ideas and receive instruction in areas such as team building. In this problem-solving exercise, OAs collaborate over a budget systems crossword puzzle. Quality control is maintained by providing efficient, state-of-the-art methods and information systems for meeting the financial needs of 1.7 million families and institutions. Knowledgeable, well-trained financial planners are backed by systems such as IDS TowerNet, a satellite broadcasting service.

QUALITY CONTROL AND PRODUCTIVITY

16

The Importance of Control
Steps in the Traditional Control
  Process

Core Management Control System

Control Approaches to Quality
Traditional Bureaucratic Control
Contemporary Clan Control

Total Quality Management
Quality Circles
TQM Techniques
TQM Success Factors

CHAPTER OUTLINE ▲

LEARNING OBJECTIVES ▼

After studying this chapter, you should be able to

- Define *organizational control* and explain why it is a key management
  function.
- Explain the four steps in the control process.
- Describe how organizational control relates to strategic planning.
- Identify the components of the core management control system.
- Describe bureaucratic and clan control approaches and the methods
  used within the organization to implement each.
- Describe the concept of total quality management and explain how
  quality circles can be used to improve quality control in organizations.
- Describe the TQM techniques of benchmarking, reduced cycle time,
  outsourcing, and continuous improvement.

In his spare time, Roger Telschow started a business by printing brochures and fliers on a tiny press in his basement. Within five years, he had transformed Ecoprint into a full-time endeavor and hired his first employee. But as the company grew to three workers, Telschow found that the only way he could ensure good quality service and profits was to do nearly everything himself. When he would tire of running the business single-handedly, he alternated between issuing ultimatums and trying to win employees over by being nice. Neither tactic seemed to work, and Telschow finally decided that he would sell Ecoprint. But before taking such a drastic step, he wondered if there were any alternatives. If you were a consultant to Telschow, what would you recommend he do? How can he best go about maintaining quality control without overseeing every aspect of the business himself?[1]

Telschow had a growing business, but it proved harder than he expected to maintain high-quality standards. Ecoprint illustrates how difficult it can be to achieve effective control. The problem of control, especially quality control, is an issue facing every manager in every organization today. Newspaper articles about the savings and loan scandal and about the enormous overdrafts by members of Congress at the House of Representatives Bank are about control. The time needed to resupply merchandise in stores, the length of time that customers must wait in check-out lines, and the number of steps to process and package a roll of film are all control concerns. Merrill Lynch's huge losses from loosely supervised traders, its 9,000-employee work force reduction, and its strategic refocus on customer service and profits are also about control. Control, including quality control, also involves office productivity, such as improved customer service, elimination of bottlenecks, and reduction in paperwork mistakes.[2]

● THE IMPORTANCE OF CONTROL

Here is a true story: Ken Jones, president of the Ontario Centre for Advanced Manufacturing, said that a few years ago IBM Canada Ltd. ordered some parts from a new supplier in Japan. The company stated in its order that acceptable quality allowed for 1.5 percent defects—a high standard in North America at that time. The Japanese sent the order, with a few parts packaged separately in plastic. Their letter said: "We don't know why you want 1.5 percent defective parts, but for your convenience we have packaged them separately."[3]

This story crystalizes the problems with control in North America. First is complacency, the assumption that our management techniques are the best in the world. Second is a top-down, pyramidal control style that is almost feudal in nature. Top management expects to control everything, making all decisions, while middle and lower managers implement decisions, and production workers do only as they are told.

This philosophy is now being stood on its head as a new control philosophy emerges. As we saw in the chapters on leadership, structure, motivation, and teams, low-level employees are being included in management and control decisions. Top management no longer decides the "right" way to do something. More and more, the people who are in control of a particular work setting are those who work within 50 feet of it. Thus at IBM Canada Ltd., *all* 11,000 employees have now been organized into participation groups. A 1.5 percent defect standard is no longer tolerable.[4]

Organizational control is defined as the systematic process through which managers regulate organizational activities to make them consistent with the expectations established in plans, targets, and standards of performance.[5] To effectively control an organization, managers (or workers) must plan and set performance standards, implement an information system that will provide knowledge of actual performance, and take action to correct deviations from the standard.

organizational control

The systematic process through which managers regulate organizational activities to make them consistent with expectations established in plans, targets, and standards of performance.

This computer "clean room" was designed for the production of computer chips at Harris Semiconductor in Melbourne, Florida. Rigid standards of cleanliness and production procedures allow managers to control errors attributable to environmental influences.

STEPS IN THE TRADITIONAL CONTROL PROCESS

Based on our definition of organizational control, a well-designed control system consists of four key steps, which are illustrated in Exhibit 16.1.

ESTABLISH STANDARDS OF PERFORMANCE.   Within the organization's overall strategic plan, managers define goals for organizational departments in specific, operational terms that include a *standard of performance* against which to compare organizational activities. A standard of performance could include "reducing the reject rate from 15 to 3 percent," "increasing the corporation's return on investment to 7 percent," or "reducing the number of accidents to 1 per each 100,000 hours of labor." American Airlines sets standards for such activities as acquiring additional aircraft for its fleet, designing discount fares to attract price-conscious travelers, improving passenger load factors, and increasing freight business. Standards must be defined in a precise way so that managers and workers can determine whether activities are on target. Standards can then be understood by the people in the organization responsible for achieving them.

MEASURE ACTUAL PERFORMANCE.   Many organizations develop quantitative measurements of performance that can be reviewed on a

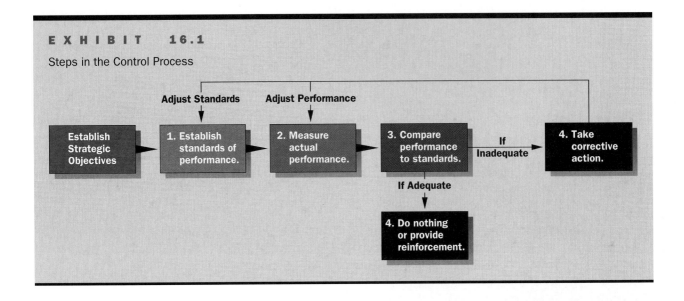

EXHIBIT   16.1

Steps in the Control Process

daily, weekly, or monthly basis. For example, Robert McDermott, CEO of USAA (an insurance and investment group), blamed his company's system of measurement, rather than employee ability, for a drop in productivity growth. A complete overhaul of USAA's measurement system resulted in creation of the family of measures (FOM), which charts and evaluates employees in four target areas: quality, quantity, timeliness, and customer service. Evaluations under the FOM system determine promotions and bonuses. USAA productivity was soon back on track and growing.[6] In most companies, however, managers do not rely exclusively on quantitative measures. They get out into the organization to see how things are going, especially for such goals as increasing employee participation and personal growth. Managers have to observe for themselves whether employees are participating in decision making and are being offered challenging opportunities for personal growth.

COMPARE PERFORMANCE TO STANDARDS.   The third step is the explicit comparison of actual activities to performance standards. Managers take time to read computer reports or walk through the plant and thereby compare actual performance to standards. In many companies, targeted performance standards are right on the computer printout along with the actual performance for the previous week and year. This makes the comparison easy for managers. A. O. Smith, manufacturer of heavy metal frames for automobiles, used comparison to determine whether it was meeting its plans to diversify products as a result of the changes in the design of automobiles. Smith's managers obtained data revealing that 20 percent of sales were from products not made five years earlier, indicating they were on target for diversification.

However, when performance falls below standard, remember that interpreting the comparison between standards and actual performance is not always easy. Managers are expected to dig beneath the surface and find the cause of the problem. If the sales goal is to increase the number of sales calls by 10 percent and a salesperson achieved an increase of 8 percent, where did she fail to achieve her goal? Perhaps several businesses on her route closed, additional salespeople were assigned to her area by competitors, or she needs training in making cold sales calls. Management should take an inquiring approach to deviations in order to gain a broad understanding of factors that influenced performance. Effective management control involves subjective judgment and employee discussions as well as objective analysis of performance data.

TAKE CORRECTIVE ACTION.   *Corrective action* should follow changes in work activities in order to bring them back to acceptable performance standards. In a traditional top-down control approach, managers exercise their formal authority to make necessary changes. Managers may encourage employees to work harder, redesign the production process, or fire employees. One Friday night, the night shift at the Toledo, Ohio, AMC Jeep plant had a 15 percent no-show rate for workers, which is above the acceptable absenteeism standard of 10 percent. Management's corrective action was to shut the plant down and send the other 85 percent of workers home without pay. In the newer, participative control approach, managers and employees together would determine the corrective action necessary, perhaps through problem-solving teams or quality circles.

In some cases, managers may take corrective action to change performance standards. They may realize that standards are too high or too low if departments continuously fail to meet or exceed standards. If contingency factors that influence organizational performance change, performance standards may need to be altered to be more realistic and provide positive motivation for employees.

Managers may wish to provide positive reinforcement when performance meets or exceeds targets. They may reward a department that has exceeded its planned goals or congratulate employees for a job well done. Managers should not ignore high-performing departments in favor of taking corrective actions elsewhere.

● CORE MANAGEMENT CONTROL SYSTEM

Research into the design of control systems across organizations has revealed the existence of a core management control system. The **core control system** consists of the strategic plans, financial forecasts, budgets, management by objectives, operations management techniques, and MIS reports that together provide an integrated system for directing and monitoring organizational activities.[7] The elements of the core control system and their relationship to one another are illustrated in Exhibit 16.2. The strategic plan and financial forecast provide guidance for the budget, management by objectives (MBO), and operations management systems used at middle management levels. The definition of each element in the core control system is as follows:[8]

core control system

The strategic plans, financial forecasts, budgets, management by objectives, operations management techniques, and MIS reports that form an integrated system for directing and monitoring organizational activities.

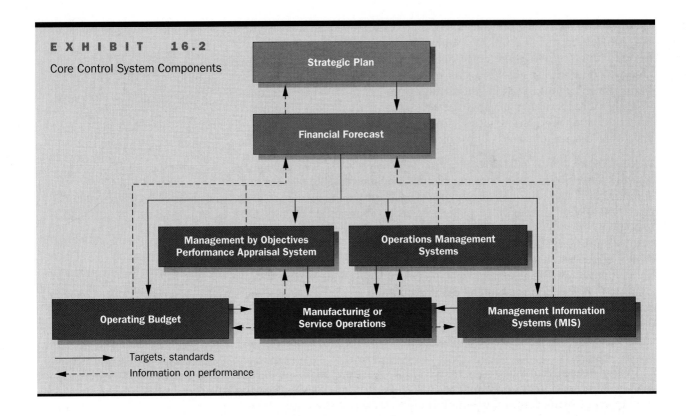

EXHIBIT 16.2

Core Control System Components

Strategic Plan

Financial Forecast

Management by Objectives Performance Appraisal System

Operations Management Systems

Operating Budget

Manufacturing or Service Operations

Management Information Systems (MIS)

→ Targets, standards

⇠ ----- Information on performance

1 *Strategic plan.* The strategic plan consists of the organization's strategic objectives, as discussed in Chapter 6. It is based on in-depth analysis of the organization's industry position, internal strengths and weaknesses, and environmental opportunities and threats. The written plan typically discusses company products, competition, economic trends, and new business opportunities.

2 *Financial forecast.* The financial forecast is based on a one- to five-year projection of company sales and revenues. This forecast is used to project income statements, balance sheets, and departmental expenditures. This is the company's financial projection based on the overall strategic plan. Companies such as W. R. Grace, Teledyne, and Union Carbide use projected financial statements to estimate their future financial positions.

3 *Operating budget.* The operating budget is an annual projection of estimated expenses, revenues, assets, and related financial figures for each operating department for the coming year. Budget reports typically are issued monthly and include comparisons of expenditures with budget targets. Budget reports are developed for all divisions and departments.

4 *Management by objectives.* Recall from Chapter 10 that performance appraisal is the formal method of evaluating and recording the performances of managers and employees. It typically includes standard forms and rating scales that evaluate employee skills and

abilities. Many companies also use management by objectives, described in Chapter 6, to direct employee activities toward corporate objectives. MBO is integrated into the performance appraisal system and enhances management control.

5 *Operations management systems and reports.* Operations management systems pertain to inventory (economic order quantity, just-in-time), purchasing and distribution systems, and project management (PERT charts).

6 *Management information system (MIS) reports.* MIS reports are composed of statistical data, such as personnel complements, volume of orders received, delinquent account ratios, percentage sales returns, and other statistical data relevant to the performance of a department or division. MIS reports typically contain nonfinancial data, whereas operating budgets contain financial data. MIS reports are issued weekly and monthly, and their exact content depends on the nature of tasks and available measures. A sales department MIS report may describe the number of new sales, whereas an assembly department report may record the number of parts assembled per hour.

Each control system component is separate and distinct from the others. The overall strategic plan is top management's responsibility and the financial forecast the controller's. The budget is concerned with the financial figures and is also the controller's responsibility. The management by objectives system is usually the responsibility of the human resource department. Operations management techniques are the responsibility of the production department. MIS reports are produced and distributed by the information system department. Although each control system element is distinct, a successful core control system combines them into an integrated package of controls.

Control systems as they are used by top and middle management levels, are illustrated in Exhibit 16.3. Top management control systems concern financial performance for the organization as a whole and include financial statements, financial analyses, and audits. Middle managers are

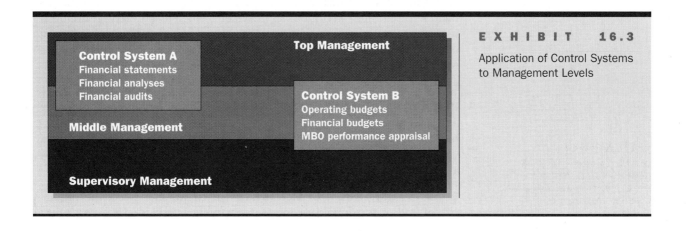

Control System A
Financial statements
Financial analyses
Financial audits

Top Management

Control System B
Operating budgets
Financial budgets
MBO performance appraisal

Middle Management

Supervisory Management

E X H I B I T   16.3

Application of Control Systems to Management Levels

responsible for departments and rely heavily on budgets and MBO systems (described in Chapter 6) for control. The components of the core control system will be discussed in Chapters 17 and 18, respectively.

● CONTROL APPROACHES TO QUALITY

An organization's approaches to quality are based on its basic philosophy of control. With many organizations moving toward participation and employee empowerment, a choice must be made between the traditional bureaucratic and contemporary clan control approaches.

These two control approaches represent different philosophies of corporate culture, which was discussed in Chapter 4. Most organizations display some aspects of both bureaucratic and clan control, but many managers emphasize one or the other, depending on the culture within their organization and their own beliefs about control.

TRADITIONAL BUREAUCRATIC CONTROL

bureaucratic control

The use of rules, policies, hierarchy of authority, reward systems, and other formal devices to influence employee behavior and assess performance.

Bureaucratic control is the use of rules, policies, hierarchy of authority, written documentation, reward systems, and other formal mechanisms to influence employee behavior and assess performance.[9] Bureaucratic control relies on the cultural value of traditional top-down control and is implemented through the organization's administrative system. It assumes that quality targets can be defined and that employees' work behavior will conform to those targets if formal rules and regulations are provided. The following control elements are typically associated with bureaucratic control.

RULES AND PROCEDURES.   Rules and procedures include the standard operating procedures and policies that prescribe correct employee behavior. Rules are based on organizational experience and indicate acceptable behaviors and quality standards for employee performance, such as a 0.5 percent defect rate.

MANAGEMENT CONTROL SYSTEMS.   Management control systems include those internal organization systems, such as budgeting, financial reporting, reward systems, operations management, and management by objectives, that monitor and evaluate performance. These systems are normally quantitative in nature and sometimes measure performance on a daily or even hourly basis.

HIERARCHY OF AUTHORITY.   Hierarchy of authority relies on central authority and personal supervision for control. Managers are responsible for the control of subordinates through direct surveillance. The supervisor has formal authority for control purposes. Lower-level employees are not expected to participate in the control process.

QUALITY CONTROL DEPARTMENT.   In conjunction with the hierarchy of authority, a quality control department is assigned responsibility

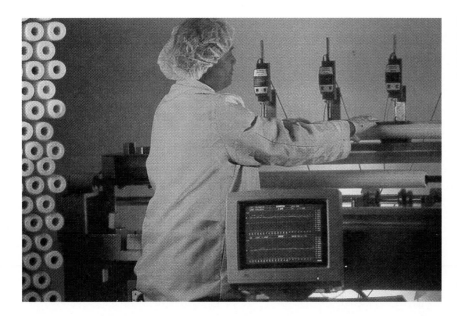

Pall Corporation uses computers to aid quality control of manufacturing processes. This technology assists in monitoring and controlling key aspects of Pall filter production.

for monitoring performance of areas such as manufacturing. Quality control inspectors make periodic checks to ensure that employees are working according to minimum standards for quality performance. Responsibility for quality rests with the quality control department rather than with employees throughout the organization.

SELECTION AND TRAINING.   Under bureaucratic control methods, selection and training are highly formalized. Objective written tests are administered to see if employees meet hiring criteria. Demographic characteristics, such as education and work experience, are quantified to see whether applicants qualify. Formalized selection procedures are intended to allow broad opportunities for employment, but they are associated with extensive paperwork.

TECHNOLOGY.   Technology extends bureaucratic control in two ways. First, it can control the flow and pace of work. In an assembly line manufacturing plant, for example, the technology defines the speed and standards at which workers must perform. Second, computer-based technology can be used to monitor employees. This occurs frequently in service firms. AT&T has a monitoring system that counts the number of seconds that elapse before operators answer each call and the number of seconds spent on each call. American Express uses electronic techniques to monitor data entry personnel who record account payments as well as operators who answer phone queries from credit cardholders. The system reports daily productivity data for each operator and each department. New systems available to organizations enable supervisors to eavesdrop on employees and count the times they call home.[10] The ethics of using electronic control devices is discussed in the Focus on Ethics box, "Is Your Boss 'Bugging' You?," on the next page.

Although many managers effectively use bureaucratic control, too much control can backfire. Employees resent being watched too closely,

IS YOUR BOSS "BUGGING" YOU?

Suspecting theft of narcotics by staff members, Holy Cross Hospital installed television cameras in the nurses' locker room. Nurses were outraged upon discovery of the monitoring equipment because, among other reasons, the only employee with access to the broadcast was the hospital's male security chief. GE's Answer Center monitors and records agents' conversations with customers. GE insists that this quality control system provides feedback and continuous improvement, pointing with pride to a 96 percent customer satisfaction rate. Safeway Stores uses dashboard computers to monitor everything from driving speed and oil pressure to idling time on each of its 782 trucks.

Because of intense competition in today's global environment, employers have stepped up efforts to control their organizations, especially in such volatile areas as inventory control, health care costs, worker negligence or crime, and customer relations. Various measures are in place from the silent monitoring of phone calls to hidden cameras, bugging devices, tailing employees, to the use of high-tech snooping through computers.

Although there is universal agreement concerning the right of employers to protect their businesses, concern is growing about the extent of surveillance and the need to control the controller. Technology enables companies to extend bureaucratic control to the extreme. Is this any way to improve quality? Critics claim that these techniques are an invasion of

privacy, and unions point to increases in stress-related complaints from employees who feel the pressure of constant surveillance.

Employers are protecting themselves from lawsuits by advising new employees of the possibility of monitoring, by having employees sign waivers to allow monitoring, and by providing written policies to employees. Employee dissatisfaction is reflected in increasing complaints, mounting lawsuits, and increased pressure for action in Congress. Observers foresee restrictions that may nudge companies to encourage employee participation rather than monitoring them. ■

SOURCE: Jeffrey Rothfeder, Michele Galen, and Lisa Driscoll, "Is Your Boss Spying on You?" *Business Week*, January 15, 1990, 74–75; and Gene Bylinsky, "How Companies Spy on Employees," *Fortune*, November 4, 1991, 131–140.

and they may try to sabotage the control system. However, too little bureaucratic control also can backfire. Finding the right level is the challenge.

CONTEMPORARY CLAN CONTROL

clan control

The use of social values, traditions, common beliefs, and trust to generate compliance with organizational goals.

Clan control represents cultural values that are almost the opposite of bureaucratic control. **Clan control** relies on social values, traditions, shared beliefs, and trust to foster compliance with organizational goals. Employees are trusted, and managers believe that employees are willing to perform correctly without extensive rules or supervision. Given minimal direction and standards, employees are assumed to perform well—indeed, they participate in setting standards and designing the control system. Clan control is usually implemented in the following areas.

CORPORATE CULTURE.   Corporate culture was described in Chapter 4 as the norms and values shared by organization members. If the organization has a strong corporate culture and the established values are consistent with its goals, corporate culture will be a powerful control device. The organization is like a large family, and each employee is committed to activities that will best serve it. Corporate traditions such as IBM's 100% Club and Mary Kay's pink Cadillac awards instill values in employees that are consistent with the goals and behaviors needed for corporate success.

PEER GROUP.   In Chapter 15, we saw that norms evolve in working teams and that cohesive teams influence employee behavior. If peer control is established, less top-down bureaucratic control is needed. Employees are likely to pressure coworkers into adhering to team norms and achieving departmental goals.

SELF-CONTROL.   No organization can control employees 100 percent of the time. Self-discipline and self-control are what keep employees performing their tasks up to standard. Most employees bring to the job a belief in doing high-quality work and a desire to contribute to the organization's success in return for rewards and fair treatment. To the extent that managers can take greater advantage of employee self-control, bureaucratic controls can be reduced. Employees high in self-control often are those who have had several years of experience and training and hence have internal standards of performance. The experience, training, and socialization of professionals provide internal standards of performance that allow for self-control.[11]

EMPLOYEE SELECTION AND SOCIALIZATION.   Clan methods of selection use personal evaluations rather than formal testing procedures. For example, companies that use clan control methods often subject employment candidates to a rigorous selection process. Tandem Computer subjects managers to 20 grueling hours of interviews. For an entry-level position at Procter & Gamble, the person is interviewed at length by line managers who have been trained to probe into the applicant's

Cost reduction, a 15 percent rise in productivity, and on-time delivery helped these Campbell Soup Company employees at Maxton, N.C., win their second company-sponsored "World Class Manufacturing Award." Campbell values clan control in its manufacturing facilities, which has led to improved productivity and keeps Campbell competitive worldwide.

qualities. Then there is a full day of one-on-one interviews at corporate headquarters and a group interview over lunch. After candidates are hired, they are subjected to intensive training in company values, standards, and traditions. Rigorous selection and socialization activities are an effective way to ensure that candidates buy into the company's values, goals, and quality traditions and hence need few rules and little supervision for control.

In summary, clan control utilizes methods different from those of bureaucratic control. The important point is that both methods provide organizational control. It is a mistake to assume that clan control is weak or represents the absence of control simply because visible rules, procedures, and supervision are absent. Indeed, some people believe that clan control is the stronger form of control because it engages employees' commitment and involvement. Clan control is the wave of the future, with more companies adopting it as part of a strong corporate culture that encourages employee involvement.

Exhibit 16.4 compares bureaucratic and clan control methods. Bureaucratic control is concerned with compliance and clan control with employee commitment.[12] Bureaucratic methods define explicit standards that translate into minimum performance and use top-down control. Compensation is based on individual performance. Employees rarely participate in the control process. With clan methods, employees strive to achieve standards beyond explicitly stated objectives. Influence is mutual, with employees having a say in how tasks are performed and even in determining standards of performance and design of control systems. Shared goals and values replace rules and procedures. Compen-

---

EXHIBIT 16.4

Bureaucratic and Clan Methods of Control

	Bureaucratic	Clan
Purpose	Employee compliance with rules	Employee commitment to quality
Techniques	Rules, formal control systems, hierarchy, QC inspectors, selection and training, technology	Corporate culture, peer group, self-control, selection, and socialization
Performance expectations	Measurable standards define minimum performance; fixed indicators	Emphasis on higher performance and oriented toward dynamic marketplace
Organization structure	Tall structure, top-down controls	Flat structure, mutual influence
	Rules and procedures for coordination and control	Shared goals, values, traditions for coordination and control
	Authority of position, QC department monitors quality	Authority of knowledge and expertise, everyone monitors quality
Rewards	Based on employee's achievement in own job	Based on group achievements and equity across employees
Participation	Formalized and narrow (e.g., grievance procedures)	Informal and broad, including quality control, system design, and organizational governance

SOURCE: Based on Richard E. Walton, "From Control to Commitment in the Workplace," *Harvard Business Review* (March–April 1985), 76–84.

sation is based on group, departmental, and organizational success rather than on individual performance. This induces individuals to help each other improve quality rather than compete against one another. Employees participate in a wide range of areas, including quality governance, objective setting, and performance standards.

An example of how far clan control can go is Marquette Electronics.

 ## MARQUETTE ELECTRONICS

Marquette Electronics makes sophisticated medical devices that doctors use to make life-or-death decisions. Considering the seriousness of its task, it is surprising to see the company characterized by disorder. Some employees wear Hawaiian shirts and have a boom box playing in the background. In the company cafeteria, employees may enjoy a beer. The day-care center takes care of employees' children, and employees can take time off to play with them. Managers at Marquette Electronics do not overcontrol. "The truth is, we're all quite bad managers," says the engineering vice-president. "Maybe we're not managers at all."

The company is well managed, but management consciously delegates important responsibilities to employees. Marquette's approach scorns policies and procedures and eschews memos and directives. The guiding philosophy, as expressed by President Mike Cudahy, follows: "People want to love their job, their boss, and their company. They want to perform. You've got to give people a voice in their jobs. You've got to give them a piece of the action and a chance to excel."

The Marquette culture is fluid and informal, but that does not mean a lack of control. People are not bound by traditional rules, but the group norms and the company culture encourage a high standard of quality. Everyone shares a simple but strong expectation: Make quality products, give good customer service, and do it all fast. This may seem an unusual approach to management, but as one former employee said, "Boy, does it work."[13] ∎

TOTAL QUALITY MANAGEMENT

About ten years ago, a *Wall Street Journal* survey confirmed the fears of U.S. managers by revealing that three-fourths of all Americans consider foreign-made products equal or superior in quality to products made in the United States. An NBC documentary entitled, "If Japan Can . . . Why Can't We?" also challenged U.S. quality standards. Executives saw the task of improving service and product quality as the most critical challenge facing their companies. Throughout the 1980s and into the 1990s, the quality revolution spread as U.S. executives saw quality improvement as the route to restoring global competitiveness, and many companies recommitted themselves to quality.[14]

The term used to describe this approach is *total quality management (TQM),* which infuses quality throughout every activity in a company.

total quality management (TQM)

A control concept that gives workers rather than managers the responsibility for achieving standards of quality.

This approach was successfully implemented by Japanese companies that earned an international reputation for high quality. As we saw in Chapter 2, much of the foundation for the Japanese system was laid by U.S. educators and consultants following World War II. The Japanese eagerly adopted the quality ideas of Americans such as Deming, Juran, and Feigenbaum.[15] The sounding of the quality alarm in North America and the publication of books such as *Quality Is Free: The Art of Making Quality Certain* by Philip Crosby and *The Deming Management Method* by Mary Walton helped reawaken managers to the need for quality throughout U.S. companies.[16]

The theme of **total quality management** is simple: "The burden of quality proof rests ... with the makers of the part."[17] In other words, workers, not managers, are responsible for achieving standards of quality. This is a revolution in management thinking, because quality control departments and formal control systems no longer have primary control responsibility. Companies that really want to improve quality are urged to stop inspecting every part and to get rid of their quality control departments. These companies are then told to train the workers and trust them to take care of quality.

This approach can give traditional executives several sleepless nights as their traditional means of control vanish. Total quality control means a shift from a bureaucratic to a clan method of control. Total quality uses clan methods to gain employees' commitment.

An outgrowth of Total Quality Management is the new emphasis on Total Quality Service (TQS). Going beyond the usual 800-numbers or "How-are-we-doing?" cards handed out to paying customers at cash registers, TQS broadens the definition of customer to also include sales people and dealers. Through TQS the customer becomes an active and trusted participant in achieving standards of product quality. Customer surveys reach beyond the traditional circled responses ("poor, good, excellent") to seek genuine feedback, and dealers are polled anonymously. Focus groups and test groups become important contributors to product development, and complaint customers are viewed as allies in the thrust toward quality. Companies such as Intuit, Inc., a maker of microcomputer software, make customer satisfaction a top priority, knowing that customers sell the product and that improved quality service translates ultimately into quality products.[18]

American Airlines is cited frequently by customers for the high quality of its service. Chairman Robert L. Crandall explains how it goes back to a policy decision to improve the traditionally adversarial relationship between labor and management.

> The airline business has historically had a strong military bent and developed as a rather rigid, procedures-based and confrontational workplace. On top of that, the industry became heavily unionized. Very early in the deregulation process, we made the decision to make a sustained, long-term effort to change the confrontational, non-cooperative, non-participative environment into an environment based on trust and mutual respect.[19]

Companywide participation in quality control requires quite a change in corporate culture values as described in Chapter 9. The mindset of both managers and employees must shift. Companies traditionally have practiced the Western notion of achieving an "acceptable quality level." This allows a certain percentage of defects and engenders a mentality that imperfections are okay. Only defects caught by a quality control department need be corrected. Total quality control not only engages the participation of all employees but has a target of zero defects. Everyone strives for perfection. A rejection rate of 2 percent will lead to a new quality target of 1 percent. This approach instills a habit of continuous improvement rather than the traditional Western approach of attempting to meet the minimum acceptable standard of performance.

Recent books and articles advocating a systematic quality effort suggest that to be successful, companywide quality control program:

1 Reflect total *commitment* to quality by management.

2 Be devoted to *prevention* rather than appraisal and correction.

3 Focus on quality *measurement* (using feedback).

4 *Reward* quality (employing incentives and penalties).

5 Focus on quality *training* at all levels.

6 Stress problem identification and *solution* (using teams).

7 Promote *innovation* and continuous *improvement*.

8 Promote total *participation*.

9 Stress high performance *standards* with zero defects.

10 Provide *calculations* and *reports* of cost savings.[20]

Quality control thus becomes part of the day-to-day business of every employee. Management needs to evaluate quality in terms of lost sales and total company performance rather than as some percentage indicator from a management control system. Each employee must internalize the value of preventing defects. When handled properly, the total quality approach really works. Standout companies using these techniques are Eastman Kodak, Ford Motor Company, Motorola, and Florida Power & Light.[21]

The implementation of total quality control is similar to that of other control methods. Targets must be set for employee involvement and for new quality standards. Employees must be trained to think in terms of prevention, not detection, and they must be given the responsibility of correcting their own errors and exposing any quality problems they discover.

Renewed U.S. commitment to quality is exemplified by the Malcolm Baldrige National Quality Award, which is discussed in the Manager's Shoptalk box on the next page.

QUALITY CIRCLES

One approach to implementing a total quality philosophy and engaging the work force in a clan approach is that of quality circles (QCs). A **quality circle** is a group of from 6 to 12 volunteer employees who meet regularly to discuss and solve problems affecting their common work activities.[22] Time is set aside during the workweek for these groups to meet,

quality circle (QC)

A group of 6 to 12 volunteer employees who meet regularly to discuss and solve problems that affect their common work activities.

THE MALCOLM BALDRIGE NATIONAL QUALITY AWARD

The motion picture industry has the Oscar, and the scientific, economic, and diplomatic communities have the Nobel Prize. For U.S. businesses, the standard of excellence is the Malcolm Baldrige National Quality Award. Established in 1987 and named for the former Secretary of Commerce, the Baldrige Award measures management systems for quality improvement programs. Awards are presented in three categories: manufacturing, service, and small business.

Two of the winners in the small-business category are Granite Rock Company and Globe Metallurgical Inc., the leading edge companies you have been reading about throughout this book. Other winners in the category include Ames Rubber Corp., Marotta Scientific Controls Inc., Marlow Industries, and Wallace Company.

Although each of the small businesses recognized by the award represents a different industry, they are part of an elite group that has managed to outperform more than 100 other applicants in the category. The Baldrige winners also have at least one other thing in common: they have proven that total quality management (TQM) can work as well for a small company as for a large corporation. In fact, TQM may work even better for small businesses because their size enables them to really get to know their customers and what it takes to satisfy them.

Marlow Industries of Dallas, for example, had the distinction of being the smallest company to ever win the Baldrige Award when it was selected for the honor in 1991. The company, which employs 160 people, manufactures thermo-electric coolers and components used by the military and in the tele-communications and aerospace industries. Because most of the company's products are custom-made, Marlow came up with a quality system that would meet the unique requirements of each of its clients.

One of the first steps in Marlow's quality program was to shift decision-making from management to employees while also switching from product inspection to process control. "We used to check the specifications and the rods' properties after they were made," says supervisor Peggy Holmes. "The good stuff we would cut up and ship to customers. And we would just toss the bad."

The company assigned process engineers to "minifactories" where worker teams were responsible for ensuring that defects did not occur. Employees also developed their own statistical process controls to track quality levels and improve efficiency. "We really dedicated ourselves to understanding our processes and finding the key variables," says Marlow's chief operating officer Chris Witzke. "All this stuff used to be black art. Now it's science."

In the four years after the quality program went into effect, Marlow cut its manufacturing cycle time by one-third and reduced order-to-shipment lead times by 37 percent. Productivity improvements have averaged 10.6 percent a year for the last six years.

Another Texas company, Houston-based Wallace Company, won the award in 1990 after initiating a quality program to ensure its survival in a struggling industry. As a supplier of the pipes, valves, and fitting used in chemical and petrochemical industries, Wallace lost half its business in the early 1980s after oil prices took a nose-dive. "The Wallaces woke up one morning and found out their pipe was worth $17 million less than it was the night before," says a company sales representative.

Wallace started a total quality program in 1985 as a way out of its dilemma. Like workers at other Baldrige Award winners, Wallace employees now have a new sense of empowerment and responsibility. However, with more sophisticated controls, the company can carry only about one-third as much inventory as it once did. Yet on-time deliveries have increased to 92 percent, a 17 percent improvement in only four years. It also has reduced the number of suppliers it deals with from 2,500 to 325 as part of its policy of building close, long-term relationship with suppliers, customers, and employees.

But while the quality program brought much-needed improvements at Wallace, it was not enough to solve all the company's financial problems. Just one year after winning the Baldrige Award, Wallace was in the red and hounded by creditors. Proponents of the Baldrige counter that quality "systems," not financial performance, are the focus of evaluation for the award.

Is the Baldrige Award the answer to how to stimulate higher quality standards in the United States? The jury is still out. However, the award has certainly focused attention on the importance of quality in businesses both big and small. ▪

SOURCE: Michael Verespel, "Marlow Industries Inc.," *Industry Week,* October 16, 1993, 45–46; Michael Barrier, "Overcoming Adversity," *Nation's Business,* June 1991, 25–29; and "Small Firms Put Quality First," *Nation's Business,* May 1992, 22–32.

identify problems, and try to find solutions. The key idea is that people who do the job know it better than anyone else and can make recommendations for improved performance. QCs also push control decision making to a lower organizational level. Circle members are free to collect data and take surveys. In many companies, team members are given training in team building, problem solving, and statistical quality control to enable them to confront problems and solutions more readily. The groups do not focus on personal gripes and problems. Often a facilitator is present to help guide the discussion. Quality circles use many of the teamwork concepts described in Chapter 15. The quality circle process as used in most U.S. companies is illustrated in Exhibit 16.5, which begins with a selected problem and ends with a decision given back to the team.

The quality circle concept spread to the United States and Canada from Japan. It had been developed by Japanese companies as a method

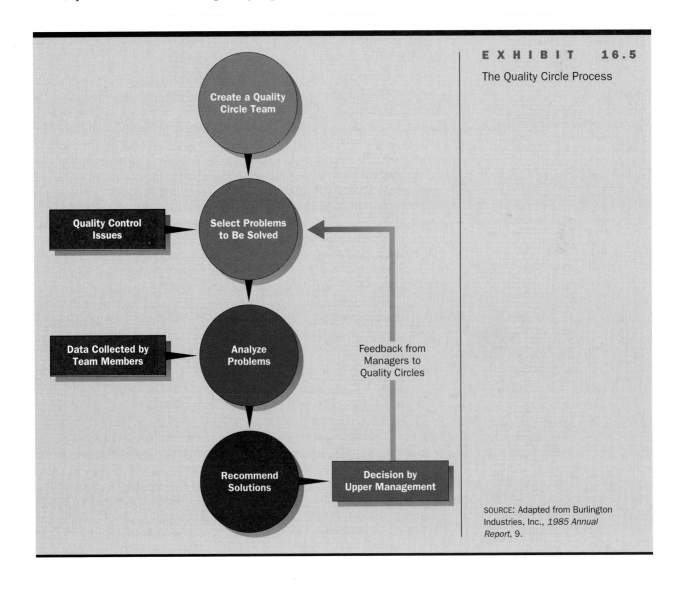

EXHIBIT 16.5

The Quality Circle Process

Create a Quality Circle Team

Quality Control Issues → Select Problems to Be Solved

Data Collected by Team Members → Analyze Problems

Recommend Solutions

Decision by Upper Management

Feedback from Managers to Quality Circles

SOURCE: Adapted from Burlington Industries, Inc., *1985 Annual Report*, 9.

of gaining employee commitment to high standards. The success of quality circles impressed executives visiting Japan from Lockheed, the first company to adopt this practice. Many other North American companies, including Digital Equipment, Martin Marietta Corporation, and Baltimore Gas & Electric Company, have since adopted quality circles. In several of these companies, managers attest to the improved performance and cost savings. Westinghouse has over 100 quality circles; a single innovation proposed by one group saved the company $2.4 million. To build on these successes, Westinghouse created the Productivity and Quality Center that assists departments throughout the company. It acts as a SWAT team of sorts to help divisions do the same work in half the time with better quality results.[23]

TQM TECHNIQUES

The implementation of total quality management involves the use of many techniques. Most companies that have adopted TQM have incorporated benchmarking, outsourcing, reduced cycle time, and continuous improvement.

benchmarking

The continuous process of measuring products, services, and practices against the toughest competitors or those companies recognized as industry leaders.

BENCHMARKING.   Introduced by Xerox in 1979, benchmarking is now a major TQM component. **Benchmarking** is defined by Xerox as "the continuous process of measuring products, services, and practices against the toughest competitors or those companies recognized as industry leaders."[24] The key to successful benchmarking lies in analysis. Starting with its own mission statement, a company must honestly analyze its current procedures and determine areas for improvement. As a second step, a company must *carefully* select competitors worthy of copying. For example, Xerox studied the order fulfillment techniques of L. L. Bean and learned ways to reduce warehouse costs by 10 percent. Companies can emulate internal processes and procedures of competitors, but with caution. For example, a small company may court failure by copying the "big boys" such as Ford or Xerox whose methods are incompatible with a small-company situation. Once a strong, compatible program is found and analyzed, the benchmarking company can then devise a strategy for implementing a new program.[25] The Seitz Corp. is one small company that found a way to use benchmarking to its advantage.

 SEITZ CORP.

Seitz Corp. decided to try benchmarking after its sales headed south. For more than three decades, the Torrington, Conn.-based business had enjoyed success supplying the gears and bearings that move paper in copiers and printers. But while the company was busy providing components for dot-matrix printers, the popularity of laser printers had begun to soar. Seitz was caught by surprise and saw its annual sales drop to $5 million in 1986, from a peak of $12 million just six years before. It had to slash its work force by two-thirds, leaving only 80 employees on the payroll.

That's when marketing manager Sharon LeGault took action. She began benchmarking Seitz's business practices with those of top companies throughout the country in all types of industries. As a result, the company adopted new techniques, such as one that boosted "just-in-time" deliveries from suppliers and reduced the inventory on hand. Seitz also initiated new practices that reduced the time it took to bring a new product to market from around two months to as little as two weeks.

It turned out to be easier to implement the new practices at a small business like Seitz than it would have been at a larger company where bureaucracy and red tape could hinder the process. In addition, the employee time commitment and expense required to successfully benchmark was more than compensated by the improvement in Seitz's financial situation. Sales started growing again and in 1992 were expected to hit a record $21 million. The number of workers also increased to 190. As LeGault says: "We attribute all of that to benchmarking."[26] ∎

OUTSOURCING.   One of the fastest-growing trends in U.S. business is **outsourcing,** the farming out of a company's in-house operation to a preferred vendor with a high quality level in the particular task area. A variety of companies, such as B. F. Goodrich, Glacxo Pharmaceuticals, Unisys, and NCNB Bank have latched on to outsourcing as a route to almost immediate savings and quality improvement. Traditional in-house operations can be farmed out to save costs on employee benefits, to reduce personnel, and to free existing personnel for other duties. For example, banks have outsourced the processing of credit cards to companies that can do it more cheaply. Large oil companies have outsourced the cleaning and maintenance of refineries. Eastman Kodak outsourced its computer operations to IBM. Manufacturing companies have outsourced the designing of new plants, and service organizations have outsourced mailrooms, warehousing, and delivery services. As with other quality systems, outsourcing is successful when care is taken in selecting the operations that can be accomplished with greater quality elsewhere and in finding the best outsourcing partner.[27]

outsourcing
The farming out of a company's in-house operation to a preferred vendor.

REDUCED CYCLE TIME.   In the book *Quality Alone Is Not Enough,* the authors refer to cycle times as the "drivers of improvement." **Cycle time** refers to the steps taken to complete a company process, such as teaching a class, publishing a textbook, or designing a new car. The simplification of work cycles, including the dropping of barriers between work steps and between departments, and the removal of worthless steps in the process, is what enables a TQM program to succeed. Even if an organization decides not to use quality circles, substantial improvement is possible by focusing on improved responsiveness and acceleration of activities into a shorter time. Reduction in cycle time improves overall company performance as well as quality.[28]

cycle time
The steps taken to complete a company process.

For example, L. L. Bean, Inc., the Freeport, Maine, mail-order firm, is a recognized leader in cycle time control. Workers have used flowcharts to track their movements and pinpoint wasted motions, shifting high-volume merchandise closer to the packing station. Improvements such as these have enabled L. L. Bean to respond with a correct shipment rate of 99.9 percent within only a few hours after the order is received.[29]

At Armstrong's Thomasville Furniture plants, cycle time is determined by order-to-shipment time. Reduced cycle time is one thrust of Armstrong's "Eighty in Five" quality program. The goal is an "80 percent reduction in nonconformances that inhibit customer satisfaction," and the target date is 1995. Employees throughout the company are pitching in to achieve these ambitious goals.

continuous improvement

The implementation of a large number of small, incremental improvements in all areas of the organization on an ongoing basis.

CONTINUOUS IMPROVEMENT.   In North America, crash programs and grand designs have been the preferred method of innovation. Yet the finding from Japanese success is that continuous improvement produces an even more effective result. **Continuous improvement** is the implementation of a large number of small, incremental improvements in all areas of the organization on an ongoing basis. In a successful TQM program, all employees learn that they are expected to contribute by initiating changes in their own job activities. The basic philosophy is that improving things a little bit at a time, all the time, has the highest probability of success. Find one small way to improve the job today and act on it. That improvement will suggest another useful piece tomorrow. No improvement is too small to implement—activities are fine-tuned all the time. In this way, innovations can start simple, and employees can run with their ideas. There is no end to the process. Improvements occur all the time, and the resulting changes give a company a significant competitive advantage.[30]

The continuous improvement concept applies to all departments, products, services, and activities throughout an organization. At South Carolina Baptist Hospital in Columbia, South Carolina, 2,500 employees have been trained in continuous improvement techniques. Managers learn a coaching role, empowering employees to recognize and act on their contributions. Baptist has learned that countless improvements require a long-term approach to building quality into the very fiber of the organization. Over time, project by project, human activity by human activity, quality through continuous improvement has become the way the hospital's employees do their work.[31] Another company that has focused on continuous improvement is Globe Metallurgical, which is featured in the Leading Edge box.

LEADING edge

GLOBE METALLURGICAL

In earlier chapters, we learned that Arden C. Sims and his fellow managers acquired Globe Metallurgical in a leveraged buyout in 1987. As they found out, improving quality was only one of many problems. Sims had his hands full simply trying to figure out ways for the firm to survive. He was managing the company's changeover from commodity to specialty metals production. Specifications were more exact, and the number of products greatly increased. He realized he had to implement a reliable quality control system to keep his customers happy. And suddenly it all came into clear focus. Total quality management wasn't just something Globe Metallurgical could apply piecemeal along with whatever other fixes seemed handy at the time. It would be the key to whether the company survived or not.

Globe's quality program earned the company a host of awards, from the Malcolm Baldrige to the Shingo Prize to excellence designations from companies that included GM, Ford, Saturn, and John Deere. The company even received the U.S. Senate Productivity Award. And all of it added up to a good deal more than a crowded trophy case. Globe's business is notoriously cyclical.

Average plant operations for the industry is under 50 percent of capacity. And even though Globe typically runs at around 90 percent of capacity, downturns are tough. So what did all the quality awards do to make this situation any better? They served as a shiny resume for Globe when Sims decided to smooth out those domestic business cycles by expanding overseas.

As he explored new markets, Sims found a couple of problems common to both Europe and the Pacific Rim. Competitors were offering three or four products and the customers were having to make them fit. Likewise, sales calls tended to consist of dropping off a price. Sims knew his product quality was superior to competitors. And he knew that his process efficiency was such that he could find out exactly what customers wanted, produce it for them, and make money while taking a greater market share. Globe grabbed off big chunks of Japanese manufacturers' business outside their own country, and made excellent inroads into Taiwan and South Korea, where he found the people very hospitable to Americans. If Sims hadn't had the highest possible product quality, his whole overseas expansion could have derailed with financially catastrophic results. As things worked out, he offered more and better products competitively priced, and his sales

force made sure the customers' needs were met.

Globe's total quality program reduced its costs almost 400 percent and increased plant efficiencies in the 30 percent range. Sims says that although that's more than he ever dreamed possible back in 1985, it is still some distance from what he now calls the company's theoretical maximum efficiency. The original inspiration was basic: the company had to remake operations if it wanted to survive. Along the way Sims discovered two important things: Doing things the right way creates its own momentum, and once underway, there's no desire to ever turn back. He also realized that eventually everyone would have to adopt the changes he instituted at Globe Metallurgical. Being one of the first small businesses to do so earned the company many awards. As for the future, total quality will become business as usual for anyone that wants to stay in the game.
■

SOURCE: Bruce Rayner, "Trial-by-Fire Transformation: An Interview with Globe Metallurgical's Arden C. Sims," *Harvard Business Review,* May–June 1992, 117–129; Charles E. Lopez, "Globe Metallurgical CEO Arden C. Sims: On Quality and Competition in World Markets," *The Quality Observer,* February 1992, 16–17; and Otis Port et al., "Quality, the Key to Growth for Small Companies and for America," *Business Week,* November 30, 1992, 66–74.

TQM SUCCESS FACTORS

Despite its promise, total quality management does not always work. A few firms have had disappointing results. A recent survey of 500 executives showed that only about one-third of the respondents believed quality programs truly improved their competitiveness. In another survey of 300 companies, two-thirds reported that a quality program had not reduced defects by more than 10 percent.

Many organizational contingency factors can influence the success of a quality circle or TQM program (see Exhibit 16.6).[32] For example, one positive contingency factor is the task skill demands on employees in the QC. When skill demands are great, the quality circle can further enhance productivity. When tasks are simple and require low skills, improved skills from TQM training will have little impact on output. TQM or QC success also increases when the program serves to enrich jobs and improve employee motivation. In addition, when the quality program improves workers' problem-solving skills, productivity is likely to increase. When the participation and teamwork aspects of TQM are used to tackle significant problems, such as how to keep metal parts free of oil film, the outcome is better. TQM or quality circles should not be used to tackle simple, routine problems, such as where to locate the water cooler. Finally, a quality program has the greatest chance of success in a corporate culture that stresses continuous improvement as a way of life.

Quality programs often have trouble when senior management's expectations are too high. Managers quickly become disaffected if they are expecting immediate jumps in quality. Quality success comes through a series of small, incremental gains. Moreover, middle- and upper-level managers sometimes are dissatisfied because problem-solving opportunities are taken from them and given to employees on the shop floor. Also, when workers are dissatisfied with their organizational lives, quality programs have a smaller chance of success. Union leaders can also upset the quality program if they feel left out of the discussions between workers and management. Finally, if the corporate culture stresses big, dramatic innovations rather than continuous improvement, the quality program has less chance of adding significant improvements to productivity and output.

When correctly applied, quality programs generate enormous savings. At Lockheed, savings of $3 million were documented. At the Norfolk Naval Shipyard, savings of $3.41 for every dollar invested in a QC program were reported over an 18-month period. Another company that succeeded with a total quality program is Tellabs Inc.

E X H I B I T 16.6 Quality Program Success Factors	**Positive Factors**	**Negative Factors**
	▪ Tasks make high skill demands on employees.	▪ Management expectations are unrealistically high.
	▪ TQM serves to enrich jobs and motivate employees.	▪ Middle managers are dissatisfied about loss of authority.
	▪ Problem-solving skills are improved for all employees.	▪ Workers are dissatisfied with other aspects of organizational life.
	▪ Participation and teamwork are used to tackle significant problems.	▪ Union leaders are left out of QC discussions.
	▪ Continuous improvement is a way of life.	▪ Managers wait for big, dramatic innovations.

TELLABS INC.

Grace Pastiak is used to breaking new ground. As plant manager in one of Tellabs Inc.'s three operating divisions, she is one of the few female managers in the manufacturing field. Pastiak considers her division's quality program so important that she handles it personally. Instead of circulating memos or following formal communication channels, Pastiak prefers to deal one-on-one with workers on the factory floor to inspire them to produce high-quality products. She also takes two full days out of each month to teach her 170-employee work force a course in what the company calls total quality commitment. About a dozen workers at a time attend the hour-long sessions, taking time out from their usual duties of assembling sophisticated telephone equipment.

Pastiak considers her time well spent. "I cannot think of anything more important that I should be doing than empowering people," she says. "I want people to have a sense of accomplishment." The quality efforts also have helped the company. Before the program went into effect, Tellabs' president uncovered serious problems during a spot check in the stockrooms. "Only 70 percent of the samples he chose performed to specs," says vice-president Edward McDevitt.

Under the new management formula, workers are trained to inspect their own work and shut down production to correct errors. When the method was first tried as part of a pilot program, overseen by Pastiak, work-in-process inventory was reduced by 80 percent and the time to fill an order went from 22 days to 2. Now that the program has been extended to all divisions, improvements have been noted companywide. In Pastiak's division, where she is director of manufacturing, production goals are met 98 percent of the time, a significant improvement over the industry average of somewhere around 90 percent.[33] ∎

SUMMARY AND MANAGEMENT SOLUTION

This chapter introduced a number of important concepts about organizational control. Organizational control is the systematic process through which managers regulate organizational activities to meet planned standards of performance. The implementation of control includes four steps: establishing standards of performance, measuring actual performance, comparing performance to standards, and taking corrective action. Control should be linked to strategic planning. Changes in the environment require that internal control systems adapt to strategic changes; control systems must not continue measuring what was important in the past.

A new approach to control being widely adopted in Canada and the United States is total quality management, which reflects clan control ideas rather than traditional bureaucratic control. TQM involves everyone in the organization who is committed to the control function. Four major techniques of TQM are benchmarking, reduced cycle time, outsourcing, and continuous improvement. Quality circles, which are teams of 6 to 12 employees who identify quality problems and discuss solutions, are one means of implementing a quality control philosophy in an organization.

Recall from the management problem that the owner of Ecoprint could only maintain quality control by overseeing every aspect of the business himself. Instead of selling the printing company, Telschow decided to try satisfying customers by working as a team with his employees. "In time, it became obvious that we had unwittingly instituted a total-quality program," he says. Telschow started out by providing more training, being more open with his workers, and letting them know he needed their help and ideas. To give employees a stake in the company's success, he began a quarterly profit-sharing bonus. Then he started paying $5 cash on the spot to any employee who found a mistake on a work order. Although the company now doles out about $300 a year in rewards, the program results in an annual savings of $5,000. What's more, customer satisfaction tops 95 percent and nearly 100 percent of jobs are delivered on time. Perhaps best of all, there no longer is any need for Telschow to do everything himself. His workers outperform the industry average by better than 50 percent and the company's sales volume has increased six times faster than competitors. In 1991, Ecoprint became the first small business in Maryland to win the state-level U.S. Senate Productivity Award, which recognizes quality efforts. "A small business can manage by using total quality methods even if the firm doesn't call them TQM," says Telschow. "The important thing is that it is people—not robots—that make a quality program work."[34]

DISCUSSION QUESTIONS

1. What is the core control system? How do its components relate to one another for control of the organization?
2. Why is control an important management function? How does it relate to the other management functions of planning, organizing, and leading?
3. Briefly describe the four steps of control. Give an example of each step from your own organizational work experience.
4. What does it mean to say that organizational control should be linked to strategic planning?
5. How might organizations use reduced cycle time, benchmarking, or outsourcing to improve the quality of products and services?
6. What is the difference between bureaucratic and clan control? Which do you think is the stronger form?
7. Which three concepts associated with successful total quality programs do you consider most essential? Explain.
8. The theme of total quality control is "The burden of quality proof rests . . . with the makers of the part." How does this differ from traditional North American approaches to quality?
9. What is a quality circle? How can it be used to improve organizational quality control?

MANAGEMENT IN PRACTICE: EXPERIENTIAL EXERCISE

● **QUALITY IMPROVEMENT QUESTIONNAIRE**

For each item circle the number that best describes your attitude or behavior on the job or at school.

	Disagree			**Agree**	
1. I recognize the practical constraints of existing conditions when someone proposes an improvement idea.	5	4	3	2	1
2. I like to support change efforts, even when the idea may not work.	5	4	3	2	1
3. I believe that many small improvements are usually better than a few big improvements.	5	4	3	2	1
4. I encourage other people to express improvement ideas, even if they differ from mine.	5	4	3	2	1
5. There is truth to the statement, "If it isn't broke, don't fix it."	5	4	3	2	1
6. I work at the politics of change to build agreement for my improvement ideas.	5	4	3	2	1
7. I study suggestions carefully to avoid change just for the sake of change.	5	4	3	2	1
8. I like to have clear objectives that support improvement, even if changes upset my efficiency.	5	4	3	2	1
9. I constantly talk about ways to improve what I'm doing.	5	4	3	2	1
10. I am able to get higher-ups to support my ideas for improvement.	5	4	3	2	1

Total Score _____

Your score indicates the extent to which you are a positive force for quality improvement. The questions represent behaviors associated with the Japanese approach to companywide continuous improvement of quality.

- 40–50: Great. A dynamo for quality improvement.
- 30–40: Good. A positive force.
- 20–30: Adequate. You have a typical North American attitude.
- 10–20: Poor. You may be dragging down quality efforts.

Go back over the questions on which you scored lowest and develop a plan to improve your approach toward quality. Discuss your ideas with other students.

CASE FOR ANALYSIS

QUALITY SCANDAL IN FRANCE

Quality is important to every consumer. But with some products, such as pharmaceuticals, food, and cars, the consequences of poor quality can be a matter of life or death. Companies have strict quality control measures and initiate recalls at the first hint that flawed merchandise has inadvertently hit the market. An exception to the rule occurred in France in the mid-1980s for blood products used in transfusions. The repercussions are still being felt today.

The story originated in the 1980s after scientists first identified acquired immune deficiency syndrome, or AIDS. When the first cases were announced by the U.S. Centers for Disease Control in 1981, the disease was believed to be limited to homosexual men. It wasn't until several cases of AIDS were confirmed in hemophiliacs in 1983 that researchers began giving serious thought to the world's blood supply.

The possibility of AIDS being transmitted through the blood supply placed hemophiliacs at particularly high risk because they rely on donated blood for key proteins that prevent uncontrolled internal bleeding. Since the 1960s, most hemophiliacs had obtained the necessary clotting proteins from a concentrated powdered formula made from the pooled blood of hundreds of donors. But by putting the clotting factors in concentrated form, one donor with contaminated blood could affect an entire batch.

As concern about a possible AIDS epidemic mounted, the International Blood Transfusion Society in Munich issued heartening news. In July 1984, it announced that heating blood products could inactivate the AIDS virus. The findings were confirmed a few months later in a published report, which said that heat killed the AIDS virus and that heated blood concentrates could prevent infection.

The news meant that manufacturers of blood products would have to incorporate the heating methods into their production system in order to avoid the spread of the HIV infection. In France, that would be the chief responsibility of the National Center for Blood Transfusions (CNTS), which produced about half of the nation's supply of blood products.

Michel Garretta, then-director of the CNTS, responded by signing a deal to license a heat treatment from the Austrian firm Immuno. But refitting the French factory would take months, and the only way to ensure the safety of the blood products in the meantime would be to import concentrates that had been heat-treated in foreign labs.

It seemed simple enough on the surface, but there were a number of problems. For starters, buying the concentrates from foreign labs violated the government's stated goal of reducing imports of blood products. There also was the question of what to do with the stocks that had already been produced. There was little doubt that existing supplies were tainted with HIV antibodies, because each batch was made from as many as 5,000 pooled donations.

In a letter to the Ministry of Social Affairs written in May 1985, Garretta outlined the economic costs associated with importing the blood concentrate and destroying contaminated stock. Importing heat-treated blood concentrate would cost about $5 million, he wrote. Destroying contaminated stocks and making up the 20 percent production loss due to the heating process would cost millions more. Later that month, Garretta met with his top officers and reiterated that recalling contaminated products would entail "grave economic consequences."

Shortly thereafter, Garretta reached an agreement with the Association of French Hemophiliacs recommending that the government ban the sale of unheated blood concentrates beginning on October 1, 1985. That would give Garretta time to refit his plant. But the agreement did not address the issue of the stocks that had already been produced. "He (Garretta) never told us that stocks of unheated (blood concentrates) were contaminated," says Francis Graeve, the association's honorary president.

The consequences of those contaminated blood products were devastating. One French official testified at an inquiry that about 200 people per month were contaminated by blood from infected donors from April through August 1985.

Although the CNTS began heat-treating all blood products in July 1985, the center continued to sell its existing stock for another three months without warning hemophiliacs of the potential risk.

Although the French health ministry earned the world's scorn for not intervening sooner, a few jumped to the country's defense. Pim van Aacken, president of the European Plasma Fractionation Association (EPFA), says the safety of heat-treated blood concentrates wasn't clear in the mid-1980s.

EPFA vice-president Johannes Leikola claimed that France was no slower than other countries in introducing heat-treatment for blood-clotting factors. He said a 1990 survey of seven leading nonprofit laboratories found that an Australian lab was the first to introduce heat-treated clotting factors in November 1984. But it wasn't until October 1986 that all of the European laboratories surveyed were marketing the heat-treated concentrate.

The arguments did not help Garretta, who was relieved of his duties at the CNTS and later charged with "deception over the basic quality of a product." In October 1992, he was sentenced to four years in prison and ordered to pay a heavy fine.

For the more than 1,000 French hemophiliacs thought to have been infected with HIV, it was little consolation.

● **Q U E S T I O N S**

1. Considering that quality standards for blood products were still being formulated in the mid-1980s, what do you think of the CNTS' actions? Who was ultimately responsible for ensuring quality control, the CNTS or the government officials that oversaw the lab?
2. What, if anything, could the CNTS have done to improve the quality of its blood products and therefore help prevent the spread of HIV among hemophiliacs?
3. If a total quality management program had been in place at the CNTS, do you think the outcome would have been different? Why or why not?

SOURCE: Mark Hunter, "Blood Money," *Discover*, August 1993, 70–78; Andrea Dorfman, "Bad Blood in France," *Time*, July 8, 1991, 48; "French Blood Scandal Echoes Across Europe," *Nature*, October 31, 1991, 781; "France's Blood Scandal Draws Blood," *Nature*, October 29, 1992, 759; "Verdict in French Blood Trial Shames Science," *Nature*, October 29, 1992, 764.

REFERENCES

1. Roger Telschow, "Quality Begins at Home," *Nation's Business,* January 1993, 6.

2. Richard J. Schonberger, "Total Quality Management Cuts a Broad Swath— Through Manufacturing and Beyond," *Organizational Dynamics* (Spring 1992), 16–28; Leah Nathans Spiro, "Raging Bull," *Business Week,* November 25, 1991, 218–221; and Ronald Henkoff, "Make Your Office More Productive," *Fortune,* February 25, 1991, 72–84.

3. "Quality: The Soul of Productivity, the Key to Future Business Growth," *Interview,* Inter-City Gas Corporation, vol. 3 (Autumn 1988), 3–5. The story was originally related by Patrick Lush in *The Globe & Mail,* Toronto, June 15, 1988.

4. Ibid.; and T. K. Das, "Organizational Control: An Evolutionary Perspective," *Journal of Management Studies* 26 (1989), 459–475.

5. Stephen G. Green and M. Ann Welsh, "Cybernetics and Dependence: Reframing the Control Concept," *Academy of Management Review* 13 (1988), 287–301; and Kenneth A. Merchant, *Control in Business Organizations* (Marshfield, Mass.: Pitman, 1985).

6. Henkoff, "Make Your Office More Productive."

7. Robert Simons, "Strategic Orientation and Top Management Attention to Control Systems," *Strategic Management Journal* 12 (1991), 49–62; and E. G. Flamholtz, "Accounting, Budgeting and Control Systems in Their Organizational Context: Theoretical and Empirical Perspectives," *Accounting, Organizations and Society 8* (1983), 153–169.

8. Richard L. Daft and Norman B. Macintosh, "The Nature and Use of Formal Control Systems for Management Control and Strategy Implementation," *Journal of Management* 10 (1984), 43–66.

9. William G. Ouchi, "Markets, Bureaucracies, and Clans," *Administrative Science Quarterly* 25 (1980), 129–141; and B. R. Baligia and Alfred M. Jaeger, "Multinational Corporations: Control Systems and Delegation Issues," *Journal of International Business Studies* (Fall 1984), 25–40.

10. Jeffrey Rothfeder and Michele Galen, "Is Your Boss Spying on You?" *Business Week,* January 15, 1990, 74–75; and Marlene C. Piturro, "Employee Performance Monitoring . . . or Meddling?" *Management Review,* May 19, 1989, 31–33.

11. Beverly H. Burris, "Technocratic Organization and Control," *Organization Studies* 10 (1989), 1–22.

12. Richard E. Walton, "From Control to Commitment in the Workplace," *Harvard Business Review* (March–April 1985), 76–84.

13. Ellen Wojahn, "Will the Company Please Come to Order," *INC.,* March 1986, 78–86; and "Honor Roll of U.S. Exporters," *Business America,* March 12, 1990, 20.

14. John Loring, "Dr. Deming's Traveling Quality Show," *Canadian Business,* September 1990, 38–42; Nancy K. Austin, "Dr. Deming and the 'Q' Factor,"

Working Woman, September 1991, 31–34; and Ross Johnson and William O. Winchell, "Management and Quality," American Society for Quality Control, 1989.

15. A. V. Feigenbaum, *Total Quality Control: Engineering and Management* (New York: McGraw-Hill, 1961).

16. Philip B. Crosby, *Quality Is Free: The Art of Making Quality Certain* (New York: McGraw-Hill, 1979); and Mary Walton, *The Deming Management Method* (New York: Dodd-Meade & Co., 1986).

17. Richard J. Schonberger, "Production Workers Bear Major Quality Responsibility in Japanese Industry," *Industrial Engineering* (December 1982), 34–40.

18. John Case, "Customer Service: The Last Word," *INC.,* April 1991, 89–93.

19. Jerry G. Bowles, "Beyond Customer Satisfaction through Quality Improvement," *Fortune,* September 26, 1988, special insert.

20. Donna Brown, "Ten Ways to Boost Quality," *Management Review,* January 1991, 5; Schonberger, "Total Quality Management Cuts a Broad Swath—Through Manufacturing and Beyond"; and Michael Barrier, "Small Firms Put Quality First," *Nation's Business,* May 1992, 22–32.

21. Schonberger, "Production Workers."

22. Johnson and Winchell, "Management and Quality"; and Edward E. Lawler III and Susan A. Mohrman, "Quality Circles after the Fad," *Harvard Business Review* (January–February 1985), 65–71.

23. Thomas A. Stewart, "Westinghouse Gets Respect at Last," *Fortune,* July 3, 1989, 92–98.

24. Howard Rothman, "You Need Not Be Big to Benchmark," *Nation's Business,* December 1992, 64–65.

25. Otis Port and Geoffrey Smith, "Beg, Borrow and Benchmark," *Business Week,* November 30, 1992, 74–75.

26. Rothman, "You Need Not Be Big to Benchmark," 64–65.

27. Donna Brown, "Outsourcing: How Companies Take Their Business Elsewhere," *Management Review,* February 1992, 16–18; and David Kirkpatrick, "Why Not Farm Out Your Computing?" *Fortune,* September 23, 1991, 103–112.

28. Philip R. Thomas, Larry J. Gallace, and Kenneth R. Martin, "Quality Alone Is Not Enough," *AMA Management Briefing* (New York: American Management Association, 1992).

29. Otis Port, John Carey, Kevin Kelly, and Stephanie Anderson Forest, "Quality: Small and Midsize Companies Seize the Challenge Not a Moment Too Soon," *Business Week,* November 30, 1992, 68–72.

30. "Beyond Total Quality," *Success,* October 1990, 48–49.

31. Robert W. Haney and Charles D. Beaman, Jr., "Management Leadership Critical to CQI Success," *Hospitals,* July 20, 1992, 64.

32. Rick Tetzeli, "News/Trends: Making Quality More Than a Fad," *Fortune,* May 18, 1992, 12–13; Thomas et al., "Quality Alone Is Not Enough"; David E.

Bowen and Edward E. Lawler III, "Total Quality-Oriented Human Resources Management," *Organizational Dynamics* (Spring 1992), 29–41; Robert Wood, Frank Hull, and Koya Azumi, "Evaluating Quality Circles: The American Application," *California Management Review* 26 (Fall 1983), 37–53; and Gregory P. Shea, "Quality Circles: The Danger of Bottled Change," *Sloan Management Review* 27 (Spring 1986), 33–46.

33. John Holusha, "Grace Pastiak's Web of Inclusion," *The New York Times,* May 5, 1991, F1.

34. Telschow, "Quality Begins at Home," 6.

MANAGEMENT CONTROL SYSTEMS

17

CHAPTER OUTLINE

LEARNING OBJECTIVES

After studying this chapter, you should be able to

- Describe financial statements, financial analysis, and financial audits used for top management controls.

- Explain the concept of responsibility centers and their relationship to operating and financial budgets.

- Explain the advantages of top-down versus bottom-up budgeting.

- Describe zero-based budgeting and how it applies to organizations.

- Describe organizational indicators of inadequate control systems.

Darren Adler started his first business in Oxfordshire when he was only 15 years old. The candy company he founded turned out to be so successful that it was featured on British television. When Adler decided he needed to devote his full attention to school, he sought the help of a top-notch accountant who put the company's books in order and helped him sell off the assets.

■ Adler's second attempt at running his own business was not nearly as successful. Like the first time around, he knew how to market himself and his product. But this time, he tried to save money on accountants' fees and didn't bother with a formal budget. Within three months, the business had failed, leaving him tens of thousands of dollars in the red. Before Adler embarked on his third business venture, he wanted to make sure he learned from his mistakes. How can Adler keep better financial control of his new business? What would you recommend he do?[1]

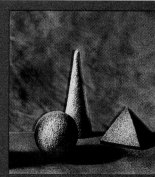

The difficulties encountered by Darren Adler illustrate a problem of control—his second business went bankrupt because he didn't have control of his finances or a proper budget. But financial management techniques do not provide a solution to every company's problems. In fact, some critics have characterized traditional techniques as inadequate and out of date in this era of rapid change and global competition. Concepts such as discounted cash flow analysis for plant and equipment purchases, for example, are abstract and theoretical. Rather than rely on such an abstract concept, many managers are learning that they are better off asking workers which piece of equipment they need to be more efficient.[2] And cost accounting systems, which are supposed to tell managers the cost and profitability of each product line, were designed 70 years ago to evaluate inventory. Today inventories are minimized, and the cost system assigns numbers that price some products too high and some too low, thereby weakening strategic competitiveness.[3] Knowing accurate costs would let managers know which product lines to expand and where to reduce prices.

Despite these weaknesses, managers need management control systems, including financial analysis, budgets, management by objectives, and other statistical reports. These control systems provide formal data and reports for management problem identification and corrective action. Control systems can be used with the clan approach to control described in Chapter 16. The Japanese pioneered quality circles and other clan approaches, and one study showed that managers in Japanese firms also had more quantitative information available from formal control systems than did managers in U.S. firms.[4]

Every organization needs basic systems for allocating financial resources, approving and developing human resources, analyzing financial performance, and evaluating operational productivity. In long-established organizations such as Cummins Engine, Lever Brothers, and Mack Trucks, the challenge for managers is to know how to use these control systems and improve them. In new, entrepreneurial firms—especially those that have grown rapidly—managers must design and implement new control systems.

The Leading Edge box illustrates how one company implemented a new control system.

● TOP MANAGEMENT FINANCIAL CONTROL

Based on the overall strategic plan, top management must define a financial forecast for the organization, perform financial analyses of selected ratios to reveal business performance, and use financial audits to evaluate internal operations. Each of these controls is based on financial statements—the building blocks of financial control.

LEADING edge

GATEWAY 2000

For Ted Waitt and Gateway 2000, the road ahead will have plenty of dangerous curves and hazards that seemingly materialize out of nowhere. We already know from Chapter 15 that IBM, Dell, and Compaq will be throwing around their considerable weight in the computer industry. Most direct-marketers will either compete on price, service, hot new technology, or some other means of separating their company from the rest of the pack. But no matter how product emphasis shakes out, one thing will likely be uniform throughout the industry. Whatever a firm decides to produce, it had better be able to do so at the lowest cost possible.

A few years back, the numbers didn't stack up well for Gateway competitors. The company's South Dakota base, with its cheap labor and no state income tax, has always been a cost advantage. A quick comparison of P&L statements shows just how tough things were. Dell's selling, general, and administrative costs amounted to about 21 percent of total expenses; Compaq spent 19.6 percent in this expense category. Gateway got by using 10.7 percent for SG&A, more than a little wiggle room when the time came to start pricing products. The gap has narrowed somewhat, but Gateway still holds a big edge.

The "necessity as the mother of invention" cliche has always applied at Gateway. The combination of starting operations in a vacant farmhouse, a lack of outside investors, and Waitt's insistence that all expenses that don't add to customer satisfaction be eliminated ingrained austerity into the company culture. Controlling inventory costs by limiting the number of components on hand combined with just-in-time assembly of product orders provided Gateway with another cost advantage. The bare bones approach enabled the company to live with lower profit margins while relying on bigger volume, yet still consistently under-pricing rivals.

Despite the fact Gateway employees are obsessed with controlling costs and actually talk about the evils of frills and overindulgence, Waitt knows of one area where too much penny pinching can cost sales. In the past, some customers have complained that the company's technical support falls short of the mark. Sensing the potential for big problems, Waitt doubled the personnel in that department. An additional 14 technicians were also added to the company's electronic bulletin-board service. The time callers spend on hold has been cut in half. Waitt still hopes to attain the goal of answering every customer call on the first ring.

For the future, Waitt plans to try grabbing off pieces of the corporate market, and making inroads into Europe. Critics at competitor Dell charge Gateway probably won't make much headway in either effort without investing more in both research and development and the kind of support personnel big cor-porations have grown to expect from suppliers. Waitt has no plans to develop technologies and thinks it can sell to the big boys without raising prices to existing customers.

One thing is for certain. Waitt won't tinker much with the low-cost formula that's gotten him this far. He'll use Gateway's size to save on purchasing. The abundant cash supply will be invested into methods of obtaining greater efficiencies. The company relocated to a 44,000-square-foot facility and organized under a cellular manufacturing plan. As a result, productivity should increase as much as 30 percent.

Waitt and Gateway 2000 have come a long way from the abandoned farmhouse, but so far they have remained true to their cost-conscious roots. Waitt isn't concerned with competitors who say stepping up to the next level will be impossible without bigger investments in technologies and support and training. He isn't expecting any Sunday drive, and he doesn't sound worried about what anyone else thinks. "Our biggest competitor is ourselves," he says. "And that keeps us busy." ■

SOURCE: Joshua Hyatt, "Betting The Farm," *Inc.*, December 1991, 36–45; John Holten, "Head 'Em Up," *Sunday World Herald*, January 23, 1994, 14A; Lois Therrien, "Why Gateway Is Racing to Answer on the First Ring," *Business Week*, September 13, 1993, 92–94; Michael Noer, "New Kid on the Block," *Forbes*, February 14, 1994, 178; Kyle Pope, "Gateway to Offer 10.9 Million Shares at $13 to $15 Each," *The Wall Street Journal*, October 22, 1993, A9; and Charles Cooper, "The Color of Money," *Computer Shopper*, February 1994, 61–78.

FINANCIAL STATEMENTS: THE BASIC NUMBERS

Financial statements provide the basic information used for financial control of a company. Two major financial statements—the balance sheet and the income statement—are the starting points for financial control.

The **balance sheet** shows the firm's financial position with respect to assets and liabilities at a specific point in time. An example of a balance sheet is presented in Exhibit 17.1. The balance sheet provides three types of information: assets, liabilities, and owners' equity. *Assets* are what the company owns and include *current assets* (assets that can be converted into cash in a short time period) and *fixed assets* (assets such as buildings and equipment that are long term in nature). *Liabilities* are the firm's debts and include both *current debt* (obligations that will be paid by the company in the near future) and *long-term debt* (obligations payable over a long period). *Owners' equity* is the difference between assets and liabilities and is the company's net worth in stock and retained earnings.

The **income statement,** sometimes called a *profit-and-loss statement,* summarizes the firm's financial performance for a given time interval, usually one year. A sample income statement is given in Exhibit 17.2. Some firms calculate the income statement at three-month intervals during the year to see if they are on target for sales and profits. The income statement shows revenues coming into the organization from all sources

balance sheet

A financial statement showing the firm's financial position with respect to assets and liabilities at a specific point in time.

income statement

A financial statement that summarizes a company's financial performance over a given time interval.

EXHIBIT 17.1

Balance Sheet

Lester's Clothiers
Consolidated Balance Sheet
December 31, 1993

Assets			Liabilities and Owners' Equity		
Current assets:			Current liabilities:		
Cash	$ 25,000		Accounts payable	$200,000	
Accounts receivable	75,000		Accrued expenses	20,000	
Inventory	500,000		Income taxes payable	30,000	
Total current assets		$ 600,000	Total current liabilities		$ 250,000
Fixed assets:			Long-term liabilities:		
Land	250,000		Mortgages payable	350,000	
Buildings and fixtures	1,000,000		Bonds outstanding	250,000	
Less depreciation	200,000		Total long-term liabilities		$ 600,000
Total fixed assets		1,050,000	Owners' equity:		
			Common stock	540,000	
			Retained earnings	260,000	
			Total owners' equity		800,000
Total assets		$1,650,000	Total liabilities and net worth		$1,650,000

EXHIBIT 17.2

Income Statement

Lester's Clothiers
Statement of Income
For the Year Ended December 31, 1993

Gross sales	$3,100,000	
Less sales returns	200,000	
Net sales		$2,900,000
Less expenses and cost of goods sold:		
Cost of goods sold	2,110,000	
Depreciation	60,000	
Sales expenses	200,000	
Administrative expenses	90,000	2,460,000
Operating profit		440,000
Other income		20,000
Gross income		460,000
Less interest expense	80,000	
Income before taxes		380,000
Less taxes	165,000	
Net income		$ 215,000

and subtracts all expenses, including cost of goods sold, interest, taxes, and depreciation. The bottom line indicates the net income—profit or loss—for the given time period.

For example, Jim Greenwood, founder of Aahs!, a specialty retailing chain in California, used the income statement to detect that sales and profits were dropping during the summer months. He immediately evaluated company activities and closed two money-losing stores. He also began a new education program to teach employees how to increase sales and decrease costs to improve net income. As a result, the Aahs! gross profit margin was 3 percent ahead of target.[5] This use of the income statement follows the control cycle described in Chapter 16, beginning with the measurement of actual performance and then taking corrective action to improve performance to meet targets.

FINANCIAL ANALYSIS: INTERPRETING THE NUMBERS

The most important numbers typically are not actual dollars spent or earned, but ratios. Any business is a set of hundreds of relationships among people, things, and events.[6] Key relationships are typically revealed in ratios that provide insight into some aspect of company behavior. These insights make manager decision making possible.

A *financial ratio* is the comparison of two financial numbers. To understand their business, managers have to understand financial ratios. For example, a small corner grocery store had plenty of customers but was losing money. The store's financial numbers looked okay, so the owners sought help. The consultant said the books looked good, except for the labor cost ratio, indicating labor costs were 18 percent of revenues. The owners did not know that a specialty food retailer typically cannot make a profit if labor exceeds 10 percent of sales. They cut labor and the store has been profitable ever since. When Paul Hawken started Smith & Hawken, he learned an absolutely vital ratio. In the catalog business, the cost of goods, the catalog, and any advertising must not exceed 70 percent of revenue. Monitoring this single ratio tells him how things are going on a weekly basis and whether to add or reduce labor.[7]

Several financial ratios can be studied to interpret company performance. Managers must decide which ratios reveal the most important relationships for their business. Frequently calculated ratios typically pertain to liquidity, activity, and profitability. Many companies compare their performance with those of other firms in the same industry as well as with their own budget targets.

liquidity ratio

A financial ratio that indicates the company's ability to meet its current debt obligations.

LIQUIDITY RATIO.   A **liquidity ratio** indicates the organization's ability to meet its current debt obligations. For example, the *current ratio* tells whether there are sufficient assets to convert into cash to pay off debts if needed. If a hypothetical company, Oceanographics, Inc., had current assets of $600,000 and current liabilities of $250,000, the current ratio is 2.4, meaning it has sufficient funds to pay off immediate debts 2.4 times. This is normally considered a satisfactory margin of safety.

activity ratio

A ratio that measures the firm's internal performance with respect to key activities defined by management.

ACTIVITY RATIO.   An **activity ratio** measures internal performance with respect to key activities defined by management. For example, *inventory turnover* is calculated by dividing total sales by average inventory. This ratio tells how many times the inventory is turned over to meet the total sales figure. If inventory sits too long, money is wasted. For Oceanographics, Inc., inventory turnover is 10, which compares favorably to industry standards. The *conversion ratio* is purchase orders divided by customer inquiries, which measures company effectiveness in converting inquiries into sales. For Oceanographics, Inc., this ratio is 50 percent, which is low compared with 60 percent for the industry. A sharp manager will infer that the number of inquiries is low or the sales force is doing a poor job closing sales. After investigation, improvements will be made either in promotional advertising or sales force training.

profitability ratio

A financial ratio that describes the firm's profits.

PROFITABILITY RATIO.   **Profitability ratios** describe the organization's profits. One important profitability ratio is the *profit margin on sales,* which is calculated as net income divided by sales. For Oceanographics, Inc., the profit margin on sales is 8 percent. Another profitability measure is *return on total assets (ROA),* which is the percentage return to investors on assets. It is a valuable yardstick of the return on investment compared with other investment opportunities. Return on total assets for Oceanographics is 13 percent, which means senior managers are making good use of assets to earn profits; thus, the owners are unlikely to sell the company and invest their money elsewhere.

Analyzing these various financial ratios can help managers of U.S. companies understand their business more clearly, especially with the increase in global competition. One company that has learned to use financial ratios to its advantage is Health Management Resources.

HEALTH MANAGEMENT RESOURCES, INC.

Larry Stifler, founder of Health Management Resources, Inc., weight-loss business, has a Ph.D. in behavioral psychology. But he also has an unusual knack for math that has helped ensure his company's revenues have increased every year since it was started in 1983. "I do everything by the numbers," Stifler says. But he doesn't mean that in the traditional sense. HMR has no budgets and shuns the standard cost-accounting approach of looking strictly at revenues and expenses. Instead, Stifler views his company as a set of relationships and uses ratios to express them.

In all, Stifler considers about 18 different ratios with net revenue being the common denominator in each category. He builds mathematical models that reflect important relationships within the business and establish appropriate targets. He then calculates the actual numbers to see how they measure up. Under Stifler's system, it doesn't matter if a cost category goes up, as long as it is the same percentage of revenues as established by the model.

For instance, Stifler measures productivity by dividing the monthly net revenues by the number of employees in the company. "If productivity is the same or better from month to month then we're OK," he says. If the figure goes down, he knows something is wrong. Sometimes the calculation is even more straightforward. If, for example, a reasonable patient-staff ratio is 50 to 1, Stifler knows that for every 50 new patients he will need a new employee, telephone, and office furniture.

Because every HMR patient who stays with the program long enough to move into the maintenance stage recommends 2.2 patients who follow suit, Stifler has come up with another all-important ratio. He figures that every dollar spent giving good care is repaid 2.2 times. "So," he says, "set up the business for quality care and it'll grow by itself."[8] ■

FINANCIAL AUDITS: VERIFYING THE NUMBERS

Financial audits are independent appraisals of the organization's financial records. Audits are of two types—external and internal.[9] An *external audit* is conducted by experts from outside the organization, typically certified public accountants (CPAs) or CPA firms. An *internal audit* is handled by experts within the organization. Large companies such as Allis-Chalmers, American Can, Boise Cascade, and Boeing have an accounting staff assigned to the internal audit function. The internal auditors evaluate departments and divisions throughout the corporation to ensure that operations are efficient and conducted according to prescribed company practices.

Both external and internal audits should be very thorough. Their purpose is to examine every nook and cranny to verify that the financial

financial audit

An independent appraisal of the organization's financial records, conducted by external or internal experts.

statement represents actual company operations. The following are some of the areas examined by auditors:

- *Cash:* Go to banks and confirm bank balances; review cash management procedures.
- *Receivables:* Obtain guarantees from customers concerning amounts owed and anticipated payments; confirm balances.
- *Inventory:* Conduct physical count of inventory and compare with financial statement; review for obsolescence.
- *Fixed assets:* Make physical observation, evaluate depreciation; determine whether insurance is adequate.
- *Loans:* Review loan agreements; summarize obligations.
- *Revenues and expenses:* Evaluate timing, propriety, and amount.[10]

USING FINANCIAL CONTROLS

Remember that the point of financial numbers is to gain insight into company relationships to identify areas out of control and take corrective action. Managers must use numbers wisely and see beneath the surface to decide exactly what is causing the problem and devise a solution. A financial performance shortfall often has several causes, and managers must be familiar with company operations and activities in order to make an accurate diagnosis. Managers can use numbers creatively and dig beneath the figures to find the causes of problems. After defining the causes, they can initiate programs that will rectify the problem and bring the financial figures back into line.

One superb example of using financial controls to bring a small company back into line occurred at Incomnet, Inc. Sam Schwartz, a major

Financial control often involves the use of computer spreadsheet programs and human analysis. Close monitoring of financial results allows managers to accurately forecast revenues and expenses for the company.

investor, took over the company after the financial statements suggested impending disaster.

 INCOMNET

Incomnet is a technology company in California that recently had annual sales of $1.2 million for its computer network that tracks used car parts for auto repair shops. Incomnet experienced extraordinary demand and overextended, growing far beyond its financial resources. Just five years old, the company had eaten up $13 million in investments without anything resembling a profit. When Schwartz took over, he interviewed everyone about problems, and he examined every line in Incomnet's woeful financial statements.

A close examination of the balance sheet showed that the current assets figure of $1.3 million was bloated because of obsolete and unsellable inventory. Moreover, accounts receivable were in disarray, with payments averaging 110 days. Further analysis and writeoffs dropped current assets to a small $180,000, but this was a number Schwartz could trust. Revamping accounts receivable led to customer payments for monthly services in advance, allowing cash flow to shift from a negative $60,000 monthly to a positive $50,000. Schwartz also found expenses too high, with "administrative expenses" out of control. Corporate overhead was $900,000 on sales of just $1.2 million. Schwartz moved to combine all corporate operations under one roof, pulled the plug on health club fees and luxury cars, and shrank the overhead figure to an acceptable $400,000 a year.

These changes were dramatic, and they changed the financial performance sharply. In two years, Incomnet saw its first profit—about $250,000 on sales of $2.7 million. Financial controls made the difference.[11] ■

MIDDLE MANAGEMENT BUDGET CONTROL

Budgets are a primary control device for middle management. Of course, top managers too are involved with budgets for the company as a whole, but middle managers are responsible for the budget performance of their departments or divisions. Budgets identify both planned and actual expenditures for cash, assets, raw materials, salaries, and other resources departments need. Budgets are the most widely used control system, because they plan and control resources and revenues essential to the firm's health and survival.[12]

A budget is created for every division or department within the organization, no matter how small, so long as it performs a distinct project, program, or function. In order for budgets to be used, the organization must define each department as a responsibility center.

RESPONSIBILITY CENTERS

responsibility center

Any organizational department under the supervision of a single individual who is responsible for its activity.

A responsibility center is the fundamental unit of analysis of a budget control system. A **responsibility center** is defined as any organizational department under the supervision of a single person who is responsible for its activity.[13] A three-person appliance sales office in Watertown, New York, is a responsibility center, as is General Electric's entire refrigerator manufacturing plant. The manager of each unit has budget "responsibility."

There are four major types of responsibility centers—cost centers, revenue centers, profit centers, and investment centers. The budget focus for each type of cost center is illustrated in Exhibit 17.3.

COST CENTER.   A *cost center* is a responsibility center in which the manager is held responsible for controlling cost inputs. The manager is responsible for salaries, supplies, and other costs relevant to the department's operation. Staff departments such as personnel, legal, and research typically are organized as cost centers, and budgets reflect the cost to run the department.

REVENUE CENTER.   In a *revenue center,* the budget is based on generated revenues or income. Sales and marketing departments frequently are revenue centers. The department has a revenue goal, such as $3,500,000. Assuming that each salesperson can generate $250,000 of revenue per year, the department can be allocated 14 salespeople. Revenue budgets can also be calculated as the number of items to be sold rather than as total revenues. For example, the revenue budget for an appliance

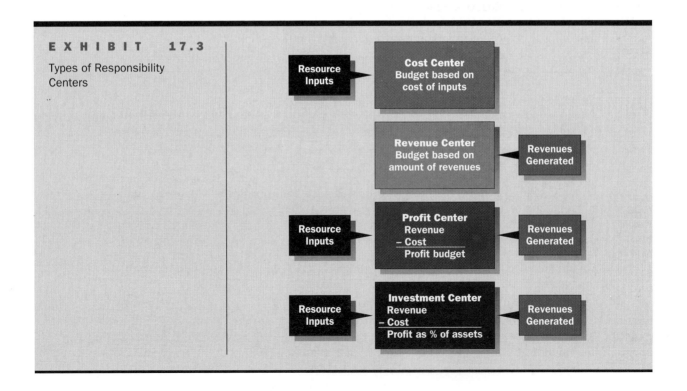

EXHIBIT   17.3

Types of Responsibility Centers

shop might include 50 refrigerators, 75 washers, 60 dryers, and 40 microwaves to be sold for 1994.

PROFIT CENTER. In a *profit center,* the budget measures the difference between revenues and costs. For budget purposes, the profit center is defined as a self-contained unit to enable a profit to be calculated. In Kollmorgen Corporation, each division is a profit center. Control is based on profit targets rather than on cost or revenue targets.

INVESTMENT CENTER. An *investment center* is based on the value of assets employed to produce a given level of profit. Profits are calculated in the same way as in a profit center, but for control purposes, managers are concerned with return on the investment in assets for the division. For example, Exxon may acquire a gasoline refinery for a price of $40 million. If Exxon managers target a 10 percent return on investment, the gasoline refinery will be expected to generate profits of $4 million a year. Exxon managers are not concerned with the absolute dollar value of costs, revenues, or profits so long as the budgeted return on assets reaches 10 percent.

RELATIONSHIP TO STRUCTURE. Responsibility centers are closely related to the types of organization structure described in Chapter 8. Cost centers and revenue centers typically exist in a functional structure. The production, assembly, finance, accounting, and human resource departments control expenditures through cost budgets. Marketing or sales departments, however, often are controlled as revenue centers. Profit centers typically exist in a divisional structure. Each self-contained division can be evaluated on the basis of total revenues minus total costs, which equals profits. Finally, very large companies in which each division is an autonomous business use investment centers. Frito-Lay and Taco Bell are investment centers for PepsiCo. PepsiCo managers are concerned with the return on investment from these companies, and each business is left alone so long as investment goals are met.

OPERATING BUDGETS

An **operating budget** is the financial plan for each organizational responsibility center for the budget period. The operating budget outlines the financial resources allocated to each responsibility center in dollar terms, typically calculated for a year in advance. The most common types of operating budgets are expense, revenue, and profit budgets.

EXPENSE BUDGET. An **expense budget** outlines the anticipated expenses for each responsibility center and for the total organization. Expense budgets apply to cost centers, as described above. The department of management at the University of Illinois may have a travel budget of $24,000; thus, the department head knows that the expense budget can be spent at approximately $2,000 per month. Three different kinds of expenses normally are evaluated in the expense budget—fixed, variable, and discretionary.

    Fixed costs are based on a commitment from a prior budget period and cannot be changed. The price of expensive machinery purchased

operating budget

The plan for the allocation of financial resources to each organizational responsibility center for the budget period under consideration.

expense budget

An operating budget that outlines the anticipated expenses for each responsibility center and for the organization as a whole.

fixed costs

Costs that are based on a commitment from a previous budget period and cannot be altered.

three years ago that is paid over a period of 10 years is a fixed cost. The same is true for the annual mortgage payments on a building amortized over 15 years.

Variable costs, often called *engineered costs,* are based on an explicit physical relationship with the volume of departmental activity. Variable costs are calculated in manufacturing departments when a separate cost can be assigned for each product produced. A variable cost budget might allocate two hours of machine time for each turbine blade or $3 in supplies for each integrated circuit board. The greater the volume of production, the greater the expense budget the department will have.

Discretionary costs are based on management decisions. They are not based on a fixed, long-term commitment or on volume of items produced, because discretionary costs cannot be calculated with precision. In the judgment of top management, an expense budget of $120,000 might be assigned to the inspection department to pay the salaries of four inspectors, one assistant, and one secretary. This budget could be increased or decreased the following year, depending on whether management feels more inspectors are needed.

REVENUE BUDGET.   A **revenue budget** identifies the revenues required by the organization. The revenue budget is the responsibility of a revenue center, such as marketing or sales. The revenue budget for a small manufacturing firm could be $3 million, based on sales of 600,000 items at $5 each. The revenue budget of $6 million for a local school district would be calculated not on sales to customers but on the community's current tax rate and property values.

PROFIT BUDGET.   A **profit budget** combines both expense and revenue budgets into one statement to show gross and net profits. Profit budgets apply to profit and investment centers. If a bank has budgeted income of $2 million and budgeted expenses of $1,800,000, the estimated profit will be $200,000. If the budget profit is unacceptable, managers must develop a plan for increasing revenues or decreasing costs to achieve an acceptable profit return.

FINANCIAL BUDGETS

Financial budgets define where the organization will receive its cash and how it intends to spend it. Three important financial budgets are the cash, capital expenditure, and balance sheet budgets.

CASH BUDGET.   The **cash budget** estimates cash flows on a daily or weekly basis to ensure that the organization has sufficient cash to meet its obligations. The cash budget shows the level of funds flowing through the organization and the nature of cash disbursements. If the cash budget shows that the firm has more cash than necessary, the company can arrange to invest the excess cash in Treasury bills to earn interest income. If the cash budget shows a payroll expenditure of $20,000 coming at the end of the week but only $10,000 in the bank, the controller must borrow cash to meet the payroll.

---

variable costs

Costs that are based on an explicit physical relationship with the volume of departmental activity; also called *engineered costs.*

discretionary costs

Costs based on management decisions and not on fixed commitments or volume of output.

revenue budget

An operating budget that identifies the revenues required by the organization.

profit budget

An operating budget that combines both expense and revenue budgets into one statement showing gross and net profits.

financial budget

A budget that defines where the organization will receive its cash and how it will spend it.

cash budget

A financial budget that estimates cash flows on a daily or weekly basis to ensure that the company has sufficient cash to meet its obligations.

CAPITAL EXPENDITURE BUDGET.   The **capital expenditure budget** plans future investments in major assets such as buildings, trucks, and heavy machinery. *Capital expenditures* are major purchases that are paid for over several years. Capital expenditures must be budgeted to determine their impact on cash flow and whether revenues are sufficient to cover capital expenditures and annual operating expenditures. Large corporations such as Navistar, Scott Paper, and Joseph E. Seagram & Sons assign financial analysts to work exclusively on the development of a capital expenditure budget. The analysts also monitor whether actual capital expenditures are being made according to plan.

BALANCE SHEET BUDGET.   The **balance sheet budget** plans the amount of assets and liabilities for the end of the time period under consideration. It indicates whether the capital expenditures and cash management, revenues, and operating expenses will mesh into the financial results desired by senior management. The balance sheet budget shows where future financial problems may exist. Financial ratio analysis can be performed on the balance sheet and profit budgets to see whether important ratio targets, such as debt to total assets or ROA, will be met.

The relationships among the operating and financial budgets are illustrated in Exhibit 17.4. All company budgets are interconnected. The revenue budget combined with the cost budget leads to the profit budget. The profit budget influences the amount of cash available, which in turn determines the amount of capital purchases the company can afford. The data from these budgets enable calculation of the balance sheet budget.

Rapid change and fluctuation in some industries makes budgeting, especially cash budgeting, extremely difficult. Trinity Computing Systems discovered how to manage its cash budget despite industry fluctuations.

capital expenditure budget

A financial budget that plans future investments in major assets to be paid for over several years.

balance sheet budget

A financial budget that plans the amount of assets and liabilities for the end of the time period under consideration.

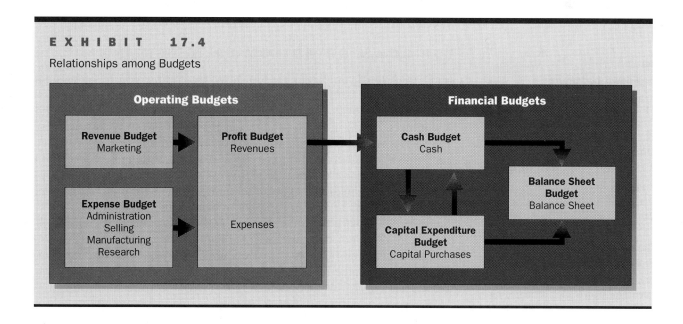

E X H I B I T   17.4

Relationships among Budgets

TRINITY COMPUTING SYSTEMS

Jim Pritchett and Dana Sellers, owners of Trinity Computing Systems, face many challenges. Their company's computers are installed in hospitals, but the average $200,000 price tag means slow payments over several months while the computer is installed and hospital personnel are fully trained. Unpredictable payments from clients, rapidly growing sales, and demands for payment from vendors created a wildly fluctuating cash flow that was handled by day-to-day crisis management. To solve the problem, Trinity went to a weekly financial cash budget, accompanied by a weekly forecast of cash coming in and flowing out, and a weekly meeting to discuss the cash situation with department heads. By collecting information on inventory, shipping dates, installation schedules, and collection dates every week, department heads could coordinate available resources and keep abreast of potential cash problems. The detailed cash budget enabled Trinity to reduce collections from 120 days to 80 days. Precise forecasting also strengthened Trinity's ability to borrow money and to buy goods on credit because the tight schedules testified to Trinity's sound management practices. Adopting a weekly cash budget literally saved Trinity from bankruptcy. As one manager said, "Without the cash-flow forecast, I doubt we would have had a product line worth selling."[14] ∎

THE BUDGETING PROCESS

The budgeting process is concerned with how budgets are actually formulated and implemented in an organization. In this section, we will briefly describe the procedure many companies use to develop the budget for the coming year.

TOP-DOWN OR BOTTOM-UP BUDGETING

top-down budgeting

A budgeting process in which middle- and lower-level managers set departmental budget targets in accordance with overall company revenues and expenditures specified by top management.

Many traditional companies use **top-down budgeting,** which is consistent with the bureaucratic control approach discussed in Chapter 16. The budgeted amounts for the coming year are literally imposed on middle- and lower-level managers.[15] The top-down process has certain advantages: Top managers have information on overall economic projections; they know the financial goals and forecasts; and they have reliable information about the amount of resources available in the coming year. Thus, the top-down process enables managers to set budget targets for each department to meet the needs of overall company revenues and expenditures.

The problem with the top-down budgeting process is that lower managers often are not committed to achieving budget targets. They are excluded from the budgeting process and resent their lack of involvement in deciding the resources available to their departments in the coming year.[16]

bottom-up budgeting

A budgeting process in which lower-level managers budget their departments' resource needs and pass them up to top management for approval.

In response to these negative outcomes, many organizations adopt **bottom-up budgeting,** which is in line with the clan approach to control. Lower managers anticipate their departments' resource needs, which are passed up the hierarchy and approved by top management. The advantage of the bottom-up process is that lower managers are able to identify resource requirements about which top managers are uninformed, have information on efficiencies and opportunities in their specialized areas, and are motivated to meet the budget because the budget plan is their responsibility.[17]

However, the bottom-up approach also has problems. Managers' estimates of future expenditures may be inconsistent with realistic economic projections for the industry or with company financial forecasts and objectives. A university accounting department may plan to increase the number of professors by 20 percent, which is too much if the university plans to increase accounting student enrollment by only 10 percent.

The result of these advantages and disadvantages is that many companies use a joint process. Top managers and the controller define economic projections and financial goals and forecasts and then inform lower managers of the anticipated resources available to them. Once these overall targets (for example, a resource increase of 4 to 7 percent) are made available, department managers can develop their budgets within them. Each department can take advantage of special information, resource requirements, and opportunities. The budget is then passed up to the next management level, where inconsistencies across departments can be removed.

The combined top-down and bottom-up process is illustrated in Exhibit 17.5. Top managers begin the cycle. They also end it by giving final approval to all departmental budgets. Departmental budgets fall within the guidelines provided by top management, and the overall company budget reflects the specific knowledge, needs, and opportunities within each department.

Quaker Oats Company employs a top-down, bottom-up approach to planning and budgeting, where the overall financial objectives, growth rates, and profits are established at the top and passed down to divisions. Specific budget plans and operating strategies within divisions, such as Quaker-Canada, are defined bottom-up.

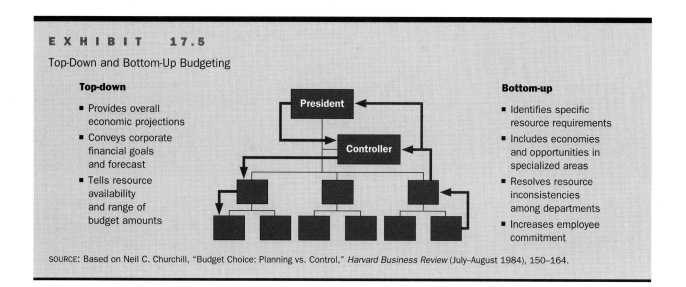

EXHIBIT 17.5

Top-Down and Bottom-Up Budgeting

Top-down

- Provides overall economic projections
- Conveys corporate financial goals and forecast
- Tells resource availability and range of budget amounts

President

Controller

Bottom-up

- Identifies specific resource requirements
- Includes economies and opportunities in specialized areas
- Resolves resource inconsistencies among departments
- Increases employee commitment

SOURCE: Based on Neil C. Churchill, "Budget Choice: Planning vs. Control," *Harvard Business Review* (July–August 1984), 150–164.

ZERO-BASED BUDGETING

█

zero-based budgeting (ZBB)

A budgeting process in which each
responsibility center calculates its
resource needs based on the coming
year's priorities rather than on the previous year's budget.

In most organizations, the budgeting process begins with the previous
year's expenditures; that is, managers plan future expenditures as an
increase or decrease over the previous year. This procedure tends to lock
departments into a stable spending pattern that lacks flexibility to meet
environmental changes. **Zero-based budgeting (ZBB)** was designed to
overcome this rigidity by having each department start from zero in calculating resource needs for the new budget period.[18] ZBB assumes that
the previous year's budget is not a valid base from which to work.
Rather, based on next year's strategic plans, each responsibility center
justifies its work activities and needed personnel, supplies, and facilities
for the next budget period. Responsibility centers that cannot justify
expenditures for the coming year will receive fewer resources or be disbanded altogether. In zero-based budgeting, each year is viewed as
bringing a new set of goals. It forces department managers to thoroughly
examine their operations and justify their departments' activities based
on their direct contribution to the achievement of organizational goals.[19]

The zero-based budgeting technique was originally developed for use
in government organizations as a way to justify cost requests for the succeeding year. The U.S. Department of Agriculture was the first to use
zero-based budgeting in the 1960s. ZBB was adopted by Texas Instruments in 1970 and by many government and business organizations during the 1970s and 1980s. Companies such as Ford, Westinghouse, Owens-
Illinois, and New York Telephone, as well as government agencies at
both the federal and state levels, use zero-based budgeting.

The specific steps used in zero-based budgeting are as follows:

1 Managers develop a *decision package* for their responsibility centers.
   The decision package includes written statements of the department's objectives, activities, costs, and benefits; alternative ways of
   achieving objectives; consequences of not performing each activity;
   and personnel, equipment, and resources required during the coming year. Managers then assign a rank order to the activities in their
   department for the coming year.

2 The decision package is then forwarded to top management for
   review. Senior managers rank the decision packages from the
   responsibility centers according to their degree of benefit to the
   organization. These rankings involve widespread management discussions and may culminate in a voting process in which managers
   rate activities from "essential" to "would be nice to have" to "not
   needed."

3 Top management allocates organizational resources based on activity rankings. Budget resources are distributed according to the
   activities rated as essential to meeting organizational goals. Some
   departments may receive large budgets and others nothing at all.

Zero-based budgeting demands more time and energy than conventional budgeting. Because it forces management to abandon traditional
budget practices, top management should develop a consensus among

participants that ZBB will have a positive influence on both the company and its employees.

ADVANTAGES AND DISADVANTAGES OF BUDGET CONTROL

Budgeting is the most widely used control system in North American organizations. It offers several advantages to managers but can also create problems. The advantages and disadvantages of budgets are summarized in Exhibit 17.6.

The first major strength of budgeting is that it coordinates activities across departments. The budget ties together resource requirements from each responsibility center into a financial blueprint for the entire firm. Second, budgets translate strategic plans into action. They specify the resources, revenues, and activities required to carry out the strategic plan for the coming year. Third, budgets provide an excellent record of organizational activities. Fourth, budgets improve communication, because they provide information to employees. Budgets let people see where the organization is going and their role in that mission. Fifth, budgets improve prudent resource allocation, because all requests are clarified and justified. Senior managers get a chance to compare budget requests across departments and set priorities for resource allocation. Finally, budgets provide a way of implementing corrective action. For example, when personal computer sales declined in 1989, the PC managers at IBM used a budget to reduce expenditures for PC manufacturing and increase budgeted resources for other computer lines. The Leading Edge box describes how one company uses budgets effectively to squeeze waste out, enabling both rapid growth and solid profits.

Budgets can also cause headaches for managers when improperly used. The major problem occurs when budgets are applied mechanically and rigidly. The budgeting process is then only an exercise in filling out paperwork, with each department getting the same percentage increase or decrease as the others. Second, when managers and employees are not allowed to participate in the budget-setting process, budgeting is

---

EXHIBIT   17.6
Advantages and Disadvantages of Budgets

Advantages	**Disadvantages**
■ Facilitate coordination across departments	■ Can be used mechanically
■ Translate strategic plans into departmental actions	■ Can demotivate employees because of lack of participation
■ Record organizational activities	■ Can cause perceptions of unfairness
■ Improve communication with employees	■ Can create competition for resources and politics
■ Improve resource allocation	■ Can limit opportunities for innovation and adaptation
■ Provide a tool for corrective action through reallocations	

LEADING edge   NO TASTE FOR WASTE

Ken Hendricks touts his ABC Roofing Supply company in Beloit, Wisconsin, as "the biggest small company in America." Repeatedly listed as one of the fastest-growing companies in the United States, with sales of $350 million and an annual growth rate of 35 percent, ABC is a stickler for details. Cost control, budget control, and waste control are not simply axioms but are values central to ABC's corporate culture. Hendricks does not believe in wasting *anything*—money, time, buildings, or people. He claims that companies lose 30 percent productivity by people wasting time and calls this waste the "biggest factor in today's business."

ABC Supply proves that waste can be controlled through proper budgeting, especially when incorporated with strategic goals. ABC's rent is 1.8 percent of sales compared to an industry average of 3.9 percent. Truck expenses are 2 percent of sales, compared to an industry average 5 percent. ABC achieves an astonishing $450,000 in sales per employee, compared to a competitor average of about $200,000 per employee. The secret? A companywide commitment to waste control.

ABC recycles everything. Stores are located in older, used buildings near the center of cities. Why? Because many potential customers are located in older sections of the city, not in the suburbs. Besides, real estate is cheaper in the city center. Hendricks scours the area for old equipment, old trucks, and so on that can be repaired for a fraction of the cost of new equipment. Moreover, Hendricks does not fire people. His policy is to utilize people, insisting it is far easier to retrain a "failed" manager than to locate and train a new manager.

The secret to waste reduction, according to Hendricks, is to study where waste is occurring and to set up strict budget standards. He advises looking at the company profit and loss statement to determine where money is being spent and to establish tough standards in those areas. At ABC Supply, every employee sees the financial numbers. Every employee understands what it costs to do business and how his or her performance fits into the overall picture. By providing monthly budget and profit figures compared to the previous year, employees can join management in finding ways to make their jobs quicker and easier. Making the money, Hendricks insists, is the *result* of good business practice, not the *goal*. ■

SOURCE: Interview with Ken Hendricks, "Waste Not, Want Not," *INC.*, March 1991, 33–42.

demotivating. If budgets are arbitrarily imposed top down, employees will not understand the reason for budgeted expenditures and will not be committed to them. A third weakness occurs when budget perceptions differ across hierarchical levels. Supervisors also may feel they did not receive a fair share of resources if top managers do not explain corporate priorities and budget decisions. Fourth, budgets may pit departments against one another. Managers may feel their own activities are essential and even resort to politics to get more resources. Finally, a rigid budget structure reduces initiative and innovation at lower levels, making it impossible to obtain money for new ideas. Some companies, such as 3M, set aside discretionary resources to prevent this problem.

Skilled managers who understand budgets and how to use them have a powerful control tool with which to attain departmental and organizational goals. Budgets also can be used effectively in small businesses. Golden Branch Interactive Productions is an example of how important good budgeting can be in the start-up phase of a company.

GOLDEN BRANCH INTERACTIVE PRO-DUCTIONS

Financial controls are essential in any company. For small businesses, however, they are especially crucial in the start-up phase when effective management control can mean the difference between bankruptcy and prosperity. Robert Gehorsam learned that lesson the hard way when he co-founded Golden Branch Interactive Productions, a business that produced interactive entertainment and educational products.

Gehorsam and a partner began with a conservative cash-flow analysis that pegged expenses high and income low. Every time they reviewed the analysis, they would pull the purse strings even tighter. They projected their first-year revenues at $225,000, and put their expenses at $180,000. As a starting point, each partner put in $5,000 for the first six months and made a commitment to invest up to twice that amount in the latter half of the year if necessary.

Despite their careful analysis, Gehorsam and his partner quickly discovered that things did not always go as planned. By the time they paid the rent, one month's security, a $1,000 phone bill, an attorney's $2,500 retainer, and $1,200 for a digital phone system, their seed money was gone. A few months later, they ran into cash flow crisis when bills were due before they had received full payment from their first client. They each made a loan to the company to tide them over and planned to pay themselves back.

Overhead turned out to be higher than planned and sales cycles were longer. But the setbacks were not enough to discourage Gehorsam and his partner. They believed that tight financial controls would eventually pay off since their business ideas were sound. "Our basic assumptions concerning industry growth, our company strengths and the type of companies we wanted to work with were right on target," Gehorsam says. With a little perseverance, they were convinced the early setbacks would be replaced by long-term success.[20] ■

SIGNS OF INADEQUATE CONTROL SYSTEMS

Financial statements, financial analysis, and budgets are designed to provide adequate control for the organization. Often, however, management control systems are not working properly. Then they must be examined for possible clarification, revision, or overhaul. Indicators of the need for a more effective control approach or revised management control systems are as follows:[21]

- Deadlines missed frequently.
- Poor quality of goods and services.
- Declining or stagnant sales or profits.
- Loss of leadership position or market share within the industry.
- Inability to obtain data necessary to evaluate employee or departmental performance.
- Low employee morale and high absenteeism.
- Insufficient employee involvement and management-employee communications.
- Excessive company debts, uncertain cash flow, or unpredictable borrowing requirements.
- Inefficient use of human and material resources, equipment, and facilities.

Management control systems help achieve overall company objectives. They help ensure that operations progress satisfactorily by identifying deviations and correcting problems. Properly used, controls help management respond to unforeseen developments and achieve strategic plans. Improperly designed and used, management control systems can lead a company into bankruptcy.

SUMMARY AND MANAGEMENT SOLUTION

This chapter introduced a number of important concepts about management control systems and techniques. Recall from Chapter 16 that organizations have a core management control system that includes the financial forecast and operating budget. Top management financial control uses the balance sheet, income statement, and financial analyses of these documents.

At the middle levels of the organization, budgets are an important control system. Departments are responsibility centers, each with a specific type of operating budget—expense, revenue, or profit. Financial budgets are also used for organizational control and include the cash, capital expenditure, and balance sheet budgets. The budget process can be either top down or bottom up, but a budget system that incorporates both seems most effective. Zero-based budgeting is a variation of the budget process and requires that managers start from zero to justify budget needs for the coming year. Finally, indicators of inadequate control systems were discussed.

The importance of the budget and financial control systems was illustrated in the management problem at the beginning of this chapter. Darren Adler's second business went bankrupt because he did not have the proper controls or budgets needed to run a business. When he founded EMR, a radio/public relations company in 1989, he took a different approach. "I wanted to be careful," Adler says. "My targets and budgets were virtually zero, just enough to get the company going." By 1993, EMR was projected to grow into a million-dollar plus business.

Adler credits strict financial controls for the company's success. "From day one we've never had an overdraft, never had to borrow money, and have always made a profit each month," he says. "The financial controls are very tight." Clients are required to make payments within 45 days of receiving EMR's services, and the company refuses to accept repeat business from those who don't pay on time. Despite the tight rein on finances, Adler says it doesn't cramp the company's style. EMR has 14 full-time staffers, who, like the 25-year-old founder, range in age from 19 to 27. Says Adler: "We want to be seen as a young, nutty, creative company."[22]

DISCUSSION QUESTIONS

1. What are the four types of responsibility centers, and how do they relate to organization structure?
2. What types of analyses can be performed on financial statements to help managers diagnose a company's financial condition?
3. Which do you think is a more important use of financial analyses: diagnosing organizational problems or taking corrective action to solve them? Discuss.
4. Explain the difference among fixed costs, variable costs, and discretionary costs. In which situation would each be used?
5. What are the advantages of top-down versus bottom-up budgeting? Why is it better to combine the two approaches?
6. According to zero-based budgeting, a department that cannot justify a budget will cease to exist. Do you think this actually happens under zero-based budgeting? Discuss.
7. Why might low employee morale or insufficient employee involvement be indicators of inadequate controls in an organization?

MANAGEMENT IN PRACTICE: ETHICAL DILEMMA

● COMPUTER SCREWUP

Ken and Barbara are coworkers in the telecommunications department of a large firm. One weekend, Ken asked Barbara and several other coworkers to help him move to a new apartment. While placing Ken's computer into its original packing, Barbara noticed that the address on the box was for their telecom office. When Barbara questioned Ken about it, he replied, "Oh, yeah, we ordered ten terminals from the manufacturer a year ago, but they accidentally shipped eleven. We didn't get charged for it." When Barbara expressed disapproval, Ken became defensive and said the boss, Dave, knew about it. "Besides, I was the one who pushed that we buy from that manufacturer, and I do

a lot of work on my home computer, so our company owes me something anyway."

● WHAT DO YOU DO?

1. Nothing. This is not your responsibility. The fault is with the two companies' control systems that let the computer slip through.
2. Try to persuade Ken to offer to pay for it. This would be the right thing for him to do even if his offer is refused.
3. Bring it up with your boss, Dave. If it's okay for your company to accept the extra computer, it should be shared with coworkers.

CASE FOR ANALYSIS

NEWSLETTER PUBLISHER

When the revelation came, it must have been sort of like what John D. Rockefeller felt when he realized that oil would eventually be the fuel that fired the engine of a nation. A new digital technology was being proposed for the country's 12,000 radio stations. Judith Gross not only was familiar with the technology, she could write clearly about it to others. She had a journalism background and had always wanted to publish a newsletter. Her clients would include station managers, researchers promoting the new technology, lobbyists, lawyers, and governmental organizations. It was a natural.

Almost. Judith found a partner, a lawyer and friend whom we'll call Jeff. She figured a newsletter pretty much involved writing stories and toting up subscribers' checks. Turns out she needed to know about mail-order techniques, printing and typesetting, and a good deal about selling. But she didn't do much research, so all of this came as quite a rude shock. She didn't turn to available publications on the topics until half a year after launch.

She naturally wanted the publication to look good, and the big logo and lots of color did that. It also cost a lot. Then there was the professional typesetters and high-dollar printing and mailing services and slick trade-show brochures. By the time Judith got down to adding up the red numbers and her projected subscribers, it dawned on her she might be a lot older before she even recouped her initial investment.

By then she had realized pricing on gut hunch was a bad way to go. A poor response to her first offering forced her to slash the cover price. Flying by the seat of her pants, she had no way of sizing up her potential market, let alone how to get renewals. She'd also failed to notice (it was about 1990), that there was a recession under way. Her targets would be cutting fat out of their budgets, and newsletters are usually one of the first casualties.

There was some other bad decision making beyond Judith's control. The company could have been set up as a partnership. And even though more than three-fourths of small businesses are run as sole-proprietorships, Jeff incorporated the company and didn't take advantage of the subchapter-S distinction. That afforded protection from lawsuits, but it meant big taxes and regulations. There were also costly filing fees involved that weren't really necessary.

Other unwelcome news came to light. Jeff had owned another business. Judith didn't find out until later that it had nearly gone bankrupt. She was discovering that having a friend and business partner weren't compatible. Jeff had picked their company's accountant. Since Jeff had old debts with the firm, he balked at forwarding financial data and other information it needed. Later, Judith also learned the firm's rates were beyond the means of her small newsletter.

Jeff did come through in a crunch, but it turned out to be a Pyrrhic victory. Judith had never written a business plan. When capital ran dry, Jeff put together one good enough to get a bank to give them a substantial loan for the newsletter. His personal guarantee on the note also played a factor. In retrospect, Judith says the personal guaranty should have sounded alarm bells. The plan looked good, but even the most conservative projections failed to materialize.

By this time flare-ups between Judith and Jeff had become more frequent. Their friendship disappeared, and so did he. He abdicated responsibilities for the company finances and ceased being concerned about the business at all. Judith found herself handling the whole operation. And she started trying to find somewhere to unload the newsletter.

A publisher picked it up at a fire-sale price that was only slightly more than the outstanding bills. Jeff nobly dropped back in and picked up the bank tab with personal funds because he didn't want a bankruptcy on his credit report. For Judith, the only payback for a lot of hard work was a lot of hard lessons. "The saddest part," she says, "is that I know it all could have been avoided, had I done my homework, taken fewer risks, and sought better advice."

● **QUESTIONS**

1. Which techniques described in this chapter would have enabled Judith to keep better financial control of her business?
2. What do you consider her most serious mistake? Why?
3. Describe some of the signs that indicated Judith's newsletter operation had inadequate control systems.

SOURCE: Judith Gross, "Autopsy of a Business," *Home Office Computing,* October 1993, 52–60.

REFERENCES

1. Flavia Hawksley, "Young, Nutty and Creative," *Accountancy*, October 1993, 52.

2. Kate Ballen, "The New Look of Capital Spending," *Fortune*, March 13, 1989, 115–120.

3. Ford S. Worthy, "Accounting Bores You? Wake Up," *Fortune*, October 12, 1987, 43–52.

4. David A. Garvin, "Quality on the Line," *Harvard Business Review* (September–October 1983), 65–75.

5. Bruce G. Posner, "How to Stop Worrying and Love the Next Recession," *INC.*, April 1986, 89–95.

6. Tom Richman, "The Language of Business," *INC.*, February 1990, 41–50, and Paul Hawken, "Mastering the Numbers," *INC.*, October 1987, 19–20.

7. Hawken, "Mastering the Numbers."

8. Tom Richman, "The Language of Business," *INC.*, February 1990, 41–50.

9. Arthur W. Holmes and Wayne S. Overmeyer, *Basic Auditing*, 5th ed. (Homewood, Ill.: Irwin, 1976).

10. John J. Welsh, "Pre-Acquisition Audit: Verifying the Bottom Line," *Management Accounting* (January 1983), 32–37.

11. Jill Andresky Fraser, "Honey, I Shrunk the Company," *INC.*, June 1990, 115–116.

12. Richard L. Daft and Norman B. Macintosh, "The Nature and Use of Formal Control Systems for Management Control and Strategy Implementation," *Journal of Management* 10 (1984), 43–66; and Robert N. Anthony, John Dearden, and Norton M. Bedford, *Management Control Systems*, 5th ed. (Homewood, Ill.: Irwin, 1984).

13. This discussion is based on Peter Lorange, Michael F. Scott Morton, and Sumantra Ghoshal, *Strategic Control* (St. Paul, Minn.: West, 1986), Chapter 4; Anthony, Dearden, and Bedford, *Management Control Systems*; and Richard F. Vancil, "What Kind of Management Control Do You Need?" *Harvard Business Review* (March–April 1973), 75–85.

14. Teri Lammers, "The Weekly Cash-Flow Planner," *INC.*, June 1992, 99–103.

15. Anthony, Dearden, and Bedford, *Management Control Systems*.

16. Participation in budget setting has been described in a number of studies, including Peter Brownell, "Leadership Style, Budgetary Participation and Managerial Behavior," *Accounting Organizations and Society* 8 (1983), 307–321; and Paul J. Carruth and Thurrell O. McClandon, "How Supervisors React to 'Meeting the Budget' Pressure," *Management Accounting* 66 (November 1984), 50–54.

17. Neil C. Churchill, "Budget Choice: Planning vs. Control," *Harvard Business Review* (July–August 1984), 150–164.

18. "Zero-based Budgeting," *Small Business Report* (April 1988), 52–57; and Peter A. Pyhrr, *Zero-Based Budgeting: A Practical Management Tool for Evaluating Expense* (New York: Wiley, 1973).

19. "Zero-Based Budgeting: Justifying All Business Activity from the Ground Up," *Small Business Report* (November 1983), 20–25; and M. Dirsmith and S. Jablonsky, "Zero-Based Budgeting as a Management Technique and Political Strategy," *Academy of Management Review* 4 (1979), 555–565.

20. Robert Gehorsam, "Start-Up Diary," *Home Office Computing*, September 1993, 52–55.

21. Based on "Controlling with Standards," *Small Business Report* (August 1987), 62–65.

22. Hawksley, "Young, Nutty and Creative."

OPERATIONS AND SERVICE MANAGEMENT

18

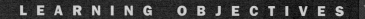

CHAPTER OUTLINE ▲

LEARNING OBJECTIVES ▼

After studying this chapter, you should be able to

- Define operations management and describe its area of application within manufacturing and service organizations.

- Explain the role of operations management strategy in the company's overall competitive strategy.

- Discuss product, process, and fixed-position layouts and their relative advantages.

- Explain why small inventories are preferred by most organizations.

- Discuss the differences between EOQ and JIT for the management of material and inventory.

- Describe productivity and statistical process control and explain their relationship to total quality management.

When Boeing came calling at Ace Clearwater Enterprises with $5 million in long-term contracts, Kellie Dodson felt a little like she had won the lottery. Her small sheet-metal-fabricating aerospace subcontractor had never worked for a firm as big as Boeing. Eight months later that had become obvious. Clearwater was 71 percent behind on Boeing's work, its rejection rate was one part in ten, and it was losing money on the account. That's when Dodson got a call from Boeing's procurement manager. In no uncertain terms, he told her that if Clearwater didn't start producing, they were history. How can Ace Clearwater design a production system that is more efficient? Considering the magnitude of the company's manufacturing problems, do you think a turnaround is possible?[1]

The problems facing Ace Clearwater Enterprises are not unusual. Many companies have discovered that strategic success is contingent on efficient manufacturing operations. In the 1990s, the manufacturing function is held in high esteem in the corporate world and is considered a key to corporate success.

- The Timken Company gambled $500 million on an ultramodern steel plant when the roller bearing industry was in decline. In the face of withering foreign competition, it invested in new technology and won changes from the steel union on staffing and work rules.[2]

- Fireplace Manufacturers, Inc. (FMI), an entrepreneurial company, hired a Japanese manufacturing expert to redesign its factory, adopting just-in-time production techniques. Hardworking immigrants were hired and given substantial say over their jobs. As a result, scrap from the manufacturing process fell nearly 60 percent, inventory costs dropped, and overall productivity jumped more than 30 percent. The average price of FMI's stoves was cut 25 percent.[3]

- In a service industry, Kmart's efforts to catch discount chain front-runner Wal-Mart include renovation and enlargement of facilities, upgrading merchandise lines, and installation of a high-tech inventory control system. In addition, Kmart is experimenting with a superstore concept—combining discount retailing and supermarkets for true "one-stop shopping."[4]

Manufacturing and service operations such as these are important because they represent the company's basic purpose—indeed, its reason for existence. Without the ability to produce products and services that are competitive in the global marketplace, companies cannot expect to succeed.[5]

This chapter describes techniques for the planning and control of manufacturing and service operations. The two preceding chapters described overall control concepts. In this chapter, we will consider the management and control of production operations. First we define operations management. Then we look at how some companies successfully bring operations into strategic decision making. Finally, we consider specific operational design issues such as plant layout, location planning, inventory management, manufacturing productivity, and structure of the operations management function.

● OPERATIONS MANAGEMENT

The topic of operations management pertains to the day-to-day management of the technical core, as illustrated in Exhibit 18.1. **Operations management** is formally defined as the field of management that specializes in the production of goods and services and uses special tools and techniques for solving manufacturing problems. In essence, operating managers are concerned with all production activities within the organization.

operations management

The field of management that specializes in the physical production of goods or services and uses quantitative techniques for solving manufacturing problems.

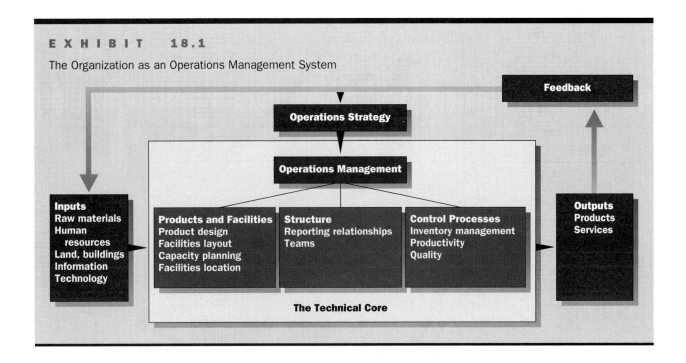

E X H I B I T   18.1

The Organization as an Operations Management System

MANUFACTURING AND SERVICE OPERATIONS

Although terms such as *production* and *operations* seem to imply manufacturing organizations, operations management applies to all organizations. The service sector has increased three times as fast as the manufacturing sector in the North American economy. Today more than one-half of all businesses are service organizations. Operations management tools and techniques apply to services as well as manufacturing.

Manufacturing organizations are those that produce physical goods. Ford Motor Company, which produces automobiles, and Levi Strauss, which makes clothing, are both manufacturing companies. In contrast, **service organizations** produce nonphysical outputs, such as medical, educational, or transportation services provided for customers. Airlines, doctors, lawyers, and the local barber all provide services. Services also include the sale of merchandise. Although merchandise is a physical good, the service company does not manufacture it but merely sells it as a service to the customer. Retail stores such as Sears and McDonald's are service organizations.

Services differ from manufactured products in two ways. First, the service customer is involved in the actual production process.[6] The patient actually visits the doctor to receive the service, and it's difficult to imagine a barber or a hair stylist providing services without direct customer contact. The same is true for hospitals, restaurants, and banks. Second, manufactured goods can be placed in inventory whereas service outputs, being intangible, cannot be stored. Manufactured products such as clothes, food, cars, and VCRs can all be put in warehouses and sold at a later date. However, a hair stylist cannot wash, cut, and set hair in advance and leave it on the shelf for the customer's arrival, nor can a

manufacturing organization
An organization that produces physical goods.

service organization
An organization that produces nonphysical goods that require customer involvement and cannot be stored in inventory.

Goglanian Bakeries, Inc., uses an old-fashioned conveyor belt process to manufacture pita bread. This manufacturing organization produces a physical good, and, therefore, determined what production process would work best.

doctor place examinations in inventory. The service must be created and provided for the customer exactly when he or she wants it.

Despite the differences between manufacturing and service firms, they face similar operational problems. First, each kind of organization needs to be concerned with scheduling. A medical clinic must schedule appointments so that doctors' and patients' times will be used efficiently. Second, both manufacturing and service organizations must obtain materials and supplies. Third, both types of organizations should be concerned with quality and productivity. Because many operational problems are similar, operations management tools and techniques can and should be applied to service organizations as readily as they are to manufacturing. Phelps County Bank is an example of a small service firm that has avoided the operational problems which plague many of its larger competitors.

 PHELPS COUNTY BANK

Many banks try to differentiate themselves with all types of alphabet accounts and other financial "products." But the average customer usually is not even aware of half of what's available. If you asked them, most customers would be satisfied if they could simply get through the teller line or drive-in bank as fast and hassle-free as possible. In the final analysis, what is usually most important to bank customers is service, and that is what they get at Phelps County Bank of Rolla, Missouri.

The difference at PCB is obvious. Customers who arrive after closing time are ushered to a secure room, and a service representative is authorized to solve problems on the spot. Instead of sending customers to customer-service personnel, tellers resolve complaints whenever possible. PCB loan officers will close loans at the customer's home if it is more convenient.

Initiating service improvements is part of the culture at PCB. Under the bank's participation/reward program, anyone can submit service enhancement ideas, with monthly awards and an annual grand prize worth $1,500. Employees also can attend bank-sponsored classes offered by both the American Banking Institute and Dale Carnegie, and seminars that put a particular emphasis on problem solving. Once staffers have a grasp of regulations and bank services, they are afforded the latitude to make decisions on their own.[7] ■

OPERATIONS STRATEGY

Many operations managers are involved in day-to-day problem solving and lose sight of the fact that the best way to control operations is through strategic planning. The more operations managers become enmeshed in operational details, the less likely they are to see the big picture with respect to inventory buildups, parts shortages, and seasonal fluctuations.[8] Indeed, one reason suggested for the Japanese success is the direct involvement of operations managers in strategic management. To manage operations effectively, managers must understand operations strategy.

Operations strategy is the recognition of the important role of operations in organizational success and the involvement of operations managers in the organization's strategic planning.[9] Exhibit 18.2 illustrates four stages in the evolution of operations strategy.

Many companies are at stage 1, where business strategy is set without considering the capability of operations. The operations department is concerned only with labor costs and operational efficiency. For example, a major electronics instrument producer experienced a serious mismatch between strategy and the ability of operations to manufacture products. Because of fast-paced technological changes, the company was changing its products and developing new ones. However, the manufacturer had installed a materials-handling system in the operations department that was efficient but could not handle diversity and change of this magnitude. Operations managers were blamed for the company's failure to achieve strategic objectives even though the operations department's capacity had never been considered during strategy formulation.

At stage 2, the operations department sets objectives according to industry practice.[10] The organization tries to be current with respect to operations management techniques and views capital investment in plant and equipment, quality control, or inventory management as ways to be competitive.

At stage 3, operations managers are more strategically active. Operations strategy is in concert with company strategy, and the operations

operations strategy
The recognition of the importance of operations to the firm's success and the involvement of operations managers in the organization's strategic planning.

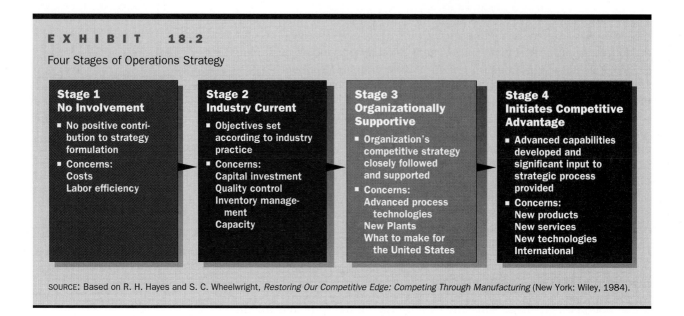

EXHIBIT 18.2

Four Stages of Operations Strategy

**Stage 1
No Involvement**
- No positive contribution to strategy formulation
- Concerns:
  Costs
  Labor efficiency

**Stage 2
Industry Current**
- Objectives set according to industry practice
- Concerns:
  Capital investment
  Quality control
  Inventory management
  Capacity

**Stage 3
Organizationally Supportive**
- Organization's competitive strategy closely followed and supported
- Concerns:
  Advanced process technologies
  New Plants
  What to make for the United States

**Stage 4
Initiates Competitive Advantage**
- Advanced capabilities developed and significant input to strategic process provided
- Concerns:
  New products
  New services
  New technologies
  International

SOURCE: Based on R. H. Hayes and S. C. Wheelwright, *Restoring Our Competitive Edge: Competing Through Manufacturing* (New York: Wiley, 1984).

department will seek new operational techniques and technologies to enhance strategy.

At the highest level of operations strategy, stage 4, operations managers may pursue new technologies on their own in order to do the best possible job of delivering the product or service. At stage 4, operations can be a genuine competitive weapon.[11] Operations departments develop new strategic concepts themselves. With the use of new technologies, operations management becomes a major force in overall company strategic planning. Operations can originate new products and processes that will add to or change company strategy.

> Why will a company that operates at stage 3 or 4 be more competitive than those that rely on marketing and financial strategies? The reason is that customer orders are won through better price, quality, performance, delivery, or responsiveness to customer demand. These factors are affected by operations, which help the company win orders in the marketplace.[12]

One example of operations strategy is the shift at General Electric's headquarters from profit growth through massive acquisitions to squeezing more profits from existing businesses. The operations strategy is to increase manufacturing productivity, which is aligned with overall corporate strategy. General Electric created the post of productivity czar to help implement the strategy change. For example, in the electrical distribution business, new products are developed with the operational goals of reducing number of parts, assembly time, and total cost of materials, thereby producing new circuit breakers that are cheaper and more profitable. Production was consolidated from six plants into one, and the number of parts needed to produce various circuit breaker models plunged from 280,000 to fewer than 100. Structure was also changed, with shop floor teams given responsibility for scheduling inventory and production rates. This strategic approach to operations management has provided the big productivity gains General Electric desired.[13]

● DESIGNING OPERATIONS MANAGEMENT SYSTEMS

Every organization must design its production system. This starts with the design of the product or service to be produced. A restaurant designs the food items on the menu. An automobile manufacturer designs the cars it produces. Once products and services have been designed, the organization turns to other design considerations, including structural reengineering, facilities layout, production technology, facilities location, and capacity planning.

PRODUCT AND SERVICE DESIGN

A big trend in the business world is toward what is called *design for manufacturability and assembly* (DFMA).[14] Engineering designers have long fashioned products with disdain for how they would be produced. Elegant designs nearly always had too many parts. One study showed that simply eliminating screws and other fasteners from products saves up to 75 percent of assembly costs. Thus the watchword is *simplicity*, making the product easy and inexpensive to manufacture.[15]

Using DFMA is ridiculously inexpensive. IBM cut assembly time for a printer from 30 minutes to only 3 minutes, achieving efficiency better than the Japanese. DFMA often requires restructuring operations, creating teams of designers, manufacturers, and assemblers to work together. For example, Hewlett-Packard got designers to work with manufacturing to develop a new low-cost computer terminal. It uses 40 percent fewer parts and can be assembled in hours versus three days previously. The new model saves 55 percent on materials and 75 percent on labor. Breakthroughs in design simplicity are making U.S. manufacturers competitive again.[16]

The notions of simplicity and DFMA translate into four concerns for product design: producibility, cost, quality, and reliability. *Producibility* is the degree to which a product or service can actually be produced for the customer within the firm's existing operational capacity.

The issue of *cost* simply means the sum of the materials, labor, design, transportation, and overhead expense associated with a product or service. Striving for simplicity and few parts keeps product and service designs within reasonable costs.

The third issue is *quality*, which is the excellence of the product or service. Quality represents the serviceability and value that customers gain by purchasing the product.

Reliability, the fourth issue, is the degree to which customers can count on the product or service to fulfill its intended function. The product should function as designed for a reasonable length of time. Highly complex products often have lower reliability because more things can go wrong.

IBM achieves these design attributes on its typewriters by putting as many of the same parts as possible in different products. Sharing parts allows IBM to maximize quality, reliability, and producibility by focusing on keeping parts count to a minimum. Its current typewriters have only one-fifth as many parts as the old Selectrics did. Screws and bolts are not allowed.[17]

In recent years, product design has also moved toward consumer-friendly products, resulting from a growing consumer alienation toward complex products. These trends are discussed in the Manager's Shoptalk box.

The design of services also should reflect producibility, cost, quality, and reliability. However, services have one additional design requirement: timing. *Timing* is the degree to which the provision of a service meets the customer's delivery requirements. Recall that a service cannot be stored in inventory and must be provided when the customer is present. If you take your friend or spouse to a restaurant for dinner, you

At Beckman Instruments, Inc., managers realize the importance of product design for manufacturability. Manufacturing staff members, such as the production supervisor pictured here, work hand-in-hand with engineering design teams, advising them on ways to simplify product assembly through reduction of parts and assembly time.

SIMPLIFY, STUPID!

I hate consulting a manual every time I use the machine.

There are so many colored lights flashing on my car dashboard, I wouldn't *know* if there was a problem.

I'm not a rocket scientist. I just want to be able to turn on the ?#!!*% thing.

The American consumer is frustrated by high-tech gizmos. Worse, consumers hate feeling like "technological illiterates" every time they purchase a new electronic product. Everything from blenders and microwaves to computers and stereos is a nightmare of buttons and dials and flashing lights. It seems that no one is spared. Tipper Gore, wife of Vice-President Al Gore, admitted placing black masking tape over her flashing VCR clock.

American product designers are finally getting the message—*simplify*, stupid! Suddenly, managers and designers in all industries are racing to find ways to simplify our lives and reduce stress. The results can be seen in a wide range of product innovations in the "Why didn't someone think of that before?" category. Many are winners of the Industrial Design Excellence Award (IDEA), sponsored by *Business Week* and conducted by the Industrial Designers Society of America.

For example, 1992 gold-medal winner Texas Instruments, Inc., designed a hand-held Audit Trading Computer for use on the hectic floor of the Chicago Board of Trade. However, not all product innovations are high tech. OXO International's Good Grips kitchen utensils by New York's Smart Design, Inc., utilize a universal big handle for such items as kitchen knives, potato peelers, and pizza cutters. The enlarged handles (which prevent cramps) and rubbery, nonslip material can be easily used by anyone from 5 to 105.

Refinement of design is often undertaken through a new approach called *product mapping*, which focuses on user needs. Careful analysis of *how* the consumer interacts with the product (hand movements, degree of difficulty in operation—pushing buttons, reading machine instructions) results in a refinement or design editing process. The result is a user-friendly product.

The future competitive success of American products depends on design innovation. Consumers in the United States and around the world will use products that offer the highest quality with the least hassle, and U.S. companies must be innovative in new product design and in refinement of old products.

Perhaps, someday, Tipper Gore and the rest of us will actually be able to set our VCR clocks! ∎

SOURCE: Zachary Schiller, "Winners: The Best Product Designs of the Year," *Business Week*, June 8, 1992, 52–57; Bruce Nussbaum, "What Works for One Works for All," *Business Week*, April 20, 1992, 112–113; and Bruce Nussbaum and Robert Neff, "I Can't Work This Thing!" *Business Week*, April 29, 1991, 58–66.

expect the meal to be served in a timely manner. The powerful push for self-service reflects the need to provide service when the customer wants and needs it. Banking by machine, pumping your own gas, and trying on your own shoes are all ways that organizations provide timely service, which is important in today's time-pressure world.[18]

For example, when Pizza Hut announced a special lunch menu that could be served in five minutes or less, the timing required that operations—the kitchen—develop a small list of special items that could consistently be made in five minutes or less. Indeed, pizzas had to be redesigned to accommodate the five-minute requirement. Each step in the delivery of pizza items to customers had to be streamlined to ensure that the timing promise was kept.

PROCESS REENGINEERING

One new approach in operations management is called **reengineering,** defined as the reconsideration and redesign of business systems that bring together all elements of a single business process, enabling managers to eliminate waste and delays. Reengineering goes beyond mere speeding up or computerization of old processes. When a company reengineers a process, management systems, job design, and work flow are reevaluated and changed. Computers often play a major role in reengineering, and major computer companies such as IBM and the struggling Wang Laboratories recognize the new market potential in providing products for reengineering systems.[19]

FACILITIES LAYOUT

Once a product or service has been designed or reengineered, the organization must plan for the actual production. The four most common types of layout are process, product, cellular, and fixed position.[20] Exhibit 18.3 illustrates these four layouts.

PROCESS LAYOUT.   As illustrated in panel (a) of Exhibit 18.3, a **process layout** is one in which all machines that perform a similar function or task are grouped together. In a machine shop, the lathes perform a similar function and are located together in one section. The grinders are in another section of the shop. Equipment that performs a similar "process" is grouped together. Service organizations also use process layouts. In a bank, the loan officers are in one area, the tellers in another, and managers in a third.

The advantage of the process layout is that it has the potential for economies of scale and reduced costs. For example, having all painting done in one spray-painting area means that fewer machines and people are required to paint all products for the organization. In a bank, having all tellers located together in one controlled area provides increased security. Placing all operating rooms together in a hospital makes it possible to control the environment for all rooms simultaneously.

The drawback to the process layout, as illustrated in Exhibit 18.3(a), is that the actual path a product or service takes can be long and complicated. A product may need several different processes performed on it and thus must travel through many different areas before production is complete.

PRODUCT LAYOUT.   Panel (b) of Exhibit 18.3 illustrates a **product layout**—one in which machines and tasks are arranged according to the progressive steps in producing a single product. The automobile assembly line is a classic example, because it produces a single product starting from the raw materials to the finished output. The product layout at Ford is so carefully tailored to each product line that Ford can make Mustangs only on the Mustang assembly line but cannot use it to make Thunderbirds. Many fast-food restaurants also use the product layout,

reengineering
The reconsideration and redesign of business systems that bring together all elements of a single business process to eliminate waste and delays.

process layout
A facilities layout in which machines that perform the same function are grouped together in one location.

product layout
A facilities layout in which machines and tasks are arranged according to the sequence of steps in the production of a single product.

EXHIBIT 18.3

EXHIBIT 18.3

Basic Production Layouts

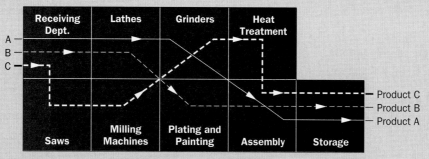

(a) Process Layout

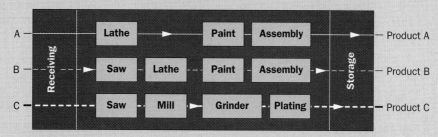

(b) Product Layout

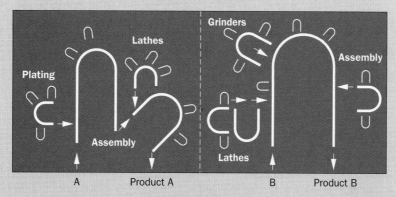

(c) Cellular Layout

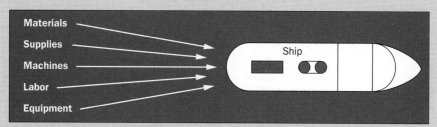

(d) Fixed-Position Layout

SOURCE: Based on J. T. Black, "Cellular Manufacturing Systems Reduce Setup Time, Make Small Lot Production Economical," *Industrial Engineering* (November 1983), 36–48; and Richard J. Schonberger, "Plant Layout Becomes Product-Oriented with Cellular, Just-in-Time Production Concepts," *Industrial Engineering* (November 1983), 66–77.

with activities arranged in sequence to produce hamburgers or chicken, depending on the products available.

The product layout is efficient when the organization produces huge volumes of identical products. Note in Exhibit 18.3(b) that two lines have paint areas. This duplication of functions can be economical only if the volume is high enough to keep each paint area busy working on specialized products.

CELLULAR LAYOUT.   Illustrated in panel (c) of Exhibit 18.3 is an innovative layout, called **cellular layout,** based on group-technology principles in which machines dedicated to sequences of operations are grouped into cells. Grouping technology into cells provides some of the efficiencies of both process and product layouts. Even more important, the U-shaped cells in Exhibit 18.3(c) provide efficiencies in material and tool handling and inventory movement. One advantage is that the workers work in clusters that facilitate teamwork and joint problem solving. Staffing flexibility is enhanced because one person can operate all the machines in the cell and walking distance is small.

FIXED-POSITION LAYOUT.   As shown in panel (d) of Exhibit 18.3, the **fixed-position layout** is one in which the product remains in one location, and tasks and equipment are brought to it. The fixed-position layout is used to create a product or service that is either very large or one of a kind, such as aircraft, ships, and buildings. The product cannot be moved from function to function or along an assembly line; rather, the people, materials, and machines all come to the fixed-position site for assembly and processing. This layout is not good for high volume but it is necessary for large, bulky products and custom orders.

PRODUCTION TECHNOLOGY

One goal of many operations management departments is to move toward more sophisticated technologies for producing products and services. New technology is sometimes called the "factory of the future." Extremely sophisticated systems that can work almost unaided by employees are being designed. For example, General Motors invested $52 million in the Vanguard plant in Saginaw, Michigan, to produce front-wheel-drive axles. Only 42 hourly workers are needed, because the work is done by robots. The product was designed to be made with supersophisticated technology. GM wants to learn whether robot technology is the most efficient way to proceed with its manufacturing operations.[21]

Two other types of production technologies that are becoming widely used in operations management are flexible manufacturing systems and CAD/CAM.

FLEXIBLE MANUFACTURING SYSTEMS.   A small or medium-size automated production line that can be adapted to produce more than one line is called a **flexible manufacturing system.**[22] The machinery uses computers to coordinate and integrate the automated machines. Functions such as loading, unloading, storing parts, changing tools, and machining are done automatically. Moreover, the computer can instruct the machines to change parts, machining, and tools when a new prod-

---

cellular layout

A facilities layout in which machines dedicated to sequences of production are grouped into cells in accordance with group-technology principles.

---

fixed-position layout

A facilities layout in which the product remains in one location and the required tasks and equipment are brought to it.

---

flexible manufacturing system (FMS)

A small or medium-size automated production line that can be adapted to produce more than one product line.

uct must be produced. This is a breakthrough compared with the product layout, in which a single line is restricted to a single product. With a flexible manufacturing system, a single line can be readily readapted to small batches of different products based on computer instructions. Cummins Engine, Caterpillar, and Rockwell have acquired FMSs.

CAD/CAM.   CAD (computer-aided design) and CAM (computer-aided manufacturing) represent new uses of computers in operations management.

CAD enables engineers to develop new-product designs in about half the time required with traditional methods. Computers provide a visual display for the engineer and illustrate the implications of any design change. For example, CAD systems have helped a sportswear manufacturer adjust to rapidly changing product lines. Products change five times a year, and each new season's line requires new production standards, new bills of material for use on the shop floor, and new cutting patterns. Engineers can use the CAD system to design the pattern layouts and then determine the manufacturing changes needed to produce new sizes and styles, expected labor standards, and bills of material.[23]

CAM is similar to the use of computers in flexible manufacturing systems. The computer is harnessed to help guide and control the manufacturing system. For example, for the sportswear manufacturer, the entire sequence of manufacturing operations—pattern scaling, layout, and printing—has now been mechanized through the use of computers. Computer-controlled cutting tables have been installed. Once the computer has mathematically defined the geometry, it guides the cutting blade, eliminating the need for paper patterns. Fabric requisitions, production orders for cutting and sewing operations, and sewing line work can also be directed by computer programs.

FACILITY LOCATION

At some point, almost every organization must make a decision concerning the location of facilities. A bank needs to open a new branch office, Wendy's needs to find locations for some of the 100 or so new stores opened each year, or a manufacturer needs to build a warehouse. When these decisions are made unwisely, they are expensive and troublesome for the organization. For example, Modulate Corporation moved its head office six times in seven years because it had incorrectly anticipated its building requirements.

The most common approach to selecting a site for a new location is to do a cost-benefit analysis.[24] For example, managers at bank headquarters may identify four possible locations. The costs associated with each location are the land (purchase or lease), moving from the current facility, and construction, including zoning laws, building codes, land features, and size of the parking lot. Taxes, utilities, rents, and maintenance are other cost factors to be considered in advance. Each possible bank location also will have certain benefits. Benefits to be evaluated are accessibility of customers, location of major competitors, general quality of working conditions, and nearness to restaurants and shops, which would be desirable for both employees and customers.

CAD

A production technology in which computers perform new-product design.

CAM

A production technology in which computers help guide and control the manufacturing system.

Once the bank managers have evaluated the worth of each benefit, total benefits can be divided by total costs for each location, and managers can select the location with the highest ratio.

Although local facilities may have some maneuverability regarding expansion and facility location, often these strategic decisions are made by the parent company with little local input.

CAPACITY PLANNING

capacity planning

The determination and adjustment of the organization's ability to produce products and services to match customer demand.

Capacity planning is the determination and adjustment of the organization's ability to produce products or services to match demand. For example, if a bank anticipates a customer increase of 20 percent over the next year, capacity planning is the procedure whereby it will ensure that it has sufficient capacity to service that demand.

Organizations can do several things to increase capacity. One is to create additional shifts and hire people to work on them. A second is to ask existing people to work overtime to add to capacity. A third is to outsource or subcontract extra work to other firms as described in Chapter 16. A fourth is to expand a plant and add more equipment. Each of these techniques will increase the organization's ability to meet demand without risk of major excess capacity.

Borden, Inc.'s cornerstone for leadership in the industry is a new pasta hyperplant at St. Louis, Missouri—the largest pasta plant in North America and the most advanced in the world. With an annual capacity of 250 million pounds, the plant can be doubled in size to meet future demand for Borden pasta.

For example, Cooper Tire & Rubber Company produces 531,000 tires a day. When expansion is necessary, Cooper refits existing plants instead of building new ones, allowing for gradual growth to fit capacity requirements. Gradual growth has increased production 40 percent over five years. Building new plants is undertaken only with major study and certainty of the demand for its products. Normally, adding people to a second shift or for overtime work increases capacity without long-term risk. Plant expansions are riskier but solve long-term capacity requirements. Such planning keeps Cooper's profitability high and adds tremendously to its corporate reputation. In rubber and plastics, Cooper ranked second only to Rubbermaid on *Fortune*'s annual ranking of America's most admired corporations in 1993.[25]

The biggest problem for most organizations, however, is excess capacity. When misjudgments occur, transportation companies have oil tankers sitting empty in the harbor, oil companies have refineries sitting idle, semiconductor companies have plants shuttered, developers have office buildings half full, and the service industry may have hotels or amusement parks operating at partial capacity.[26] The challenge is for managers to add capacity as needed without excess. One company that owes much of its success to its ability to manufacture products that match customer demand is Spartan Motors, profiled in the Leading Edge box on the next page.

● INVENTORY MANAGEMENT

A large portion of the operations manager's job consists of inventory management. **Inventory** is the goods the organization keeps on hand for use in the production process. Most organizations have three types of inventory—finished goods prior to shipment, work in process, and raw materials.

Finished-goods inventory includes items that have passed through the entire production process but have not been sold. This is highly visible inventory. The new cars sitting in the storage lot of an automobile factory are finished-goods inventory, as are the hamburgers and french fries waiting under the lamps at a McDonald's restaurant. Finished-goods inventory is expensive, because the organization has invested labor and other costs to make the finished product.

Work-in-process inventory includes the materials moving through the stages of the production process that are not completed products. Work-in-process inventory in an automobile plant includes engines, wheel and tire assemblies, and dashboards waiting to be installed. In a fast-food restaurant, the french fries in the fryer and hamburgers on the grill are work-in-process inventory.

Raw materials inventory includes the basic inputs to the organization's production process. This inventory is cheapest, because the organization has not yet invested labor in it. Steel, wire, glass, and paint are raw materials inventory for an auto plant. Meat patties, buns, and raw potatoes are the raw materials inventory in a fast-food restaurant.

inventory

The goods that the organization keeps on hand for use in the production process up to the point of selling the final products to customers.

finished-goods inventory

Inventory consisting of items that have passed through the complete production process but have yet to be sold.

work-in-process inventory

Inventory composed of the materials that are still moving through the stages of the production process.

raw materials inventory

Inventory consisting of the basic inputs to the organization's production process.

SPARTAN MOTORS

George Sztykiel, whom you read about in Chapters 4 and 9, spent 18 years watching Chrysler Corporation mass produce truck chassis using inflexible, redundant methods—and losing money doing it. Sztykiel did not need a crystal ball to predict that a couple of things were about to happen. A glutted truck market at home and abroad was going to hurt big assembly line manufacturers. But smaller, more flexible outfits could identify niches, produce specialty truck components customers wanted, and earn a premium for their trouble. With this in mind, Spartan Motors was born.

Spartan does not use any automated lines in its fire truck, cab painting, or motorhome and bus/specialty chassis assembly lines. Instead, the company employs a series of work stations where employees perform a number of tasks. When one station's objectives are met, the work in process moves to the next station. In the fire-truck factory, it is pushed by hand; Sztykiel does not want anything that resembles standardization.

That does not mean that Spartan's employees are likely to fall victim to burnout because of too much rote work. Employees who handle cab/engine setting can also mount engines and cabs, put radiators and transmissions in place, and even install electrical and plumbing systems if necessary. The ability to fill in at several work stations maximizes manpower utilization, and adds to one of Spartan's biggest competitive advantages: flexibility.

That advantage is particularly evident when you consider a typical day at the fire-truck factory. Two-person work stations dot the floor, and they seldom see two chassis in a row requiring remotely similar specifications. Workers may install a 350-horsepower engine with four-speed transmission and double person cab, followed by a 450-horsepower engine manufactured by another company that uses a multispeed electronic transmission and has a cab that holds ten people. "We don't have to shut down the plant to change tools and production fixtures," says William Courtney, operations director. "We just take the new specifications in stride and go right on building the truck."

Spartan actually goes out of its way to produce whatever customers want. Its Gladiator line features 300 options, including 10 different transmissions, 12 engine types, and 30 rear-axle and suspension systems. Customers can choose from 45 cab models and pick one of 57 colors of red for the paint job.

All the specialty features mean Spartan has to stay flinty-eyed about costs. A custom fire engine chassis costs twice as much as mass-produced models. But they last longer. The company also has to maintain extremely cordial relations with its 900 suppliers. To accommodate RV customers, Spartan will accept modifications as late as 10 days before production begins. That means Spartan purchasers often must go hat in hand asking for parts on very short notice, which has led to an innovative approach by Sztykiel. He convinced Cummins Engine Company of Columbus, Indiana, to store inventory near one of Spartan's plants. Other suppliers have done the same, saving on costs in this area.

At Spartan, Sztykiel has combined product and service design with his own customized process engineering and facilities layout to create products tailored to the specific needs of customers. Keeping all the balls in the air can be tricky at times, but the company continues to add employees and increase earnings. ■

SOURCE: Edward O. Welles, "The Shape of Things to Come," *INC.*, February 1992, 66–74; Richard S. Teitelbaum, "Spartan Motors," *Fortune*, December 28, 1992; "In-house Payroll Gives HR More Control," *Personnel Journal*, November 1992, 80L; Michael Selz, "Small Manufacturers Display the Nimbleness the Times Require," *The Wall Street Journal*, A1 and A2; and company annual report and Form 10-K.

THE IMPORTANCE OF INVENTORY

Inventory management is vitally important to organizations, because inventory sitting idly on the shop floor or in the warehouse costs money. Many years ago, a firm's wealth was measured by its inventory. Today

Inventory management can be problematic for companies with perishable goods. Employees at Brothers Gourmet Coffees of Boca Raton, Florida, constantly review the inventory to ensure that fresh coffee beans are shipped to customers.

inventory is recognized as an unproductive asset in cost-conscious firms. Dollars not tied up in inventory can be used in other productive ventures. For example, "power retailers" such as Wal-Mart, Toys 'R' Us, Home Depot, or Circuit City understand the relationship between inventory and competitive pricing. State-of-the-art information systems allow tight inventory control with the capacity to meet customer needs "on demand." No excess inventory is needed. Suppliers such as Whirlpool have refined their delivery systems so that retail giants receive only the products needed to meet customer purchases.[27]

The Japanese analogy of rocks and water describes the current management attitude toward the importance of inventory.[28] As illustrated in Exhibit 18.4, the water in the stream is the inventory in the organization. The higher the water, the less managers have to worry about the rocks, which represent problems. In operations management, these problems apply to scheduling, plant layout, product design, and quality. When the water level goes down, managers see the rocks and must deal with them. When inventories are reduced, the problems of a poorly designed and managed production process also are revealed. The problems then must be solved. When inventory can be kept at an absolute minimum, operations management is considered excellent.

Ed Heard, a consultant who specializes in inventory management, has the following message:

> The best criterion for gauging the effectiveness of a manufacturing operation is inventory. If you have a lot of it sitting on the floor, you are probably not doing as good a job as you could be. Inventory is simply the best indicator

EXHIBIT   18.4

Large Inventories Hide Operations Management Problems

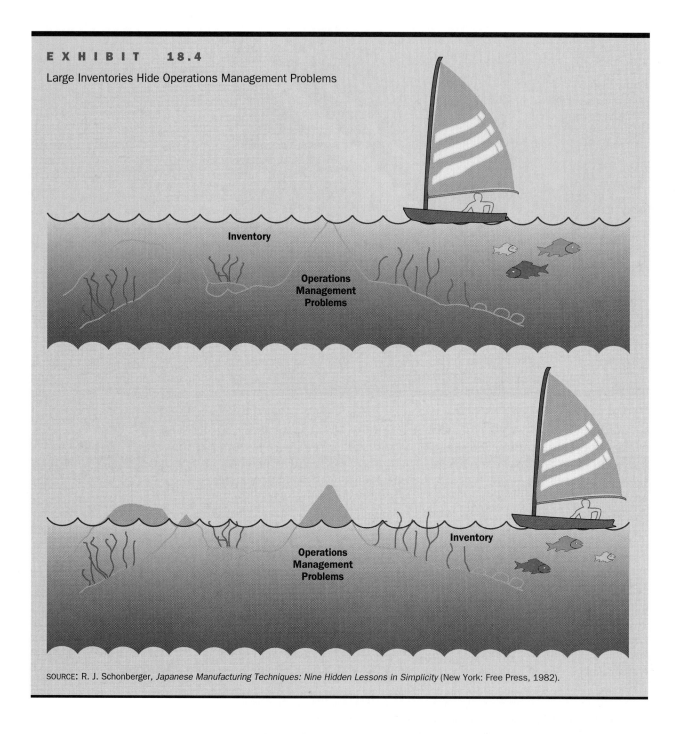

SOURCE: R. J. Schonberger, *Japanese Manufacturing Techniques: Nine Hidden Lessons in Simplicity* (New York: Free Press, 1982).

of manufacturing performance that we have. There is no problem, no screw-up, that doesn't show up in the inventory number. Both raw materials and work-in-process are supposed to be where they are needed in the right quantity at the right time. Too much too soon and money invested in inventory is wasted. Too little too late and the production process is held up waiting for more inventory.[29]

ECONOMIC ORDER QUANTITY

Two basic decisions that can help minimize inventory are how much raw material to order and when to order from outside suppliers.[30] Ordering the minimum amounts at the right time keeps the raw materials, work-in-process, and finished-goods inventories at low levels. One popular technique is **economic order quantity (EOQ),** which is designed to minimize the total of ordering costs and holding costs for inventory items. *Ordering costs* are the costs associated with actually placing the order, such as postage, receiving, and inspection. *Holding costs* are costs associated with keeping the item on hand, such as storage space charges, finance charges, and materials-handling expenses.

economic order quantity (EOQ)

An inventory management technique designed to minimize the total of ordering and holding costs for inventory items.

The EOQ calculation indicates the order quantity size that will minimize holding and ordering costs based on the organization's use of inventory. The EOQ formula includes ordering costs (C), holding costs (H), and annual demand (D). For example, consider a hospital's need to order surgical dressings. Based on hospital records, the ordering costs for surgical dressings are $15, the annual holding cost is $6, and the annual demand for dressings is 605. The following is the formula for the economic order quantity:

$$EOQ = \sqrt{\frac{2DC}{H}} = \sqrt{\frac{2(605)(15)}{6}} = 55.$$

The EOQ formula tells us that the best quantity to order is 55.

The next questions is when to make the order. For this decision, a different formula, called **reorder point (ROP),** is used. ROP is calculated by the following formula, which assumes that it takes three days to receive the order after the hospital has placed it:

reorder point (ROP)

The most economical level at which an inventory item should be reordered.

$$ROP = \frac{D}{\text{Time}} \text{ (Lead time)} = \frac{605}{365}(3) = 4.97, \text{ or } 5.$$

The reorder point tells us that because it takes three days to receive the order, at least five dressings should be on hand when the order is placed. As nurses use surgical dressings, operations managers will know that when the level reaches the point of 5, the new order should be placed for a quantity of 55.

This relationship is illustrated in Exhibit 18.5. Whenever the reorder point of 5 dressings is reached, the new order is initiated, and the 55 arrive just as the inventory is depleted. In a typical hospital, however, some variability in lead time and use of surgical dressings will occur. Thus, a few extra items of inventory, called *safety stock,* are used to ensure that the hospital does not run out of surgical dressings.

JUST-IN-TIME INVENTORY

Just-in-time (JIT) inventory systems are designed to reduce the level of an organization's inventory to zero. Sometimes these systems are referred to as *stockless systems, zero inventory systems,* or *Kanban systems.* Each system centers on the concept that suppliers deliver materials only at the exact moment needed, thereby reducing raw material inventories to zero. Moreover, work-in-process inventories are kept to a minimum

just-in-time (JIT) inventory systems

An inventory control system that schedules materials to arrive precisely when they are needed on a production line.

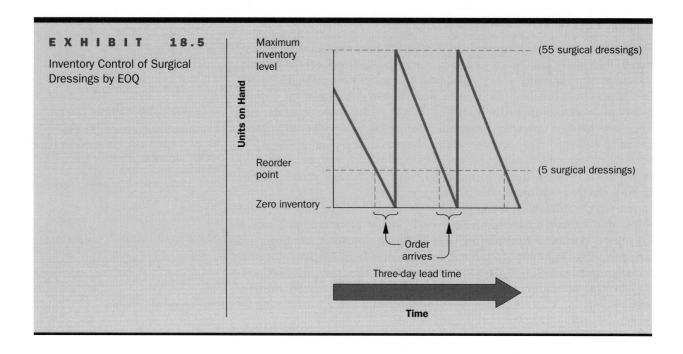

E X H I B I T   18.5

Inventory Control of Surgical Dressings by EOQ

because goods are produced only as needed to service the next stage of production. Finished-goods inventories are minimized by matching them exactly to sales demand.

Recall the Japanese analogy of the rocks and the water. To reduce inventory levels to zero means that all management and coordination problems will surface and must be resolved. Scheduling must be scrupulously precise. For example, Woodbridge Foam Corporation's plant in Saint-Jerome, Quebec, makes automobile seats just hours before they are installed in automobiles at GM's nearby Saint-Therese plant. GM electronically relays seat requirements based on the assembly line's car sequence. The Woodbridge plant uses the car sequence to quickly load the trucks for the 20-kilometer drive. As seats are unloaded in the proper order, assembly is completed without missing a beat.[31] Another company that has mastered the just-in-time inventory system is Schafer Bros.

 S C H A F E R   B R O S .

When Schafer Bros. furniture company decided to cease operations in 1989, Janette Fling thought she saw the opportunity of a lifetime. She had worked as a representative for the firm's office-furniture line known throughout the industry for its quality and craftsmanship. But if she had talked to industry experts, they might have warned her away. The office-furniture sector was shrinking. And Schafer's offerings were high-end furnishings of the sort big law firms and insurance companies favored. Before its bankruptcy, Schafer Bros. had had as much as $4 million languishing in inventory. Not one to be scared away by a challenge, Fling decided to bank on a turnaround by investing her life savings in the company. With $70,000 of her own money and another $225,000 in bank loans, she won the rights to the Schafer Bros. name and designs.

Fling had started out by reviewing the company's financial history, sales records, and market trends to determine where to focus her efforts. She decided to avoid retailers and target the old company's primary market of higher-end goods. She scaled back the factory and got production under way at what she termed "controlled growth." But the most critical component of Schafer Bros.' comeback, according to Fling, was the adoption of a just-in-time manufacturing and inventory system.

Instead of building hundreds of chair and sofa frames, the strategy that had heaped big costs on her predecessors, she used a "lean and mean" operational approach that was more like a custom-built furniture manufacturer. Suppliers were notified of materials needs and reacted with deliveries only after customer orders had been written up. Factory craftsmen completed work that was immediately ready for shipment. "JIT is the single most important thing that has allowed this company to survive," Fling says. "I even consider the suppliers part of the team."[32] ∎

● MANAGING PRODUCTIVITY

During the 1980s, globalization and increased competition from Japan and Europe created a sense of urgency among Americans regarding U.S. growth and productivity. Productivity is significant because it influences the well-being of the entire society as well as of individual companies. The only way to increase the output of goods and services to society is to increase organizational productivity.

MEASURING PRODUCTIVITY

What is productivity, and how is it measured? In simple terms, **productivity** is the organization's output of goods and services divided by its inputs. This means that productivity can be improved by either increasing the amount of output using the same level of inputs or reducing the number of inputs required to produce the output. For example, May Department Stores gauged productivity as sales per square foot. Sales was the measure of output, and floor space was a summary measure of inputs. During one year, sales per square foot were $123, up 35 percent in three years, which meant that productivity was improving. May executives then designed new stores to have twice the productivity of old stores.

Typically, the accurate measure of productivity is more complex than dividing sales by square feet, which is a single measure of outputs and inputs. Two approaches for measuring productivity are total factor productivity and partial productivity.[33] **Total factor productivity** is the ratio of total outputs to the inputs from labor, capital, materials, and energy:

$$Total\ factor\ productivity = \frac{Output}{Labor + Capital + Materials + Energy}$$

productivity

The organization's output of products and services divided by its inputs.

total factor productivity

The ratio of total outputs to the inputs from labor, capital, materials, and energy.

■
partial productivity

The ratio of total outputs to the inputs from a single major input category.

Total factor productivity represents the best measure of how the organization is doing. Often, however, managers need to know about productivity with respect to certain inputs. **Partial productivity** is the ratio of total outputs to a major category of inputs. For example, many organizations are interested in labor productivity, which would be measured as follows:

$$Productivity = \frac{Output}{Labor\ dollars}$$

Calculating this formula for labor, capital, or materials provides information on whether improvements in each element are occurring. However, managers are often criticized for relying too heavily on partial productivity measures, especially direct labor.[34] Measuring direct labor misses the valuable improvements in materials, manufacturing processes, and work quality. Labor productivity is easily measured but may show an increase as a result of capital improvements. Thus managers will misinterpret the reason for productivity increases.

TOTAL QUALITY MANAGEMENT

Recall from Chapter 16 that total quality management (TQM) improves quality and productivity by striving to perfect the entire manufacturing process. Under TQM, employees are encouraged to participate in the improvement of quality. Quality and productivity teams are created. Training budgets are increased. Statistical techniques are used to assist in spotting defects and correcting them. Moreover, TQM stresses coordination with other departments, especially product design, purchasing, sales, and service, so that all groups are working together to enhance manufacturing quality and productivity.

In the United States, operations managers traditionally have resisted spending money to improve quality, believing that productivity would suffer. In the new way of thinking, also discussed in the Manager's Shoptalk box, improvements in quality have a positive impact on productivity. One reason is that dollars spent on improved quality dramatically reduce waste. Poor quality causes huge delayed costs, such as the cost to rework defective products, the cost of maintenance, the cost of dissatisfied customers who do not buy additional products, and the time involved in dealing with dissatisfied customers and returned products.[35] One operations management technique for improving quality and productivity is statistical process control.

STATISTICAL QUALITY CONTROL

Quality is not just an abstract concept. It must be measured if a TQM system is to be successful. But measurement is by workers, not top managers or formal control systems. Workers must be given the training and tools to use statistical techniques to evaluate their tasks and make improvements as needed. The use of statistical measurements is a powerful weapon in the drive to improved quality.

statistical quality control

The application of statistical techniques to the control of quality.

Statistical quality control refers to the application of statistical techniques to the control of quality. The best known is called **statistical**

PRODUCTIVITY OR CUSTOMER SERVICE?

William H. Davidow and Bro Uttal, coauthors of *Total Customer Service: The Ultimate Weapon,* classify firms into two groups. The first group includes firms that promote quality and customer service regardless of the cost, such as IBM. Big Blue's machines are designed so they are easy for hardware and software designers to work with, and the company has invested in a reputation for service.

The second group includes firms that cut costs in an effort to maximize profits. For example, past chairman Ray McDonald of the now defunct Burroughs Corporation considered customer service "a skirmish between Burroughs and its customers." Cost-cutting efforts saved Burroughs money, but savings from omitting special hardware to diagnose machine failures were offset by lost sales, hundreds of lawsuits, and a damaged reputation.

Davidow and Uttal suggest that firms can increase productivity, quality, and customer service at the same time by looking hard at six components.
1. Develop a strategy for customer service. Determine customer expectations, and develop a plan to provide products and services they desire.
2. Communicate the importance of the service strategy and have leaders make personal visits to customers. Executive leadership is essential to provide an example of service.
3. Push authority and responsibility down to those employees so they can respond to customer demands quickly. Real customer service occurs when customers interact with frontline employees.
4. Design products and services with customer service in mind.
Poor service often can be traced back to an engineer who failed to listen to customer demands or field technicians when designing the product.
5. Restructure to create special teams devoted to a product or service for the sole purpose of looking after customer needs and wants.
6. Measure company performance on customer service. Involve employees in developing goals for customer service and analyze customer service records for feedback.

In an environment of complex manufacturing technology, investing in quality enhances both productivity and customer service. Investing wisely in operations management is the key to company survival. ■

SOURCE: Based on Christopher Elias, "Putting the Customer First Again," *Insight,* October 16, 1989, 40–41.

---

process control (SPC), the application of statistical techniques to the control of work processes to detect production of defective items.[36] In addition, workers are often trained in traditional statistical concepts such as frequency distributions, regression and correlation, acceptance sampling, and tests of significance. These techniques are widely used in manufacturing departments, because production activities can be measured and analyzed.

For example, employees can be trained to use charts as graphic representations of work processes. A statistical process control chart measures a specific characteristic, as illustrated in Exhibit 18.6. In this particular chart, workers take a sample of five parts each hour, where the production rate is approximately 100 per hour. The diameters of the five parts are measured, and the sample mean is calculated and plotted on the chart. If the upper control limit or lower control limit is exceeded, the variation is too great and is not due to chance alone. If either limit

statistical process control (SPC)

A type of managerial control that employs carefully gathered data and statistical analysis to evaluate the quality and productivity of employee activities.

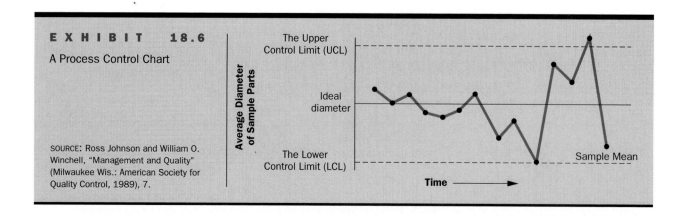

EXHIBIT 18.6

A Process Control Chart

SOURCE: Ross Johnson and William O. Winchell, "Management and Quality" (Milwaukee Wis.: American Society for Quality Control, 1989), 7.

is exceeded, the operation is stopped and the cause determined. In the case illustrated in Exhibit 18.6, the tool had become loose, and so it was reset.

Procedures have been developed for implementing statistical quality control, which include the following steps.

1 *Define the characteristics of a high-quality output.* The output can be a hamburger produced by a Wendy's restaurant, a job description written by an employee in the human resource department, or a radial tire produced at a Firestone plant. The supervisor must provide an exact definition of a high-quality output or service.

2 *Decompose the work activities into the discrete elements required for producing a high-quality output.* For making a hamburger, one discrete element is forming the raw hamburger patty, a second is cooking it, and a third is garnishing it. The quality associated with each discrete element must be defined.

3 *Have a standard for each work element that is current and reasonable.* If standards for work elements are not already available, they must wsaabe developed. The standard is the basis for comparison of worker performance.

4 *Discuss specific performance expectations for every job with workers.* Each worker must understand what is expected with respect to his or her work elements and quality outputs. Workers should participate in decisions about how their performances will be measured.

5 *Make checksheets and collect data for each task element.* Written documents must be developed that reflect performance, and machine operators must be taught to collect data and assess whether their performances are up to standard. Likewise, supervisors can monitor departmental performance by gathering data on team outputs.

6 *Evaluate employee progress against standards at frequent intervals.* In some manufacturing situations, the output records should be checked for every worker several times during the day. If employees are involved in running several different batches of material, different standards will apply. If planned quality standards are not met, adjustments can be made before the end of the work period.

For example, Tridon Ltd., an Oakville, Ontario, manufacturer of wind-shield wiper blades, implemented an SPC program when it discovered that 25 percent of the output from the rubber extrusion line was defective. The rubber could not be reworked and thus was lost. To set up its program, Tridon conducted a feasibility study to identify the dimensions of high-quality parts. After defining standards for performance, it taught operators how the production line functioned and how to collect data that would indicate whether quality standards were being met. Setting up the SPC program cost almost $30,000 for studies, analysis, and training. Since implementing the SPC program, Tridon's scrap rate has decreased 10 percent. Now each part is higher quality but actually costs less to produce. Customers are happy and owners are, too.[37]

IMPROVING PRODUCTIVITY

Quality problems plague many firms. One Ford engine plant had so much variation in pistons for the same engine that they were classified into 13 sizes. Quality improvements over five years reduced the sizes to three and then to one. Now any piston fits any engine block, as do those made in Japan.[38]

When an organization decides that improving productivity is important, there are three places to look: technological productivity, worker productivity, and managerial productivity.

Increased *technological productivity* refers to the use of more efficient machines, robots, computers, and other technologies to increase outputs. The flexible manufacturing and CAD/CAM systems described earlier in this chapter are technological improvements that enhance productivity. Robots are another example.[39]

Increased *worker productivity* means having workers produce more output in the same time period. Improving worker productivity is a real challenge for American companies, because too often workers have an antagonistic relationship with management. At Corning Glass, workers are formed into temporary "corrective action teams" to solve specific problems. Employees also fill out "method improvement requests," which are promptly reviewed. Zebco, a manufacturer of fishing reels, got its workers involved by taking them to a trade show to see how good the Japanese reels were. With workers' efforts, Zebco's productivity doubled in four years.[40]

Increased *managerial productivity* simply means that managers do a better job of running the business. Leading experts in productivity and quality have often stated that the real reason for productivity problems in the United States is poor management.[41] One of these authorities, W. Edwards Deming, proposed specific points for telling management how to improve productivity. These points are listed in Exhibit 18.7.

Management productivity improves when managers emphasize quality over quantity, break down barriers and empower their employees, and do not overmanage using numbers. Managers must learn to use reward systems, management by objectives, employee involvement, teamwork, and other management techniques that have been described throughout this book. For example, in the mid-1980s, a comparison

E X H I B I T   1 8 . 7

Deming's 14 Points for Management Productivity

SOURCE: Deming's 14 Points (January 1990 revision) reprinted from *Out of the Crisis* by W. Edwards Deming by permission of MIT and W. Edwards Deming. Published by MIT, Center for Advanced Engineering Study, Cambridge, MA 02139. Copyright 1986 by W. Edwards Deming.

1. Create and publish to all employees a statement of the aims and purposes of the company or other organization. The management must demonstrate constantly its commitment to this statement.
2. Learn the new philosophy, top management and everybody.
3. Understand the purpose of inspection, for improvement of processes and reduction of cost.
4. End the practice of awarding business on the basis of price tag alone.
5. Improve constantly and forever the system of production and service.
6. Institute training.
7. Teach and institute leadership.
8. Drive out fear. Create trust. Create a climate for innovation.
9. Optimize toward the aims and purposes of the company the efforts of teams, groups, staff areas.
10. Eliminate exhortations for the work force.
11. a. Eliminate numerical quotas for production. Instead, learn and institute methods for improvement
    b. Eliminate MBO. Instead, learn the capabilities of processes, and how to improve them.
12. Remove barriers that rob people of pride of workmanship.
13. Encourage education and self-improvement for everyone.
14. Take action to accomplish the transformation.

between Honda and Jeep automobile assembly plants in Ohio revealed a dramatic difference in quality and productivity. The Honda plant produced 870 cars a day with 2,423 workers, and the Jeep plant produced 750 cars with 5,400 workers. The greater productivity in the Honda plant was attributed to better management.[42]

SUMMARY AND MANAGEMENT SOLUTION

This chapter described several points about operations management. Operations management pertains to the tools and techniques used to manage the organization's core production process. These techniques apply to both manufacturing and service organizations. Operations management has a great impact when it influences competitive strategy. Areas of operations management described in the chapter include product and service design, structural reengineering, location of facilities, facilities layout, capacity planning, and the use of new technologies.

The chapter also discussed inventory management. Three types of inventory are raw materials, work in process, and finished goods. Economic order quantity and just-in-time inventory are techniques for minimizing inventory levels.

Another important concept is that operations management can enhance organizational productivity. Total factor productivity is the best measurement of organizational productivity. Total quality management is an approach to improving quality and productivity of operations. Managers can improve both quality and productivity through statistical process control, technology, management, and work-force improvements.

As described in the management problem at the beginning of this chapter, Ace Clearwater had been given an ultimatum from Boeing: either improve the quality and productivity of its operations, or lose the aerospace company's account.

Dodson realized that if Ace Clearwater was to satisfactorily complete work for companies like Boeing, it would have to adopt updated technologies and management practices. As things stood, the family-owned company had no production-control process. When customers called, there was no way to tell them the status of their order because there was no system in place to find out. Dodson moved to remedy the situation by first putting some punch in her management team, hiring key people including a manufacturing director, a comptroller, an accounting manager, and a materials manager to direct purchasing and production control. She also brought everyone up to speed with across-the-board training. Both hourly and management employees attended on-site courses on Total Quality Management and Statistical Process Control. All 175 employees became aware of Ace Clearwater's overall operations strategy and the role they could play in helping the company achieve its objectives. A few months after issuing its ultimatum, Boeing was so impressed with the improvements at Ace Clearwater that it picked the company to receive its supplier of the year award.[43]

DISCUSSION QUESTIONS

1. What is the difference between manufacturing and service organizations? Which has the greater need for operations management techniques?
2. Briefly explain the difference between process and product layout. What do you see as the advantages and disadvantages of each?
3. If you were asked by a local video store owner to help identify a location for a second video store, how would you proceed? How might you help the owner plan for the new store's capacity?
4. What are the three types of inventory? Which of these is most likely to be affected by the just-in-time inventory system? Explain.
5. Many managers believe that improvements in product quality reduce plant productivity. Why do you think managers feel this way? Are they correct?
6. Assume that a local manufacturing manager asks you about ways to improve productivity. What would you advise the manager?
7. What is the appropriate strategic role for operations management? Should operations management take the initiative in influencing competitive strategy?
8. What are the structural issues relevant to process reengineering? How might reengineering influence operations strategy?

MANAGEMENT IN PRACTICE: ETHICAL DILEMMA

● A STINKY SITUATION

At 3:30 A.M., Jacob Schilden, industrial relations manager, walked into the fuel tank assembly plant four hours earlier than usual. Jacob was called in because Sam Harding, a skilled welder, was threatening to walk off the job. Schilden was responsible for resolving conflicts between the managers, workers, and union representatives.

The problem involved a new process of dipping two metal halves of fuel tanks into an anticorrosion agent before welding them together. The design engineers said the agent was known to be highly toxic as a liquid but was safe after drying on the metal. Unfortunately, it created horrible fumes during welding, which was Sam's job.

The ventilation system installed by the engineers did not decrease the smell. Sam threatened to walk off the job unless the fumes were eliminated. Union representatives questioned whether safety standards were in jeopardy, saying perhaps the agent was toxic in gaseous form.

Management was trying to maintain high quality, which Schilden supports. Employee involvement teams had made a real difference, and Schilden did not want to alienate them. However, manufacturing management refused to stop the line to deal with this problem, because the gas tanks went to a car assembly plant ten miles away. The auto plant had no tanks in inventory, depending on just-in-time delivery from this assembly plant. Shutting down the tank assembly line would also shut down the car assembly plant. As of this moment, union representatives and management are in a heated argument about whether Sam should continue working.

● WHAT DO YOU DO?

1. Support Sam Harding and ask that the line be stopped. It is unethical to endanger Sam's health, and supporting the workers will enhance quality over the long term.
2. Support management's position of keeping the line going. Explain to Sam and the union representatives that the engineers studied the anticorrosion agent carefully. Management will work on improving ventilation first thing in the morning.
3. Propose an intermediate solution. Perhaps give Sam longer breaks than usual, set up fans in the area, or encourage worker rotation until the fumes can be removed.

CASE FOR ANALYSIS

GITANO GROUP INC.

In a way, the Gitano Group's story typifies everything good about opportunities in the American melting pot and how anyone from anywhere can come ashore and make it big. But it also provides some hard lessons about what it takes to achieve long-term survival in business. If the founding family had put in place the right operations strategy and organizational controls initially, Gitano could have been a thoroughbred. Instead, it turned out to be more like a one-trick pony.

Back in the 1980s, brothers Haim and Isaac Dabah could do little wrong. Haim's marketing touch, centered around high-fashion ads that established Gitano's young, slick, and sassy image, was virtually unerring. While Isaac took care of production, Haim established the label in department stores, along with its Gloria Vanderbilt and Regatta Sport brands. The company started earning nice profit margins by grabbing off customers who shunned big-ticket designers like Calvin Klein, but who still wanted the glitz of a label on their jeans. In 1989, Gitano netted $31 million on sales of around $600 million.

The kind of success the brothers were enjoying made them complacent. "Everything we touched turned good," Haim says, "I figured things would stay that way." They didn't. The company had no business plan, no budget, and no organized system to keep up with materials purchases or inventory. When orders were streaming in it didn't matter much. But when Haim decided to begin selling to discounters like Wal-Mart, and the economy took a nosedive, things tightened up. Wal-Mart bargains hard with suppliers, and Gitano's big margins became a thing of the past. And, when the 1990 recession kept customers away, Haim found himself in a predicament. "Imagine flying a plane without instruments," he says. "That's basically what happened."

Isaac wasn't helping matters much. He was the driving force in the company's acquisition of plants in Mississippi, Guatemala, and Jamaica. But he wasn't very skilled at designing systems to control them. The plant in Jamaica was wasting 20 percent of materials, or five times the industry average. No controls existed to determine where apparel was in the production process. The plants sometimes shipped out the wrong merchandise, weeks or even months behind schedule. Many thousands of dollars worth of apparel simply disappeared. Instead of reworking jeans that had been dyed the wrong colors, workers threw them away.

Because Gitano was eager to respond quickly to orders, Isaac ordered the factories to run at full capacity with no thought to actual demand. "At any given time in 1989, we had at least three years' worth of jeans in storage," says one former employee. Without any sort of forecasting, Gitano ended up in a situation where excess inventory was costing big money. Haim decided to solve the problem by plunging into retail. Over a four-year period, the company opened nearly 100 stores. If anything, this decision only made the situation worse. Buyers and designers worked independently from private agendas. New inventory poured in and was piled on older merchandise that hadn't sold. Eventually, the stores were so backlogged everything had to be marked down below cost to get rid of it.

Gitano ran into problems at Wal-Mart as well when the Arkansas retailer ordered its vendors to begin tagging merchandise with bar codes. That meant Wal-Mart could easily compare every pair of jeans against what it had actually ordered. But it also meant the end of Gitano's practice of making substitutions for the sake of filling orders. Haim convinced Wal-Mart that the company was developing a bar-coding system. In the meantime, Gitano continued its practice of substituting snap-front jeans if button-front jeans weren't available. Says one former Gitano manager: "We knew it would take us years to correct the factories, so that they would consistently produce what we really ordered. It was that messed up."

At the urging of their bankers, the brothers brought in an experienced executive, Robert E. Gregory. He formerly was president and chief operating officer of VF Corporation, maker of Lee jeans and a respected figure in the industry. His first priority was to establish the badly needed control systems the company lacked. He moved to downsize the business and eliminate several divisions and six of seven Manhattan showrooms. He also announced that the company would concentrate on marketing, while retailers manufactured under the Gitano label.

But even his best efforts at saving the company failed after the Dabah brothers pleaded guilty in December 1993 to a scheme to avoid import quotas and agreed to pay $2 million in fines. The repercussions were swift and far-reaching. Wal-Mart pulled its Gitano account, saying it would not do business with a company that broke customs regulations. A few months later, Gitano announced it was filing for Chapter 11 bankruptcy protection and selling its assets to Fruit of the Loom Inc. for $100 million. Gregory offered an accurate assessment of the rise and fall of Gitano: "They were so good at marketing and that allowed them to be successful for a long time because in the 1980s you could succeed with marketing."

● **Q U E S T I O N S**

1. Which of the operations management systems described in this chapter could have helped Gitano avoid the manufacturing problems it encountered?
2. How could the company have better managed productivity and inventory?
3. What lessons can other companies learn from what happened to Gitano?

SOURCE: Teri Agins, "Gitano Jeans' Fall Is Saga of Corruption and Mismanagement," *The Wall Street Journal*, February 18, 1994, A1 and A4; Agins, "Gitano Put on Block as Company Loses Wal-Mart Business," *The Wall Street Journal*, February 20, 1994; "Gitano to Be Sold to Fruit of the Loom," *The Wall Street Journal*, March 2, 1994; Ron Stodghill, "Is This Any Way to Run the Family Business?" *Business Week*, August 24, 1992, 48–49; Maryellen Gordon, "Gregory's Plans for Revitalizing Gitano," *Women's Wear Daily*, March 3, 1993, 11; Adam Bryant, "Founder of Gitano Resign Company Posts," *The New York Times*, December 10, 1993, D4; Suzanne Oliver, "Your Best Loss Is Your First Loss," *Forbes*, May 27, 1991, 356–358; and Gretchen Morganson, "Greener Pastures?" *Forbes*, July 6, 1992, 48.

REFERENCES

1. William H. Miller, "Boeing Gives Credence to Clearwater's Revival," *Industry Week*, January 17, 1994, 40–42.

2. John Holusha, "Beating Japan at Its Own Game," *The New York Times*, July 16, 1989, sec. 3, 1, 7.

3. Joel Kotkin, "The Great American Revival," *INC.*, February 1988, 52–63.

4. David Woodruff, "Attention Kmart Shop . . . Hey, Where Is Everybody?" *Business Week*, January 18, 1993, 38.

5. Everett E. Adam, "Towards a Typology of Production and Operations Management Systems," *Academy of Management Review* 8 (1983), 365–375.

6. Gregory B. Northcraft and Richard B. Chase, "Managing Service Demand at the Point of Delivery," *Academy of Management Review* 10 (1985), 66–75; and Richard B. Chase and David A. Tansik, "The Customer Contact Model for Organization Design," *Management Science* 29 (1983), 1037–1050.

7. John Case, "Total Customer Service," *INC.*, January 1994, 52–61.

8. Harlan C. Meal, "Putting Production Decisions Where They Belong," *Harvard Business Review* (March–April 1984), 102–111.

9. Everett E. Adam, Jr., and Paul M. Swamidass, "Assessing Operations Management from a Strategic Perspective," *Journal of Management* 15 (1989), 181–203.

10. W. Skinner, "Manufacturing: The Missing Link in Corporate Strategy," *Harvard Business Review* (May–June 1969), 136–145.

11. R. H. Hayes and S. C. Wheelwright, *Restoring Our Competitive Edge: Competing through Manufacturing* (New York: Wiley, 1984).

12. T. Hill, *Manufacturing Strategy: The Strategic Management of the Manufacturing Function* (London: Macmillan, 1985).

13. Todd Vogel, "Big Changes Are Galvanizing General Electric," *Business Week*, December 18, 1989, 100–102.

14. Otis Port, "Pssst! Want a Secret for Making Superproducts?" *Business Week*, October 2, 1989, 106–110.

15. Otis Port, "The Best-Engineered Part Is No Part at All," *Business Week*, May 8, 1989, 150.

16. Jonathan B. Levine, "How HP Built a Better Terminal," *Business Week*, March 7, 1988, 114; and Bruce Nussbaum, "Smart Design," *Business Week*, April 11, 1988, 102–108.

17. Zachary Schiller, "Big Blue's Overhaul," *Business Week*, Special Issue on Innovation, 1989, 147.

18. Claudia H. Deutsch, "The Powerful Push for Self-Service," *The New York Times*, April 9, 1989, sec. 3, 1, 15.

19. John A. Byrne, "Management's New Gurus," *Business Week*, August 31, 1992, 44–52; and John W. Verity and Gary McWilliams, "Is It Time to Junk the Way You Use Computers?" *Business Week*, July 21, 1991, 66–69.

20. Barbara B. Flynn and F. Robert Jacobs, "An Experimental Comparison of Cellular (Group Technology) Layout with Process Layout," *Decision Sciences* 18 (1987), 562–581; Richard J. Schonberger, "Plant Layout Becomes Product-Oriented with Cellular, Just-in-Time Production Concepts," *Industrial Engineering*, November 1983, 66–77; and Jack R. Meredith and Marianne M. Hill, "Justifying New Manufacturing Systems: A Managerial Approach," *Sloan Management Review* (Summer 1987), 49–61.

21. William J. Hampton, "GM Bets an Arm and a Leg on a People-Free Plant," *Business Week*, September 12, 1988, 72–73.

22. Sumer C. Aggarwal, "MRP, JIT, OPT, FMS?" *Harvard Business Review* 63 (September–October 1985), 8–16; and Paul Ranky, *The Design and Operation of Flexible Manufacturing Systems* (New York: Elsevier, 1983).

23. Kurt H. Schaffir, "Information Technology for the Manufacturer," *Management Review* (November 1985), 61–62.

24. Suren S. Singhvi, "A Quantitative Approach to Site Selection," *Management Review* (April 1987), 47–52.

25. Jennifer Reese, "America's Most Admired Corporations," *Fortune*, February 8, 1993, 44–72.

26. Marvin B. Lieberman, "Strategies for Capacity Expansion," *Sloan Management Review* (Summer 1987), 19–27.

27. Zachery Schiller, Wendy Zellner, Ron Stodghill II, and Mark Marmont, "Clout! More and More, Retail Giants Rule the Marketplace," *Business Week*, December 21, 1992, 67–73.

28. R. J. Schonberger, *Japanese Manufacturing Techniques: Nine Hidden Lessons in Simplicity* (New York: Free Press, 1982).

29. Craig R. Waters, "Profit and Loss," *INC.*, April 1985, 103–112.

30. Henry C. Ekstein, "Better Materials Control with Inventory Cardiograms," *Small Business Report* (March 1989), 76–79.

31. John Lorinc, "Inventory: Taking Stock," *Canadian Business*, April 1991, 46–52.

32. David T. Bottoms, "She Bought the Store," *Industry Week*, January 18, 1993, 11–12.

33. E. E. Adam, Jr., J. C. Hershauer, and W. A. Ruch, *Productivity and Quality: Measurement as a Basis for Improvement*, 2d ed. (Columbia, Mo.: Research Center, College of Business and Public Administration, University of Missouri–Columbia, 1986).

34. W. Bouce Chew, "No-Nonsense Guide to Measuring Productivity," *Harvard Business Review* (January–February 1988), 110–118.

35. Hank Johansson and Dan McArther, "Rediscovering the Fundamentals of Quality," *Management Review* (January 1988), 34–37.

36. Ross Johnson and William O. Winchell, "Management and Quality" (Milwaukee, Wis.: American Society for Quality Control, 1989).

37. Sherrie Posesorski, "Here's How to Put Statistical Process Control to Work for You," *Canadian Business*, December 1985, 163.

38. Jeremy Main, "Detroit's Cars Really Are Getting Better," *Fortune*, February 2, 1987, 90–98.

39. Kimberly J. Studer and Mark D. Dibner, "Robots Invade Small Businesses," *Management Review* (November 1988), 26–31.

40. Maggie McComas, "Cutting Costs without Killing the Business," *Fortune*, October 13, 1986, 70–78.

41. W. E. Deming, *Quality, Productivity, and Competitive Position* (Cambridge, Mass.: Center for Advanced Engineering Study, MIT, 1982); and P. B. Crosby, *Quality Is Free* (New York: McGraw-Hill, 1979).

42. J. Merwin, "A Tale of Two Worlds," *Forbes*, June 16, 1986.

43. Miller, "Boeing Gives Credence to Clearwater's Revival."

The topic of careers is important to both individuals striving to succeed in organizations and organizations that want to assist the careers of their employees. The right fit between person and career makes a difference. For example, a survey of vice-presidents found that the most important criterion for career success is love of work: "People don't get to the top unless they really love what they are doing and are willing to work very, very hard."[1] Sometimes a career causes problems. Suzanne P. is so obsessed with career success that she blocks out all aspects of her life other than work. She is cool, impersonal, aloof, attractive, and has easily reached the upper middle management of a major corporation, but she is really not happy. Media coverage of such career problems highlights career burnout and mid-career crises.

This appendix explores the topic of career management in organizations. First we examine the scope of career issues in today's organizations. Then we discuss individuals' career planning, including steps for self-analysis and career selection, stages in a successful career, and how to cope with stress. We also examine career management strategies from the organization's perspective, including career development systems, job matching, career paths, and succession planning. Finally, we will examine the special career problems of women, minorities, dual-career couples, and plateaued employees.

● CHANGING SCOPE OF CAREERS

CAREER VERSUS JOB

What does it mean to have a career? Most people do not want to just "go to work"; they want to "pursue a career." To some people, having a career requires successful movement up the corporate ladder, marked by boosts in salary and status. To others, a career means having a profession—doctors and professors have careers, whereas secretaries and blue-collar workers have jobs. Still others will tell you that no matter what the occupation, the difference between a career and a job is about 20 hours a week—that is, people who have careers are so involved in their work that they extend beyond its requirements. For these people, it is psychological involvement in their work that defines a career.

A **job** is a specific task performed for an organization. A **career** is the sequence of jobs a person holds over a life span and the person's attitudes toward involvement in those job experiences.[2] A career has a long-term perspective and includes a series of jobs. Moreover, to understand careers, we must look not only at people's work histories or résumés but also at their attitudes toward their work. People may have more or less money or power, be professional or blue collar, and vary in the importance they place on the work in relation to the rest of their lives—yet all may have careers.

A CAREER DEVELOPMENT PERSPECTIVE

Career development refers to employee progress or growth over time as a career unfolds. Career development is the result of two important activities: career planning and career management. *Career planning* emphasizes individual activities helpful in making career-related decisions. *Career management* focuses on organizational activities that foster employees' career growth.[3]

A career management perspective means adopting a "big picture" of work in the total context of people's lives and recognizing that each person's work experiences add up to a career. More importantly, as long as people are employed with an organization, they have an *organizational career,* which is the sequence of work-related activities and experiences they accumulate during their time with the organization.

A CAREER IN MANAGEMENT

Managers are responsible for developing people and helping manage their careers. But what about a career in management? What steps can a person take to become a manager? Recall from Chapter 1 that employees typically start out in organizations with a *technical skill* in an area such as finance, accounting, advertising, human resources, or computers. Most people get promoted into management positions after they become proficient in a technical skill area.

At some point, individuals will face the choice of whether to remain a technical specialist or take on supervisory and management responsibility. Examples of people who may choose to remain technical special-

job

A unit of work that a single employee is responsible for performing.

career

A sequence of work-related activities and behaviors over a person's life span viewed as movement through various job experiences and the individual's attitudes toward involvement in those experiences.

career development

Employee progress or growth over time as a career unfolds.

ists are securities traders, lawyers, teachers, and investment bankers. More typically, at a company such as Kmart or Sears, recent college graduates start out without management responsibilities. The first jobs provide basic training in store sales or merchandising. Successful employees then are given the opportunity to move into first-level management positions such as sales supervisor, visual sales manager, convenience center manager, or sales support supervisor. From there, a person's career may lead to higher-level positions such as regional merchandise manager, store operating manager, store manager, general merchandise manager, or operating manager for geographical area.

Those people who choose to move into management must be willing to shift away from reliance on technical skills toward reliance on *human skills*. As described in Chapter 1, human skill is the person's ability to work with and through other people and to participate effectively as a team member. This skill is demonstrated by the ability to motivate, facilitate, coordinate, lead, communicate, get along with others, and resolve conflicts. Human skills can be developed through practice, by taking courses and seminars, and by entering jobs that require superb human skills. For example, product manager or brand manager jobs at a consumer products company require excellent human skills.

Brand managers were called *integrating managers* in Chapter 8. Recall that an integrating manager has the responsibility to coordinate across several functions, but without formal authority. A brand manager for Fritos, Tide, or M&Ms coordinates all functions necessary to produce the product, which is a lot like running his or her own small company. The brand manager uses human skills to persuade people to perform activities necessary for product success. The brand manager also practices *conceptual skills* such as planning the advertising, retail, and trade promotions; developing a new product or packaging; and developing ways to increase sales. Companies such as Procter & Gamble, General Mills, General Foods, Ralston Purina, and M&M-Mars use brand management systems. Some 18 percent to 20 percent of graduating classes from some universities go into brand management to acquire experience useful to management careers.[4]

● INDIVIDUAL CAREER PLANNING

"Work hard and you will be rewarded." When it comes to your career, the advice to work hard makes sense, but it is not enough. Although many organizations take great interest in the management of their employees' careers, you cannot expect to work hard and let the organization take care of your career. The responsibility for your career is yours alone. People who plan their careers improve their chance of having successful ones. Perhaps the title of a recent book by General Electric Chief Executive Jack Welch says it best: *Control Your Destiny or Someone Else Will*.

Career planning is the self-assessment, exploration of opportunities, goal setting, and other activities necessary for making informed career-related choices. It is a crucial step in linking your personal needs and

career planning

The self-assessment, exploration of opportunities, goal setting, and other activities necessary to make informed career-related decisions.

capabilities with career opportunities. Career planning involves systematic thinking and attention to short-term and long-term career goals. It is an ongoing activity, not something limited to high school and college graduates making an initial job choice. Because the world and organizations change, a periodic review of your career plans and progress is a must.[5]

STEPS IN CAREER PLANNING

There are five steps involved in career planning.

1 **Self-Assessment.** The first step is gathering data on yourself—your values, interests, skills, abilities, and preferred activities. You must learn to see yourself clearly and objectively. Consider what makes you happy in work, how closely your self-image is tied to your occupation, and rewards that are important to you. Richard K. Bernstein, a corporate vice-president for a housewares company, answered the following question as part of a self-assessment: "If you had two million dollars, how would you spend it?" Bernstein immediately pictured himself in medical school. Despite being 45 years old, he knew what he wanted and went on to study medicine and specialize in research and teaching on diabetes.[6]

2 **Explore Opportunities.** Step 2 involves gathering data on your opportunities and potential choices both within and outside your organization. Evaluate the job market and economic conditions. Also, find out about training and development opportunities offered by your organization, including chances to move into different jobs and departments. For example, when Sharon Burklund wanted to move from communications research into sales, her superiors were not interested. So, she used an industry directory and called possible employers directly. Through direct contact, she discovered some opportunities. Sharon got her big break when she talked to the head of a trade paper who was about to launch a new publication and needed help in sales.

3 **Make Decisions and Set Goals.** Once you have evaluated yourself and available opportunities, you must make decisions about short-term and long-term goals. What do you want to accomplish in the next year? To which areas of the organization do you desire exposure? What skills do you want to acquire? Decide which target jobs or departments will help you get the necessary exposure and accomplish your goals. Define projects and work assignments that will provide growth opportunities.

4 **Action Planning.** This is the "how-do-I-get-there" part of career planning. It involves setting deadline dates, defining needed resources, and making plans to get around barriers. For example, when Sharon Burklund could not get the sales job in her own organization, she made action plans to find out about opportunities in other companies.

5 **Follow Up.** Once your plan is in place, periodic review and updating are needed. Take it out every six months and ask yourself,

"How am I doing? Am I growing? Did I accomplish what I wanted? Are there new target jobs or work assignments that would be better for me?"

AVOIDING OVERPLANNING

Career planning should not be rigid, narrow one's options, or chart a single course at the expense of unexpected opportunities. No one can see 10 to 15 years into the future. The point of the plan is to assess yourself and chart a course consistent with your strengths.

Walter B. Wriston, who served 14 years as CEO of Citibank, calls life a series of accidents. People must be prepared for opportunities. A big part of having a successful career is the corner you are standing on when the bus comes. If an organization is so static and employees so rigid that they know where they will be in five years, their jobs are not worth much. Every job Wriston had at the bank before becoming CEO did not exist when he joined it.[7] Likewise, the student newspaper of a large midwestern university ran the headline "Students Shouldn't Plan Their Careers" based on an interview with the university president. The president cautioned students against deciding too early on just one interest area and closing off other options.

The policy of paying careful attention to career planning is intended to do just the opposite. Career planning enables you to consider a broad range of options, identify several that will be satisfying, and choose the path that seems best at the time. Career planning provides you with self-insight to help you adjust your plans as you go along. Career planning gives you a criterion against which to evaluate unplanned opportunities so that you will know which ones to accept.

STAGES OF CAREER DEVELOPMENT

As their careers unfold, people pass through stages that signify the course of career development over time. Most careers go through four distinct stages, each associated with different issues and tasks. Dealing successfully with these stages leads to career satisfaction and growth.[8]

STAGE 1: EXPLORATION AND TRIAL. The **exploration and trial stage** usually occurs between the ages of 15 and 25. A person accepts his or her first job and may try several jobs, some part-time. People must decide whether to stay with an organization or try a job with another company. Job training, developing an image of a preferred occupation, job interviews, and early job challenges and feedback are all part of the learning process associated with this stage.

STAGE 2: ESTABLISHMENT AND ADVANCEMENT. During the **establishment and advancement stage**—typically from age 25 to 45— people experience progress within the organization. They are transferred and promoted, establish their worth to the organization, and become visible to those at higher levels. Many people form a specific career strategy, decide on a field of specialization, and find a mentor to support them. A person may receive offers from other organizations.

exploration and trial stage
The stage of career development during which a person accepts his or her first job and perhaps tries several jobs.

establishment and advancement stage
The stage of career development during which the individual experiences progress with the organization in the form of transfers, promotions, and/or high visibility.

mid-career stage

The stage of career development characterized by growth, maintenance, or decline.

disengagement stage

The stage of career development during which the person prepares for retirement and begins to disengage from both the organization and the occupation.

mentor

A senior employee who acts as a sponsor and teacher to a newer, less experienced employee.

STAGE 3: MID-CAREER.   The **mid-career stage** often occurs from ages 45 to 65. Mid-career may move in three directions. If characterized by *growth,* the individual continues to progress, receiving promotions and increasing responsibility. The person may have a feeling of "making it" but fear stagnation and thus seek new challenges. If mid-career is characterized by *maintenance,* the person tends to remain in the same job or be transferred at the same level. The individual has job security and is loyal to the organization but stops progressing up the hierarchy. He or she enjoys professional accomplishments and may become a mentor. The person may also consider a second career. If the mid-career stage is characterized by *decline,* the individual is not valued by the organization. As a "surplus" employee, demotion is possible. Decline is characterized by insecurity, crisis, a feeling of failure, and possible early retirement.

STAGE 4: DISENGAGEMENT.   The **disengagement stage** comes toward the end of every career. The person prepares for retirement and begins to disengage from both the organization and the occupation. In today's uncertain economic environment, many older workers believe that their job security and futures are threatened as companies scale back employees and retirement benefits. During the disengagement stage, a person may polish job skills through refresher courses, establish networks inside and outside the company, and develop interests and a "nest egg" for life after work. Older employees may also prove their value to the company by offering their skills as mentor to younger employees or by offering their services as a half-time worker or as a consultant.[9]

MENTOR RELATIONSHIPS

A **mentor** is a senior employee who acts as a sponsor and teacher to a newer, less experienced protégé.[10] The concept of mentor is derived from Greek mythology. Odysseus trusted the education of his son Telemachus to Mentor, a trusted counselor and friend. In today's organizations, mentors are senior, experienced employees who help newer ones navigate the organization. A mentor relationship typically lasts from two to five years and goes through periods of initiation, cultivation, and separation.[11] The *initiation stage* is a period of six months or so during which mentor and protégé get to know each other. *Cultivation* is the major period, during which the mentor "supports, guides, and counsels the new employee." During this period, the mentor-protégé relationship can be described by terms such as "master-apprentice" and "teacher-student." During the *separation* period, which lasts six months or so, the protégé may no longer want guidance, and the mentor is likely to move on to other junior employees.

Mentoring has career and social implications. The relationship often goes beyond coaching and training to become a close, personal friendship that includes mutual respect and affection, helping the protégé understand organizational norms, using power on the protégé's behalf, and taking the protégé along when the mentor moves to a new position. The mentor is a friend, counselor, and source of support.

A survey of top executives found that nearly two-thirds had a mentor at some point in their careers. The benefits of a mentoring relationship to an aspiring manager are substantial. Executives who had mentors received higher total compensation than did those who had not.[12] Mentors can be an important source of career development because they help new managers learn the ropes and benefit from the mentor's experience.[13]

Although mentoring relationships are valuable, they are not without problems. A study in Canada revealed a number of differences in the approach to mentoring by women and men. Among the findings: Men view having a mentor as a way of learning how to perform their jobs more effectively; women tend to use the mentor relationship to gain knowledge about corporate culture and thus bypass traditional barriers to their advancement. The study also revealed potential complications, especially those found in mixed (male/female) mentoring relationships, including gossip about them and charges of favoritism. Perhaps the most difficult and painful aspect is the ending of a mentoring relationship when the junior person is ready to progress on his or her own. The most successful mentoring efforts are usually found within companies that establish a voluntary mentoring program with trained mentors and the full support of the company.[14]

Senior managers generally initiate mentoring relationships, but there are steps that young managers can take to develop a mentoring relationship with experienced managers:

1 Determine who is successful and well thought of, and get to know him or her professionally and socially.

2 Seek out opportunities for exposure and visibility—committees and special projects—that will provide opportunities to work with experienced, successful people.

3 Inform experienced colleagues of your interests and goals; let your activities and successes be known to these people; seek specific feedback on your performance from experienced colleagues other than your boss.

4 Keep in mind that it may not be necessary to find a single, powerful senior manager to fulfill the mentor role. You may be able to develop mentoring relationships with a variety of experienced managers, including peers, during your career.[15]

Acquiring a mentor has made a difference in many careers. For example, Nancy Lane, executive producer at CNN News, was fortunate to have Mary Alice Williams, now NBC news anchor, as her mentor. Senator Bill Bradley saw special ability and skills in Betty Sapoch and took the time to help her gain confidence and skills necessary to become executive director of his election campaigns.[16]

● MANAGING CAREER STRESS

Recall from Chapter 1 that managerial work is characterized by brevity, variety, and discontinuity. In other chapters, we have seen that managers are responsible for organizing, controlling, and

■
stress

The physiological and emotional
response to demands, constraints, and
opportunities that create uncertainty
when important outcomes are at stake.

leading the organization. Successful managers are action oriented and responsible for high performance. Considering the nature of managerial work, stress is part of the job—indeed, many people have a stereotype of executives as harried, stressed-out, coronary-prone individuals.

Stress is defined as the physiological and emotional response to demands, constraints, and opportunities that create uncertainty when important outcomes are at stake.[17] A key notion concerning stress is that people perceive the situation as taxing or as beyond their resources for responding appropriately.[18] Thus, you experience stress if your workload is too heavy for the available time, a deadline is rapidly approaching and you need more information to make a decision, or your boss is dragging his feet on approving a project important to your career. Many life events, such as a promotion, a death in the family, marriage, divorce, or a new baby, can induce stress because of the adjustments they require.[19]

SOURCES OF STRESS

There are many sources of stress for managers. Some common ones are listed in Exhibit A.1. Factors such as work overload, erratic schedules, job instability, and cutthroat competition influence the level of stress.[20] Managers also feel stress in the transition from one career stage to the next. Turbulence and uncertainty associated with the establishment and mid-career stages can be great, especially if the career is perceived as not going well or if there is no mentor relationship.

In recent years, much has been published about the "Type-A" personality as a potential source of stress.[21] People with Type-A behavior patterns demonstrate many potential leadership qualities and are viewed as competitive, action-oriented individuals. However, they are also prime targets for stress and stress-related diseases, such as high blood pressure, heart disease, and ulcers. Typical Type-A characteristics include the following:

- Impatience when standing in a line at the bank, store, or a restaurant.
- Excess energy and a tendency to have many projects going at once.
- Burning the candle at both ends.
- Irritability and a "hair trigger."
- Excessive need to lead in any group or organization.

By pacing themselves and by learning control and intelligent use of their natural tendencies, Type-A men and women can become powerful forces for innovation and leadership within their companies without creating stress-related problems for themselves.

An emerging source of stress for middle managers has been turbulence in the external environment, such as the threat of termination brought about by downsizing, shifts in corporate strategy based on global competition, and mergers and acquisitions. The fear and uncertainty surrounding possible job loss often create stress as great as that from actual job loss. Job insecurity and job loss due to rapid environ-

---

E X H I B I T   A . 1

Sources of Management Stress

- Work overload, excessive time demands, and "rush" deadlines
- Erratic work schedules and take-home work
- Ambiguity regarding work tasks, territory, and role
- Constant change and daily variability
- Role conflict (e.g., with immediate supervisor)
- Job instability and fear of unemployment
- Negative competition (e.g., "cutthroat," "one-upmanship," "zero-sum game," and "hidden aggression")

- Type of vigilance required in work assignments
- Ongoing contact with "stress carriers" (e.g., workaholics, passive-aggressive subordinates, anxious and indecisive individuals)
- Sexual harassment
- Accelerated recognition for achievement (e.g., the Peter Principle)
- Detrimental environmental conditions of lighting, ventilation, noise, and personal privacy

SOURCE: Based on K. R. Pelletier, *Healthy People in Unhealthy Places: Stress and Fitness at Work* (New York: Dell, 1984).

---

mental changes and global competition will continue as major sources of manager stress through the 1990s.

One example of externally caused stress occurred at Phillips Petroleum Company. Due to a takeover attempt and a decline in the oil industry, 6,800 employees were laid off over several years in Bartlesville, Oklahoma, the company headquarters. The stress from job loss produced negative family consequences. Requests for assistance from a local shelter and counseling center for abused families shot up 69 percent. Women attending support groups for battered wives increased 41 percent. The number of children in counseling groups rose 74 percent. Emotional consequences were also felt by Phillips employees who did not lose their jobs.[22]

However, despite the negative consequences of severe stress, not all stress is bad. Hans Selye, one of the originators of stress research, observed that the only people who have no stress are dead![23] A moderate amount of stress has a positive effect on performance, but extremely high stress contributes to performance decline. Extended periods of high stress can lead to **burnout,** which is the emotional exhaustion arising from overexposure to stress.[24] Moderate job stress is a natural part of managerial work. Although executives may complain of stress, few want lower-pressure jobs.

burnout

The emotional exhaustion resulting from extended periods of stress.

SYMPTOMS OF STRESS

How do managers manifest too much stress? Common stress symptoms are anxiety and tension, depression, and physical disorders such as headache, low back pain, hypertension, and gastrointestinal problems. Behavioral symptoms include difficulty sleeping, loss of creativity, compulsive eating, and alcohol or drug abuse.[25] For example, after General Motors took over Hughes Aircraft, Robert Hearsch experienced a stress situation. A successful manager at Hughes, he was put in charge of buying pens and pencils. He worked hard but under the new system received constant criticism. He lost 20 pounds, his marriage hit the skids, and he suffered a minor nervous breakdown. A coworker handled his stress in another way, showing up at the office brandishing a handgun.[26]

COPING WITH STRESS

Research on effective ways of coping with managerial stress is just now emerging, but some trends have been identified. For example, ways to cope include learning to relax through meditation or regular exercise. Managers can learn to say no to unacceptable work overloads, stand up to the boss, and delegate responsibility to subordinates. Requesting resources needed to remove the cause of stress often helps.[27] Other effective behaviors are building resistance to stress through regular sleep, good eating and health habits, and discussing the stressful situation with coworkers, family, and friends.

Recent data indicate that factors under managerial control, such as performance feedback and clear job expectations, job decision latitude, and social support, are key factors in helping subordinates cope effectively with job stress.[28] In the end, however, each person must find his or her own strategies for coping with stress. For example, a survey of senior executives revealed a variety of techniques, including having other interests, maintaining a sense of humor, keeping in shape, keeping a balance in their lives, deciding not to let things bother them, and not taking matters too seriously.

At the company level, managers can ease employee stress by adopting sound corporate practices such as these:

- Implementing stress audits to determine factors that contribute to stress (including boredom as well as overwork, noise, danger, etc.).
- Utilizing employee assistance programs and wellness programs.
- Improved matching of employees with jobs and job rotation.
- Empowering employees, giving them a greater sense of control over their situation.
- Developing trauma contingency plans to assist employees in dealing with crises that may occur in the workplace.
- Improving educational, training, and information programs.[29]

ORGANIZATIONAL POLICIES FOR CAREER MANAGEMENT

Up to this point, we have been dealing with career planning from the viewpoint of the individual employee. Now we turn to career management policies and strategies that organizations can use to promote effective employee career development.

Career management refers to organizational activities designed to promote employees' career development. These activities should func-

career management

Organizational activities designed to promote employees' career development.

tion as a system designed to meet individual needs for job advancement, extension of skill, or the enhancement of human experience on the job and to relate these needs to the future requirements of the organization.[30] A career development system is created by coordinating various human resource functions, such as recruitment, performance appraisal, and staffing, while providing a variety of special policies and programs focusing specifically on employee career development.

Exhibit A.2 illustrates the key components and functions of a career development system. The formal responsibility for career development is usually housed in the human resource management/personnel department. As with most human resource management programs, however, the success of career development depends on line managers' adoption of a career development perspective on a cooperative relationship with the human resource staff. The two dimensions in Exhibit A.2 are career planning and career management. As described earlier, career planning emphasizes individual actions, whereas career management emphasizes organizational initiatives. Moreover, as the arrows in Exhibit A.2 indicate, individual and organizational activities should jointly influence career development. Employees are more likely to do systematic career planning if the organization provides opportunities and structure for this purpose. Organizationally prescribed performance feedback and discussion of career potential are an important impetus to individual efforts. Organizations can provide career planning programs such as workshops

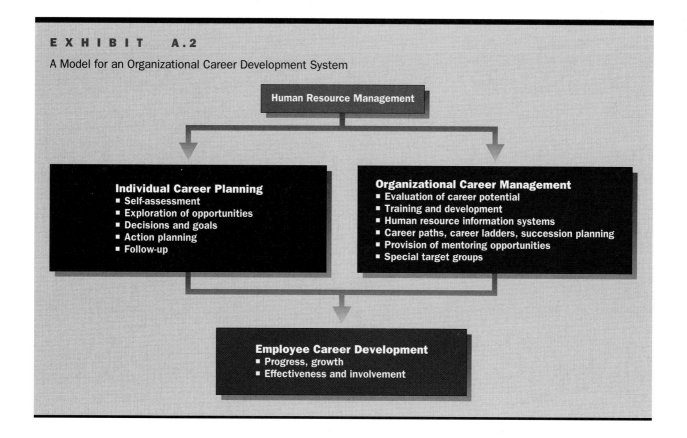

E X H I B I T   A . 2

A Model for an Organizational Career Development System

Human Resource Management

Individual Career Planning
- Self-assessment
- Exploration of opportunities
- Decisions and goals
- Action planning
- Follow-up

Organizational Career Management
- Evaluation of career potential
- Training and development
- Human resource information systems
- Career paths, career ladders, succession planning
- Provision of mentoring opportunities
- Special target groups

Employee Career Development
- Progress, growth
- Effectiveness and involvement

and counseling, but individuals must choose to invest energy and time in action planning and follow-up if career development is to take place.

The major components of the organization's career management system are an evaluation of potential, training and development, human resource information systems, career paths, career planning programs, and provision of mentoring opportunities.

EVALUATION OF CAREER POTENTIAL

A critical input into career development is the performance appraisal process described in Chapter 10. Feedback on job performance is important in all aspects of individual career planning, providing valuable data on skills and strengths and assisting employees in identifying realistic future goals.

The appraisal process also helps the organization assess future potential—the individual's probability of moving upward in the organization. Organizations may use a variety of tools to assess potential, such as commercially prepared tests and inventories, internally developed questionnaires, succession planning, or an assessment center. Often, however, it is the manager's role to determine future career potential using personal judgment. A section of the formal performance appraisal rating form can ask the manager to rate the employee's "future potential" or "promotability."

TRAINING AND MANAGEMENT DEVELOPMENT

The backbone of a career management program is organizational commitment to training and employee development. *Training* programs focus on the immediately applicable, technically oriented skills required for the next level of job. *Management development* suggests a longer-term view of expanding a person's confidence and growth. Many organizations have a wide range of training and development programs that employees can attend. Some new managers attend management training programs sponsored by universities and the American Management Association to develop their human and conceptual skills.

Another important aspect of training and development involves internal job moves. The most frequently used job moves for broadening and increasing an employee's potential for advancement are vertical and horizontal:

- *Vertical:* Moving up and down the organizational pyramid; job moves in this category involve changes in rank or organizational level.
- *Horizontal:* Lateral movement to a different function, division, or product line in the organization, such as from sales to marketing or from human resources to public relations.

HUMAN RESOURCE INFORMATION SYSTEMS

Effective career development systems depend on information. Data on organizational human resource planning and individual career planning must be available to managers and employees. These data usually come from job analysis and job matching systems.

JOB ANALYSIS.   *Job analysis* was referred to in Chapter 10 as the systematic collection of information about the purpose, responsibilities, tasks, knowledge, and abilities needed for a job. Data are collected by the personnel staff through interviews with job incumbents and supervisors.

HUMAN RESOURCE INVENTORY.   The **human resource inventory** is a data base that summarizes individuals' skills, abilities, work experiences, and career interests. These data are made available to both managers and personnel specialists.

human resource inventory

A data base that summarizes individuals' skills, abilities, work experiences, and career interests.

JOB MATCHING SYSTEMS.   The component for bringing together both job data and human resource interests is a **job matching system,** which links individuals with career opportunities within the organization. The job matching system brings together the human resources inventory as well as the job characteristics, descriptions, and profiles derived from the job analysis. The job matching system searches through all potentially qualified or interested employees and matches them with present or future openings.

job matching system

A method that links qualified individuals with career opportunities within the organization.

One type of matching system developed by Gannett Company, Inc., is the Talent Tracking System. The system is a computerized job matching network managed by the corporate news staff in Arlington, Virginia, for all of the company's newspapers. Over 1,500 names have been logged into the system, and top editors from around the country use a computer to review the credentials of job prospects. The system works like a giant cookie jar, with top managers able to select and recruit employees from around the Gannett system.[31]

CAREER PATHS, CAREER LADDERS, AND SUCCESSION PLANNING

Career paths are job progression routes along which employees can advance through the organization. Career paths typically are developed for specific employees, or they may be drawn up by the organization as general routes for employee advancement. They consist of a series of target jobs or functional areas that indicate future job moves appropriate for the individual's career. Career paths may include horizontal moves and an occasional downward move in order to obtain the needed experience.

career path

A job progression route along which an employee can advance through the organization.

Career ladders are formalized job progression routes based on jobs that are logically connected. Career ladders tend to be more precisely and objectively determined than career paths. Career ladders are based on data collected through job analysis and examination of personnel records showing historical patterns of employee job moves. An example of a career ladder for Link Flight Simulator Division of the Singer Company is illustrated in Exhibit A.3. This career ladder charts the normal progression for engineers. After an engineer advances through the first four stages, a decision must be made. The person can concentrate on

career ladder

A formalized job progression route based on logically connected jobs.

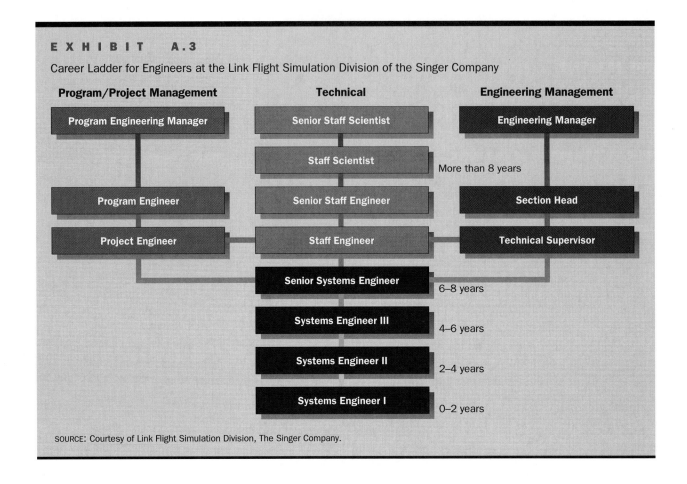

EXHIBIT A.3

Career Ladder for Engineers at the Link Flight Simulation Division of the Singer Company

Program/Project Management	Technical	Engineering Management
Program Engineering Manager	Senior Staff Scientist	Engineering Manager
	Staff Scientist	More than 8 years
Program Engineer	Senior Staff Engineer	Section Head
Project Engineer	Staff Engineer	Technical Supervisor
	Senior Systems Engineer	6–8 years
	Systems Engineer III	4–6 years
	Systems Engineer II	2–4 years
	Systems Engineer I	0–2 years

SOURCE: Courtesy of Link Flight Simulation Division, The Singer Company.

technical challenges and remain in the staff engineering track, or he or she may decide to pursue a management track.

There are two ladders associated with management—functional management within the engineering department and program management that involves the coordination of entire projects. The decision to pursue a specific track will be based on the individual's self-assessment and interest in becoming either a staff scientist or a manager.

Succession planning is the process used to create a plan for moving people into the higher levels of the organization. Succession planning applies to a specific group of employees who have the development potential to become top-level managers. "Top level" usually is defined as two to four levels below the CEO. Organizations with progressive career development systems have extended succession planning for all professional and managerial positions.

Succession planning defines both present and future job requirements and determines the availability of candidates and their readiness to move into top jobs.[32] It also uses *employee resource charts* to identify likely successors for each management position. This system suggests possible career paths and career ladders for a set of managers and managerial jobs. The succession planning time horizon is usually 12 to 36 months

succession planning

The process of creating a plan for moving people into higher organizational levels.

and is periodically updated. The appropriate emphasis in succession planning is on developing a pool of talent rather than selecting a "crown prince" to assume a top position.

CAREER PLANNING PROGRAMS

Career planning programs offered by the organization can take the form of career planning workshops and individual career counseling sessions. Group workshops can be conducted by personnel department staff or outside consultants. The workshops take employees through the systematic steps of individual career planning by using individual assessment exercises, holding small-group discussions, and providing information on organizational opportunities.

Individual career counseling may be provided by the personnel department, but a major part takes place during career planning discussions with supervisors. Supervisors must be trained and knowledgeable about career planning and opportunities. Career counseling requires that a manager assume the role of coach and counselor. Sometimes it is difficult to do career planning during a performance appraisal session because employees become defensive. Some organizations resolve this problem by asking supervisors to hold separate sessions—the first for performance evaluation and the second for creating a career plan.[33]

MENTORING OPPORTUNITIES

As we discussed earlier, mentoring provides many advantages to the career development of junior managers. Although mentoring is something that junior managers can undertake on their own, mentor relationships can be an important organizational tool for employee career development.

One approach organizations can use to encourage and facilitate mentoring is education.[34] Educational programs help senior managers understand mentoring and its importance in career management and help establish norms and cultural values in support of mentoring. Other changes that facilitate mentoring include adjusting the reward system to place greater emphasis on mentoring, modifying the work design, adapting performance management systems, and even introducing a formal mentoring program. In this way, senior managers can be encouraged and rewarded for mentoring and may even be assigned junior managers to support and assist. Organizational efforts to facilitate mentoring are important because informally developed, one-to-one relationships may not be available to all promising junior managers. One outcome of mentoring programs is to foster multiple developmental relationships between junior managers and more experienced senior people.

Small entrepreneurial companies often have a difficult time developing managers because they cannot afford formal training programs. General Alum & Chemical Corporation invented its own in-house mentoring system to solve this problem. To socialize new managers and train them into the corporate culture, senior executives were assigned to a handful of developing managers. The junior managers had great potential but lacked experience. The mentor relationship enabled these young men and women to learn about subtle aspects of management, including human and conceptual skills. Formally assigning mentors made sure that all potential managers had this positive experience.[35]

● SPECIAL CAREER MANAGEMENT PROBLEMS

Because of current social, economic, and legal pressures, organizational career management strategies may be focused on the unique needs of special target groups. Concerns about career development for women and minorities is a direct outgrowth of equal employment opportunity legislation. Although women and minorities are advancing within corporations, they are still underrepresented in middle- and top-level management.[36] The increasing number of dual-career couples has pressured organizations to solve the problems unique to this group of employees. Further, as organizations face increasing competition and are forced to streamline management structures, many management employees find they have plateaued because there are fewer opportunities to move up the hierarchy.

EMPLOYEE DIVERSITY

Because of common issues faced by women and minorities, recommended career development management strategies often consider these two target groups together. Organizations must confront issues related to assimilating and developing these two groups. For example, because minorities and women have only recently entered management ranks, they may have difficulty developing the social networking and mentoring helpful to career development. Recall from Chapter 1 that work-force diversity is a major issue facing organizations in the 1990s. White males will make up a smaller proportion of the management work force in future years.

WOMEN. Issues that women face include balancing multiple roles of career and family and dealing with sexual harassment.[37] A recent survey found that nearly one out of three women who received MBAs from the nation's top business schools ten years ago have left the managerial work force.[38] Because many of these women left to devote more time to their families, some companies are experimenting with innovative programs that respond to family pressures and offer more flexibility for both men and women.

Because only women have babies and often are responsible for child care, some female managers and professionals are leaving the fast track for what has been called the *mommy track.* These women devote time to raising a young family rather than devoting all their energies to career advancement. Some women dislike the notion of a mommy track, believing it identifies female employees as separate and unequal and may permanently derail women's careers, making them second-class citizens. Taking time to raise a family as well as work may confirm prejudices of male executives and contribute to perception of the glass ceiling. So-called mommy trackers are less likely to be considered for promotion to highly responsible positions.[39]

Many companies encourage women to take time for their children because it allows the company to retain valued employees. These employees may be given extended leave, flexible scheduling, or opportunities for job sharing and telecommuting that enable them to raise a family. These managers come back to regular work when the children are older. For example, Mellon Bank allows women to work flexible hours, work at home, and engage in job sharing. At KMPG Peat Marwick, women can opt for a lighter client load and a less than 40-hour workweek for two to three years. Procter & Gamble gives women eight weeks' paid maternity leave and six months' unpaid child care leave to either parent.[40]

MINORITIES. Despite a large and growing black middle class, the progress of blacks in U.S. corporations has been disappointing to blacks and whites alike. According to statistics from the Equal Employment Opportunity Commission, only 9.5 percent of all managers are minorities. One discouraged manager said, "The U.S. is in a global trade war and we're trying to fight without all our troops."[41]

The biggest barrier facing minorities, especially black managers, is advancement into upper management. Minorities must learn the "difficult, lonely and threatening way to navigate in a basically white environment." This environment is characterized by white executives' discomfort with nonwhites as well as the tendency to promote managers with backgrounds similar to their own. A recent survey of black managers revealed that many of them perceived the organizational climate for black managers in their organization as indifferent, patronizing, and reluctant to accept blacks. On the positive side, some organizational climates were seen as encouraging, supportive, and trusting.[42] Although the percentage is small, an increasing number of blacks have triumphed in corporate careers, becoming successful managers in major companies.

Recommendations for addressing the unique needs of women and minorities include providing them with access to information, allowing nontraditional career moves, enforcing affirmative action, and providing better assessment and coaching skills for potential managers. Organizations should pay particular attention to assisting women and minorities in identifying and examining career paths and the requirements for advancement. Training programs should emphasize the job skills that women and minorities need as well as the unique problems they face when advancing within the corporation.

DUAL-CAREER COUPLES

The growing number of dual-career couples has prompted organizational career management programs to focus on the corporate problems posed by this expanding group of employees.[43] Traditionally, it was assumed that if a wife worked, her own career took second place to her husband's. Today women are increasingly likely to place equal importance on their career involvement and are no longer expected to fit their careers to their husbands' career needs. As a result, more couples face the issue of having both a committed personal relationship and careers that are central to each spouse.

Dual-career relationships involve trade-offs, and both employees and managers are realizing that most people cannot "have it all"—happy marriage, children, charming home, many friends, and intense commitment to a career. Organizations are concerned because the pressures experienced by dual-career couples may harm productivity or morale and can pose difficulties when recruiting new employees or transferring current employees to new locations.[44]

There is a strong link between the career problems facing women and the problems of dual-career couples. Women MBAs who left the work force did so because of work-family conflicts. In the final analysis, in most families the responsibility for balancing work and family responsibilities falls disproportionately on the woman.[45]

These issues are difficult to resolve. Suppose, for example, that you have just been promoted to manager of market development for a fast-growing computer software firm in Chicago. Your spouse is offered a big promotion that requires a move to Dallas. What criteria would you use to decide whether to give up your new position or make your spouse pass up the promotion? Will you consider a commuting relationship? If so, for how long?

Corporations are finding ways to help dual-career couples eliminate stress and to help the company retain competent people. One change is dropping antiquated "antinepotism" rules that prevented husbands and wives from working together. Universities, law firms, publishing houses, newspapers, and corporate offices are just a few of the organizations to have realized that top men and women in the field meet and marry. Recruiting high-quality people increasingly means hiring both spouses in the same discipline or department.[46] Other career management programs directed at dual-career couples include flexible work schedules, transfer policies, career planning assistance, and local support services such as day care for children.

PLATEAUED EMPLOYEES

career plateau

A point in a career from which the opportunities for further promotion are scarce.

A **career plateau** is "a point in a career from which the likelihood of additional hierarchical promotion, in the judgment of the organization, is very low."[47] Due to the high value most people place on upward mobility, plateauing has come to be viewed by organizations as a problem and may lead to the employee being written off or ignored with respect to career development opportunities. As a practical matter, there is nothing inherently negative about reaching a career plateau. It is a natural consequence of the narrowing pyramid shape of organizations, and many employees experience a career plateau somewhere during mid-career.

Plateaued employees can fall into one of two categories. "Solid citizens" are plateaued employees rated as performing satisfactorily. "Deadwood" are plateaued employees whose performance has fallen below the satisfactory level.[48] Many plateaued employees are effective performers, and they should not be stereotyped as unmotivated or performing inadequately. Indeed, many companies want to keep plateaued employees and their accumulated knowledge. Many people have spent their entire careers in excellent organizations such as IBM, GE, Eastman Kodak, Westinghouse, and Hewlett-Packard, even after they had no prospect of further advancement.[49]

Many organizations anticipate a larger number of plateaued employees in the future. Fewer promotional opportunities will be available because of leaner management staffs. This may also mean that plateauing will occur earlier than mid-career for some employees. Most managers will have plateaued employees and will need to devote attention to developing and maintaining these people's competence.

One study found that plateaued managers performed better when they and their bosses agreed on clear performance objectives and when the managers received feedback on specific tasks and overall performance. Other factors that helped plateaued employees' performances were whether they knew the basis on which their performances were being evaluated and whether they had challenging, satisfying, and clearly defined jobs that were important to the company.[50]

A number of career management techniques exist that organizations can use to help plateaued employees. One is to enhance job challenge and task accomplishment opportunities. This can be done through transfers or by changing the scope of the present job. Other techniques include job changes, training programs that provide mentoring and career counseling, and managerial and technical updating.[51]

● CAREER DEVELOPMENT IN FOUR STAGES

To make career development more effective, the organization can focus on employee career stages. Rather than provide one program for all employees, the firm can offer several programs, each of which can match the needs of specific employee groups. Examples of career management strategies associated with each of the four career stages described earlier are illustrated in Exhibit A.4.

In the exploration/trial stage, one concern is how to deal with *reality shock*, which is the upsetting experience and stress brought about by unmet expectations of organizational newcomers.[52] Reality shock can lead to early career dissatisfaction and high turnover. Thus, one career management strategy is to give new recruits *realistic job previews* that present job interviewees with the full picture of the organization without selling or "sugar coating" job opportunities. Other strategies during the early career stage are to provide varied job activities, opportunities for self-exploration, and opportunities to gain organizational knowledge.

For employees in the establishment/advancement stage, career management should focus on helping them gain competence in a specialty and develop personal creativity and innovation skills. People at this level should be encouraged to gain familiarity with different organizational areas, possibly through horizontal transfers. They should also be given

mid-career renewal strategies

A strategy designed to provide advancement opportunities for deserving mid-career employees while maximizing the contributions of plateaued employees who continue to perform satisfactorily.

preretirement program

A strategy designed to assist employees in coping with the stress of the transition from work to retirement.

an opportunity to develop and display their skills and expertise for potential mentor relationships and promotability.

For employees in mid-career, the organization should provide **mid-career renewal strategies,** which are designed to provide upward mobility for those who merit it while maximizing the contributions of plateaued employees who continue to perform satisfactorily. For employees who experience mid-career crises, planning workshops and support groups can help redirect career goals. The organization also can help managers combat obsolescence by providing technical and managerial skill training programs.

For employees in the disengagement stage of their careers, an increasingly popular career management strategy is to provide preretirement programs. **Preretirement programs** assist employees in managing the stress of transition from work to retirement. Some educational areas that facilitate the transition are financial planning, leisure activities, work/career alternatives, and health.[53] Other ways to keep disengaging managers contributing to the organization are to help them shift from a role of power and decision making to one of consultation, guidance, and development of key subordinates. The organization can also help disengaging people find meaningful activities outside the organization.

Focusing on employees' needs relative to their career stages coordinates the organization's career management strategies with the varied needs of all personnel. The potential bottom-line payoffs to the organization for effective career management are substantial. Productivity, satisfaction, retention, and commitment of valued employees, stress reduction, and a flexible work force will help the organization remain competitive in our global economy.

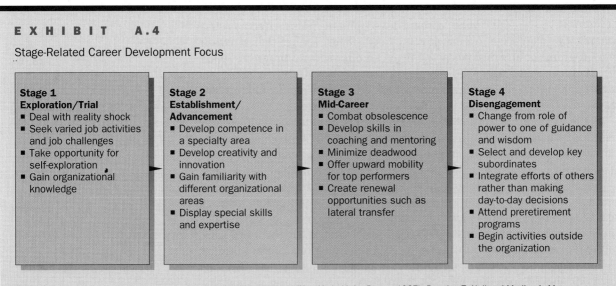

EXHIBIT A.4

Stage-Related Career Development Focus

Stage 1
Exploration/Trial
- Deal with reality shock
- Seek varied job activities and job challenges
- Take opportunity for self-exploration
- Gain organizational knowledge

Stage 2
Establishment/Advancement
- Develop competence in a specialty area
- Develop creativity and innovation
- Gain familiarity with different organizational areas
- Display special skills and expertise

Stage 3
Mid-Career
- Combat obsolescence
- Develop skills in coaching and mentoring
- Minimize deadwood
- Offer upward mobility for top performers
- Create renewal opportunities such as lateral transfer

Stage 4
Disengagement
- Change from role of power to one of guidance and wisdom
- Select and develop key subordinates
- Integrate efforts of others rather than making day-to-day decisions
- Attend preretirement programs
- Begin activities outside the organization

SOURCE: Adapted from T. Gutteridge, *Career Planning and Management* (New York: Little, Brown, 1987); Douglas T. Hall and Marilyn A. Morgan, "Career Development and Planning," in *Contemporary Problems in Personnel*, rev. ed., W. Clay Hammer and Frank Schmidt (Chicago: St. Clair Press, 1977), 205–225; and Edgar H. Seatin, *Career Dynamics* (Reading, Mass.: Addison-Wesley, 1978), 40–46.

SUMMARY

This appendix covered several important issues about the management of careers. Career management was discussed from two perspectives: the individual who wants to have a successful career and the organization that wishes to provide career opportunities for its employees.

Individual career planning normally entails five steps—self-assessment, exploring opportunities, making decisions and setting goals, action planning, and follow-up. Individual careers follow predictable stages that include exploration and trial, establishment and advancement, mid-career, and disengagement. Other issues of concern to individual career planning are mentors and coping with stress.

Organizational career management involves several systems and techniques. These include evaluation of career potential, training and development programs, human resource information systems, career paths and succession planning, career planning programs, and facilitation of mentoring. Other organizational concerns pertain to women and minorities, dual-career couples, and plateaued employees. Dealing effectively with these target groups can enhance the organization's human resource base. Finally, effective career management programs target individuals' needs at each stage in their career.

REFERENCES

1. R. Ricklafs, "Many Executives Complain of Stress, but Few Want Less-Pressure Jobs," *The Wall Street Journal,* September 29, 1982, 1.

2. Daniel C. Feldman, "Careers in Organizations: Recent Trends and Future Directions," *Journal of Management* 15 (1989), 135–156.

3. T. Gutteridge, *Career Planning and Management* (Boston: Little, Brown, 1987).

4. Janet Bamford, "Climb Quickly or Get Out Fast," *Forbes,* November 3, 1986, 224–226.

5. Mona Melanson, "Career Self-Assessment," *National Business Employment Weekly,* June 25, 1989, 9.

6. Scott Bronestein, "Past Forty and Back to Square One," *The New York Times,* October 20, 1985, 6F.

7. "Expert View," *Working Woman,* October 1985, 154.

8. The discussion of career stages is based on M. London and S. A. Stumpf, "Individual and Organizational Development in Changing Times," in *Career Development in Organizations,* ed. Douglas T. Hall and associates (San Francisco: Jossey-Bass, 1986).

9. Kenneth Labich, "Take Control of Your Career," *Fortune,* November 18, 1991, 1991, 87–96.

10. Kathy E. Kram, *Mentoring at Work: Developmental Relationships in Organizational Life* (Glenview, Ill.: Scott, Foresman, 1985).

11. Kathy E. Kram, "Phases of the Mentor Relationship," *Academy of Management Journal* 26 (1983), 608–625.

12. William Whitely, Thomas W. Dougherty, and George F. Dreher, "Relationships of Career Mentoring and Social Economic Origin to Managers' and Professionals' Early Career Progress," *Academy of Management Journal* 34 (1991), 331–351, and G. R. Roche, "Much Ado about Mentors," *Harvard Business Review* (January–February 1979), 14–28.

13. Kathy E. Kram and L. Isabella, "Mentoring Alternatives: The Role of Peer Relationships in Career Development," *Academy of Management Journal* 28 (1985), 110–132.

14. John Lorinc, "The Mentor Gap, Older Men Guiding Younger Women: The Perils and Payoffs," *Canadian Business,* September 1990, 93–94.

15. Rosabeth Moss Kanter, *Men and Women of the Corporation* (New York: Basic Books, 1977).

16. Aimee Lee Ball, "Mentors & Protégés," *Working Woman,* October 1989, 134–142.

17. T. A. Beehr and R. S. Bhagat, *Human Stress and Cognition in Organizations: An Integrated Perspective* (New York: Wiley, 1985).

18. R. S. Lazarus and S. Folkman, *Stress, Appraisal and Coping* (New York: Springer, 1984).

19. T. Homes and R. Rahe, "The Social Readjustment Rating Scale," *Journal of Psychosomatic Research* 11 (1967), 213–218.

20. K. R. Pelletier, *Healthy People in Unhealthy Places: Stress and Fitness at Work* (New York: Dell, 1984).

21. Daniel C. Ganster and John Schaubroeck, "Work Stress and Employee Health," *Journal of Management* 17 (1991), 235–271.

22. Emily T. Smith, "Stress: The Test Americans Are Failing," *Business Week,* April 18, 1988, 74–76.

23. Hans Selye, *The Stress of Life* (New York: McGraw-Hill, 1956).

24. Brian Dumaine, "Cool Cures for Burnout," *Fortune,* June 20, 1988, 78–84, and Jeannie Gaines and John M. Jermier, "Emotional Exhaustion in a High Stress Organization," *Academy of Management Journal* 26 (1983), 567–586.

25. Sana Siwolop, "The Crippling Ills That Stress Can Trigger," *Business Week,* April 18, 1988, 77–78.

26. Annetta Miller, "Stress on the Job," *Newsweek,* April 25, 1988, 40–45.

27. Ibid.

28. J. C. Latack, R. J. Aldag, and B. Joseph, "Job Stress: Determinants and Consequences of Coping Behaviors" (Working paper, Ohio State University, 1986), and R. A. Karasek, Jr., "Job Demands, Job Decision Latitude, and Mental Strain: Implications for Job Redesign," *Administrative Science Quarterly* 24 (1979), 285–308.

29. Alan Farnham, "Who Beats Stress Best—And How," *Fortune,* October 7, 1991, 71–86.

30. Jeffrey A. Sonnenfeld and Maury A. Peiperl, "Staffing Policy as a Strategic Response: A Topology of Career Systems," *Academy of Management Review* 13

(1988) 588–600; "Career Development Programs," *Small Business Report* (November 1987), 30–35; and E. H. Burack, *Career Planning and Management: A Managerial Summary* (Lake Forest, Ill.: Brace-Park Press, 1983).

31. Molly Badgett, "Computerized Talent Files Broaden Editors' Reach for New Employees," *Gannetteer*, published by Gannett Company, Inc. (June 1989), 4–5.

32. M. London, *Developing Managers* (San Francisco: Jossey-Bass, 1985).

33. D. T. Wight, "The Split Role in Performance Appraisal," *Personnel Administrator* (May 1985), 83–87, and A. H. Soerwine, "The Manager as Career Counselor: Some Issues and Approaches," in *Career Development in the 1980s*, ed. D. H. Montross and C. J. Shinkman (Springfield, Ill.: Charles C. Thomas, 1981).

34. Kram, *Mentoring at Work.*

35. Lisa R. Sheeran and Donna Fenn, "The Mentor System," *INC.*, June 1987, 136–142.

36. Anne B. Fisher, "Where Women Are Succeeding," *Fortune*, August 3, 1987, 78–86.

37. Felice N. Schwartz, "Management Women and the New Facts of Life," *Harvard Business Review* (January–February 1989), 65–76.

38. A. Taylor, "Why Women Managers Are Bailing Out," *Fortune*, August 18, 1986, 16–23.

39. Elizabeth Ehrlich, "The Mommy Track," *Business Week*, March 20, 1989, 126–134.

40. Taylor, "Women Managers."

41. Colin Lolinster, "Black Executives: How They're Doing," *Fortune*, January 18, 1988, 109–120, and Joel Dreyfuss, "Get Ready for the New Work Force," *Fortune*, April 23, 1990, 165–181.

42. L. Riebstein, "Many Hurdles, Old and New, Keep Black Managers Out of Top Jobs," *The Wall Street Journal*, July 10, 1986, 1.

43. U. Sekaran, *Dual Career Families: Implications for Organizations and Counselors* (San Francisco: Jossey-Bass, 1986).

44. Colin Lolinster, "The Young Exec as Superdad," *Fortune*, April 25, 1988, 233–242.

45. D. T. Hall, "Career Development in Organizations: Where Do We Go from Here?" in *Career Development in Organizations*, ed. Douglas T. Hall and associates (San Francisco: Jossey-Bass, 1986).

46. Fran Schumer, "The New Nepotism: Married Couples Are Working Together All Over," *New York*, November 19, 1990, 46–50.

47. J. A. F. Stoner, T. P. Ference, E. K. Warren, and H. K. Christensen, *Managerial Career Plateaus: An Exploratory Study* (New York: Center for Research and Career Development, Columbia University, 1980).

48. Ibid.

49. Judith M. Bardwick, "How Executives Can Help Plateaued Employees," *Management Review* (January 1987), 40–46.

50. J. P. Carnazza, A. K. Korman, T. P. Ference, and J. A. F. Stoner, "Plateaued and Non-Plateaued Managers: Factors in Job Performance," *Journal of Management* 7 (1981), 7–25.

51. J. M. Bardwick, "Plateauing and Productivity," *Sloan Management Review* (Spring 1983), 67–73.

52. J. P. Wanous, *Organizational Entry: Recruitment, Selection, and Socialization of Newcomers* (Reading, Mass.: Addison-Wesley, 1980).

53. W. Arnone, "Preretirement Planning: An Employee Benefit That Has Come of Age," *Personnel* 61 (1982), 760–763.

MANAGEMENT SCIENCE AIDS FOR PLANNING AND DECISION MAKING

B

In Chapters 6 and 7 we saw how good managers are distinguished from poor ones by how effectively they set goals, develop plans with which to meet those goals, and make the necessary decisions. This appendix introduces quantitative techniques that can serve as valuable decision aids and planning tools. Management science techniques are especially effective when many factors affect a problem, when problems can be quantified, when relationships among factors can be defined, and when the decision maker can control the key factors affecting performance outcomes.[1]

This appendix describes some of the more common management science techniques that are applicable to managerial planning and decision making. It discusses quantitative approaches to forecasting, breakeven analysis, linear programming, PERT charting, and the decision aids of payoff matrix and decision tree. These techniques are not covered in depth; managers need to understand only the basic approach and be able to communicate with management science experts.

● THE NATURE AND ROLE OF MANAGEMENT SCIENCE

Management science techniques are designed to supplement managerial planning and decision making. For many decisions, management science leads to better answers. For example, in today's organizations, it is not uncommon to find experts who use mathematical and statistical analyses to help managers make capital budgeting decisions; decide whether to open a new factory; predict economic trends or customer demands; determine whether to rent or buy a new computer system; schedule trucks, ships, or aircraft; decide among several proposals for research and development projects; and assess whether a new-product introduction is likely to be profitable.

management science

A set of quantitatively based decision models used to assist management decision makers.

Management science is defined as a set of quantitatively based decision models used to assist management decision makers. There are three key components in this definition.

First, *management science is a set of quantitative tools.* Mathematically based procedures impart a systematic rigor to the decision process. Certain types of data must be gathered, put into a specific format, and analyzed according to stringent mathematical rules.

Second, *management science uses decision models.* A *model* is a simplified representation of a real-life situation. For example, small-scale physical models were constructed for every set in the movie *Raiders of the Lost Ark* to diagnose filming problems before constructing the real sets. In a mathematical model, key elements are represented by numbers. Mathematical models are difficult for many students and managers because they use a language that is abstract and unfamiliar. However, outcomes from mathematical models can still aid in decision making.

Third, *quantitative models assist decision makers; they cannot substitute for or replace a manager.*[2] Management science models are simply one of many tools in a manager's tool kit. The manager's role is to provide information for use in the models, interpret the information they provide, and carry out the final plan of action.

Sometimes proponents of management science techniques oversell their value for managerial decision making. Conversely, managers who are unfamiliar with mathematics may resist the use of management science techniques and hence fail to take advantage of a powerful tool. The best management approach is to attempt to understand the types of problems to which management science aids apply and then work with specialists to formulate the necessary data and analytical procedures. For example, using models, a severity index was developed to enable physicians to predict survival time for persons diagnosed with AIDS. The index enables hospital administrators to anticipate necessary resources for patients, including beds, and to assess the effectiveness of the care program.[3]

● FORECASTING

Managers look into the future through forecasts. *Forecasts* are predictions about future organizational and environmental circumstances that will influence plans, decisions, and goal attainment. Forecasts are a basic part of the SWOT analysis described in Chapter 6. Virtually every planning decision depends on assumptions about future conditions.

Four types of forecasts are frequently used by managers.

1 Sales forecasts predict future company sales. Sales forecasting is critical, because it defines customers' demands for products or services. Sales forecasts determine production levels for three months, six months, or one year into the future. Managers use them to hire necessary personnel, buy needed raw materials, make plans to finance an expansion, and arrange needed transportation services. Medium- and large-size companies such as Sound Warehouse and Monsanto use sales forecasts to plan production activities.

2 Technological forecasts attempt to predict the advent of technological changes, especially major technological breakthroughs that could alter an organization's way of doing business. Companies forecast technological changes to avoid building plants or acquiring equipment that is out of date and noncompetitive. Watch manufacturers tracked developments from a company called AT&E Corporation that found a high-tech way to transform a standard wristwatch into a paging device.

3 Demographic forecasts pertain to the characteristics of society, including birthrates, educational levels, marriage rates, and diseases. For example, the baby boomlet of the 1980s will permit managers in schools and companies that make children's clothing and toys to plan for increased product demand in the near future.

4 Human resources forecasts predict the organization's future personnel needs.[4] When AT&T predicted a decrease of several thousand employees during the late 1980s, its human resources department arranged for early retirements and helped displaced employees find jobs elsewhere. Likewise, companies in rapidly growing industries must initiate employee recruitment programs and urge the location of new plants in areas where employees are available.

Forecasts provide information that reduces uncertainty in decision making. Several specific techniques, both quantitative and qualitative, help managers derive forecasts for use in their planning and decision making. Exhibit B.1 illustrates some of the forecasting techniques, their possible applications, and their degree of accuracy.

Let us now examine both the quantitative and qualitative techniques more closely.

QUANTITATIVE FORECASTING TECHNIQUES

Quantitative forecasts start with a series of past data values and then use a set of mathematical rules with which to predict future values.[5] Quantitative techniques have become widely used by managers for two reasons. First, the techniques have repeatedly demonstrated accuracy, especially in the short and intermediate term, thus earning managers'

sales forecast

A forecast of future company sales based on projected customer demand for products or services.

technological forecast

A forecast of the occurrence of technological changes that could affect an organization's way of doing business.

demographic forecast

A forecast of societal characteristics such as birthrates, educational levels, marriage rates, and diseases.

human resources forecast

A forecast of the organization's future personnel needs.

quantitative forecast

A forecast that begins with a series of past data values and then applies a set of mathematical rules with which to predict future values.

E X H I B I T   B . 1

Forecasting Techniques Used by Organizations

Quantitative Techniques	Sample Application	Accuracy		
		Short Term	**Intermediate Term**	**Long Term**
Time series analysis	Sales, earnings, inventory control	Excellent	Good	Good
Regression analysis	Sales, earnings	Excellent	Excellent	Fair
Econometric models	GNP, sales, demographics, economic shifts	Excellent	Good	Fair
Qualitative Techniques				
Delphi	Product development, technological predictions	Good	Good	Good
Sales force composite	Sales projections, future customer demand	Fair	Fair	Poor
Jury of opinion	Sales, new-product development, earnings	Good	Fair	Poor

SOURCE: Adapted from J. Chambers, S. Mullick, and D. Smith, "How to Choose the Right Forecasting Technique," *Harvard Business Review* (July–August 1971), 55–64.

---

confidence as a planning aid. Second, improvements in computer hardware and software have increased the efficiency and decreased the expense of using quantitative techniques. A large number of variables can be incorporated into the analysis, and statistical refinements have improved the techniques' ability to meet the forecasting needs of company managers.

Quantitative forecasting techniques can be subdivided into two categories: time series analysis and causal models. Time series analysis projects past behavior into the future. Causal modeling attempts to unearth past causes of behavior as a way of projecting into the future.[6]

time series analysis

A forecasting technique that examines the patterns of movement in historical data.

TIME SERIES ANALYSIS.   The forecasting technique called **time series analysis** examines the patterns of movement in historical data. It defines patterns in terms of one of four categories.

1 Secular trends   **3** Seasonal variation

2 Cyclic patterns   **4** Random variation

A *secular trend* is the general behavior of a variable over a long period of time. Panel (a) of Exhibit B.2 shows a set of data with an upward trend in unit sales each year. The demand for this company's sales is growing regularly, and managers project sales for 1993 based on this growth.

A *cyclic pattern* involves a recurring up-and-down movement that is periodic in nature. The pattern extends over several years and cannot always be counted on to repeat with precise regularity. Cyclic patterns are related to general business cycles of growth and recession, which managers find extremely valuable to predict. Panel (b) of Exhibit B.2 shows units sold over a typical business cycle of several years.

Seasonal variation is a regular variation in behavior that recurs within a period of one year or less. Climatic changes and social and religious customs can cause seasonal variation. For example, the coordinator for

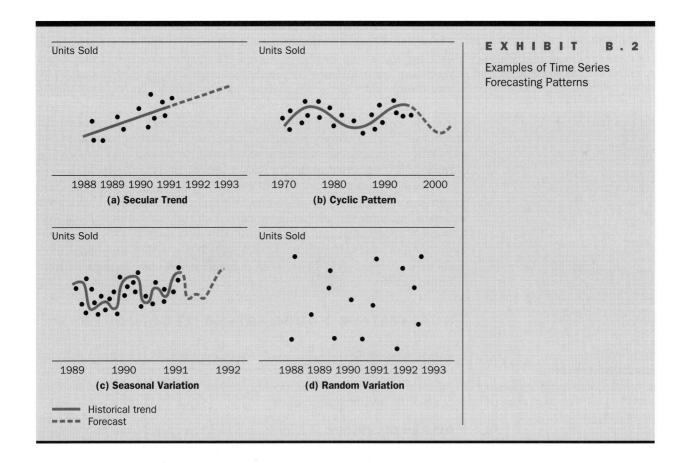

Montreal ambulances found seasonal variance in ambulance use, with higher winter demand for increased emergency use and hospital transfers, but a substantial decrease in the summer.[7]

In another example, bicycle sales normally peak in November and December—prior to Christmas—decline in the winter months, rise in the spring and summer, and decline again in the fall. Panel (c) of Exhibit B.2 shows a seasonal pattern of units sold that would help a manager predict future sales.

Random variation is not a pattern at all. *Random variation* means that there are changes in units sold, but they are unpredictable. These movements might be caused by random factors such as a strike, natural disaster, or changes in government regulations. Panel (d) of Exhibit B.2 shows data that have random variation. Managers are unable to use random variation to predict the future.

Time series analysis is used to predict both short-term and intermediate-term behavior. Its power is its ability to account for seasonal changes as well as long-run trends. Time series analysis works best when the business environment is relatively stable, that is, when the past is a good indicator of the future. In environments in which consumer tastes change radically or random occurrences have a great impact on sales, time series models tend to be inaccurate and of little value.

causal modeling

A forecasting technique that attempts to predict behavior (the dependent variable) by analyzing its causes (independent variables).

CAUSAL FORECASTING MODELS. The forecasting technique called **causal modeling** attempts to predict behavior, called the *dependent variable,* by analyzing its causes, called *independent variables.* Thus, causal modeling may attempt to predict sales (the dependent variable) by examining those factors that cause sales to increase or decrease including amount of advertising expenditure, unit price, competitors' prices, and the overall inflation rate (independent variables). This technique differs from that of simply projecting future sales based on past sales.[8]

When choosing between time series predictions and causal modeling, managers should realize that time series predictions are better at describing seasonal sales variations and predicting changes in sales direction, and causal models provide better information on how to influence a dependent variable such as units sold. Both time series and causal forecasting approaches can produce reliable forecasts if they start with proper data and assumptions. Managers using causal or time series models may wish to work closely with management science experts for maximum benefit.

QUALITATIVE FORECASTING TECHNIQUES

qualitative forecast

A forecast based on the opinions of experts in the absence of precise historical data.

Delphi technique

A qualitative forecasting method in which experts reach consensus about future events through a series of continuously refined questionnaires rather than through face-to-face discussion.

Qualitative techniques are used when quantitative historical data are unavailable. **Qualitative forecasts** rely on experts' judgment. Three useful forms of qualitative forecasting are the Delphi technique, sales force composite, and jury of opinion.

DELPHI TECHNIQUE. A process whereby experts come to a consensus about future events without face-to-face discussion is called the **Delphi technique.**[9] The Delphi procedure was described in Chapter 7 as a means of group decision making. It is especially effective for technological forecasts, because precise data for predicting technological breakthroughs are not available. Technological experts fill out a questionnaire about future events, and the responses are summarized and returned to participants. They then complete a new questionnaire based on their own previous responses and the estimates of other experts. The process continues until a consensus is reached. The Delphi technique promotes independent thought and precludes direct confrontations and participants' defensiveness about their ideas. Its biggest advantage is that experts with widely different opinions can share information with one another and reach agreement about future predictions.[10]

sales force composite

A type of qualitative forecasting that relies on the combined expert opinions of field sales personnel.

SALES FORCE COMPOSITE. Another technique, called the **sales force composite,** relies on the combined expert judgments of field sales personnel. Experienced salespeople know their customers and generally sense fluctuations in customers' needs and buying patterns before these changes are reflected in quantitative data. Salespeople are polled about their customers' expected purchases in the coming time period. Each estimate is reviewed by a district or regional sales manager, who combines these estimates and makes adjustments for expected changes in economic conditions. Findings by Dun and Bradstreet suggest that businesspeople are good forecasters except in times of unexpected or deep recession. During especially bad periods, both managers and salespeople tend to be overly optimistic about the future.[11]

JURY OF OPINION.   A third technique is the **jury of opinion,** sometimes called the *jury of executive opinion,* which averages the opinions of managers from various company divisions and departments. It is similar to a Delphi procedure in that jury members need not meet face to face. Because opinions come from several people, the forecast is less risky than it would be if conducted by a single individual. The method is quick and inexpensive and does not require elaborate statistical analysis. It takes advantage of management's knowledge of the environment based on past experience and good judgment. Jury of opinion was used to forecast the 1990s glut of new automobiles. Experts saw that new plants built in the United States by Japanese and American carmakers would lead to overcapacity by 6 million units. Based on this forecast, some companies curtailed expansion plans.[12]

All forecasting is based on historical patterns, and qualitative techniques are used when precise, historical data are unavailable. If managers feel that experts' biases are affecting forecast accuracy, they can correct future forecasts through instructional feedback. As managers or other experts see that their forecasts are too high or too low, they learn to forecast more accurately in future periods.[13]

● QUANTITATIVE APPROACHES TO PLANNING

Once a sales forecast is developed, managers incorporate that information into their planning for the firm's future actions. Many quantitative techniques are available to help managers plan. Three of these techniques tell managers how many units must be sold before a product is profitable (breakeven analysis), which combination of products can minimize costs (linear programming), and how to schedule complex projects to be completed in the shortest amount of time (PERT). The following discussion illustrates how these techniques assist planning in some situations.

BREAKEVEN ANALYSIS

Breakeven analysis is a quantitative technique that helps managers determine the levels of sales at which total revenues equal total costs and, hence, the firm breaks even.[14] Breakeven analysis portrays the relationships among units of output, sales revenue, and costs, as illustrated in Exhibit B.3. This analysis is an important tool for small business and can answer such questions as: What would happen to sales volume and profits if fixed costs rise 10 percent and prices are held constant? What can we do if our competitor cuts prices 10 percent and our sales volume drops 5 percent? What increase in sales volume must be gained to justify a 15 percent increase in the advertising budget? At what point should company operations simply be shut down?[15] These questions can be answered using the following variables of breakeven analysis:

jury of opinion
A method of qualitative forecasting based on the average opinions of managers from various company divisions and departments.

breakeven analysis
A quantitative technique that helps managers determine the level of sales at which total revenues equal total costs.

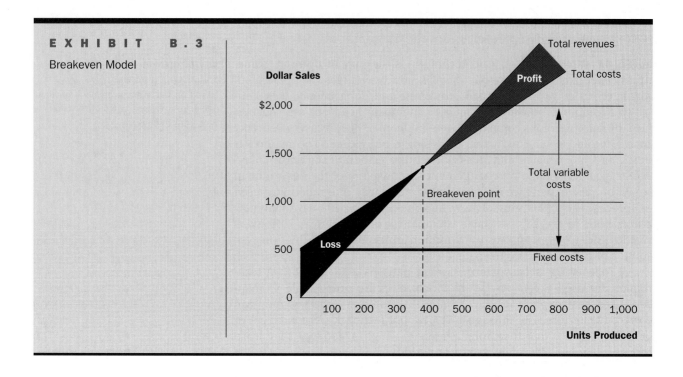

E X H I B I T   B . 3

Breakeven Model

1 *Fixed costs:* Costs that remain the same regardless of the level of production, such as the payment on the building's mortgage. Fixed costs, represented by the horizontal line in Exhibit B.3, remain at $500 whether production is low or high.

2 *Variable costs:* Costs that vary with the number of units produced, such as the cost of raw material. These costs increase as production increases and are the difference between total costs and fixed costs in Exhibit B.3.

3 *Total costs:* The sum of fixed and variable costs, illustrated by the diagonal line in Exhibit B.3.

4 *Total revenues:* Total revenue dollars for a given unit of production, as illustrated by the steep diagonal line in Exhibit B.3. Total revenues are calculated as units sold times unit price.

5 *Breakeven point:* The production volume at which total revenues equal total costs, illustrated by the crossover of the two diagonal lines in Exhibit B.3. As the dashed line indicates, the breakeven point in this particular case is about 380 units.

6 *Profit:* The amount by which total revenues exceed total costs. In Exhibit B.3, profit occurs at a production volume greater than the breakeven point.

7 *Loss:* The amount by which total costs exceed total revenues, which occurs at a production volume less than the breakeven point in Exhibit B.3.

LINEAR PROGRAMMING

Linear programming applies to such planning problems as allocating resources across competing demands or mixing things together efficiently. Farmers want to blend the cheapest feeds to provide enough nutrition to fatten chickens. Oil companies must decide whether to make more jet fuel or heating oil at a refinery, depending on the costs of crude oil and market prices. Airlines must decide what mix of planes to put on routes, depending on fuel costs and passenger loads. Manufacturing managers must decide whether their profits can be maximized by producing more of product A and less of product B, or vice versa. Linear programming is a technique for solving these kinds of problems.[16] For example, linear programming was used to model the planning and management of New Zealand forest, including the amounts and types of trees to harvest, trees to replace, and estimated cash flow.[17]

Linear programming is a mathematical technique that allocates resources to optimize a predefined objective. Moreover, linear programming assumes that the decision maker has limited resources with which to attain the objective.

The nontechnical manager needs to understand only the three basic steps in formulating a linear programming problem:

- **Step 1:** Define the relevant decision variables. These variables must be controllable by the manager.
- **Step 2:** Define the objective in terms of the decision variables. There can be only one objective; thus, it must be chosen carefully.
- **Step 3:** Define the resource restrictions or constraints *first* as word statements and then as mathematical statements.

The following example demonstrates the three steps used in formulating a linear programming model.

linear programming

A quantitative technique that allocates resources to optimize a predefined organizational objective.

WICKER CLASSICS

Wicker Classics makes wicker baskets and seats. Both products must be processed by soaking, weaving, and drying. A basket has a profit margin of $3.25 and a seat a profit margin of $5. Exhibit B.4 summarizes the number of hours available for soaking, weaving, and drying and the number of hours required to complete each task. The question confronting Wicker Classics' managers is: How many baskets and seats should Wicker make per day to maximize profits?

	Soaking Time (Hours)	Weaving Time (Hours)	Drying Time (Hours)	Profit	
Per basket	0.2	0.4	0.3	$3.25	**E X H I B I T B . 4**
Per seat	0.4	0.4	0.8	5.00	Resource Requirements for Wicker Classics
Available hours	60.0	90.0	108.0		

Step 1 is to define the decision variables. What can Wicker managers control in the production process? Two readily controllable variables are the number of baskets and seats to be produced. Thus, we can let X_1 = Number of baskets to produce and X_2 = Number of seats to produce.

Step 2 is to define an objective function. The objective is clear: Maximize profits. This objective can be described mathematically by using the two decision variables. The profit for each basket is $3.25, or 3.25X_1$. Similarly, the profit for each seat produced is $5, or 5X_2$. Total profits for the firm will be the sum of these two components:

$$\text{Maximize profits} = \$3.25X_1 + \$5.00X_2.$$

Step 3 is to define resource constraints. This is the most difficult step in formulating a linear programming model. Wicker is constrained by three scarce resources, expressed in words as appears on the following page.

1 Soaking time cannot exceed 60 hours.

2 Weaving time cannot exceed 90 hours.

3 Drying time cannot exceed 108 hours.

These constraints enable us to state in mathematical terms that total soaking time must be less than or equal to 60 hours. Every basket takes 0.2 hours of soaking time and every seat 0.4 hours. The total production of baskets and seats cannot exceed 60 hours; therefore, our mathematical statement can be

$$0.2X_1 + 0.4X_2 \leq 60.$$

The remaining constraints can be described in similar fashion. Weaving time cannot exceed 90 hours, which is expressed as

$$0.4X_1 + 0.4X_2 \leq 90.$$

Drying time cannot exceed 108 hours, which is expressed mathematically as

$$0.3X_1 + 0.8X_2 \leq 108.$$

A final constraint for keeping the mathematical calculations in the correct range is that neither seats nor baskets can be produced in a volume of less than zero. This is expressed mathematically as

$$X_1 \geq 0$$
$$X_2 \geq 0.$$

The completed problem formulation looks like this:

- Maximize profits = $3.25X_1 + 5X_2$
- Subject to
  Soaking time: $0.2X_1 + 0.4X_2 \leq 60$
  Weaving time: $0.4X_1 + 0.4X_2 \leq 90$
  Drying time: $0.3X_1 + 0.8X_2 \leq 108$
  Nonnegativity: $X_1 \geq 0, X_2 \geq 0$

Exhibit B.5 graphs the constraints for Wicker Classics. Each constraint defines a boundary called the *feasibility region,* which is that region

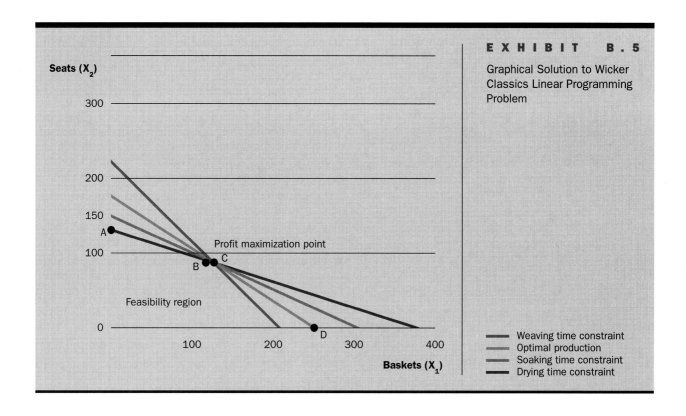

bounded by a resource restriction. The optimal solution for maximizing profits is found at the intersection of two or more constraints at the edge of the feasibility region. Those intersections are at point A, B, C, or D.

Management science specialists use computers and sophisticated software to solve linear programming problems. For a simple problem such as Wicker Classics, the solution can be defined on the graph in Exhibit B.5. Profit maximization is formally defined as the point (A, B, C, or D) that lies farthest from the origin (0) and through which a line can be drawn that has only one point in common with the feasibility region. In Exhibit B.5 this is point C, because it is farthest from the origin and the green line drawn through point C touches the feasibility region at only one point. Thus, the production mix to maximize profits is 125 baskets and 85 seats.[18] ∎

PERSONAL COMPUTERS. Linear programming may seem complicated, but it has many applications in small business. With the advent of personal computers and new software such as *"What's Best!"* small businesses can use this powerful tool for planning and decision making. A user simply sets up the information on costs and other constraints on a computerized spreadsheet program, and the computer will calculate what should be optimized. The cost for software is inexpensive, ranging from $200 to $1,000 depending on complexity. Hawley Fuel Corporation, for example, uses a personal computer to make the cheapest blend of coal that meets utility customers' demands for a particular sulfur content, ash content, and heating value. Even small-business managers who do not understand the underlying mathematics can use PCs and linear programming software for decision making.[19]

PERT

Organizations often confront a situation in which they have a large project to complete for which a complicated, single-use plan is developed. A large project may consist of many interrelated activities. In 1958, the U.S. Navy was confronted with the enormous task of coordinating thousands of contractors to build the Polaris nuclear submarine. The Program Evaluation and Review Technique (PERT) was developed to manage the building of submarines.

PERT allows managers to decompose a project into specific activities and to plan far in advance when it is to be completed. PERT can pinpoint bottlenecks and indicate whether resources should be reallocated. It also provides a map of the project and allows managers to control its execution by determining whether activities are completed on time and in the correct sequence.

There are four basic steps required in the use of PERT:

1 Identify all major activities (tasks) to be performed in the project.

2 Determine the sequence in which the tasks must be completed and whether tasks can be performed simultaneously.

3 Determine the amount of time required to complete each task.

4 Draw a PERT network for controlling the project.

A PERT network is a graphical representation of a large project. *Activities* are the tasks that must be completed in order to finish the project. Each activity must have a discrete beginning and ending. Activities are illustrated as solid lines on a PERT network. *Events* represent the beginning and ending of specific activities. Events are represented on the PERT network as circled numbers. *Paths* are strings of activities and events on a network diagram. Project managers determine the sequence of activities that must be performed in order to complete the entire project. A *critical activity* is one that if delayed will cause a slowdown in the entire project. The path with the longest total time is called the **critical path** and represents the total time required for the project.[20]

The application of PERT can best be seen through an illustration.

PERT

The Program Evaluation and Review Technique; consists of breaking down a project into a network of specific activities and mapping out their sequence and necessary completion dates.

critical path

The path with the longest total time; represents the total time required for the project.

 CAREER RESOURCES, INC.

Career Resources, Inc., is a consulting firm that provides training seminars for companies all around the country. Planning these seminars can be a difficult project, because each company's requirements are different and a number of factors must be brought together in a timely fashion. Doug Black is director of Executive Training Programs, and he decided to develop a PERT network for the next training seminar. He began by listing all activities to be completed and determined whether each had to be done before or after other activities, as illustrated in Exhibit B.6.

E X H I B I T   B . 6

Activities Required for Designing a Training Program

| | | | Estimated Time (Weeks) | | | |
| | | | Optimistic | Most Likely | Pessimistic | Expected |
Activity	Description	Immediate Predecessor(s)				
A	Determine topic	—	3.0	4.0	5.0	4.0
B	Locate speakers	A	4.0	5.0	12.0	6.0
C	Find potential meeting sites	—	2.0	4.0	6.0	4.0
D	Select location	C	3.0	4.0	5.0	4.0
E	Arrange speaker travel plans	B, D	1.0	2.0	3.0	2.0
F	Finalize speaker plans	E	2.0	4.0	6.0	4.0
G	Prepare announcements	B, D	2.0	4.0	12.0	5.0
H	Distribute announcements	G	2.0	3.0	4.0	3.0
I	Take reservations	H	6.0	8.0	10.0	8.0
J	Attend to last-minute details	F, I	3.0	4.0	5.0	4.0

Doug's next step was to determine the length of time required for each activity. To do this, he and two other managers decided on an optimistic, most likely, and pessimistic estimate of how long each activity would take. The optimistic time indicates how quickly the activity will be completed if there are no problems or obstacles. The pessimistic time indicates the amount of time required if everything goes wrong. The most likely time is the estimate assuming that only a few routine problems will occur.

The expected time is a weighted average of the three estimates. The most likely time is weighted by four. The estimated time is calculated as shown in the following formula:

$$\text{Estimated time} = \frac{\text{Optimistic} + (4)\,\text{Most likely} + \text{Pessimistic}}{6}$$

The expected time for completing each activity is shown in the right-hand column of Exhibit B.6.

Based on the information listed in Exhibit B.6, Doug drew the PERT network illustrated in Exhibit B.7. This network shows when activities must be completed in order to move on to the next activity. The critical path is the longest path through the network, which for Doug's project is A-B-G-H-I-J. Thus, the project is expected to take 4 + 6 + 5 + 3 + 8 + 4 = 30 weeks to complete. ■

PERSONAL COMPUTERS.   Doug Black of Career Resources, Inc., drew the PERT chart by hand, but microcomputers have made PERT charting much easier. More than two dozen project-planning software packages are now on the market. These packages provide an easy method of charting and following any kind of task. For example, Rick Gehrig, production coordinator at Westuff Tool & Die, St. Louis, can

EXHIBIT B.7

PERT Network for Designing a Training Program

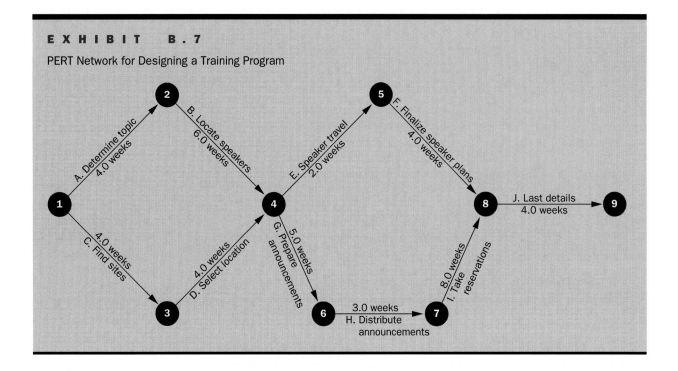

coordinate 80 different projects at once, printing out charts and schedules for each one, on his IBM PC. He even links the projects together in one big schedule to show resource needs for the whole plant. Nuvatec, Inc., located in Downers Grove, Illinois, manages 50 consulting projects with a microcomputer. The tasks and times required for each step in a consulting project are plugged into the computer, which provides a nice method for reporting the status of consulting projects to customers as well as forestalling unpleasant surprises.[21]

● QUANTITATIVE APPROACHES TO DECISION MAKING

Now we turn to quantitative techniques that help managers make choices under conditions of risk and uncertainty. Recall from Chapter 7 that managerial decision making follows six steps: problem definition, diagnosis, development of alternatives, selection of an alternative, implementation, and evaluation/feedback. Decision aids focus on the fourth step—selecting an alternative. First we will examine two quantitative decision approaches: the payoff matrix and the decision tree. Then we will discuss simulation models, an extension of the two decision approaches.

PAYOFF MATRIX

To use the **payoff matrix** as an aid to decision making, a manager must be able to define four variables.

payoff matrix

A decision-making aid comprising relevant strategies, states of nature, probability of occurrence of states of nature, and expected outcome(s).

STRATEGIES.   *Strategies* are the decision alternatives. There can be two strategies or ten, depending on the number of alternatives available. For example, a manager wanting to open a new store might consider four different locations, or a university considering an expansion of its football stadium might consider three expansion alternatives of 8,000, 15,000, and 20,000 seats.

STATES OF NATURE.   Future events or conditions that are relevant to decision outcomes are called **states of nature.** For example, the states of nature for a new store location could be the anticipated sales volume at each site, and those for expanding the football stadium could be the number of additional paying fans at football games.

state of nature

A future event or condition that is relevant to a decision outcome.

PROBABILITY.   *Probability* represents the likelihood, expressed as a percentage, that a given state of nature will occur. Thus, the store owner may calculate the probability of making a profit in location 1 as 20 percent, in location 2 as 30 percent, and in location 3 as 50 percent. A probability of 50 percent would be listed in the payoff matrix as 0.5. University administrators would estimate the probability of filling the stadium under each condition of 8,000, 15,000, and 20,000 additional seats. The probabilities associated with the states of nature must add up to 100 percent.

OUTCOME.   The outcome is the payoff calculated for each strategy given the probabilities associated with each state of nature. The outcome is called the **expected value,** which is the weighted average of each possible outcome for a decision alternative. For example, the store owner could calculate the expected profit from each store location, and the university administrators could calculate the expected returns associated with each construction alternative of 8,000, 15,000, and 20,000 seats.

expected value

The weighted average of each possible outcome for a decision alternative.

To illustrate the payoff matrix in action, let us consider the problem facing Sanders Industries' managers, who are trying to decide how to finance the construction of a new plant and its equipment.

SANDERS INDUSTRIES

The senior managers at Sanders Industries wish to raise funds to finance the construction and new machinery for a new plant to be located in Alberta, Canada. They have determined that they have three alternative funding sources: to issue common stock, bonds, or preferred stock. The desired decision outcome is the net dollars that can be raised through each financing vehicle. The state of nature that affects the decision is the interest rate at the time the securities are issued, because interest rates influence the firm's ability to attract investment dollars. If interest rates are high, investors prefer bonds; if interest rates are low, they prefer stocks. Sanders' financial experts have advised that if interest rates are high, a common stock issue will bring $1 million, bonds $5 million, and preferred stock $3 million. If interest rates are moderate, common stocks will yield $3.5 million, bonds $3.5 million, preferred stock $3 million. If interest rates are low, common stock will return $7.5 million, bonds $2.5 million, and preferred stock $4 million. The financial experts also have estimated the likelihood of low interest rates at 10 percent, of moderate interest rates at 40 percent, and of high interest rates at 50 percent.

Sanders' senior managers want to use a logical structure to make this decision, and the payoff matrix is appropriate. The three decision alternatives of stock, bonds, and preferred stock are shown in Exhibit B.8. The three states of nature—low, moderate, and high interest rates—are listed across the top of the exhibit. The listing of strategy on one side and of states of nature on the other side composes the payoff matrix. The probability associated with each interest rate is also included in the exhibit.

The decision outcome as defined by the managers is to gain the highest expected monetary value from issuing a security. Thus, the managers must calculate the expected monetary return associated with each decision alternative. The calculation of expected value for each decision alternative is performed by multiplying each dollar amount by the probability of occurrence. For the figures in Exhibit B.8, the expected value of each strategy is calculated as follows:

$$
\begin{aligned}
\text{Expected value of common stock} = {} & (0.1)(7.5 \text{ million}) \\
& + (0.4)(3.5 \text{ million}) \\
& + (0.5)\ (1 \text{ million}) \\
& = \$2,650,000
\end{aligned}
$$

$$
\begin{aligned}
\text{Expected value of bonds} = {} & (0.1)(2.5 \text{ million}) \\
& + (0.4)(3.5 \text{ million}) \\
& + (0.5)(5 \text{ million}) \\
& \$4,150,000
\end{aligned}
$$

$$
\begin{aligned}
\text{Expected value of preferred stock} = {} & (0.1)(4 \text{ million}) \\
& + (0.4)(3 \text{ million}) \\
& + (0.5)(3 \text{ million}) \\
& = \$3,100,000
\end{aligned}
$$

From this analysis, the best decision clearly is to issue bonds, which have an expected value of $4,150,000. Although managers cannot be certain about which state of nature will actually occur, the expected value calculation weights each possibility and indicates the choice with the highest likelihood of success. ∎

E X H I B I T   B.8

Payoff Matrix for Sanders Industries

Strategy (Decision Alternative)	Event (Interest Rate Level/ State of Nature)		
	Low (0.1)	Moderate (0.4)	High (0.5)
Common stock	$7,500,000	$3,500,000	$1,000,000
Bonds	2,500,000	3,500,000	5,000,000
Preferred Stock	4,000,000	3,000,000	3,000,000

DECISION TREE

Management problems often require that several decisions be made in sequence. As the outcome of one decision becomes obvious or as additional information becomes available, another decision is required to correct past mistakes or take advantage of new information. For instance, a production manager analyzing the company's product line may decide to add a new product on a trial basis. If customers buy the product, the manager must then decide how to increase production to meet demand. Conversely, if the new product fails to generate sufficient demand, the manager must then decide whether to drop the product.

This type of decision is difficult to structure into a payoff matrix because of the decision sequence. **Decision trees** are an alternative to payoff tables for decision situations that occur in sequence. The objective of decision tree analysis is the same as for payoff tables: to select the decision that will provide the greatest return to the company. The decision tree approach requires the following variables:

1 The decision tree, which is a pictorial representation of decision alternatives, states of nature, and the outcomes of each course of action.

2 The estimated probabilities of each outcome occurring.

3 The payoff (profit or loss) associated with each outcome.

4 The expected value, which is calculated based on the probabilities and conditional payoffs along each branch of the decision tree.

The decision tree consists of a series of nodes and connecting lines. A square node, called a *decision fork,* represents the alternative strategies available to the decision maker *at that time.* From a decision fork, the decision maker must choose one branch to follow. A round node, called a *chance fork,* represents states of nature over which the decision maker has no control. For branches emanating from a chance fork, the decision maker cannot choose which path to follow and must wait until after the decision has been made to see which state of nature occurred.

The use of a decision tree for decision making can be illustrated by the risks and uncertainties associated with the decision to use fire in contemporary forest management.

decision tree

A decision-making aid used for decision situations that occur in sequence; consists of a pictorial representation of decision alternatives, states of nature, and outcomes of each course of action.

 NATIONAL FOREST SERVICE

Forest management personnel often use fires under controlled conditions to reduce natural fire hazards and enhance the wildlife habitat. However, decision uncertainties are inherent in the use of fire. For example, the decision to commit personnel and equipment to the burn site and to actually initiate the burn must be made before weather conditions and fire behavior can be determined with certainty.

A specific burn has two basic alternatives, as illustrated in Exhibit B.9. Decision fork 1 shows that forest managers can either (1) commit resources to the burn or (2) postpone the burn. Two uncertainties are

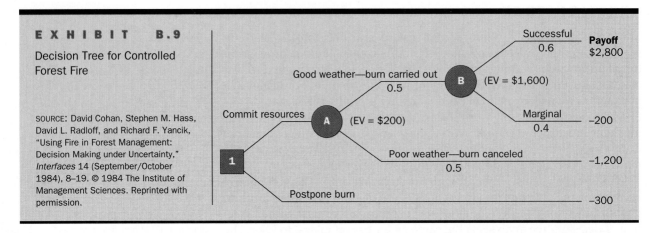

EXHIBIT B.9

Decision Tree for Controlled Forest Fire

SOURCE: David Cohan, Stephen M. Hass, David L. Radloff, and Richard F. Yancik, "Using Fire in Forest Management: Decision Making under Uncertainty," *Interfaces* 14 (September/October 1984), 8–19. © 1984 The Institute of Management Sciences. Reprinted with permission.

central to this decision. The first is the actual weather conditions on the day of the burn, illustrated in chance fork A. There is a 50 percent likelihood that the weather will be poor, in which case the burn will have to be canceled. The second results from the decision to carry out the burn: Will the objectives be met, or will the burn be only marginally successful? This decision is illustrated by chance fork B in Exhibit B.9. The experts have estimated a 60 percent probability of a successful burn and a 40 percent probability of a marginal burn in that situation.

Given the uncertainties facing National Forest Service managers, should they decide to commit the resources or postpone the burn to await better information? The payoff value of each outcome is listed on the far right in Exhibit B.9. If everything is successful, the benefit to the forest service will be $2,800. If a marginal burn occurs, there will be a loss of $200. If the burn is canceled after resources have been committed, there will be a loss of $1,200. If the burn is postponed indefinitely, there will be a loss of $300 in management costs.

The way to choose the best decision is through a procedure known as *rollback*. The rollback procedure begins with the end branches and works backward through the tree by assigning a value to each decision fork and chance fork. A fork's value is the expected return from the branches emanating from the fork. Applying the rollback procedure to the data in Exhibit B.9 produces the following outcomes: The expected value (EV) of chance fork B is $(0.6)(2,800) + 0.4(-200) = \$1,600$; the expected value of chance fork A is $(0.5)(1,600) + 0.5(-1,200) = \$200$.

These figures provide the information needed for the decision. If the managers decide to commit resources, there is a positive expected value of $200. If they postpone the burn, there is a certain loss of $300. Thus, it is worthwhile to go ahead with the planned burn despite management's uncertainty about the weather and possible outcomes.[22] ∎

Decision tree analysis is one of the most widely used decision analysis techniques.[23] As with linear programming and PERT charting described earlier, excellent software programs are available. General managers and small-business managers can use decision tree analysis without hiring a staff specialist. This technique can be used for any decision situation in which probabilities can be estimated and decisions occur in sequence, such as those concerning new-product introduction, pricing, plant expansion, advertising campaigns, or even acquiring another firm.

SIMULATION MODELS

Another useful tool for management decision makers is a simulation model. **Simulation models** are mathematical representations of the relationships among variables in real-life organizational situations.[24] For example, simulations are popular for the risky business of new-product innovations. For, say, a new bar of soap, managers can feed data into a computer about where the soap will be introduced, how much money will be spent on advertising, and what kind of promotion will be done. Data from past new products are in the computer, providing comparisons. The simulation model can predict the new soap's yearly sales. Simulation would take no more than 90 days and cost around $50,000, compared with a minimum 9 months and $1 million dollars to test a real product. Simulations will not always be accurate, however, especially for highly innovative products that have no historical base, but simulations have become very accurate where firms have compiled new-product case histories.[25]

simulation model

A mathematical representation of the relationships among variables in real-world organizational situations.

● STRENGTHS AND LIMITATIONS OF MANAGEMENT SCIENCE AIDS

When selectively applied, management science techniques provide information for improving both planning and decision making. Many businesses have operations research departments in which experts apply management science techniques to organizational problems. And with the use of microcomputers and the many available software programs, management science aids can also be used by small-business managers. Whether using these techniques in small businesses or large businesses, however, managers should be aware of their basic strengths and limitations.

STRENGTHS

The primary strength of management science aids is their ability to enhance decision effectiveness in many situations. For example, time series forecasting helps predict seasonal sales variations. Causal models help managers understand the reasons for future sales increases or decreases. Decision trees, payoff matrices, and PERT networks are valuable when data can be organized into the framework the model requires.

Another strength of management science techniques is that they provide a systematic way of thinking about and organizing complex problems. Managers may use these models intuitively, perhaps sketching things out to clarify their thinking. Moreover, new software packages ask all the right questions so managers will provide the correct data. The computer helps managers organize their thinking and reach the best decision.

Still another strength is that the models promote management rationality when fully applied. They help managers define a problem, select alternatives, gauge probabilities of alternatives' success, and understand the trade-offs and potential payoffs. Managers need not rely on hunch or intuition to make a complicated, multidimensional decision.

Finally, management science aids are inexpensive compared with alternatives such as organizational experiments. If an organization actually had to build a new plant to learn whether it would increase profits, a failure would be enormously expensive. Management science models provide a way to experiment with the decision without having to build the plant.

LIMITATIONS

The growth of management science has led to some problems. First—and perhaps most important—management science techniques do not yet fit many decision situations. Many management decisions are too ambiguous and subjective. For example, management science techniques have little impact on the poorly structured strategic problems at the top levels of corporations.

A second limitation is that they may not reflect the reality of the organizational situation. The management science model is a simplification, and the outcome can be no better than the numbers and assumptions fed into the model. If these numbers are not good or important variables are left out, the outcome will be unrealistic.

A third limitation is overhead costs. The organization may hire management science specialists and provide computer facilities. If these specialists are not frequently used to help solve real problems, they will add to the organization's overhead costs while providing little return.[26]

Finally, management science techniques can be given too much legitimacy. When managers are trying to make a decision under uncertainty, they may be desperate for a clear and precise answer. A management science model may produce an answer that is taken as fact even though the model is only a simplification of reality and the decision needs the interpretation and judgment of experienced managers.

SUMMARY

This appendix described several important points about management science aids for managerial planning and decision making. Forecasting is the attempt to predict behavior in the future. Forecasting techniques can be either quantitative or qualitative. Quantitative techniques include time series analysis and causal modeling. Qualitative techniques include the Delphi method, sales force composite, and jury of opinion.

Quantitative aids to management planning include breakeven analysis, linear programming, and PERT. Breakeven analysis indicates the volume at which a new product will earn enough revenues to cover costs. Linear programming helps managers decide which product mix will maximize profits or minimize costs. PERT helps managers plan, monitor, and control project progress.

Management science aids to decision choices also were described. The payoff matrix helps managers determine the expected value of various alternatives. The decision tree is a similar procedure that is used for decisions made in sequence. Simulation models use mathematics to evaluate the impact of management decisions. Microcomputers and new software make all of these techniques accessible to managers, but managers should remember that management science aids have limitations as well as strengths.

REFERENCES

1. David R. Anderson, Dennis J. Sweeney, and Thomas A. Williams, *Quantitative Methods for Business,* 4th ed. (St. Paul, Minn.: West, 1989), and H. Watson and P. Marett, "A Survey of Management Science Implementation Problems," *Interfaces* 9 (August 1979), 124–128.

2. For further explanation of management science techniques, see B. Render and R. Stair, *Quantitative Analysis for Management,* 2d ed. (Boston: Allyn & Bacon, 1985), and S. Lee, L. Moore, and B. Taylor, *Management Science* (Dubuque, Iowa: W. C. Brown, 1981).

3. Farrokh Alemi, Barbara Turner, Leona Markson, Richard Szorady, and Tom McCarron, "Prognosis after AIDS: A Severity Index Based on Expert's Judgments," *Interfaces* 21 (May–June 1991), 109–116.

4. Thomas H. Stone and Jack Fiorito, "A Perceived Uncertainty Model of Human Resource Forecasting Technique Use," *Academy of Management Review* 11 (1986), 635–642.

5. S. C. Wheelwright and S. Makridakis, *Forecasting Methods for Management* (New York: Wiley, 1973).

6. Ibid.

7. Jean Aubin, "Scheduling Ambulances," *Interfaces* 22 (March–April, 1992), 1–10.

8. Dexter Hutchins, "And Now, the Home-Brewed Forecast," *Fortune,* January 20, 1986, 53–54.

9. N. Dalkey, *The Delphi Method: An Experimental Study of Group Opinion* (Santa Monica, Calif.: Rand Corporation, 1969).

10. Bruce Blaylock and L. Reese, "Cognitive Style and the Usefulness of Information," *Decision Sciences* 15 (Winter 1984), 74–91.

11. J. Duncan, "Businessmen Are Good Sales Forecasters," *Dun's Review* (July 1986).

12. Alex Taylor III, "Who's Afraid in the World Auto War," *Fortune,* November 9, 1987, 74–88.

13. M. Moriarty, "Design Features of Forecasting Systems Involving Management Judgments," *Journal of Marketing Research* 22 (November 1985), 353–364, and D. Kahneman, B. Slovic, and A. Tversky, eds., *Judgment under Uncertainty: Heuristics and Biases* (Cambridge, Mass.: Cambridge Press, 1982).

14. M. Anderson and R. Lievano, *Quantitative Management: An Introduction,* 2d ed. (Boston: Kent, 1986).

15. "Break-Even Analysis: Analyzing the Relationship between Costs and Revenues," *Small Business Report* (August 1986), 22–24.

16. Anderson and Lievano, *Quantitative Management;* J. Byrd and L. Moore, "The Application of a Product Mix Linear Programming Model in Corporate Policy Making," *Management Science* 24 (September 1978), 1342–1350; and D. Darnell and C. Lofflin, "National Airlines Fuel Management and Allocation Model," *Interfaces* 7 (February 1977), 1–16.

17. Bruce R. Manley and John A. Threadgill, "LP Used for Valuation and Planning of New Zealand Plantation Forests," *Interfaces* 21 (November–December 1991), 66–79.

18. P. Williams, "A Linear Programming Approach to Production Scheduling," *Production and Inventory Management* 11 (3d Quarter 1970), 39–49.

19. William M. Bulkeley, "The Right Mix: New Software Makes the Choice Much Easier," *The Wall Street Journal*, March 27, 1987, 25.

20. W. J. Erikson and O. P. Hall, *Computer Models for Management Science* (Reading, Mass.: Addison-Wesley, 1986).

21. Nancy Madlin, "Streamlining the PERT Chart," *Management Review* (September 1986), 67–68.

22. David Cohan, Stephen M. Haas, David L. Radloff, and Richard F. Yancik, "Using Fire in Forest Management: Decision Making under Uncertainty," *Interfaces* 14 (September–October 1984), 8–19.

23. J. W. Ulvila and R. V. Brown, "Decision Analysis Comes of Age," *Harvard Business Review* (September–October 1982), 130–141.

24. Render and Stair, *Quantitative Analysis for Management.*

25. Toni Mack, "Let the Computer Do It," *Forbes*, August 10, 1987, 94.

26. T. Naylor and H. Schauland, "A Survey of Users of Corporate Planning Models," *Management Science* 22 (1976), 927–937.

GLOSSARY

accommodative response A response to social demands in which the organization accepts—often under pressure—social responsibility for its actions to comply with the public interest.

accountability The fact that the people with authority and responsibility are subject to reporting and justifying task outcomes to those above them in the chain of command.

activity ratio A ratio that measures the firm's internal performance with respect to key activities defined by management.

adjourning The stage of team development in which members prepare for the team's disbandment.

administrative model A decision-making model that describes how managers actually make decisions in situations characterized by nonprogrammed decisions, uncertainty, and ambiguity.

administrative principles A subfield of the classical management perspective that focused on the total organization rather than the individual worker, delineating the management functions of planning, organizing, commanding, coordinating, and controlling.

affirmative action A policy requiring employers to take positive steps to guarantee equal employment opportunities for people within protected groups.

ambiguity The objectives to be achieved or the problem to be solved is unclear, alternatives are difficult to define, and information about outcomes is unavailable.

application form A device for collecting information about an applicant's education, previous job experience, and other background characteristics.

assessment center A technique for selecting individuals with high managerial potential based on their performance on a series of simulated managerial tasks.

authority The formal and legitimate right of a manager to make decisions, issue orders, and allocate resources to achieve organizationally desired outcomes.

autocratic leader A leader who tends to centralize authority and rely on legitimate, reward, and coercive power to manage subordinates.

balance sheet A financial statement showing the firm's financial position with respect to assets and liabilities at a specific point in time.

balance sheet budget A financial budget that plans the amount of assets and liabili-

ties for the end of the time period under consideration.

behavior modification The set of techniques by which reinforcement theory is used to modify human behavior.

behavioral sciences approach A subfield of the human resource management perspective that applied social science in an organizational context, drawing from economics, psychology, sociology, and other disciplines.

behaviorally anchored rating scale (BARS) A rating technique that relates an employee's performance to specific job-related incidents.

benchmarking The continuous process of measuring products, services, and practices against the toughest competitors or those companies recognized as industry leaders.

birth stage The phase of the organization life cycle in which the company is created.

bottom-up budgeting A budgeting process in which lower-level managers budget their departments' resource needs and pass them up to top management for approval.

boundary-spanning roles Roles assumed by people and/or departments that link and coordinate the organization with key elements in the external environment.

bounded rationality The concept that people have the time and cognitive ability to process only a limited amount of information on which to base decisions.

brainstorming A decision-making technique in which group members present spontaneous suggestions for problem solution, regardless of their likelihood of implementation, in order to promote freer, more creative thinking within the group.

breakeven analysis A quantitative technique that helps managers determine the level of sales at which total revenues equal total costs.

bureaucratic control The use of rules, policies, hierarchy of authority, reward systems, and other formal devices to influence employee behavior and assess performance.

bureaucratic organizations A subfield of the classical management perspective that emphasized management on an impersonal, rational basis through elements such as clearly defined authority and responsibility, formal recordkeeping, and separation of management and ownership.

burnout The emotional exhaustion resulting from extended periods of stress.

business incubator An innovation that provides shared office space, management support services, and management advice to entrepreneurs.

business-level strategy The level of strategy concerned with the question: "How do we compete?" Pertains to each business unit or product line within the organization.

business plan A document specifying the business details prepared by an entrepreneur in preparation for opening a new business.

CAD A production technology in which computers perform new-product design.

CAM A production technology in which computers help guide and control the manufacturing system.

capacity planning The determination and adjustment of the organization's ability to produce products and services to match customer demand.

capital expenditure budget A financial budget that plans future investments in major assets to be paid for over several years.

career A sequence of work-related activities and behaviors over a person's life span viewed as movement through various job experiences and the individual's attitudes toward involvement in those experiences.

career development Employee progress or growth over time as a career unfolds.

career ladder A formalized job progression route based on logically connected jobs.

career management Organizational activities designed to promote employees' career development.

career path A job progression route along which an employee can advance through the organization.

career planning The self-assessment, exploration of opportunities, goal setting, and other activities necessary to make informed career-related decisions.

career plateau A point in a career from which the opportunities for further promotion are scarce.

cash budget A financial budget that estimates cash flows on a daily or weekly basis to ensure that the company has sufficient cash to meet its obligations.

causal modeling A forecasting technique that attempts to predict behavior (the dependent variable) by analyzing its causes (independent variables).

cellular layout A facilities layout in which machines dedicated to sequences of production are grouped into cells in accordance with group-technology principles.

centralization The location of decision authority near top organizational levels.

centralized network A team communication structure in which team members communicate through a single individual to solve problems or make decisions.

ceremony A planned activity that makes up a special event and is conducted for the benefit of an audience.

certainty All the information the decision maker needs is fully available.

chain of command An unbroken line of authority that links all individuals in the organization and specifies who reports to whom.

change agent An OD specialist who contracts with an organization to facilitate change.

changing A step in the intervention stage of organizational development in which individuals experiment with new workplace behavior.

channel The carrier of a communication.

channel richness The amount of information that can be transmitted during a communication episode.

charismatic leader A leader who has the ability to motivate subordinates to transcend their expected performance.

clan control The use of social values, traditions, common beliefs, and trust to generate compliance with organizational goals.

classical model A decision-making model based on the assumption that managers should make logical decisions that will be in the organization's best economic interests.

classical perspective A management perspective that emerged during the nineteenth and early twentieth centuries that emphasized a rational, scientific approach to the study of management and sought to make organizations efficient operating machines.

closed system A system that does not interact with the external environment

cluster organization An organizational form in which team members from different company locations use CBIS such as electronic mail to solve problems.

coalition An informal alliance among managers who support a specific goal.

code of ethics A formal statement of the organization's values regarding ethics and social issues.

coercive power Power that stems from the leader's authority to punish or recommend punishment.

collectivism A preference for a tightly knit social framework in which individuals look after one another and organizations protect their members' interests.

committee A long-lasting, sometimes permanent team in the organization structure created to deal with tasks that recur regularly.

communication The process by which information is exchanged and understood by two or more people, usually with the intent to motivate or influence behavior.

compensation Monetary payments (wages, salaries) and nonmonetary goods/commodities (fringe benefits, vacations) used to reward employees.

compensatory justice The concept that individuals should be compensated for the cost of their injuries by the party responsible and also that individuals should not be held responsible for matters over which they have no control.

competitors Other organizations in the same industry or type of business that provide goods or services to the same set of customers.

completeness The extent to which information contains the appropriate amount of data.

computer-based information system (CBIS) An information system that uses electronic computing technology to create the information system.

conceptual skill The cognitive ability to see the organization as a whole and the relationship among its parts.

conflict Antagonistic interaction in which one party attempts to thwart the intentions or goals of another.

consideration A type of leader behavior that describes the extent to which a leader is sensitive to subordinates, respects their ideas and feelings, and establishes mutual trust.

content theories A group of theories that emphasize the needs that motivate people.

contingency approach A model of leadership that describes the relationship between leadership styles and specific organizational situations.

contingency plans Plans that define company responses to specific situations such as emergencies or setbacks.

contingency view An extension of the human resource perspective in which the successful resolution of organizational problems is thought to depend on managers' identification of key variables in the situation at hand.

continuous improvement The implementation of a large number of small, incremental improvements in all areas of the organization on an ongoing basis.

continuous reinforcement schedule A schedule in which every occurrence of the desired behavior is reinforced.

controlling The management function concerned with monitoring employees' activities, keeping the organization on track toward its goals, and making corrections as needed.

coordination The quality of collaboration across departments.

coordination costs The time and energy needed to coordinate the activities of a team to enable it to perform its task.

core control system The strategic plans, financial forecasts, budgets, management by objectives, operations management techniques, and MIS reports that form an integrated system for directing and monitoring organizational activities.

corporate-level strategy The level of strategy concerned with the question: "What business are we in?" Pertains to the organization as a whole and the combination of business units and product lines that make it up.

corporation An artificial entity created by the state and existing apart from its owners.

cost leadership A type of competitive strategy with which the organization aggressively seeks efficient facilities, cuts costs, and employs tight cost controls to be more efficient than competitors.

countertrade The barter of products for other products rather than their sale for currency.

creativity The development of novel solutions to perceived organizational problems.

critical path The path with the longest total time; represents the total time required for the project.

cross-functional team A group of employees assigned to a functional department that meets as a team to resolve mutual problems.

culture The set of key values, beliefs, understandings, and norms that members of an organization share; the shared knowledge, beliefs, values, behaviors, and ways of thinking among members of a society.

culture gap The difference between an organization's desired cultural norms and values and actual norms and values.

customers People and organizations in the environment who acquire goods or services from the organization.

cycle time The steps taken to complete a company process.

data Raw, unsummarized, and unanalyzed facts.

debt financing Borrowing money that has to be repaid in order to start a business.

decentralization The location of decision authority near lower organizational levels.

decentralized network A team communication structure in which team members freely communicate with one another and arrive at decisions together.

decision A choice made from available alternatives.

decision making The process of identifying problems and opportunities and then resolving them.

decision tree A decision-making aid used for decision situations that occur in sequence; consists of a pictorial representation of decision alternatives, states of nature, and outcomes of each course of action.

decode To translate the symbols used in a message for the purpose of interpreting its meaning.

defensive response A response to social demands in which the organization admits to some errors of commission or omission but does not act obstructively.

delegation The process managers use to transfer authority and responsibility to positions below them in the hierarchy.

Delphi group A group decision-making format that involves the circulation among participants of questionnaires on the selected problem, sharing of answers, and continuous recirculation/refinement of questionnaires until a consensus has been obtained.

Delphi technique A qualitative forecasting method in which experts reach consensus about future events through a series of continuously refined questionnaires rather than through face-to-face discussion.

democratic leader A leader who delegates authority to others, encourages participation, and relies on expert and referent power to manage subordinates.

demographic forecast A forecast of societal characteristics such as birthrates, educational levels, marriage rates, and diseases.

departmentalization The basis on which individuals are grouped into departments and departments into total organizations.

descriptive An approach that describes how managers actually make decisions rather than how they should.

devil's advocate A decision-making technique in which an individual is assigned the role of challenging the assumptions and assertions made by the group to prevent premature consensus.

diagnosis The step in the decision-making process in which managers analyze underlying causal factors associated with the decision situation.

differentiation A type of competitive strategy with which the organization seeks to distinguish its products or services from competitors'.

direct investing An entry strategy in which the organization is involved in managing its production facilities in a foreign country.

discretionary costs Costs based on management decisions and not on fixed commitments or volume of output.

discretionary responsibility Organizational responsibility that is voluntary and guided by the organization's desire to make social contributions not mandated by economics, law, or ethics.

discrimination The hiring or promoting of applicants based on criteria that are not job relevant.

disengagement stage The stage of career development during which the person prepares for retirement and begins to disengage from both the organization and the occupation.

distributive justice The concept that different treatment of people should not be based on arbitrary characteristics. In the case of substantive differences, people should be treated differently in proportion to the differences between them.

diversity awareness training Special training designed to make people aware of their own prejudices and stereotypes.

divisional structure An organization structure in which departments are grouped based on similar organizational outputs.

downsizing The systematic reduction in the number of managers and employees to make a company more cost efficient and competitive.

downward communication Messages sent from top management down to subordinates.

dual role A role in which the individual both contributes to the team's task and supports members' emotional needs.

economic dimension The dimension of the general environment representing the overall economic health of the country or region in which the organization functions.

economic forces Forces that affect the availability, production, and distribution of a society's resources among competing users.

economic order quantity (EOQ) An inventory management technique designed to minimize the total of ordering and holding costs for inventory items.

effectiveness The degree to which the organization achieves a stated objective.

efficiency The use of minimal resources—raw materials, money, and people—to produce a desired volume of output.

employee stock ownership plan (ESOP) A motivational compensation program that gives employees part ownership of the organization.

encode To select symbols with which to compose a message.

entropy The tendency for a system to run down and die.

equity A situation that exists when the ratio of one person's outcomes to inputs equals that of another's.

equity financing Financing that consists of funds that are invested in exchange for ownership in the company.

equity theory A process theory that focuses on individuals' perceptions of how fairly they are treated relative to others.

establishment and advancement stage The stage of career development during which the individual experiences progress with the organization in the form of transfers, promotions, and/or high visibility.

ethical dilemma A situation that arises when all alternative choices or behaviors have been deemed undesirable because of potentially negative ethical consequences, making it difficult to distinguish right from wrong.

ethics The code of moral principles and values that govern the behaviors of a person or group with respect to what is right or wrong.

ethics committee A group of executives assigned to oversee the organization's ethics by ruling on questionable issues and disciplining violators.

ethics ombudsman An official given the responsibility of corporate conscience who hears and investigates ethics complaints and points out potential ethical failures to top management.

ethnocentrism A cultural attitude marked by the tendency to regard one's own culture as superior to others.

ethnorelativism The belief that groups and subcultures are inherently equal.

excellence characteristics A group of eight features found to typify the highest-performing U.S. companies.

executive information system (EIS) An interactive CBIS that retrieves, manipulates, and displays information serving the needs of top managers; also called *decision support system*.

exit interview   An interview conducted with departing employees to determine the reasons for their termination.

expatriates   Employees who live and work in a country other than their own.

expectancy theory   A process theory that proposes that motivation depends on individuals' expectations about their ability to perform tasks and receive desired rewards.

expected value   The weighted average of each possible outcome for a decision alternative.

expense budget   An operating budget that outlines the anticipated expenses for each responsibility center and for the organization as a whole.

expert power   Power that stems from the leader's special knowledge of or skill in the tasks performed by subordinates.

exploration and trial stage   The stage of career development during which a person accepts his or her first job and perhaps tries several jobs.

exporting   An entry strategy in which the organization maintains its production facilities within its home country and transfers its products for sale in foreign markets.

extrinsic reward   A reward given by another person.

feedback   A response by the receiver to the sender's communication.

femininity   A cultural preference for modesty, caring for the weak, and quality of life.

financial audit   An independent appraisal of the organization's financial records, conducted by external or internal experts.

financial budget   A budget that defines where the organization will receive its cash and how it will spend it.

finished-goods inventory   Inventory consisting of items that have passed through the complete production process but have yet to be sold.

first-line manager   A manager who is at the first or second management level and directly responsible for the production of goods and services.

fixed costs   Costs that are based on a commitment from a previous budget period and cannot be altered.

fixed-position layout   A facilities layout in which the product remains in one location and the required tasks and equipment are brought to it.

flat structure   A management structure characterized by an overall broad span of control and relatively few hierarchical levels.

flexible manufacturing system (FMS)   A small or medium-size automated production line that can be adapted to produce more than one product line.

focus   A type of competitive strategy that emphasizes concentration on a specific regional market or buyer group.

force field analysis   The process of determining which forces drive and which resist a proposed change.

formal communication channel   A communication channel that flows within the chain of command or task responsibility defined by the organization.

formal team   A team created by the organization as part of the formal organization structure.

forming   The stage of team development characterized by orientation and acquaintance.

franchising   A form of licensing in which an organization provides its foreign franchisees with a complete assortment of materials and services; an arrangement by which the owner of a product or service allows others to purchase the right to distribute the product or service with help from the owner.

free rider   A person who benefits from team membership but does not make a proportionate contribution to the team's work.

functional-level strategy   The level of strategy concerned with the question: "How do we support the business-level strategy?" Pertains to all of the organization's major departments.

functional manager   A manager who is responsible for a department that performs a single functional task and has employees with similar training and skills.

functional structure   An organization structure in which positions are grouped into departments based on similar skills, expertise, and resource use.

gain sharing   A motivational compensation program that rewards employees and managers when predetermined performance targets are met.

general environment   The layer of the external environment that affects the organization indirectly.

general manager   A manager who is responsible for several departments that perform different functions.

glass ceiling   Invisible barrier that separates women and minorities from top management positions.

global outsourcing   Engaging in the international division of labor so as to obtain the cheapest sources of labor and supplies regardless of country; also called *global sourcing*.

goal   A desired future state that the organization attempts to realize.

grapevine   An informal, person-to-person communication network of employees that is not officially sanctioned by the organization.

groupthink   A phenomenon in which group members are so committed to the group that they are reluctant to express contrary opinions.

halo error   A type of rating error that occurs when an employee receives the same rating on all dimensions regardless of his or her performance on individual ones.

Hawthorne studies   A series of experiments on worker productivity begun in 1924 at the Hawthorne plant of Western Electric Company in Illinois; attributed employees' increased output to managers' better treatment of them during the study.

hero   A figure who exemplifies the deeds, character, and attributes of a corporate culture.

hierarchy of needs theory   A content theory that proposes that people are motivated by five categories of needs—physiological, safety, belongingness, esteem, and self-actualization—that exist in a hierarchical order.

high-context culture   A culture in which communication is used to enhance personal relationships.

homogeneity   A type of rating error that occurs when a rater gives all employees a similar rating regardless of their individual performances.

horizontal communication   The lateral or diagonal exchange of messages among peers or coworkers.

horizontal linkage model   An approach to product change that emphasizes shared development of innovations among several departments.

horizontal team   A formal team composed of employees from about the same hierarchical level but from different areas of expertise.

human relations movement   A movement in management thinking and practice that emphasized satisfaction of employees' basic needs as the key to increased worker productivity.

human resource inventory   A data base that summarizes individuals' skills, abilities, work experiences, and career interests.

human resource management (HRM)   Activities undertaken to attract, develop, and maintain an effective work force within an organization.

human resource perspective A management perspective that emerged around the late nineteenth century that emphasized enlightened treatment of workers and power sharing between managers and employees.

human resource planning The forecasting of human resource needs and the projected matching of individuals with expected job vacancies.

human resources forecast A forecast of the organization's future personnel needs.

human skill The ability to work with and through other people and to work effectively as a group member.

hygiene factors Factors that involve the presence or absence of job dissatisfiers, including working conditions, pay, company policies, and interpersonal relationships.

idea champion A person who sees the need for and champions productive change within the organization.

individualism A preference for a loosely knit social framework in which individuals are expected to take care of themselves.

individualism approach The ethical concept that acts are moral when they promote the individual's best long-term interests, which ultimately leads to the greater good.

infrastructure A country's physical facilities that support economic activities.

implementation The step in the decision-making process that involves the employment of managerial, administrative, and persuasive abilities to translate the chosen alternative into action.

income statement A financial statement that summarizes a company's financial performance over a given time interval.

informal communication channel A communication channel that exists outside formally authorized channels without regard for the organization's hierarchy of authority.

information Data that are meaningful and alter the receiver's understanding.

information system A mechanism for collecting, organizing, and distributing data to organizational employees.

initiating structure A type of leader behavior that describes the extent to which a leader is task oriented and directs subordinates' work activities toward goal achievement.

integrating manager An individual responsible for coordinating the activities of several departments on a full-time basis to achieve specific project or product outcomes.

interactive leader A leader who is concerned with consensus building, is open

and inclusive, and encourages participation.

internal environment The environment within the organization's boundaries.

international dimension Portion of the external environment that represents events originating in foreign countries as well as opportunities for American companies in other countries.

international management The management of business operations conducted in more than one country.

intrinsic reward A reward received as a direct consequence of a person's actions.

intuition The immediate comprehension of a decision situation based on past experience but without conscious thought.

inventory The goods that the organization keeps on hand for use in the production process up to the point of selling the final products to customers.

invisible minorities Individuals who share a social stigma that is not visibly recognizable.

job A unit of work that a single employee is responsible for performing.

job characteristics model A model of job design that comprises core job dimensions, critical psychological states, and employee growth-need strength.

job description A listing of duties as well as desirable qualifications for a particular job.

job design The application of motivational theories to the structure of work for improving productivity and satisfaction.

job enlargement A job design that combines a series of tasks into one new, broader job to give employees variety and challenge.

job enrichment A job design that incorporates achievement, recognition, and other high-level motivators into the work.

job evaluation The process of determining the values of jobs within an organization through an examination of job content.

job matching system A method that links qualified individuals with career opportunities within the organization.

job rotation A job design that systematically moves employees from one job to another to provide them with variety and stimulation.

job simplification A job design whose purpose is to improve task efficiency by reducing the number of tasks a single person must perform.

joint venture A variation of direct investment in which an organization shares costs and risks with another firm to build a manufacturing facility, develop new prod-

ucts, or set up a sales and distribution network; a strategic alliance or program by two or more organizations.

jury of opinion A method of qualitative forecasting based on the average opinions of managers from various company divisions and departments.

justice approach The ethical concept that moral decisions must be based on standards of equity, fairness, and impartiality.

just-in-time (JIT) inventory systems An inventory control system that schedules materials to arrive precisely when they are needed on a production line.

labor market The people available for hire by the organization.

law of effect The assumption that positively reinforced behavior tends to be repeated and unreinforced or negatively reinforced behavior tends to be inhibited.

leadership The ability to influence people toward the attainment of organizational goals.

leadership grid A three-dimensional leadership theory that measures a leader's concern for people and concern for production.

leading The management function that involves the use of influence to motivate employees to achieve the organization's goals.

legal-political dimension The dimension of the general environment that includes federal, state, and local government regulations and political activities designed to control company behavior.

legitimate power Power that stems from a formal management position in an organization and the authority granted to it.

licensing An entry strategy in which an organization in one country makes certain resources available to companies in another in order to participate in the production and sale of its products abroad.

linear programming A quantitative technique that allocates resources to optimize a predefined organizational objective.

liquidity ratio A financial ratio that indicates the company's ability to meet its current debt obligations.

listening The skill of receiving messages to accurately grasp facts and feelings to interpret the genuine meaning.

low-context culture A culture in which communication is used to exchange facts and information.

LPC scale A questionnaire designed to measure relationship-oriented versus task-oriented leadership style according to the leader's choice of adjectives for describing the "least preferred coworker."

lump-sum bonus A motivational compensation program that rewards employees with a one-time cash payment based on performance.

management The attainment of organizational goals in an effective and efficient manner through planning, organizing, leading, and controlling organizational resources.

management by objectives A method of management whereby managers and employees define objectives for every department, project, and person and use them to control subsequent performance.

management by wandering around (MBWA) A communication technique in which managers interact directly with workers to exchange information.

management information system (MIS) A form of CBIS that collects, organizes, and distributes the data managers use in performing their management functions.

management science A set of quantitatively based decision models used to assist management decision makers.

management science perspective A management perspective that emerged after World War II and applied mathematics, statistics, and other quantitative techniques to managerial problems.

manufacturing organization An organization that produces physical goods.

market entry strategy An organizational strategy for entering a foreign market.

masculinity A cultural preference for achievement, heroism, assertiveness, and material success.

matching model An employee selection approach in which the organization and the applicant attempt to match each other's needs, interests, and values.

matrix approach An organization structure that utilizes functional and divisional chains of command simultaneously in the same part of the organization.

matrix boss A product or functional boss, responsible for one side of the matrix.

maturity stage The phase of the organization life cycle in which the organization has become exceedingly large and mechanistic.

mechanistic structure An organizational structure characterized by rigidly defined tasks, many rules and regulations, little teamwork, and centralized decision making.

mediation The process of using a third party to settle a dispute.

mentor A senior employee who acts as a sponsor and teacher to a newer, less experienced employee.

merger The combination of two or more organizations into one.

message The tangible formulation of an idea to be sent to a receiver.

mid-career renewal strategies A strategy designed to provide advancement opportunities for deserving mid-career employees while maximizing the contributions of plateaued employees who continue to perform satisfactorily.

mid-career stage The stage of career development characterized by growth, maintenance, or decline.

middle manager A manager who works at the middle levels of the organization and is responsible for major departments.

midlife stage The phase of the organization life cycle in which the firm has reached prosperity and grown substantially large.

mission The organization's reason for existence.

mission statement A broadly stated definition of the organization's basic business scope and operations that distinguish it from similar types of organizations.

monoculture A culture that accepts only one way of doing things and one set of values and beliefs.

moral-rights approach The ethical concept that moral decisions are those that best maintain the rights of those people affected by them.

motivation The arousal, direction, and persistence of behavior.

motivators Factors that influence job satisfaction based on fulfillment of higher-level needs such as achievement, recognition, responsibility, and opportunity for growth.

multinational corporation (MNC) An organization that receives more than 25 percent of its total sales revenues from operations outside the parent company's home country; also called *global corporation* or *transnational corporation.*

multiple advocacy A decision-making technique that involves several advocates and presentation of multiple points of view, including minority and unpopular opinions.

network structure An organization structure that disaggregates major functions into separate companies that are brokered by a small headquarters organization.

neutralizer A situational variable that counteracts a leadership style and prevents the leader from displaying certain behaviors.

new-venture fund A fund providing resources from which individuals and groups draw to develop new ideas, products, or businesses.

new-venture team A unit separate from the mainstream of the organization that is responsible for developing and initiating innovations.

nominal group A group decision-making format that emphasizes equal participation in the decision process by all group members.

nonparticipator role A role in which the individual contributes little to either the task or members' socioemotional needs.

nonprogrammed decision A decision made in response to a situation that is unique, is poorly defined and largely unstructured, and has important consequences for the organization.

nonverbal communication A communication transmitted through actions and behaviors rather than through words.

norm A standard of conduct that is shared by team members and that guides their behavior.

normative An approach that defines how a decision maker should make decisions and provides guidelines for reaching an ideal outcome for the organization.

norming The stage of team development in which conflicts developed during the storming stage are resolved and team harmony and unity emerge.

obstructive response A response to social demands in which the organization denies responsibility, claims that evidence of misconduct is misleading or distorted, and attempts to obstruct investigation.

on-the-job training (OJT) A type of training in which an experienced employee "adopts" a new employee to teach him or her how to perform job duties.

open system A system that interacts with the external environment.

operating budget The plan for the allocation of financial resources to each organizational responsibility center for the budget period under consideration.

operational goals Specific, measurable results expected from departments, work groups, and individuals within the organization.

operational plans Plans developed at the organization's lower levels that specify action steps toward achieving operational goals and support tactical planning activities.

operations management The field of management that specializes in the physical production of goods or services and uses quantitative techniques for solving manufacturing problems.

operations strategy The recognition of the importance of operations to the firm's success and the involvement of operations managers in the organization's strategic planning.

opportunity A situation in which managers see potential organizational accomplishments that exceed current objectives.

organic structure An organizational structure that is free flowing, has few rules and regulations, encourages employee teamwork, and decentralizes decision making to employees doing the job.

organization A social entity that is goal directed and deliberately structured.

organizational change The adoption of a new idea or behavior by an organization.

organizational control The systematic process through which managers regulate organizational activities to make them consistent with expectations established in plans, targets, and standards of performance.

organizational development (OD) The application of behavioral science techniques to improve an organization's health and effectiveness through its ability to cope with environmental changes, improve internal relationships, and increase problem-solving capabilities.

organizational environment All elements existing outside the organization's boundaries that have the potential to affect the organization.

organization chart The visual representation of an organization's structure.

organization life cycle The organization's evolution through major developmental stages.

organization structure The framework in which the organization defines how tasks are divided, resources are deployed, and departments are coordinated.

organizing The management function concerned with assigning tasks, grouping tasks into departments, and allocating resources to departments; the deployment of organizational resources to achieve strategic objectives.

outsourcing The farming out of a company's in-house operation to a preferred vendor.

P → E expectancy Expectancy that putting effort into a given task will lead to high performance.

P → O expectancy Expectancy that successful performance of a task will lead to the desired outcome.

paper-and-pencil test A written test designed to measure a particular attribute such as intelligence or aptitude.

paradigm A mind-set that presents a fundamental way of thinking, perceiving, and understanding the world.

partial productivity The ratio of total outputs to the inputs from a single major input category.

partial reinforcement schedule A schedule in which only some occurrences of the desired behavior are reinforced.

partnership An unincorporated business owned by two or more people.

path-goal theory A process theory that proposes that individual motivation depends on the leader's ability to clarify the behavior necessary for task accomplishments and rewards.

pay for knowledge A motivational compensation program that links employee's salary with the number of tasks performed.

pay for performance A motivational compensation program that rewards employees in proportion to their performance contributions.

payoff matrix A decision-making aid comprising relevant strategies, states of nature, probability of occurrence of states of nature, and expected outcome(s).

pay survey A study of what other companies pay employees in jobs that correspond to a sample of key positions selected by the organization.

pay-trend line A graph that shows the relationship between pay and total job point values for determining the worth of a given job.

perception The process of making sense out of one's environment.

perceptual organization The categorization of an object or stimulus according to one's frame of reference.

perceptual selectivity The screening and selection of objects and stimuli that compete for one's attention.

performance The organization's ability to attain its goals by using resources in an efficient and effective manner.

performance appraisal The process of observing and evaluating an employee's performance, recording the assessment, and providing feedback to the employee.

performance appraisal interview A formal review of an employee's performance conducted between the superior and the subordinate.

performance gap A disparity between existing and desired performance levels.

performing The stage of team development in which members focus on problem solving and accomplishing the team's assigned task.

permanent team A group of participants from several functions who are permanently assigned to solve ongoing problems of common interest.

PERT The Program Evaluation and Review Technique; consists of breaking down a project into a network of specific activities and mapping out their sequence and necessary completion dates.

plan A blueprint specifying the resource allocations, schedules, and other actions necessary for attaining goals.

planning The management function concerned with defining goals for future organizational performance and deciding on the tasks and resource use needed to attain them; the act of determining the organization's goals and the means for achieving them.

pluralism The organization accommodates several subcultures, including employees who would otherwise feel isolated and ignored.

point system A job evaluation system that assigns a predetermined point value to each compensable job factor in order to determine the worth of a given job.

political activity Organizational attempts, such as lobbying, to influence government legislation and regulation.

political forces The influence of political and legal institutions on people and organizations.

political risk A company's risk of loss of assets, earning power, or managerial control due to politically motivated events or actions by host governments.

power The potential ability to influence others' behavior.

power distance The degree to which people accept inequality in power among institutions, organizations, and people.

preretirement program A strategy designed to assist employees in coping with the stress of the transition from work to retirement.

proactive response A response to social demands in which the organization seeks to learn what is in its constituencies' interest and to respond without pressure from them.

problem A situation in which organizational accomplishments have failed to meet established objectives.

problem-solving team Typically 5 to 12 hourly employees from the same department who meet to discuss ways of improving quality, efficiency, and the work environment.

procedural justice The concept that rules should be clearly stated and consistently and impartially enforced.

process layout A facilities layout in which machines that perform the same function are grouped together in one location.

process theories A group of theories that explain how employees select behaviors with which to meet their needs and determine whether their choices were successful.

product change A change in the organization's product or service output.

productivity The organization's output of products and services divided by its inputs.

product layout A facilities layout in which machines and tasks are arranged according to the sequence of steps in the production of a single product.

product life cycle The stages through which a product or service goes: (1) development and introduction into the marketplace, (2) growth, (3) maturity, and (4) decline.

profitability ratio A financial ratio that describes the firm's profits.

profit budget An operating budget that combines both expense and revenue budgets into one statement showing gross and net profits.

programmed decision A decision made in response to a situation that has occurred often enough to enable decision rules to be developed and applied in the future.

project manager A manager who coordinates people across several departments to accomplish a specific project.

proprietorship An unincorporated business owned by an individual for profit.

qualitative forecast A forecast based on the opinions of experts in the absence of precise historical data.

quality The degree to which information accurately portrays reality.

quality circle (QC) A group of 6 to 12 volunteer employees who meet regularly to discuss and solve problems that affect their common work activities.

quantitative forecast A forecast that begins with a series of past data values and then applies a set of mathematical rules with which to predict future values.

raw materials inventory Inventory consisting of the basic inputs to the organization's production process.

realistic job preview (RJP) A recruiting approach that gives applicants all pertinent and realistic information about the job and the organization.

recruiting The activities or practices that define the desired characteristics of applicants for specific jobs.

reengineering The reconsideration and redesign of business systems that bring together all elements of a single business process to eliminate waste and delays.

referent power Power that results from leader characteristics that command subordinates' identification with, respect and admiration for, and desire to emulate the leader.

refreezing A step in the reinforcement stage of organizational development in which individuals acquire a desired new skill or attitude and are rewarded for it by the organization.

reinforcement Anything that causes a given behavior to be repeated or inhibited.

reinforcement theory A motivation theory based on the relationship between a given behavior and its consequences.

relevance The degree to which information pertains to the problems, decisions, and tasks for which a manager is responsible.

reorder point (ROP) The most economical level at which an inventory item should be reordered.

responsibility The duty to perform the task or activity an employee has been assigned.

responsibility center Any organizational department under the supervision of a single individual who is responsible for its activity.

revenue budget An operating budget that identifies the revenues required by the organization.

reward power Power that results from the leader's authority to reward others.

risk A decision has clear-cut objectives, and good information is available, but the future outcomes associated with each alternative are subject to chance.

risk propensity The willingness to undertake risk with the opportunity of gaining an increased payoff.

role A set of expectations for one's behavior.

sales force composite A type of qualitative forecasting that relies on the combined expert opinions of field sales personnel.

sales forecast A forecast of future company sales based on projected customer demand for products or services.

satisfice To choose the first solution alternative that satisfies minimal decision criteria regardless of whether better solutions are presumed to exist.

schedule of reinforcement The frequency with and intervals over which reinforcement occurs.

scientific management A subfield of the classical management perspective that emphasized scientifically determined changes in management practices as the solution to improving labor productivity.

search The process of learning about current developments inside or outside the organization that can be used to meet a perceived need for change.

selection The process of determining the skills, abilities, and other attributes a person needs to perform a particular job.

self-managing team A team consisting of 5 to 20 multiskilled workers who rotate jobs to produce an entire product or service, often supervised by an elected member.

semantics The meaning of words and the way they are used.

service organization An organization that produces nonphysical goods that require customer involvement and cannot be stored in inventory.

simulation model A mathematical representation of the relationships among variables in real-world organizational situations.

situation analysis Analysis of the strengths, weaknesses, opportunities, and threats (SWOT) that affect organizational performance.

situational theory A contingency approach to leadership that links the leader's two-dimensional style with the task maturity of subordinates.

size The organization's scope or magnitude, typically measured by number of employees.

skunkworks Small, informal, and sometimes unauthorized groups that create innovations.

slogan A phrase or sentence that succinctly expresses a key corporate value.

social facilitation The tendency for the presence of others to influence an individual's motivation and performance.

social forces The aspects of a culture that guide and influence relationships among people—their values, needs, and standards of behavior.

social responsibility The obligation of organization management to make decisions and take actions that will enhance the welfare and interests of society as well as the organization.

sociocultural dimension The dimension of the general environment representing the demographic characteristics, norms, customs, and values of the population within which the organization operates.

socioemotional role A role in which the individual provides support for team members' emotional needs and social unity.

span of management The number of employees who report to a supervisor; also called *span of control.*

special-purpose team A team created outside the formal organization to undertake a project of special importance or creativity.

spin-off An independent company producing a product or service similar to that produced by the entrepreneur's former employer.

stakeholder Any group within or outside the organization that has a stake in the organization's performance.

state of nature A future event or condition that is relevant to a decision outcome.

statistical process control (SPC) A type of managerial control that employs carefully gathered data and statistical analysis to evaluate the quality and productivity of employee activities.

statistical quality control The application of statistical techniques to the control of quality.

stereotype A widely held generalization about a group of people that assigns attributes to them solely on the basis of a limited number of categories.

storming The stage of team development in which individual personalities and roles, and resulting conflicts, emerge.

story A narrative based on true events that is repeated frequently and shared by organizational employees.

strategic goals Broad statements of where the organization wants to be in the future; pertain to the organization as a whole rather than to specific divisions or departments.

strategic management The set of decisions and actions used to formulate and implement strategies that will provide a competitively superior fit between the organization and its environment so as to achieve organizational objectives.

strategic plans The action steps by which an organization intends to attain its strategic goals.

stress The physiological and emotional response to demands, constraints, and opportunities that create uncertainty when important outcomes are at stake.

structural change Any change in the way in which the organization is designed and managed.

substitute A situational variable that makes a leadership style redundant or unnecessary.

subsystems Parts of a system that depend on one another for their functioning.

succession planning The process of creating a plan for moving people into higher organizational levels.

superordinate goal A goal that cannot be reached by a single party.

suppliers People and organizations who provide the raw materials the organization uses to produce its output.

survey feedback A type of OD intervention in which questionnaires on organizational climate and other factors are distributed among employees and the results reported back to them by a change agent.

symbol An object, act, or event that conveys meaning to others.

symbolic manager A manager who defines and uses signals and symbols to influence corporate culture.

synergy The concept that the whole is greater than the sum of its parts.

system A set of interrelated parts that function as a whole to achieve a common purpose.

systems theory An extension of the human resources perspective that describes organizations as open systems that are characterized by entropy, synergy, and subsystem interdependence.

tactical goals Objectives that define the outcomes that major divisions and departments must achieve in order for the organization to reach its overall goals.

tactical plans Plans designed to help execute major strategic plans and to accomplish a specific part of the company's strategy.

tall structure A management structure characterized by an overall narrow span of management and a relatively large number of hierarchical levels.

task environment The layer of the external environment that directly influences the organization's operations and performance.

task force A temporary team or committee formed to solve a specific short-term problem involving several departments.

task specialist role A role in which the individual devotes personal time and energy to helping the team accomplish its task.

team A unit of two or more people who interact and coordinate their work to accomplish a specific objective; a group of participants from several departments who meet regularly to solve ongoing problems of common interest.

team building A type of OD intervention that enhances the cohesiveness of departments by helping members to learn to function as a team.

team cohesiveness The extent to which team members are attracted to the team and motivated to remain in it.

technical skill The understanding of and proficiency in the performance of specific tasks.

technological dimension The dimension of the general environment that includes scientific and technological advancements in the industry and society at large.

technological forecast A forecast of the occurrence of technological changes that could affect an organization's way of doing business.

technology change A change that pertains to the organization's production process.

Theory Z A management perspective that incorporates techniques from both Japanese and North American management practices.

time-based competition A strategy of competition based on the ability to deliver products and services faster than competitors.

timeliness The degree to which information is available soon after events occur.

time series analysis A forecasting technique that examines the patterns of movement in historical data.

top-down budgeting A budgeting process in which middle- and lower-level managers set departmental budget targets in accordance with overall company revenues and expenditures specified by top management.

top leader The overseer of both the product and the functional chains of command, responsible for the entire matrix.

top manager A manager who is at the top of the organizational hierarchy and responsible for the entire organization.

total factor productivity The ratio of total outputs to the inputs from labor, capital, materials, and energy.

total quality management (TQM) A control concept that gives workers rather than managers the responsibility for achieving standards of quality.

trade association An association made up of organizations with similar interests for the purpose of influencing the environment.

traits The distinguishing personal characteristics of a leader, such as intelligence, values, and appearance.

transactional leader A leader who clarifies subordinates' role and task requirements, initiates structure, provides rewards, and displays consideration for subordinates.

transformational leader A leader distinguished by a special ability to bring about innovation and change.

two-boss employee An employee who reports to two supervisors simultaneously.

uncertainty Managers know what objective they wish to achieve but information about alternatives and future events is incomplete.

uncertainty avoidance A value characterized by people's intolerance for uncertainty and ambiguity and resulting support for beliefs that promise certainty and conformity.

unfreezing A step in the diagnosis stage of organizational development in which participants are made aware of problems in order to increase their willingness to change their behavior.

upward communication Messages transmitted from the lower to the higher level in the organization's hierarchy.

utilitarian approach The ethical concept that moral behaviors produce the greatest good for the greatest number.

valence The value or attraction an individual has for an outcome.

validity The relationship between an applicant's score on a selection device and his or her future job performance.

variable costs Costs that are based on an explicit physical relationship with the volume of departmental activity; also called *engineered costs*.

venture capital firm A group of companies or individuals that invests money in new or expanding businesses for a share of ownership and potential profits.

vertical team A formal team composed of a manager and his or her subordinates in the organization's formal chain of command.

Vroom-Jago model A model designed to help managers gauge the amount of subordinate participation in decision making.

whistle-blowing The disclosure by an employee of illegal, immoral, or illegitimate practices by the organization.

wholly owned foreign affiliate A foreign subsidiary over which an organization has complete control.

work-force diversity Hiring people with different human qualities who belong to various cultural groups.

work-in-process inventory Inventory composed of the materials that are still moving through the stages of the production process.

work redesign The altering of jobs to increase both the quality of employees' work experience and their productivity.

work specialization The degree to which organizational tasks are subdivided into individual jobs; also called *division of labor*.

youth stage The phase of the organization life cycle in which the organization is growing rapidly and has a product enjoying some marketplace success.

zero-based budgeting (ZBB) A budgeting process in which each responsibility center calculates its resource needs based on the coming year's priorities rather than on the previous year's budget.

● PHOTO CREDITS

CHAPTER 1

Page **6** © John Abbott. Page **10** Courtesy of the *Los Angeles Times*. Page **11** Reprinted with permission of Compaq Computer Corporation. All Rights Reserved. Page **25** Courtesy of Reynolds Metals Company. Page **29** Courtesy of Dow Chemical Company.

CHAPTER 2

Page **41** From the collection of Walter and Naomi Rosenblum. Used with permission. Page **44** Frederick W. Taylor Collection, S. C. Williams Library. Stevens Institute of Technology. Page **45** Courtesy of Ronald G. Greenwood. Page **46** Courtesy of German Information Center. Page **47** Courtesy of Ronald G. Greenwood. Page **59** Courtesy of The Stanley Works. Al Ferreira, photographer.

CHAPTER 3

Page **78** Photo courtesy of Otis Communications World Headquarters. Page **82** Courtesy of J. B. Hunt Transport, Inc. Photo by Dan Bryant. Page **84** Courtesy of Pan-Pacific Hotel San Diego. Page **90** Mark Tuschman/The Upjohn Company.

CHAPTER 4

Page **105** Courtesy of Bumble Bee Tuna. Page **111** Courtesy of The Stanley Works. Page **113** Courtesy of the *San Diego Union-Tribune*. Page **116** Courtesy of First Security Corporation.

CHAPTER 5

Page **135** Copyright Dave Morrison for Florida Progress Corporation. Page **142** Cray Research, Inc. Page **152** Courtesy of The Stride Rite Corporation. Page **155** Courtesy of Rohm and Haas Company.

CHAPTER 6

Page **170** *San Diego Union-Tribune*. Page **180** © Copyright British Telecommunications plc. Page **189** © Tom Tracy for Dreyer's Ice Cream. Page **191** Courtesy of Toys "R" Us.

CHAPTER 7

Page **207** Courtesy of Quad/Photo. Page **209** © 1994 Manhattan East Suite Hotels. Page **218** Courtesy of Boeing. Page **223** Courtesy of PictureTel.

CHAPTER 8

Page **245** © 1992 Steven Pumphrey. All rights reserved. Page **249** Courtesy of Brown-Froman Beverage Company. Page **259** © Ed Wheeler. Reprinted by permission of Philip Morris Companies, Inc.

CHAPTER 9

Page **275** TAKASHIMAYA Annual Report. Courtesy of TAKASHIMAYA Co., Ltd. Page **279** © Michael Melford 1992. Page **293** © Alen MacWeeney 1991.

CHAPTER 10

Page **304** Courtesy of MagneTek, Inc. Page **307** © Christina M. Freitag for Louisville Gas & Electric Company. Page **322** © Jay Dickman.

CHAPTER 11

Page **339** Courtesy of Consumers Gas Company Ltd., Toronto, Canada. Page **343** © Wayne Sorce. Page **346** © Charles Moore/Black Star.

CHAPTER 12

Page **376** Allan Brinback, photographer, and ASARCO Incorporated. Page **380** © Cameron Davidson/Tony Stone Images. Page **390** AP/Wide World.

CHAPTER 13

Page **409** Courtesy of *Frontline Magazine*, published by Taco Bell Public Affairs Department. Page **414** Courtesy of Mary Kay Cosmetics. Page **423** Courtesy of Creative Learning Systems, Inc.

CHAPTER 14

Page **445** Courtesy of Securities Department, Ito-Yakado Co., Ltd. Page **450** Richard Mitchell. Page **457** Courtesy of Flowers Industries, Inc. Photographer: Ovak Arslanian, New York. Page **459** © Chuck Keeler/Tony Stone Images.

CHAPTER 15

Page **472** © Michael O'Neill. Page **490** Courtesy of Gilbane Building Company. Page **494** G. Robert Nease for Marshall Industries.

CHAPTER 16

Page **509** Chip Henderson/Tony Stone Images. Page **515** Courtesy of Pall Corporation, East Hills, New York. Page **517** Courtesy of Campbell Soup Company. Page **526** Courtesy of Armstrong World Industries, Inc.

CHAPTER 17

Page **544** © Don Smetzer/Tony Stone Images. Page **551** Courtesy of the Quaker Oats Company.

CHAPTER 18

Page **564** Photo courtesy of Goglanian Bakeries, Inc. Page **568** Courtesy Beckman Instruments, Inc. Photograph by Ken Whitmore. Page **574** Courtesy of Borden, Inc. Page **577** Courtesy of Brothers Gourmet Coffees, Inc.

COMPANY INDEX

● SUBJECT INDEX